AF446734

# LEGITIMACY, LEGAL DEVELOPMENT AND CHANGE

*For Kim, for patience.*

# Legitimacy, Legal Development and Change
## Law and Modernization Reconsidered

*Edited by*

DAVID K. LINNAN
*Law & Finance Institutional Partnership (LFIP), Indonesia*
*University of South Carolina School of Law, US*
*Asian Law Centre, Melbourne, Australia*

ASHGATE

Published by
Ashgate Publishing Limited
Wey Court East
Union Road
Farnham
Surrey, GU9 7PT
England

Ashgate Publishing Company
Suite 420
101 Cherry Street
Burlington
VT 05401-4405
USA

www.ashgate.com

**British Library Cataloguing in Publication Data**
Legitimacy, legal development and change : law and
   modernization reconsidered.
   1. Law reform. 2. Sociological jurisprudence.
   I. Linnan, David K., 1953-
   340.3-dc23

**Library of Congress Cataloging-in-Publication Data**
Linnan, David K., 1953-
   Legitimacy, legal development, and change : law and modernization
reconsidered / by David K. Linnan.
      p. cm.
   Includes bibliographical references and index.
   ISBN 978-0-7546-7728-4 (hardback) -- ISBN 978-0-7546-9445-8 (ebook)
1. Law--History. 2. Rule of law. 3. Law reform. I. Title.

   K150.L56 2011
   340'.115--dc23

2011049377

ISBN 9780754677284 (hbk)
ISBN 9780754694458 (ebk)

Printed and bound in Great Britain by the
MPG Books Group, UK

# Contents

## PART III: *SHARI'AH*, CUSTOMARY AND SECULAR NATIONAL LAWS' INTERPLAY IN THE WORLD'S MOST POPULOUS ISLAMIC COUNTRY



## PART IV: JAPAN'S ONCE AND FUTURE LEGAL MODERNIZATION NARRATIVE



## PART V: LATIN AMERICA, POST CONFLICT AND THE JUDICIARY

## PART VI: RUSSIA AND THE STATE: A WINDOW ON MODERNIZATION



## PART VII: INTERNATIONAL LAW AS LEGAL DEVELOPMENT SUBJECT

# List of Figures and Tables

**Figures**



**Tables**

# List of Contributors

**Tarak Abdallah** is an Associate Professor at the Institute for Islamic World Studies at Zayed University, UAE. He studied economics at the Universities of Tunis (BS 1985) and Paris X Nanterre (MA 1987; PhD 1992) and sociology at the University of Quebec (PhD 1999). His research interests include Islamic economics, waqf and social institutions, as well as civil society in the Arab world. Beyond his academic role, he has advised a variety of charitable institutions in the Middle East and Southeast Asia as well as the UNDP.

**Kent Anderson** is a comparative lawyer specializing in Japan. He joined the University of Adelaide in 2012 as Pro Vice-Chancellor (International) and Professor of Law in the Adelaide Law School. He has an eclectic background doing his tertiary studies in Japan, US, and the UK. Kent first worked as a marketing manager with a US regional airline in Alaska, then as a practicing commercial lawyer in Hawaii, and subsequently joined academia as associate professor at Hokkaido University School of Law. For the decade before joining the University of Adelaide, he held a joint appointment at the Australian National University College of Law and Faculty of Asian Studies, where he was Director from 2007–2011.

**Edgardo Buscaglia** is a Senior Scholar in Law and Economics at Columbia University; the Director of the International Law and Economics Development Centre and the President of the Institute for Citizens Action in Mexico. He has served also as Director of the International Law and Economic Development Center at the University of Virginia School of Law, a visiting Professor of Law and Economics at the Mexican Autonomous Insitute of Technology (ITAM, Mexico), University of Virginia, Georgetown University, and has served as a fellow at the Hoover Institution, Stanford University, between 1991 and 2008, as well as an adviser to the United Nations and vice president of the Inter-American Law and Economics Association. He received his legal postdoctoral training in the Jurisprudence and Social Policy Program at the University of California at Berkeley Law School. He also received a master's in law and economics and a PhD in economics from the University of Illinois at Urbana-Champaign. Dr. Buscaglia studies the impact of legal and judicial frameworks on economic development, initially in Latin America but now more broadly. His current research focuses on the economic and legal analysis of transnational organized crime and private/public sector corruption. He has published widely on these subjects.

**Robin Bush** is a Senior Research Fellow in the Religion and Globalization Cluster within the Asia Research Institute (ARI) at the National University of Singapore. She studied political science at the Universities of South Carolina (BA) and Washington (PhD 2002), and international affairs at Ohio University (MA). Her research interests revolve around the interface between Islam, politics, and development, particularly in Indonesia and Southeast Asia. Prior to joining ARI in December 2011, she spent 11 years at The Asia Foundation's Indonesia office. She directed its programs on Islam for the first six years, and served first as Deputy and then Country Representative for the last five years. She has published a book entitled *Nahdlatul Ulama and the Struggle for Power in Islam and Politics in Indonesia* (2009), and is the author of numerous other articles on Islam in Indonesia.

**Liu Dongjin** is an Associate Professor of Peking University Law School and General Secretary of the Beijing International Law Society. He studied economic law (LLB 1985) and international economic law (LLM 1987) at Peking University and has visited at the University of Minnesota Law School and the National University of Singapore (as ASLI Fellow). His interests include international economic law and intellectual property law, international investment law, law on international transfer of technology, WTO law and private international law. He also teaches legal practice and is a part-time legal consultant.

**Peter J. Haas** serves as chair of the Department of Religious Studies at Case Western University in Cleveland, Ohio. He studied Ancient Near East History at the University of Michigan (BA 1970) and received his PhD in Jewish Studies from Brown University (1980). He has taught courses in Judaism, Jewish ethics, the Holocaust and Western religion, and his most recent work is on the relationship between science and moral discourse.

**John O. Haley** is director emeritus of the Whitney R. Harris Institute for Global Legal Studies, Washington University Law School in St. Louis, Missouri, and former director of the Asian Law Program at the University of Washington in Seattle. He received his AB degree at Princeton University (1964) and studied law at Yale University (LLB 1969) and the University of Washington (LLM 1971). He has taught and lectured at Aoyama Gakuin University, Kobe University and Tohoku University in Japan and Tuebingen University in Germany. His research interests encompass comparative law, contracts, Japanese law and transnational litigation. His most recent book, *Antitrust in Germany and Japan: The First Fifty Years, 1947–1998* is the first comparative study of German and Japanese antitrust law in English.

**Andrew Harding** is Professor of Law and Director of the Centre for Asian Legal Studies at the National University of Singapore. He received his MA from Oxford in 1974, his LLM from the National University of Singapore in 1984, and his PhD from Monash University in 1987. He is a leading scholar in Asian comparative law, having served as Head of the School of Law and Professor of Law at the School of Oriental and African Studies (SOAS) at the University of London, and Director of the Centre for Asia-Pacific Initiatives at the University of Victoria, BC Canada. He has previously taught at Harvard Law School, Melbourne Law School, and several other universities across the world. He co-founded and serves as Co-Editor of the series "Constitutional Systems of the World" (Hart). His interests are in Asian legal studies, comparative public law, law and development, comparative law theory and environmental law. His recent publications include *The Constitutional System of Thailand: A Contextual Analysis* (with Peter Leyland, 2011) and *New Courts in Asia* (edited with Pip Nicholson, 2010).

**Darminto Hartono** is a rising economic law scholar teaching at Diponegoro University (UNDIP) Faculty of Law in Semarang, Indonesia. He studied law at UNDIP (SH), Harvard University and Boston University (LLM), and the economic law program at the University of Indonesia, Jakarta (PhD). His area of special expertise is capital markets, bankruptcy and tax law. He has been active as a legal consultant particularly in workouts and insolvency practice since the 1997 Asian Financial Crisis.

**Eugene Huskey** is the William R. Kenan, Jr. Chair and Director of Russian Studies at Stetson University. He studied history and politics at Vanderbilt (BA 1974), politics at the University of Essex (MA 1976) and London School of Economics and Political Science (PhD 1983). His expertise is in Soviet and post-Soviet Russian law. He has held teaching positions at Bowdoin College, Colgate University and Stetson University.

**Joseph M. Isanga** is a faculty member at Ave Maria School of Law in Naples, Florida and former postdoctoral research associate at the University of Notre Dame's Center for Civil and Human Rights. He is a widely published scholar on human rights in Africa and has expertise in international law, jurisprudence, law, ethics and public policy. He is a priest from the Diocese of Jinja, Uganda. He received a BPhil from the Pontifical Urban University in Rome; a BD and LLB from Makerere University in Kampala, Uganda; a Diploma in Legal Practice from Law Development Center in Kampala, Uganda; and an LLM and JSD from the University of Notre Dame, Indiana.

**Peter Kirby** is a graduate student and research assistant at The Australian National University currently completing a thesis on the jury system in Japan. He studied education (BEd) and law (LLB) at the University of Canberra. His scholarly interests include Japanese law, criminal procedure and the rights of indigenous peoples. He is a member of the Wiradjuri Nation of Australian indigenous peoples.

**Michael Kubiciel** is a rising criminal law scholar, who is currently writing his Habilitation at the University of Regensburg Faculty of Law, Germany. He studied law at the Universities of Bonn and Freiburg i.Br. (PhD 2002), Germany as well as Granada, Spain. He is associated as lecturer and senior research assistant with the Chair for Criminal Law, Procedure and Legal Philosophy at Regenburg, and acts as a consultant and expert for the Council of Europe and various United Nations bodies in the corruption area.

**Peter Leyland** is professor of public law at London Metropolitan University and Professorial Research Associate at SOAS, University of London teaching in the areas of administrative law, constitutional law, comparative public law, LLM research methods, and penal policy. He has also been a visiting professor at Bologna, Ferrara, Padua, Rome, Milan, Vienna and Bangkok. His research interests are mainly in British constitutional and administrative law, and comparative constitutional and administrative law with particular focus on France, Italy, Thailand and Southeast Asia. Peter is co-editor of the series "Constitutional Systems of the World" (Hart Publishing), and his recent publications include *The Constitutional System of Thailand: A Contextual Analysis* (with Andrew Harding, 2011) and *The Constitutional System of the United Kingdom: A Contextual Analysis* (2012).

**David K. Linnan** is a scholar of comparative, economic and public international law with a special interest in Asian law. He studied humanities at Emory University (BA 1976) and law at the University of Chicago (JD 1979) and the University of Freiburg i.Br., Germany. He has held research or teaching appointments at the University of South Carolina-Columbia (currently in the School of Law and School of the Environment), the University of Washington-Seattle, the Australian National University in Canberra (RSPAS and Faculty of Law), the University of Melbourne, the University of Indonesia Faculty of Law and Graduate Law Program in Jakarta (separately), and the Max-Planck-Institut (Strafrecht), Freiburg i.Br., Germany. Since 2000 he has been the program director for the Law & Finance Institutional Partnership (www.lfip.org), a legal and financial sector reform project run from Jakarta now as an academic consortium of Indonesian and foreign universities. Since 2007 he has been an associate of the Asian Law Centre, University of Melbourne, Australia.

**Lily Zakiyah Munir** was an Islamic feminist and leading Indonesian Moslem human rights activist who passed away as this book went to press. Following a traditional Islamic secondary education, she studied management at Northern Illinois University and anthropology at the University of Amsterdam. Her research focused on issues of Islam, politics and gender, and she was the founding director of the Centre for Pesantren and Democracy Studies. She was also a national board member of Muslimat Nahdlatul Ulama, the women's wing of Nahdlatul Ulama, the world's largest mass-based Islamic organization with over 30 million members within Indonesia. She visited at the University of South Carolina Law School January–February 2006 to teach in an intensive course entitled "Women's & Human Rights Under Islam."

**Angelika Nußberger** is a sitting judge representing Germany at the European Court of Human Rights in Strasbourg since January 1, 2011. Prior to that, she was a Professor at the Faculty of Law of the University of Cologne, Germany, serving since 2002 as director of its Institute for Eastern European Law. She studied Slavic languages (MA 1987) and law at the Universities of Munich (1984–9), Strasbourg (Diploma in Comparative Law 1988) and Würzburg (PhD 1991). She was formerly an academic researcher at the Max Planck Institute for Foreign and International Social Welfare Law in Munich (1993–2001) and still serves as a member of the Committee of Experts on the Application of Conventions and Recommendations of the International Labour Organisation. She is also a substitute member of the Venice Commission (Commission for Democracy through Law) of the Council of Europe. She has worked as a visiting researcher at Harvard University (1994–5) and as a Legal Counsellor at the Council of Europe in Strasbourg (2001–2). Her research interests encompass public law in Eastern Europe, especially Russia, public international law's effects on legal development of social welfare law in Central and Eastern Europe, and more generally legal development in Central and Eastern Europe.

**Erman Rajagukguk** is a professor of the University of Indonesia Faculty of Law and dean of the Al Azhar Indonesia Faculty of Law who specializes in international and economic law. He studied law at the University of Indonesia (SH) and the University of Washington (LLM, PhD). He also served as Deputy Cabinet Secretary (WASESKAB) of the Republic of Indonesia 1999–2005, and continues to serve as an advisor to the Indonesian Ministry of Justice. The WASESKAB's closest institutional analogue is Legal Counsel to the President in the US governmental system, and he served as the chief lawyer in the Indonesian executive branch responsible under four presidents for legal reform during a period of significant institutional, political and legal change as Indonesia emerged from its authoritarian New Order period 1965–98.

**Joel H. Samuels** teaches law at the University of South Carolina Law School. He studied political science at Princeton University (BA 1994) and law (JD 1999) and Russian & East European Studies (MA 2003) at the University of Michigan. He has worked as visiting faculty member at University of Michigan Law School and also at the World Bank in both Washington and Zimbabwe. His interests encompass Russian law, civil procedure and arbitration as well as public and private international law generally.

**Gordon B. Smith** is Professor of Political Science and Director of the Walker Institute of International and Area Studies at the University of South Carolina. Professor Smith studied journalism and international relations at Iowa State University (BS 1971), and political science at Indiana University (MA 1974; PhD 1976). He also has served as Associate Dean of the College of Liberal Arts at the University of South Carolina (1997–2001), Interim Dean of the College of Liberal Arts (1998–9) and Associate Provost and Dean of the Graduate School (2001–4). Dr. Smith has been a fellow of the Harvard University Davis Russian Research Center, the Kennan Institute for Advanced Russian Studies (Washington, DC), and Russian Studies centers in England and Japan. He was a delegate to the World Justice Forum in 2009 and serves on the International Advisory Board of the Rule of Law Index project.

**Julia Suryakusuma** (www.juliasuryakusuma.com) is an Indonesian social commentator, author, independent scholar and one of her country's first feminists. She studied psychology at the University of Indonesia in Jakarta and then social sciences at the City University, London (BSc), and the politics of development at the Institute of Social Studies in The Hague (MA). Julia is the author of "Sex, Power and Nation: an anthology of writings 1979-2003" (Metafor, 2004). An Indonesian version entitled "*Seks, Agama dan Kekuasaan*" (Sex, Religion and Power), with four additional chapters, was published by Komunitas Bambu in 2012. Her collection of columns, "Julia's Jihad" was published in Korean in 2009, Indonesian in 2010 and English in 2012. Her MA thesis "State Ibuism: the Social Construction of Womanhood in New Order Indonesia", considered a classic for almost a quarter of a century, was published as a bilingual book (in English and Indonesian) in 2011, also by Komunitas Bambu. Her columns, which she has been writing in the English language daily *The Jakarta Post* since 2006, are known for their insight, wit and humour.

**Veronica L. Taylor** is the Director of the School of Regulation, Justice and Diplomacy at Australian National University, Canberra (ANU) and Professor in the Regulatory Institutions Network (RegNet) at ANU. Her work focuses on socio-legal approaches to commercial law in Asia, applied regulatory theory, and rule of law promotion. She has 20 years' experience designing rule of law interventions in Asia and has directed multiyear legal reform projects in Afghanistan and rural China. Her most recent book, edited with Per Berling and Jenny Ederlöf, is *Rule of Law Promotion: Global Perspectives, Local Applications* (Iustus Förlag, 2009) In 2010 she was the inaugural Hague Visiting Professor in Rule of Law at the Hague and the Van Vollenhoven Institute, University of Leiden. She holds degrees in Law and Japanese Studies from Monash University, Australia and an LLM in Asian and Comparative Law from the University of Washington.

**Lydia Brashear Tiede** is an Assistant Professor in the Political Science Department at the University of Houston. She studied History and French at the University of Michigan (BA 1987), Law at American University (JD 1991), Latin American studies at the University of California at San Diego (MA 2002), and received her doctorate in Political Science from the University of California at San Diego (PhD 2008). Her research focuses on American and comparative judicial politics with specific emphasis on the impact of legal and judicial reforms on courts and case outcomes. She also conducts research on judicial independence, the rule of law, and constitutional courts in Latin America and other countries.

**Marsudi Triatmodjo** is Dean of the Faculty of Law, Gadjah Mada University and a scholar of public international law. He studied law at Gadjah Mada University (SH 1984; PhD 2001) and Dalhousie University-Canada (LLM 1990). He has been a researcher and teacher at leading Indonesian institutions of higher education and for the Indonesian government in the areas of public international law, the law of the sea and international environmental law. Most recently he participated in the government-sponsored drafting committee for statutory reform of Indonesian higher education, to move toward autonomous institutions of higher education. He is now implementing the concept in practice.

**Alexei Trochev** is an Associate Professor at the School of Humanities and Social Sciences at Nazarbayev University in Astana, Kazakhstan. Prior to that, he taught at the University of Wisconsin-Madison, Queen's University in Kingston, Canada and the Pomor State University in Arkhangelsk, Russia. His articles on post-Soviet law and politics have appeared in Post-Soviet Affairs, Demokratizatsiya, American Journal of Comparative Law, Law & Society Review, I-CON: International Journal of Constitutional Law, and East European Constitutional Review. His book, "Judging Russia: Constitutional Court in Russian Politics" (Cambridge University Press, 2008) is now available in paperback. His other research projects explore how socialist legacy impacts criminal justice and how political competition simultaneously helps and hurts judicial independence in post-communist countries.

**Raul A. Sanchez Urribarri** is a Lecturer in Legal Studies at LaTrobe University in Melbourne, Australia. For three years prior to that, he was a visiting Assistant Professor at the Political Science Department of Tulane University, New Orleans. He is a graduate of the Universidad Catolica's Law School in Caracas, Venezuela (LLB 1997), Cambridge University (LLM 1999) and the University of South Carolina (PhD 2011). Before studying political science, Raul practiced law as an assistant clerk at the Venezuelan Supreme Court for five years and worked as a part-time instructor and lecturer of law in Caracas. His research is in the field of judicial politics (both domestic and comparative) and the study of politics in Latin America.

# Acknowledgments

Lily Zakiyah Munir (alm.), who contributed the chapter "Rules and Behavior in Judging *Shari'ah*: A Woman's Perspective," passed away too early as this book went to press. She will be missed dearly by her friends and family in Indonesia, Afghanistan and elsewhere.

Angelika Nussberger's chapter entitled "Rebuilding the Tower of Babel—The European Court of Human Rights and the Diversity of Legal Cultures" is based on a paper presented at the Constitutional Forum in Moscow in 2006 which was dedicated to the subject "European Convention on Human Rights and Fundamental Freedoms in the XXI Century: Problems and Prospects of Implementation." A slightly different version of the text was published in Russian in *Sravnitel'noe Konstitucionnoe Pravo* 2007, No. 2, pp. 71–9.

Veronica Taylor's chapter entitled "Japan's Legal Technical Assistance Efforts: A Different Modernization Narrative?" is adapted from "Rule of Law Assistance Discourse and Practice: Japanese Inflections," in *Law in Pursuit of Development: Principles into Practice?*, edited by Amanda Perry-Kessaris (Abingdon: Routledge-Cavendish, 2009), pp. 161–79.

# Chapter 1

# Introduction to Legal Development and Change

David K. Linnan

This book explores overlapping themes, asking how legal development and change actually work. We approach the questions in comparative, empirical terms, searching for answers in specific legal system examples, rather than pursuing theory in the abstract. Thus we ask questions about traditional schools like "modernization theory" or "Law and Development," but we do so within a framework of 23 country chapters. There are now non-Western legal development alternatives, so we need a better way to ask comparable questions of different approaches.

At a practical level, we tackle the problem of "law in the books" versus "law in action." Legal change is embedded in modernization, but presents an underlying "chicken or egg" question. Can law be employed to shape behavior as a form of social engineering, or must social behavior change first, relegating legal change to follow as a form of ratification or reinforcement of changed behavior? The problem is that most legal development efforts simply assume an instrumental effect. Yet that may be only the first in a series of issues. The hidden concern may be the relationship between legitimacy and instrumentalist approaches to legal development. But we also speak as though contemplating an ahistorical, homogenous society as subject, yet matters are rarely so simple. Meanwhile, if legitimacy is the bridge to social change through legal development, how do we conceptualize and examine social change when its motivating values may not be our own?

Legitimacy itself requires unpacking too, since it traditionally presumes in Western views of legal development certain relationships between government, civil society, citizens and growth. In a nutshell, how to understand the overlap in the context of legal development between the legal and economic fields, more or less in parallel with the overlap between the legal and political (democratization) fields? There are indeed values seemingly embedded in Western rule of law (ROL) work, particularly when examined at the level of ideas concerning the proper relationship between human rights, democracy and economic growth. But how shall we validly measure and evaluate ROL beyond comfortable Western boundaries?

Is a growing emphasis on non-Western alternatives the natural counterweight to the modernization concept's implicit assumption of secular, national law as part of economic and social development? How then shall we deal with legal pluralism as feature of many developing countries? Modernization theory as the social science-based development concept of the 1960s addressed to traditional society in lower income countries was one thing, yet "modernization" is an ongoing process also in middle income countries in most of the globalized, developing world. But *whose* version of modernization will predominate absent a Western monopoly on change? And what is legal development's source of legitimacy, if not modernization?

The acute focus from an American perspective is currently on the "failed state" phenomenon and, separately, the Islamic world. Meanwhile, among developing countries, Asia is broadly recognized as representing successful economic development worthy of emulation. The implicit disconnect is that the developing world may look to Asia as an economic success story, but American views of legal development currently look backwards to the transitional economies of culturally Western, formerly Socialist Europe in the 1990s. The practical question becomes how to bridge the gap to understand legal development and change in the non-Western setting.

Thematically, we first examine different approaches to the general problem of understanding legal development in empirical rather than ideological terms. We then shift to a more pointed inquiry targeting the overlap between customary, religious and secular law in legal development, including weighing the implicit question whether mostly conservative social views present in *shari'ah* law in particular are a product of religious views or social conservatism (tribalism). Finally, we look at several different countries and international law to address special aspects.

## Changing the Rule of Law Narrative

Part I (of seven) of our book commences with five chapters addressing general aspects of legal development, legitimacy and modernization. Under differing points of view, donor-driven legal transplantation may encompass anything from traditional development assistance focused on economic growth, democratization and governance assistance, through trade facilitation technical assistance, to pre-/post-conflict and security sector, as well as generic rule of law assistance focused on law enforcement. Our own interest is directed more narrowly at legal development as part of traditional development, while still recognizing that law's role in development changed when development itself began to target private foreign investment. The US government's high profile working ROL concept in conflict and post-conflict countries (3C, or courts, cops and corrections) is somewhat misleading as pursued, but that same usage is paralleled in UN peacemaking/ keeping/building activities. Such activity may serve foreign policy purposes, but is hardly legal development in any ordinary sense. Meanwhile, non-Western competition now exists in ordinary legal development, looking in particular to Asian examples.

David Linnan notes a surprising lack of attention to the empirical question whether and how legal development actually works. He raises the chicken or egg question addressing instrumentalist assumptions underlying Law and Development approaches, or, more recently, American ROL work generally. The question is whether today's ROL efforts are simply a continuation of early 1960s modernization theory and the Law and Development approach in "old wine, new bottles" terms, harking back to questions about "liberal legalism," argued links between democracy and economic development, and an intellectual partnership between American foreign policy and academic social science. A new form of modernization theory can rescue some of its earlier insights, but it should be equally applicable to non-Western legal development concepts also, focusing on demographic trends and the degree of urbanization present, and a renewed focus on social psychology (because of legitimacy concerns), in a change from the pure new institutional economics IFI focus since the 1990s. It also requires closer attention to individual behavior in adapting to ROL changes, since instrumental behavior is visible there. The problem with simple conclusions, however, is that the developing world itself is beginning to push the arguable bounds of ROL work from domestic to international law, pushing back in many ways independent of traditional formulations such as an assumed relationship between democracy and economic growth (e.g., in connection with climate change).

Joseph Isanga notes that, from the African perspective, ROL is understood as Westernization and a continuation of the Washington Consensus. Further, ROL approaches have not led to much economic improvement in Africa's circumstances. They do not address well the reality that an overwhelming majority of Africans still live in rural (traditional) society, while even in urban areas traditional attitudes to authoritarian leadership have been carried forward. Some African leaders manipulate ROL and democracy claims to buttress their own political positions with the donor community (and anti-corruption laws being employed opportunistically to attack political opponents is not solely an African phenomenon). From an African perspective, more attention should be paid to issues like education as a precondition to real development, since democratic choice and governance are hollow concepts if exercised by poorly educated majority rural populations on the basis of ill-suited Western categories. Exemplary African leaders pursuing an African vision do exist, but they tend to be underappreciated in the West.

Andrew Harding and Peter Leyland examine the contradictions now visible in acutely polarized Thai law and society, particularly in Thailand's juxtaposition of political stalemate and repeated governmental flip-flops between the (pro-Shinawatra, traditional rural-based) "Red Shirts" versus (nominally monarchist, modern Bangkok-based) "Yellow Shirts" in the Thai parliament and on Bangkok's streets. The ultimate problem may be whether Thailand's true constitution is an unwritten one based upon concepts of the Thai people like *chat* (nation), *satsana* (religion) and *mahakesat* (monarchy) as civic religion, versus Western categories of constitution-making incorporating the received formal categories like separation of powers and the judiciary. The current level of discourse challenging even principles like "one man, one vote" raises the question whether legal reforms were ever adopted on a principled basis, as opposed merely to serve the political interests of their proponents. So, in chicken or egg terms, what is the message about constitutionalism as applied within Thai society? Can legal and constitutional institutions overcome deep social divisions and divergent political outlooks (and a political culture focused more on individuals than policies)? Judging by Thailand's example, social consensus must precede law.

Darminto Hartono addresses the empirical question of whether and how individuals learn to operate in a new, ROL-inspired legal environment. On the example of Indonesian corporate reorganizations following significant changes in insolvency law, the answer is that individuals are observed to learn, but behave instrumentally in pursuing new legal forms to their own ends. Here the object lesson is that legal development may change observed behavior, but that does not necessarily mean that it shapes underlying beliefs. Instead, compared to implicit ROL views verging on law as self-implementing norm, actors in the (changed) legal system navigate the changes to serve their own self-interest. This behavior is not unlike that of sophisticated parties in Western countries pursuing litigation among a portfolio of business strategies. At the empirical level, current instrumentalist views generally may overlook the idea that legal development in creating modern "commercial rules" may simply represent one more theater of action for commercial parties. And on the evidence of Isanga's discussion of African leaders manipulating ROL efforts, Hartono's perception of self-interested actors within a changing legal environment may not be limited to the commercial sphere.

Liu Dongjin describes changes in Chinese economic law dating back to the 1949 founding of the People's Republic of China. Rather than following ROL lines, his presentation is a road map of practical experimentation in the service of China's economic development in moving since the 1980s toward a market-based economy. To that extent, it is probably best viewed in the tradition of Japan's nineteenth-century embrace of (Western) law as a means of modernization and development. Borrowings have come from many different external sources, while internal experimentation is chronicled over time. On a doctrinal level, China appears to share the Korean and Japanese experience of borrowing more in a technical sense from Civil Law rather than Common Law legal systems. Meanwhile, Liu notes that the Chinese distinguish between differing economic approaches within the West, finding the European (social democratic) approach to a market-based economy more congenial. China's economic success calls into question the common assertion of an automatic link between democratization, modernization and rule of law raised also in David

Linnan's historical examination of the original modernization concept. This Chinese affinity for the European approach to the market implicitly entails a rejection of the Washington Consensus. This raises the issue in the ROL context of a "Beijing Consensus" offering a differing approach to markets (differing or alternate views of capitalism have been a staple of Asian economic development for decades). Liu's description of the Chinese experience ultimately constitutes a counterexample for the Law and Development approach understood as "liberal legalism."


## Religious Law as Religious and Social Form

Part II of our book shifts its focus to the specific area of religious law encompassing in a practical sense both religious and social beliefs. The question is the extent to which rules may be claimed as religious imperatives, while actually representing effectively social or "tribal" norms. Implicitly the emphasis is on relatively sophisticated theological or theoretical discussion. Part III addresses how things work on the ground in a key Muslim majority developing country, specifically Indonesia. Assuming high legitimacy of religious views in many settings, how beyond theological disputation can we separate out tribal from truly religious norms and what is the relevance for our basic chicken or egg question?

Tarak Abdallah opines that modernization was originally based upon concepts of economic growth following the West. Meanwhile, conceptually development was shaped by neoclassical economic views, particularly IFIs attempting to implement the Washington Consensus. Within the Islamic world, conceptually modernization is typically interpreted as Westernization. The Islamic vision has been focused on the human dimension within societies at a level recalling more economic sociology than law. Those outside the Islamic tradition struggle with recognizing any concept of "law" in such discussions.

The Islamic view is that questions of governance surrounding social and economic relations lie at the heart of laws, compared to concepts like charity and endowment which play an analogous role to civil society under Western governance concepts (providing distance to the state). The ultimate result is a rejection of "market fundamentalism" under Islamic approaches as regulating mechanism (including the idea of a perfectly rational "economic man"), because it incorporates pure efficiency and utility-based approaches. Turning to discussions of modernization in the context of "traditional" versus "modern" societies, the problem from an Islamic viewpoint is the reductionism of Western economic thought which traditionally denies any value to economic history outside of capitalism and neoclassical economics apart from limited nascent discussion of concepts like "sustainable development." The idea of a chicken or egg problem and instrumental approaches can be posed in the Islamic context insofar as the development of law is tied to development of institutions and human relationships.

Lily Zakiyah Munir initially distinguishes doctrinally between *shari'ah* as religious law and *fiqh* as its context bound human interpretation via *ijtihad* or consideration by Islamic scholars. *Fiqh* brings with it the frailties of any human interpreter including also its potential incorporation into secular law in modern Muslim majority societies, typically via a constitutional requirement of secular law's "consistency" with Islamic principles. So how does one derive applicable principles in the Islamic context? The Islamic version of the chicken or egg problem is probably best understood in conjunction with two competing approaches to interpretation.

This involves a traditional preference for textual interpretation (via *ahlul hadith*, or people of the text) over ethically or rationally based interpretation (via *ahlur ra'yi*, or people of ratio). Textual approaches predominate in Islamic practice, with constant reference made to historical texts in a literal interpretive mode, as opposed to ethical modes of interpretation where the attempt is made to separate the general principles of a text like a Qur'anic passage from its historical framework on the Arabian Peninsula. Those pursuing strictly textual interpretive approaches to *shari'ah* seemingly assume that articulating textually derived rules will change behavior. Meanwhile, those believing that *shari'ah* should follow an ethical or moral interpretation seemingly believe that ethical beliefs must underpin social behavior, rendering it a precursor to changing behavior (behavior only follows ethical precept). This kind of division is particularly visible in the treatment of women under the differing approaches, but represents a wider interpretive pattern.

Peter Haas examines the problem of social change and legal development from a historical perspective via the reform of Jewish legal status in nineteenth-century Europe, particularly in France (1806–7) and Germany (1820–50). Since the Middle Ages, Jews residing in European countries typically had a semi-autonomous status under the local monarch allowing for the application of Jewish religious law (*halacha*) in a manner comparable to consular jurisdiction. The legal history of their formal emancipation lies buried in questions like the original significance of legal "capacity" for citizens under the Code Civil of Napoleonic France (abolishing all outmoded personal status forms like serfdom in favor of the autonomous republican citizen). The so-called Jewish question of the period was whether the historically separate community of Jews (a "nation" in nineteenth-century terminology) should be fully incorporated into the new French and German nations (assimilated in legal terms). The question of legal development and change arose in addressing whether and how Jews could lose their special status in favor of full citizenship; whether *halacha* would continue to apply to the Jews, or whether secular national law should take its place (bearing in mind the pattern of civil marriage generally, under which to this day the only "legal" marriage ceremonies are secular and take place at city hall—*la Mairie* in France, *das Standesamt* in Germany—while parallel religious ceremonies are deemed mere cultural exercises).

Formally speaking, the French example seems to support the proposition that French Jews could be made into French citizens in the eyes of broader French society by the social engineering exercise of top-down articulation of secular law. On the other hand, the German example appears to support the idea that social change must come first from the bottom up, since the legal assimilation question itself fractured the German Jewish community into competing segments based upon views of the relative legitimacy of *halacha* versus secular law.

### *Shari'ah*, Customary and Secular National Laws' Interplay in the World's Most Populous Islamic Country

Part III of our book shifts the focus from religious versus social views at a higher theoretical level to the question of how legal development works on the ground in modern Southeast Asia as non-Western environment. We focus the inquiry on Indonesia as the world's most populous Muslim developing country with circa 240 million inhabitants, of which approximately 89 percent are Muslims, even though Indonesia is not a sectarian or Islamic state in technical terms. Indonesia itself is a legally pluralistic environment, importantly recognizing for our purposes traditional ethnic or tribally-based customary law (*adat*), Islamic (*shari'ah*) and secular national law. To that extent it is a veritable laboratory for questions of legitimacy and legal development in the non-Western setting.

To provide the necessary depth of understanding of Indonesia's complex law and society, Part III's three chapters are intended to be read cumulatively. Robin Bush's chapter provides a historical framework for the political and legal interplay between Islamic forces and Indonesian nationalism at the constitutional level reaching back to the colonial period. Julia Suryakusuma's chapter is written from the modern female Muslim social commentator's viewpoint, addressing issues of conservative Muslim religious groups' voice, religious influence on women's place in society in the wake of Indonesia's veritable democratic explosion since 1998, and controversial anti-pornography legislation with differing significance for different social groups. Suryakusuma speaks implicitly from the position of "modern" Indonesia, meaning here Jakarta as major urban area comparable in size and sophistication to New York or Tokyo. Erman Rajagukguk's chapter is a legal ethnographic work addressing the interplay between *adat, shari'ah* and secular national law in women's inheritance matters among the *Sasak* ethnic group on Lombok Island, a more traditional rural society (although now exposed to tourism, since Islamic Lombok lies close by Hindu Bali with comparable beaches).

Robin Bush addresses Islam and constitutionalism in Indonesia. Nationalist and religious elements have coexisted in Indonesian politics under varying degrees of tension since late colonial times. To avoid threatened secession by the Christian majority islands of Eastern Indonesia, something of a grand bargain was struck at independence under which religion was recognized as important constitutionally, but Islam as such was specifically not given any special or superior status. For the next 50+ years much of Indonesia's Islamic religious and political leadership periodically tried to revisit and reverse this grand bargain in the name of recognizing some kind of special status or treatment for Indonesia's Muslim majority.

Tracing electoral results over time, however, a majority of Indonesian Muslims have aligned themselves with nationalist rather than Islamic parties (and at this point it would appear that fewer than one in three Indonesian Muslims votes for Islamic parties). Thus, a majority of the population has seemingly embraced a pluralist, nationalist identity, but that does not entail any embrace of secularism as such. There are geographic exceptions such as the introduction in Aceh of *kanun* or local Islamic law as part of the 2005 resolution of Aceh's long-running insurgency. However, a relatively high proportion of the Indonesian population has "voted with their feet" by implicitly rejecting Islamic political party proposals in recent electoral campaigns for the general introduction of *shari'ah* law (in voting for nationalist parties, a majority of whose members may be Muslims, but who would reject such changes as a threat to national unity). But the very act of periodically revisiting the appropriate role of Islam within Indonesia's political and legal system speaks to the complexity of Indonesian attitudes toward religion and its proper place within their society. There seems currently strong political will for increased public expression of Islam, and for the increased integration of "Islamic values" into the political system. This ongoing process of integrating Islamic values seems a prime example of the chicken or egg question in non-Western legal development.

Julia Suryakusuma addresses current legal developments and Indonesian politics as they affect women in particular. Her focus is on the controversial recent enactment of Indonesia's Anti-Pornography Law No. 44 of 2008, which was strongly supported by conservative Islamic groups and politicians, but drew equally strong opposition from women's advocacy, progressive and non-Muslim groups generally. How could women's groups in particular oppose any measures against pornography?

A comparison is drawn between the role of the Christian and Muslim right wings in American and Indonesian politics, creating moral panics under which religious groups embrace a conservative social agenda, to the general detriment of women. The definition of pornography is broad enough to regulate women's dress and behavior, which is viewed as problematic. The political fight casts those who speak against the law as being in favor of pornography, while in the face of general non-enforcement it would appear that the law's stance is more symbolic than real. This is

regarded as evidence of "Arabization" of Indonesian Islam, understood as encroachment of Middle Eastern (typically *Salafist*) views that differ from traditional Islam within Indonesia, and the use of religion for political purposes. The question is whether this represents an effort at non-Western modernization (insofar as it represents an attempt to change social norms, and in Suryakusuma's view is undertaken by a small number of activists).

At the political level, the democratic flowering which followed the 1998 end of authoritarian government freed not only the progressives, but also resuscitated traditional leadership on the local level of society, including socially conservative Islamicists. Julia Suryakusuma sees the social debate growing in complexity and extending over time, paralleling the sentiment expressed by Robin Bush of increasing integration of Islamic views into the political system. The question within Indonesian Islam, however, is *whose* Islamic views?

Erman Rajagukguk approaches the problem of legal change in women's inheritance rights among Lombok's *Sasak* ethnic group as a legal ethnographic problem tracing the overlap of *adat*, *shari'ah* and secular national law. He has the eye of someone who has been responsible for legal development within the executive branch of the Indonesian government, and as the responsible (Muslim) lawyer within government considered the technical details surrounding introduction of *kanun* or local Islamic law consistent with international human rights law pursuant to the 2005 Helsinki MOU ending the Acehnese insurgency. For his chapter, however, he traveled the rural back roads of Lombok, interviewing ordinary people about the resolution of inheritance disputes (also often outside the court system), reading local court decisions, and talking with elders about changes in the customary law community. He captures women's inheritance as demonstrating the process of legal change, documenting evolution toward a plurality of legal resolutions among which individuals may choose presumably based upon legitimacy concerns.

Lombok's Muslim *Sasak* ethnic community divides into three groups in inheritance matters. The first represents a continuation of the traditional *Sasak* patriarchal customary law rule under which women are ineligible to receive any inheritance in the form of real property or similar core family goods. This group has been reduced to small numbers, but traditional *adat* can retain its authoritative status within rural villages where inheritance matters never go to court (and challenging the traditional rules amounts to electing out of the customary law community, which may go so far as to exclude in and out-marriage). The second community group represents those Muslims who accept the Islamic legal principle that a daughter should receive half the inheritance portion of her brother. Government religious courts in Lombok always firmly adhere to that principle, which is sometimes implemented also under an alternative dispute resolution (ADR) approach when inheritance complaints are brought to respected local Islamic scholars as mediators in lieu of going to court. The third community group represents that part of the Muslim *Sasak* community willing to bring their inheritance disputes to the secular district courts, where social change has been recognized to the extent that both the traditional customary law resolution of no inheritance by women, and the traditional Islamic law resolution of half inheritance shares for women, are rejected in favor of equal inheritance by women on the basis of equal protection principles in modern Indonesian law and society.

There are two notable aspects to this tripartite resolution given our focus on legitimacy. The first is that, despite having appellate (cassation) jurisdiction over both the religious and secular district courts, the Indonesian Supreme Court has been willing to postulate changes in women's status only in reviewing decisions from the (secular) district courts technically applying *adat* or national law. It has never exercised its review power to change distributions determined in the religious courts. Thus, the Supreme Court seems very cautious if confronted with traditional Islamic law argued in terms of Qur'anic text and hadiths. The second is the implicit question of why and how a potential claimant chooses between the district and religious courts (or chooses ADR also via leadership of the customary law community versus Islamic scholars), which coexist in Lombok's relatively traditional, rural or small town devout Muslim communities.

In ordinary economic terms, it seemingly would make no sense for *Sasak* women in Lombok to accept less than a full inheritance share (so the assumption is that they should always choose the secular district court as dispute resolution venue in the classic ROL sense). However, living in Lombok, recognized within Indonesia as a relatively devout Islamic region, and living within the *Sasak* ethnic group with its own customary law, it would appear that many if not most women seek greater legitimacy in challenging the traditional "no female inheritance" *Sasak* customary law rule under the tenets of Islamic law, where they have the benefit of the "female half inheritance share" rule. The perception that Islamic law enjoys special social legitimacy is reinforced by the idea that not only many women elect to resolve the disputes under religious law in choosing the religious court or Islamic scholars for ADR purposes, but the Indonesian Supreme Court implicitly has chosen to "modernize" customary or secular national law, but seemingly hesitates to do the same when faced with Islamic law.

In terms of our chicken or egg question, in the context of Lombok's mostly traditional society, it would appear that social beliefs must change, as under Islam versus presumably pre-Islamic customary law, before merely changing law changes behavior. But the most striking aspect may be that social legitimacy affects individual decisions, since in a pluralistic legal setting the individuals implicitly choose their own rules in choosing to pursue dispute resolution through different venues applying the differing legal resolutions. This echoes Darminto Hartono's observation at the individual level of instrumental behavior by debtors learning the ropes in corporate reorganizations carried out under Indonesia's new insolvency law (so instrumentalist behavior is not just present in commercial law cases). Those looking at cultural or institutional explanations of behavior presumably note that the "mental map" in legitimacy involves choice among multiple, sometimes conflicting, legal sources, which infers that there is arguably more than one appropriate choice in legitimacy terms, since the women in question choose their own outcomes based upon their venue choices.


## Japan's Once and Future Legal Modernization Narrative

Part IV of our book shifts the focus to Japan as the original nineteenth-century Asian development success story, and one of the new Asian alternate sources for legal development support. Japan presents an equally complex law and society, so Part IV's three chapters are intended again to be read cumulatively.

Veronica Taylor presents the status of Japan's ongoing legal technical assistance efforts generally in Asia. Japanese lawyers are specifically agnostic toward the Washington Consensus (economics plays little role in Japanese legal education, and its professionals otherwise are standoffish toward US Law and Development efforts generally). Japan seemingly desires to replicate Japan's Civil Law nineteenth-century legal development experience in countries like Cambodia, Vietnam and portions of Central Asia. The Japanese approach both emphasizes its Asian credentials and alternative character, since Japan is the original locus of the claim, understood in opposition to transaction cost minimization economic analysis, that ROL as such is not crucial for development ("law" being understood for these purposes as a strong legal framework at the level of private rights under neoclassical economic approaches, as opposed to "policy-oriented" government actions under alternate views of capitalism). Instead, Japan's own legal development efforts are driven within Asia by a combination of perceived complementarities with developing Asia and leadership competition with China (as another prominent alternative legal development model).

John Haley addresses the idea that, while Japan is currently portrayed as moving toward a "rights-based society," with a view toward our chicken or egg question, due to a different legal history, it is unclear whether the rights concept is fully transferable. The basic conceptual issue is that, in the Sino-legal tradition, law is more a means of steering behavior under communitarian assumptions via criminal and administrative law, rather than representing individual claims of moral or legal right. As such, the missing conceptual underpinning in a traditional sense is the Western conception of rights as morally-based, legally enforceable claims between private parties (private rights), and separately again against the state (public or civil rights). Instead, litigation seems more often part of a broader strategy to spur government action, in a manner analogous to environmental litigation being pursued in the United States as part of an integrated political strategy, rather than with an eye to winning a judgment on the merits to remediate environmental problems.

We note that this indirectly raises again differences of opinion concerning human rights visible elsewhere between American views of civil and political rights, which it supports strongly as "law," versus foreign prominence often given to economic and social rights, which the American government regards more as aspirational and "political" in nature (this may represent a coming source of tension with developing countries in areas like climate change). This indicates why "liberal legalism" could be merely an American rather than international aspiration if underlying social values place a higher priority on communal rather than individual well-being. The insight at the level of our chicken or egg inquiry is that, in the absence of a shared technical conception of rights, instrumental use of law may be a one-way street in which citizen actions are shaped, but more often as part of a chiefly political rather than legal process. And in the absence of a strong private rights framework, transaction cost economics-based explanations of the role of law in development hardly make sense.

Kent Anderson and Peter Kirby's chapter provides an illustrative counterpoint. They look at the recent reintroduction into Japanese criminal procedure of jury trials for serious criminal offenses. "Reintroduction" because a similar effort to establish criminal jury trials failed to take root 1920–40 in Japan, with the resultant question being why the introduction of jury trials failed the first time (and what that says about current prospects for successful reintroduction). The surprising aspect is that the jury sought to be introduced is more analogous to the American jury, rather than the lay judges of Continental criminal procedure (meaning the *Schöffengericht* of German criminal procedure, which otherwise shaped much of Japanese law). So the question is the extent to which a system to encourage lay participation in the Japanese criminal justice system is reconcilable with the kinds of structural differences to which John Haley alludes. The answer remains open because the reintroduction is still very recent, but may indicate whether Japan can succeed in its stated goal of becoming a rights-based society. But what constitutes "rights," assuming with John Haley an historical emphasis on communalism, and social rather than legal control?


**Latin America, Post Conflict and the Judiciary**

Part V of our book focuses on the peculiar problem that law and legal norms require implementation via the judicial system, sometimes referred to as the problem of law "in the books" versus "in action." Reform of judicial systems has been a longtime ROL focus, particularly in Latin America, so that here we are introduced to the complication that legal development includes also a bureaucratic or administrative component (including political science approaches exploring views of elites versus ordinary citizens via such means as public opinion surveys and quantitative analysis). In broader ROL terms, Latin America was also the original center of transitional justice, as human rights endeavor, so that we also look to transitional justice's overlap with legal development. The three chapters largely focus on public law like the criminal justice system, rather than private law matters, but in the context of Latin America's middle income, arguably culturally more "Western" countries.

Edgardo Buscaglia seeks necessary conditions for effective implementation of laws, looking to reduce the gap between law in the books versus law in action as his approach to the chicken or egg question. He applies jurimetrics and economic analysis in a law and economics of development approach, seemingly accepting instrumentalist assumptions typically rejected by other chapter authors. Looking initially to the top-down versus bottom-up question of law-making from a civilian viewpoint, he notes that the top-down method may divorce the formal legal system from custom or commercial practice, driving large segments of the population to pursue informal means to address grievances. He then examines legal transplants through the lens of responses to organized crime (Palermo Convention) and its connection with weak ROL in terms of judicial effectiveness.

There is a link between court ineffectiveness and legal implementation, while addressing problems like administrative weaknesses and politicized judicial appointments has shown relative success in improving judicial performance. The problem is that many lower and middle income countries grossly underfund the judicial system, particularly as compared with police, so that prosecutorial and judicial systems are simply unable to implement law in combating organized crime. So instrumentalist assumptions collide with underfunding with the result that the formal law does not work. Judicial accountability and independence exist in a complicated balance, which requires more attention to political balance rather than formal accountability at the constitutional level (judging by the fact that leading industrialized countries without such constitutional protections for judicial independence nonetheless enjoy it).

Raul Sanchez Urribari approaches the effectiveness question from the perspective of judicial politics, drawing specifically on Latin American examples to explore the mismatch of formal judicial independence within particularistic political systems (which describes many, if not most, lower and middle income countries in which politics may be more personally than programmatically oriented, including Andrew Harding and Peter Leyland's chapter touching on Thai politics). Rather than the institutional efficiency focus stressed by Edgardo Buscaglia, he sees persistent judicial loyalties having a negative effect on judicial quality and explains why certain reform initiatives have failed. The problem is not how judges reach decisions in normal cases, but rather how informal connections influence those cases in which the judiciary is called upon as supposedly neutral arbiters to rein in unruly political actors. This analysis applies to both democratic and non-democratic regimes.

The apparent surge of judicial power within Latin America is portrayed in an unreservedly positive light in typical ROL analysis, but the empowerment of courts and the politicization of the judiciary are not mutually exclusive. Looking at judicial effectiveness in light of the chicken or egg problem, however, the key is that formal institutions affecting inter-branch relations will be poor predictors of actual behavior in (developing) countries where the gap between formal and informal politics is prominent. This leads us theoretically back to the idea missing from typical ROL analysis, already highlighted in conjunction with Darminto Hartono and Erman Rajagukguk's chapters, of a self-interested or public choice element in the instrumental behavior of actors within the legal system. This illustrates why formal institutions may matter less than political and social culture, while ROL analysis typically focuses exclusively on institutions (because "politics" is perceived as inconsistent with "law" for ROL purposes, at least insofar as "liberal legalism" is concerned).

Lydia Brashear Tiede addresses legal change in Chilean criminal justice, examining developments over a 20+ year period dating back to the authoritarian Pinochet regime's 1990 handover of power (up to the current day's democratic government; so a successful experiment in democratization). She examines in the longer term what may become of transitional justice, exploring also differences of outlook between elites and ordinary citizens in their differing estimations of human rights-based "due process" versus public safety-oriented "crime control" models of criminal justice. These outcomes manifested themselves over time as the Chilean truth and reconciliation commission first emphasized a human rights-inspired reform of Chile's colonial era criminal procedure code to increase defendants' rights to something comparable to modern Western European criminal procedure ("international standards," in ROL terminology, albeit in the Continental public law or Civilian tradition). Chile originally enacted such reforms during the 1990s in pursuing a "due process" model of criminal justice rooted in ideals of democracy and ROL, followed by subsequent legislatures starting in 2003 to cut back on defendants' rights under a "crime control" approach when faced from conservative political forces with a drumbeat campaign of (arguably unfounded) claims in the mass media about rising ordinary criminality.

In terms of the chicken or egg question, Tiede emphasizes that legal reforms are a longer term effort, capturing the "push–pull" nature of reforms in a media-driven, relatively democratic environment. So social engineering could hardly take place over a short period of time. In a democratic environment, as memories of the bad old days fade and in response to "law and order" rhetoric concerning rising crime rates, citizens may push political leaders to cut back on criminal defendants' rights (with the chief surprise being how short a time period may be required for the flip-flop in social views). In the case of Chile as middle income country, however, there was no substantial evidence of views differing between urban and rural areas. So is the proper interpretation for purposes of our chicken or egg inquiry that middle income countries are generally already "modernized," or that middle income Latin American countries, in comparison to Africa or Asia, consists of "Western" societies anyway (or both)?


**Russia and the State: A Window on Modernization**

Part VI of our book focuses on the peculiar status of post-Soviet Russia as a locus of continuing "modernization" efforts over time. Russia itself presents an equally complex law and society, so Part VI's four chapters are intended again to be read cumulatively. Russia is regarded in Western ROL circles as somewhat problematic due to a perception of post-Soviet democratization efforts waxing and waning. At the same time, however, Russia vigorously pursued economic liberalization and the development of economic law in a fashion that seemingly drew from the IFI standard playbook. So middle income Russia may simply be pursuing its own version of a "Beijing Consensus," including heavy state involvement in the natural resource economy as counterweight to oligarchy; notwithstanding the traditional Western linkage between democratization and economic development modeled on the Washington Consensus.

Gordon Smith explores the idea that post-Soviet Russian legal development efforts targeting "international standards" are simply the third or fourth cycle of what we would consider Russia's modernization efforts. The Soviet Union's dilemma in the early Perestroika period as an industrialized country (hence already modern and developed under traditional views, albeit ambiguously "Westernized") reflected a split between those favoring the values of an independent legal system following "international standards" to replace socialist legality, and others favoring policy over law as a powerful instrument supporting the state's efforts to implement yet another plan of modernization and social engineering. So our chicken or egg problem as duality has seemingly deep roots in Russian society and history.

Tsar Alexander II, under the reforms of 1864, introduced modernizing measures modeled on German law (analogously to Meiji Japan), but subsequent economic and political issues snuffed out those reforms in favor of competing revolutionary and utopian concepts of legality through the 1917 revolution. The early post-revolutionary days knew two countervailing trends, neither of which drew upon Weberian views which arguably still underpin ROL as concept. The first was the Marxist, utopian trend which stressed the withering away of law and the state under socialism, and the creation of popular, informal tribunals to administer revolutionary justice. The second, Leninist or dictatorial trend perceived law as a powerful social engineering tool to be subordinated to revolutionary goals of the party (capturing the converse of "liberal legalism" in the idea that all law had a class character, with the result that, if it did not serve the Bolsheviks' purposes, it would serve counter-revolutionary purposes).

The dictatorial approach won out under Stalin who, for all his well-documented crimes before World War II, industrialized and coincidentally urbanized what was by Western standards still a traditional society (the rural peasantry of Tsarist Russia) as part of the Soviet modernization plan. Gone were ideas about the withering away of the state, and the hyper-centralized state bureaucracy Stalin designed in creating a state-owned economy still lives on in many ways. But, looking solely to the chicken or egg question, the Soviet Union under Stalin actively pursued a vision of social engineering to produce the New Soviet Man and succeeded at industrialization via "law" (but certainly not in the sense of ROL's "liberal legalism"; here we recall the thick versus thin rule of law debate). This parallels also John Haley's observation about the paucity of "rights" analysis in Sino-legal historical terms, with the current legal development question being whether this time those in Russia favoring rule *of* law rather than rule *by* law will succeed. To the extent ROL now does succeed as another approach to Russian legal development it would represent presumably the view that law can only ratify changed social concepts. In practical terms, to a great extent Russians already have drawn away from the concept of social engineering through law, due to a perception that they have been the subject too often of social experiments lately.

Looking to the three remaining chapters, they concern ROL interpretation and document aspects of bureaucratic or institutional resistance to change. As such they are representative of more general patterns in legal development at the lower and middle income country level. The issues may be summed up in the question whether such resistance to implementation of reforms based in particular upon IFI economic views represents: (1) a corruption problem (petty officialdom extorting rents); (2) an ideological problem (individual officials having a principled disagreement with government policy in transitioning to a market-based, capitalist economic system, or challenging governance approaches like decentralization as likely to lead to chaos); or (3) an envy problem (pique at the newly rich entrepreneurial classes running up against relatively poor *nomenklatura* still in control of the machinery of government).

What is their significance for our chicken or egg inquiry? The corruption explanation is probably best viewed as a specific example of the public choice or instrumentalist point of view for actors in the (new) legal system in which manipulation simply goes outside the legal system (recalling Joseph Isanga, Darminto Hartono and Erman Rajagukguk's chapters). The ideological problem is probably best understood as a specific example of the view that social behavior must change first, and legal change can only follow as form of ratification or reinforcement of changed behavior (recalling Peter Haas and Andrew Harding and Peter Leyland's chapters). The envy problem is probably best understood as another variation on the public choice or instrumentalist point of view for actors in the (new) legal system. The notable absence of the social engineering explanation may illustrate its arguable non-applicability to the institutional or bureaucratic side of legal development (so under conditions of legal development, this argues that the bureaucratic side of government is ordinarily resistant to change).

Alexei Trochev argues that judges *are* recognizing citizen rights against the government in the new Russia. The problem with the standard ROL picture of an empowered and independent judiciary upholding citizens' rights is that the executive branch of Russian government at an enforcement level has simply refused to pay judgments against the government in a timely fashion, with the result that citizens increasingly regard the courts as ineffective. Eugene Huskey discusses the (non-) implementation in Russian practice of deregulatory laws intended to limit the bureaucracy's authority in an effort to help small businesses. Joel Samuels traces the wide reaching recentralization of Russia's government under Putin, notwithstanding the Russian Federation's 1993 constitution providing for federalism arguing that Russia's ethnic and geographic diversity threatens chaos if the center loses too much control over the periphery.

All seemingly stand for a counterfactual to arguments about social engineering via law, that, regardless of society's openness to change, it would be difficult to achieve social engineering's results in the face of institutional resistance at the bureaucratic level of government. This may in turn call into question the standard picture of relationships between state, individual and civil society pursued on the democratization and governance side of ROL, which stresses the judiciary as core of democratic governance (following Common Law models, meanwhile ignoring to a great extent the bureaucracy which constitutes the modern regulatory state as well as more modest Civilian expectations of judges). Here the history of Stalin's (successful) Soviet modernization plan indicates perhaps that social engineering as legal development goal can succeed, but hardly in democratic terms (no wonder, since who seeks social engineering at the majority level, and for what purpose?).


## International Law as Legal Development Subject

Part VII of our book focuses on international law, while legal development in the ROL tradition is normally restricted to domestic or national law despite links to substantive law like human rights, at least under thick rule of law versions. This raises questions in at least two concrete situations. The first involves the minimum standards problem now raised where an international body or tribunal reviews national law for compliance with an international standard (for example, Angelika Nußberger on the European Court of Human Rights and the diversity of European legal cultures). The second involves related problems in the formation and implementation of international law. In the alternative, these are present in (1) the problem of states agreeing to an international standard or goal by treaty in a specified area of international law, which then must be implemented in national law via legislation (often via the criminal law), raising enforceability issues in the absence of a social consensus in the implementing state (for example, Michael Kubiciel on international legal development against corruption), or (2) formation of customary international law based on state behavior, in the absence of strong social views, given that the influence on states' positions via domestic lobbying (for example, Marsudi Triatmodjo on the precautionary principle from a developing country perspective). But the most interesting question may be why such questions arise only now?

Angelika Nußberger, moving in the opposite direction from Erman Rajagukguk before, approaches the problem of the European Human Rights Convention (Convention) and legal diversity from a (formerly) academic perspective, but with the eye of someone who now sits as a judge on the European Court of Human Rights (ECHR). Her perspective as legal specialist of the former Soviet bloc countries is specifically on their re-inclusion within the sphere of broader shared European views of human rights. One should not underestimate the practical challenge of harmonizing legal cultures under a regional human rights system, even within Europe. In terms of legitimacy, she sees the ECHR's challenge as defending the common values of "the Europeans," if not the common values of the world community. Concerning our chicken or egg question, the ECHR seeks to enforce a minimum standard rather than harmonizing different legal cultures, meanwhile recognizing real differences in institutions and values.

Surveys within Europe reflect very different attitudes and value judgments concerning such basic questions as the role of religion, the concept of the family, and the roles of men and women in society. And geographic patterns (Eastern versus Western Europe, plus Turkey and Russia additionally) can be established on the basis of sociological data, with differences correlated to the relevant society's degree of modernization, per capita GNP, educational levels and life expectancy (largely paralleling Human Development Index scores). Nonetheless, the European human rights system places the individual in the center of its protections as social being, but focuses on civil and political rights to the exclusion of economic and social rights, protecting it under the combination of a basic text and more flexible additional protocols (for example, protecting private property or outlawing capital punishment) to broaden the human rights protection system without endangering the bedrock of the original compromise.

At the same time, there is an interplay between the ECHR and national constitutional courts, reflected negatively sometimes in the place of the Convention in national law (monism versus dualism), and possibly incomplete implementation of necessary changes under national law following the ECHR's finding of a violation of the Convention (resistance at the national legislative level). On the positive side, the ECHR's jurisprudence may be incorporated over time by national constitutional courts referencing it with increasing frequency. Concerning the chicken or egg question, not all ECHR judgments are accepted universally, but there exists rather a reinforcing exchange between legal cultures, leaving the impression that legal change can only follow as form of ratification or reinforcement of changed behavior, at least within Eastern and Western Europe, consisting of middle and upper income countries, the underlying diversity of which still remains broad. And, recalling John Haley's chapter, here we take notice of very basic differences in the technical concept of "rights." Concerning the timing question, these matters arise only now largely as a direct result of the former Soviet bloc and now also Muslim majority countries like Turkey seeking (re)integration into (Western) Europe.

Michael Kubiciel approaches the international law ROL problem chiefly from the perspective of reincorporating middle income Eastern European countries into the broader European community, but also observing the behavior of certain low income African developing countries, in the special area of the adoption of legal frameworks to address corruption. He writes as a German criminal law scholar, stressing individual responsibility and community standards, rather than utilitarian positivism approaches to law. Kubiciel stresses the dual stages of first the factors leading to the veritable explosion of international anti-corruption instruments since the early 1990s, followed by the issue of whether and how such international law conventions can lead to normative and social changes on the national level (typically in theory via criminalization under national law of the corrupt behavior). The problem of importance to our "chicken or egg" inquiry is the extent to which technocrats typically overestimate the effectiveness of social engineering via formal law. This raises questions about the effectiveness of simple deterrence approaches under the criminal law to change behavior, with the result that formal legal changes must be linked with social approaches to energize the fight against corruption on the national level.

The practical problem is that, given many Eastern European countries' desire to join the EU, they may accede to international legal instruments combating corruption as a practical condition of EU accession, even where certain Western European EU member states have not so joined. Similarly, certain African developing states have acceded to international anti-corruption agreements, apparently to qualify themselves for broader development assistance unavailable absent formal anti-corruption efforts, even where there is no social consensus against corruption within their own society. The problem is that, absent such a social consensus, legal effectiveness will be lacking because the enactments will likely remain "law in the books" as opposed to enjoying enforcement "in action." So the real rationale for middle and low income states joining in anticorruption instruments and formally changing their national law is raw self-interest under *de facto* conditionality. Meanwhile, the checkered history of IFI conditionality tied to access to loans, etc. counsels caution.

The practical approach to raising compliance with new prohibitions on corruption is particularly necessary in the former Soviet bloc countries. Their citizens were accustomed to party functionaries using law in a purely instrumental fashion, as has been explored already by Gordon Smith's chapter, rather than following any morally or community-oriented concept. The most common approaches link attempts to undercut the necessity of bribe-taking (for example, by raising government officials' salaries), with steps to reduce their willingness to take bribes (for example, by emphasizing law generally as representing society's moral standard of behavior). These steps typically involve adoption of things like codes of ethics, creation of a critical social climate, and a social awareness-raising program generally. Here we should note the overlap between ethical (morally wrong) and economic (undercutting transition to a market-based economy) rationales for combating corruption, and that criminal law can only stabilize those norms which are generally accepted by society. Ultimately, all this points to the position under the chicken or egg question that the weight of the evidence is that criminal law in particular only ratifies a change in social behavior, instead of forcing changes in that behavior directly. It may sometimes appear that a change in formal law will coincide with a change in behavior, but only insofar as actively supported by programmatic actions to support changes in underlying social beliefs.

Marsudi Triatmodjo addresses the problem of international legal development in the context of the formation of customary law, or in the alternative general principles of law, specifically concerning the precautionary principle from a developing country perspective. The substantive argument recognizes the plurality of opinions concerning the precautionary principle as "law," but focuses on two collateral matters. The first is the implicit asymmetry from a developing country perspective, given that climate change adaptation and effects are anticipated to have their greatest negative consequences in the tropics (where developing countries are concentrated), while perceived economic self-interest in developed temperate countries like the United States motivates resistance to climate change-related regulation which could negatively affect businesses. The second is the *sic utere* principle recognized under the *Trail Smelter* proceeding brought by the United States itself, however, which backstops with liability the possibility of harm behind the precautionary principle.

The relevance of the chicken or egg inquiry here concerns the question of how states reach their positions concerning the formation and desirability of new customary law based upon domestic politics (crassly put, in the American setting via specific industry lobbying activities, although the business community is not monolithic), versus conviction at the level of government and science concerning consequences like global warming being tied to issues like atmospheric carbon levels (more of an expert than popular activity, so it remains hard to invoke social standards absent experts' designation as the agents of "society"). Admittedly, substantial portions of the world's population are blissfully unaware of the entire climate change controversy, but that does not mean that they will not suffer its consequences or that current arguments about lack of scientific certainty will lead to absolution from liability under something like *sic utere*.

Despite sovereignty-based objections to the precautionary principle, the underlying issue arguably presents itself as a pay me (some) now, or pay me (more) later problem. This rationale applies regardless whether cast in terms of the international community as such, or as a grouping of sovereign nations, but the current developing country emphasis on the precautionary principle is linked to the asymmetry of vulnerability of their populations, coupled with ideas about their own economic development. The common (or uncommon) link, depending upon states' perspectives on climate change in particular, may lie in differing ideas at the technical level of economics (what to make of negative externalities like pollution), but also social and economic rights. Fitting such substantive concerns under ROL may seem a bridge too far, but a generation ago the same was said about human rights generally (which ROL now seeks to uphold).


## Conclusion

We return to our initial questions before launching into the body of our book. The weight of the evidence is that social engineering via formal law is exceptional, if not unlikely. Thus, in legal development terms, simple enactment of formal laws ("law in the books") does not lead to effective laws ("law in action"). To the extent a legal enactment appears to change behavior, such a change is probably best accounted for by parallel supporting efforts to change social behavior (for example, via socialization of the underlying concept, rather than relying upon criminal law deterrence linked to any formal enactment).

Instead, social behavior must change first, and legal change thereafter follows as a form of ratification or support for the social norm. In a particular society, the choices made will reflect ideas about social legitimacy, rather than any formal prohibition. The older modernization concept of the 1960s seemed to assume Westernization, but upon close inspection its original theorists did not tie it to democratization as such. The problem now is in understanding an updated modernization concept, at least for lower income countries, where the substantive content may reflect a tug of war at least at the donor level. Given the presence of non-Western alongside Western models for legal development, *whose* modernization concept becomes the operative question.

The temptation is great to try to influence non-Western modernization, but it borders on incendiary to tinker with others' ideas of social legitimacy, as witnessed by current US difficulties in the Islamic world (where problems often involve trying to influence religious views, even if they may incorporate "tribal" alongside "theological" elements). The other possibility is the superficial adoption of ROL approaches in the non-Western setting, perhaps including the full articulation of a sophisticated constitutional system, which may come to naught when push comes to shove if the real local "constitution" bears little relation to the imported model. So in a broader sense, the question may be what is the proper response to countries pursuing non-Western modernization?

One set of interesting questions may arise in examining behavior in societies harboring multiple choices (legal pluralism), since social legitimacy there seems to drive the choice among different legal "pathways" (which does not always lead to obtaining the highest value in economic terms for claims, reinforcing the importance of legitimacy as such, which indicates that ideas about efficiency and economic analysis underlying much ROL work may be misplaced under certain circumstances). This raises a whole set of questions about economic views in development (IFI Washington Consensus), since some of the non-Western legal development models at the very least call it into question in a technical sense. And beyond the technical questions lie issues to be explored further, including both differing ideas about social and economic rights, as well as the differing underlying structure of "rights" in some legal cultures. These are not purely theoretical questions, given that the G-20 countries are seeking to end sole control by Europe and the United States of IFI leadership positions.

Another set of interesting questions may arise in a closer examination of how parties may change their behavior in the face of legal development, which may reflect more instrumental views on individuals' part concerning how to use the (new) law, rather than any changes in social beliefs. So "build it and they will come" approaches implicit in much ROL work seem misplaced, whenever they assume that formal legal norms enforce themselves. Instead, ROL work requires a more sophisticated view of public choice and similar complications, particularly in dealing with bureaucratic reform in both low and middle income countries.

Moving into the institutional side of law reform, ROL's customary heavy reliance on the work with the judiciary may also mislead. One problem is that "governance" in reliance on the judiciary may simply be an attempt to render legal what is more properly a political process (and should be admitted to be one). In the alternative, it ignores the bureaucratic side of government, and simultaneously may overestimate the role and functional independence of the judiciary under particularistic political systems. Beyond democratization, the formal concept of governance is often understood to include judicial review, so governance as anchor of development practice under approaches like the World Bank's Comprehensive Development Framework (CDF) and those of bilateral donors presents problems beyond original compatibility issues at the IFI constitutional level.

Our challenge is to contemplate the legitimacy and change questions outside the context of cultural relativism. As an example, this book touches on legal development within the Islamic world, where the underlying instrumentalist premises are surprisingly similar in arguments about promoting purely secular (Western) law incorporating ideas about liberal democracy, versus promoting some version of Islamic law as a way to achieve a more perfect (Islamic) society. Both share the same premise about the utility of law as an instrument of social engineering, namely that enacting positive law will change behavior (rather than the position that behavior must change first, which new social standards are merely "ratified" after the fact by subsequent legal changes). So what is at stake for us, how does law and legal change function empirically, and who may seize the reins in instrumental terms (or let them drop, if law is an imperfect tool for social engineering)?

# PART I
## Changing The ROL Narrative

# Chapter 2
# The New, New Legal Development Model

David K. Linnan

Rule of law (ROL) practitioners note a surprising lack of attention to the empirical question of whether and how legal development works. This is true even in core areas like the institutional development of courts and the judiciary (Jensen and Heller 2003). Additionally, development approaches of international financial institutions (IFIs) like the World Bank (under its Comprehensive Development Framework or CDF), or bilateral development agencies like the United States Agency for International Development (USAID), typically seem informed more by independent policy positions or normative ideology.[1] Meanwhile, as attention has shifted toward the software exercise of capacity-building under policy-based lending, views of "development," as opposed to "legal development," have in many ways collapsed modern legal development into the whole development concept.

"Legal development" is employed as a neutral term to designate the creation and reform of law and legal institutions in the developing country context. We employ it positively to escape continuing normative questions surrounding the terminology of ROL and governance, namely whether they are simple shorthand for "legal liberalism" or the Law and Development tradition, including an assumed link between democracy and economic growth.[2] The issue involves an arguable repetition of 1960s developments in which normative liberalism mixed with American perceptions of national interest yielded the modernization paradigm in a process commingling academic social science and governmental interests (subjected recently to several historians' critical post mortems: Ekbladh 2010; Gilman 2003; Latham 2000). "Modernization" as a social

---

1   Regarding ROL and ideology, see Taylor (2007); development economics and ideology, see Bayliss et al. (2011); liberalism and ideology, see Tamanaha (2008). Even the UN, not always critically focused, has raised the effectiveness question specifically in conjunction with its own ROL assistance as it has become progressively more involved in such work since the early 2000s (see UN Report of the Secretary-General 2008: para. 59–64). The UN's own ROL approach betrays its origins in peacekeeping and transitional justice, but ultimately may be less ideologically oriented in a formal sense than many bilateral donor or IFI ROL programs, noting: "The international community has sometimes underestimated the extent of political will necessary to support effective rule of law development and invested inadequately in political dialogue on rule of law promotion. Rule of law activities take place in neither an economic nor a political void, and require changes in the legal framework and institutional structures of governance and their functioning. Rule of law development, like all national reforms, generates winners and losers. They are therefore political questions as well as technical ones. Rule of law assistance has often overemphasized technical dimensions and paid less attention to political and strategic considerations" (see Guidance Note of the Secretary-General: UN Approach to Rule of Law Assistance, April 2008).

2   Compare Tamanaha (2008) about legal liberalism as mixed blessing. Theoretically, querying how legal development operates in an empirical sense implicitly invokes a larger discussion about legal positivism and values. In practice, this raises questions about the overlap between politics and law, understood as an argument about legal liberalism which normally surfaces in the academic setting under the rubric critical legal studies. This draws it away from empiricism, but still underlies much ROL theorizing (compare Kennedy 2006b; Trubek 2006).

science concept largely fell into disrepute post-1960s as a result. The theoretical issue is to what extent, beyond economic development, current intellectual fashions focused on the overlap between economic progress and the rule of law, governance, and Western-focused concepts like civil society in opposition to the state are best understood as an old wine, new bottles phenomenon paralleling the 1960s modernization discussion, particularly if regarded from a non-Western perspective.[3] Meanwhile, there are now budding non-Western legal development efforts (for example, Chapter 13, this volume, describing Japanese efforts).

The direction of the chicken or egg inquiry which our book pursues, however, sidesteps normative or definitional ROL and development debates in favor of the empirical question whether and how legal development typically viewed as (instrumentalist) social engineering actually works, looking at both historical examples and ongoing processes (and what part "legitimacy" may play in the process). The key insight here is that, if we now recognize competing (non-Western) legal development efforts, it presumably makes sense to question the manner and feasibility of implementation in "chicken or egg" terms. This should be separated from normative judgments concerning whose legal development efforts will be more suitable/have a greater impact in the non-Western setting. The broader question is how to conceptualize and examine social change when its motivating values may not be our own.

## Past as Prologue

The roots of our problem conceptualizing social change lie buried in the 1960s. They reach back to foundational disputes about modernization, dependency and worldview political development approaches at the height of the Cold War. This was long before ROL concerns entered development discussions. Thereafter, during the 1970s–90s, heavy emphasis was laid upon economic approaches, particularly the Washington Consensus as the epitome of neoclassical economics (followed by ideas like the new institutional economics or NIE, and transaction cost minimization to encompass law's role in economic development).[4] More recently, democratic or political development is rolled into economic growth concepts, often *sub silentio* under governance concepts (compare Linnan 2007).

There is a recent focus on the supposed measurement of results to justify legal development expenditures (Taylor 2007), but those closest to the process recognize that the measures are almost invariably formalistic (e.g., whether new regulations or laws are enacted, not whether and how they are implemented; so in our chicken or egg terms, they assume instrumentality or that

---

3   Development as an operational concept, and modern legal development in particular, now have a history spanning 50+ years. This is merely the modern history, not to mention a colonial "pre-history" also encompassing nineteenth-century legal modernization as in the case of Japan (as discussed in Chapter 13), and a Western tradition dating back at least to the Scottish Enlightenment (Muller 2002). Meanwhile, underlying Western sociological assumptions concerning the centrality of rationality and law to economic development arguably have remained constant from Max Weber to Douglas North.

4   This coincidentally faded in the wake of the 1997 Asian Financial Crisis; still less has been heard about the Washington Consensus during the West's financial sector crisis since 2008. The practical difficulty lies presumably in development policy's traditional technical focus on financial sector development for mobilization of investment capital, linked now with a visible hesitancy in some countries at the G-20 level, perceiving the financial sector as a sometime sorcerer's apprentice (compare Birdsall and Fukuyama 2011). Critical voices in development policy speak of a "financialization fetish" (Bayliss et al. 2011).

simply enacting "law" already changes behavior).[5] But anyone seriously involved in ROL work recognizes the difference between law on the books and in practice. This is nothing new, because the distinction reaches back at this point two generations to 1960s Law and Development and at least a full generation beyond that to Legal Realism.

The practical problem is that ROL work reintroduces the state *sub silentio*, at least under Weberian approaches which still lie hidden behind American ROL discourse focusing particularly on the assumed overlap between economic growth, and democracy and governance.[6] The practical confusion may lie in a parallel rhetorical emphasis on private law for economic growth purposes (e.g., in the name of transaction cost economies) linked with efforts like privatization to force the state out of the economy, while pushing back against the "rule by law" developmental state in the name of democracy and governance via civil society (which amounts to a public law and political action emphasis). Arguably, legitimacy is assumed in this context, if not in the state then in civil society as government's idealized fraternal twin. The problem is that "civil society" in the non-Western context may be oriented entirely differently from the "legal liberalism" construct, however, not just speaking of the state.

There is a renewed economic argument about state-centered versus "free market" capitalism (repositioned as the "Beijing Consensus"), which refocuses on political and legal questions like the role of the state recognizable in scholarly disputes about "thin" versus "thick" ROL versions (or procedural versus substantive interpretations, see Peerenboom 2003, 2004). The economics profession itself stresses a limited understanding of the nature and causes of economic progress (compare Kohn 2009 with Williamson 2005a, 2005b, 2000; and Granovetter 2005, 1985),[7] which perhaps accounts for a certain black box character to NIE approaches anchoring IFI views on a technical level since the 1990s.[8] Meanwhile, policy focus has been shifting toward an ill-defined

---

5 There is an argument that US legal views tend toward instrumentalism generally (see Tamahana 2006), and that Law and Development in particular assumed it on a theoretical level (see Tamahana 2010), even while decrying its effect on liberal legalism (see Tamahana 1995). Here we might distinguish on a practical level between measures employed in the development donor setting, versus approaches now visible in military and interagency circles, since the operational rule of law evaluations are directed more toward mapping domestic law content to determine applicable law, and what additions might be needed. That may be formalistic in its own way, but the basic orientation is different insofar as the operational evaluation by its nature is more a functional checklist.

6 There is some evidence, however, that state infrastructure is not absolutely necessary to economic activity judging by private sector activity in Somalia as poster child failed state (Coyne 2008: 153–4; Nenova and Harford 2004). Somalia is hardly a leading example for governance and democracy purposes. In the modern setting, in East Asia, there is similar evidence that the absence of ROL does not substantially interfere with private sector activities (Linnan 2008). None of this is surprising, since it is entirely consistent with ideas expressed as new institutional economics in the context of historical development.

7 Granovetter's social network ideas are arguably visible in the "pre-law" setting in terms of reputational interests and family or ethnic networks permitting the enforcement of contracts outside a legal framework (see Linnan 2008), which are otherwise viewed by Williamson himself as critical commentaries on transaction cost economics itself, while others point to China as evidence that economic development may require that a state not appropriate private wealth, but does not necessarily require functioning courts for those purposes (Clarke 2007). But a detailed exploration of the economists' own internal debates, employing the evidence available on a comparative law basis, is beyond this chapter's scope. The ultimate problem, however, may lie in the issue how to conceptualize markets (as formalistic price-setting mechanisms in the sense of neoclassical economics' assumptions, versus as social institutions, compare Swedberg 1994).

8 Some would tie the lack of attention to technical details to the notion that legal development in the form of ROL has become an independent goal, as opposed to the idea reaching back to Max Weber that a functioning

"post-Washington Consensus," understood more in opposition to neoclassical economics and Anglo-American capitalism post 2008 financial crisis, rather than articulating any clear policy stance (see Birdsall and Fukuyama 2011). Those with a longer term perspective have begun to discuss the "death" of the development concept, in favor of measurable targets on the order of the Millennium Development Goals (MDGs) stressing anti-poverty goals (Rist 2008: 226–64). The practical problem is how does one know when development in any sphere has succeeded, if there is no agreement on what to measure (Linnan 2010a: 236–7)?

Beyond Orientalism, how should we approach the issue of legal development in a non-Western setting? Here the complication arises with concerns about states themselves (including failed states and non-state actors), and finds its expression in ideas about conflict or post-conflict societies and "nation-building." Again politically, there is a tendency to conflate ROL with the nation-building exercise itself, arguably confusing "law and order" with the question whether an effective state or nation exists at all.[9] "Nation-building" is itself a controversial topic, but one which tends to blur the legitimacy question (typically in the midst of permissive foreign intervention, who is building what for whom, in whose image, and why?). Meanwhile, there seems to be a disregard for the legitimacy question, particularly in the non-Western context (and the state or nation presumably must precede effectively its own secular law).

Modernization theory is remembered for its opposition of "traditional" to "modern" societies (rather than states). This dualistic view of societies effectively frozen in time appears empirically doubtful. As examples, Chapters 3 and 12 in this book contemplate separately in Southeast Asia and Africa multiple sources of law regarded positively by various members of local societies (secular or national law, religious-based law—typically *shari'ah* in Muslim majority societies— and customary or "tribal" law; not to mention the possibility of human rights law anchored, in the alternative, in domestic or international law). The key to understanding what distinguishes them is the idea that they may affect behavior (or not, as the case may be) based largely on their perceived differing levels of local legitimacy. Furthermore, both religious-based and customary law evince change over time in response to social changes. The frozen or fixed characteristics imputed to traditional society under classical modernization theory are not borne out in practice, while this interplay of changing law and changing social behavior is particularly suited to our chicken or egg inquiry. Under classical modernization theory, "traditional society" was largely a straw man opposed to modern, Western society. However, this simplistic general opposition has become increasingly difficult as certain non-Western societies seemingly have achieved success in development terms (meaning, typically, in terms of economic growth).

---

legal system is necessary to secure economic growth (which was the underlying conceit for economists like North advancing ideas about engendering institutions in the development context) (for example, arguing that Sen's focus on freedom or choice really represented elevation of ROL to a goal of development itself, see Kennedy 2006a: 156–7). However, this seems simply to play the "what is development" definitional game in treating ROL as a state, and simply assuming it can be achieved, rather than inquiring how to achieve it. The value is not clear in trading one black box explanation for another, at least not in empirical terms.

9   This genre of ROL work is perhaps best represented by Stromseth et al. (2006), coming out of the normatively based human rights community, as opposed to ROL inquiry more positively based in the Asian or comparative law community represented by discussions about "thick" versus "thin" versions of the rule of law, for example, Peerenboom (2003, 2004). What actually occurs may lie closest in spirit to security sector reform, at least once military operations cease.

**Legal Development in a Once and Future Perspective: PRTs, Peacebuilding, Modernization and Climate Change**

We now approach these questions initially by examining activities seemingly viewed as "ROL work" in the United States (considered part of peacebuilding in the United Nations context), which go beyond legal development. This is followed by an examination first of the economic growth concept as the crossroads of lawyers, political scientists and economists on the boundaries of the "legal origins" controversy, then the classical modernization concept itself and how we can build upon it currently. Finally, we touch upon the scope of substantive law covered by the legal development or ROL concepts, inquiring whether it should now include areas beyond domestic law concerns (e.g., climate change beyond human rights). The underlying issue is the extent to which ROL views increasingly may go beyond domestic law to incorporate international law beyond human rights, implicitly doubling back on economic growth concerns under climate change.

*American ROL Views: Militarization of Development?*

Under divergent points of view, donor-driven legal transplantation may encompass anything from traditional development assistance focused on economic growth, democratization and governance assistance, through trade facilitation technical assistance, to pre-/post-conflict and security sector, as well as generic rule of law assistance focused on law enforcement. The definition of ROL has been expanded in American and international (UN) practice seemingly to embrace military operations ordinarily viewed as counterinsurgency or similar work within peacekeeping and stability operations (or equally, law enforcement anti-narcotics efforts). Here we refer primarily to the position that provincial reconstruction teams or PRTs are engaged in "rule of law" work in Iraq and Afghanistan, which stretches almost beyond recognition the traditional ROL concept as part of development. In essence, counterinsurgency or anti-drug trafficking operations may have their place in the armed conflict or law enforcement setting, but are not the same as ROL work.[10] However, this may also be said of the broader blurring of distinctions inherent in the concept of muscular humanitarian interventions with substantial interagency involvement, following US government terminology,[11] or problems of peacekeeping/making/building in conflict and post-

---

10   This does not even take into account that the US military itself would now recognize stability military operations in particular "in support of the Rule of Law," as an ambiguous concept. Without getting too deeply into a discussion concerning the law of armed conflict and military operational typology, stability operations (as a step beyond peacekeeping) are understood to reach both the use of force in Panama (Noriega's displacement) and counterinsurgency in Afghanistan. Additionally, much ROL work is funded typically as anti-narcotics rather than "development" work with funding flowing via the State Department's Bureau or International Narcotics and Law Enforcement Affairs (INL) into police, corrections and criminal justice system operations. As an example, INL heads up civilian US government legal reform efforts in Afghanistan as part of its anti-poppy cultivation efforts. This effort includes support of legal education in Afghanistan, so INL's efforts extend far beyond traditional law enforcement.

11   The further problem is represented by specific concerns in a functional sense with recent military and law enforcement-based American ROL approaches. Here we mean not only Iraq and Afghanistan, but also Africa in the shape of Africom (regarding related civil-military structures, see Reed 2008). Most recently, the focus is on dealing with post-conflict societies via coordinated activities with the Department of State's Office for the Coordinator of Reconstruction and Stabilization (S/CRS), but also more generally with American ROL approaches reaching further back. S/CRS was created under 2004 legislation in the wake of problems encountered when the United States took control of Iraq (chaos and looting in Baghdad, etc.). Its aim was to coordinate foreign assistance programs within the State Department to better respond to post- 9/11 security

conflict situations, following the UN terminology.[12] The underlying normative conceit seems to be that stabilization efforts addressing the "failed state" or conflict problem constitute ROL efforts in fact. US and UN perspectives have been converging recently as a result of the broadening of the concept of threats to international peace and security from the UN perspective, particularly since the UN 2005 World Summit introduced the concept of "responsibility to protect," even as UN ROL activities are on the increase (compare UN Report of the Secretary General 2008: para. 7-9).

There is a broader re-examination of development generally underway in American government, notably under the September 22, 2010 Presidential Policy Directive 7 on global development (PSD-7) and most recently under the US State Department's first Quadrennial Diplomacy *and Development* Review (QDDR; my italics).[13] These appear not to challenge the underlying instrumental view, that development assistance is part of American foreign policy, alongside diplomacy and military force. This now indirectly crosses over into questions concerning the extent to which democracy promotion and economic growth continue to be paired. In the traditional development community outside the United States, and certain other Western bilateral donors, democracy promotion is regarded at best with suspicion, even beyond the militarization issues (Carothers et al. 2010). And, beyond democracy promotion as such, IFI ROL practice such as the World Bank, which treats governance within the CDF, presents old wine in new bottles problems analogous to the American position that economic growth and democracy are inseparable (compare Ginsburg 2000 with Trubek and Santos 2006: 1–18).

There are several closely related issues coinciding in recent developments. The first, within the American government, is reconsideration of the place of development in foreign policy, linked with a failure to appreciate effects on legitimacy of a double instrumentalism approach on ROL.

---

demands. National Security Presidential Directive-44 (2005) sought to "promote the security of the United States through improved coordination, planning, and implementation for reconstruction and stabilization assistance for foreign states and regions at risk of, in, or in transition from conflict or civil strife." The directive included the basic responsibilities of the Office of Coordination for Reconstruction and Stabilization, while also stating that any of the foreign assistance programs currently in existence, including USAID, were to be under the directive and to work in cooperation with the new S/CRS. S/CRS aspires to integrate at a planning level both the civil and the military aspects of foreign assistance, and as such has a broader formal function than USAID, although internally it draws upon USAID know-how (since the stabilization and reconstruction in question presumably takes place within the developing world). Concerning the place of development in American foreign policy, this is both a current matter at the level of PSD-7 "A New Way Forward on Global Development" (Presidential Policy Directive on Global Development, signed September 22, 2010), plus the recently completed State Department Quadrennial Diplomacy and Development Review (QDDR), and specific questions have been raised about S/CRS's future in connection with these reviews (Hall 2010). There are longer term issues considered at the level of the history of USAID, as well as still on-going development of the elusive "interagency" national security concept following the Cold War's end, now including the S/CRS and Civilian Response Corps (see Department of State 2011). This is a subject of continuing tension between the Departments of Defense and State within US government, but also within the Department of State to the extent of underlying questions about partially undoing post 9/11 organizational changes (whether USAID recovers an independent character as development rises in importance following PSD-7, see Landler 2010).

12   Its related character is clear in earlier documents like the UN Report of the Panel on United Nations Peace Operations (2000), the UN Report of the Secretary-General (2004), the World Summit Outrcome Report (2005), the UN Report of the Secretary General (2006) and the Guidance Note of the Secretary-General: UN Approach to Rule of Law Assistance (April 2008).

13   The PSD-7 itself is not public, and implementation remains an open question, see MacDonald (2010). The QDDR is the Department of State's initial attempt to introduce long-term strategic planning at the departmental level in emulation of the US Department of Defense's quadrennial review process.

Double instrumentalism here is the idea in terms of our chicken or egg formulation that American ROL views seemingly assume that changing law will change behavior directly, but also that advancing ROL itself is an instrument of American foreign policy (perhaps paralleling reflections in Chapter 13 on self-interest in Japanese legal development efforts).[14] Meanwhile, the Bush Administration's Global War on Terror had a distinctly negative effect overseas concerning the US government's reputation in the areas of democracy, human rights and rule of law (Abu Ghraib, Guantanamo, etc.).

The immediate underlying difficulty reaches completely outside the traditional ROL sphere, because it reflects ongoing post-Cold War changes with an armed conflict emphasis on "Military Operations Other Than War" (MOOTW in military doctrine, for example, Govern 2008; JFSC 2000; the active 1990s changes really reach back to the Clinton era humanitarian—military—interventions in places like the former Yugoslavia, rather than the post-9/11 Bush era "War on Terror"). Rather than high intensity international armed conflict, current military activity focuses on low intensity intra-state armed conflict at the level of non-state actors and insurgencies. These are termed generically in US military usage "stability operations," which typically incorporate nation-building aspects (hence the ROL connection; see Center for Law and Military Operations 2010; Dept of the Operational Army 2009a, Appendices C–E; Dept of the Army 2009b; US Institute of Peace and PKSOP 2009), although in the specific context of Iraq and Afghanistan "counterinsurgency operations" (Dept of the Army 2006).

Such stability operations, at least as conducted by the United States,[15] call for interagency cooperation and involvement of a broad spectrum of civilian agencies within the US government (Department of State, USAID, Department of Justice, Department of Agriculture, etc.; now under S/CRS formal leadership) under a whole-of-government approach more or less as a form of aggressive peacekeeping or peacebuilding operations, to employ the equivalent UN terminology.[16]

---

14 Advancement of democracy, human rights and the rule of law figures prominently in the US National Security Strategy of May 2010, but to appearances mostly in the international human rights law sphere, rather than development. The emphasis would be on civil and political, as opposed to economic and social, rights.

15 They are not solely American in doctrinal terms, compare CDEF 2007 (French military doctrine), and presumably must now be accepted more generally within NATO because of ISAF's non-US elements including PRTs.

16 The US military traditionally had a limited or temporary capacity to perform limited support efforts to military operations within civil affairs units, which served to interface with local civilians and civil government (traditionally observing the armed conflict law distinctions between combatants and non-combatants in high intensity armed conflict, with the development now that they function also in MOOTW). Civil affairs itself has been subject to its own functional reorganization within the military in line with MOOTW adjustments (since its original duties were more in the nature of occupation government), and ROL elements seemingly have been taken over more directly within the US military by the Judge Advocate General Corps (JAGC, or military lawyers generically) based apparently upon affinity ideas (and because as ROL operations became more important within MOOTW, the Judge Advocate General Corps as the larger element seemingly desired to assume responsibility for the function as it grew in importance). See CLAMO 2010. Civil affairs units are largely reserve units with personnel possessing "civilian" skills, while formal leadership in such assistance to host country governments has now passed to the civilian side in terms of the interagency "country team" under the leadership of the US Ambassador (theoretically, the US President's personal representative in-country). PRTs themselves now exist also under non-US NATO militaries in Afghanistan as part of the International Security Assistance Forces (ISAF), but there are apparent differences of opinion among different NATO members concerning the true character of PRTs as "military" versus "development" entities, particularly as may affect their integration in counterinsurgency efforts. Compare Walther (2007) with Save the Children (2004) (and, for implicit comparison to the Vietnam-era CORDS program, Leepson 2000). The significance is

The problem is that rebuilding courthouses, guarding judges against assassination, and revamping antiquated corrections systems (MOOTW ROL's "3C" trinity of courts, cops and corrections) as civilian adjunct to military operations lies far beyond ideas about legal development work outside the United States. Thus, designating it as ROL work may devalue the concept and effectiveness of traditional legal development work targeting economic growth and governance. US government civilian agency guidance itself disavows performing development work in the stability operations setting; the emphasis instead is on stopping or preventing conflict (US Institute of Peace and PKSOP 2009: 1.4.2; but see, from the military side, Johnson et al. 2011).

The underlying problem is that the concept of "stability operations" from a military perspective is aimed relatively short term at restoration of some kind of order in the wake of chaos, contemplating the possibility of active military operations to defeat a military force or criminal gangs, followed by the establishment of civil order in a vacuum (looking to Kosovo as a recent example in the context of humanitarian intervention). The concept of "counterinsurgency operations" is aimed at defeating an insurgency, that is to say intervening in a low intensity intra-state armed conflict (e.g., civil war) on the side of the host country government. The goals are military suppression of the insurgency, but equally building the legitimacy of the host country government (through a traditional "hearts and minds" strategy, recently exemplified in Afghanistan). Meanwhile, merely replacing uniformed military with substantial contingents of "security contractors" hardly alters the legitimacy analysis (and may worsen it, if locals consider them mercenaries).

This is not a purely American outlook. It embodies the humanitarian (unilateral) intervention strain somewhat weakened in international eyes in the aftermath of US intervention in Iraq, paralleled on the multilateral side by UN peacekeeping and peacebuilding approaches which contemplate UN ROL work in conflict and post-conflict societies under the authority of Security Council resolutions (see UN Report of the Secretary General 2004; UN Report of the Panel on United Nations Peace Operations 2000). More recently, as a result of recognition of the principle of responsibility to protect populations from genocide, war crimes, ethnic cleansing and crimes against humanity in the so-called World Summit Outcome Report (2005: para. 138–9; see as precursor UN Report of the Secretary-General 2005: para. 133–9), some have interpreted this to expand the case for

---

that US military materials describe ROL operations effectively as part of counterinsurgency (as with its Civil Development and Rural Development Support Program or CORDS), at least in Iraq and Afghanistan, while German-led ISAF PRTs consider themselves more engaged in traditional development work for which the military merely provides security. In Iraq and Afghanistan, however, in American practice, the complaint was that civilian agencies (in particular the Department of State) were unable to provide civilian personnel for the PRTs. Anecdotally, "civilian contractors," hired typically via USAID to perform such work, were more often than not retired civil affairs personnel (so ex-military with the result that viewing them as "civilian" personnel may not be entirely accurate). On a secondary level, the Department of Defense has moved in bureaucratic budgetary terms to appropriate more of the interagency process (Williams 2010), against a still confused background where there have been suggestions (and proposed legislation) to both formalize interagency national security personnel education (Hall and Larkin 2010) as well as a civilian intervention reserve cadre for stabilization and similar purposes. These specific problems have played themselves out in the PRT context in Iraq and Afghanistan (see Perito 2005; Ruiz 2009; USAID 2007) but represent more generally the still unfolding adjustment of the US military and government to a post-Cold War world of low intensity intra-state conflicts and humanitarian interventions, as opposed to a focusing on high intensity armed conflict. In that sense, the developments commence in the 1990s with humanitarian interventions in the former Yugoslavia (Kosovo), if not already with the First Gulf War (relief operations for the Kurds), against the background of the Rwandan genocide as the mooted humanitarian intervention not taken by the Clinton Administration, which has colored the contemplation of potential interventions up to and including Libya, and now Syria. They reflect a human security emphasis, not coincidentally.

unilateral invention (Bannon 2006). In the conflict/post-conflict/humanitarian intervention sphere this has played out post-Arab Spring specifically in the opposition between handing of the Libya and (so far) the Syria situations. The problem is, apart from issues of unilateral versus multilateral intervention, from the ROL viewpoint things look largely the same.

This includes intervention with the consent of a host government, as in the case of foreign support against an insurgency. The UN's peacebuilding focus on reform of policing, judicial, penal and legal systems in the conflict or transitional justice setting tracks the US ROL focus in Iraq and Afghanistan on the 3Cs (cops, courts and corrections). While the UN formally rationalizes ROL assistance as having three levels (ROL at the international level tying into institutions like the ICC; ROL in conflict and post-conflict situations; and ROL in long-term development), it stresses equally that ROL for long-term development efforts closely mirrors activities undertaken in the context of conflict and post-conflict societies (see UN Report of the Secretary-General 2006: para. 37–42). Meanwhile, any ICC element of ROL at the international level automatically ties it into conflict situations. In practical terms, what constitutes counterinsurgency work in the PRT context bears a not coincidental likeness to peacebuilding work in the marginal or failed state context under the authority of UN Security Council resolutions.

By opposition, the traditional concept of legal development is aimed at economic and social development of an underdeveloped country which is neither in the throes of armed conflict, nor civil chaos. This means they are unlikely to invite intervention, even if the question may be considered close in the case of so-called failed or failing states suffering endemic violence (looking to a variety of African states as recent examples, returning to the question of humanitarian intervention). The separate concepts of ROL as adjunct to military operations and in traditional legal development are simply apples and oranges. They share the idea that host governments and their governance (also ROL) must be strengthened, but are legally an uneasy fit to the extent that host state governments' legitimacy and hence longer term political effectiveness remains a standing issue for military interventions (the delicacy of which is witnessed by recent events in Libya and Syria).

Finally, under a whole-of-government approach, US government actors' technical skill set for ROL work is often wrong because not all "law" is created equal for legal development purposes, particularly in the interagency context. Here the problem lies less with military civil affairs specialists or JAGC officers cast as ROL actors by operational commanders, who traditionally are very short-term players in stability operations, and whose role may be minimized in the counterinsurgency setting (because of the interagency concept, when civilian government "experts" should come to the fore). The typical problem is more the mismatch between Common Law-trained domestic Department of Justice lawyers and similarly USAID contractors, or Civilian Response Corps members trying to navigate technically Civil Law-based secular legal systems in countries like Iraq, overlaid with even more significant Islamic and tribal law elements there and in countries like Afghanistan.[17] This problem has existed since the 1960s Law and Development involvement

---

17  S/CRS's *Guiding Principles for Stabilization and Reconstruction* as civilian counterpart to the Department of the Army's FM 3-07 *Stability Operations* downplays differences between Civil Law and Common Law systems, making the correct observation that in practice approaches are now hybrid (see US Institute of Peace and PKSOP 2009: 7.5.21). The problems in practice, however, are typically not just with substantive principles, but also lie in a real lack of understanding concerning basic differing structural elements within legal systems (compare Linnan 2010b, commenting on problems with donor lack of understanding concerning Civil Law versus Common Law judicial career paths, and the resulting mismatch leading to failure). The underlying difference of opinion is whether you need "local expertise" for anything that resembles ROL work, or whether this is a social science exercise in the nature of peacebuilding and studies so that the details do not matter. More to the point in addressing non-Western settings, *Guiding Principles'*

in Civil Law-based Latin American legal systems (concerning differences in judicial, prosecutorial and police systems, compare Linnan 1984, 2010b), but is exacerbated as ROL work has moved into non-Western environments.[18] This raises questions concerning the basis for an affinity for Civil Law or Continental public law in such non-Western societies beyond (colonial) historical accident. But the technical point is simply that, lacking familiarity with Civil Law structures and approaches, there is a tendency for US legal development assistance to pursue less effective legal transplantation strategies as opposed to really working within existing local legal structures, in what is already an environment inviting legitimacy challenges.[19] This coincidentally works also against the idea of donor cooperation at the detail level as approach to avoiding duplication and maximizing impact via combination of effort. So indirectly, the recently adopted US whole-of-government approach, together with "the usual suspects" as USAID contractors, may tend to decrease aggregate legal development impacts.

We ultimately face the problem of the military national security (or multilateral peace and security) tail wagging the civilian development dog. Within the US government, traditional

---

ROL definitions contemplate a traditional modern state with complete legal system which has descended into chaos as a function of conflict (US Institute of Peace and PKSOP 2009: 7.0–7.5). So its apparent ROL picture of the future implicitly contemplates situations like in the former Yugoslavia, which for our purposes would still count as a Western setting despite the religious composition problems. They simply do not contemplate anything like the rural traditional society and legitimacy problem in which, on the example of Afghanistan, secular national law and its institutions may stand third behind religious (Islamic) law and tribal institutions. Accepting *Guiding Principles* on its own terms, the appropriate question is whether they are correct in anticipating stabilization operations will occur in a basically "Western" setting.

18    There were actually parallel prior changes at the personnel level within USAID dating back to the early 1990s, since it was originally created as an economic development agency with a focus on economic growth including legal development work, until at the Cold War's end emphasis increased on democracy promotion as part of governance (and USAID regarded judicial review in whatever form as part of governance, restraining the executive), so that USAID's legal development efforts were split between economic growth, and democracy and governance programs. Economic Growth (EG) was itself treated as a commercial or business law reform program under economists' supervision as development assistance mostly for the formal legal implementation of ideas behind the Washington Consensus. Democracy and Governance (DG) was the governance element, understood, however, as mostly engaged in encouraging the development of civil society (as opposed to government work). EG personnel in the form of development economists were de-emphasized in hiring terms (to the extent it occurred, the hires were more so-called private sector experts, meaning with some experience in business), and DG hiring for civil society positions tended to draw more upon the activist or political science communities. Now, 20 years later, there are relatively few experienced economists left in the system, so that technical capacity interfacing with economic institutions in foreign governments is limited on the EG side, while DG personnel, even those involved in ROL work, are typically not lawyers and otherwise are concerned typically about democratic consolidation. Meanwhile, the Department of Justice, and to a lesser extent the Department of the Treasury, are now inserting themselves into ROL work within the interagency process, but suffer from the lack of technical skills on the ROL side in dealing now in Civil Law-based, non-Western legal system environments.

19    A typical example would be that US Department of Justice lawyers have a tendency when giving advice in a Civil Law country concerning reform of the criminal justice system literally to try to recast inquisitorial (Civil Law) criminal procedure systems as adversarial (Common Law) systems, as opposed to modernizing them by instead patterning advice on modern inquisitorial criminal justice systems like Germany or France. This is not a new problem, since it was present already in Eastern Europe in the 1990s. Judging Eastern Europe as the second wave of law reform, with the possible exception of Russia, despite major American efforts the Eastern Europeans largely settled upon Civil Law (typically German) models (see Berkowitz et al. 2003: 164–7).

ROL work located on the civilian side of government has been harnessed to appearances' sake for defense and law enforcement purposes via problematic reorganization on the civilian side of government (as part of the interagency process). Beyond the occasional humanitarian intervention, this may be best understood as the American expression of the security sector reform movement, originally focused on European efforts in Africa to improve civil–military relations. These have expanded to encompass work with police and the criminal justice system also as a result of the fluid boundaries between military and police functions in developing countries' views of internal security.[20] So seeming security sector reform efforts have floated between the US military and civilian government agencies in Iraq and Afghanistan under a whole of government approach, while being designated with great fanfare ROL work (see US Joint Forces Command 2011). Meanwhile, structures within the civilian side of the American government (e.g., the Reconstruction Coordinator within the Department of State or S/CRS) have moved away from traditional legal development. The practical issue is that such a broad view of ROL truly raises ghosts in the form of modernization theory's Cold War roots, because they are tied to military operations, whether humanitarian interventions or otherwise.[21]

Our final concern grows out of a certain abiding ill-ease in the development community relating to the cross-over between development assistance targeted at economic growth versus democracy promotion (Carothers et al 2010).[22] Meanwhile, the same community exercises fairly pointed

---

20   The security sector reform movement apparently originated in British government policy (DFID) (see OECD 2007), but the US military's long-standing DILS program, and elements of its current Africom program aim at the civil–military question (see USAID, US Dept of Defense and US Dept of State 2009).

21   The problematic operational aspect on the civilian side is that USAID had served as institutional repository within the US government of development know-how since the early 1960s. USAID itself was formed in 1961 under Executive Order as independent agency to implement the Foreign Assistance Act, but was from the beginning involved in Vietnam in something recognizable as the 1960s version of interagency counterinsurgency work (under the CORDS program; see Leepson 2000), even while engaging in ROL work in Latin America. USAID was never popular in US politics as part of the foreign aid bureaucracy, and in 1999 Congress consolidated foreign policy agencies organizationally into the Department of State, shortly before 9/11, following which USAID as development-focused institution was caught up in the Bush Administration's ensuing shift to a security emphasis. But development work itself took on a political tinge as part of the Bush Administration's "Global War on Terror." Meanwhile, USAID as "know-how" repository lost institutional control in a management sense to the Department of State, seeking control via S/CRS. The inherent mismatch lay in treatment of development directly as a problem for political and strategic analysis, rather than an operational exercise in areas like capacity building. Instead, control was placed via S/CRS in the Department of State's mid-level foreign policy apparatus, which itself was struggling operationally with staffing up PRT and similar operations in Iraq and Afghanistan. In some ways, the hidden tug of war between USAID as repository of development know-how and the Department of State as diplomacy operation parallels the new MOOTW debate within the US military between the civil affairs function as traditional repository of civil governmental interface and know-how, versus the Judge Advocate General Corps as operational legal advisors. The hidden agenda is a general concern with legal development and views of ROL, but they are cast specifically in the American context as a debate about the direction and prospective institutional structures for support of US foreign policy.

22   That discussion reflects at least three distinct problems on background. The first is the historical problem that the 1960s "developmental state" espoused the view that authoritarian approaches were necessary to favor capital accumulation and suppress undue (labor) claims in the early stage of development, which was challenged by democracy proponents in challenging the "developmental state" itself following the 1960s (compare Bauzon 1992). The second involves a more recent, general challenge whether there is any effective link between economic growth and democracy (compare Ramaswamy and Cason 2003). The third simply addresses the wisdom of democracy promotion itself, typically based upon questions whether political

criticism of USAID's operations (see Carothers 2009), which ultimately returns to the question of what will be the outcome as PSD-7 and QDDR unfold? There is a sense that development efforts constantly involve consultation in governance terms, but that in the context of the ongoing review "governance" activities at the level of democracy promotion could either be reformed in place within USAID, or, more radically, largely moved out of the development function within USAID and into a more focused substantive bureau within the traditional Department of State (for example, the Bureau of Democracy, Human Rights and Labor or DHL; see Carothers et al. 2010). This would constitute recognition of its character as political activity, rather than attempting neutrality due to a claimed linkage to economic development.[23] This would coincidentally indicate the need for a re-examination of its character also by IFIs, such as the World Bank (which includes governance under the CDF), meanwhile raising the question of other influences going forward, particularly as the G-20 and similar groupings challenge traditional American and European dominance of IFI leadership. How will the BRIC countries (Brazil, Russia, India, China) view such matters, and what is the significance of asking the question for legal development as our interest?

*Economic Growth, the Legal Origins Hypothesis, and Correlation versus Causation*

Confusion sometimes arises since disparate branches of the social sciences (economics, political science, anthropology, psychology and law) conduct seemingly independent discussions of the complex of problems related to development, economic growth, democratization and legal development. Rarely, if ever, do the twain meet in disciplinary terms.

The recent legal origins hypothesis presents an exception which arose from quantitatively-oriented economic research. It initially claimed that legal origins at the level of legal families as exogenous framework worked significant effects over time on economic growth (exogenous because law in many countries reflected a historical transplantation process, for example, from metropolitan countries like England and France to their colonies). Thus, the claim was made that the Common Law was better than the Civil Law for economic growth (La Porta et al. 1997, 1998), resulting in a relatively rare spillover between economics, law and development policy of interest to ordinary legal scholars (for the view from traditional comparative law, see Michaels 2009). Similarly, the issue whether democracy is necessary to economic growth versus the idea that it may merely coincide presents another (the problem of correlation versus causation, employing

---

conditionality in foreign aid makes sense, with strong proponents on the American side in the 1990s push to democratize Eastern Europe, matched against equally strong opponents claiming a variety of problems in the developing country setting (compare Crawford 2001; Cox et al. 2000; Muravchik 1991; Stokke 1995).

23   If most democracy activities were moved out of USAID, it might effectively represent a return to an older organizational orientation in USAID as development institution. It would be closer to that which prevailed before the Berlin Wall came down and Eastern Europe opened up at the end of the Cold War (and might be better suited to increasing work in the non-Western world). It would have organizational consequences within USAID's ROL work, in particular moving more ROL work formally back into its economic growth section, ultimately de-emphasizing civil society-based ROL work, while emphasizing re-engagement with government actors. It is less clear whether such an emphasis might push ROL work again in the direction of traditional work with judges and prosecutors, or rather would lead to more of an emphasis on ROL work focused upon elements of the modern regulatory state in terms of independent agencies and commissions of the executive branch. Based upon the US National Security Strategy (May 2010), it would appear that activities like stabilization operations may continue at an undiminished pace since the basic US foreign policy orientation is unchanged. However, we would gain a clearer division between what currently are claimed as ROL mixed civil and military shorter term operations in conjunction with conflict societies, versus traditional legal development work in the longer term setting.

the political science terminology; West 2002). Both raise technical concerns because they focus on the overlap between the legal and economics fields, more or less in parallel to the overlap between the legal and political science fields that underlies Law and Development approaches traditionally assuming a causal relationship between democracy and economic growth. The economic discussion plays out against broader questions opposing policy-prescriptive, normative neoclassical economics positions largely in the form of the Washington Consensus, to analytical, positive NIE ideas, understood for our purposes as anchored in the concept that:

> Institutions are the humanly devised constraints that structure political, economic and social interaction. They consist of both informal constraints (sanctions, taboos, customs, traditions, and codes of conduct), and formal rules (constitutions, laws, property rights). Throughout history, institutions have been devised by human beings to create order and reduce uncertainty in exchange. (North 1991: 97)

NIE was adapted to development in the 1990s as part of the shift to a "software" approach to development in the form of policy lending to build institutional capacity, and we approach law institutionally for these purposes. We pose questions concerning change via legal development, but this parallels intimations of "legitimacy" also underlying economists' general understanding of institutional change (see North 1981: 45–58), which echoes political scientists' consideration of the same (see Lipset 1959: 86–7).

The initial direction of the economic growth and development debate within the economics profession since the late 1990s was whether economic development is more heavily influenced by geography (European mortality under tropical disease versus settlement in temperate climates; compare Easterly and Levine 2003) as opposed to institutions or policy (compare Acemoglu et al. 2001, 2002, 2005, 2006; Dollar and Kraay 2003; Hall and Jones 1999; Roderik et al. 2004). This position argues that native population density and relatively higher mortality for Western European colonists in tropical environments, particularly in Africa, affected local governance and colonial institutions. It produced large-scale, often absentee-owned plantations worked with indigenous labor that were effectively expropriated.

This extractive approach to tropical colonial economies is juxtaposed against European migration to relatively temperate climates like North America and Australia that absorbed large numbers of Europeans. The European settlers brought comparatively higher technology and levels of education, plus the seeds of institutions like limited government. The assumption is that whatever effect predominated was carried forward via path determinism. The hidden question for the economic growth literature is whether higher human capital (chiefly educational levels) associated with European settlement under a policy analysis caused superior growth, or whether the Europeans' political institutions (limited government) under an institutional analysis caused superior growth thereafter.

So the political interpretation of institutionalism may transmute the economists' growth discussion into one about the proper relationship between democracy and economic growth. Explanations based upon geography versus institutions in particular overlap, given a combination of differing economic and governance structures historically conceived of as the boundary of economic possibilities under specific local circumstances. The overlap extends informally beyond economic growth potentially to political effects as by-product (e.g., coloring democratization), given that the relative concentration of wealth and education levels arising under exploitative institutions affect social structure also in the long run.

The opinion expressed in the debate by the original legal origins economists was that there was essentially no causal connection between economic growth and institutions understood as limited government or democracy (see Glaeser et al. 2004). Instead superior economic growth associated with European settlement was best accounted for by superior human capital (education) as factor. The legal origins economists seemed slightly uncomfortable with this result (Glaeser et al. 2004: 293–6; having established the lack of a causal connection, they proceeded to praise the independent value of democracy). But they specifically reach into the political science (and older modernization) literature in singling out a leading original modernization theorist (Lipset) for the view that higher incomes led to the creation of better institutions, rather than vice versa. This is a correlation rather than causation view, and ties via the institutional explanation for economic growth into the related current (minority) political science viewpoint undercutting assumptions about democratization embedded in Law and Development views (compare Wucherpfennig and Deutsch 2009). They are obviously conscious of the implications for what we raise as alternate sources of legal development, discussing the idea that a seeming democracy deficit in countries like Singapore and China did not negatively affect their economic growth (as long as they made the right "policy" decisions, understood here from the neoclassical viewpoint).

The legal origins hypothesis itself emerged from a small group of economists with practical economic reform experience after the Berlin Wall came down, aiming specifically at a quantitative evaluation of capital markets protections. They initially posited better investor protection in Common Law than Civil Law jurisdictions, criticizing members of the French Civil Law family (see La Porta et al. 1997), subsequently expanded to include creditors' rights and limited aspects of enforcement (see La Porta et al. 1998). The crucial point was that they treated "law" as an exogenous framework affecting long-term economic performance but which presumably was subject to change, so law was also effectively an instrument of economic policy.

The initial legal origins work led to an explosion of literature seemingly abandoning econometric and similar modeling approaches to the macroeconomic problem of growth in order to pursue broader social science explanations employing historically based hypotheses using datasets that rarely extended more than 50 years into the past (notwithstanding which, the hypotheses typically were explained in terms of patterns and effects extending back to colonial times and further). Application of quantitative methodology to legal origins datasets merely followed disciplinary conventions among economists, but it encountered comparative lawyers unaccustomed to such approaches. All along, legal origins' frame of reference was not primarily developing countries as source of data, but, much as the original modernization theory in its day, drew upon developed Western countries as models implicitly to explain how legal development might affect economic growth in the developing world.

So how to characterize the dataset underlying the original legal origins work? Their approach is best understood against the background of the 1990s "big bang"-style economic reform in Eastern European countries. The quantitative work's initial coding style focused on a checklist of specific legal provisions as would have been recommended for any new capital market or similar economic law at the time. This extended a mindset under which the enforcement of law was simply assumed to accompany enactment. Economic law reform at this time in Eastern Europe seemingly was pursued via enactment of pattern or model statutes borrowed from other jurisdictions containing the recommended provisions. Little attention was paid to local, historical legal sources, which in any case lay further back in time, having been displaced for 40–70 years by Socialist legality (although such approaches were eventually reincorporated at local insistence, compare La Porta et al. 2008: 288).

At this level of the growth discussion, "institutions," also including law, are best understood to reflect an NIE orientation, while "policy" is usually shorthand for a neoclassical, efficiency-based orientation (in the developing country setting, typically in the form of free trade policy). This whole approach may be criticized as treating newly enacted economic law fashioned according to "international standards" as a kind of passive endowment (compare Milhaupt and Pistor 2008). However, it is probably better understood also in the legal origins context as reflecting the "policy" as opposed to "institutional" approaches to law and economic growth, albeit one overlaid with assumptions about greater flexibility in responding to changes by Common Law rather than Civil Law judges. Legal origins proponents drew upon Hayek's views relatively early as embodying the idea that distinctions between the Common Law and Civil Law reflected mostly underlying differences in approaches to the state (see Mahoney 2001), stressing that the real distinction between Common Law and Civil Law lay not in substantive rules, but rather in how they approached the state's views of property and the role of government in the economy.

Is this really a philosophy of government issue, or can legal origins justifiably claim under the NIE definition of institutions otherwise that, once "law" is understood institutionally to incorporate a certain frame of reference via existing legal institutions and analytical habits of those trained in a particular system, such views about the state still constitute "law" with effects across time? Looking to Civil Law approaches, at least under Continental (German) public law this level of distinction in terms of choice of the form of government and state under *Staatsrecht* still are viewed as law. However, it would seem that Common Law approaches would treat this instead as political philosophy beyond law (stressing Locke on property rights, etc.). The ultimate issue is whether the legal origins discussion, now refocused on the role of the state in the economy (compare La Porta et al. 2008), is not simply a hidden, slightly more philosophical version of deregulatory arguments about whither neoclassical economics and the Washington Consensus? To that extent, it may be no less ideologically freighted than IFI "policy" approaches (see critically, Bayliss et al. 2011).

Law over differing durations may seem "policy" to the extent it effects change as part of an exogenous framework, while an "institutional" approach to law would render it part of an endogenous framework reflected in the idea that "*[i]nstitutions* [NB, including law] *are the humanly devised constraints that structure political, economic and social interaction*" (North 1991: 97). Its "policy" character is evident in the use of the legal origins thesis and related literature to drive the World Bank's *Doing Business* reports aimed at the upper reaches of government and the private sector. The goal was to spur efficiency-based reform (via country rankings aimed at foreign investors), even to the extent that related positions on deregulation including labor flexibility attracted criticism from the ILO among others on the basis that certain indicators employed were inconsistent with World Bank policies (leading to changes as of the *Doing Business* 2010 report, see Michaels 2009: 771–5).

The legal origins hypothesis generated its own large and often critical literature which we need not explore further in detail (for cumulative survey purposes, see Dam 2006; Michaels 2009; Roe and Siegal 2009). Instead, we focus on final criticisms of particular importance to our examination of legal development, plus its own originators' reformulation in a 2008 publication attempting a unified (re-)interpretation of the literature after a decade (La Porta et al. 2008). The most basic criticism from a legal development standpoint is that the legal origins literature is based on a fairly static interpretation of "law on the books," largely ignoring legal change and law in action problems also evident in legal transplantation issues. It also assumes uniform transplanted national secular law in terms of "law on the books," while we see from Chapters 3 and 12, in particular, that customary and religious law under legal pluralism are often part of the formal legal system of former colonies, now developing countries. It repeats the original modernization theory's pattern of explaining (legal) development in non-Western countries in terms of how they would follow Western models, focusing on the state. This seems implicitly to follow Weberian models of legal development focused on the state, despite a perception in modern international relations that current issues lie outside the bounds of the traditional state (on the downside the failed state problem, and on the upside globalization; this is also indirectly the impetus for the human security approach to development subsequently discussed).

Legal origins' data focus, typically limited to circa 50 years post-World War II, presented a relatively short historical span prior to recent growth spurts in the developing world linked with financial crises in the West, rendering problematic claims about legal families' longer term exogenous effects.[24] Meanwhile, in Islamic countries, *shari'ah* finance and economic law are increasingly important, not least because of a growing international market for *shari'ah* compliant investments, driven internationally by Middle Eastern oil revenues and investor preferences (and, as seemingly clear in reading Chapter 7, post-Arab Spring economic reform in the Middle East is unlikely to be inspired by "policy" neoclassical, efficiency-based approaches). *Shari'ah* compliant laws seemingly fit the revised legal origins identification of a legal family with an ideology or culture (see La Porta et al. 2008: 307–8) for the Islamic world as important part of the non-Western world, but legal origins would potentially overlook the existence of something that may affect up to 25 percent of the world's population (because it fits well into neither the Civil Law nor Common Law families). And the immediate policy context for post-Arab Spring economic development efforts renders this more than a simple academic debate.

One critical explanation for discrepancies at the level of law on the books is phrased in terms of the difference between origin and transplant countries lying in a "demand for law," implying that transplanted law developed elsewhere might be less legitimate in local terms (who needs it?), with the result that it simply does not fit (see Berkowitz et al. 2003; see also Milhaupt 2009; Milhaupt and Pistor 2008; Pistor 2009). Another focuses more on legal change aspects, challenging the legal origins characterization of law as exogenous, seeing instead legal systems being endogenous as shaping, and reciprocally being shaped by, their legal and political environment (Armour et al. 2009). This really does not fully explain how the interchange should work, but borders on the institutional view (compare La Porta et al. 1999: 233). Both the "demand for law" and "endogeneity" explanations are directed seemingly only at the economic law context following on the underlying economic growth focus of the legal origins hypothesis.

Also, legal origins' unfavorable evaluation of the Civil Law generally is targeted largely at countries deemed to belong to the French Civil Law family (among developing countries meaning normally in Africa and South America as a matter of colonial history). There is some suggestion that German Civil Law systems may produce better economic growth recently than even Common Law systems (La Porta et al. 2008: 301–2), but a further issue exists whether said superior performance is a product rather of such countries' relatively higher human capital levels rather than their legal origin (a correlation versus causation question, since relatively higher wealth is generally associated with better investment climate and legal enforcement). But prominent and economically successful Asian developing countries deemed to belong to the German Civil Law

---

24	There is a special problem in the legal origins evaluations ignoring cyclicality and financial crises while relying on financial sector development measures in conjunction with datasets organized around variables concerning investor protection and creditors' rights (problems of ahistoricity, but also what financial sector development really means; compare Reinhardt and Rogoff 2009). Later legal origins analyses note that twentieth-century economic growth was markedly more rapid in the Common Law than Civil Law countries, but one suspects that is particularly reliant on periods measured given the interplay of growth spurts and financial crises.

family were largely downplayed (for example, Japan, Korea and China, which modeled their own legal modernization largely on German law). The problem is that economically successful Asian countries apparently coded under the German Civil Law category now constitute potential leading sources for non-Western legal development. Meanwhile, they are seemingly neglected under the legal origins hypothesis focused chiefly on distinguishing effects of the Common Law from French Civil Law. This is presumably because they are considered too few or growth spurts seem too recent for statistical analysis purposes. But that simply raises the issue whether the whole legal origins effort is ultimately a data-mining exercise directed at what is easily accessible, rather than a full universe of information. Meanwhile, large-scale quantitative studies examining perceived economic effects of the French Civil Law system were hardly necessary to demonstrate that the vast majority of African and South American countries were underperforming economically. The real question remains why, and, in policy terms, what can be done to change this, bearing in mind that our focus is limited to attempting to understand how legal development works on the ground?

The prospective direction of legal origins work is visible also since 2003 in a broader theoretical effort of its originators (see Djankov et al. 2003). This piece reformulated the post-World War II field of comparative economics, formerly understood as an approach comparing market-based capitalism to plan-based socialism, into one more generally addressing the social regulation of business under differing market-based approaches. The emphasis was on the security of property rights, but both from the depredations of private parties (private disorder, recalling Hobbes' war of all against all, or public order as central state concern) and from the taking of property rights by the government (with public attacks on property termed dictatorship, recognizing that any government powerful enough to control private disorder could itself become a threat). Too much of either dictatorship or private disorder creates problems, so that the fundamental problem of institutional design is trade-offs to address the conflict. Legal origin is here already understood as proxy for the strategy of social control of business (Djankov et al. 2003: 612), which leads to ideas about appropriate institutions as choices from a limited number of possibilities of different countries at different stages of development.

This thought is then carried forward in the formal effort of legal origins' founders to reformulate their hypothesis (see La Porta et al. 2008). They articulate a broad conception of legal origin as a style of social control of economic life, in its strong form arguing that the Common Law stands for a strategy of social control that seeks to support private market outcomes, whereas Civil Law seeks to replace such outcomes with state-desired allocations (La Porta et al. 2008: 286). Strikingly, however, they substantially soften up legal origins claims concerning economic growth insofar as they admit that "it is less clear that legal origins predict aggregate growth" (La Porta et al. 2008: 302). This is of particular interest in our legal development context, because of the accompanying idea that one explanation may be that, in the long run, there are periods that may advantage Civil Law regimes (such as state-led growth; La Porta et al. 2008), and separately that the general evidence on legal or regulatory reform is just beginning to come in and is largely confined to the developed world (La Porta et al. 2008: 326). Having restated the legal origins hypothesis at the very general level of the state's involvement in economic life, questioned the existence of developing country evidence, and taken exceptions that seem to apply to the very Asian countries constituting non-Western sources of legal development, they rephrase their question in terms of the close relationship of legal origins to types of capitalism. Their question is restated as: "what kind of capitalism is likely to prevail in the long run? Will it be more market-focused Anglo-Saxon capitalism, or the more state-centered capitalism of Continental Europe *and perhaps Asia*?" (La Porta et al. 2008: 327; my italics). So the original legal origins' proponents seemingly recognize that the general thrust of legal origins now seems to border on traditional "policy" advice stressing deregulation and markets. But, poignantly, they may now have to differentiate on the Civil Law side between Asian capitalism as potential source of non-Western legal development and, post European banking and state lending crisis (2008 to date), Continental Europe. So, concerning our special interest at the level of legal development, particularly distinguishing traditional Western sources from now visible non-Western sources, it would appear that legal origins proponents themselves would recognize the limited utility of their theory for our purposes. Speaking as economists, however, they have at least rejected a claimed causal link between democracy and economic growth such as Law and Development traditionally assumed.

*Modernization Revisited*

Modernization theory is "the process by which economic and technological change leads to the transformation of the institutions and values of society" (Vassilev 1999). Classical modernization theory was rooted in circumstances following World War II, including the need to conceptualize the process of nation building in newly independent colonies (Pye 1979). As such, its focus was on the sociological transformation from many traditional (often tribal) societies into a single, unified modern one within the theoretical framework of a modern nation state. So how did we exchange the precepts of modernization for rule of law?

On the academic side, development's eventual perceived failure in places like Africa called forth dependency theory and world-system theory as alternate Marxist macro-level explanations that developing countries were at the mercy of external forces. The corollary, that developing countries were not the masters of their own destinies, called in turn into question the efficacy of internal institutional change as endogenous path to economic growth and development success. The higher level theoretical discussion is largely absent from current ROL practice, but one should note that generic ROL ideas as applied in the non-Western setting arguably are a comfortable fit within the modernization theory camp.

But what were the tenets of classical modernization theory? In summary form, its original underlying assumptions were that it (compare Linnan 2008: 608–9):

- involves distinct phases of social development (also understood at the individual or psychological level);
- involves homogenization or convergence among societies;
- represents a Westernization process;
- is an irreversible and progressive process; and
- works consistently across a traditional society to transform existing social systems by replacing traditional structures and values with "modern" ones, with a change in one social sphere triggering related changes in other social spheres (for example, raising educational levels for women indirectly affects women's social status, family structures, plus economic and reproductive activities).

Rather than the above, more recent legal development policy in a globalizing world tends to focus on ROL, democracy theory or other approaches linking democracy to economic growth, simply assuming the picture of a modern "state." This may have been acceptable pursuing legal development work in Eastern Europe after the fall of the Berlin Wall. However, in the field, in non-Western settings like Iraq, Afghanistan and Africa, Westerners have rediscovered linkages among the problems of legal development, legitimacy and traditional society.

In the Afghan setting, for example, it is now commonplace to question whether the country itself should even be considered a modern state. Instead, Afghanistan is conceived of as more of a loose tribal confederation; hence the idea that Afghanistan's president is best characterized as the mayor of Kabul (since the writ of the modern state famously extends not very far beyond its municipal boundaries). Beyond Kabul's bounds, representatives of the central government are typically constrained to attempt to give advice to the traditional local governance bodies (*jirgas* and *shuras*) on how in a modern Afghanistan disputes should be settled. Practical power, much less legitimacy, still resides in traditional local ethnic customary law and institutions first, perhaps Islamic law second (the order of priority between customary and Islamic law is subject to dispute generally within the Islamic world; compare El-Ansary and Linnan 2010: 11, with Chapter 12, this volume), and secular national law an often distant third.

But this spectrum is not peculiar to Afghanistan, as witnessed by Chapter 12 addressing the relationship on Lombok Island, Indonesia, among those same three sources for legal development purposes. Recently, the UN estimated in presenting its own ROL work that in many developing countries, such "informal systems" are estimated to handle 80 percent of the cases (UN Report of the Secretary-General 2009: para. 37).[25] It is probably most accurate to speak in positive terms of all three co-existing, rather than adopting the normative Western assumption that under modernization theory customary law simply withers away with time, against which idea, in parallel to Chapter 12, Chapter 3 covering African conditions argues, and otherwise caricaturing *shari'ah* law as simply to be avoided. The practical problem is that, in rural areas within the Islamic world in particular, in terms of legitimacy only Islamic law can compete with customary or ethnic law in areas like family law (and following inherited colonial legal pluralism patterns, such highly "political" areas of law may be consigned to religious law anyway). So there, the normative advantage lies with either religious or customary law; here legitimacy is the normative determinant. The writ of national secular law, on which ROL work focuses, applies more in urban areas where traditional groupings may be submerged in a hodge-podge of in-migrated ethnic and tribal groups.[26] The real

---

25   The United Nations' "informal system" characterization itself may mislead, because that is the language of a unitary secular law system not recognizing legal plurality. Meanwhile, many former colonies incorporate ethnic or religious law as source into their (legally pluralistic) national legal systems, in which case it is unquestionably part of the formal system. In instances where an attempt may be made to displace traditional legal sources with unitary modern, national secular law, or where gender-oriented challenges may be based in human rights law as international law, the informal system characterization may seem more accurate on its face. The jurisprudential problem is whether the formal enactments constitute "law" if they are simply disregarded by much of the population in favor of the traditional "law" that they nominally replaced. The same issues are visible in questions whether that which the locals apply should be called "custom" or "customary law," assuming locals conform their behavior to traditional practices because they are regarded as more legitimate. UN ROL work is somewhat unusual in its acknowledgement of this problem, even while being potentially inconsistent in insisting that ROL requires equality before the law, meanwhile stipulating that the administration of justice involves "both formal judicial and informal/customary/traditional mechanisms" (Guidance Note of the Secretary-General 2008: 1). The problem with much customary and religious law is that it applies only to members of specified religious or ethnic groups under something analogous to a "conflict of laws" analysis, but the result departs from equality before the law in any normal sense. Instead, it resembles nineteenth century consular jurisdiction, or in this work Chapter 9 describing the application of *halacha* in European Jewish communities through the eighteenth century.

26   Even here customary and religious law creates practical problems. The argument may be made that customary or Islamic law classically only apply to certain legal areas like family law and inheritance, hence the national or secular law focus should serve for economic growth and similar purposes. The problem is that Islamic law is being pushed also in commercial areas (e.g., *shari'ah* complaint finance), while, for example,

difference between them involves the question of legitimacy visible in which system locals call upon for dispute resolution and similar purposes. Life in rural areas may simply be different from urban settings in terms of which version of "law" is legitimate in locals' eyes, although traditional culture may also color behavior in the urban setting as reviewed in Chapter 3. The demography of rural–urban migration thus becomes a hidden concern for ROL debates (which sets normative expectations). It is no accident that relatively lower urbanization rates seemingly predominate in non-Western settings presenting ROL challenges.[27]

Current ROL approaches to law in non-conflict rural areas typically overlook most customary or similar legal questions in favor of simply trying to establish a new (statutory) system of land tenure and land titles, as a way of establishing farmers' access to credit (e.g., to allow them to pledge "their" land to financial institutions as collateral). This follows the strain of development economics that poverty results from the poor's inability to access capital, hence law's contribution in rural areas should be chiefly to establish individual small farmer titles to land to provide access to capital via secured lending, and presumably to pursue micro-lending in urban areas (Desoto and the Grameen Bank).[28] Land law is the typical topic of customary law in a traditional society (compare Chapter 12 describing land and inheritance law in Lombok), however, this demonstrates

---

customary law remains in place in Indonesia in the form of *adat* and *hukum antargolongan* or conflicts principles between the customary law of different ethnic groups applicable to real property (with the indirect result for modern financings in the large scale Jakarta commercial real estate market that it is practically impossible to get unqualified legal opinions on ownership of major real estate parcels that foreign banks might demand in connection with financing an office building; the businessman's response more often than not is to see if you can get the state to acquire the underlying property as a way of cleaning up a confusing *adat* law chain of title reaching back to colonial times).

27   Original modernization theory's emphasis was somewhat different, seemingly because of the assumption that traditional society was by definition "rural," so that modern society was "urban." The current disconnect is that (non-American) legal development professionals doing work in non-Western settings increasingly are trying to increase knowledge of, and expressly incorporate, tribal and religious law into legal development work without clearly confronting the implications of their roots in traditional societies (e.g., that they may disadvantage whole groups like women). To the extent they focus on religious law, they simply avoid the question of whether viewpoints concerning the law's requirements represent true theological dictates, versus mere conservative social views. Meanwhile, the American approach to ROL largely assumes away modernization theory's dichotomy between traditional and modern society also in the non-Western setting. Instead, its practitioners tend to work in relative isolation among English speakers at the ministry level in the capital or major provincial cities, and have typically only been forced to confront the problem of "applicable" law in fact in rural as opposed to urban settings in places like Afghanistan (where the PRTs function as development focus in a potentially hostile non-urban environment). The generic American response at the civil society level of democracy and governance work has been implicitly to choose sides in what are essentially mixed doctrinal and social arguments within religion (for example, advocating "progressive Islam" against more traditional views within the religion), a problematic approach for any number of reasons. Beyond the technical first amendment issues (advocating for a religious view, see Mansfield 2008), the difficulty is that it would be analogous to Muslim governments advocating in a Christian country for Protestantism over Catholicism because of a dislike for the doctrine of papal infallibility. It is reasonably foreseeable that all stripes of Christians would perceive such religious advocacy of a foreign government as an affront, and it could engender a more active response from true religious extremists. In that light, it is unsurprising that the American government has significant problems in the Islamic world, while facing claims that its own actions may enable terrorist recruitment.

28   Although in sub-Saharan Africa, the tiller has swung yet again in a different direction since customary law is now sometimes favored for policy reasons to govern land law, raising a new set of issues (see Tripp 2004).

precisely how problems of legitimacy may arise. This is a particular problem when financial institutions dispossess customary law's traditional, often collective, ownership first via rural land reform, and then later may move traditional property out of local ownership completely via sales or foreclosures, etc.

The last time there was serious social science-style focus beyond economic doctrine on detailed empirical aspects of development's "how to" question was under modernization theory's aegis. Meanwhile, something has been lost in terms of insight into economic activity and social change occurring (and sometimes not occurring) on the ground, particularly in non-Western lower and middle income countries. So we turn to trace modernization theory's original tenets in an attempt to see how much we can recover of its empirical insights for legal development into problems like the dualistic vision of traditional versus modern society. We have effectively already passed beyond certain of classical modernization's premises. First is the idea that modernization equates to Westernization. Second is that modernization involves homogenization or convergence among societies. This follows from the recognition that there are now competing non-Western attempts at, or sponsorship of, legal development. But approaching legal development from a positive, empirically informed view of modernization seems more promising than ideology or definitional ROL approaches (the heart of the "thick" versus "thin" rule of law debates).

During the 1950s–60s, the writings of six theorists defined early modernization theory (Arat 1988). Almond and Verba discussed education as a key component of modernization. Deutsch and Pye indicated that formulation of a mass communication system was essential to modernization. Lerner believed that urbanization would lead to advancements in education, and advancements in education would lead to media growth. Lipset focused on economic and social conditions as they related to effectiveness and stability of the political system for the developing society. While Lipset famously noticed a relationship between economic development and democracy in the nature of correlation (Lipset 1959: 80), he mainly focused on what conditions were necessary for a stable political system (Lipset 1964). He further observed that modernization of a society was a necessary condition for democracy (Arat 1988).

Scholars in the 1960s used examples from Western Europe, including Italy, France, Germany and Spain, to support their theory. The observation was that modernization in European factories went hand in hand with urbanization (Lipset 1964). As a nation industrialized, morale of the working class increased, and workers indicated that they felt happier in their jobs. Members of the working class indicated that they believed that competent individuals had the ability to rise socially. Lipset linked technological modernization with increased social mobility and increased earnings for employees in industry due to increases in employment levels (Lipset 1964: 284). Lipset also noted that as a country industrialized, people began to show loyalty to multiple social groups (meaning, in practical terms, beyond traditional society). He associated loyalty to one social group with early stages of development, and loyalty to many social groups with advanced stages of development (1964: 281).

The loyalty to multiple social groups could be explained partially by the view that high degrees of urbanization and industrialization correlated with lowered levels of ideological conflict within society.[29] Lipset observed that de Tocqueville recommended "widespread support for secondary

---

29 Lipset (1964: 281). From a political standpoint during the 1960s, Lipset observed that, generally, countries with large communist parties tended to be less modern (1964: 288). Studies in Italy showed that as a specific factory became more "modern," fewer workers were members of the communist party (1964: 284). However, higher levels of industrialization and urbanization coincided with more men in big cities sympathizing with leftist views (1964: 284). Scholarship during the Cold War-focused 1960s tended to discuss political issues related to modernization theory in terms of communism and democracy. Theorists noted

associations" as a necessary part of the social infrastructure required for democracy (1964: 281). In other words, an increase in the number of citizens who associated themselves with multiple social groups (again, implicitly moving beyond traditional society) as a society grew more modern was necessary for a democratic government. However, Lipset suggested that democracy was nothing more than a potential consequence of modernization, rather than its inevitable result. Lipset emphasized that as a country grew more urban and industrialized, a society would grow more stable no matter what the character of its political system (1964: 285).

Lipset subsequently discussed the importance of tertiary education to modernization of a country. He believed higher education could contribute to the modernization of a country pre-World War II (before modernization theory, looking backwards into pre-independence colonial conditions). Lipset first observed that in underdeveloped countries, universities would be essential in providing trained workers to form the elite members of society (Lipset 1966). Further, universities in underdeveloped countries must be able to train their students in order to ignite change within society and foster a national culture. Lipset supported his assertions by citing university students in China in 1911 who were instrumental in overthrowing the Manchu dynasty and gaining independence, and university students in Africa who were instrumental in ending colonialism (1966: 132–3; see also Chapter 3, this volume, since he would place renewed emphasis on education over ROL).

Scholars in the early 1970s continued to discuss predictions of modernization theory. For example, writers predicted that as a society grew more modern, religious institutions around secular universities would modernize as theology became "a subbranch of the broader intellectual life" (Dobson and Lipset 1972). By the late 1970s, however, modernization theory had fallen out of vogue, and its creators were reduced to speculating as to why the theory faded from view.[30] After the Bay of Pigs, modernization theory shifted from a focus on bringing technology to underdeveloped countries, and instead focused on changing the politics and society of established Latin American societies (which arguably was the indirect impetus for the original Law and Development movement, namely "liberal legalism's" engagement with Latin America in the context of Cold War anticommunism, also in terms of legal development; Lipset 1972) (Pye 1979: 30; compare Trubek and Galanter 1974). The Law and Development movement simply assumed that changing law would change and shape behavior as part of the development process.

At the same time that its original theorists were hypothesizing why their theory faded, other scholars in the late 1970s attacked and disproved various assumptions of modernization theory. An assumption was made by modernization theorists that dimensions of life such as acculturation and socio-economic status would advance at the same rate (Tessler and Hawkins 1979). In some

---

correlations between modernization and preferred type of government without stating that modernization went hand in hand with any specific form of government.

30    Pye suggested that the Bay of Pigs fiasco, the Vietnam War, and the formation of OPEC combined to bring about the end of modernization theory (Pye 1979: 30). The Vietnam War was accompanied by an American sensitivity to what its role should be in determining the direction of other countries. As a result of the first oil shock, American interest in foreign aid declined. At the same time, oil producing countries suddenly grew wealthy, while other underdeveloped nations grew poorer (and subject to structural adjustment). The formation of OPEC called into question the idea that first world nations could help modernize underdeveloped nations when an historical event out of the control of developed nations could affect the economic climate of underdeveloped nations. Pye did note that modernization theory as it was conceived in the 1950s–60s was meant to be a dynamic process with no end to the progress that nations made (1979: 35). Other theorists writing in the 1970s echoed Pye's belief that the Vietnam War and the situation in Cuba coupled with changing American beliefs about our role in foreign policy helped undercut modernization theory.

countries such as Jamaica, Mexico and Brazil, this assumption proved true (1979: 477). However, in other countries like Tunisia, acculturation and socio-economic status changed independently of one another. Acculturation was defined as "the degree to which [a person] has had experiences and acquired skills that expose him to ideas and behavior patterns that are foreign to his immediate social environment" (Tessler and Hawkins 1979). The conclusion was that in some underdeveloped countries, universities educated more people than the economy could support. These graduates had to accept lower level jobs than they might have received otherwise, and had a high level of acculturation with a low socio-economic status. Conversely, in some countries, students entered the workforce where labor was needed and became wealthy with a low level of acculturation. So "build it and they will come" has never been particularly successful as a modernization approach.

The 1980s saw little discussion of modernization theory. However, in 1984 Lipset as one of modernization theory's founders traveled to China (Lipset 1984). He observed an openness to capitalism and a commitment to modernization and industrialization. Interestingly, Lipset noticed frequent references to Hong Kong, Singapore, Taiwan and South Korea; PRC Chinese believed that modernization in these areas indicated that modernization could succeed in China (Lipset 1984). This reference to modernization in Asian countries was an early indication that the model of modernization in Western Europe might not interest non-Western developing countries as much as modernization of other societies within their geographic or cultural spheres (so non-Western development models, appropriately enough, are of special interest to non-Western societies).[31] And as previously noted, broader political science debates concerning Lipset's conclusions about causation versus correlation in the relationship between economic development and democracy were already visible in the early 1990s (see Diamond 1992) and continue (Wucherpfennig and Deutsch 2009).

The 1990s saw an apparent resurgence in the popularity of modernization theory; however, modernization theorists of the 1990s saw democracy as the inevitable end to modernization in society (Pereira 1993). Theorists acknowledged that education, industrialization and economic development were integral to modernization (Vassilev 1999: 568). Meanwhile Vassilev, a theorist who focused on Eastern Europe and Bulgaria in particular, also stated that "socio-economic development, producing increased income, secularization and widespread literacy, promotes democracy by encouraging socially dispossessed groups to choose political bargaining and moderation over radicalism and revolution" (1999: 568). He explicitly tied modernization to democracy despite no explicit link between the two concepts appearing in the original conceptualization of modernization theory. So to that extent, linking modernization theory to democratization was an anachronism presumably resulting from the foreign policy linkage of democratization to economic growth.[32] Anachronism was an easy step, however, to the extent Eastern Europe was still culturally "Western," and Eastern European countries specifically embraced "Westernization" in the case of targeting EU accession as ultimate political goal. Changing focus to Eastern Europe from non-Western development also

---

31    Meanwhile, the absence of Japan from the list of cited models might be interpreted in the alternative as the idea that the sharing of (at least) the written Chinese language played a role, or that memories of World War II still periodically visible in Sino-Japanese relations militated against making Japan a model. It is noteworthy that Japanese legal development efforts discussed in Chapter 13, this volume, are focused away from its former colonies (Korea and Taiwan) and the Chinese core of East Asia.

32    Vassilev acknowledged, however, that modernization theorists of his time saw democracy as the final point in the modernization process, whereas Bulgaria became a democracy at a midpoint of economic development (Vassilev 1999: 574). Vassilev's acknowledgment regarding Bulgaria's development inadvertently may illustrate why others in the 1990s attacked modernization theory: the anachronistic model ending in democracy rarely seemed to work as predicted.

coincidentally removed concerns about traditional versus modern societies since Socialist states were already "modern." Changes to Socialist states instead combined economic changes in the form of the embrace of the market over central planning with a movement away from "people's" and toward "liberal" democracy.

Other 1990s theorists attacked modernization theory as overly simplistic and inaccurate. Specifically, theorists noted that modernization and economic success did not necessarily end with a transition to democracy, and democracy could result from any number of processes that were not modernization (Prezeworski et al. 2000; Przeworski and Limongi 1997). Very poor countries with authoritarian governments had stable authoritarian regimes, while countries with a high per capita income also had stable governments, whether that government was authoritarian or democratic (Przeworski and Limongi 1997: 159–60). Countries with an intermediate per capita income were most likely to transition from an authoritarian government to a democratic government; the necessary implication of this statistic was that, if a country were likely to transition to democracy at all, it would do so at an intermediate level of development rather than at the end of development. Furthermore, a country could be modern despite its governmental structure (also providing justification for non-Western modernization). The study demonstrated that a modern country with a high per capita income had a stable government no matter what the government type, which interestingly reaffirms Lipset's 1960s prediction. However, political scientists attempting via statistical analysis to disprove the notion that modernization theory inevitably ended in democracy failed to differentiate between the original 1960s version of modernization theory as it developed through the anachronistic modernization theory of the 1990s.

Around 2000, and with increasing frequency post-9/11, in a renewed shift away from the 1990s focus on "Western societies," political scientists employed the term "democratization" and attempted to discern why democracy was not widespread in the Middle East. The majority of scholars decried modernization theory as a failure and, to bolster their argument, highlighted studies about per capita income relative to government structure similar to the 1990s scholarship. Theorists favoring modernization theory constituted a minority and blamed lack of democratization on poor socio-economic conditions (Jamal 2006). Furthermore, these theorists defined education as a factor in explaining support for democracy in the Middle East. Others noted that while modernization theory predicted secularization, religious leaders in the Middle East rather than secular leaders appeared more prominent in terms of social change (Eickelman 2000). The vast majority of post-2000 scholarship acknowledged democratization as the end result of now anachronistic modernization theory (compare Wucherpfennig and Deutsch 2009). The metamorphosis was complete as scholars began to identify modernization theory as an endogenous theory of democratization. That not coincidentally also offers easy accommodation of the position that economic growth and democracy are inseparable.

So how much of original modernization theory's insights survive and are useful in understanding legal development as empirical matter? The classical modernization theorist who has worn the best over time is Lipset. He was one of the original agnostics on claims of reciprocal causal links between economic growth and democracy, and has made an appearance again most recently in the legal origins debate (as its economist instigators opted for the minority political science position that correlation rather than causation is the correct understanding of the relationship between economic growth and democracy; see Glaeser et al. 2004). Our first realization is that modernization's picture of evolution at the social level is helpful, but needs to be recast. What we can focus on is the importance of demography and rural–urban shifts in the context of how the legitimacy of different sources of law may alternate. The spectrum ranges from a relatively homogenous traditional rural village setting to the heterogeneous society of mixed ethnic and social groups now to be found in a typical teeming developing country megalopolis (including extensive intermarriage at a certain social level, with populations also showing evidence of a political focus on successfully building national unity in the wake of independence, etc.).

The problem lies in a realization that, even in the megalopolis setting, the (modern) society formed is not necessarily Western (visit Shanghai, Singapore or Jakarta to see for oneself). The assumptions behind an implicit focus on legal liberalism are probably misplaced, to the extent an Asian society may be presumed to be both non-Western and modern (and that point may be embedded in its economic views too, as witnessed by specifically Islamic views visible in Chapter 7). In fact, the question is whether Lipset's 1980s view was right in asserting that a country like China evinced more interest in modernization as carried out by its Asian cultural cousins, rather than seeking out Western models as such (the current discussion in development circles is whether an element of the so-called post-Washington Consensus is an increasing attention to non-Western success stories; see Birdsall and Fukuyama 2011). Modernization theory is not a theory of democratization, and any "Beijing Consensus" would clearly separate economic growth from democracy.

We can turn the demography point to additional use in ROL terms. If one wishes to make an early judgment on how successful legal development will be over an extended period in a particular country, perhaps the single most telling indicator may be its demographic trends. In that regard, Asia is rapidly urbanizing, while Africa and the Middle East less so. So the relative demographic pressures of rural–urban migration and degree of urbanization may be more useful than any in-depth social science study in predictive terms to judge the relative receptivity of a country or society for legal development in its own terms (equating to modernization on its own terms).

The aspect that perhaps transfers the best for purposes of understanding how legal development works in practice may be simply a focus also at the individual or social psychological level (which was present in much early modernization theory work; Gilman 2003; Latham 2000). This understanding should be opposed to a focus at the institutional level per se, which has accompanied IFI emphasis on economic growth under NIE precepts since the 1990s. A link does exist between institutions and change, implicitly challenging rational man and efficiency-based explanations of legal development, to the extent that legitimacy would be the keystone of institutions' acceptance under any change theory (see North 1981: 45–58). Legitimacy concerns require less of a bird's eye view in general, since the evidence visible in Chapters 3 and 12 illustrates that traditional law does not simply fade away, but rather continues to co-exist with religious and modern secular law. Legitimacy (at the social as well as individual levels) then may dictate which body of law actually governs how an individual behaves (which is consistent with legal transplantation-based challenges to the original legal origins claims; see Berkowitz et al. 2003). So the legitimacy question is seemingly where to orient our chicken or egg query in practical terms? If legitimacy is found to be lacking at the individual level, the social engineering or instrumental approach to law presumably will fail. So do individuals consciously choose, and shall we regard change and the multiple sources of law problem visible in legal pluralism as being about questions of degree rather than kind in the legitimacy context?

Following on the emphasis at an individual level, what should be added to traditional modernization analysis is also a sense of instrumentalist behavior at the individual level (compare the iterative view of the relationship between law and markets, Milhaupt and Pistor 2008). The example is to be found in Chapter 5 reviewing the Indonesian corporate insolvency context (see also Linnan 2010b). It is possible to observe individuals learning how to navigate a brave new world of insolvency proceedings to their advantage. In that sense, ROL may assume automatic normativity of "new" law, while actors at the individual level engage in something analogous to public choice analysis. They will adopt the new legal framework implicitly when it suits their own purposes, but not simply because it is "law" in a public interest sense (also rejecting the idea that compliance may follow due to ideas about any Weberian state monopoly on force, etc.). And this is not a surprising result, to the extent it describes the behavior of sophisticated private parties engaged in dispute resolution in industrialized countries where the rule of law is unquestioned. They use courts and litigation where necessary, but litigation is more a tactical tool than ideal dispute resolution (Linnan 2008).

Meanwhile, ROL approaches' seeming concentration on the judiciary as central focus for legal development efforts, the crux since 1960s Latin America, is probably misplaced. The tension is exemplified in this book in the formal assumptions of Chapter 16 concerning the judiciary (essentially traditional law and economics assumptions including instrumentalism), versus Chapter 17's insistence that formalism is not enough in dealing with the judiciary under conditions of particularistic politics. Instrumentalism at the individual level entails an element of "horses for courses," so a dispute may be better resolved outside the formal legal system (compare Linnan 2008). The secular or national focus of "law" may lie equally in the regulatory state in modern practice (as under Continental public law, attractive historically in Asia), with the traditional attractiveness of judicial and court reform for ROL presumably saying more about the mindset of ROL donors from Common Law-based legal systems, rather than local priorities. This coincidentally calls into question revised views of the legal origins hypothesis' flexibility focus that the Common Law's advantage lies in its judicial institutions, rather than any substantive rules.

At a social level, foreigners targeting truly exogenous development of legal institutions (a functional description of much ROL work under legal transplant analysis) is theoretically possible, but very, very difficult in practice. Modernization as Westernization is of doubly doubtful utility as a result for the non-Western world. Facially neutral "international standards" approaches may succeed, but perhaps as private replacement for an absent state (compare Nenova and Harford 2004), rather than "modernization" of the state itself, or as proof of legal convergence. International standards approaches may thus be a reaction to dysfunctionality, and so instead a curious variant of endogenous response. The interesting speculation would be the extent to which this might explain much about responses to endemic corruption, where "international standards" (or, equally, ethics in religion in opposition to corruption, as the argument may run in Islamic societies) may be a battle cry to displace the whole of local practice and legal institutions. But it may be conceived of equally as recreating extra-legal norms and enforcement systems as envisioned in historical terms by NIE proponents. Such may also be the practical backstop for formal law, as reflected by Chapter 24.

## Industrialization, Climate Change and Legal Development

The further question is whether simply reworking views of modernization involving legal development suffices going forward. The answer is arguably no, to the extent the broader economic framework has been changing too. Climate change and related greenhouse gas concerns are hardly incorporated into traditional ideas about development as such, nor ROL concepts, despite their impending impacts on industrialization as preferred development strategy (looking to East Asia as example). In economic terms, this may constitute the insight that growth may be less a result of endogenous factors in terms of institutional development or (historical) human capital, and more the result of exogenous factors like access to external markets (under export-led development strategies, which economists could interpret simply as producing gains keyed to increasing scale of production; compare Krugman 1994). And what does this tell us potentially about the relative importance of (endogenous) institutional development, which is where legal and economic development is currently understood to meet under American views? There is much talk of "sustainable development" as political concept, but there exists a basic disconnect between technical economic concepts like externalities, pollution and growth as they relate to economic development.[33]

This question is posed against the background of a distinct shift in international relations or political science approaches, from traditional concepts of state-centered "national security" to so-called "human security" approaches since 1990. This is also visible in definitional approaches to development, in particular in discussions surrounding the Human Development Report (HDR) of the United Nations Development Program (UNDP) and its related Human Development Index (HDI, which adds social indicators like life expectancy and education levels to traditional economic indicators like GDP per capita). The 1994 Human Development Report defined the human security approach in terms of "freedom from fear" (physical security) and "freedom from want" (economic security), while the human security approach is now the basis for conceptualizing non-traditional security threats such as AIDS (public health) and climate change (UNDP 2010). The 2011 Human Development Report is still in progress, but promises to focus on patterns of human development at national and global levels, focusing on the growing evidence of inequality and environmental threats.[34] The traditional link to economically oriented development policy is that even its proponents admit that the Washington Consensus may increase domestic economic inequality (under traditional Gini coefficient measures), while industrialization's pollution effects are generally recognized.

Development has so far been accomplished worldwide via pollution-heavy industrialization. Countries that experienced rapid growth of productivity and living standards over the past 200 years have done so via industrialization. The story is largely the same, whether the countries in question were eighteenth-century Britain, or nineteenth-century America and Japan, or twentieth-century Korea and China (see Murphy et al. 1989). Industrialization historically is linked to environmental degradation, and such damage has been endemic to the development process. Resource extraction, factory production, population concentration, and the disposal of unwanted by-products all generate pollution in some form (for example, Lofdahl 1998; Newell 1997). Greenhouse gas emissions are now recognized as a significant form of atmospheric pollution, both in developed and developing countries and the problems are not new since they lay behind the 1992 Rio Declaration on the Environment and Development, and, for that matter, the 1972

---

33 Determined assertions are made concerning the primacy of human rights law and democratization (understood here as the civil and political rights branch of human rights law), meanwhile there is at least a logical inconsistency in disclaiming legal change in the climate change setting based upon traditional sovereignty-based arguments. Treated as a source of law question, human rights law's articulation seemingly results more as a matter of general principles of law, rather than customary law approaches. Meanwhile, the US position seems to be that any climate change law can only be made via treaty, in terms of traditional sources doctrine. Without intending to pursue a rights-based approach to international environmental law, what is the underlying basis for differentiating so sharply between human rights and climate change law on the technical level of formation of law, given ROL's seeming human rights emphasis?

34 See *Human Development Report 2011: Sustainability and Equity: A Better Future for All*, http://hdr. undp.org/en/reports/global/hdr2011/. Meanwhile, to appearances, current (military) intervention into Libya with the express justification of protecting civilians may represent application of the human security approach to traditional security threats.

Stockholm Declaration on the Human Environment (both considered foundational documents in international environmental law).[35]

"Sustainable development" as legal nexus is typically understood as representing the overlap between economic, environmental and human rights law, in the face of a perceived conflict between environmental protection and economic growth imperatives. It is not a sharply defined concept, and may simply equate to human security's "freedom from want" on the economic side (so more aspirational goal, rather than providing a map to concrete policy). Our interest is the more direct conflict between export-oriented growth linked to industrialization as preferred strategy of successful (mostly Asian) developmental states and climate change. The effects of this conflict are already visible in the Kyoto Protocol's failure, to the extent developing countries refused to accept limitations on their greenhouse gas emissions, understanding it as a limitation on their economic development. The problem in practical terms is that limiting emissions is perceived as limiting industrialization itself as preferred development strategy. Some would point to other potential paths to economic development (tourism, or services more generally), but these exceptions may be easier to argue at the level of a single country than at the global level where more than half of humanity might be trying to raise living standards at the same time. Where our question leads is whether and how public international law on the environmental side may insert itself as legal development subject into the (normative, meaning thick rather than thin) ROL discussion too.

If current scientific thinking about the impending effects of anthropogenic climate change is correct, then a substantial roadblock may be raised to development.[36] The premise is that developed countries, having already made significant economic headway, are becoming increasingly concerned with global environmental degradation and that "[t]hey would like poor states to avoid adopting the same form of industrialization by which they themselves became rich" in order to

---

35   Carbon dioxide is now commonly identified as a major greenhouse gas raising the concern that "the uncontrolled emission of greenhouse gases … into the atmosphere [will give] rise to the 'greenhouse effect' which scientists predict could lead to global warming and climatic change" (Dzidonu and Foster 2003: 321). While the absolute volume of carbon dioxide emissions in developing countries may be lower than their Western counterparts, the rate of emission growth is substantially higher. By way of example, member countries of the Association of Southeast Asian Nations (ASEAN), which have been widely regarded as export-led development success stories, are prime examples. Between 1990 and 2007, the volume of carbon dioxide emitted in Indonesia has increased by 165.5 percent, in Thailand by 189.6 percent, and in Malaysia by 243.6 percent. The rate of growth was much smaller in the Philippines (59.2 percent) but was still substantially higher than in most industrialized Western nations. See The World Bank, CO2 Emissions (kt) (2007) (during the same time period some European countries experienced a reduction in the total rate of carbon dioxide emissions: the United Kingdom saw a decrease of 5.4 percent, France 6.8 percent, and Germany 18.0 percent. Some countries experienced a moderate growth in emissions: the United States increased its emission rate by 19.9 percent and Canada increased by 23.8 percent. Even the poorer developing areas of Europe experienced emission rate increases substantially lower than those in most Southeast Asian developing countries: Greece 34.9 percent increase and Spain 57.8 percent increase. Moreover, the total volume of carbon dioxide emissions in some ASEAN countries is beginning to become comparable to the European countries that led the world in industrialization (compare 2007 carbon dioxide kiloton emission levels (in millions) in Indonesia (396,818.53), Thailand (277,284.19), and Malaysia (194,316.58) with the UK (539,175.92), France (371,452.66) and Germany (787,291.01)). The problem is all the more acute in China which has passed the United States as the leading emitter of greenhouse gases.

36   The problem circles back on itself in part in conjunction with the "what is development" question, but comparison of trends over time in the 2010 Human Development Report yields the conclusion that it is comparatively much easier to raise social components of the HDI like public health or education indicators, as compared with per capita GDP.

avoid exponential growth in the emission of atmospheric pollutants (Shue 1999). Even for those countries that are in the process of industrializing, any cap-and-reduce approach to greenhouse gas emissions would almost certainly require emission reductions on their part. Estimates for even modest versions of such plans in high carbon dioxide producing countries like China and India are predicted to cause a 9–11 percent decline in manufacturing exports (Mattoo et al. 2009). The evidence in collateral disputes like once and future controversies concerning yuan exchange rates demonstrates how such countries may believe that such a measure resulting in a decline in manufacturing exports invariably will be unacceptable for domestic political reasons.[37]

This facet of the problem is seemingly a form of catch-22: development can generally only be achieved by industrialization and acceptance of economic systems, which can no longer be embraced. It may eventually need to be prevented by the countries that have both already industrialized and encouraged the traditional neoclassical economic paradigm which underlies also ROL efforts (that good governance leads to economic development; and law is supposedly necessary to both good governance and economic development). Resolving this catch-22 is beyond our scope, but note the centrality of those concerns to developing countries and their engagement in legal development on the public international law side. Thus, Chapter 25 addresses the precautionary principle, considered part of sustainable development law.[38] For our purposes, it is enough to register that developing countries now take matters like climate change and global warming seriously, and so are interested in articulating law. So much as Western countries were once accused of pushing human rights law against the developmental state, the developing countries are increasingly pushing back in the opposite direction on greenhouse gas and climate change concerns in a legal setting.

Beyond attention to traditional sources doctrine, the creation of international law in such areas is now an active part of what developing countries may consider to be part of ROL (perhaps a different take on the thick versus thin "rule of law" debate, but which could draw in the alternative on UN ROL views that ROL involves both international and domestic law; see UN Report of the Secretary General 2009). And interest in development and the role of international law as part of ROL is a broader concern also on the European side, as witnessed by Chapter 23 looking at the European Human Rights Convention's effects in Eastern Europe, or Chapter 24 exploring international and national legal change concerning corruption also in Eastern Europe. What seems to be changing is that legal development concerns are expanding arguably beyond national into

---

37   Sustainable development and technological innovations are commonly offered as solutions to the underlying problem of ameliorating industrialization's challenges. First, concerning new technologies, there is the necessity to develop these prophesized technologies, even before confronting the "who pays" question (with developing countries claiming they could not afford the technology, so industrialized countries should provide it gratis as "technology transfer"). Second, there is a broader aspect of cost. Sustainable development through utilization of renewable energy and installation of state of the art technologies will be more expensive than following traditional industrialization. This added cost may well serve to undercut the export dependent markets that have thus far proved successful for development. Moreover, using higher cost technologies and modes of production runs contrary to the neoclassical economic concepts underlying views like the Washington Consensus (Haque 1999). While one hears less in development circles about the Washington Consensus than 10 years ago, its emphasis on deregulation and keeping costs low militate towards the industrialization practices that are threatening climate change (Haque 1999).

38   Under ILA Res. 3/2002, "New Delhi Declaration on Principles of International Law Relating to Sustainable Development," accessible at www.cisdl.org/pdf/ILAdeclaration.pdf. The general character of sustainable development as legal concept is problematic, particularly whether it has acceded to the status of customary law (compare Lowe 1999: 23 with Sands 2003: 254–5). There is a much broader argument, however, concerning sustainable development's status in legal terms or even as a policy norm based upon the idea that it functions almost like a Rorschach test: everyone looking at the concept sees something different.

international law, if taken at face value (or, in the alternative, it is difficult for IFIs and developed countries to make governance arguments only at the national level as under American ROL approaches while maintaining that they are value-neutral). Not coincidentally, this surfaces issues about ROL's proper place alongside liberalism and redistributive concerns (compare Tamanaha 2008: 541–7), which might help to bridge understanding as with views expressed in Chapter 7.

Looking backwards, this is a further step beyond the liberal legalism of Law and Development, legal origins' comparative analysis of how states relate to the market, or our analysis of how a new articulation of modernization in conjunction with legitimacy concerns may better address empirically how legal development actually works in practice. The "chicken or egg" problem is reflected differently in each. Law and Development as well as legal origins reflect generally assumptions that legal development works instrumentally because they tend to focus in practice on "law on the books." Modernization in its new, revised form addresses this via a focus on legitimacy, absent which behavior will not change. Finally, legitimacy is the touchstone for developing states pressing the issue whether ROL now extends beyond domestic to international law. This takes us at least two steps beyond Law and Development, including its embedded assumptions about a causal relationship between democracy and economic growth.

## References

Acemoglu, Daron, Simon Johnson and James Robinson. December 2001. The Colonial Origins of Comparative Development: An Empirical Investigation. *American Economic Review*, 91(5), 1369–401.

Acemoglu, Daron, Simon Johnson and James Robinson. 2002. Reversal of Fortune: Geography and Development in the Making of the Modern World Income Distribution. *Quarterly Journal of Economics*, 117(4), 1231–94.

Acemoglu, Daron, Simon Johnson and James Robinson. 2005. A Response to Albouy's "A Reexamination Based on Improved Settler Mortality Data." Available at: http://econ-www.mit.edu/files/203.

Acemoglu, Daron, Simon Johnson and James Robinson. 2006. Reply to the Revised (May 2006) Version of David Albouy's "The Colonial Origins of Comparative Development: An Investigation of the Settler Mortality Data." Available at: http://econ-www.mit.edu/files/212.

Al Jazeera. 2010. US Unveils New Security Strategy: Document Downplays Fears the US is "at War" with Islam. Press Release, May 28, 2010 (commenting on May 2010 release of US National Security Strategy). Available at: http://english.aljazeera.net/news/americas/2010/05/2010527124921463370.html.

Arat, Zehra R. 1988. Democracy and Economic Development: Modernization Theory Revisited. *Comparative Politics*, 21(1), 21–36.

Armour, John, Simon Deakin, Viviana Mollica and Mathias Siems. 2009. Law and Financial Development: What We Are Learning from Time-Series Evidence. *Brigham Young University Law Review*, 1435–500.

Bannon, Alice L. 2006. The Responsibility to Protect: The U.N. World Summit and the Question of Unilateralism. *Yale Law Journal*, 115, 1157–65.

Bauzon, Kenneth E., ed. 1992. *Development and Democratization in the Third World: Myths, Hopes, and Realities*. Washington, DC: Crane Russak.

Bayliss, Kate, Ben Fine and Elisa Van Waeyenberge, eds. 2011. *The Political Economy of Development: The World Bank, Neoliberalism and Developmental Research.* London: Pluto Press.

Berger, Mark T. 2004. *The Battle for Asia: From Decolonization to Globalization.* London and New York: RoutledgeCurzon.

Berkowitz, Daniel, Katharina Pistor and Jean-Francois Richard. 2003. The Transplant Effect. *American Journal of Comparative Law,* LI(1), 163–203.

Birdsall, Nancy and Francis Fukuyama. 2011. The Post-Washington Consensus: Development after the Crisis. *Foreign Affairs,* 90(2), 45–54.

Carothers, Thomas. 2009. Revitalizing U.S. Democracy Assistance: The Challenge of USAID. Washington, DC: Carnegie Endowment for International Peace. Available at: www. carnegieendowment.org/files/revitalizing_democracy_assistance.pdf.

Carothers, Thomas, Scott Hubli, Brian Levy and Marc F. Plattner. 2010. The Elusive Synthesis: Exploring the Changing Relationship Between Democracy Support and Development Aid. Washington, DC: Carnegie Endowment for International Peace, October 10 (event video). Available at: www.carnegieendowment.org/events/index.cfm?fa=eventDetail&id=3038.

Centre de Doctrine d'Emploi des Forces. 2007. *FT-01 (ENG) Winning the Battle, Building the Peace: Land Forces in Present and Future Conflicts.* Paris: Centre de Doctrine d'Emploi des Forces.

Center for Law and Military Operations. 2010. *Rule of Law Handbook: A Practitioner's Guide for Judge Advocates.* 4th edn. Charlottesville, VA: CLAMO (institute and publication of the Judge Advocate General's Legal Center and School). Available at: www.loc.gov/rr/frd/Military_Law/ pdf/rule-of-law_2010.pdf.

Clarke, Donald C. 2007. What Kind of Legal System is Necessary for Economic Development? The China Puzzle, in *Law Reform in Developing and Transitional States,* edited by T.C. Lindsey. Oxford: Routledge, 65–82.

Coyne, Christopher. 2008. *After War: The Political Economy of Exporting Democracy.* Stanford: Stanford University Press.

Cox, M.G., J. Ikenberry and T. Inoguchi, eds. 2000. *American Democracy Promotion: Impulses, Strategies, and Impacts.* Oxford: Oxford University Press.

Crawford, Gordon. 2001. *Foreign Aid and Political Reform: A Comparative Analysis of Democracy Assistance and Political Conditionality.* Basingstoke and New York: Palgrave.

Dam, Kenneth W. 2006. *The Law-Growth Nexus: The Rule of Law and Economic Development.* Washington, DC: Brookings Institution Press.

Department of the Army. 2006. FM 3-24 (MCWP 3-33.5) *Counterinsurgency.* Washington, DC: Headquarters, Department of the Army, December. Available at: www.scribd.com/doc/9137276/ US-Army-Field-Manual-FM-324-Counterinsurgency.

Department of the Army. 2009a. FM 1-04 (27-100) *Legal Support to the Operational Army.* Washington, DC: Headquarters, Department of the Army, April. Available at: www.fas.org/irp/ doddir/army/fm1-04.pdf.

Department of the Army. 2009b. FM 3-07 *Stability Operations.* Washington, DC: Headquarters, Department of the Army, April. Available at: http://usacac.army.mil/CAC2/Repository/FM307/ FM3-07.pdf.

Department of State. 2011. Leading Through Civilian Power, First Quadrennial Diplomacy and Development Review. Available at: www.state.gov/s/dmr/qddr/.

Diamond, Larry. 1992. Economic Development and Democracy Reconsidered, in *Reexamining Democracy: Essays in Honor of Seymour Martin Lipset*, edited by Larry Diamond and Gary Marks. Newbury Park: Sage Publications, 93–139.

Djankov, Simeon, Edward Glaeser, Rafael La Porta, Florencio Lopez-de-Silanes and Andrei Shleifer. 2003. The New Comparative Economics. *Journal of Comparative Economics*, 31, 595–619.

Dobson, Richard and Seymour Martin Lipset. 1972. The Intellectual as Critic and Rebel: With Special Reference to the United States and the Soviet Union. *Daedelus*, 101, 137–98.

*Doing Business 2010: Reforming Through Difficult Times (Comparing Regulation in 183 Economies)*. 2009. Washington, DC, New York and Basingstoke: World Bank, IFC and Palgrave Macmillan.

Dollar, David and Aart Kraay. 2003. Institutions, Trade and Growth. *Journal of Monetary Economics*, 50, 133–62.

Dzidonu, C.K. and Foster, F.G. 1993. Prolegomena to OR Modeling of the Global Environment-Development Problem. *Journal of Operational Research Society*, 44, 321–31.

Easterly, William and Ross Levine. 2003. Tropics, Germs, and Crops: How Endowments Influence Economic Development. *Journal of Monetary Economics*, 50, 3–39.

Eickelman, D.F. 2000. Islam and the Languages of Modernity. *DAEDALUS*, 129(1), 119–35.

Ekbladh, David. 2010. *The Great American Mission: Modernization & the Construction of an American World Order*. Princeton and Oxford: Princeton University Press.

El-Ansary, Waleed and David K. Linnan. 2010. Narrative Introduction, in *Muslim and Christian Understanding: Theory and Application of "A Common Word,"* edited by W. El-Ansary and D.K. Linnan. New York: Palgrave Macmillan, 1–14.

Gilman, Nils. 2003. *Mandarins of the Future: Modernization Theory in Cold War America*. Baltimore: Johns Hopkins University Press.

Ginsburg, Tom. 2000. Does Law Matter for Economic Development? Evidence from East Asia. *Law and Society Review*, 34(3), 829–56.

Glaeser, Edward L., Rafael La Porta, Florencio Lopez-de-Silanes and Andrei Shleifer. 2004. Do Institutions Cause Growth? *Journal of Economic Growth*, 9, 271–303.

Govern, Kevin H. 2008. The Legal Way Ahead Between War and Peace, in *Enemy Combatants, Terrorism and Armed Conflict Law: A Guide to the Issues*, edited by David K. Linnan. Westport: Praeger Security International, 280.

Granovetter, Mark. 1985. Economic Action and Social Structure: The Problem of Embeddedness. *American Journal of Sociology*, 91(3), 481–510.

Granovetter, Mark. 2005. The Impact of Social Structure on Economic Outcomes. *Journal of Economic Perspectives*, 19(1), 33–50.

Guidance Note of the Secretary-General: UN Approach to Rule of Law Assistance. April 2008. Available at: www.unrol.org/files/RoL%20Guidance%20Note%20UN%20Approach%20FINAL.pdf.

Hall, Laura A. 2010. Stimpson Brief: The Future of S/CRS. Budgeting for Foreign Affairs and Defense Blog, June 29. Available at: http://apps.stimson.org/budgeting/pdf/Stimson_Brief_%20 The_Future_of_S_CRS.pdf.

Hall, Laura A. and Jonathan M. Larkin. 2010. No Civilian Left Behind: Educating the Elusive "Interagency." The Will and the Wallet: Budget Insights for Foreign Affairs and Defense Policy Blog, October 6. Available at: http://thewillandthewallet.org/2010/10/06/no-civilian-left-behind-educating-the-elusive-%e2%80%9cinteragency%e2%80%9d/.

Hall, Robert E. and Charles I. Jones. 1999. Why do some Countries Produce so much more Output per Worker than Others? *Quarterly Journal of Economics*, 114(1), 83–116.

Haque, M. Shamsul. 1999. The Fate of Sustainable Development under Neo-Liberal Regimes in Developing Countries. *International Political Science Review*, 20(2), 197–218.

Jamal, Amaney A. 2006. Reassessing Support for Islam and Democracy in the Arab World? *World Affairs*, Fall, 51.

Jayasuriya, Kanishka, ed. 1999. *Law Capitalism and Power in Asia: The Rule of Law and Legal Institutions*. London and New York: Routledge.

Jensen, Erik G. and Thomas C. Heller, eds. 2003. *Beyond Common Knowledge: Empirical Appraoches to the Rule of Law*. Stanford: Stanford University Press.

Johnson, Gregory, Vijaya Ramachandran and Julie Walz. September 2011. The Commanders Emergency Response Program in Afghanistan: Refining U.S. Military Capabilities in Stability and In-Conflict Development Activities. Center for Global Development WP 265. Available at www.cgdev.org/files/1425397_file_Johnson_Ramachandran_Walz_CERP_FINAL.pdf.

Joint Forces Staff College (JFSC). 2000. *The Joint Staff Officer's Guide 2000*. Norfolk: JFSC, E-1 (JFSC Pub 1) (Appendix E: The Military in Operations Other than War). Available at: www.au.af.mil/au/awc/awcgate/pub1/introduction.pdf.

Kennedy, David. 2006a. The "Rule of Law," Political Choices, and Development Common Sense, in *The New Law and Economic Development: A Critical Appraisal*, edited by David M. Trubek and Alvaro Santos. Cambridge: Cambridge University Press, 95–173.

Kennedy, Duncan. 2006b. Three Globalizations of Law and Legal Thought: 1850–2000, in *The New Law and Economic Development: A Critical Appraisal*, edited by David M. Trubek and Alvaro Santos. Cambridge: Cambridge University Press, 19–73.

Kohn, Meir. 2009. Economic Development and Growth: A Survey. *Cato Journal*, 29(2), 237–46.

Krugman, Paul. 1994. The Fall and Rise of Development Economics, in *Rethinking the Development Experience: Essays Provoked by the Work of Albert O. Hirschman*, edited by L. Rodwin and D. Schon. Washington, DC: Brookings Institution, 39–58.

Landler, Mark. 2010. The Saturday Profile: Curing the Ills of America's Top Foreign Aid Agency. *New York Times*, October 22. Available at: www.nytimes.com/2010/10/23/world/23shah.html?_r=2&ref=agency_for_international_development.

La Porta, Rafael, Florencio Lopez-de-Silanes and Andrei Shleifer. 2008. The Economic Consequences of Legal Origins. *Journal of Economic Literature*, 46(2), 285–332.

La Porta, Rafael, Florencio Lopez-de-Silanes, Andrei Shleifer and Robert W. Vishny. 1997. Legal Determinants of External Finance. *Journal of Finance*, 52(3), 1131–50.

La Porta, Rafael, Florencio Lopez-de-Silanes, Andrei Shleifer and Robert W. Vishny. 1998. Law and Finance. *Journal of Political Economy*, 106(6), 1113–55.

La Porta, Rafael, Florencio Lopez-de-Silanes, Andrei Shleifer and Robert Vishny. 1999. The Quality of Government. *Journal of Law, Economics & Organization*, 15(1), 222–79.

Latham, Michael E. 2000. *Modernization as Ideology: American Social Science and "Nation Building" in the Kennedy Era*. Chapel Hill and London: University of North Carolina Press.

Leepson, Marc. 2000. The Heart and Mind of USAID's Vietnam Mission. *American Foreign Service Association*, April. Available at: www.afsa.org/fsj/apr00/leepson.cfm.

Linnan, David K. 1984. Police Discretion in a Continental Administrative State: The Police of Baden-Wuerttemberg in the Federal Republic of Germany. *Law and Contemporary Problems*, 47(4), 185–223.

Linnan, David K. 2007. Like a Fish Needs a Bicycle: Public Law Theory, Civil Society and Governance Reform in Indonesia, in *Law Reform in Developing and Transitional States*, edited by Timothy Lindsey. London: Routledge, 268–90.

Linnan, David K. 2008. Commercial Law Enforcement in Indonesia: The Manulife Case, in *Indonesia: Law and Society*, edited by T. Lindsey. 2nd edn. Singapore and Sydney: ISEAS and the Federation Press, 596–619.

Linnan, David K. 2010a. A Common View of Development: Richer Versus Better, and Who Decides?, in *Muslim and Christian Understanding: Theory and Application of "A Common Word,"* edited by W. El-Ansary and D.K. Linnan. New York: Palgrave Macmillan, 235–57.

Linnan, David K. 2010b. Reading the Tea Leaves in the Indonesian Commercial Court: A Cautionary Tale, but for whom?, in *New Courts in Asia*, edited by A. Harding and P. Nicholson. Oxford: Routledge, 56–79.

Lipset, Seymour Martin. 1959. Some Social Requisites of Democracy: Economic Development and Political Legitimacy. *American Political Science Review*, 53(1), 69–105.

Lipset, Seymour Martin. 1964. The Changing Class Structure and Contemporary European Politics. *DAEDALUS*, 271–303.

Lipset, Seymour Martin. 1966. University Students and Politics in Underdeveloped Countries. *Comparative Education Review*, 10(2), 132–62.

Lipset, Seymour Martin. 1984. China in Transition: A Travel Memoir, May-June 1984. *PS*, Autumn, 765–77.

Lofdahl, Corey L. 1998. On the Externalities of Global Trade. *International Political Science Review*, 19(4), 339–55.

Lowe, Vaughn. 1999. Sustainable Development and Unsustainable Arguments, in *International Law and Sustainable Development: Past Achievements and Future Challenges*, edited by A. Boyle and D. Freestone. Oxford: Oxford University Press, 19–38.

MacDonald, Lawrence. 2010. Tempered Optimism on New U.S. Development Policy: Connie Veillette. Center for Global Development. Available at: http://blogs.cgdev.org/global_prosperity_wonkcast/2010/09/27/tempered-optimism-on-new-u-s-development-policy-connie-veillette/.

Mahoney, Paul G. 2001. The Common Law and Economic Growth: Hayek Might be Right. *Journal of Legal Studies*, 30, 503.

Mansfield, John H. 2008. Promotion of Liberal Islam by the United States, in *Enemy Combatants, Terrorism, and Armed Conflict Law: A Guide to the Issues*, edited by David K. Linnan. Westport and London: Praeger Security International, 85–91.

Mattoo, Aaditya, A. Subramanian, Dominique van der Mensbrugghe and Jianwu He. 2009. *Can Global De-Carbonization Inhibit Developing Country Industrialization?* Washington, DC: World Bank.

MDGs and Theories of Change. 2010. Aid on the Edge of Chaos, October 5 (Blog). Available at: http://aidontheedge.info/2010/10/05/mdgs-and-theories-of-change/.

Michaels, Ralf. 2009. Comparative Law by Numbers? Legal Origins Thesis, Doing Business Reports, and the Silence of Traditional Comparative Law. *American Journal of Comparative Law*, LVII(4), 765–95.

Milhaupt, Curtis J. 2009. Beyond Legal Origin: Rethinking Law's Relationship to the Economy-- Implications for Policy. *American Journal of Comparative Law*, LVII(4), 831–45.

Milhaupt, Curtis J. and Katharina Pistor. 2008. *Law and Capitalism: What Corporate Crises Reveal about Legal Systems and Economic Development around the World*. Chicago and London: University of Chicago Press.

Muller, Jerry Z. 2002. *The Mind and the Market: Capitalism in Western Thought*. New York: Anchor Books.

Muravchik, Joshua. 1991. *Exporting Democracy: Fulfilling America's Destiny*. Washington, DC: AEI Press.

Murphy, K.M., A. Shleifer and R.W. Vishny. 1989. Industrialization and the Big Push. *The Journal of Political Economy*, 97(5), 1003–26.

Nenova, Tatiana and Tim Harford. 2004. *Anarchy and Invention: How Does Somalia's Private Sector Cope without Government?* Washington, DC: World Bank November (Public Policy for the Private Sector Note No. 280).

New Directions in Development Economics: Theory or Empirics? 2005. *Economic and Political Weekly*, Symposium Issue, August.

Newell, Edmund. 1997. Atmospheric Pollution and the British Copper Industry, 1690–1920. *Technology and Culture*, 38(3), 655–89.

North, Douglas C. 1981. *Structure and Change in Economic History*. New York and London: W.W. Norton & Co.

North, Douglas C. 1991. Institutions. *Journal of Economic Perspectives*, 5(1), 97–112.

Organisation for Economic Cooperation and Development. 2007. OECD DAC Handbook on Security System Reform: Supporting Security and Justice. Available at: www.oecd.org/dataoecd/43/25/38406485.pdf.

Peerenboom, Randal P. 2003. Competing Conceptions of the Rule of Law in China, in *East Asian Law: Universal Norms and Local Cultures*, edited by A. Rossett, L. Cheng and M.Y.K. Woo. London: RoutledgeCurzon, 51–84.

Peerenboom, Randall P., ed. 2004. *Asian Discourses of Rule of Law: Theories and Implementation of Rule of Law in Twelve Asian Countries, France and the U.S.* London: RoutledgeCurzon.

Pereira, Anthony W. 1993. Economic Underdevelopment, Democracy and Civil Society: The North-east Brazilian Case. *Third World Quarterly*, 14(2), 365–80.

Perito, Robert M. 2005. The U.S. Experience with Provincial Reconstruction Teams in Afghanistan: Lessons Identified. Washington, DC: United States Institute of Peace, October (USIP Special Report). Available at: www.usip.org/publications/us-experience-provincial-reconstruction-teams-afghanistan-lessons-identified.

Pistor, Katarina. 2009. Rethinking the "Law and Finance" Paradigm. *Brigham Young University Law Review*, 1647–70.

Pistor, Katarina and Phillip A. Wellons. 1999. *The Role of Law and Legal Institutions in Asian Economic Development, 1960–1995*. Oxford and New York: Oxford University Press.

Presidential Policy Directive 7 on Global Development. 2010. (White House factsheet, as PPD 7 itself is classified). Press release available at: www.whitehouse.gov/the-press-office/2010/09/22/fact-sheet-us-global-development-policy.

Przeworski, A. and L. Fernando. 1997. Modernization: Theories and Facts. *World Politics*, 49(2), 155–83.

Przeworski, Adam, Michael E. Alvarez, Jose Antonio Cheibub and Fernando Limongi. 2000. *Democracy and Development: Political Institutions and Well-Being in the World, 1950–1990*. Cambridge: Cambridge University Press.

Pye, Lucien W. 1979. Political Modernization: Gaps Between Theory and Reality. *Annals of the American Academy of Political and Social Science*, March, 28–39.

Ramaswamy, Sunder and Jeffrey W. Cason, eds. 2003. *Development and Democracy: New Perspectives on an Old Debate*. Hanover and London: University Press of New England.

Reed, Clifton D. 2008. The Battle Within: DOD and Interagency Coordination for Regional Conflicts—AFRICOM and the Interagency Management System as Models. Research Report, Air Command and Staff College, Air University, Maxwell Air Force Base, AL, April.

Available at: www.afresearch.org/skins/rims/display.aspx?moduleid=be0e99f3-fc56-4ccb-8dfe- 670c0822a153&mode=user&action=downloadpaper&objectid=8eac006c-48e2-47f5-afad-86570261b7ba&rs=PublishedSearch.

Reinhardt, Carmen M. and Kenneth S. Rogoff. 2009. *This Time is Different: Eight Centuries of Financial Folly*. Princeton: Princeton University Press.

Rist, Gilbert. 2008. *The History of Development: From Western Origins to Global Faith*. 3rd edn. London and New York: Zed Books (trans. Patrick Camiller).

Roderik, Dan, Arvind Subramanian and Francesco Trebbi. 2004. Institutions Rule: The Primacy of Institutions Over Geography and Integration in Economic Development. *Journal of Economic Growth*, 9, 131–65.

Roe, Mark and Jordan Siegal. 2009. Finance and Politics: A Review Essay Based on Kenneth Dam's Analysis of Legal Traditions in The Law-Growth Nexus. Harvard Law Scool John M. Olin Center for Law, Economics and Business Discussion Paper 625. Available at: http://lsr.nellco.org/harvard_olin/625.

Ruiz, Moses. 2009. *Sharpening the Spear: The United States' Provincial Reconstruction Teams in Afghanistan, Applied Research Project*. San Marcos: Texas State University. Available at: http://ecommons.txstate.edu/arp/297.

Sands, Philippe. 2003. *Principles of International Environmental Law*. 2nd edn. Cambridge: Cambridge University Press.

Santos, Alvaro. 2006. The World Bank's Use of the "Rule of Law" Promise in Economic Development, in *The New Law and Economic Development Model: A Critical Appraisal*, edited by D.M. Trubek and A. Santos, Cambridge: Cambridge University Press, 253–300.

Save the Children UK. 2004. *Provincial Reconstruction Teams and Humanitarian-Military Relations in Afghanistan*. London: Save the Children.

Shue, Henry. 1999. Global Environment and International Inequality. *Royal Institute of International Affairs*, 75(3), 531–45.

Stokke, Olav, ed. 1995. *Aid and Political Conditionality*. London and Geneva: Frank Cass and EADI.

Stromseth, J., D. Wippman and R. Brooks. 2006. *Can Might Make Rights? Building the Rule of Law After Military Interventions*. New York: Cambridge University Press.

Swedberg, Richard. 1994. Markets as Social Structures in *The Handbook of Economic Sociology*, edited by Ned Smelser and Richard Swedberg. Princeton: Princeton University Press, 255–82.

Tamahana, Brian Z. 1995. The Lessons of Law-and-Development Studies. *American Journal of International Law*, 89(2), 470–86.

Tamahana, Brian Z. 2006. *Law as a Means to an End: Threat to the Rule of Law*. New York and Cambridge: Cambridge University Press.

Tamahana, Brian Z. 2008. The Dark Side of the Relationship Between the Rule of Law and Liberalism. *NYU Journal of Law & Liberty*, 3, 516–47.

Tamahana, Brian Z. 2010. The Primacy of Society and the Failures of Law and Development: Decades of Stubborn Refusal to Learn. Washington University St Louis School of Law Faculty Research Paper No. 10-03-02. Available at: http://ssrn.com/abstract=1406999.

Taylor, Veronica. 2007. The Law Reform Olympics: Measuring the Effects of Law Reform in Transition Economies, in *Law Reform in Developing and Transitional States*, edited by T.C. Lindsey. Oxford: Routledge, 83–104.

Tessler, M.A. and Linda L. Hawkins. 1979. Acculturation, Socio-Economic Status, and Attitude Change in Tunisia: Implications for Modernization Theory. *The Journal of Modern African Studies*, 17(3), 473–95.

Tripp, A.M. 2004. Women's Movements, Customary Law and Land Rights in Africa: The Case of Uganda. *African Studies Quarterly*, 7(4). Available at: www.africa.ufl.edu/asq/v7/v7i4a1.htm.

Trubek, D.M. 2006. The "Rule of Law" in Development Assistance: Past, Present, and Future, in *The New Law and Economic Development: A Critical Appraisal*, edited by D.M. Trubek and A. Santos. Cambridge: Cambridge University Press, 74–94.

Trubek, D.M. and M. Galanter. 1974. Scholars in Self-Estrangement: Some Reflections on the Crisis in Law and Development Studies in the United States. *Wisconsin Law Review*, 1974(4), 1062–102.

Trubek, D.M. and A. Santos. 2006. Introduction: The Third Moment in Law and Development Theory and the Emergence of a New Critical Practice, in *The New Law and Economic Development: A Critical Appraisal*, edited by David M. Trubek and Alvaro Santos. Cambridge: Cambridge University Press, 1–18.

United Nations Development Program 2010. Human Development Report 2010: The Real Wealth of Nations: Pathways to Human Development. Available at: http://hdr.undp.org/en/reports/global/hdr2010/chapters/ (also published by Palgrave Macmillan, November 2010).

United Nations Report of the Secretary-General. 2004. The Rule of Law and Transitional Justice in Conflict and Post Conflict Societies. S/2004/616* (August 23, 2004). Available at: www.unrol.org/files/2004%20report.pdf.

United Nations Report of the Secretary-General. 2005. In Larger Freedom: Towards Development, Security and Human Rights for all. A/59/2005/Add. 3 (May 26, 2005). Available at: http://unrol.org/files/A.59.2005.Add.3%5B1%5D.pdf.

United Nations Report of the Secretary-General 2006. Uniting our Strengths: Enhancing United Nations Support for the Rule of Law. A/61/636-S/2006/980 (December 14, 2006). Available at: http://unrol.org/files/2006%20Report.pdf.

United Nations Report of the Secretary-General 2008. Strengthening and Coordinating United Nations Rule of Law Activities. A/63/226 (August 6, 2008). Available at: http://unrol.org/doc.aspx?d=2132US.

United Nations Report of the Secretary-General. 2009. Annual Report on Strengthening and Coordinating United Nations Rule of Law Activities. A/64/298 (August 17, 2009). Available at: http://unrol.org/files/A-64-298%20Annual%20SG%20report%20on%20strenghtening%20and%20coordinating%20UN%20RoL%20act.pdf.

United Nations Report of the Panel on United Nations Peace Operations. 2000. (Brahimi Report). A/55/305-S/2000/809 (August 21, 2000). Available at: www.un.org/peace/reports/peace_operations/.

United States Agency for International Development. 2007. *Iraq PRTs: Provincial Reconstruction Teams: Training Provincial and Local Governments: Fostering Economic Development; Promoting Reconciliation*. Washington, DC: USAID, Fall. Available at: www.usaid.gov/iraq/pdf/iraqprts_1007.pdf.

United States Agency for International Development, US Department of Defense and US Department of State. 2009. *Security Sector Reform*. Washington, DC: USAID, November. Available at: www.usaid.gov/our_work/democracy_and_governance/publications/pdfs/SSR_JS_Mar2009.pdf.

United States Department of State. 2010. A Look Back: Ambassador Herbst Retires. *Civilian Response*. Washington, DC: S/CRS, Summer(11), 3. Available at: www.state.gov/documents/organization/149326.pdf.

United States Institute of Peace and US Army Peacekeeping and Stability Operations Institute. 2009. *Guiding Principles for Stabilization and Reconstruction*. Washington, DC: USIP Books, November. Available at: www.usip.org/files/resources/guiding_principles_full.pdf.

United States Joint Forces Command. June 13, 2011. *Handbook for Military Support to Rule of Law and Security Sector Reform* (Unified Action Handbook Series Book 5). Available at: www.dtic.mil/doctrine/doctrine/jwfc/ruleoflaw_hbk.pdf.

Vassilev, Rossen. 1999. Modernization Theory Revisited: The Case of Bulgaria. *East European Politics & Societies*, 13(3), 566–99.

Walther, Horst. 2007. The German Concept for Provincial Reconstruction Teams: The Army's Principles of Employment and Experience in Matters of Peace Stabilization, 104–107.

West, Mark D. 2002. Legal Determinants of World Cup Success. Ann Arbor: Michigan Law and Economics Research Paper # 02-009. Available at: http://ssrn.com/abstract=318940 or doi:10.2139/ssrn.318940.

White House. 2010. National Security Strategy. Available at: www.whitehouse.gov/sites/default/files/rss_viewer/national_security_strategy.pdf.

Williams, Rebecca. 2010. This Old House: Tear Down or Remodel? Trends in Security Assistance and how we got here. The Will and the Wallet: Budget Insights for Foreign Affairs and Defense Policy Blog, October. Available at: http://thewillandthewallet.org/2010/10/22/this-old-house-tear-down-or-remodel/.

Williamson, Oliver E. 2000. Empirical Microeconomics: Another Perspective. University of California, Berkley, Working Paper. Available at: http://groups.haas.berkeley.edu/bpp/oew/emap14edw.pdf.

Williamson, Oliver E. 2005a. The Economics of Governance. *The American Economic Review*, 95(2), 1–18 (Richard T. Ely Lecture, Papers and Proceedings of the 117th Annual Meeting of the American Economic Association, Philadelphia, PA, January 7–9, 2005).

Williamson, Oliver E. 2005b. Why Law, Economics, and Organization? *Annual Review of Law and Social Science*, 1, 369–96.

The World Bank, CO2 Emissions (kt) (2007). Available at: HTTP://DATA.WORLDBANK.ORG/INDICATOR/EN.ATM.CO2E.KT.

World Summit Outcome Report. 2005. A/RES/60/1 (October 24, 2005). Available at: http://daccess-dds-ny.un.org/doc/UNDOC/GEN/N05/487/60/PDF/N0548760.pdf?OpenElement.

Wucherpfennig, Julian and Franziska Deutsch. 2009. Modernization and Democracy: Theories and Evidence Revisited. *Living Reviews in Democracy*, 1, 1–9.

Chapter 3

# Rethinking the Rule of Law as Antidote to African Development Challenges

Joseph M. Isanga

Since the 1990s, many African countries have carried out legal reforms—adopting new constitutions and bills of rights, meanwhile implementing judicial review of legislative and executive acts. These were in response to the rule of law promptings and international financial institution (IFI) conditionality, which were part of a concerted international effort to rid Africa of biting and seemingly intractable poverty. Those efforts, however, affected only a modicum of political, legal, and human rights improvements on the continent. International actors justified their support for the rule of law initiatives by citing studies that demonstrated the importance of functioning, fair, and accessible justice institutions to ensure social cohesion and combat poverty. For example, the World Bank's 2000 *Voices of the Poor* report pointed to the negative role played by the police, which it considered corrupt and responsible for harassing small traders (Piron 2006). Indeed, it is expected that the absence of the rule of law would impede investment efforts. The above simply assumes away our "chicken or egg" inquiry, attributing all African evils to an apparent shortage of "law," presumably to be remedied by legal and institutional reform in the abstract.

Yet, the promise of an economically bright future continues to elude many African countries that have made significant progress in establishing the rule of law. These countries continue to lag economically behind similarly situated Asian nations that hardly implemented such measures. East Asian countries are distinguished by their rapid economic growth, which is increasingly understood to be proof that formal laws and legal institutions are not central determinants of a country's economic development (compare Chapter 13). Informal mechanisms that recognize and protect private property rights and ensure performance of contracts are often effective substitutes (Davis 2008). Meanwhile, then International Monetary Fund (IMF) Managing Director, Dominique Strauss-Kahn, conceded "[w]e understand that we need to change the way we work with Africa" (International Monetary Fund 2009). The Obama Administration, while acknowledging the historical priority of human rights and good governance in international trade and financial assistance programs, seems to have de-emphasized the role of human rights in US–China relations (Spencer 2009).[1] Even in Africa, there are cases of economic growth not directly linked to democratic reforms, often as a result of Africa's continuing reliance on primary industries. For example, disregarding foreign aid, Togo owed its relative prosperity in the 1980s not exclusively to its governance, but rather to external factors, such as soaring prices for its major export commodity (Kohnert 2008).

---

1   US Secretary of State, Hillary Clinton, said the United States would continue to press China on issues such as human rights and Tibet, but also stated: "Our pressing on those issues can't interfere on the global economic crisis, the global climate change crisis and the security crisis" (Spencer 2009). This is not a suggestion that the rule of law played no role in Chinese economic growth. It has been observed that China conducted legal modernization efforts, although this did not go hand in hand with fundamental political reform (Ohnesorge 2007).

Undoubtedly, human rights and the rule of law will continue to remain important in addressing a host of international issues. But, when it comes to development on the African Continent, the need to seek broader solutions has never been more urgent. Africa's development challenges are extremely complex as they involve deep historical, geographic, ethnic, social, economic, and legal issues that call for multi-faceted approaches and will continue to defy monolithic solutions (Davis 2008). Seizing upon indicators of opportunity, some important international actors, such as the United States, may now be more willing to engage in broader approaches. This chapter first critically evaluates the rule of law in the development of Africa. Next, it offers insights into the complex nature of the African society and why broader approaches now seem necessary.

To confront clearly a continuing specter, Africans largely understand both traditional modernization theory and more recent efforts targeting the rule of law to be targeted at Westernization of Africa. The practical problem is that both modernization theory and rule of law approaches assume a picture of a predominantly urban society under a modern national state that is simply inapplicable to the vast majority of Africans. Our focus differs from traditional modernization and rule of law ideals in three ways. First, modernization theory was premised largely on industrialization and, implicitly, urbanization. Meanwhile, Africa remains predominantly rural, and customary law under traditional authority largely controls in rural areas over modern national law under secular, central government authorities (and this seems unlikely to change through the medium term despite standing rural–urban migration). Second, modernization and perceived rule of law concepts predicated on a strong, liberal state may have worked unintended consequences when laid over the gap between Africa's "modern" urban capitals and still predominantly rural "traditional" societies. Third, modernization's focus on national leadership and tertiary education to the detriment of secondary education (viewed as necessary to national development particularly in Asia) may have unwittingly exacerbated the yawning urban–rural divide. We call for a reinvigorated attention to mostly secondary educational programs in order radically to transform and ultimately sustain mostly rural African communities, while remaining mindful of the imperative of authentic development rooted in contemporary African traditions, sensibilities, and social realities.

## Rule of Law, Social Engineering, and Economic Development

A common argument is that the rule of law is a condition *sine qua non* for sustainable economic development (Druckman 1992). While the rule of law certainly may influence development, the effort and focus devoted to its promotion has arguably resulted in more important factors being overlooked. Some have even suggested that, when humanity ought to be cultivating new attitudes consistent with a new horizon or world order, the emphasis on the rule of law risks disingenuously resuscitating the long discredited colonial insistence on the "modernization" of Africa and ultimately promoting an uncritical transplantation of Western models. Others have a more favorable view of the connection between rule of law, development, and modernization as an effective means of establishing modern market systems. A leading proponent of the Law and Development school states that law is necessary to the establishment of markets because law provides universal and predictable rules (Trubek 1972). Along the same lines, others argue that where the "rule of law is absent or weak, property rights will be fragile, markets dysfunctional, and economic performance most likely unsustainable" (Amavilah 2008).

However, some suspect in these arguments an ulterior economic advantage for the advocates of market systems that do not necessarily result in progress for Africa. For instance, it is argued that good governance is an imposition of the Western, industrialized nations and international agencies, and the "underlying aim of this push for market governance is that of increasing the role of the private sector as the engine for economic growth and releasing market forces from what ware considered to be the constraints or clutches of government-imposed regulatory controls" (Gathii 1999). Scholars further argue that the economic development of Africa should not be predicated on the "Westernization"[2] of African societies, although this is to a significant extent precisely what has historically happened.

To this day, the African state continues to retain a high dosage of "Western" characteristics. Postcolonial African states have strived to fashion themselves in the image of the Western liberal state with limited success. The primary reason for this is that the Western liberal conception of states and democracy does not fit in Africa. The term "modern state" is usually meant for polities with three independent organs – the legislature, the executive, and judiciary. The Western multiparty system presumes the existence of a modern state, a fully functioning civil society, a free press, and constitutions grounded on the soil and clearly defined powers, rights, and responsibilities of all participants. However the African state, which is multicultural, significantly differs from the Western state, which is why wholesale transfers of legal structures into the African setting without appropriate adaptations cannot readily translate into development. Colonialism imposed boundaries on existing ethnic communities and called them "modern states," but that could easily create "imagined political communities" without the necessary cohesiveness and communion that was necessary to create a state. The boundaries of current African states do not coincide with the geographic extensions of ethnic entities (Smith 1991). It is no surprise that tribalism, nepotism, ethnic strife, and corruption continued to thrive in the African state. It was simplistically presumed that Western law would create a modern state out of these ethnic groups. But, despite the many years since colonialists imposed Western law, ethnic norms and structures of traditional authority persist, which is why they are recognized in several constitutions (Udombana 2003).

*The History of Rule of Law on the African Continent*

Certainly, it was necessary for the African state to shed some of its postcolonial autocratic and predatory attributes, which thrived on the Cold War divide. The colonial experience was never a plausible justification for mistakes and atrocities committed by postcolonial administrations during that time. That is precisely why the end of the Cold War precipitated the demise of most brutal dictatorships in Africa and unleashed a wave of democratization, constitutionalism, and rule of law emphases beginning in 1991 with the democratic elections in Benin. Throughout the 1990s and beginning of the new millennium, these reforms, often promoted by development actors as the antidote to Africa's economic challenges, seemed to hold the key to a political, legal, and economic dispensation in Africa. As part of this process, many African states ratified international human rights instruments that expanded the freedoms of their constituencies, particularly through the right of every individual to take part in the conduct of public affairs, directly or indirectly through

---

2   This view seems to have some credibility in light of African colonial history. European colonialists understood that they had to change the culture if their colonial experiment was to succeed. There was a deliberate attempt by some colonial masters to introduce British, French, and Portuguese culture through assimilation. Thus Colonel Trentinian, the governor of French Sudan in 1897 sent this circular to his subordinate: "Here in the Sudan, we confront a population which has been defeated militarily, it must now be conquered intellectually and morally. We must therefore draw the people to us, work with them constantly so that we can curb their spirit, impose our ideas upon them, and brand them with our particular stamp" (Skinner 1989).

freely chosen representatives.[3] It was hoped that the single-minded and consistent pursuit of the rule of law and good governance principles would automatically and instrumentally turn African economies around. This seemed to make sense in light of the preceding postcolonial experience.

However, almost two decades into the rule of law experiment, only a few countries in the region can claim to have really made any significant gains on the economic front. Africa is the only continent that has grown poorer over the last three decades. All regions of the world have experienced tremendous economic growth,[4] except for Africa, which continues to have the slowest growth (USAID 2008).

*The Insufficiency of Rule of Law*

The vital question is whether Western style democracy and rule of law can instrumentally produce an economic miracle in Africa, or whether it is now time for African states and international actors to broaden their outlook and try new approaches.[5] Critics argue that the insistence on the rule of law is no more than an exercise in nomenclature and semantics with the underlying substantive ideology remaining unchanged. They see the plan as essentially recycled, already discredited Bretton Woods institution (IMF and World Bank) strategies masquerading as a new approach (Pearce 2001). Critics further point out that the IMF and the World Bank, with a sense of vindication and leverage of Western economic systems, used structural adjustment programs forcing humbled former authoritarian regimes to deregulate their economies and restructure public administration.

––––––––––––––––––––

3   An overwhelming majority of African states signed and ratified the International Covenant on Civil and Political Rights (1966) which entered into force in 1976. Article 13 of the African Charter on Human and Peoples' Rights (1981) also provides for the right to participate freely in government. The African Commission on Human and Peoples' Rights had the opportunity to affirm this right in *Constitutional Rights Project and Civil Liberties Organization v. Nigeria* (1993), where the court held that the annulment of election results – reflecting "the free choice of the voters" – by the military government was in effect a violation of Article 13.1 of the Charter. In addition, the Commission's decision in *Legal Resources Foundation v. Zambia*, Communication (1998) held that Article 13 of the Charter included the freedom of everybody to compete for elective office. Indeed, the African Commission also adopted a Resolution on Electoral Process and Participatory Governance (1996), asserting that "elections are the only means by which the people can elect democratically the government of their choice in conformity to the African Charter on Human and Peoples' Rights."

4   For example, while the share of Africa's population earning less than US $1 per day fell by 1.4 percentage points over the 1990–8 period, it declined by 4 percentage points in South Asia and by 12.3 percentage points in East Asia. This meant that sub-Saharan Africa's share of the world's population living below US $1 per day increased from 19 percent to 24 percent in 1998 (Moser and Ichida 2001).

5   Some have even been highly critical of attempts to use Western style rule of law and democratization as attempts to draw attention away from the onslaught and prepare the way for neo-imperialism or to legitimize it. That is, the African state or public apparatus is made to retreat so that global capital can replace it in the name of private (read "foreign") capital (Kostenniemi 1996). Another scholar essentially argues that insistence on good governance principles is an attempt to promote, legitimate, and refashion the world in the interests of global capital (Marks 1998). Certainly, the rule of law and good governance are universal, not merely Western, values applicable to all humanity. It should be noted that some African scholars actually subscribe to the view that establishment of rule of law itself will generate development. Professor Ndulo, for instance, argues for this position. Ndulo does not advocate for the transplanting of foreign models into Africa, and also rejects the opposite view which advocates for "African solutions to African problems." This course, he charges as a pretext for perpetuation of peculiar variants of democracy in Africa, which essentially endeavor to consolidate political power (Ndulo 2000).

These impositions never really died away. Moreover, they seem to continue under the guise of the rule of law. The outcome has been the privatization of failing state enterprises, removal of price controls and subsidies for social services, and reduction of public expenditure. Critics suggest the problem is that these reforms were imposed top down and lacked a domestic African constituency. In spite of this, several African leaders adopted the reforms because they had limited options with respect to IFIs (Prempeh 2007). Critics maintain that after many years of such experiments, these programs ultimately proved to be ineffective as evidenced by the massive layoffs, unemployment, and civil strife. As a response, the Bretton Woods institutions merely shifted their strategies by insisting that African leaders adopt the rule of law without changing the substance of the underlying Washington Consensus ideology.

Notwithstanding such criticism, for several years the number of international development actors engaged in rule of law[6] projects with the aim of effecting social change proliferated.[7] Performance with regard to governance and the rule of law became the primary benchmarks to measure progress toward economic development (Alence 2004). Indeed, the African Union itself bought into this logic by providing that the Union would be premised on the principles of "respect for democratic principles, human rights, the rule of law, and good governance" (Art. IV. Constitutive Act of the African Union 2000). In addition, the African Union adopted the African Charter on Democracy, Elections and Governance, which provides that States Parties "shall commit themselves to promote democracy, the principle of the rule of law and human rights."[8] Not long after, the New Partnership for Africa's Development (NEPAD), operating under the auspices of the African Union, adopted the Declaration on Democracy, Political, Economic and Corporate Governance. This instrument provides that member states commit themselves to promote and protect democracy, human rights, and rule of law in their respective countries and regions, by developing clear standards of accountability, transparency and participative governance (NEPAD 2005).

*Judicial Review and Deferential Courts*

In order to promote the rule of law, numerous countries in Africa experiencing democratic transitions tried to institutionalize judicial review.[9] Many of the courts in these countries borrowed the jurisprudence of Western courts in order to fit the image of countries where the rule of law

---

6    The principles for evaluating rule of law include: 1. The government and its officials and agents are accountable under the law; 2. The laws are clear, publicized, stable and fair, and protect fundamental rights; 3. The process by which the laws are enacted, administered, and enforced is accessible, fair, and efficient; and, 4. The laws are upheld and access to justice is provided by competent, independent, and ethical law enforcement officials, attorneys or representatives, and judges who are of sufficient number, have adequate resources, and reflect the make up of the communities they serve (Agrast et al. 2008).

7    e.g., Aspen Institute Justice and Society Program, ABA Rule of Law Initiative, International Network to Promote the Rule of Law, International Rule of Law; available at Rule of Law Resource Center http://law. lexisnexis.com/webcenters/RuleoflawResourceCenter.

8    The instrument is yet to come into force. The charter provides that the instrument will come into force after the deposit of 15 instruments of ratification. As of May 12, 2009, only two countries had filed instruments of ratification – Ethiopia and Mauritania.

9    In *Marburry v. Madison* (1803) 1 Cranch 137 Justice Marshall observed that the US Constitution was the fundamental law of the nation. It follows from this that any law repugnant to the Constitution is void. In addition, it was the particular duty of the courts to interpret the law. Therefore, it falls to the courts to pass judgment upon the constitutionality of a law alleged to run counter to its norms. Otherwise, the legislature would be omnipotent and able to do what is expressly prohibited.

prevails.[10] Predictably, the West has tended to focus on the relatively successful experiment in the constitutional jurisprudence of South Africa while failing to appreciate the positive developments elsewhere on the continent (Prempeh 2007). Given a new constitution with an entrenched bill of rights, significant checks and balances or limits on governmental power, and guarantees of judicial independence, the assumption was that judicial review would lead to a liberal-democratic jurisprudence[11] and the rule of law almost as a matter of course.[12]

As it turned out, establishing judicial review was surprisingly easy. Actually exercising this power, however, proved far more difficult. Indeed, very few courts were able to stand up to omnipotent executives, whose power the constitutional clauses providing for judicial review had tried to tame. In some countries the executive branch of government compelled the judiciary to only issue decisions that would not "destabilize" their nations and, by extension, derail the country's march to development. Warnings were sometimes given to the judiciary that if they dare issue decisions contrary to the wishes of the executive, the military might intervene to ensure that peace and development prevail. As a result, some judiciaries have balked and subscribed to self-censorship, in turn fostering an unrestrained and dominant executive.

The Ugandan and Ghanaian cases exemplify this trend. While as Kwasi Prempeh noted, the Ghanaian Constitution contains generous provisions on freedom of expression, the Supreme Court of Ghana ruled that a seditious libel statute, first enacted during the colonial period and later re-enacted without much modification during the one-party era of the 1960s, did not violate the Constitution (Prempeh 1999). This ruling would pave the way for the criminal prosecution of journalists and certain influential public figures charged with defamation of the government.

Similarly, in *Kizza Besigye v. Y.K. Museveni and the Electoral Commission* (2006) UGCC 1, where a Ugandan citizen challenged the 2001 presidential election of the Ugandan nation, the country's Supreme Court held that "[t]he fact that these malpractices were proved to have occurred is not enough … the petitioner had to go further and prove their extent, degree, and the *substantial* effect they had on the election" (emphasis added). This was the case even though, according to the relevant electoral law, certain malpractices were sufficient to invalidate the election if found to have been committed. The Court admitted these malpractices were proven. Thus, the Ugandan judiciary creatively navigated past the constitutional courts, or simply reined them in, in order to protect the interests of the ruling elites. In the end, exclusive reliance on either judicial review of executive and legislative acts *or* rule of law for the purposing of ushering in social change, liberation from authoritarian rule, and economic development, can prove futile and illusory.

---

10   Thus, in *Charles Onyango Obbo and Andrew Mujuni Mwenda v. The Attorney General* (2004) UGSC 1, the Uganda Supreme Court argued that "engagement in comparative constitutional jurisprudence by emerging democracies is a sign of hope because the process of sustained exposure to principles evolved in more democratic countries provides lessons and challenges which cannot be ignored especially if foreign judgments can only be ignored for good reason." In *State v. Makwanyan* (1995) 6 BCLR 665, South Africa's Chaskalson P. referred to a plethora of foreign decisions and justified the decision on the ground that the Constitution of the Republic of South Africa permitted the use of public international law and comparable foreign case law.

11   Under classical (conservative) liberalism, the rule of law is understood as liberty understanding law (Tamanaha 2008). Classical liberalists argue that "the first condition of free government is government not by the arbitrary determination of the ruler, but by fixed rules of law, to which the ruler himself is subject" (Hobhouse cited in Tamanaha 2008).

12   H. Kwasi Prempeh for example observed that "judicial review, though widely celebrated by democrats and constitutional architects in transitional democracies, is not quite the unmitigated virtue it is frequently made out to be" (Prempeh 1999).

Instances where the courts of judicial review have stood up to the executive can be attributed to factors specific to those particular countries. The generous provisions of the Constitution or statutes are not alone sufficient, and judicial review cannot be relied upon like a magic wand. Why Benin's,[13] Ghana's,[14] Namibia's, Malawi's,[15] Mali's, Zambia's, Botswana's, and South Africa's[16] constitutional courts have been successful in their judicial review where other country's courts have failed may have less to do with their respective constitutions or statutes and more to do with the socio-political conditions existing in their respective countries. As these costumes demonstrate, society's condition must change before legal institutions can be truly effective, which is an African take on the chicken or egg problem.

*The Rise of African Leadership*

Many African leaders have been viewed by some in the international community as a "new breed" of African leaders because of their rule of law reforms. Meanwhile, they cleverly navigated the new constitutional configurations[17] to extend their hold on power. This also demonstrates the limits of insisting that rule of law in Africa is the engine for economic development. Leaders often legitimize their actions by conducting referendums so the majority of the population, primarily a rural or

---

13   In 1993, the Constitutional Court of Benin stood its ground against government attempts to restrict the right to freedom of association. In Benin, democratic reforms were due to a confluence of social, economic, and political conditions where grassroots, homegrown, and popular movements, which consisted in nationwide demonstrations, rejected authoritarian rule (Rotman 2004).

14   In *New Patriotic Party v. Attorney–General* (1995) S. Ct. G.L.R. 1, Ghana's Supreme Court held that the celebration of public-funded anniversary of a *coup d'état* would be inconsistent with the Constitution.

15   In *State v. President of Malawi* (Ex parte Malawi Law Society) (2002) ICHRL 15, Malawi's court held that the banning of public protests regarding a proposed constitutional amendment to extend a two-term presidential limit was constitutional.

16   These countries' courts of judicial review have been strikingly less deferential to the executive branch than others in sub-Saharan Africa (Prempeh 1999).

17   There are a number of presidents who changed their nations' constitutions to extend their presidential terms or eliminate them completely. Algerian lawmakers in November 2008 approved lifting presidential term limits to let President Abdelaziz Bouteflika stay in office for life. Burkina Faso's Blaise Compaore, who seized power in 1987, removed a term limit in 1997. Cameroon's Paul Biya had Cameroon's national assembly adopt a a constitutional bill in April 2006 removing a two-term presidential limit to allow Biya to extend his 25-year rule in the central African country past 2011. Chad's Idriss Deby, who took power in a coup in 1990, won a third term in 2006 after a referendum the year before removed a two-term limit. Gabon's Omar Bongo, who came to power in 1967, Africa's longest-serving ruler, secured a change in the law in 2003 so he can seek re-election as many times as he wanted. Guinea's Lansana Conte won disputed elections in 1993, 1998, and 2003 after a change in the Constitution allowed him a third term, Namibian president Sam Nujoma, Tunisia's Zine el-Abidine Ben Ali-Ben Ali, who took office in 1987, won nearly 100 percent approval for 2002 reforms to let him keep standing for re-election. Uganda's Yoweri Museveni, in power since 1986, won re-election in February 2006 after he changed the constitution in 2005 to let him stand for a third term. Other leaders do not have to worry about changing their constitutions because they simply do not provide for any term limits (Reuters AlertNet Nov. 12, 2008). Scholar Okoth-Ogendo argues that provisions "limiting the tenure of office of the President have never been, nor are they likely, to be successful" (Okoth-Ogendo 1993). While that may be an overstatement, there have been many cases where they failed to work. They certainly worked in the case of Malawi's Bakili Muluzi, Kenya's Daniel Arap Moi, Zambia's Frederick Chiluba, and Nigeria's Olesegun Obasanjo, but by far, the defaults outstrip the cases where the term limits were respected.

ethnic constituency, appears to ratify their actions.[18] Specifically, according to the World Bank, from 2003 to 2005, the rural population in African nations could range anywhere between 90.3 percent of the total population of Burundi to 40.2 percent of the total population of the Republic of the Congo (2008). Most African nations have a rural population that makes up over 60 percent of the total population. Quite often, the rural populations still living in traditional societies relate to and lend support to leaders who are inclined toward authoritarianism.[19] Some of those countries continue to be lauded for their economic progress, even when it appears marginal compared to similarly situated nations in other regions of the world.

Criticisms have only increased recently regarding the extent the rule of law should be pushed by policymakers in order to effect supposed social change as a precondition for "modernization."[20] The broad Western democratization and economic liberalization agendas of the past two decades, including the advocacy for rule of law, has had uneven success across Africa. The results have been modest[21] with economic growth more affected by commodity prices than institutional frameworks (Arbache and Page 2008).

However, it is still important to explore the merits, if any, of the rule of law initiatives that may affect economic growth and general governance. It is imperative to assess the theoretical assumptions that undergird the appeal to rule of law as an instrument of social engineering. The issue is the theory that law can effect social change or behavior. If law is capable of influencing social norms and thus development, then rule of law should be strengthened in states where it is weak (Cao 2000).

*Law as a Tool to Order Society*

What does rule of law mean as a function of social change and development? First, the rule of law can bring about desired change because, at its core, it requires government officials and citizens to be bound by and act consistently with the law. The basic requirements entail a set of minimal characteristics: law must be set forth in advance (be prospective), made public, be general, clear, stable, certain, and must be applied to everyone according to its terms (Tamanaha 2007). In authoritarian states, the ruling authority would be restrained from using the law to do as it desires (Tamanaha 2007).

---

18   In Uganda for example, the Uganda Constitutional Court invalidated a referendum law and by implication questioned the legality of the system of government put in place and elections subsequent to that referendum. President Museveni responded that the result was "totally unacceptable," arguing, "[i]f we are to go by the ruling, it will land the country in a lot of problems." Instead of looking to the judiciary, Museveni said "I will count on the support of Parliament and the population. We shall bring you some issues to decide on. Once the people have spoken in a referendum, nobody on earth can question it except God" (Osike et al. 2004).

19   Robert Rotberg argues that both Sir Seretse Kharma of Namibia and Sir Seewoosagur Ramgoolam, the founding prime minister of Mauritius, "could have obtained support within their young nations for authoritarianism" (Rotberg 2007). In Zimbabwe, for some time urban Zimbabweans were demonstrably discontented while rural Zimbabweans continued to support and believe in Robert Mugabe as the "father of the nation" and tolerated his corrupt regime (Rotberg 2007).

20   Modernization theory was criticized in the 1970s and 1980s but it did not disappear. It quietly found its way into applied fields and undergirded numerous development programs especially when focusing on cultural institutions that did not fit Western models (Pearce 2001).

21   Despite billions of dollars in aid law and development programs have not been successful. Thomas Carothers observed that despite a "multimillion-dollar effort to promote the 'rule of law' in the Russian Federation" problems facing legal-development programs seemed immense and intractable (Carothers 1998).

The second function of the rule of law is to maintain order and coordinate behavior and transactions among citizens. This aspect of the rule of law means that a legal framework's rules govern social behavior. Advocates of the rule of law concede that this function does not entail that the entire realm of social behavior must be governed by state legal rules, as it is neither possible nor desirable. Multiple normative orders exist within every society. These can include customary norms, moral norms, religious norms, family norms, norms of social etiquette, workplace norms, and norms of business interaction. In some societies or regions, state law has a marginal or negligible role in social ordering, usually when state law is relatively weak. Disputes there are resolved primarily through social institutions (Tamanaha 2007).

Proponents argue the rule of law promotes liberty because its benefits include certainty, predictability, and security. Predictability is critical to liberty because it enables fellow citizens to interact with one another knowing in advance the rules that will be applied to their conduct should a problem or dispute arise. Predictability furthers their ability to make choices and to engage in conduct with others (Tamanaha 2007).

It is widely thought that market-based economic systems benefit from these qualities with respect to contracts and property. First, economic actors can better predict in advance the anticipated costs and benefits of prospective transactions enabling them to make more efficient decisions. One can enter into a contract with some assurances of the consequences that will follow if the other party fails to live up to the terms of the contract. This encourages the creation of contracts with strangers or parties at a distance, which expands the range and frequency of commercial interactions, increasing the economic pie. Second, the protection of property (and persons) conferred by legal rules offers an assurance that the fruits of one's labor will be protected from expropriation by others.

These economic benefits conferred by the rule of law have been identified in connection with capitalism on local and global levels. But one must examine both the law and the relationship between the law and the system of economic exchange in a given situation to determine whether and to what extent these claims are borne out (Tamanaha 2007). People must believe in and be committed to the rule of law. They must take it for granted as a necessary, proper, and existing part of their political-legal system. From this shared political ideal a cultural belief can be formed. Once this cultural belief is pervasive, the rule of law becomes resilient and spans generations. If the cultural belief is not pervasive, the rule of law will be weak or non-existent (Tamanaha 2007). In order for this cultural belief to be viable, people must identify with the law and perceive it as worthy of obedience. General trust in law must be earned, and it takes time to become what is tantamount to a cultural view about law passed on through socialization (Tamanaha 2007).

*The Relevance of Sociological Jurisprudence*

The jurisprudential or legal theories most commonly associated with law in relation to its social functions require exploration. When law is viewed as serving social needs, an instrumentalist or goal-oriented concept and development view of law becomes the focus. Advocates of this approach insist it is possible to use law as a vehicle to direct social change because law fosters a set of behavioral norms (Potts 1982). Sociological jurists such as Rudolf Von Jhering, Eugen Ehrlich, and Roscoe Pound postulate that no true study of law can be made without an understanding of the social milieu which the law governs. Moreover, to be binding, efficacious, and respected, law has to be dictated by the social life of the community. Roscoe Pound argued that where change is needed but society itself has not considered or demanded it, then the role of legislation in changing social norms should be conceded. Pound's theory of social engineering, which calls for ordering human relations through the action of a politically organized society, has contributed to the development of a sociological jurisprudence. Proponents of this theory argue that sociological jurisprudence seems to be particularly appealing to developing African societies because of their diverse ethnicity. Coexistence among individual citizens, tribal and other groups means when the interests of these groups and individuals come into conflict, it is only through law that social compromises can be made.[22] The rule of law and development advocates insist law can mold norms and be a catalyst for social change.

Still, the recognition is emerging that changes in the law may not yield the desired results because mere legal reforms without change in the underlying, concrete condition of the people lack legitimacy. The adequacy of the change will depend on the extent to which it is rooted in the fundamental historical, economic, cultural, or political life on the ground. African societies have steadfastly resisted top-down attempts at reform (Davis 2008). The legal process will only be effective if it is compatible with the populace's pre-existing concepts of justice and is relevant to their real life conditions (Potts 1982). Empirical literature has documented a large variability in the quality of rule of law across democracies (Barro 2000). Theories of democratization postulate either a positive relationship between democracy and economic development, or leave open whether democracy implies better economic institutions (Acemoglu and Robinson 2005). In the 1990s, democratization was even read retrospectively into the original 1960s version of modernization theory. Significantly though, the effect of interactions between inequality and democracy on the quality of legal institutions has not been explored (Sunde et al. 2007).

According to another view, law is a dependent variable in the nexus of social processes. Scholars of law and social change generally assert that legal change and social change may flow in either direction (Aubert and Dror 1959 cited in Potts 1982). Law, in other words, emerges as a product of other social processes. Sociologists, such as Emile Durkheim, saw law as a representation of the community consensus on both the need and the acceptable procedures for conflict resolution. They viewed the primary service of law as being a mechanism for preserving community integrity in the face of conflicting interpretations of proper and improper conduct and individual incidents of norm violation. In their view, the social norm precedes and legitimizes the legal procedures. Thus, law derives from principles previously developed in non-legal spheres of action. Accordingly, legal change follows, but does not initiate, social change (Potts 1982).

*An African Perspective on Law*

The role of law in shaping the development of African nations needs to be understood from a specifically African rather than non-African perspective because law must be responsive to the actual social needs of each particular society (Mwalimu 1986). This is one important reason why broader approaches to African development ought to be considered given the complex situation of the African setting. In many African countries there are two kinds of laws in play as a result of legal pluralism: national statutory law and local or ethno-religiously based customary law. This distinction, which may parallel in part urban and rural divides, is simply hidden in traditional modernization theory focused on industrialization (assuming urbanization *sub silentio*). Statutory law is written down and binds all members of society. Customary law, on the other hand, is unwritten, but governs the relationships of people living according to traditional patterns

---

22    Roscoe Pound postulated that the end of law is the satisfaction of different society interests, which are categorized as individual interests, public interests, and social interests and that it is the task of law to achieve a balance and harmony among all of these interests (Mwalimu 1986).

of behavior. Customary laws are basically reflections of social practices, as they emanate from (traditional) society and not from a sovereign or legislature. Customary law is based often also on traditional authority rather than ideas about modern governance (e.g., the tribal chief or elders instead of a national government following separation of powers ideals) and is a distinct social phenomenon.

According to this view, sociological jurisprudential top-down approaches would need to be complemented by some aspects of legal realism. Legal realism is based on the premise that law cannot be understood without reference to the realities of human social life. One of those realities is that judges conversant with historical, economic, and social aspects of life will define the true state of the law. From this understanding, some theorists urge that the maximum utility of law would be achieved by the use of techniques or processes that would assure the harmonious coexistence of old customary laws with new statutory ones, at least at the local level. Emphasizing the utilization of past cultures in understanding and improving the present cultures is particularly well suited for the circumstances of developing nations in Africa (Mwalimu 1986).

However, law may still be relevant in educating people as to what runs contrary to development goals in traditional culture. This could include targeting cultural practices, beliefs, general inclinations, and values that do not positively contribute to economic development. Examples of these include customs restricting the education of girls, requiring too much time spent on funeral ceremonies, relating to inheritance law, and regarding wealth as opposition to individual initiative. For education on these issues to occur, African states must go beyond simply passing a few necessary laws and introduce to society norms that improve the culture. Japan adopted precisely this strategy in its Ministry of Education campaigns that directed reform of norms and habits of the poor (Garon 1997). Japan involved community leaders, religious groups, civic organizations, media, motion pictures, and other groups in its education campaigns. Molding the cultural norms via socialization into conformance with the law is essential, because development efforts are likely to fail if the underlying cultural norms are foreign or imposed. This may look like norm-shaping or manipulation, but if this process is guided through persuasive and non-coercive methods by accepted social leaders, there should be no question of legitimacy.

Nevertheless, there may still be some intangibles that elude even the most careful good-faith efforts to measure the rule of law from an objective standpoint. As one scholar acknowledges:

> An analysis of legal and judicial institutions within a country or across countries must take into account variations that stem from many factors, including ethnic, cultural and religious differences, socio-economic status and geographic conditions. A particular concern is the role played in many countries, and particularly developing countries, by traditional or "informal" systems of law— including traditional tribal and religious courts and community-based systems for resolving disputes. These systems play a large role in many cultures in which formal legal institutions fail to provide effective remedies for large segments of the population. (Agrast et al. 2008)

**Affirmation of (Traditional Society's) Culture in Development**

The cultural complexity of African societies cannot be overemphasized or dismissed as a thing of the past.[23] African societies are predominantly rural, living under a moral as opposed to a formal

---

23    Sub-Saharan Africa alone contains approximately 2,000 ethnic groups and 1,200 languages (Merriam 1961).

economy, in a prior stage according to modernization theory (Shimada 2004). This contributes to the persistence of customary law, which continues to guide the behavior of Africans in rural areas that exist outside the formal structures of the state. In these settings, customary law regulates virtually every facet of life, marriage to divorce, land tenure to trade, and the rules of inheritance (Miles 2006). Even the concept of human rights has roots in customary law.[24] Moreover, it is important to address the persistence of certain biases toward customary law and traditional institutions, which have been essentially a colonial legacy subsumed under modernization theory.

*Customary Law and Colonialism*

Colonial regimes acknowledged the persistence of customary life, as they made conscientious efforts to leave in place most customary laws.[25] Thus, colonial regimes were themselves the original inventors of the system of legal pluralism that persists to this day. Colonial acknowledgment of customary law, however, also involved the nullification of some of its aspects via repugnancy clauses. These were used to impose limitations on the extent and content of customary law, usually targeting aspects of custom which Europeans found irreconcilable with their own culture. Some of these clauses stated that customary rules must not be "repugnant to natural justice, equity and good conscience." As a result, marriage consideration (bride price) was declared repugnant,[26] along with a host of other African norms. The ambiguity in the repugnancy clauses allowed colonial leaders and jurists to impose their own European standards. For example, in 1938, a British judge in a Tanzanian case admitted: "I have no doubt whatever that the only standard of justice and morality which a British court in Africa can apply is its own British standard" (*Gwao bin Kilimo v. Kisunda bin Ifuti* 1938).

After achieving independence from colonial occupation, many African administrations rushed to modify the repugnancy clauses believing that certain aspects of African customary law remained valid and legitimate. Others, however, enshrined in their constitutions some standard by which they could limit customary law. One way countries did this was by stating that a rule of customary law was void if it was inconsistent with the constitution or human dignity.[27] While not intrinsically dangerous, as imperfect customary law itself must be subject to critique, these actions may have created the perpetuation of attitudes which subordinate customary law to systems of law regarded "modern" in relation to the development of African society. Which society should be

---

24   One scholar uses customary law to argue for the existence of the individual and group rights, such as the right to life and security, freedom of expression, freedom of religion, freedom of movement (Motala 1989).

25   Customary law is defined as rules of custom, morality, and religion that the indigenous people of a given locality view as enforceable either by the central political system or authority or various social unities such as the family. If custom emanates from the people, there could be as many customary laws as there are different communities. The modern state was not present in nineteenth-century African communities (Ocran 2006).

26   For instance, in *R v. Amkeyo* (1917) 7. E.A.L.R. 14, the court condemned the institution of bride price stating that the African customary marriage at issue appeared to have all the elements of "wife purchase," the description given to an African customary marriage.

27   Most African constitutions continue to void some aspects of customary law which are inconsistent with human dignity. E.g., the Uganda Constitution (1995) Art. 2(2) providing that "if any other law or any custom is inconsistent with any of the provisions of this Constitution, the Constitution shall prevail, and that other law or custom shall, to the extent of the inconsistency, be void." The South African Constitution (1996) provides that everyone has the right to participate in the cultural life of his or her choice provided that no one exercising this right does so in a "manner inconsistent with any provision of the Bill of Rights."

the target – urban society assumed by modernization theory or traditional rural society where the majority of Africans still live? Certain leaders and jurists in Africa continue to regard customary law as a relic of the past that with time will die away and should not be allowed to develop or thrive.[28] Indeed, jurists who have exhibited this tendency view customary law as inimical to development and would rather "modify customary law in aid of modernization" (Ocran 2006). Unsurprisingly, these same jurists would uncritically prescribe the rule of law and development approach without first paying sufficient attention to how such an antidote would respond to the complex realities of Africa.

*Accommodation and Affirmation of Traditional Institutions*

Attention to pre-existing concepts of justice is critical to fostering authentic African development. For the foreseeable future and until a sufficiently homogenous society emerges necessitating a unified legal system, African societies will remain characterized by a pluralistic legal system composed of "traditional" customary law and "modern" national statutory law. Similarly, customary law will presumably predominate in more homogeneous rural areas as the heartland of traditional society, while national law will predominate in more heterogeneous urban areas where traditional society has lost control. Some analysts see this duality as unsolvable dilemma, as African polities seem to be at once modern and traditional, urban and rural, modern state and ethnic nation (Shimada 2004). Many African states indeed seem to harbor two worlds. On one hand, many envision a world largely urban and characterized by modernization, evident in terms of the impact of the constitution, Western-oriented laws, relatively developed infrastructure, education, health, and modern amenities. On the other hand, the Africa that exists is predominantly rural, where a majority of the population is hardly touched by the first world and customary law prevails (McKinnon 2006). However, does this plurality undermine development? If so, how can the seemingly problematic chasm be bridged in order to avoid these apparently parallel realms?

Indigenous institutions need not be expunged in order to promote development, as modernization theory would have it, and the majority of the population presently lives under such institutions. Even if the majority of the poor in developing nations often live in an isolated world defined by a different set of norms, only the pro-development aspects of that world need to be embraced and affirmed (Cao 2006). On that basis, there can be engagement across the cultural divide. The sudden appeal to the rule of law, especially if meant to sideline authentic African values, would be ill-advised.

It is important to allow development to grow from within, which enables local populations to take charge and ownership of their destiny. This means being attentive and adaptive to local conditions in order to avoid unnecessary social stress. Each country has a unique cultural, political, and economic history that guides it when determining issues of legitimacy. But in far too many countries, there has been a real failure to promote homegrown customary institutions to take charge of development. It seems to be shortsighted and counterproductive to exclude formal structures of local government that command habitual allegiance and are familiar to a significant number of the

---

28　In *Mabuza v Mbatha* (2003), (4) SA 218, 227–28(C), Hlope JP commented on the application and development of customary law arguing that "if one accepts that African customary law is recognised in terms of the Constitution and relevant legislation passed thereunder … there is no reason, in my view, why the Courts should be slow in developing African customary law" and that African law is should not be "recognised only when it does not conflict with the principles of public policy or natural justice" because "the Courts have a constitutional obligation to develop African customary law."

population.[29] Glossing over norms that guide a whole group of the nation's population ignores the reality of Africa's largely rural citizenry (Mazrui 2001).

The rule of law rhetoric gives the impression, in the words of one author, that Africa is a "lawless world" (Dudziak 2003), but it is important to consider the local conditions of legitimacy. A reasonable course of action would accommodate traditional features of African states not only because they are deeply entrenched but also because they represent legitimacy.[30] Thus, it is necessary to examine attributes of every culture that may impede economic development. Some have suggested that diminishing the significance of diverse cultural loyalties is important for promoting national unity. Yet, African indigenous cultures still play an important role in many people's socialization and economic and political lives, forming a large part of their identity. Some have argued that cultural diversity can enhance the sense of nationhood and is not necessarily antidevelopment. Even conceding that nationhood can coexist with cultural pluralism (Wani 1991) on the African continent, cultural diversity is at the root of many of its problems (Merriam 1961).

While cultural diversity may itself constitute the identity of a particular nation, such as the cases of the United States or Switzerland (Wani 1991), pluralism can pose serious challenges. Nationhood or nationalism cannot be legislated. It is something that evolves from perceptions of common identity and aspirations. As long as there are shared values, it will not matter if the nation is fundamentally multicultural. Cultural diversity becomes problematic only when manipulated or used as the basis for the allocation and distribution of political power and economic resources (Wani 1991). It is possible to have complementary loyalties in a single state, as long as the central authorities adhere to respect for equality, fairness, and justice. Because of this opportunity, it is important to give more serious attention to studying, appraising, and engaging cultures and traditions. Studies show that culture is an important factor in economic development. In addition, some have asserted that culture plays a primary role, "mak[ing] almost all the difference" (Landes 2000).

The international community should be able to work with various regimes to bring about social change while respecting each country's social traditions, history, and challenges. This means that there should be a focus on the community and not just the state and its law institutions (Cao 2006). Furthermore, traditional institutions should be incorporated because they are probably viewed as more legitimate[31] than the modern (untraditional) institutions. One example of this is seen in an African country's paramount chief or king, who embodies authority, and continues to play a significant role in development. An often present danger after colonialism was justification of tight centralized control with little or no participatory elements on the basis of creating national unity. The outcome tended to result in authoritarianism and negative economic growth.

Africa's postcolonial elites objected to multiparty politics arguing in part that it was based on class-stratified societies of industrialized Western economies. Since African societies were supposedly "classless" and preindustrial, political parties served no constructive function, but instead, divided people along the unconstructive lines of identities of ethnicity and religion. The

---

29   Kwasi Prempeh argues that "Africa's newly emergent democracies have failed to emulate the successful example of Botswana, one of only two African countries with an unbroken record of postcolonial democracy, and one that has had a postcolonial policy of making selective use of traditional customary institutions at the basic or community level of its system of local administration" (Prempeh 2007).

30   South Africa, for example, despite its being highly urbanized about 60 percent of its people live in rural areas under traditional leaders (Ndulo 2000).

31   The success of law in achieving its intended objectives often depends on the popular support of the changes brought about by law. Thus, societal input in the formulation of the law is of utmost importance (Mwalimu 1986).

single party was seen as the means for uniting the African polity and focusing the meager resources on national development. Similar arguments were used to undermine the legitimacy of traditional leadership structures because national considerations had to trump all local and subnational sentiments considered subversive to national interest and identity. It became fashionable to suggest economic development fast, democratization later (Lipset 1959; Prempeh 2007). Many leaders in Africa justified one-party rule on the need to maintain unity "in the face of ethnic, linguistic, and cultural differences" (Kpundeh 1992).

Some nations have already begun recognizing and affirming traditional institutions, but more must be done. In addition, there are a few constitutions that recognize local centers of authority,[32] which vary among ethnic groups. In Uganda for instance, the constitution provides for decentralization and traditional leaders. Decentralization is particularly suitable to many African nations because they are composed of a large number of groups maintaining their specific traditional structures. Accommodating them allows people to take charge of their destiny and affirm their operations through familiar structures (Bois de Gaudusson 1989). Decentralization means respectful adaptation to the local particularities (Bois de Gaudusson 1989) in addition to focusing on responses attuned to local needs (Ndulo 2000). Also, decentralization's ability to encourage development through participatory methods is important (Rajagopal 2002). Local administrations may mirror some of those traditional authority frameworks to some extent.

Not everything in a culture may be pro-development. It is precisely for this reason to consider efforts challenging a culture to change. Indeed, with the forces of globalization, no culture is

---

32    The following are examples of this from the constitutions of various African countries. The Angola Constitution 1992, Art. 90 (k), provides that the National Assembly shall have "relative sole legislative powers" on, among others, the "participation of traditional authorities and citizens in local government." The Constitution of Cameroon 1972, Art. 1 (2), provides that Cameroon "shall recognize and protect traditional values." The Republic of Congo Constitution 1992, Art. 35, provides that "[c]itizens shall possess a right to culture and to the respect of their cultural identity." The Ethiopia Constitution 1983, Art. 39 (2) provides that "[e]very nation [in Ethiopia], nationality and people shall have the right to speak, write and develop its language and to promote its culture, help it grow and flourish, and preserve its historical heritage." In the Gambia Constitution 1997, Art. 32, every person has the right to practice their tradition. The Constitution of Kenya 1998, Art. 26[1], recognizes culture as the "foundation of the nation, the cumulative civilization of the Kenyan people and communities" and "affirms the values and principles of the communities of Kenya, their tradition," and Art. 178(3) provides that "the use of traditional courts, where appropriate, shall be promoted." The Constitution of Lesotho 1966, Art. 35: "Lesotho shall endeavour to ensure that every citizen has an opportunity to freely participate in the cultural life of the community and to share in the benefits of scientific advancement and its application." Malawi, Art. 110(3), Parliament may "make provision for traditional local courts presided over by lay persons or chief." The Constitution of Mozambique 1990, Art. 53, states it "shall promote the development of national culture and identity, and shall guarantee free expression of the traditions and values of Mozambican society." The Constitution of Namibia 1992, Art. 102, recognize centers of traditional authority and provides for a "Council of Traditional Leaders" to "advise the President on the control and utilization of communal land and on all such other matters as may be referred to it by the President for advice." The Nigeria Constitution 1999, 7(2), provides that local authority must be prescribed with regard to the "traditional authority of the community in the area." The Constitution of Sierra Leone 1999, Art. 12, states the government shall "recognize traditional Sierra Leonean institutions compatible with national development." The Constitution of South Africa 1996, Arts. 211 and 212 recognize traditional leadership with respect to matters affecting local communities and the application of customary law when that law is applicable. The Uganda Constitution 1995, Art. 246, provides for the existence of the institution of traditional leader or cultural leader in any area, Uganda. Art. 126 provides that judicial power must be exercised in conformity with the norms of the people and Art. 127 provides that "parliament shall provide for the participation of the people in the administration of justice by the courts."

immune from change. However, change can only be advanced when it is preceded by a legitimate process that is not threatening to the integrity and identity of the community, and does not appear to be imposed from outside. Years of exposure to foreign law and cultures has left Africa with a mosaic of cultures, comprised of indigenous, Arabic, Islamic, Western European, and Christian, among others (Wani 1991). This legacy has undoubtedly enriched African culture. Still, some cultures need to change with regard to women's rights. Also, self-consciousness and over-attachment to each one's ethnic group can be a source of tension, intolerance, disunity, and lack of cohesiveness. Therefore, it is vital for African states to move their varying cultures toward a sense of accommodation regarding diversity and inclusiveness (Ndulo 2000). Efforts aimed at affecting such change should involve both legal and non-legal approaches.[33]


**Rule of Law: An Antidote to Corruption?**

Accommodating culture is important because development should involve grassroots participation. However, in an age of globalization, culture cannot remain pure or monolithic (Cao 2006). In an increasingly urbanized Africa attention should also be given to mediating sub-cultures. They are neither strictly traditional nor strictly "modern," in the ordinary sense of the word, but are pre-modern to the extent that old attitudes survive while traditional authority does not. Sub-cultures accept something from both worlds; the old and the new. Members of these sub-cultures, for instance, are likely to accept all the modern amenities that modern life brings. Thus, they will transpose some models of traditional authority to modern forms of authority. These members tend to resist liberal ideologies of democracy insisting on a less than critical attitude of the authority. Moreover, they tend to hold a positive opinion of the authorities. Many government leaders seem drawn to sub-cultures. It is against this backdrop that the intractableness of corruption, clientelism, and political patronage in many African states can be understood.[34] These entrenched inclinations have facilitated the tendency among many African leaders to be patriarchal and imperial and to appear as personifications of the state.[35] As a result, personal rule and personality cult become legitimate, even normal. By relying on the military and members of this sub-culture, African leaders are empowered to further this political dispensation. Therefore, corruption seems to be and likely will continue to be the greatest and most stubbornly intractable challenge to African development.

The rule of law is thought to be closely connected to the prevention and combating of corruption. After all, rule of law approaches target official conduct. But can the rule of law, factoring in both

---

33   Lan Cao, for example, argues that although the formalistic approach emphasizing rule of law and market development is necessary it is far from sufficient, "[m]uch more attention needs to be paid to the non-law framework—norms and culture—that influence the efficacy of formal laws" (Cao 2006).

34   A more recent example is the newly elected leader of South Africa, Jacob Zuma. In spite of allegations of corruption (formerly dropped) and confessed sexual misconduct, he was overwhelmingly elected President of South Africa, following his party's landslide victory in the national elections. A self-described "farm boy" known to don traditional garb – including leopard skins and a spear – at ceremonial events, Zuma puts a different face on the South African leadership than Mandela, the attorney imprisoned under segregationist apartheid rule, and the Western-educated Thabo Mbeki, his predecessors in office (CNN, April 25, 2009).

35   The African leader sees himself in some respects as the continuation of the former kings. A recent example is Libyan leader, Muammar Gaddafi, who allowed himself to be proclaimed "King-of-kings of Africa," by over 200 traditional leaders from all over Africa. Gaddafi, who has been insistent that African revolutionary leaders should never retire, invited traditional leaders to join his cause for a United States of Africa, believing that they represent the grassroots that legitimates his cause (BBC News 2008).

its own limitations relating to social change and the vast cultural complexities of Africa, really stem corruption in Africa? Some have argued that any serious movement for social change cannot treat the legal process or the rule of law as a mere sham because it is the only way to make corrupt leaders accountable (Gathii 1999). Nevertheless, the insistence on rule of law must be tempered by the reality that only in enforcement of those laws can the rule of law become instrumental in a practical sense. Legal reforms alone, although important, will not suffice. Indeed, one scholar has argued that although "the rule of law reforms are significant for reducing opportunities for abuse of public office, they do not necessarily guarantee or entail … substantive outcomes" (Gathii 1999). Thus, here is another important area where broader approaches become necessary.

Efforts within the realm of law have not been lacking. In the wake of the United Nations Convention Against Corruption, the African Union adopted the Convention on Preventing and Combating Corruption. The Convention's foremost objective is promoting development through preventing, detecting, and punishing acts of corruption. To this end, state parties to the convention are recommended to adhere to "democratic principles and institutions, popular participation, the rule of law, and good governance."[36] Thus, the African Convention on Preventing and Combating Corruption takes a good governance approach to the problem of corruption. While this is a significant step, it remains to be seen what, if any, impact it will have. In fact, in many African countries, statutes aimed at combating corruption have been on the law books for many decades. Kenya, for example, has had the Prevention of Corruption Act since 1956. Yet, Kenya is one of the most corrupt countries in the world according to Transparency International, ranking 147th in its 2008 Corruption Perceptions Index (transparency.org 2008). In many African countries, corruption is pernicious in the judiciary, the very institution expected to uphold the rule of law. Sadly, on much of the African continent, corruption has become endemic and part of the culture.

*The Necessity of Cultural Engagement and Education*

Engaging culture itself with broad approaches is paramount. Cultural perceptions are important because a population's acceptance of corruption as a fact of life and despondency or complacency toward it matters. When corruption is so endemic, it is doubtful that the mere enactment of laws will root it out. This is especially the case when the enforcement officials themselves are corrupt. Africa, indeed, has unique challenges with regard to corruption.[37] Thus, the drafters of the Convention on Preventing and Combating Corruption incorporated and emphasized traditional notions of justice (Snider and Kidane 2007). When a state faces endemic levels of corruption, it becomes generally accepted as a part of life. In such a situation, much more needs to be done than simply appeal to the rule of law (Khemani 2009). Necessary to the task is engaging with the citizenry regarding attitudes toward corruption and changing cultural perceptions toward corruption and the rule of law. It is important to create a culture of intolerance toward corruption. Implementation of awareness activities (Khemani 2009) help change the culture of complacency and helplessness toward corruption. Once people are sufficiently motivated and aware, the underlying support for corrupt leadership disappears. In some countries the pressure of public opinion coupled with a sufficiently empowered population has been enough to undermine corrupt leadership (Pope 1994).

---

36    The African Union Convention on Preventing and Combating Corruption, Art. 3(1) was adopted by the 2nd Ordinary Session of the Assembly of the Union Maputo, July 11, 2003, and entered into force August 5, 2006. As of May 14, 2009, 29 countries had ratified the convention and 43 had signed it (Smith 2008).

37    In some countries, this even led to what has been described as a culture of corruption due to high levels of popular tolerance of corruption.

The rule of law, in order to be an effective instrument in combating corruption, must be preceded by a society-wide internalization process of norms that are decidedly anti-corruption.

Finally, any meaningful and legitimate struggle to end corruption must acknowledge the underlying substantive social and historical inequities. The origin of the problems could lie, after all, in the laws themselves. Laws are often prone to be instruments of the wealthy and powerful, even when they appear to be neutral. Facial neutrality of the laws is not enough, as outcomes could be unequal or fail to redress underlying institutional, historical, and structural circumstances (Gathii 1999). Because substantive fairness is a prerequisite for legitimacy, laws that lack it must change.


**Moving Beyond Rule of Law and Development**

IFIs and major development donors, such as the United States, are reconsidering or even adopting new and broader approaches to dealing with Africa's development challenges. New approaches must be considered. First, it is not that legal reforms are unnecessary, but they should be considered as only one of the means to achieve a desired end (Davis 2008). The rule of law is not a panacea, as it sometimes appears. Second, emphasis and efforts should be placed on affirming and socializing African leaders who are positive role models and exhibit authentic leadership. One hopes the examples take hold. Lastly, special attention should be given to educating the citizenry in order to affirmatively develop elements of African traditions that are pro-development.

Whatever measure of growth has taken place in Africa in recent years can be attributed in large part to better leadership, which for these purposes is grounded in politics (political leadership, normally via the executive in a parliamentary system).[38] These leaders have encouraged full participation and accountability, stemmed corruption, and propelled their countries toward development. African leaders are more inclined to look to their African peers than to "outsiders," whom they often continue to blame for the colonial legacy and persisting inequalities in the international system. Africa has many models of distinguished and development-oriented leadership. South African Nelson Mandela laid the groundwork for future leaders of his country. Botswana's Sir Seretse Kharma, followed by Sir Ketumile Masire, and Festus Mogae, were all exemplary democratic leaders credited with establishing inclusive, participatory values (Rotberg 2007). They each set in place a tradition within those countries which law could have taken years, if ever, to create. Other African leaders too have made similar strides, such as Benjamin Mkapa of Tanzania, Abdoulaye Wade of Senegal, and John Kufuor of Ghana. Despite the visibility of some other brazenly dictatorial, ruthless, and autocratic leaders, such as Robert Mugabe of Zimbabwe, the number of positive leaders is increasing.

Once exemplary leadership is in place (coincidentally, in a role not inconsistent with modernization theory's original emphasis on building leadership via a focus on tertiary education), it becomes easier to use the human and physical resources, with which so many African nations are incredibly endowed, to propel development. For example, Botswana discovered diamond wealth about the same time it had sensible leadership. This enabled the country to manage the resources, not for individuals in the leadership, but for the nation as a whole. This did not happen in Nigeria and Congo, despite their incredible mineral resource base, because these countries maintained authoritarian regimes. Many institutions of good leadership are already in place but they need

---

38   Some argue that the current acceleration of growth is due in part to improved governance under the African Union and the New Partnership for Africa's Development Initiatives, which insist on good practices in governance (Arbache et al. 2008).

greater international support and resources to make them effective. The African Leadership Council as well as the voluntary African Peer Review Mechanism (APRM),[39] under the auspices of the New Partnership for African Development (NEPAD), are positive developments in support of a culture of good leadership. Present also are improvements in construction of a development oriented leadership profile on the African continent, as they represent an attempt to recognize, affirm, reinforce, and make visible the positive role models around the continent. Additionally, the African Union has been promoting good leadership by condemning *coup d'états* on the continent.[40]

## Cultivation of an Informed Citizenry

The programs aimed at development, however, should pay particular attention to education. The conventional conception of rule of law in support of market-based economic development is merely procedural, that is, the performance of the state is assessed based on the extent to which it fulfills a predetermined role or follows principles, as opposed to a predetermined end. There is need to move to a conception of rule of law that is substantive in nature; one that measures the performance of the state from the extent to which it incorporates and delivers on specific public policy goals, such as public education, housing, or health programs (Gathii 1999). Meaningful democracy requires reciprocity.[41] An educated and enlightened population is the strongest foundation of development, not just the rule of law or good governance. Insisting on only civil and political rights in Africa and ignoring economic, social, and cultural rights will not provide a recipe for success in Africa. As Professor Oloka-Onyango observes:

> [I]t is just as futile to speak of the right of participation in conditions where basic human necessities, such as food, shelter, and water are beyond the reach of the majority of the population. What is the meaning of the 'right to vote' when the voter may be too weak from disease and hunger to exercise his or her franchise? … In sum, for a human to be considered whole, he or she must be able to enjoy both civil and political rights and economic, social and cultural rights as well. (Oloka-Onyango 2000)

Indeed, some have argued that international concern should be focused on human welfare rather than establishing a civil and political human rights record popular with Western donors because a government with limited resources would rather seek to enhance the capabilities of its population through investment in education, health, and infrastructure. Development assistance would be provided only to states that show progress with regard to human welfare (Posner 2008). Because knowledge is power, it is vital that the people understand what will affect them and promote their health as a precondition for their participation in development efforts.

---

39 As of June 29, 2008, APRM counted 29 states members as follows: Algeria, Angola, Benin, Burkina Faso, Cameroon, Djibouti, Egypt, Ethiopia, Gabon, Ghana, Kenya, Lesotho, Malawi, Mali, Mauritania, Mauritius, Mozambique, Nigeria, Republic of Congo, Rwanda, Sao Tome & Principe, Senegal, Sierra Leone, South Africa, Sudan, Tanzania, Togo, Uganda, and Zambia (uneca.org 2008).

40 Article 30 of The Constitutive Act of the African Union provides that "Governments which shall come to power through unconstitutional means shall not be allowed to participate in the activities of the Union." But, of course, this says nothing about those leaders that amend the constitution to perpetuate themselves in power. Nevertheless, the AU was instrumental in reversing the coup in Togo in 2005, and pressing others to hold democratic elections.

41 Rita Abrahamsen notes that the birth of democracies in Africa did not "incorporate the poor majority in any meaningful way" (Abrahamsen 2000).

Nevertheless, it ultimately means very little to have an enlightened free media in the urban centers with a vibrant civil society targeted typically by the donor community when a majority of the people live in rural settings and are not in a position critically to evaluate matters of great importance. Lack of education hinders them from meaningfully participating in governance and making decisions vital to their well-being under such circumstances. To begin by insisting on democracy and the rule of law without first having in place a properly educated populace puts the cart before the horse, even if we recognize that generally raising education levels in a country may take an entire generation.[42] Only a population able to understand the implications of the political, legal, and policy choices to be made can meaningfully contribute to public discourse and development and be protected from the political manipulation by ruling elites. If democracy and the rule of law means putting a set of policy choices and controlling the use of power of elected leaders through a rational system of checks and balances, then the population should first be in a position to understand those policies, operations, and outcomes of their system of checks and balances. Otherwise, transparency and accountability, which are so critical to development, will not be effectively promoted. Any meaningful approach to development must first focus on ensuring that the population is in a position to be informed.

Raising literacy levels to critical mass is a particularly urgent component of this process. Research has shown that the accumulation of human capital, specifically knowledge, is a key factor in explaining the growth experiences of countries (Lucas Jr. 1998). A study on Asian economies found that an increase in investment in secondary education was significant in achieving high rates of investment and high per-capita GDP growth (Mchahon 1998).[43] Although there are some who would disagree,[44] the impact of education on human capital accumulation is well-established and well-accepted by policymakers.[45] Many development donors have not placed enough emphasis on this component. Critics even argue that this lack of focus on education is because international aid is usually tied to the purchase of the donor country's products, which tends to favor physical, rather than human, capital investment (Koh and Leung 2003). However, if development actors are serious about their interventions in Africa, focus on education seems to be a precondition for technological innovations. Without technological innovations, few countries have made any significant economic advancement. Quality of education matters: universal primary and secondary educations are important as a first step. Attainment at the primary level turns out not to be significantly related to growth rates (Barro and Lee 1996). Much more needs to be done to expand university education in Africa. Moreover, there should be efforts aimed at inculcating attitudes and creating the skills tailored to the unique challenges of the particular or specific social and cultural milieu. Education should create a consciousness regarding the positive attributes of cultural diversity that at once values the underlying commonality of national ideals rather than the differences that distinguish one cultural group from another.

---

42    The United Nations acknowledges and affirms that "basic education for all is essential for achieving the goals of eradicating poverty, reducing child mortality, curbing population growth, achieving gender equality and *ensuring sustainable development, peace and democracy*" (General Assembly Resolution on Education for All 1999; emphasis added).

43    But an influential and much-cited cross-national econometric study by Lant Pritchett suggests that increases in education capital resulting from improvements in the educational attainment of the labor force have had little impact on the growth rate of output per worker (Pritchett 1996).

44    For example, Amavilah (2008) argues that with respect to economic performance, investment plays the most important part and education (knowledge) as a component of human capital plays a modest part.

45    Some have observed that inadequate education and poor health are two other explanations of poor long-term growth performance in Africa (Johnson et al. 2007).

## Recognition and Preservation of African Communities

The affirmation and development of positive cultural values is a prerequisite to sustainable and authentic human development, and should be part of the broad approaches strategy. There are a plethora of positive African cultural values, but it suffices to highlight by way of example a few of them with particular relevance to development. Whereas the liberal view of the rule of law is based on individualism rather than a set of shared values, in many African societies, bonds of social obligation remain strong because culture and tradition continue to provide sources of norms that are solidaristic and communal (Gathii 1999). Some argue that rule of law programs are based on an individualistic bias, which presupposes the priority of individuals instead of the community. That proposition would be mostly an inaccurate and inauthentic prescription for most African societies (Gathii 1999a). It is precisely because of this that every effort should be made to "adapt African indigenous law to make it a tool of socio-economic development" (Ocran 2006). Authentic African development would require the preservation of African values, such as the idea of being each other's keeper and the notion that the development of the individual person is indeed a condition for the development of everybody. Each person, according to African communitarian values, is connected to every other person, thus defining existence and integrating authentic development along with it. As Professor Mbiti says, for the African, the guiding existential philosophy is "I am because We are, and since we are, therefore I am" (Mbiti 1989).[46] Certainly, these values have not remained intact in light of a creeping sense of individualism derived from globalization and modern life. This is visible particularly in urban Africa where individual achievement and status symbols are highly revered. The urban people, composed of students, laborers, business people, and civil servants, tend to have different characteristics from their rural counterparts. Traditional constraints of family, class, and religion do not fully apply to them (Haile 1984), which is why they transpose models of traditional authority on modern forms of government. However, those urban values do have some inbuilt costs which are not difficult to delineate. As Mbiti notes, at every turn of his life, the African individual in the city and under modern change discovers constantly that he is alone (1989), an outcome that authentic African development would try to avoid.

With regard to customary law itself, it is important particularly in rural places to continue affirmatively to recognize community-based models of customary or popular justice.[47] These can be important mechanisms in empowering local movements toward development and challenging manifestations of individualism, such as abuse of office and corruption. One basic flaw of liberal legalism[48] that underpins the rule of law ideal is the assumption that the role of the state is merely to support basic rights and liberties without affirming any particular social and economic goals (Gathii

---

46　Etounga-Manguelle (2000) argues these African values are anti-development because they subordinate the individual to the community and thus suppress individual initiative.

47　It is conceded that the received Western European judicial system would overhaul the African setting especially because of its adversarial character, complex rules of evidence, and its procedure, which is intelligible only to the initiated and experienced. In addition, the tendency to proceed in a slow and costly fashion would make it available only to a few people in the African setting as poverty dominates (Gyandoh Jr. 1988).

48　Klare (1979; cited in Gathii 1999) argues that the institutional and cultural practice embodied in the rule of law ideal is liberal legalism. Some argue that as the liberals see it, the task of the state consists solely and exclusively in guaranteeing the protection of life, health, liberty, and private property against violent attacks (von Mises, cited in Tamanaha 2008). Pure or classical liberalism would oppose the social welfare state because it would lay burdens on property rights in order to achieve greater social justice. Advocates of the social welfare state observe that genuine liberty is defeated by social and economic conditions beyond the

1999). The assumption is that as long as individuals have their basic rights and liberties, they can choose the type of economic or social arrangements they desire. But critics of this view, especially communitarians, question the underlying individualism as well as the separation of the individual from any social engagement. Prescriptions for fighting for justice and development should not be based on abstract theories of justice that claim universal truth or application irrespective of history and context (Gathii 1999).

## Conclusion

For over four decades the international community has attempted to promote development of the African continent through approaches that are, in many cases, foreign to African cultural, historical, social, and political milieux. With hindsight, it is safe to say that modernization theory failed as predicted in the first few decades. The more recent insistence on the rule of law and strong reliance on market-based neoclassical economics following the Washington Consensus has produced minimal results, even if it remains an important component of development efforts. Now, it seems, international development partners are recognizing, once again, that some of the approaches that have been tried for so long and at such a high price, have not been particularly effective and seem poised to rethink their strategies. It may well be important to take into account approaches tailored to the specific needs of Africa and to focus less on models that seem to have worked elsewhere (in Asia, but less so in Latin America) but perhaps are less appropriate to the African setting. This may imply adopting broad, multi-faceted approaches, which would give due attention to issues beyond the rule of law, including non-legal issues such as education of the African populace, health programs, and the affirmation of African traditions that are pro-development. None of this is necessarily opposed to the rule of law. It is rather a question of emphasis, but the implicit message in "chicken or egg" terms is that merely emphasizing the formal rule of law by passing new statutes will not change social conditions involving ignorance, disease, or the general African framework of rural predominance over urban settings.

## References

Abrahamsen, R. 2000. *Disciplining Democracy: Development Discourse and Good Governance in Africa*. New York: Zed Books.

Acemoglu, D. and Robinson, J. 2005. *Economic Origins of Dictatorship and Democracy*. Cambridge: Cambridge University Press.

The African Charter on Human and Peoples' Rights (adopted June 27, 1981, OAU Doc. CAB/ LEG/67/3 rev. 5, 21 I.L.M. 58 (1982), entered into force October 21, 1986).

Agrast, M.D., Botero, J.C., Ponce-Rodriguez, A., and Dumas, C. 2008. *The World Justice Project Rule of Law Index: Measuring Adherence to the Rule of Law around the World*. Presented at the World Justice Forum, Vienna, Austria [July 3, 2008].

Alence, R. 2004. Political Institutions and Developmental Governance in Sub–Saharan Africa. *The Journal of Modern African Studies*, 42, 163–87.

---

control of individuals, thus government has the obligation to address circumstances that defeat the exercise of liberty.

Amavilah, V. 2008. *Domestic Resources, Governance, Global Links, and Economic Performance of Sub-Saharan Africa.* Available at: http://ssrn.com/abstract=1359944.

Arbache, J., Go, D.S. and Page, J. 2008. Is Africa's Economy at A Turning Point? Growth, Aid, and External Shocks. *World Bank Policy Research*, 955, 13–85.

Arbache, S.A. and Page, J. 2008. *Is Africa's Recent Growth Robust?* Available at: http://ssrn.com/abstract=1090274.

Aubert, V. and Dror, Y. 1959. Law and Social Change. *Tulane Law Review*, 33(4), 787–802.

Barro, R. 2000. Rule of Law, Democracy, and Economic Performance, in *2000 Index of Economic Freedom*, edited by M. Miles. Washington, DC: The Heritage Foundation, 31–49.

Barro, R.J. and Lee, J. 1996. International Measures of Schooling Years and Schooling Quality. *American Economic Review*, 86(2), 218–23.

BBC News. 2008. *Gaddafi: Africa's "King of Kings."* Available at: http://news.bbc.co.uk/2/hi/africa/7588033.stm.

Bois de Gaudusson, J. 1989. Administrative Decentralization in Former French Africa: New Hallucinations or a New Policy. *Third World Legal Studies*, 105.

Cao, L. 2006. *Culture Change.* Available at: http://ssrn.com/abstract=906767.

Carothers, T. 2006. The Problem of Knowledge, in *Promoting the Rule of Law Abroad: In Search of Knowledge*, edited by T. Carothers. Washington, DC: Carnegie Endowment, 15–30.

Carothers, T. 1998. The Rule of law Revival. *Foreign Affairs*, 95 (March/April).

*Constitutional Rights Project and Civil Liberties Organization v. Nigeria*, Communication 102/1993.

Constitutive Act of the African Union (2000), Art. 4(m). Available at: www.au2002.gov.za/docs/key_oau/au_act.htm.

Davis, K. 2008. The Relationship Between Law and Development: Optimists Versus Skeptics. *The American Journal of Comparative Law*, 56(4), 895–946.

Druckman, D. 1992. Assessing Progress Towards Democracy and Good Governance: Summary of a Workshop. *National Research Council.*

Dudziak, M. 2003. Who Cares About Courts? Creating a Constituency for Judicial Independence in Africa. *Michigan Law Review*, 101(6), 1622–34.

Economic Commission for Africa. 2012. *African Peer Review Mechanism.* Available at: www.uneca.org/aprm/CountriesStatus.asp.

Etounga-Manguelle, D. 2000. Does Africa Need a Cultural Adjustment Program?, in *Culture Matters*, edited by S. Huntington and L. Harrison. New York: Basic Books, 65–78.

Garon, S. 1997. *Molding Japanese Minds.* Princeton: Princeton University Press.

Gathii, J. 1999. Corruption and Donor Reforms: Expanding the Promises and Possibilities of the Rule of Law as an Anti-Corruption Strategy in Kenya. *Connecticut Journal of International Law*, 14(2), 407–54.

Gathii, J. 1999a. Representations of Africa in Good Governance Discourse: Policing and Containing Dissidence to Neo-Liberalism. *Third World Legal Studies*, 18, 65–108.

General Assembly Resolution on Education for All, A/54/595 of the 54th session of the United Nations General Assembly, October 1999.

Gyandoh Jr., S. 1988. Popular Justice and the Development of Constitutional Orders in Sub-Saharan Africa. *Third World Legal Studies*, 139–60.

Haile, M. 1984. Human Rights, Stability, and Development in Africa: Some Observations on Concept and Reality. *Virginia Journal of International Law*, 24(3).

Hobhouse, L. 1964. *Liberalism.* Oxford: Oxford University Press.

International Covenant on Civil and Political Rights, G.A. res. 2200A (XXI), 21 U.N. GAOR
  Supp. (No. 16) at 52, U.N. Doc. A/6316 (1966), 999 U.N.T.S. 171, entered into force March
  23, 1976, Art. 25.

International Monetary Fund. 2009. *Africa Conference Debates Way Forward Amid Crisis.*
  Available at: www.imf.org/external/pubs/ft/survey/so/2009/car031309a.htm.

Johnson, S., Ostry, J.D., and Subramanian, A. 2007. The Prospects for Sustained Growth in Africa:
  Benchmarking the Constraints. International Monetary Fund Working Paper, 07(52).

Khemani, M. 2009. *The Role of Anti–Corruption Commissions in Changing Cultural Attitudes
  Towards Corruption and the Rule of Law.* Available at: http://ssrn.com/abstract=1386496.

Koh, W.T.H. and Leung, H.M. 2003. *Education, Technological Progress and Economic Growth.*
  Available at: http://ssrn.com/abstract=637462.

Kohnert, D. 2008. *Does Democratic Transition in Africa Enhance Economic Performance? The
  Case of Togo.* Available at: http://ssrn.com/abstract=1210865.

Kostenniemi, M. 1996. "Intolerant Democracy": A Reaction. *The Harvard Law Journal*, 37(1), 231.

Kpundeh, J. 1992. *Democratization in Africa: African Views, African Voices.* Washington, DC:
  National Academies Press.

Landes, D. 2000. *Culture Makes Almost All the Difference*, in *Culture Matters*, edited by
  S. Huntington and L. Harrison. New York: Basic Books, 2–13.

*Legal Resources Foundation v. Zambia*, Communication 211/1998.

Lipset, S. 1959. Some Social Requisites of Democracy: Economic Development and Political
  Legitimacy. *American Political Science Review*, 53(1), 69–105.

Lucas Jr., R.E. 1988. On the Mechanics of Economic Development. *Journal of Monetary
  Economics*, 22(1), 3–42.

Mabuse, N. 2009. *CNN, African National Congress Scores Landslide Win in South Africa.*
  Available at: www.cnn.com/2009/WORLD/africa/04/25/south.africa.elections.results/index.
  html?iref=newssearch.

Marks, S. 1998. Democratic Celebration, Democratic Melancholy. *Finnish Yearbook of
  International Law*, 9, 73–79.

Mazrui, A. 2001. Constitutional Change and Cultural Engineering: Africa's Search for New
  Directions, in *Constitutionalism In Africa: Creating Opportunities, Facing Challenges*, edited
  by J. Oloka-Onyango. Kampala: Fountain Publishers.

Mbiti, J.S. 1989. *African Religions and Philosophy.* London: Heinemann Educational Publishers,
  219.

Mchahon, W.W. 1998. Education and Growth in East Asia. *Economics of Education*, 17(2), 159–72.

McKinnon, D. 2006. The Rule of Law in Today's Africa. *Commonwealth Law Bulletin*, 32(4),
  349–58.

Merriam, A. 1961. Traditional Cultures of Africa and Their Influence on Current Problems.
  *American Society of International Law Proceedings*, 55(Fourth Session), 146–52.

Miles, J. 2006. Customary and Islamic Law and Its Development in Africa. *African Development
  Bank Law for Development Review*, 1, 81.

Mises, L. 2005. *Liberalism: The Classical Tradition.* Indianapolis: Liberty Fund.

Moser, G. and Ichida, T. 2001. Economic Growth and Poverty Reduction in Sub-Saharan Africa.
  International Monetary Fund Working Paper.

Motala, Z. 1989. Human Rights in Africa: A Cultural, Ideological, and Legal Examination. *Hastings
  International Law and Comparative Law Review*, 12(2), 373–410.

Mwalimu, M. 1986. The Need for A Functionalist Jurisprudence for Developing Countries in
  Africa. *Third World Legal Studies*, 39, 39–52.

Ndulo, M. 2000. The Democratic State in Africa: The Challenges for Institution Building. *The National Black Law Journal*, 16(1), 70–101.

NEPAD. 2005. *commit4africa.org*. Available at: www.commit4africa.org/declarations/34/-/AU/ Gender.

Ocran, M. 2006. Clash of Legal Cultures: The Treatment of Indigenous Law in Colonial and Post–Colonial Africa. *Akron Law Review*, 39(2), 465–82.

Ohnesorge, J. 2007. *The Rule of Law from Social Science Research Network*. Available at: http:// ssrn.com/abstract=1006093.

Okoth-Ogendo, H. 1993. Constitutions without Constitutionalism: Reflections on an African Political Paradox, in *Constitutionalism and Democracy: Transitions in the Contemporary World*, edited by D. Greenberg and S. Katz. Oxford: Oxford University Press.

Oloka-Onyango, J. 2000. Human Rights and Sustainable Development in Contemporary Africa: A New Dawn, or Retreating Horizons? *Buffalo Human Rights Law Review*, 6(1), 39–76.

Osike, F., Candia, S., and Museveni, Y.K. 2004. *The New Vision* from *Disputes Referendum*. Available at: www.newvision.co.ug/D/8/12/368947/Referendum%20museveni.

Pearce, T. 2001. Human Rights and Sociology: Some Observations from Africa. *Social Problems*, 48(1), 48–56.

Piron, L. 2006. Time to Learn, Time to Act in Africa, in *Promoting the Rule of Law Abroad: In Search of Knowledge*, edited by T. Carothers. Washington, DC: Carnegie Endowment.

Pope, J. 1994. Corruption in Africa: The Role for Transparency International. *Commonwealth Law Bulletin*, 20(4), 1468–73.

Posner, E. 2008. *Human Welfare, Not Human Rights*. Available at: http://ssrn.com/abstract=1105209.

Potts, L. 1982. Law as a Tool of Social Engineering: The Case of the Republic of South Africa. *Boston College International and Comparative Law Review*, 5(1), 1–50.

Prempeh, K. 1999. A New Jurisprudence for Africa. *Journal of Democracy*, 10(3), 135.

Prempeh, K. 2007. Africa's "Constitutionalism Revival": False Start or New Dawn? *International Journal of Constitutional Law*, 5, 469.

Pritchett, L. 1996. Where Has All the Education Gone?. Policy Research Working Paper 1581, The World Bank.

Rajagopal, B. 2002. From Modernization to Democratization: The Political Economy of the "New" International Law, in *Reframing the International Law: Law, Culture, Politics*, edited by R.B.J. Walker and L. Ruiz. London: Routledge, 136.

Resolution on Electoral Process and Participatory Governance (1996) (ACHPR /Res.23(XIX)96) at its Nineteenth Ordinary Session at Ouagadougou in Burkina Faso in 1996.

Reuters. 2009. *Factbox–Africa's Third Term Presidents*. Available at: www.alertnet.org/thenews/ newsdesk/LC738182.htm.

Rotberg, R. 2007. Africa's Troubled Leadership and What To Do About It. *The Fletcher Forum of World Affairs*, 31(2), 49.

Rotman, A. 2004. Benin's Constitutional Court: an Institutional Model for Guaranteeing Human Rights. *The Harvard Human Rights Journal*, 17, 281–314.

Rule of Law Resource Center. Available at: http://law.lexisnexis.com/webcenters/ RuleoflawResourceCenter.

Shimada, B. 2004. Is Market Capitalism Possible Under the Moral Economy of Africa: How the IFIs Can Help. Working Paper Series American University of Nigeria. Available at: http://ssrn. com/abstract=587222.

Skinner, E. 1989. Development in Africa: A Cultural Perspective. *The Fletcher Forum of World Affairs*, 13(2), 205–16.

Smith, A. 1991. *National Identity: (Ethnonationalism in Comparative Perspective)*. Nevada: University of Nevada Press.

Smith, D. 2008. *A Culture of Corruption: Everyday Deception and Popular Discontent in Nigeria*. Princeton: Princeton University Press.

Snider, T. and Kidane, W. 2007. Combating Corruption Through International Law in Africa: A Comparative Analysis. *Cornell International Law Journal*, 40(3), 691–748.

Spencer, R. 2009. *Hillary Clinton: Chinese Human Rights Secondary to Economic Survival*. Available at: www.telegraph.co.uk/news/worldnews/asia/china/4735087/Hillary-Clinton-Chinese-human-rights-secondary-to-economic-survival.html.

Sunde, U., Cervellati, M., and Fortunato, P. 2007. Are All Democracies Equally Good? The Role of Interactions Between Political Environment and Inequality for Rule of Law. Working Paper Series, IZA Discussion Paper No. 2984. Available at: http://ssrn.com/abstract=1012340.

Tamanaha, B. 2007. A Concise Guide to the Rule of Law. Social Science Research Network. Available at: http://ssrn.com/abstract=1012051.

Tamanaha, B. 2008. The Dark Side of the Relationship Between the Rule of Law and Liberalism. *New York University Journal of Law and Liberty*, 33(3), 516–47.

Trubek, D. 1972. Toward a Social Theory of Law: An Essay on the Study of Law and Development. *Yale Law Journal*, 82(1), 7.

Udombana, N. 2003. Articulating the Right to Democratic Governance in Africa. *Michigan Journal of International Law*, 24, 1209.

USAID Africa: Economic Growth. 2008. Available at: www.usaid.gov/locations/sub-saharan_africa/sectors/eg/index.html.

Wani, I. 1991. Cultural Preservation and the Challenges of Diversity and Nationhood: The Dilemma of Indigenous Cultures in Africa. *University of Missouri–Kansas City Law Review*, 59(3), 611–44.

# Chapter 4

# The Color of Thailand's (Un)Constitutional Reforms: Red, Yellow, or Orange?

Andrew Harding and Peter Leyland

> To my knowledge red and yellow makes orange. And orange stands for innovation.
> – Abhisit Vejjajiva, Prime Minister of Thailand, in an interview with *The Star*, Kuala Lumpur, June 13, 2009

Constitution building has become a major industry in these times of good governance, emergent democracy, sustainable rule-of-law-based economic growth, and reconstruction of failed states.[1] The experience of Thailand over the last 12 years since the major constitutional reforms of 1997 is a cautionary tale in this context (Harding 2001; Harding and Leyland 2011; McCargo 2002a). Thailand is one of Asia's rapidly industrializing tiger economies, has a buoyant civil society, plus a political system based on what Thais and Thai constitutions refer to as "the democratic regime with the King as head of state," or in other words constitutional monarchy, which has been Thailand's constitutional system since the overthrow of the absolute monarchy in 1932.

Major constitutional reforms in 1997 seemed a promising start toward resolving most of Thailand's difficulties. Thailand, however, suffers from a serious urban–rural divide that has problematic social and political consequences. This may echo the division between African urban and rural social and political views (partially "modern" versus "traditional" attitudes) discussed in Chapter 3. Thailand may therefore represent a version of the "chicken or egg" problem under which a constitutional system imposed on a partially transformed society may prove problematic, particularly when the majority, comprising mainly rural "traditional society" dwellers, claim political power on a one man, one vote basis. Thailand's 1997 constitutional reforms have unfortunately unraveled, perhaps not completely, but nonetheless to a significant extent, since 2001 (Ginsburg 2009; Kuhonta 2008; McCargo and Pathamanand 2005; Pongsudhirak 2003).[2] This chapter therefore addresses the highly complex and problematic phenomenon of constitutional reform in Thailand in the opening years of the twenty-first century. At a certain level, the issue is whether and how a formal constitution can overcome deep social divisions and divergent political outlooks, and a political culture in which political parties are focused more on individuals than policies. Fundamentally, the question is why has Thailand gone to the trouble of adopting as many as 18 constitutions *seriatim*, viewed potentially as a series of "eggs" in terms of our "chicken or egg" question (or better regarded as eighteen refinements of the same egg)?

The colors in the chapter's title refer to the acute polarization which has afflicted political life, in Bangkok in particular, but also elsewhere in Thailand, since 2005 (Funston 2009). "Red" denotes the mostly rural-based supporters of former Prime Minister Thaksin Shinawatra. "Yellow" denotes his mostly urban-based opponents. "Orange"[3] refers not to any clearly identified group

---

1 See, for example, Horowitz (2008).

2 For an Asian comparative analysis, see Harding (2008b: 5–37).

3 On August 29, 2009 *The Economist* ran an article entitled, "Orange, Anyone?" about the need for the red and yellow factions to "call it quits." The title of this chapter was, the authors beg to point out, settled

of people but to the bare possibility of a view of the constitution, held by at least some Thais (including apparently, if we construe correctly the quotation at the head of this chapter, the last prime minister, whose favorable references to reconciliation have been repeated, as this chapter goes to press, by the incoming Prime Minister Yingluck Shinawatra). Their apparent hope is to find middle ground and take Thailand beyond confrontation toward something more akin to the period of intensive reform during 1997–2001.

After examining the reforms and their unraveling against the background of what we can call Thailand's "constitutional cycle," since the 1930s, of constitutions and coups, this chapter examines what can be salvaged from the apparent collapse of the reforms, sketching a possible constitutional path out of the current difficulties.


**The Constitutional Cycle**

We first examine the nature and reasons for continuing constitutional instability in Thailand. As a point of departure, one should understand Thailand's "constitutional cycle" since the 1930s as involving an oscillation between extra-constitutional changes in government, and steady political progress under a democratic (and intended at least to be permanent) constitution. Thailand has been ruled under a system of constitutional government since 1932. Nonetheless, it would be inaccurate to characterize the system as liberal-democratic in the sense understood in the West, or even Japan. The original displacement of absolute monarchy in the 1932 insurrection engineered by Pridi Banomyong was not so much a rejection of kingship or of the Chakri dynasty, but rather an attack on the privilege and exclusivity which stood in the way of Siam's progress (Baker and Phongpaichit 2000). The first constitution may have declared that "[t]he supreme power in the country belongs to the people," and the constitution did introduce universal suffrage. It did not, however, tackle the practical task of building an elected parliament based on representative political parties and less than 5 percent of the population exercised their right to vote.

Given that Thailand was an overwhelmingly rural nation with a very small middle class, it was not surprising that the nation's version of democracy was not established from the bottom up but from the top down, frequently characterized as a struggle between elites (Wyatt 2003). Since the end of absolute monarchy in 1932, Thailand[4] has lacked a stable system of constitutional rule. In fact the nation has experienced the adoption of a total of 18 new (including interim) constitutions, encompassing also the present constitution which came into effect in August 2007. On 17 occasions also in the last 77 years since the end of the absolute monarchy, most recently on September 19, 2006, a military coup has brought existing constitutional arrangements to an end and inaugurated the emplacement of further constitutional arrangements.

These coups have usually cited national security, often along with other aspects of public interest, such as widespread government corruption or constitutional breakdown, as the justification for intervention in the political system (Harding 2009a; Tan 2009). Without exception the leaders of such military coups (if successful) have acted under retrospective legal immunity for their actions, which only the institution of a new legal order under a new constitution could provide. Anything short of this would potentially entail serious criminal consequences for the coup leaders,

---

much earlier than either the interview with the Thai PM quoted below the title, or *The Economist*'s article, and was the title of a talk given by Andrew Harding at Singapore Management University in May 2009.

4   For an historical introduction see Baker and Phongpaichit (2005); for constitutional history see Wongtrangan (1990: 287–321).

since overthrowing the government constitutes treason under Thai law. Indeed, when the issue of legality of a coup first arose in the courts it was decided in effect that a successful coup begets its own legality.[5]

In the most recent instance in 2006, the military junta was able to enjoy complete immunity in respect of all of its actions.[6] The 2006 coup was peaceful, but the same principle applies even where those concerned have been guilty of gross human rights abuses (Harding 2006). A cycle developed over the years, especially after World War II, in which weak and often corrupt coalition governments were dismissed by a parliamentary "no-confidence" motion or a military coup, the latter usually leading to an Interim Constitution followed by a new constitution-drafting episode. This in turn led to elections and a weak coalition government, commencing the cycle over again. The influence of the generals was challenged by popular demonstrations in 1973 and 1976, and a brief flowering of genuine democracy between those events was suppressed with killing of protesters in the streets of Bangkok. However, the popular revolution of October 1973 remained a clear statement by students, workers, and others of a desire for parliamentary democracy. Many protesters fled to join the communist party in the jungles along the borders.

A period of post-World War II expansion and then economic boom during the 1980s and 1990s ended with a spectacular collapse of the financial system, which started the Asian currency crisis (Baker and Phongpaichit 1998).[7] During the 1980s Thailand moved further toward national reconciliation and constitutional stability, but a military coup in 1991 led to further mass street demonstrations which were also brutally suppressed in what became known as "Black May" (1992), in which the official death toll exceeded 50 (and the unofficial toll of deaths and disappearances was much higher). The Bangkok business and urban class demanded a restoration of civilian rule. The king eventually intervened to force the military out of office and appointed a civilian prime minister. Widespread calls for political reform (Baker and Pongpaichit 1998) were a result of this episode.

In 1995, influenced by the ideas of Thai liberal intellectuals and civil society activists, a 99-member Constitutional Drafting Assembly (CDA), representing all the 76 provinces of Thailand together with 23 experts, set about the task of drafting a new constitution. In this instance the drafting of a new constitution was provided for by amendments to the previous constitution of 1991, under which parliament had no power to amend, but only to reject or ratify the draft. The

---

5　"The high court held that it was immaterial how a government came into being and that the only real test of its legitimacy was whether in fact it could rule" (Blanchard 1958: 202, referring to a decision relating to the 1947 coup). The reasoning is also familiar in common law jurisdictions, cf. Mahmud (1994).

6　Constitution of the Kingdom of Thailand 2007 states at s.309: "Any act whose legality and constitutionality has been recognised by the Constitution of the Kingdom of Thailand (Interim), BE 2549 [2006], including all acts related therewith committed whether before or after the date of promulgation of this Constitution shall be deemed constitutionally valid under this Constitution." The Interim Constitution stated at s.37: "All acts performed on account of the Acts of the seizure and control of State governing power on 19 September 2006 of the Chairperson of the Council for Democratic Reform, including all acts of persons incidental to such performance or of persons entrusted by the Chairperson or the Council for Democratic Reform or of persons ordered by persons entrusted by the Chairperson or the Council for Democratic Reform whereby such acts have been done for the benefit of the above mentioned performance, irrespective of their legislative, executive or judicial force as well as punishments and other official administrative acts and irrespective of whether those acts have been done as a principal, abettor, agent provocateur or commission agent and whether those acts have been done on, before or after the aforesaid date, if those acts are offences under the laws, the persons who commit those acts shall be entirely discharged from such offences and liabilities."

7　For further economic and political analysis see Sulistiyanto (2003: Chapter 3, particularly 103ff.).

proposals which emerged were strongly resisted by entrenched elements such as some military and police generals, MPs, senators, and the higher judiciary. The judiciary was in particular opposed to the creation of a Constitutional Court. However, it was the sudden economic crisis in mid-1997 which prompted the adoption of the CDA's constitutional reform proposals. Diverse groups, ranging from monks to the Democratic Party in parliament, recognized that Thailand needed to strengthen its internal institutions if was going to survive and prosper (Baker and Phongpaichit 1998). The radically improved environment of good governance and accountability offered by the CDA's draft offered an impressive and ambitious new way forward.[8]

The 1997 Constitution contained comprehensive measures designed to guarantee democracy and human rights, exclude military influence in the political process, provide for strong and legitimate governments, and eliminate corruption in elections and in public life generally. It has acquired iconic status in Thai constitution-making history, despite its obliteration by the 2006 coup (Ginsburg 2009). First, it resulted from genuine public consultation, in consequence of which it appeared to have wider support than previous constitutions. It was indeed dubbed "the people's constitution" (Burns and Uwanno 1999–2000).[9] Second, it was an impressive document in its own right with carefully conceived measures designed to tackle the endemic corruption and abuse of power that had been so prevalent and so destabilizing, especially during the mid-1970s and early 1990s. The 1997 constitution simply represented a revolution in Thai politics. It was a bold attempt at conferring greater power to the Thai people than had ever been granted before (Chambers 2002).

Thailand has remained a constitutional monarchy throughout all the post-1932 changes, with the king as head of state at the apogee of power (mainly symbolically but also with limited capacity to intervene in certain circumstances, as in 1992).[10] The 1997 Constitution displayed much more sagacity and seriousness than its 16 predecessors in modifying the electoral system, changing the composition of both Houses of Parliament, and reforming the structure of the courts. As well as recasting the shape of the main institutions, a prime objective was also to provide a basis for a stable government and political party system, tackle corruption, exclude the military from having a constitutional role, and to protect basic human rights effectively.

To achieve these objectives one significant innovation was the establishment of several new or newly reformed independent agencies or "watchdog" organizations. The Election Commission of Thailand, the National Counter-Corruption Commission, the Anti-Money Laundering Office,[11] and the State Audit Commission were each designed to tackle particular aspects of malfeasance and corruption associated with the political process. The National Human Rights Commission (Harding 2006, 2007) was intended to deal with abuses of group rights and individual human

---

8   One of the present co-authors commented then that it was "hard to imagine a more comprehensive attempt to change social facts by law" (Harding 2001: 24–48).

9   See, further, Klein (1998).

10   The Constitution of Thailand 2007, Chapter II, recognizes the king as head of state, as nominal head of the armed forces and confers on him powers to appoint Privy Councillors and officials of the Royal Household. He has the prerogative power under section 116 to dissolve the House of Representatives precipitating an election. Under Section 94 the king has the power to refuse the Royal Assent to legislation for up to a 90-day period. After which the matter will be referred back to the National Assembly. It will require a two-thirds majority of the members present for the bill to be presented again for the Royal Assent. However, the king has intervened, for example during the 1992 crisis and the crisis over the elections of April 2006. In the former instance he secured the strictly unconstitutional appointment of a prime minister who was not a member of parliament. For analysis of the role of the monarchy in the political system, see Suwannathat-Pian (2003).

11   This particular agency was only statutory rather than entrenched in the Constitution.

rights. In the domain of law and administration, a system of Administrative Courts (Leyland 2006, 2009a, 2009b) and an Ombudsman (Leyland 2007a) were introduced for the first time, to further protect citizen rights by extending the range of remedies available. A special chamber of the Supreme Court was also set up to deal with criminal cases of corruption against holders of public office. Finally, the boundary of the entire constitutional scheme was to be patrolled by a new institution of paramount status: the Constitutional Court (Harding 2009b). The independence of these nine watchdogs was guaranteed by a set of uniquely interesting and novel devices. The members of each agency were to be chosen by a selection committee set up especially for the purpose, and the selection committee's composition was set out in the Constitution to avoid the possibility of government interference with the appointment process. Moreover the Senate, to which only non-members of political parties could be elected, would guarantee the independence of the appointments to the watchdogs by having the final choice from twice the required number of appointees who had been nominated by the selection committee (Leyland 2007b, 2008).

The Constitution was passed in October 1997. Most members of the Thai parliament had reasons to oppose this, since it tended to work against their personal interests as sitting members under the previous constitutional arrangements. However, they were constrained by the circumstances to ratify it.


## Political Culture and Constitutional Engineering

There are strands of Thai society which still remain resistant to democratic values. This is so notwithstanding developments in the 1990s and the incorporation of many of the principles evident in the 1997 Constitution, in some form at least, in virtually all of the various constitutions since 1932. Vote-buying, for example, has been long identified as a fundamental problem in the political process. It is disturbing to note that even in local elections as recently as September 2009 there was evidence of rampant vote-buying according to the Election Commission of Thailand (ECT) itself, with votes being bought for 100–500 baht or 2,000 baht in tightly fought districts (*The Nation* 2009).[12] Voting remains compulsory for all Thai citizens and measures may be taken against a person who fails to vote without good reason under the Organic Act on the Election of Members of the House of Representatives and Senators 2009.[13] The purpose of this measure, introduced in 1997 (Constitution of Thailand 1997: s. 68 and Organic Act on the Election of Members of the House of Representatives and Senators 2009), was to make vote-buying more difficult by increasing the numbers of votes that would need to be bought to make a difference to the result. Ensuring fair elections has proven, however, to be an enduring problem because corruption is considered to riddle governance, business and elections, and corruption scandals define the entire political process (Thornton 2000).

The ECT as a fully independent electoral body was conceived as an essential weapon against abuse under the 1997 Constitution, and the verdict on its initial performance was positive. One commentator opined:

> In the Senate Elections of 2000 and the House of Representative Elections of 2001 it is apparent
> that the new Election Commission of Thailand has provided unprecedented succour to the cause

---

12　One candidate was said to have borrowed 500,000 baht from a loan shark.

13　This recent Act replaced the Organic Act on the Election of Members of the House of Representatives and Senators 1998.

> of reform. In punishing scores of recalcitrant and corrupt politicians by ordering new elections the
> EC is striking a blow against old style electioneering. (Connors 2002)[14]

This, however, was provisional and may have been too optimistic an assessment of the ECT's achievement.[15] The opposing view focuses more on politicians' behavior in these terms: "[a]t best, Thai electoral politics can qualify as democracy in form only. From the point of view of almost all Thai politicians involvement in politics is the best way to access wealth" (Phatharathananunth 2002). Entry into politics has mainly provided already wealthy individuals the opportunity to gain election, and thereby to obtain further enrichment. Election candidates in many parts of Thailand would expect to gain the vote of local constituents by offering individual electors a cash payment. The lack of truly representative parties in a society with a traditionally Buddhist social hierarchy poses deeper questions about the degree of genuine political participation as opposed to merely voting. Moreover, the phenomenon of vote-buying is not universally regarded as wrongful conduct but as a reciprocal return of favours (see Laothamatas 1996).

Despite the existence of the secret ballot and explicit attempts to stamp out vote-buying, the practice has been pervasive and taken for granted. One influential commentator observed that:

> Vote-buying, a longstanding Thai practice, was actually exacerbated by new legislation passed at
> the end of the 1970s, intended to clean up elections and restructure political parties. By the 1995
> and 1996 elections it had reached epidemic proportions: to stand a serious chance of winning a
> typical up-country seat, a basic investment equivalent to nearly 1 million US dollars was required.
> (McCargo 2002a)

At the root of this phenomenon are the prevailing attitudes to democracy itself. Another commentator observed in the 1980s:

> [That] the Thai middle strata also fear the "turmoil" a more open society might lead to. And the
> experience of the democratic years, 1973 to 1976 reinforces this fear. Like the established members
> of the nineteenth century European middle classes, they believe that the "masses" are not ready
> for democracy; they are too ignorant, short-sighted and too easily swayed by emotions to obey its
> rules and make it work. (Girling 1981)

A similar point was elaborated more recently in a frequently quoted piece entitled "A Tale of Two Democracies: Conflicting Perception of Elections and Democracy in Thailand" (Laothamatas 1996):[16]

> [V]oting in farming areas is not guided by political principles, policy issues, or what is perceived
> to be in the national interest, all of which is [regarded as] the only legitimate rationale for citizens
> casting their ballots in a democratic election. The ideal candidates for rural voters are those who
> visit them often, address their immediate grievances effectively, and bring numerous public works
> to their communities. [These candidates are however regarded by the middle classes as] parochial

---

14   As an index of the ECT's "zero tolerance" approach, in the province of Samut Prakan in the Senate elections of 2000 five elections had to be held before a winner was declared. Unfortunately in many cases the candidates found by the ECT to have cheated were actually finally elected, indicating that ECT intervention was not necessarily in practice a political setback for the candidates concerned. See, further, Bureekul (2002).

15   Compare, Nogsuan (2006: 103) and McCargo and Pathmanand (2005: 99ff.).

16   See also LoGerfo (1996: 904–23) and Chotiya and Samudavanija (1998).

> in outlook, boorish in manner, and too uneducated to be competent lawmakers or cabinet members … Ideally, patron-client ties might be replaced by a more responsive and effective system of local government. On top of that, voters are [yet] to be convinced that principle-or-policy-oriented voting brings them greater benefits than what they may get from local patrons.

In similar vein, a study of rural northern Thai political attitudes refers to "a larger attitudinal complex that enables locally influential figures, often involved in illegal business activities, to win elections and engage in corruption of all kinds so long as they continue to deliver the goods to their constituencies."[17] It goes on to show that in the rural north there is

> more support for a more restricted, military-based model of democracy consisting of a political role for the armed forces,[18] limited participation for societal groups, a strong Senate, weak local government, and restrictions on press freedom … [and] because of their overwhelming numbers, rural Thais determine which party will control the government, but because of their economic weight and political importance, the urban middle classes have significant influence over the government's viability.

A kind of "Thai-style democracy" on the model of ASEAN soft authoritarianism which claims legitimacy in economic development has been advocated by an influential strand of the "yellow" movement. Such a view has been repeatedly asserted since the early 1960s Sarit Thanarat regime by the Thai establishment against demands for liberal democratic institutions and the redistribution of wealth and privilege. This strongly elitist view eschews granting the franchise and civil liberties to what it sees as an uneducated rural peasantry. Instead, it would revert to representation by the father-leader who visits his "children" around the nation, listening to their concerns and then interpreting their demands. The "one person, one vote" approach to democracy is thus characterized as a foreign import. Somewhat cynically, "[t]he monarchy remains inviolate and immune from even the most benign criticism. Unelected institutions can still impose their will on people's representative; when elected politicians refuse to play along, they are accused of being 'corrupt,' 'immoral,' and hence 'worthy of removal via coups d'états endorsed by his Majesty the King'." (Ferrara 2010).

The "two democracies" approach can still be clearly discerned. It has taken on even more (and disturbing) significance during the current period of extreme political polarization of Thailand before and following the military coup of September 2006. The coup ousted from government Prime Minister Thaksin Shinawatra (2001–6) and his Thai Rak Thai (TRT) Party, which had been recently re-elected by a very large majority in an election contest boycotted by opposition parties. He had been opposed by huge and hostile demonstrations in Bangkok during 2005–6, following many allegations of corruption, culminating in the controversial sale of Shin Corp, a leading telecommunications company owned by his Shinawatra family. This sale, on which no capital gains tax had been paid, was widely regarded as blatantly corrupt as well as detrimental to national interests. A technocrat government installed by the military junta supervised the drafting of what became the 2007 Constitution.

The January 2008 return to elected government, under the 2007 Constitution, saw the election of the People Power Party (PPP) under Prime Minister Samak Sundaravej. This party was

---

17　Above n. 4.

18　Of course this has changed in recent years as Thaksin emerged as the perceived champion of their interests and was then ousted by the military.

undoubtedly close to Thaksin who broadcasted frequent messages to his "red shirt" supporters in the governing coalition, and this again prompted huge demonstrations by the People's Alliance for Democracy (PAD, or yellow shirts) which effectively brought the Thai government and economy to a standstill during 2008. Samak was eventually forced to resign as prime minister following an adverse Constitutional Court ruling in September 2008. His successor Somchai Wongsawat fared no better as the occupation of the prime minister's office was extended to Bangkok's Suvarnabhumi international airport causing massive disruption. He was forced from office in December 2008 when his party PPP was dissolved, again as a result of a ruling of the Constitutional Court (Harding and Leyland 2008). Defections of members of parliament previously loyal to Thaksin who were lured by a better offer from the opposition then enabled the Democrat Party under Prime Minister Abhisit Vejjajiva to take power without an election in December 2008. The supporters (red shirts) of the pro-Thaksin parties, which were in opposition, also in turn mounted huge demonstrations against the government, demanding new elections. The red shirts rested their case on a clear electoral majority in the general elections of January 2008. The yellow shirts, consistently with the observation above, have stated a policy objective of *removing* the vote from the 70 percent of the electorate who live in rural areas. In their view, they are unready for democracy and their votes are simply bought.[19] The red protests were brought to an abrupt end with the crackdown in central Bangkok in May 2010. This event left the main shopping area on fire and about 90 citizens dead. Despite this, or perhaps because of it, the general election of July 2011 was won by the red party Pheua Thai, and in August 2011 Thaksin's younger sister, Yingluck Shinawatra, took office as Prime Minister.

Political parties themselves present further difficulties. The wider project to entrench democracy is not simply about granting citizens the right to vote. Unlike, for example, Malaysia and Singapore, Thailand lacks an established political tradition in which political parties organize from the grassroots up to the national level on the basis of a consistent set of policies. Ironically TRT itself was in some respects precisely such an "ideal" party, because it had a national support base, campaigned on the basis of a clear set of policies, and actually implemented them while in power; unfortunately in all other respects it was precisely the kind of party which constitution-makers envisage only in their worst nightmares.

Thai political parties tend to be many, representing a range of positions and interests which do not embrace any clear ideology. They are usually in essence personal followings, having purely regional interests and electoral base. Again TRT looks typical in some respects, being the personal creation of Thaksin and also primarily though not exclusively based on support in the north and east of Thailand. They also tend to be coalitions of factions, any of which might at any time switch party for some advantage to the faction or its leaders. Changes in government due to no-confidence motions and military interventions have made even controlling the office of Prime Minister much less attractive as an object of party organization than in most countries. Most prime ministers have stayed in office only for one or two years and have had little impact on actual policy.[20] It was therefore one of the challenges of the 1997 drafting process to find a means of ensuring that party politics would become less fractious or breakaway oriented, and more centripetal. The goal was that governments would be more likely to consist of one party, or at least a reasonably firm coalition of parties.[21] Hence restrictions on no-confidence motions were introduced, although these have been

---

19   See, for example, Arghiros (2002).

20   As of August 2011, there have been six prime ministers in the last five years and 29 altogether since 1932 (several held office more than once). See, further, Bunbongkarn (1987: 61).

21   Ironically, the object of attaining one-party government for a full parliamentary term was achieved in 2001, but at the expense of entrenching a government (Thaksin's TRT) which would doubtless have horrified

slightly watered down in the 2007 Constitution.[22] In addition the single-member constituency was introduced to strengthen ties between MPs and their constituencies (this too has been changed back to a multi-member constituency system under the 2007 Constitution).

The powers of the Constitutional Court have proved very controversial, but the problem arguably lies more in the underlying dynamics of the Thai political system. In particular the power to dissolve political parties has been exercised drastically, although with little impact on the political parties themselves. The idea of punishing the party for the misdeeds of individual members can be called into question. The Court is also itself dragged into the very heart of the political process in performing its constitutional duty by disbanding parties for the malfeasance of their members. Even more to the point, this approach has been ineffective both in stamping out corruption and in eliminating the underlying movements represented by these parties. TRT was dissolved in May 2007, but was in effect merely converted into the PPP and the successor of that party as Phuea Thai (For Thais Party) when the PPP in turn was dissolved.

Critically, a decision of the ECT to allow the general election held on April 2, 2006 was challenged successfully in the Constitutional Court, which held the election invalid in May 2006 (Shawl 2006). During the election itself, there were the customary allegations of widespread vote-buying.[23] The ECT failed to uphold objections to the results, and the Constitutional Court initially confirmed individual results which had been called into question. Although TRT won the election, it had been boycotted by opposition parties (this lack of the required level of participation, along with some technical issues, resulted in the unconstitutionality of the elections as was eventually held by the Constitutional Court).

In an unprecedented move the king intervened on April 26, 2006 by addressing the judges of the Constitutional and Administrative Courts directly. He suggested in typically oblique royal language that they should assert their authority under the constitution to invalidate the election, which had been boycotted by opposition parties. This virtual instruction (given the authoritative nature of royal pronouncements in Thai culture) resulted in the Constitutional Court's subsequent decision. Further investigation of the conduct of the political parties (TRT and the Democrat Party) in the election was expedited by the military government after the September 2006 coup, resulting in the dissolution of TRT, but not the Democrat Party, as a result of the May 2007 decision by the Constitutional Tribunal set up under the provisions of the 2006 Interim Constitution.[24] The

---

the constitution-makers of 1997 in every other respect, not least the fact that TRT was set up only weeks before the election.

22   For example, under the Constitution of Thailand 2007, Article 158, at least one-fifth of the members of the House of Representatives are needed to submit a motion for the purpose of passing a vote of no confidence in the prime minister but members are restricted to presenting one motion per session. The alternative prime minister must be named in the motion and an allegation of corruption therein must be accompanied by an impeachment motion. Compare Constitution of Thailand 1997, s.185, where two-fifths of MPs were required to submit a motion of no confidence.

23   These led to the Constitutional Tribunal's decisions of 30 May 2007 dissolving the Thai Rak Thai Party: see below.

24   See *Summary of the Decision of the Constitutional Tribunal Case Group 1* and *Summary of the Decision of the Constitutional Tribunal Case Group 2*. The Constitutional Tribunal replaced the Constitutional court which was abolished by the Interim Constitution; however, existing cases in the court were transferred to the Constitutional Tribunal. Thai Rak Thai was unanimously found guilty on all charges, together with three minor parties which were also dissolved. In particular, the verdict was based on the fact that a few high-ranking party members were directly involved in bribing several small parties into competing in constituencies that were bases of the former opposition parties, in order to ensure that the minimum 20 percent turnout requirement was met; the Court dissolved Thai Rak Thai and banned 111 members of its executive committee,

institutional dissonance from a customary liberal democratic separation of powers perspective is clear, to the extent the judiciary was effectively put on notice by the (constitutional) monarch that they should intervene to address the political contest.

Another method of controlling political parties which emerged in 1997 was the "90-day rule" which, having been included in the 1997 Constitution,[25] survived the 2007 drafting process in modified form. Under this rule a candidate for election to the House of Representatives must be a member of any and only one political party, for a consecutive period of not less than 90 days, up to the date of applying for candidacy in an election. However, under the 2007 Constitution the period drops to 30 days should the lower house be dissolved (Constitution of the Kingdom of Thailand 2007).[26] The point of this provision is to prevent opportunistic party-hopping prior to an election. Although this can be seen as controlling the behavior of individual politicians, it also encourages parties to hold together (recalling the fractious nature of Thai political parties). On this issue the constitutional "engineers" seem to have sold the pass by allowing a brief window of 30 days for opportunistic party-hopping.[27]

Constitutional provisions also require candidates to have a solid connection with the *changwat* or district in which they stand for election (i.e., being born in it, having lived in it for five years immediately before candidacy, or having held public office in it, or studied in it for five years). The connection of the candidate with the constituency is indeed a matter fraught with difficulty. The paucity of funding for parties means that they tend to recruit wealthy candidates with local influence rather than vice versa; or that wealthy individuals set up their own parties. It is thus local networks of influence that ultimately matter rather than the courting of individual voters. Indeed it is often reported that members display little interest in their constituencies after being elected (LoGerfo 1996), preferring advancement through Thailand's complex factional parliamentary politics.

One possible remedy to several of the problems here outlined is of course to have party-list elections in addition to, or instead of, constituency elections. The 1997 Constitution provided for party lists for the first time, but they were designed to fill only 100 of the 500 parliamentary seats. The main purpose of this was not simply to consolidate national parties but to ensure that the best people could be appointed to the Cabinet without the need for a by-election in each case. This would otherwise be needed given the required separation of the executive from the legislature after a general election, under which members of the government had to resign their parliamentary seats. This proved one of the problematical issues in the 2007 drafting process. One group wanted a 400-seat house equally divided between constituency and party-list seats. Another wanted a house comprising entirely of constituency-elected members. The result was a compromise: 320 constituency and 80 party-list seats, with the nuance that the latter is to consist of eight lists of 10

---

including Thaksin himself, from politics for a period of five years. It was also ruled that there was inadequate evidence supporting the charge that the Democrats bribed small parties into exposing some high-profile Thai Rak Thai party members' involvement in election fraud in a series of by-elections in April 2006; and that the Democrat Party did not defame Thaksin or urge voters to cast a "no" vote in the election. Accordingly this party avoided dissolution.

25   For a discussion of the unintended impact of this rule see Kuhonta (2008).

26   See Kuhonta (2008). Reducing the period to 30 days in the event of a dissolution would appear to defeat the purpose of the original rule, namely, to prevent the formation of new parties at short notice from existing MPs tempted by short-term inducements. The decision to slash the period to 30 days appears to have been a compromise reached as part of the constitutional drafting process.

27   The 90-day period was longer, but the 30-day period shorter, than the prescribed notice period for a general election.

based on eight regions of Thailand, thus maintaining some local connection even for the party-list members.

Despite all these facts of political life in Thailand, there remains a conviction that constitutional "engineering" is required and will be effective to ensure that politicians will be "good and capable" (Nelson 2007). The argument is that national political parties will both become more viable and will be less corrupt, and act more in the national interest. Most of the constitutional and legal engineering essayed during the past 20 years appears to have been directed towards trying to solve this intractable problem of political culture. At this point of democratic development, while there seems to be agreement that in some sense political parties and politicians are quintessentially "the problem," there seems to be very little evidence to support the conviction that their behavior can actually be "improved" by legal engineering. As has already been noted decisions of the Constitutional Court dissolving political parties, for example, are easily trumped by the setting up of new parties. Even the nuclear option of a military coup demolishing the government and the entire constitutional apparatus has been shown by the events of 2006–8 to be ineffective. Thaksin's government was dismissed only to see its simulacrum elected to office a mere 16 months later (hence the resort to the no-confidence motion and the proposals for restricting the franchise). Constitutional reform at this point begins to resemble obsessive testing of smoke detectors while one's house burns.


## Thai Constitutionalism: Ce n'existe pas?

It has already been observed that, despite the drafting of 18 Thai constitutions since 1932, there is a family resemblance between them. Many provisions are identical from one document to the next.[28] It would therefore be a mistake to see each new constitution as the substitution of a new "*grundnorm*" or basic norm. Instead, we should rather regard each constitution as a statement of the governance system as it has developed to that particular point.[29] We have to look further for the *grundnorm* in the true sense. If we were to stitch together all the constitutional Preambles since that of 1932, we would see that they constitute something like a developing essay on Thai constitutional jurisprudence. These Preambles could, it is suggested, hardly be clearer in concept. Paraphrased, we obtain something like the following narrative.

In 1932 there was an axial constitutional moment in which the monarchy was changed from an absolute to a constitutional monarchy. Although there have been many constitutions since then, which reveal some differences, there is a thread running through them, which involves the following major propositions. First, the constitution may change from time to time, as the king deems expedient on the advice of the legislature or other body drafting the constitution, and reflecting the changing needs of the kingdom. Second, these changes do, and must, always reflect the central political fact that there is a democratic regime with the king as Head of State and that the previously exclusively royal power to legislate, execute, and judge is now exercised respectively by the National Assembly, the Council of Ministers, and the judiciary. How these bodies relate to each other and to other issues such as the electoral system and other forms of representation, accountability, and governance, will differ somewhat from constitution to constitution. The essential point is that we can see in terms of institutional design, beyond the responses to particular

---

28   See, for example, Harding (2009a), discussing the emergency powers provisions in the last three constitutions.

29   Ginsburg (2009) argues, however, for the "constitutional afterlife" of the 1997 constitution.

events, an overall movement toward a democratic, constitutional system of government.[30] However, despite the fact that civilian rule has predominated in recent years the pervasive influence of the military which still exists beyond formal constitutional and legal arrangements is perhaps the most serious obstacle to reaching this goal.

All of Thai constitutional history since 1932 could be explained in these terms, despite the fact that there were periods of dictatorship under various military leaders. The consequence of this would be that, consistently with an analysis of the *grundnorm* in terms of the last paragraph, neither the constitutional monarchy, nor the democratic and parliamentary form of government, nor the independence of the judiciary, can be abolished in a constitution-making process—not at least without forfeiting all forms of legitimacy based on Thai jurisprudence and historical experience and precedent. However, the precise relationship between the executive and the legislature could be changed from time to time, providing democracy is in general maintained, at least as an objective. By this means we can see that, despite 18 constitutions, there are fundamental principles which have continued to apply since 1932 and which themselves represent a continuous thread of reform whose origins can be traced back to the modernization process commended by Rama IV and brought to its culmination by Rama V, Rama VI, and Rama VII (Harding 2008a).

One possible objection to this analysis is that these considerations are irrelevant if the military can intervene and dismiss the elected government and abrogate the constitution at any time. However, this is clearly an overstatement. The coup of 2006 was peaceful, accompanied by images of monks, office girls, and flowers welcoming or adorning the tanks, and announced by a celebrity former model on television. It was carried out in the name of constitutional reform rather than, as previously, to prevent it. It required the appointment of a technocrat government rather than a military one. It targeted both a new constitution and democratic elections within a short period, but was seen as having decreasing legitimacy: notably it failed to deal effectively with economic problems. It was ultimately an unsuccessful attempt to prevent Thaksin's supporters returning to power. The military coup as a violent assertion that power flows from the barrel of a gun is probably now therefore recognized by many senior military figures as ineffective. Even as a mere constitutional adjustment device, it is very nearly obsolete. While it will always be possible to envisage a situation where the military could intervene to prevent a breakdown of law and order, this by its very nature becomes an exercise of martial law or emergency rule, not a constitutional device (Harding 2008a).

Seen in this light, the notion put forward by Ginsburg that the 1997 Constitution enjoys a "constitutional afterlife"[31] may have value. It may ultimately be remembered as a decisive moment of reform, rather than an unsuccessful attempt to change Thai political culture. Clearly much has to occur before this can be asserted with any great confidence—in particular a way out of the present polarized political situation. But one can imagine that the signal reforms of 1997, the creation of the watchdog agencies, the entrenchment of the Constitutional Court (Harding and Leyland 2008), and the extensive articulation of new fundamental rights (Muntarbhorn 2006)—these are features which will see development in future and will not simply disappear from the landscape along with the 1997 Constitution itself. It is notable that the coup did not result in the abolition of the watchdog agencies, except for the Constitutional Court, which was immediately recreated in the form of the Constitutional Tribunal under the Interim Constitution 2006, and then in the form of the Constitutional Court provided for by the 2007 Constitution. The Senate could also be seen as

---

30   This is the heavily implicit "foundation myth" as one might call it, of the Preambles. It is not however being suggested here that this is necessary a complete or wholly correct analysis.

31   Above n. 5.

an institution which is progressively entrenched even though its configuration (elected/appointed) may change from time to time.

## The 2007 Constitution

Under the 2006 Interim Constitution, the Drafting Assembly for the 2007 Constitution was required in finalizing the draft to indicate in what ways and why the 2007 differed from the 1997 Constitution. Moreover, if the draft was not approved at the referendum which followed (in fact it was approved by a majority of 58 percent), then the government was empowered to nominate "any previous constitution" (probably code for the 1997 Constitution) and introduce that with appropriate amendments (Interim Constitution 2006: Article 26). This is further evidence of the unusual status of the 1997 Constitution and its "afterlife" in Thai constitution-making. In fact, the 2007 Constitution made many changes, which were largely attempts to plug alleged loopholes in the 1997 Constitution. Given this situation, the question arises why the 1997 Constitution could not simply have been amended? This possibility was of course forestalled by the coup which abrogated it and the problem of immunity from suit referred to earlier. Conversely, if the problem of legal immunity could be dealt with by rendering the grant of immunity legally invalid under any restored or recreated constitutional regime, then the military might think twice about intervening again in future except to enforce martial law or emergency provisions.[32]

The 2007 Constitution to prevent Thaksin or a figure like him from establishing a predominant position limits the term of the prime minister to eight consecutive years, a familiar and often controversial feature of presidential as opposed to parliamentary systems. It reduces somewhat the restrictions on no-confidence motions introduced in 1997, as is discussed above. It also changes the composition of the Senate into a half elected/half appointed body, abandoning (perhaps unfortunately) the attempt to isolate the Senate from political party influence. The 2007 Constitution goes some distance beyond the 1997 Constitution in combating corruption. It requires for public officeholders a statement of ethical standards, extension of the definitions of conflict of interest and declaration of assets, provision for blind trusts, and makes it easier to remove from office individuals in breach of its provisions.

One further result of several changes under the 2007 Constitution is an increase in power of the judiciary—giving rise to what has in other contexts been labeled "jurocracy." The powers of the Constitutional Court have been increased rather than diverted away from the regulation of political parties. The new model of selection committee for the watchdog agencies as we see below entails an extraordinary high level of judicial involvement in scrutinizing nominations for appointments to these agencies—an executive function which is not normally given to judges.

The all-important Constitutional Court (Mark II) is an example of how the 2007 Constitution seeks to protect the protective mechanisms against political interference. The judges are now nine as opposed to 15 in number and enjoy a single term of nine instead of six years. The judges comprise three Supreme Court Judges elected by the Supreme Court Judges from amongst their own number; two Supreme Administrative Court Judges elected by the Supreme Administrative Court Judges from amongst their own number; four others, two lawyers and two persons qualified

---

32   One possible way to accomplish this might be to enact a "snow white" clause, i.e. a clause which would invalidate a abrogation of the constitution, allowing it to be merely "put to sleep" during a brief period of military rule. Whether however such a clause could or would be recognized juridically as having such effect would be in interesting issue.

in political science, public administration, social sciences, who must have held high office under Constitution, or else be a lawyer of 30 years standing or a professor, as the case may be, and not have been member of political party for the previous three years. The selection committee for choosing these four persons comprises the President of the Supreme Court, President of the Supreme Administrative Court, the President of the House of Representatives, the Leader of Opposition, and the President of one of the watchdog bodies.

Crucially, the selection committee system has been reformed so as to render these committees less amenable to political interference, which had been a problem under the 1997 Constitution. There the selection committees, although structured so as to avoid government interference, were nonetheless open to manipulation by political party representatives and Senate committees. The other selection committees under the 2007 Constitution are constituted similarly to that for the Constitutional Court judges in what seems to be a clear attempt to narrow the base of representation on these committees (with the precise aim of restricting the ways in which the committees could be subjected to political interference). There is also one other important difference from the selection committee model under the 1997 Constitution. The Senate still approves and can return nominees, but it is now the selection committee and not the Senate that has the power to confirm the nominees. In other words, the selection committee can veto the Senate's objections.

These powers are in addition to extensive and increased powers now enjoyed by the judiciary qua judiciary. They can review validity of legislation as before, but in the face of many more opportunities for bringing cases to court. The 2007 reforms broaden human rights guarantees and provide for an individual right of petition to the Constitutional Court which allows a citizen to raise directly in the Constitutional Court an allegation that his or her human right has been violated (previously this could only be done indirectly by reference from an ordinary court or via an official with standing such as the Ombudsman or the President of the House of Representatives).

There can be no doubt that the Thai judiciary is worried about this change. The unfortunate aspect of the new jurocracy is that, while many people regard the judges as uniquely reliable and dependable, giving them too much power could destroy judicial independence and the proper separation of powers. The fear is that it might attract to the hitherto independent judiciary a measure of political interference, as occurred with the Senate under the 1997 Constitution (McCargo and Pathmanand 2005).


**Prospects for the Future**

The bloody end to the red shirt demonstration and occupation of central Bangkok in May 2010 with the arrest of the red shirt leaders allowed the city to return to a state of apparent normality. The many casualties added to the sense of grievance felt by the demonstrators, however, and an accommodation of the opposed camps has not been achieved (McCargo 2010). Clearly the constitutional impasse in which Thailand now finds itself is an unenviably complex one in which there seems to be neither the possibility of referring to an accepted, and legitimated set of rules, nor the possibility on agreeing what those rules might be for the future. The extent of constitutional tinkering has been so great as to degrade even the notion of stable and respected rules which carry a weight quite distinct from the merits of their actual content. The best, but only a vague, idea to come out of current discourse is that a broad based agreement could be brokered between the two sides which would offer a political agreement on the way forward constitutionally. The basis of this might be seen in the military's apparent acceptance of the red victory in the July 2011 election on the basis that vociferous red shirt activists were omitted from the Cabinet, and the new prime minister's reported acceptance that the government would not interfere with the military, as Thaksin had indeed done.

One problem in taking any proposals forward is a vacuum of leadership. Who should represent the respective factions? Another problem is who might act as peace broker? It will be apparent that once again, under the present king, the monarchy has occupied a very special place in Thailand. To a considerable extent King Bhumibol has acted as a stabilizing influence because of the respect he has personally commanded. In this capacity he has been able to defuse conflict on a number of occasions. With age he is obviously indisposed and unable to intervene. Further, the manifest failure of the Crown Prince, as his named successor, to take on this mantle during the crisis of May 2010 has clearly intensified anxiety of many Thais over the succession. This problem also demonstrates that the monarchy as an institution must be neutral if it is to continue to enjoy universal respect, and thus arguably should not assume such a forceful role in the future.

Constitutions are often adopted after a political process of negotiation which results from momentous events ranging from war, revolution, independence, or regime change. A new constitution is anticipated to work precisely because such an agreement is in place. On the other hand, a constitution which lacks a high degree of consensus among the main players might appear as an instrument by which a dominant political faction attains victory over the main opposition. One problem is that the 2007 Constitution has been subject to contestation, so that the idea of a set of neutrally arrived at constitutional rules which are binding in practice has been degraded. This makes the prospect of a lasting agreement and its implementation hard to envisage under present circumstances.

Given the experience of so many constitutional changes, the idea that the present set of constitutional rules could now be subjected to broad and open-ended discussion seems exactly the opposite of what Thailand needs. Rather, there needs to be a commitment to a form of constitutionalism already embraced by the 1997 and 2007 Constitutions to achieve a stable political future. This boils down to an agreement to actually observe the existing constitution (whatever that happens to be) in spirit as well as in letter. Constitutions become entrenched because they have an authority which transcends the reputation and actual outcomes of individual rules. The arrangements work because the main protagonists accept that operating through the constitutional process is actually the right way to debate constitutional issues, even if there is a perception that the rules in force are unfair, outmoded, or even completely lacking in justification.

The constitutional puzzle of contemporary Thailand is that constitutional rules and changes are constantly under discussion, and yet at the most basic level they do not seem to matter in themselves. They carry legitimacy and are adhered to only so far as they serve the immediate advantage of those who advocate them. Constitutional rules still seem to be worth a good deal of haggling over, but only because they confer some kind of a marginal advantage in the larger project of achieving total victory over one's opponents. The most obvious way beyond this is for each side to recognize the possibility that the other side might have some valid arguments to make and valid interests to protect, and that a compromise is the only possible solution.

A prominent regional element has emerged as another dimension to the present conflict, and a lasting solution might need to take account of this. The strongholds of the red shirt movement are the rural north around Chiang Mai and Chiang Rai and the north-east of Thailand, whereas the yellow shirts tend to gain support from the south and from the elites and the emerging Bangkok middle classes. The struggle for power and advantage with this regional element should be viewed against the background of a highly centralized state. Victory at an election has a winner-takes-all effect in Thailand. To put it somewhat differently, local government is weak and Bangkok is able to impose its administrative will over distant provinces. Under Thaksin's premiership this power was used deliberately to sweeten the rural population. It is suggested that a substantial devolution of power to the regions with new elected institutional structures might fundamentally change the political balance and, at the same time, address this issue. In effect, there would be the prospect of a degree of power sharing with the north and north-east under the control of the Reds, while the South and Bangkok would be in the hands of the yellows. However, one might ask how would the "traditional" or rural society of the north be governed in comparison to the "modernized" or urban society of the south?

At least some of the following elements will have to be addressed.

First, must the constitution as it stands be adhered to simply because it is law? The rule of law, which has been so much abused in recent times by elements of both the political factions as well as the military and the government, has to be agreed to be a basic principle. Extra-constitutional mechanisms should be disavowed. These include protest movements which go beyond protest to actually disrupting the operation of government and the economy and posing a risk to public order. The military coup must specifically be disavowed as a quasi-constitutional instrument. The military must clearly be seen to be subject to the constitution and the law and intervention should take place only where the civil authority invokes its aid in a lawful fashion for legitimate reasons.

Second, should a limited range of constitutional amendments sensibly form part of an agreed package of reforms? For example, the power of the Constitutional Court to dissolve political parties could be revoked in return for stronger and more effective methods of punishing individual transgressors and new elected regional institutions.

Third, are there other ways in which a negotiated settlement might work? The red faction might be seen to be correct to demand an end to legal immunity for mounting a coup and the reform of the lèse majesté law which has increasingly been deployed as a weapon against them (Leyland 2010), but might have to accept progressive restriction of the kind of vote-buying that has largely favored their interests. The yellow faction on the other hand might be seen to be correct to demand legal accountability for abuses of power, but might have to abandon its regressive view of the right to vote.

Fourth, it is regularly stated that political parties and the party system need to be reformed. This is undoubtedly the case, as we seen above, but given the political culture of Thailand, which seems to be immune to improvement via legal enactment (legal engineering approaches), one has to doubt whether meaningful reforms could be achieved in a short space of time. A few rays of hope might be discerned here. Perhaps the very polarization of current political discourse could result in the emergence of at least two strong and stable parties with a national base and a clear policy orientation. Given the problem of the two democracies, perhaps it would prove fruitful to debate how to bridge the gap between the two democracies in terms of flattening out Thailand's uneven development. This raises again the question whether steering behavior via law works better in modern rather than traditional society, and what are the potential political and legal development implications beyond urban migration's general effects? Political scientists examining the politics of the north and east of Thailand appear to agree that empowerment and proper representation, not disenfranchisement, of the rural masses is essential to this process.[33] Democracy is indeed historically the result of the demand for participation and recognition, rather than an ideology imposed from above.

It has been often stated that what holds Thailand together is not the constitution but the civic religion, involving the relationship between *chat* (nation), *satsana* (religion), and *mahakesat* (monarchy). This would seem to favor the view that shared values produce legal principles, rather

---

33   See, for one example among many, Ungpakorn (2002: 191–205).

than vice versa. Perhaps the constitutional stability which has eluded Thailand in recent years can only be achieved, however, when the constitution under the rule of law can with conviction be added as a fourth element. Meanwhile the uncertainty surrounding this element threatens the integrity of that which is held together by the other three.

# References


Arghiros, D. 2002. Political reform and civil society at the local level: Thailand's local government reforms, in *Reforming Thai Politics*, edited by D. McCargo. Copenhagen: NIAS, 223–46.

Baker, C. and Phongpaichit, P. 1998. *Thailand's Boom and Bust!* Chiang Mai: Silkworm Books.

Baker, C. and Phongpaichit, P. 2000. *Pridi by Pridi: Selected Writings on Life, Politics and Economy*. Chiang Mai: Silkworm Books.

Baker, C. and Phongpaichit, P. 2005. *A History of Thailand.* Cambridge: Cambridge University Press.

Blanchard, W. 1958. *Thailand: its People, its Society, its Culture*. New Haven: HRAF Press.

Bunbongkarn, S. 1987. Political institutions and processes, in *Government and Politics of Thailand*, edited by S. Xuto. Singapore: Oxford University Press.

Bureekul, T. 2002. *Citizen Participation in Politics: The Senate Elections 2000 Case*. Nonthaburi: KPI.

Burns, W. and Uwanno, B. 1999–2000. The Thai Constitution of 1997: sources and processes. *UBC Law Review*, 32, 227–47. Available at: hwww.thailawforum.com/articles/constburns1.html.

Chambers, P. 2002. *Good Governance, Political Stability and Constitutionalism in Thailand*. King Prajadhipok's Institute, August 10.

Chotiya, P. and Samudavanija, C. 1998. Beyond transition in Thailand, in *Democracy in East Asia*, edited by L. Diamond and M. Plattner. Baltimore: Johns Hopkins University Press, 150–67.

Connors, M. 2002. Framing the people's constitution, in *Reforming Thai Politics*, edited by D. McCargo. Copenhagen: NIAS, 37–55.

Constitution of the Kingdom of Thailand 2007.

Ferrara, F. 2010. *Thailand Unhinged*. Jakarta: Equinox Publishing.

Funston, J. (ed.). 2009. *Divided Over Thaksin: Thailand's Coup and Problematic Transition*. Singapore: ISEAS.

Ginsburg, T. 2009. Constitutional afterlife: the continuing impact of Thailand's postpolitical constitution. *International Journal of Constitutional Law*, 7(1), 83–105.

Girling, J.L.S. 1981. *Thailand: Society and Politics*. Ithaca: Cornell University Press.

Harding, A.J. 2001. May there be virtue: "new Asian constitutionalism" in Thailand. *Australian Journal of Asian Law*, 3(3), 24–48.

Harding, A.J. 2006. Thailand's reforms: human rights and the national commission. *Journal of Comparative Law*, 1(1), 88–100.

Harding, A.J. 2007. Buddhism, human rights and constitutional reform. *Asian Journal of Comparative Law*, 2(1), 1–25.

Harding, A.J. 2008a. The eclipse of the astrologers: King Mongkut, his successors, and the reformation of law in Thailand, in *Examining Practice, Interrogating Theory: Comparative Legal Studies in Asia*, edited by P. Nicholson and S. Biddulph. Leiden: Martinus Nijhoff.

Harding, A.J. 2008b. New Asian constitutionalism: myth or reality?, in *Constitution Reform: Comparative Perspectives*, edited by A. Harding and T. Bureekul. Bangkok: KPI.

Harding, A.J. 2009a. Emergency powers with a moustache: special powers and evolving constitutionalism in Thailand, in *Emergency Powers in Asia*, edited by V.V. Ramraj and A. Thiruvengadam. Cambridge: Cambridge University Press, Chapter 13.

Harding, A.J. 2009b. A turbulent innovation: the Constitutional Court of Thailand, 1998–2006, in *New Courts in Asia*, edited by A.J. Harding and P. Nicholson. Abingdon: Routledge.

Harding, A.J. and Leyland, P. 2008. The constitutional courts of Thailand and Indonesia: two case studies from South East Asia. *Journal of Comparative Law*, 3(2), 118–37.

Harding, A.J. and Leyland, P. 2011. *The Constitutional System of Thailand: A Contextual Analysis*. Oxford. Hart Publishing.

Horowitz, D.L. 2008. Constitution-drafting in post-conflict states symposium: conciliatory institutions and constitutional processes in post-conflict states. *William and Mary Law Review*, 49(4), 1213–48.

Interim Constitution 2006.

Klein, J.R. 1998. The Constitution of the Kingdom of Thailand, 1997: A Blueprint for Participatory Democracy. Working Paper no. 8. Asia Foundation.

Kuhonta, E.M. 2008. The paradox of Thailand's 1997 "People's Constitution": be careful what you wish for. *Asian Survey*, 48(3), 373–92.

Laothamatas, Anek. 1996. A Tale of Two Democracies: Conflicting Perceptions of Elections and Democracy in Thailand, in R.H. Taylor (ed.), *The Politics of Elections in Southeast Asia*. New York: Cambridge University Press, 201–23.

Leyland, P. 2006. "Droit Administratif" Thai style: a comparative analysis of the administrative courts in Thailand. *Australian Journal of Asian Law*, 8(2), 121–54.

Leyland, P. 2007a. The Ombudsman principle in Thailand. *Journal of Comparative Law*, 2(1), 137–51.

Leyland, P. 2007b. Thailand's constitutional watchdogs: dobermans, bloodhounds or lapdogs? *Journal of Comparative Law*, 2(2), 151–77.

Leyland, P. 2008. Appointment processes reviewed and compared, in *Constitution Reform: Comparative Perspectives*, edited by A. Harding and T. Bureekul. Bangkok: KPI, 213–42.

Leyland, P. 2009a. The emergence of administrative justice in Thailand under the 1997 Constitution, in *Administrative Law and Governance in Asia*, edited by T. Ginsburg and A. Chan. Abingdon: Routledge, 230–57.

Leyland, P. 2009b. The genealogy of the administrative courts and the consolidation of administrative justice in Thailand, in *New Courts in Asia*, edited by A.J. Harding and P. Nicholson. Abingdon: Routledge, 231–51.

Leyland, P. 2010. The struggle for freedom of expression in Thailand: media moguls, the king, citizen politics and the law. *The Journal of Media Law*, 2(1), 115–39.

LoGerfo, J. 1996. Attitudes toward democracy among rural northern Thais. *Asian Survey*, 36(9), 904–23.

Mahmud, T. 1994. Jurisprudence of successful treason: coup d'etat & common law. *Cornell International Law Journal*, 27, 49–131.

McCargo, D. 2002a. Introduction: understanding political reform in Thailand, in *Reforming Thai Politics*, edited by D. McCargo. Copenhagen: NIAS, 1–18.

McCargo, D. (ed.). 2002b. *Reforming Thai Politics*. Copenhagen: NIAS.

McCargo, D. 2010. Bangkok's savage conflict may be a mere dress rehearsal. *The Telegraph*, May 19. Available at: www.telegraph.co.uk/news/worldnews/asia/thailand/7738887/Bangkoks-savage-conflict-may-be-a-mere-dress-rehearsal.html.

McCargo, D. and Pathamanand, U. 2005. *The Thaksinization of Thailand*. Copenhagen: NIAS.

Muntarbhorn, V. 2006. Human rights in the era of "Thailand Inc," in *Human Rights in Asia: A Comparative Legal Study of Twelve Asian Jurisdictions*, edited by R. Peerenboom, C. Petersen, and A. Chen. London: Routledge, 346–63.

Nelson, M. 2007. *A Proportional Election System for Thailand*, KPI Politics Update No. 2. Bangkok: KPI.

Nogsuan, S. 2006. Party elites in the business of conglomerate model of Thai political parties, in *Eyes on Democracy: National and Local Issues*, edited by N. Rathamarit. Nonthaburi: KPI, 103–37.

Organic Act on the Election of Members of the House of Representatives and Senators BE 2550 (2009).

Phatharathananunth, S. 2002. Civil society and democratization in Thailand: a critique of elite democracy, in *Reforming Thai Politics*, edited by D. McCargo. Copenhagen: NIAS, 125–42.

Pongsudhirak, T. 2003. Thailand: democratic authoritarianism. *South East Asian Affairs* 2003. Singapore. Institute of South East Asian Studies, 277–90. Shawl, J. 2006. *Thailand Constitutional Court Voids Election Results*. Available at: http://jurist.law.pitt.edu/paperchase/2006/05/thailand-constitutional-court-voids.php.

Sulistiyanto, P. 2003. *Thailand, Indonesia and Burma in Comparative Perspective*. Aldershot: Ashgate.

Suwannathat-Pian, K. 2003. *Kings, Country and Constitutions: Thailand's Political Development, 1932–2000*. Richmond: RoutledgeCurzon.

Tan, K.Y.L. 2009. From Myanmar to Manila: a brief study of emergency powers in Southeast Asia, in *Emergency Powers in Asia*, edited by V.V. Ramraj and A. Thiruvengadam. Cambridge: Cambridge University Press.

Thornton, L. 2000. *Combating Corruption at the Grassroots: The Thailand Experience 1999–2000*. National Democratic Institute for International Affairs.

Ungpakorn, J.G. 2002. From tragedy to comedy: political reform in Thailand. *Journal of Contemporary Asia*, 32(2), 191–205.

Wongtrangan, K. 1990. Executive power and constitutionalism in Thailand, in *Constitutional and Legal Systems of ASEAN Countries*, edited by C.V. Sison. Philippines: Academy of Asean Law and Jurisprudence, University of Philippines Law Complex, 287–312.

Wyatt, D. 2003. *Thailand: A Short History*. 2nd Edition. New Haven: Yale University Press.

Chapter 5

# Debtor and Creditor Learning: Changes Over Time in Indonesian Bankruptcy Reorganization Approaches

Darminto Hartono

How does the sophisticated local business community learn to use new legal structures resulting from donor-supported rule of law (ROL) work in developing countries? Do they adopt them because the rule of law is part of the general environment (or will theoretically increasingly become so)? Or do they need to see some short-term personal or business advantage and approach things in an instrumental sense? What does it mean if private sector adoption of the rule of law is chiefly an instrumental exercise (the "what's in it for me" question), rather than being motivated by abstract principles or the concept that it represents their government's or society's (new) official policy? How does this bear on our "chicken or egg" question, namely whether changing law changes behavior in terms of social engineering, versus the idea that social views have to change before legal changes can be introduced to support the new consensus (except here we are talking more about the use of new institutional structures, rather than following new substantive standards[1])? And for commercial law reform, is the proper "society" even the business community (domestic or foreign investors), or the local public at large?

This chapter explores these questions by looking at changes in debtor and creditor behavior over time in Indonesian insolvencies, tracing debtors' conduct in particular from the period immediately prior to the 1997 Asian Financial Crisis (circa the early 1990s to 1997), through the extremely depressed economic conditions in Indonesia during what Indonesians refer to as their "multidimensional crisis" (circa 1998 to 2003–4), and after Indonesian economic conditions began to improve substantially (circa 2005 to date). The evidence reveals debtor behavior with the legal framework seemingly changed over time in the sense that reorganizations are now being commenced by a few sophisticated debtors. This is despite the fact that they were largely unknown before the financial crisis, and resisted de facto in judicial proceedings during the multidimensional crisis. Why did it take so long, and what does this mean?

**Indonesian Insolvency Law and Institutions' Development**

*Economic Conditions*

Indonesia has undergone rapid change in economic circumstances and government during the past 20 years. During the early 1990s era of the "Asian Tigers" (e.g., Singapore and Hong Kong) and

---

1   This could be a functional distinction in different areas of donor work, since typically commercial law reform efforts seem tied to the creation of new substantive law, while general judicial and court or governmental reform targets institutions and procedures. However, private ordering systems like contracts must assume an enforcement mechanism somewhere.

"Newly Industrialized Economies" (e.g., Korea and Taiwan), Indonesia's economy grew under the authoritarian New Order Suharto government at a respectable pace but was in the second tier in terms of Asian growth. Its economy was based to a large extent on cronyism in terms of favoritism shown private sector companies with good connections, plus subsidies for state-owned enterprises, while exports drew upon a combination of natural resources and cheap labor.

Following the 1997 Asian Financial Crisis, the comparative stability of the New Order ended when President Suharto was forced to resign in May 1998 in the midst of widespread public disturbances after 32 years in office. Then, Indonesia's "multidimensional crisis" commenced in earnest. The banking system collapsed due to the combination of the currency crisis and unrealistic, affiliate lending over a longer period of time. Foreign portfolio and direct investment stopped and at the same time, the political system entered an extended transition (exacerbated by depression-like economic conditions). Almost the entire domestic formal business sector became insolvent simultaneously. Local debt problems are illustrated by the fact that non-performing loans (NPLs) in Indonesia already stood at around 13 percent before the crisis (the financial system problems were papered over pre-crisis by loans being rolled over continuously). During the crisis, NPLs rose quickly to 80 percent as the Indonesian rupiah plummeted in value from IDR 2,500 to as low as IDR 17,000 to U$1 in 1997–8 (and 12 years later the exchange rate hangs around IDR 9,000 to 10,000 to U$1) (Golin 2001). The joke was that Indonesia had gone directly from being an emerging economy to being a submerging one, even while the so-called Asian "miracle" economies had changed from being one, to needing a miracle (McLeod and Garnaut 1998).

There were substantial structural reforms carried out under IMF conditionality, including commercial law reform (even while the judiciary and other legal system institutions were and are still subject to continuing reform efforts; areas like corruption continue to be problematic). Unlike most Asian economies, Indonesia's economy did not recover until 2003–4, leaving enormous non-performing loans in place as a banking sector problem for more than five years (despite the introduction of new insolvency legislation relatively early in 1998). The insolvency legislation, originally perceived largely as having been introduced for the benefit of foreign creditors, was pronounced a failure during this period (Linnan 2010).

By 2005–6, Indonesian economic conditions were perceived as having changed for the better, on a broader regional basis, notwithstanding a variety of continuing challenges. There were competitive challenges from China in manufacturing affecting a variety of industries (e.g., textiles post-phase out of the Multi-fibre Agreement), even while regional trade was expanding (e.g., the ASEAN–China Free Trade Agreement fully phasing in as of 2010). The commercial real estate market finally showed some life post-1997 Financial Crisis so that collateral values for commercial real estate improved, although many NPLs dating back pre-1997 Financial Crisis still have not yet been resolved. Indonesia has benefited during this period from Western investors' enthusiasm for Asian investment destinations, particularly since the Western economies slowed down following their own 2008 financial and banking crisis (however, such investment seems to be more portfolio than direct in nature). Much like the early 1990s, there is talk again about all the action being in emerging economies, and Indonesia, as G-20 member, is being touted in the international press as potentially belonging to the next generation of "BRIC" countries (only this time, potentially belonging in the "first league").

*Insolvency Law Changes*

Indonesia did have colonial era insolvency law in place at the commencement of the 1997 Asian Financial Crisis. Colonial era insolvency law was carried forward post-Independence under a

Bankruptcy Ordinance (*Verordening op het faillsesment en de surseance van betaling*, published in Staatsblad 1905 Number 217 juncto Staatsblad 1906 Number 348) that had rarely been used by debtors and creditors to settle debts (Lindsey 2000). According to the contemporaneous opinion of a foreign legal adviser to the IMF:

> The research showed that in the preceding year [meaning immediately pre-1997 Asian Financial Crisis] only some 20 applications had been made in the Jakarta Court of first instance for a declaration of bankruptcy. Almost all of these applications were filed by the debtors themselves; most of them were small shopkeepers in the inner city of Jakarta. As far as could be determined from the public records, no application had been filed in the past few years for the bankruptcy of major commercial enterprises. It was therefore concluded in the meeting that there would be little merit in pursuing an extensive discussion on the ramifications of the insolvency laws of Indonesia since real life showed that the Bankruptcy Ordinance, although still on the Books, was in fact a dead letter. (Hoff 1999)

A similar view was also stated by Professor Sudargo Gautama, as perhaps Indonesia's leading commercial law scholar that Indonesian companies simply stayed away from the courts at the time:

> According to our experience in law practice, if a company that has a huge sum of debt [owed] to a debtor, and who also has many other creditors, it simply does its best to avoid bankruptcy on account of debts owed to its debtor.[2]

Thus, prior to 1998, bankruptcy law simply did not exist for all practical purposes, therefore debt settlements or reorganizations were arranged via negotiation and out of court settlements as a business matter. That was not surprising, since the local business community typically tried to avoid the Indonesian court system completely, relying instead on informal dispute resolution mechanisms (Linnan 2008). The problem from the donor or IFI perspective was perceived as a lack of modern substantive insolvency law or "law in the books," rather than asking questions about "law in action." Thus, the supposed solution to resolve insolvencies at the donor or conditionality level was enactment of a new and improved bankruptcy law, which happened under emergency regulation in lieu of law (PERPU No. 1/1998) in the second half of 1998, that eventually became Law No. 4/1998. In our "chicken or egg" terms, this seemed simply to assume implementation if and when the law were enacted. Meanwhile, this ignored the problematic general effect of what amounted to an economic depression, bearing in mind that insolvency law works differently when an isolated business enterprise fails in a generally good economy (presumably due to bad business decisions, etc.), versus economic activity generally grinding to a halt in a general financial or banking crisis. The standard ROL approach also failed to confront the question whether people (businessmen in particular) automatically conform their behavior to abstract legal precepts for the greater good, versus asking the question how to behave tactically under the new norms for personal gain (essentially a public choice exercise).

In 1998, both donors and the Indonesian government recognized the economic side of Indonesia's multidimensional crisis required a broad response. In the insolvency area, this would

---

2   In the original: "Pengalaman kami dalam praktek hukum adalah bahwa sebagai perusahaan yang mempunyai tagihan besar terhadap seorang debitur yang ternyata mempunyai banyak penagih-penagih hutang lain, telah berusaha sekuat tenaga untuk jangan sampai terjadi pailisemen dari orang yang berhutang padanya."

consist of not only renewing the colonial era bankruptcy law but also introducing a voluntary debt renegotiation forum modeled roughly on the London Approach (Linnan 2007). Thus, the Indonesian government also established the Jakarta Initiative (also referred to as the JITF, because it was based on the Jakarta Initiative Task Force) as a voluntary, government sponsored non-judicial debt settlement forum for creditors and debtors to meet under facilitation. According to a foreign insolvency expert:

> JITF was founded to encourage debtors and creditors to settle their debt based on win–win solutions with the assumption that a business is more valuable as a going concern than when subject to a forced sale, and there was an incentive for the management and the shareholder did not lose control of the process. (Hoff 2000)

The JITF was staffed jointly with high-level financial sector experts from the Indonesian government (for example, its chairman was a former head of the Indonesian Capital Markets Regulatory Agency or Bapepam). Using donor funding, the JITF employed staff at levels ranging from sophisticated locals to experienced foreign professionals who assisted in negotiations. Beyond facilitation, the approach was for the Indonesian government to offer a variety of "carrots," while it was understood that, once agreement was reached between a debtor and its creditors, the government would make sure that agreements would be honored via the "stick." In practice, it constituted an administrative alternative to judicial proceedings.

In terms of insolvency law reform, the biggest change was the creation of an entirely new commercial court (*Pengadilan Niaga*) to house insolvency proceedings, alongside a coterie of more sophisticated local bankruptcy trustees and administrators to work with the judges assigned to the new court. Most of the trustees and administrators were drawn from the commercial world, or at least commercial law practice, unlike the judges. Much effort and many resources were expended training the new court's judges, due to a perception that doctrinally oriented Civil Law jurists with typically little experience in economic law were not in a position to understand modern commercial finance practices, which had brought down the economic house during the Asian Financial Crisis (for example, derivatives, offshore bank and capital market borrowings, the whole problem of foreign exchange exposure, complex financial contracts in foreign languages, etc.) (Linnan 2010). In theory, the judges, trustees and administrators were given substantial powers as a matter of formal authority to direct a debtor's business, but in practice debtor managements remained in control of their businesses. Judges, trustees and administrators largely deferred to their plans, changed or unchanged, for the businesses. The problem was that many debtor managements representing controlling shareholders were not eager to rationalize their businesses, which had failed, instead apparently only wanting to discuss debt haircuts as a possibility provided for under the law.

In substantive terms, changes to existing insolvency law were more *de minimis* in the nature of bringing the (Dutch) colonial law up to date in terms of modern (Dutch) insolvency law. The new insolvency law provided for two basic kinds of legal proceedings. First, there was the possibility of bankruptcy as a liquidation proceeding. Second, there was a voluntary debt compromise proceeding amounting to a relatively weak reorganization approach. It was premised seemingly on the picture of a debtor facing a short-term liquidity squeeze dealing with unsecured creditors (although it was recognized that continuing to operate a business would lead to recovery of more value to creditors, as opposed to simple liquidation value). There were provisions within the law allowing proceedings under a variety of circumstances to be converted, particularly from bankruptcy liquidation into voluntary debt compromise proceedings at the behest of different parties. Additionally, voting rules permitted unwilling creditors to be bound by specific majorities. At the time Law No. 4/1998 was enacted, however, more attention was probably paid to the idea that bankruptcy proceedings were a way to force debtors into negotiations, rather than focusing on judicial proceedings as means to dispose of insolvencies under either of the liquidation or debt compromise approaches.

Following Civil Law principles, the position of secured creditors was largely unchanged. Since they retained the right as a matter of law to take back their collateral (in which they were considered to have a continuing property interest as doctrinal matter), they were largely uninvolved in the voluntary debt compromise proceedings. However, they were subject to the Indonesian equivalent of the bankruptcy stay during insolvency proceedings, thought to last not more than nine months. No legal provision was made for common reorganization approaches like debt for equity swaps, or for approaches other than liquidating versus literally compromising debts despite modern reorganization approaches like debt–equity swaps and work-outs being recognized in the upper levels of Indonesian businesses, which were active internationally. The explanation for such omissions offered at the donor expert level at the time was that the legal provisions hardly mattered, since parties would work out reorganizations as a matter of voluntary negotiation. This view was based upon the idea that such reorganizations were conducted under a similar statute in the Netherlands. At the same time, it should be recognized that other European Civil Law jurisdictions had, in recent decades, introduced broader reorganization provisions patterned on US Chapter 11 bankruptcy reorganizations which provided more of a roadmap for work-outs. On the Indonesian side, the law stayed close to the older models also as a result of lobbying from banking counsel who did not want to lose their preferred secured creditor position due to changes in legal treatment of collateral. Therefore, the apparent concept, at least in the donor community, was that private ordering would work, if only a bare substantive rights framework were given to define debtor and creditor "legal positions" as parameters for reorganization negotiation purposes.

The new bankruptcy law was criticized for a variety of reasons. Then, following a relatively contentious six-year trial, relatively minor amendments were made under Law No. 37/2004 (standardizing certain key definitions, granting voting rights to secured creditors in voluntary debt compromise proceedings—although not by class, and refining the trigger for bringing bankruptcy proceedings). But by 2004, the changes seemed almost beside the point, however, to the extent that the foreign creditor community had long since abandoned judicial insolvency proceedings after they concluded, in the wake of their experience from 1998 to 2003–4, that pursuing insolvency proceedings in the courts merely wasted time and money.

**Effects Under the Law of Unintended Consequences?**

What actually happened in the wake of Law No. 4/1998's enactment? It was in part a study in diversion and incentives under the law of unintended consequences. First, the Jakarta Initiative as a voluntary negotiating forum was successful in attracting those local corporate debtors who wished to settle their debt problems quickly. Such debtors presumably had made a prior decision that it was important for their enterprises to be able to access international capital markets again. Thus, Indonesian corporate debtors eager to settle their debts by negotiation for business reasons hardly ever entered the commercial court. However, some later filed in the commercial court after negotiating their voluntary reorganizations in order to make them enforceable against non-cooperative creditors (in the Indonesian equivalent of a prepackaged bankruptcy).

While corporate debtors who desired a quick resolution for their own purposes went to the JITF, many if not most Indonesian corporate debtors faced the problem of their businesses being deeply under water as a result of either foreign currency loans which now had to be repaid from devalued rupiah sources of income, or because they simply could not refinance their short-term debts now due (which had been extended previously as a matter of course on a rollover basis, but by early 1998 credit sources dried up). Such debtors were described in Jakarta at the time as simply no longer answering their telephone even while maintaining control of their businesses as a kind of denial exercise, since they essentially refused to talk with creditors at all during a period of combined political turbulence and economic stress. These non-responsive debtors were the group against whom foreign creditors eventually commenced bankruptcy proceedings, largely in an attempt to force them to the negotiating table (Lindsey 2000). So there was substantial adverse selection at work, since those debtors forced into judicial proceedings were specifically those who had decided not to negotiate with creditors. Unsurprisingly, they tried everything possible to derail judicial proceedings that they regarded as designed to dispossess them.

Additionally, these mostly family-controlled corporate debtors were also so far under water, given that Indonesian borrowers under the crony system were highly leveraged even before 1998, that they had negligible to negative equity. Controlling families typically did not wish to surrender control of their companies in terms of changing debt into equity, or otherwise diluting themselves, even while retaining management control of the corporate debtors. So, debtors remained in possession, but managements simply did not change. The creditors did not complain about management-controlled debtor business plans in the ordinary course but rather about the controlling shareholders possibly diverting assets into affiliated or overseas companies.

The frame of reference and nature of creditor banks created its own variety of difficulties in conjunction with both Jakarta Initiative and judicial insolvency proceedings. Japanese and Korean banks in particular were constrained in their actions as creditors due to financial problems in their home jurisdictions arising out of the 1997 Asian Financial Crisis. Their constraint was an inability to recognize losses for fear of capital impairment at home. Thus, such creditors simply acquiesced in stretching out of debt repayment as long as no formal recognition of loss was necessary, despite the fact that rescheduled debts at reduced, extremely low interest rates represented a substantial economic loss.

Similarly, Indonesian state banks faced the peculiar problem that if they reduced a borrower's principal repayment obligations, this too might be deemed a loss, and individual bankers involved might be subject to corruption charges or personally liable for the "loss" of state assets. So, state banks, for different reasons, resisted write-offs, even though agreeing to rescheduled debts at reduced, extremely low interest rates represented an economic cost. Meanwhile, because of the simultaneous banking crisis, the Indonesian government through state banks was involved also as an indirect principal in many, if not most, larger restructurings and often held a large enough share of debt to have a veto power over any resolution.

The problem, in both cases, was that the creditors themselves were hardly trying to recognize true economic value, which would render realistic reorganizations harder. If one studies the voluntary debt compromise plans from a business point of view, it is often clear that all parties effectively colluded in simply "kicking the can down the road," and it appears judges approving such plans did not understand their economic aspects. There were many such plans approved where it was seemingly clear that the debtor's business would either remain insolvent or become insolvent again within the foreseeable future.

## Patterns of Changing Behavior

Starting in 1998, creditors began filing bankruptcy petitions against unwilling debtors who were "not answering their telephones." The response from debtors was twofold as rule of law problems came to the fore. Sometimes debtors would try to use claims about unpaid debts to put creditors themselves into bankruptcy, as in the *Manulife* case (Linnan 2007), or when it came time to vote on debt compromise plans, suspicious claims would be discovered of "fictitious" creditors, who would then outvote the real creditors to approve a debt compromise plan against the creditors' own interest, as in the *Panca Overseas Finance* case (Linnan 2007). Voluntary debt compromise proceedings were largely launched as a lever simply to stop bankruptcy liquidation proceedings. Real reorganizations in an economic sense simply did not occur. According to OECD Proceedings, "Insolvency Systems in Asia: An Efficiency Perspective":

> A Related concern regards the pace and depth of corporate restructuring. While change is occurring very rapidly and governments have established special agencies (such as the Corporate Debt Restructuring Committee (CDRC) in Malaysia, Corporate debt Restructuring Advisory Committee (CDRAC) in Thailand, and the Jakarta Initiative task Force (JITF) In Indonesia) to facilitate out of court restructuring, progress has been slow and the restructurings undertaken so far have not been very successful. Participants noted certain debtors and creditors have engaged in "band-aid reconstruction" by only rescheduling debts without attempting real restructuring. In addition, certain participants question whether the newly created asset management companies promote or impede the required long-term restructuring. (OECD 2001)

Instead, voluntary debt compromises were conducted simply as part of debtor controlling shareholder opposition to losing control of their businesses. So, insolvency law clearly did not "shape" behavior among businessmen. Instead, the key factor was simply the economic situation, and the business parties that used, or more often misused, insolvency law as a sword to fight their own battles in instrumental terms. Personal advantage clearly took precedence over any sense of obligation to follow the law, for which the legitimacy was cleverly undermined in debtors arguing that it was solely for the benefit of foreign creditors. In fact, most creditors were domestic parties and banks that the Indonesian government eventually had to take over due to the banking crisis. As a result, vast amounts of private debt were socialized when the Indonesian government "saved" the banks in taking over individual banks and recapitalizing the banking system generally.

By 2003–4, there were some successfully completed reorganizations, but those were largely the ones which went through the Jakarta Initiative process and, therefore, probably made only a token appearance in judicial proceedings at the end as the Indonesian equivalent of "prepackaged" bankruptcies. Such debtors had gone to the JITF originally because they had business reasons to resolve their debt problems. As such, it seems glib to assert that the changed insolvency law played a substantial role in successful reorganizations in providing a framework for negotiations. Instead, the framework was the Jakarta Initiative itself, geared more to negotiating business reality again for the debtor's instrumental reasons.

By 2005–6, a new phenomenon appeared. Debtor behavior changed as many seemed to want to settle their debts as the economy came back. For the first time, debtors initiated the suspension of payment and voluntary debt compromise, apparently as a real form of reorganization. When debtors initiated a voluntary debt compromise including initial suspension of payments under the equivalent of the bankruptcy stay, this behavior seemingly resembled using a prepackaged bankruptcy approach as in the US Bankruptcy System (the Jakarta Initiative had been wound down by that point in time because it was a time-bound administrative response to the Asian Financial Crisis) (Baird 2001). Debtors and creditors compromised on the composition plan outside of the commercial court. Then the debtor submitted the agreed upon composition plan to the commercial court. The purpose of submission of the composition plan to the commercial court was to formalize agreements already reached in order to bind all creditors and to prevent any creditors from filing a bankruptcy petition. For a variety of structural and institutional reasons, it arguably continues to be practically impossible to force any reorganization under the relatively weak voluntary debt compromise process by going to the commercial court before a deal exists between the debtor and a sufficient number of creditors.

Debtors and creditors could make a compromise in 2005 because in that year economic conditions were markedly better than 1998 to 2004. Therefore, general economic conditions may be what empowered the parties to negotiate a reorganization, not the mere fact that a new insolvency statute had been adopted 6–7 years before. The debtors who reorganized starting in 2005 as a result of improving economic conditions included PT Ciputra Development Tbk (Ciputra), PT Argo Pantes Tbk (AP), PT Purinusa Eka Persada and PT Jababeka Industrial Estate Tbk. We discuss the Ciputra and AP cases later in more detail.

Recall that Law No. 4/1998, as amended by Law No. 37/2004, has two basic options: first, to settle debts, by liquidating debts through by the debtor by filing a bankruptcy petition, and second to restructure debts by filing a suspension of payment. Among the most interesting changes made to the law between Law No. 4/1998 and Law No. 37/2004 concerned the specific role of creditors. Creditors originally had no right pursuant to Law No. 4/1998 to apply for a voluntary debt compromise. However, Law No. 37/2004 specifically empowered creditors to apply for a voluntary debt compromise. This amendment between Law No. 4/1998 and Law No. 37/2004 resulted from the practice of debt settlements carried out in the Jakarta Initiative itself.

Under Law No. 37/2004, the role of the creditor is not limited only to applying for a voluntary debt compromise, but creditors may also conduct voting in order to approve or disapprove any voluntary debt compromise petition under article 229 of Law No. 37/2004, and approve or disapprove any resulting composition plan suggested by the debtor as specified in article 281 of Law No. 37/2004. In other words, under Law No. 37/2004, the rights of creditors now not only include the right to force liquidation in bankruptcy, but also the right to restructure in order to settle debt. The changing law may not have a direct impact on the behavior of debtors and creditors in settling their debts, but now, creditors begin to have some tools. Let us look at a few successful reorganizations to discover the factors which caused debtors and creditors to settle the debt through a voluntary debt compromise proceeding implemented initially in a suspension of payments.

During the period after Law No. 4/1998 was enacted in the Jakarta commercial court, secured creditors rarely, if ever, tried to recover their debt through participation in the voluntary debt compromises or suspension of payment proceedings. In other words, the secured creditors preferred to use the security underlying their debt to recover what was owed them by the debtor. This was so even though they had an economic interest in the proceedings, and the debts owed often substantially exceeded the value of collateral security during the 1998–2004 period. Therefore, they were simultaneously unsecured creditors, to the extent of the shortfall. The role of secured creditor in the Civil Law tradition, as mentioned before, was somewhat different and outside the voluntary debt compromise process. So from 1998 to 2004 their debt settlement was achieved by enforcing their security rights under a pro-creditor regime, such as in *PT Gemilang vs. PT Sejahtera Bank Umum* (in Liquidation) (2000) and *PT Jakarta International Trade Fair vs. Jakarta Development Corporation* (2002).

According to data from the district court of Jakarta from 1998 to 2002, the secured creditors involved in a suspension of payment process would eventually seek liquidation (bankruptcy) rather than restructuring. Why did this happen? The factors causing the secured creditor to choose liquidation rather than a restructuring are:

- The debtor was not be able to complete a (business) restructuring process because the creditors did not offer any cash to strengthen the weak cash flow of the debtor's company due to the depressed economic conditions generally from 1998 to 2002 (the bad business conditions problem); and
- The secured creditor just wanted to liquidate because the creditor itself had only a limited term of continued survival. For example, the creditor bank was itself being liquidated in conjunction with government takeovers of banks as a result of the banking crisis, as in PT Sejahtera Bank Umum, eventually closed down by the government.

As mentioned above, the role of the secured creditor changed under Law No. 37/2004. The secured creditor was basically put on a par with unsecured creditors in being able to apply for a voluntary debt compromise and approving any voluntary debt compromise petition and composition plan. This similarity is a new phenomenon in Civil Law terms. Under the Civil Law tradition, the applicable right of a secured creditor, when a debt owed is due and payable, is to liquidate the debt by asserting its creditor's right of possession (*hak tanggungan*) in the collateral. This legal right is a property right of possession under Civil Law approaches to be asserted via self-help in seizing collateral, rather than an inchoate security right in the sense of a Common Law mortgage recognized via enforcement in a judicial proceeding in order to change legal ownership of the collateral.

However, pursuant to Law No. 37 /2004, the role of secured creditors changed to restructuring by voting whether to approve fixed voluntary debt compromise petitions, the composition plans arranged by the debtors.

According to Remy Sjahdeini, as one of Indonesia's leading banking law and insolvency law scholars, corporate debtors may reasonably consider restructuring if:

> Debtor still has good business prospects to be able to settle its debts if the company is granted a debt payment moratorium for a certain period of time, with or without dispensation of terms and conditions, or continuing debt accruals, or new financing. In the past, the Jakarta Initiative stipulated that period of time for a debt repayment moratorium of not more than 8 years;

> In addition, the debtor's debt shall be considered eligible for restructuring if the creditor shall receive a greater benefit for a debt settlement with restructuring than if debtor is declared bankrupt.

Therefore, debtors engaged in a voluntary debt compromise initiated by the suspension of payments because their concern value was higher than their liquidation value as mentioned in the below cases.

## What Did Businesses Learn?

As discussed in *PT Ciputra Development* (2005), *PT Argo Pantes Tbk vs. Indo Plus BV* (2006), and *PT Indo Veneer Utama vs. CV.Indo Jati* (2006), debtors began post-2004 to restructure voluntarily rather than simply reacting against a bankruptcy petition filed by creditors.

*PT Ciputra Development Tbk*

PT Ciputra Development (Ciputra) was established October 22, 1981 under the name of PT Citra Habitat Indonesia. It was one of the companies founded by Ir. Ciputra, the "Donald Trump" of Indonesia's property market, who has been involved in the local commercial real estate development business since 1961. Ciputra's business activities are in multiple property sectors, covering residential, shopping centers, hotels, apartments, office buildings, golf courses and the related facilities. Ciputra offered shares in the Jakarta capital markets (1994) and on the Surabaya Stock Exchange (1996) as part of its plan to become a public company (Indonesia Stock Exchange 2006).

Ciputra encountered financial difficulties for external reasons when the Indonesian government increased fuel prices during 2005, and inflation reached a very high level (the rate approached 16.2 percent per annum on a short-term basis). The property sector suffered negative impacts including Ciputra. When Ciputra got into difficulties, it tried to restructure by offering its composition plan on May 9, 2005. Then Bank Indonesia as central bank lowered interest rates, inflation dropped successively from 9.75 percent to 5.5 percent on an annual basis, so the property sector was again resurgent in 2006–7. Ciputra revenues in 2006 amounted to Rp.1,185,718 million, an increase of 13 percent compared with Rp.1,049,896 million in 2005. Revenues consist of (1) net sales, which are derived from residential business activities and (2) operating revenues, which are derived from property, commercial and other business activities. For the years 2006 and 2005, net sales contributed 73 and 74 percent of total revenues, respectively.

Ciputra had total liabilities or debt amounting IDR of 1,781,371,441,803.00 with seven unsecured creditors and other secured creditor(s). In order to settle the debt, Ciputra applied for a voluntary debt compromise, not in reaction to any creditor-filed bankruptcy petition as was the practice in 1998 to 2005. During the voluntary proceeding, Ciputra submitted a composition plan to its creditors. The objective of the composition plan was to reorganize the debts that are arranged in the composition plan in final settlement of debts settlement and in order to maximize the value that will be received by the participating creditors, either unsecured or secured. For Ciputra, the composition plan was also prophylactic in the sense that it was to be used to protect against any bankruptcy petition filed by Ciputra's creditors. In other words, Ciputra wanted to formalize arrangements in order to bind all of its creditors under the composition plan.

The composition plan issued by Ciputra as debtor contained the following terms of restructuring:

- Ciputra's total liabilities were IDR 1,781,371,441,803, as of May 9, 2005.
- The terms of restructuring would provide for debt to equity swaps, debt to asset exchanges, and debt rescheduling.

*Ciputra's Financial Condition Pre-Restructuring 2005*

**Table 5.1 Liquidation pre-restructuring 2005**

| Liquidation | Debt/Asset | (ROI) | Asset (mill) | Liability (mill) | Equity (mill) |
|---|---|---|---|---|---|
| 60% | 84% | 16.8% | 5,306,702 | 14,489,036 | (98,427) |

Before restructuring, Ciputra's solvency ratio was as high as 84 percent, meaning almost all assets of Ciputra Development were required to cover the debt of 84 percent. So, its debt to equity ratio was approximately six to one. Supposing that Ciputra were to be liquidated, the liquidation value would be only 60 percent. This liquidation value was low enough that Ciputra's shareholders might not receive anything if liquidation took place.

*Ciputra's Financial Condition Post-Restructuring 2006*

**Table 5.2 Liquidation post-restructuring 2006**

| Liquidation | Debt/Asset | ROI | Asset (mill) | Liability (mill) | Equity (mill) |
|---|---|---|---|---|---|
| 93.38% | 25% | 8.4% | 5,153,111 | 1,303,269 | 2,844,824 |

Ever since restructuring, the pattern is that the assets and account receivables have decreased even while equity has increased. One result was that the solvency ratio improved from 84 percent to become 25 percent, so the debt to equity ratio was cut in half. Additionally, on the assumption that assets offered in debt settlement were assets that were not liquid, that liquidation valuation increased from 60 percent to 90 percent. This reduced the risk for present creditor or potential creditors so that Ciputra became eligible again for new credits and financial resources as a newly solvent enterprise. So, they could relaunch themselves in the property development business with new projects.

On the other hand, Ciputra's return on investment (ROI) was previously enjoyed by the original stockholders, but following the reorganization, as a matter of dilution, it dwindled from 16.8 percent to 8.4 percent. This is due to the debt conversion. It diluted equity in increasing the number of shares against which results are measured, so equity increased from negative equity to positive equity. Even though the ROI decreased from the original ratio of 16.8 percent to become 8.4 percent, the ratio change is not as dramatic as it might appear because the dilution of earnings is offset by interest expenses saved as the result of the conversion of debt to equity so that the share of profits is increasing. Debt conversion effects on interest expenses should be higher, along with the interest rate that is borne by CD as company. The higher the interest rate borne by the company, the bigger the gain obtained by the company from this debt conversion. In general, this stock conversion reduces the risk level that they have to bear and harms the stockholders who have to receive lesser profit proportions due to the increase in the amount of stock. Nonetheless, these stockholders would have been more harmed by a bankruptcy resolution if the restructuring offer were rejected because they would not have received any residual value at all from their investment due to negative equity pre-reorganization.

In other words, following restructuring, creditors and stockholders were better off compared to before restructuring. Creditors enjoyed increased security value (reclaiming value theoretically at the time of liquidation). Before restructuring, the liquidation value was 60.05 percent, but after restructuring, the liquidation value became 93 percent. The debt to equity ratio of Ciputra became lower after restructuring, decreasing from 84 percent to 25 percent. The original stockholders still own their stock, although suffering from dilution due to the increase of equity resulted from debt conversion. Before restructuring, its equity was negative (IDR 98,427 billion), but that becomes positive (IDR 2,844,824 billion) after the restructuring.

The restructuring process in Indonesia is different from Chapter 11 reorganization in the United States. In the United States, the debtor's assets are effectively going to be sold to the creditors, not to the third parties as mentioned by Thomas Jackson:

> The conceptual keys differ between reorganization and liquidation that in reorganization the firm's assets (or most of them) are sold to the creditors themselves rather than to third parties ... The key distinction between reorganization and liquidation is who are the new owner of the assets; third parties or the former claimants. (Jackson 1986)

Under US approaches, the process of restructuring should result in splitting the bad and good debtor assets, appointment of a new management, and payment of creditors, often including former shareholders who lost control as a result of restructuring, such as General Motors. Under the Indonesia bankruptcy proceeding or voluntary debt compromise process, usually the controlling shareholder/management still maintains control before and after restructuring, and the creditors do not get paid immediately. In this case, often, the benefit of restructuring comes to the debtor's company in order to get a new financing to strengthen the liquidity and its business prospects going forward, as in the case of Ciputra and AP.

I deduce that the following factors are key in causing the debtor to enter a voluntary debt compromise proceeding (involving a temporary suspension of payments) to settle its debt, as follows:

- The debtor must enter into a suspension of payments without previously facing a bankruptcy petition. This suspension of payment is as an instrument against any creditor's actions. It signals that the debtor as a reputable business person intends to act before any bankruptcy petition were filed by creditors.
- The debtor wants a suspension of payment as a medium to make an accord with its creditors, in order to formalize arrangements already to be worked out to bind all its creditors. It is better off to settle through a reorganization rather than to settle its debt through liquidation indicated by the financial ratios as mentioned above.
- Indonesian economic conditions since 2006 have been improving; therefore, these favorable economic conditions can stimulate an increase in the value of the property business in the future.

*PT Argo Pantes Tbk*

PT Argo Pantes (AP) is one of the largest integrated cotton and blended cotton textile companies in Indonesia. The company was established in 1997, and its shares were listed on the Jakarta and Surabaya Stock Exchanges since 1991. In 2005, the company's direct export sales reached 67.59 percent of its production, and the remaining sales were to local markets for re-export.

AP had total liabilities or debts amounting to U\$268,953,804.82, which was owed to 16 unsecured creditors in the amount of U\$104,072,853.32 and to four secured creditors in the amount of U\$106,516,552.30. In order to settle the debt, AP filed a voluntary debt compromise petition in reaction to a bankruptcy petition filed by Indo Plus BV as creditor (so following the 1998–2004 pattern, except AP sought a real reorganization rather than just trying to throw a wrench into the bankruptcy liquidation process). During the mandatory quiet period, AP had submitted a composition plan to its creditors. The objective of the composition plan was to reorganize the debts that were arranged in the composition plan to give the optimum value to the creditors and save the jobs of 3,828 employees. AP, as a state owned company, clearly was focused on workers as constituency, too.

The composition plan issued by AP as debtor contained the terms of restructuring as follows:

- The total liability was U$268,953,804.82, as of April 11, 2006.
- The terms of restructuring involved debt to equity conversion, shorter-term debt being changed into bonds as conversion and rescheduled with the term of 25 years.

According to Pro forma Financial Information as of December 31, 2005, the pre- and post-restructuring figures were as follows (Capital Market Reference Centre 2007).

**Table 5.3 Pro Forma Financial Information (December 31, 2005)**

|  | Pre-restructuring IDR (000) | Post-restructuring IDR (000) |
|---|---|---|
| Current assets | 450,262,177 | 450,262,177 |
| Fixed assets | 1,411,049,653 | 1,411,049,653 |
| Other assets | 93,334,472 | 93,334,472 |
| Total assets | 1,954,646,302 | 1,954,646,302 |
| Current liabilities | 1,573,533,497 | 651,723,849 |
| Fixed liabilities | 596,585,595 | 870,079,373 |
| Own equity | (215,472,790) | 432,843,080 |
| Total liabilities and own equity | 1,954,646,302 | 1,954,646,302 |

*Pre-Restructuring 2005*

**Table 5.4 Liquidity pre-restructuring 2005**

| Liquidity | Solvency Ratio | Asset (mill) | Liability (mill) | Equity (mill) |
|---|---|---|---|---|
| 28% | 111% | 1.954.646 | 2,170,119 | (215,472,790) |

Before restructuring, AP's solvency ratio was extremely bad in the amount of 111 percent. It meant that all assets of AP were not enough to cover the debt up to 111 percent, so the debt to equity ratio was effectively negative. Assume that unsecured debt in the amount of U$67,569,134.68 was to be converted into equity at the exchange rate of IDR9,915=U$1. The liquidity ratio, consisting of current assets divided by current liabilities, was bad, in the amount of 28 percent. It meant that the liquid assets of the company were only 28 percent, which was not enough to cover liabilities.

*Post-Restructuring 2005*

**Table 5.5 Liquidity post-restructuring 2006**

| Liquidity | Solvency Ratio | Asset | Liability | Equity |
|---|---|---|---|---|
| 69% | 77% | 1.954.646 | 1.521,803 | 432,843,080 |

As a result of restructuring, liabilities were lessened, while equity increased or became positive. One result was that the solvency ratio improved from 111 percent to become 77 percent, which was still not great as debt to equity ratio but better. This reduced the risk for present or potential creditors, so AP became more financially stable and able to raise more capital than before.

This was due to a debt conversion diluting the share of profit to be received by the original stockholders, diluted by the number of equity shares that increased. Liquidity consists of current assets divided by current liabilities, and is better after restructuring, increasing up to 69 percent. It means that the assets of the company are more than 50 percent, or in the amount of 69 percent, to cover more liabilities. This improved liquidity ratio would increase supplier or trade financing to support AP's business.

In this case, the previous shareholders were only being diluted 21.1 percent based on the composition plan dated April 11, 2006. The previous owner still controlled the management of AP. Debt conversation effects on interest expenses were higher, as was the interest rate borne by the company. The higher the interest rate borne by the company, the bigger the gain to be obtained by the company from any debt conversion.

In general, this stock conversion benefited them by reducing the risk level they have to bear, balanced against any harm the stockholders who are diluted in receiving lesser profit proportionally due to the increased amount of stock outstanding. Nonetheless, these stockholders would be more harmed by the bankruptcy decision if the restructuring offer were rejected, because they would not receive any value at all from their investment. In other words, if all the assets of AP were sold, the proceeds would not be enough to pay its liabilities. Therefore, the shareholders would not receive anything under a liquidation scenario.

After restructuring, the creditors and stockholders are in a better position compared to before restructuring. Creditors enjoy increased security values, potentially reclaiming value if liquidation occurs. Before restructuring, the solvency ratio was 111 percent, while after restructuring, the solvency ratio became 77 percent, and the ability of the assets of AP to bear its liability became stronger after restructuring. The (original) stockholders still own their stock or control AP as company, although they suffered a dilution due to the increase of equity resulted from debt conversion.

A comparison between AP and Ciputra reveals similarities and differences. Similarly, both companies suffered from negative equity before restructuring, but after restructuring, both companies have positive equity. The solvency ratio also improved after restructuring. This means creditors are better off after restructuring than before restructuring. The difference between Ciputra and AP involves the prospects of AP's textile industry being more fragile compared with Ciputra's property business (chiefly because of Chinese competition specifically in the textile industry). This means that the converted creditors face a higher risk in textile business compared with in the property business.

The factors surrounding a decision by the debtor to commence a voluntary debt compromise, including suspension of payments in order to settle its debts rather than to liquidate and pay off its debts, are:

- The creditors of AP consist mostly of state owned companies (BUMN), which do not want to recognize losses. If the secured creditors wanted to execute on their collateral, they would have received in value less than if the restructuring of the debt took place (indicated by the financial ratios above).
- The secured creditors of AP may have considered that when they liquidate their security, they may not have received anything because the solvency ratio is 111 percent and the nature of AP business is manufacturing, not real property. AP's assets mostly consist of machines (personal property), and the value of machines always deteriorates over time, in opposition to real property.
- The secured creditor as a state-owned enterprise sometimes is designated to be an agent of development assigned by the government, therefore the secured creditor as a state-owned company would prefer to restructure AP because to liquidate AP's business would presumably have increased unemployment. In other words, the restructuring of AP's debt was done in large part in order to save jobs rather than targeting profit and loss, as in the private sector.

## Conclusion

Factors that cause a change in the behavior of debtors to commence a voluntary debt compromise process as reorganization without previously facing a bankruptcy petition were:

- The debtor really intends that a voluntary debt compromise constitutes a reorganization to improve the business' financial condition treated as a tool against any credit risk. It means that the debtor wants to prevent its creditors from filing a bankruptcy petition (as mentioned above, this behavior resembles a prepackaged bankruptcy under the US bankruptcy system). This behavior may be categorized as a transplantation of law in changing the traditional voluntary debt compromise for debtors facing a liquidity squeeze, as well as the position of secured creditors, into a full-fledged corporate reorganization. In other words, the debtor wants all its creditors to be bound by a composition plan.
- As mentioned in the cases of Ciputra and AP, Indonesian economic conditions in 2005 stimulated the work-out process. In other words, the bankruptcy law is only workable when economic conditions become more favorable compared to 1998–2004 (so there are external limits imposed by general business conditions on any reorganization's prospects).
- General financial conditions were much better in 2005 compared with 1998, so that the banking sector itself had more liquidity to provide financing for restructuring their debt. External conditions include the general creditor financial position, too.
- The nature of the business makes a difference. Under the current economic conditions, the debt of a property business is easier to restructure compared to the debt of a textile manufacturing business because the property business can create more income in the future.

The textile business is under significant competitive pressure, especially from Chinese products.
- When the creditor is a state-owned company, they try to settle their debts through restructuring process rather than liquidating process in consideration of the public benefit of saving jobs, so debt should be settled through restructuring rather than liquidation, especially in the case of AP.
- Unless the original owner might lose control of management of debtor's company even though the former owner might be diluted in a debt to equity conversion, they still may agree to restructure by entering reorganization rather than a bankruptcy liquidation process.
- Debtors use the voluntary debt compromise process also without first receiving a creditor's bankruptcy petition in order to formalize pre-negotiated arrangements and to prevent any other creditors who might want to file a bankruptcy petition. "Formalization" means that any compromise negotiated by a sufficient majority of debtors and creditors is made binding on the other creditors via running it through the judicial process.
- When business conditions become better, the debtor's behavior changes and may become proactive toward restructuring by entering the voluntary debt compromise (suspension of payment) process without having previously filed a bankruptcy petition. However, the impetus must come from the debtor still in practice, since the judicial framework does not lend itself well to reorganizations beyond prepackaged bankruptcies. This is on top of any economic gains, a desire to formalize its composition plan in order to bind any creditors, and other factors such as what kind of creditor is involved (whether it is a state-owned company or not).

A cursory examination of the above reveals that debtors and creditors may require a bit of common understanding, but in terms of our "chicken or egg" question just enacting the law had little or no effect on behavior. The biggest influence was again an external one, the idea that the economy picked up generally. The institutional mechanisms were used instrumentally to produce positive results in an economic sense, not due to any broader social engineering or compulsion. Here, it would seem that the "society" is also the business community (debtors and creditors together), rather than society at large, although some consideration of broader interests may be present if parties in a reorganization are state-owned. So, society at large may derive some benefit from assets being used more efficiently in a business venture. However, the better economic results, in terms of the profit motive, seem really just focused on the relationships of debtors and creditors. My ultimate conclusion, based on the evidence of Indonesian insolvency practice, is that the private sector at least approaches law reform and legal implementation purely on an instrumental basis. Once a new law or legal institutions exist, there is a learning process as they explore how best to turn the new substantive law or institutional structures to their advantage. However, if their self-interest is somehow opposed to the new law and institutions, depending upon the stakes, the private sector may vigorously oppose implementation. And the "what's in it for me" question tends to contemplate a short time horizon.

# References


Baird, D.G. 2001. *Elements of Bankruptcy*. New York: Foundation Press.

Capital Market Reference Centre. 2007. Notice to Shareholders, PT. Argo Pantes. Tbk, Domiciled in Jakarta, the Business Activities Cover Integrated Textile Industry. March 8, Jakarta.

Golin, J. 2001. *The Bank Credit Analysis*. Singapore: John Wiley & Sons.

Hoff, J. 1999. *Indonesian Bankruptcy Law*. Jakarta: Tata Nusa.

Jackson, T. 1986. *The Logic and Limits of Bankruptcy Law*. Cambridge, MA: Harvard University Press.

Jakarta Stock Exchange. 2006. *Capital Market Reference Centre Annual Report*.

Lindsey, T. 2000. *Indonesia Bankruptcy, Law Reform & the Commercial Court*. Sydney: Desert Pea Press.

Linnan, D. 2007. Insolvency Law and Institutions in Indonesia, in *Insolvency Law in East Asia*, edited by R. Tomasic. London: Ashgate, 355–73.

Linnan, D. 2008. Commercial Law Enforcement in Indonesia: The Manulife Case, in *Indonesia: Law & Society*, Second Edition, edited by T. Lindsey. Singapore and Sydney: Federation Press and INSEAS, 596–619.

Linnan, D. 2010. Reading the Tea Leaves in the Indonesian Commercial Court: A Cautionary Tale but for whom?, in *New Courts in Asia*, edited by A. Harding ans P. Nicholson. Oxford: Routledge, 56–79.

McLeod, R. and Garnaut, R. 1998. *East Asia in Crisis: From Being a Miracle to Needing One?* London: Routledge.

OECD 2001, *Insolvency Systems in Asia, An Efficiency Perspective*.

*PT Argo Pantes Tbk vs. Indo Plus BV*. 2006. No. 03/PKPU/2006/PN.Niaga.Jkt.Pst Jo. No.05/Pailit/2006/PN.Niaga.Jkt.Pst.

*PT Ciputra Development*. 2005. No.05/PKPU/2000/PN.Niaga.Jkt.Pst No.02/PKPU/2005/PN.Niaga.Jkt.Pst.

*PT Gemilang vs. PT Sejahtera Bank Umum*. 2000. No.05/PKPU/2000/PN.Niaga.Jkt.Pst.

*PT Indo Veneer Utama vs. CV.Indo Jati*. 2006. No.04/PKPU/2006/PN.Niaga.Jkt.Pst Jo. No.11/Pailit/2006/PN.Niaga.Jkt.Pst.

*PT Jakarta International Trade Fair vs. Jakarta Development Corporation*. 2002. No.01/PKPU/2003/PN.Niaga.Jkt.Pst Jo.No.38/pailit/2002/PN.Niaga.Jkt.Pst.

# Chapter 6
# China's Economic Legal System in Changing Times

Liu Dongjin

Times are changing faster than ever, and China too has been engulfed in the wave of change sweeping the world. Especially in the last 20 years, the rapid development of China's economy has greatly influenced patterns in the global economy. The 2006 best-seller, *When China Changes the World*, authored by the French economist Erik Izraelewicz, explored the deep impact made by China on the world economy. However, China itself is the subject of profound changes, particularly the Chinese legal system as it relates to the economy, so the world has, in turn, changed China. This chapter describes such change through a Chinese legal scholar's eyes in approaches to the Chinese economic law system: policy guidance, drawing on international rules, the promotion of social practices and cultural traditions, etc. These are the mechanics of how change has affected Chinese law.

As a point of departure, however, the terminology of "economic legal systems" or "economic law" has always been a controversial concept in Chinese legal circles. It can have two kinds of meanings in a broader or narrower sense. The broad economic law system refers to all parts of the legal system concerning economic activities, including economic administrative law, property law, and commercial law. In effect, we borrow the German concept of *Wirtschaftsrecht* when we speak in these terms. Meanwhile, the narrow sense of economic legal system typically refers only to those parts of the legal system concerning government intervention, management, and supervision of economic activity. There we tend more to focus on ideas about controlling the economic system, so it looks much more like traditional ideas preceding China's more recent social market-orientation. Fully exploring ideas behind Chinese views of the market as economic matter are beyond the scope of this chapter about legal development per se, but foreign readers should be aware that we probably find more resonance in Continental ideas about a "social market economy" rather than so-called Anglo-Saxon neo-liberalism. This chapter takes the broader perspective, but regards as a work in progress what the Chinese version of a social market economy approach may precisely look like at journey's end.

## Implementation of "Reform and Opening" Policy—Reconstruction of China's Economic Law System on the "Ruins"

On October 1, 2009, the People's Republic of China celebrated the sixtieth anniversary of its founding. The past 60 years can be divided into two phases from the Chinese perspective. The initial 30 years represented a system damage period,[1] basically when China was, as an ideological

---

1 Here "system destructive phase" is only a symbolic description. In the 1949–1978 years, there were some laws in China, such as the Constitution, the Organic Law of the various government agencies, the Marriage Law, as well as some regulations related to social law and order, and economic-related law was limited to a few tax regulations. However, the number of the laws was small, and operation of the state relied

matter, "taking the concept of class struggle as outline" as official policy. In 1978, a great debate was launched in political theory circles of China under the rubric "practice is the only touchstone to test truth." So, the argument was at a certain level about placing practice over theory. As an important consequence of the debate, the Chinese Communist Party held the Third Plenary Session of its Eleventh Central Committee Meeting at the end of that year. At that time, the country changed its central focus, as we would say, to "economic construction." As a result, the policy of "reform and opening" was put forward as basic change in orientation. At the session, proposals to "promote socialist democracy" and "improve the socialist legal system" were introduced by Deng Xiaoping, who opined:

> The trouble now is that our legal system is incomplete, with many laws yet to be enacted. Some people often take what leaders say as a "law," not in favor of the leaders say is called "illegal." When the leadership speaks out for change, the "law" must also change. So, we should focus on enacting Criminal Law, Civil Law, Procedural Law, and other necessary law, for instance, Factory Law, People's Commune Law, Forest Law, Grassland Law, Environmental Protection Law, Labor Legislation, Foreigner Investment Law, and so on. (Xiaoping 1978)

Thus commenced the three decades of our "system construction period," or, as you would say it, since we have been building a legal system in earnest. In 1999, we finally wrote into our Constitution the concepts of "implementation of the rule of law, and creation of a socialist country ruled by law." Hence, "the rule of law" instantly became an important legal principle and officially part of China's development goals ever since.

Economic law system construction is one of China's legislative priorities. According to the author's statistics, in only the first five years of "reform and opening" (1979–1984), there were 30 pieces of legislation concerning economic law approved by the National People's Congress and its Standing Committee, which accounted for one-third of the total 91 pieces of legislation passed during that period.

Since 1982, our Constitution has been amended four times (Chinese Constitution 1988, 1993, 1999, 2004), involving a total of 31 provisions. Each of the four amendments and a total of 15 provisions have been involved somehow with matters touching on our economic system. Matters covered included such concepts as the transferability of land tenure, the system of labor and distribution, the status and character of all kinds of economic organizations, the market economy system, social security, the protection of private property rights and the private sector economy, expropriation and compensation of land, and so on. Among them, the establishment of a market economy system, the protection of private property rights and the private sector of the economy, creating transferrable land use rights, and some other provisions are of a "revolutionary nature," because they play an important role in inspiring people to "pursue [their own self-]interest," thus promoting the rapid development of the Chinese economy. So now we too look to individual initiative to drive economic development.

As of January 1, 2008, China's statutes in force totaled 229 (National People's Congress 2008), of which nearly half directly or indirectly involved our economic system. Beginning in August 2008, the National People's Congress conducted clean-up work on existing laws on the basis that our "socialist legal system with Chinese characteristics has basically taken shape," to "ensure the formulation of socialist legal system with Chinese characteristics by 2010," and to "identify the

---

more on the policy documents (commonly known as "official documents") created by administrative organs at all levels as well as a variety of programs.

clearly existing uncoordinated and unsuitable responses to problems, which should be prioritized, classified and dealt with as the case may be" (Yeung 2008). So, at the highest levels, we are starting to try to harmonize statutes enacted in somewhat piecemeal fashion during the past 30 years.

The rule of law is well established in many Western developed countries, a very important reason for which is the continuity of the rule of law in their history. But, China did not undergo the same historical path of development, notwithstanding the idea that China constituted one of the great truly ancient civilizations and over time developed an indigenous Chinese legal system (State Council Information Office 2008).[2] Following the Opium War of 1848, however, China unfortunately passed through a century-long period as a semi-colonial, semi-feudal country. We were essentially at war constantly during this period prior to the 1949 founding of the People's Republic. During this chaotic period, there was no uniform implementation of law in the country.[3]

Since 1949, China's legal system has had to overcome two gaps or disturbances in terms of continuity. The first one involved the 1949 abolition of the Chinese Nationalist government's "Six Codes" based upon the Japanese model of German law and "pseudo-legitimacy,"[4] understood as part of the political struggle between the Chinese Communist Party and Kuomintang at the time, and the establishment of a Socialist legal and economic system modeled on the former Soviet Union, characterized by "public ownership" within a "planned economy" (Poumin 2004; Xianjue 2007). This is probably best understood as flowing from the then current Soviet-influenced view that as a matter of legal succession, a country's legal system must change with a change in its social and economic systems.[5]

---

2  According to the expression of the White Paper entitled China's Efforts and Achievements in Promoting the Rule of Law (2008), as early as the twenty-first century BC, China had produced the customary law of slavery. In the Spring and Autumn period (770 BC–221 BC), China began to develop statutory law and a self-contained statute book emerged. During the Tang Dynasty (618–907 AD), China formed a fairly complete feudal code, which was inherited and developed by the later ancient feudal dynasties. Chinese law became the world's unique legal system. It was also an important contribution to human civilization as the rule of law made by the ancient Chinese.

3  Despite the fact that of the "central government" developed a series of laws at different stages, they could not be effectively implemented.

4  Concerning the abolition of "pseudo-legal system," it originated from the political struggle between the Chinese Communist Party and the Kuomintang. On New Year's Day of 1949, when the "Republic of China President" Chiang Kai-shek issued a "Happy New Year message," the proposal of "not break Republic of China's legal system" was one of the conditions of negotiations that were put forward to the Communist Party. On January 4 and 14, 1949, Mao Tse-tung, respectively, released the "Assessments of suing for peace from the war criminals" and "A statement on the current situation," and took the "abolition of pseudo-legitimacy" as one of the conditions of the negotiations. In February 1949, the CPC Central Committee issued the "Directions of the abolition of the Six Codes of the Kuomintang and the confirmation of judicial principles in the liberated areas," drafted by Wang Ming, the far-left thinker of the Legal Committee of the CPC Central Committee. It was reported that Chou En-lai had instructed at that time: "For the old legal provisions, you can also use individually and modify some of them critically in the new democratic spirit of the law, rather than basic use. We still need some of them for future judicial work. This point could be added by comrade Wang Ming," but it was not adopted. Later, the abolition of the pseudo-legal system and "Six books" became a political campaign in the judicial field, continued into the "judicial reforms" in 1952 and "anti-rightist" in 1957. In recent years, scholars have questioned the extension from repealing the "pseudo-legal system" to the repeal of "the Six Codes."

5  Abolition of the old legal system was also the practice adopted by the former Soviet Union. Lenin once pointed out: "proletariat of the Socialism must always remember that … the struggle will destroy the entire law system of the bourgeois society doomed to extinction" (Lenin 1910: 309). This may be the reason why Wang Ming drafted "Directions of the abolition of the Six Codes of the Kuomintan and the

The second gap arose during the period of the Great Proletarian Cultural Revolution (1966–1976), when the predominant political slogan was "smash the public security organs" as part of an internal political struggle in which certain individuals whipped up public sentiment against police, prosecution authorities, and the courts (Easy Web, PRC Official Government Web Site 2008).[6] During the Cultural Revolution, the judicial system established following 1949 suffered enormous damage, and all the institutions and institutionalized processes were basically overthrown. China was in a "lawless" state and what had been the legal system degenerated into the "rule of man" as opposed to the rule of law.

Experience tells us that it is far more difficult to build on ruins rather than a vacant lot, because you have to remove debris and clear up the foundation of old buildings. In 1979, China began to rebuild the rule of law, not by a "revolution," which we experienced during the Cultural Revolution, but rather through "reform" to restore law and order. Some "ruins" needed to be removed, and some "ruins" needed to be retained, so the reconstruction was even more difficult. The challenge was how to remain true to what we considered Chinese principles while borrowing various legal approaches from other countries. On one hand, we had to adhere to what we considered "the Socialist road," while, on the other hand, we had to learn from the experience of developed countries. On one hand, we must develop and remain true to our inherited characteristics, while on the other hand, we had to face internationalization and globalization trends to be in line with international practice.

It can be said that rule of law is a new road for China, without much precedent in our terms, and so constitutes an "exploration" and "adventure." It is precisely because of this reason that after 30 years' development the Chinese legal system is still a work in progress.

## The Effect of International Rules on China's Economic Law System

One of the objectives of China's reform and opening up to the world is to synchronize with and integrate international standards, which are not only reflected in the market economy system, but also in our approach to legal development in terms of the rule of law. We strove to make as much progress as we could quickly in a new setting, rather than delaying to search for perfect answers

---

confirmation of judicial principles in the liberated areas," who was long nurtured by the dogmatism of the former Soviet Union.

6    The so-called "smash the public security organs" slogan involved Lin Biao, Jiang Qing, and others calling for the common people to persecute politically the personnel in police, prosecution, and court system during the "Cultural Revolution" period, so that these institutions would be paralyzed. If the "abolition of the pseudo-legal system and the Six Codes" is only an attack in the history of the legislation and the rule of law tradition, then "smashed public security organs" would entail collapse of the entire law enforcement and the judicial system. The initial cause of the "smash the public security organs" was Jiang Qing suspecting she was monitored by the public security organs, so she assigned Xie Fuzhi and instructed "Red Guards" to take over the Public Security Bureau of Xicheng District, Beijing at the end of 1966, and gradually spread throughout the whole police, prosecution, and court system. In March 1967, Lin Biao proposed to destroy the police and legal system "in politics, in theory, and the organization" completely at the meeting of military system. In August of the same year, Xie Fuzhi, then-Minister of Public Security, publicly advocated "smashed public security organs" in a assembly of all staff in the Ministry of Public Security.

The impact of "smash the public security organs" on the court system was mentioned in the Supreme People's Court Work Report to National People's Congress in 1983, made by Jianghua, the sixth president of the Supreme People's Court: "During the decade of civil strife, Lin Biao, Jiang Qing counter-revolutionary group frantically implemented 'smash the public security organs' and other crimes, bringing down organizations of the people's court, persecuting the judicial cadres, and sabotaged the socialist legal system."

to our challenges. In the first decade or so of reform and opening up, the guiding ideology was "better than none" and "coarse is better than fine,"[7] which must be understood in connection with our lack of experience engaging in a market economy. So the legislation produced was essentially broad-brush in China in terms of getting some rules on the books as a practical matter. Therefore, we often grafted the relevant international rules from and took the international treaties or international conventions directly into the texts of the relevant laws to make up for deficiencies in the legislation itself.

For example, the Foreign Economic Contract Law (1985),[8] the Civil Law (1986),[9] the Administrative Procedure Law (1989),[10] and the Civil Procedure Law[11] which passed in 1991 and revised in 2007, all specified that in dealing with foreign relations, if the international treaties concluded or acceded by China are different from this law (or Chinese laws), the application should follow the international treaties, but the reservation clause which China has declared is not included. In the Foreign Economic Contract Law and the Civil Law, they also separately provide that if the Chinese law has not specified a rule to govern the outcome, then it can call upon international practices to supply a rule of resolution. And if there is no stipulation in Chinese law and in the international treaties which China concluded or participated, it can apply the international customs.

The approach to adoption of law here is seemingly "lazy" in working more or less via unspecified incorporation by reference, and so has significant shortcomings. The problem is that the specific rules recognized by the relevant international treaties or international conventions can only be applied in legal relations between foreign and Chinese parties, rather than the more common legal relationship between two domestic Chinese parties. Thus, there is a lack of consistency in domestic party relations, which leads to the phenomenon of different legal treatments within China under domestic law between two purely domestic parties, and in China or abroad in relations between Chinese and foreign parties. So the rules were not universal and sometimes even led to discrimination against Chinese citizens, because of the duality caused by differing rules used in solely domestic versus mixed foreign economic relationships.[12]

This phenomenon changed significantly after 1999 as a result of conflicts of law principles. For example, in March 1999 the new contract principles no longer stipulated the application of special unitary foreign-related contracting rules, but directly stated that foreign-related contractors may choose the applicable law to govern contractual disputes, except as otherwise provided. If foreign-related contractors did not have this option, the applicable law that should be used is the domestic law with the closest relationship to the contract.[13] In addition, the law does not re-employ the concept of "international practice," but rather uses the term "transaction practices," which it

---

7    Ibid., note 5.

8    See Article 6 of the Act. With the enforcement of "Contract Law" in October 1, 1999, the Act and the "Economic Contract Law" and "Technology Contract Law" were all abolished.

9    See Article 142 of the Act.

10    See Article 72 of the Act.

11    See Article 236 of the Act.

12    For example, in the early time of "reform and opening," foreign natural persons can invest or engage in international trade in China, while Chinese natural persons cannot; foreign-invested enterprises can enjoy a lower tax rate and a variety of tax incentives, while Chinese enterprises cannot enjoy the same treatment. Even contract law applied, there was "Foreign Economic Contract Law" applicable to the contract signed with foreign countries, while "Economic Contract Law" was applied in the domestic context, and so on.

13    See the first paragraph, Article 126 of the Act.

takes as a commonly used rule in contract formation,[14] performance,[15] etc. The important reason for this change is that as a matter of law the relevant rules in international treaties (for example, in the 1980 United Nations Convention on International Sale of Goods) had been converted into domestic law rules by the terms of treaty adoptions. In the 2004 Foreign Trade Law amendments, Chinese individuals were also permitted to engage in foreign trade activities. As of 2005, the rules concerning the payment of the registered capital under Company Law were also brought closer to those governing the foreign-invested enterprises legal regulation. Under the 2007 Enterprise Income Tax Law, the treatment of foreign-funded enterprises and domestic enterprises was unified. In this sense, the international rules not only promoted market economy and legal system in China, but also promoted China's economic democratization process as the rules were often extended from governing foreign or mixed foreign and domestic enterprise relationships to governing dealings between purely domestic enterprises.

China's accession to the World Trade Organization (WTO) had a very significant impact on the transformation of the international rules into domestic law generally. China entered into the WTO in 2001, and the effects were almost immediately felt in areas like intellectual property and investment law. Thereafter, the Patent Law, Trademark Law, Sino–Foreign Cooperative Enterprises and the Foreign Law (2000), Sino–Foreign Joint Enterprise Law (2001), and a series of laws had been amended to meet the requirements of the Agreement on Trade-Related Aspects of Intellectual Property Rights (TRIPs) and the Trade-Related Investment Measures Agreement (TRIMs) and other requirements under the WTO agreements. In 2001, China published a series of legal rules related to trade in goods, such as the Anti-Dumping Rules, the Countervailing Duties Regulations[16] and Safeguard Regulations, in accordance with WTO agreements relating to trade in goods (as opposed to areas like trade in services under the General Agreement on Trade in Services or GATS). In 2004, China made further amendments to the Foreign Trade Law and the aforementioned rules to bring them more into line with the relevant rules of the WTO.

The impact from international rules on China's economic law system is not only from international treaties, but also draws upon the developed market economies. China's two major legislative organs, the Legislative Affairs Committee of the National People's Congress Standing Committee and the Legislative Affairs Office of the State Council, are both not only in part specialized agencies for studying foreign legislation,[17] but also form delegations to study abroad and conduct extensive exchanges with foreign legislative organs, law enforcement agencies, and courts as well as other related business institutions, universities, and legal research institutions. As example, consider the Anti-Monopoly Law known as "Economic Constitution." Wang Xiaoye,

---

14   For example, the first paragraph of Article 26 of the Act: "commitment to be effective when notice reached the offeror. Commitment does not require notification, shall entry into force as the commitment act was done according to the transaction practices or requirements of offer."

15   For example, the second paragraph of Article 60 of the Act provides that: "The parties should follow the principle of good faith, fulfill notification, assistance, confidentiality obligations according to the nature of the contract, purpose and transaction practices." Article 61 of the Act also provides that: "The contract after the commencement, the parties may agree to add agreements on the quality, price, or pay, discharge location not contained in the agreement or the agreement is not clear, those cannot reach a supplementary agreement, shall be determined in accordance with the relevant provisions of the contract or transaction practices."

16   Prior to this, anti-dumping and countervailing duties problems were treated in the same ordinance, namely, the 1997 Anti-Dumping and Countervailing Duties Regulations.

17   For example: the Research Office of Commission of Legislative Affairs of the NPC Standing Committee, the Laws and Regulations Examining Department and the Foreign Affairs Department of the State Council Legislative Affairs Office all have the function of compiling foreign law materials.

a legal scholar who participated in drafting the law, considers the law to draw on advanced experiences represented by competition policies of developed countries and regions, especially of the United States and European countries (Xiaoye 2009). Article 45 of the Law was built on the Commitment of the EU competition law, while the 2nd clause of Article 46 draws on the experience of Forgiveness Policy from the US anti–trust laws.[18] In addition, the cartel exemption provisions, and the factors that determined market dominance as well as on market dominance inference, were drawn from German law.[19]

## Developments Driven by Social Practice to Change China's Economic Law System

If one thinks that the imperative to bring Chinese law and regulation into line with international standards is the external driver for the establishment and refinement of China's market economic law system, then the development of Chinese social practice ought to be the internal force driving change. The "all–round contract,"[20] which was signed by 18 farmers at the end of 1978 secretly to divide communal land into individual plots in Xiaogang Village, Anhui Province (Nanlan 2008), led in promoting the formation of China's reform and opening policy based upon individual initiative. From then on, both in terms of policy and in building the legal system, the tactic called "crossing the river by feeling the stones" was progressively formed. It focused on local experimentation, in that first we should select some experimental locality to test the program in order to examine the effects, and then draw up laws and regulations that could be carried out universally based upon the limited experiment's outcome.

China's creation of forms of business enterprises serves as another example in the absence of Company Law, the joint-stock company as a form of business enterprise in China first emerged in the early 1980s. By 1992, the number of joint-stock companies in the whole of China had reached 3,220 (not a large number, considering the country's size). In 1984, the first company to offer shares to the public was established, and that first company's stock started trading in September 1986 (SCRE & SCPO 1992). On the basis of the full pilot experience, the State Economic Restructuring Commission printed and distributed "Opinions on Standards for Stock Limited Company" and "Opinions on Standards for Limited Liability Company" in May 1992. On that basis, the Fifth Meeting of the Standing Committee of the Eighth National People's Congress finally passed the Company Law at the end of 1993. (The Act was further amended in 1999, 2004, and 2005, so the experimentation and refinement continues.) This kind of approach in which first an experimental "pilot" of the new legal provision was undertaken on a limited basis and then generalized by enactment into national law once proven successful, is still being used today.

As a current example, China is now experimenting with the concept of margin trading in its securities markets. On January 27, 2010, the Securities Association of China announced the "Rules of Professional Evaluation of Implementation of Pilot Program of Margin Trading Services of Securities Firms" and two other relevant pilot margin trading documents (Lu 2010). So economic legal development in China tends not to be a "big bang" exercise or driven by ideology

---

18   Xiaoye (2009).

19   Ibid.

20   China's "Constitution" provides that rural land is collectively owned. Prior to 1978, China's rural land was collectively farmed by production teams, and crops were also allocated uniformly by the same production teams. However, 18 farmers in Xiaogang Village tried the way of "sub-fields households" and "household contract management" by signing an agreement, which at that time put them at risk of being thrown in jail.

(remembering the switch from ideology to practice as watchword for legal reforms as far back as 1978), but rather a series of limited or local experiments which are enacted into national law once authorities feel their usefulness has been proven.

The development of law driven by social practice in China's economic law system not only comes from the Chinese government, but also stems from civil society and academic circles. The most typical example of these varying inputs can be followed in the progress of drafting and formulation of China's Property Law. That law took 13 years from its drafting to its adoption as a statute, and this socially sensitive law was the subject of public advice and comment (verifications, in Chinese terminology) eight times (Ping 2007). Scholars played a significant role in formulating the law. The Property Law was created originally in the form of an "academic draft" by experts and scholars commissioned by China's supreme legislative body. Two of China's best known Civil Law experts[21] led two groups who completed separate drafts in 1999 and in 2000, which then became the basis of a generally accessible exposure draft.

In July 2005, the Property Law (Draft) was approved by the Standing Committee of the National People's Congress, and a third public advice and comment was announced to collect input from the public. The same year, August 12, 2005, a university professor published an open letter via the Internet, arguing that the draft was "contrary to the Constitution and departed from the basic principles of socialism" (Xiantian 2007), which caused a huge reaction among the public and raised intensive discussions and arguments about the constitutionality of the draft in China's academic community (Zhu 2007). As the result of the incident and the resulting controversy, the original plan to vote on the Property Rights Act at the March 2006 National People's Congress was delayed for a year. After more than a year of careful discussion, the law was passed in March 2007. So, the creation of statutes can also become a high profile public process involving expert and public disputes over controversy in society.

Growing out of the Property Law controversy, in December 2009, five Peking University Law School scholars made waves again. They submitted a document entitled "Suggestion to Review the 'Urban Housing Demolition Management Regulations'" to the Standing Committee of the National People's Congress. These scholars argued that the eponymous Ordinance issued by the State Council in 2001 conflicted with the Constitution, the Property Law, and the Real Estate Management Law. This conflict resulted in distortion of the proper understanding of urban development and the protection of private property (Haiyan 2009). These scholars were driven to make suggestions on account of the many policy contradictions and social conflicts caused by demolition of houses in the rapid development of China's urban areas. Feelings had run so high that some extreme events occurred (i.e., self-immolation as public statement, which form of suicide as protest has a special social history in Asia). These scholars' proposals attracted great attention in the legislature, and became a strong impetus in the process of relevant legislative reform (State Council Legislative Affairs Office 2010).[22]

---

21   Liang Huixing, researcher at the Institute of Law of the Chinese Academy of Social Sciences, and Wang Liming, Professor of the Law School of Renmin or the Chinese People's University in Beijing.

22   According to Article 41 of the draft, "City House Demolition Management Regulations" will be annulled simultaneously in implementation of new regulations.

## Effects of Traditional Culture on the Reform of China's Economic Law System

As discussed above, the reform of China's economic law system has both external drivers (international standards) and internal impetus (social changes), yet the influence of a certain traditional cultural factor cannot be ignored. From the author's point of view, concerning contemporary China, traditional culture here involves two aspects. The first is a mindset or outlook of which Confucianism is representative, and it was formed in our feudal history over several thousand years. The second is the historical experience of the Chinese Communist Party. Both aspects may represent an influence or restriction on the performance of the legal system.

In various feudal dynasties of ancient China, favoring farmers over merchants was emphasized in their version of industrial policy. In terms of relations among the social class, in descending order the ranking was "scholar, farmer, artisan, and merchant"; scholars were ranked at the top, while merchants were on the bottom of the social pyramid. In the public's view, prejudice exists like "an honest merchant does not exist," and merchants "always put their honor aside and only pursue profits." So every merchant was viewed as existing on par with used car salesmen, a group not famous for business ethics in contemporary Western terms.

Such traditional thought is also reflected in the economic law system nowadays, which pays more attention to "management" or "supervision"[23] in regulatory terms, and there are extensive processes of government approval and supervision. As the market economic system has been established and perfected gradually, the Chinese government places more emphasis on the "transformation of government functions" which is from the "management-oriented government" to "service-oriented government" (presumably within a market structure). Confucianism stresses "the rule of rites" and advocates "governance by virtue" while emphasizing the "rule of man." It deemed the ruler as the center of all things (implying ideological loyalty to the emperor), which is incorporated in the traditional idea that "official rank [was] considered to be the sole criterion of one's worth." In dealing with problems, the methods of "[Golden] Mean" and "Harmony" are emphasized.

These kinds of principles can be respected in the performance of the economic law system and other types of Chinese law. Specifically, it can be described as stressing "the balancing of interests" or "accommodating the interests of all sides" in legislation,[24] and the avoidance of extremes while "maintaining stability." Meanwhile, as a result of history, Chinese culture, in which the culture of the Han Dynasty is its main body, has shown a readiness for "inclusion and incorporation." Consequently, it receives and accepts external things easily in terms of assimilation. It should be said that the traditional ideology has both positive and negative effects to the reform of Chinese economic law system. How to combine our inherited tradition with learning from the West are dual imperatives that need to be explored continuously.

Concerning the Chinese Communist Party's own historical experience, the prevalence of administrative guidance is the issue. The Party has paid great attention to the effectiveness of administration (administrative efficiency) both during times of war before it obtained political

---

23    For example, in the Chinese legal database of www.chinalawinfo.com, when "management" is used as the keyword in searching the index, there will be 41,097 formal documents while using "supervision" produces 1,594 items.

24    The process of Chinese legislation often needs balance and coordination between different government bodies, administrative bureaus, and judicial departments as well as different classes of interest. Legislators usually have to investigate through various forms and hear the voice of every aspect. When it is difficult to coordinate different interests, legislation is often postponed or bypasses questions so that the formulation of important laws, from draft to approval, typically requires around 10 years.

power and during the peace and reconstruction time after obtaining political power. It is also good at "appealing" or "campaign" methods as ways of approaching the public. Therefore, in the process of the management of economic activities by government, it often may take the easy road in pursuing immediate effects by using its administrative power while downplaying the functions of law. The best typical example is that it adopts the methods of issuing a "notice" or "urgent notice."[25] This indicates that the function of law has not been fully internalized, and the idea of "abiding by the law" has not struck its root in the hearts of people. In other words, market, the "the invisible hand," has to yield its place to government, "the visible hand," and the legal authority is unable to exceed government power.

To sum up, in the context of economic globalization, China's economic law system is evolving toward a market orientation and is undergoing change. We consider this part of modernization in terms of China's economic development. This change began in the change in policy as early as 1978. International standards and rules as well as social practice and traditional culture play prominent and sometimes restrictive roles in varying degrees within the economic law system. China's market economy system is learning from the West but does not copy the West. It has its own characteristics. From the "rule of law" point of view, China's economic legal system is far from perfect. There is still a long way to go, but our progress made since 1978 is striking.

## References


Chinese Constitution. 1988, 1993, 1999, 2004.

Haiyan, Z. 2009. The Petition to People's Congress to Amend Demolition Regulations Proposed by Five Scholars of Peking University. *People's Network*. Available at: http://npc.people.com. cn/GB/14840/10553850.html.

Lenin, V. 1910. *The Collected Works of Lenin* (Chinese version), Vol. 16. People's Press [1959].

Lu, W. 2010. Professional Evaluation of the Securities Financing Pilot Program will Commence Shortly. *Financial Times*, January 27.

Nanlan, W. 2008. Reform and Opening Up: The Xiaogang Village Story. *Peoples Daily Online Edition*, March 6. Available at: http://english.people.com.cn/90002/95607/6531490.html.

National People's Congress. 2008. *The Law in Force (by Year Statistics)*. Available at: www.npc. gov.cn/npc/xinwen/lfgz/2008-03/26/content_1421575.htm.

Ping, J. 2007. A Number of Issues of the Formulation and Implementation of the "Property Law." *Guangdong Learning Forum*, 42.

Poumin, J. 2004. Before and After the Repeal of the Six Codes. *Chinese Legal Culture Network*. Available at: www.law-culture.com/shownews.asp?id=7314.

SCRE & SCPO. 1992. *State Commission for Restructuring the Economy, the State Council Production Office of the Experimental Work on the Joint-Stock Enterprises Forum Report*. Available at: http://news.xinhuanet.com/ziliao/2005-02/17/ content_2586502.htm.

State Council Information Office. 2008. *White Paper of "China's Efforts and Achievements in Promoting the Rule of Law."* Available at: http://news.xinhuanet.com/legal/2008-02/ 28/ content_7687348.htm.


---

25   The simplest example is available via standard search terms. In the Chinese legal database www. chinalawinfo.com, if one uses the term "notice" as the keyword in a title search, 61,803 results can be obtained; meanwhile during the period January 1 2010 to February 1 2010, the number of "notice" entries issued by government bodies amounted to 1,830, or almost 60 items per day.

State Council Legislative Affairs Office. 2010. *Expropriation and Compensation to State-owned Land and Housing Ordinance (Draft) and Notice of Collecting Public Comment.* Available at: http://yijian.chinalaw.gov.cn/lismsPro/law_download/fulltext/1264721763296.doc.

Supreme People's Court Work Report. 1983. Available at: www.gov.cn/test/2008-03/27/content_929837.htm.

Xianjue, X. 2007. Origins and Impacts of the Repeal of The Six Codes. *Yanhuang Spring and Autumn.* Available at: http://zf007.fyfz.cn/blog/zf007/index.aspx?blogid=310568.

Xiantian, G. 2007. A Violation of the Constitution and the Departure from the Basic Principles of Socialism "Property Law (Draft)"—the Open Letter for the Abolition of Article 12 of the Constitution and Article 73 of Civil Law (1986). *Peking University Law Information Network.* Available at: http://article1.chinalawinfo.com/Article_Detail.asp?ArticleID=32266.

Xiaoping, D. 1978. Emancipating One's Mind, Seeking Truth from Facts, Uniting as One in Looking to the Future. *Financial Network.* Available at: www.caijing.com.cn/zmb/zmtt/2008-01-04/44207.shtml.

Xiaoye, W. 2009. The Economic Reform and Anti-Monopoly Law in China. *Oriental Law*, 3.

*Xie Advocated Openly in the Cultural Revolution.* 2009. Available at: http://history.163.com/07/0505/09/3DNJK26700011247.html.

Yeung, W.H. 2008. To Create and Constantly Improve the Socialist Legal System with Chinese Characteristics, NPC Law Committee Deployed Clean-up Work of Law. *Legal Daily*, August 1.

Zhu, W. 2007. Notes from the Topic "Property Law (Draft)" Constitutional Crisis—the Observation and Evaluation of the Academic to "Unconstitutional Storm." *Chinese Civil and Commercial Law Network.* Available at: www.civillaw. com.cn / Article / default.asp? id = 31715.

# PART II
# Religious Law as Religious and Social Form

# Chapter 7
# Economy and Society: A Qur'anic Perspective

Tarak Abdallah

Modernization theory was originally based upon concepts of industrialization underpinning economic growth following the West, while the modern study of development is shaped typically by economics.[1] This is seemingly the case of legal development as viewed by the international financial institutions (IFIs, in particular the World Bank and IMF) tied in particular to implementation of the Washington Consensus. So we shall talk about law and society in the modernization context in questioning certain economic "articles of faith," since even in the West some scholars now speak of "market ideology" or "market fundamentalism." But the deeper problem is that, under current circumstances, within the Islamic world "modernization" as concept seems inapposite to the extent that it is interpreted as Westernization.

The overlooked issue is often whether such legal and economic principles are valid as basis for (legal) development for all times and societies. Meanwhile, even stating the question in this fashion may puzzle many Western scholars. However, law incorporates social values and beliefs, so when scholars in the Islamic world talk about law or *Shari'ah* law (or technically *fiqh* as human interpretation of *Shari'ah*), they emphasize the concept of Islamic views of economics or finance as part of their view of a proper society. We do not necessarily share all the same values, particularly since we believe that "efficiency" or utilitarianism are not necessarily the "be all and end all" in human relations, even when dealing with problems like economic scarcity. And we think the West may recently be coming around to this view, also in the development area, when one considers current concepts like "sustainable development" as recognition that the world may have already reached capacity limits on ideas like industrialization as preferred development strategy (due to climate change concerns) (El-Ansary and Linnan 2010).

**Economics, Law and Society**

The rise of economics as a social science is strongly linked to the development of capitalism. Moreover, classical economists tried to explain the rules by which the economy operated in the shadow of Newtonian mechanical laws. The search for the scientific criteria to explain economic

---

1   In spite of the diverse polemical debate that permeates sociology circles over the crisis of modernism and the different specialties of those involved in it, the debate revolves in one way or another around the elements mentioned in Charles Taylor's book *Grandeur et Misère de la Modernité* in which he points out three main indicators for the crisis. The first indicator is what we can call the loss of destination or the absence of ethical horizons of the modern Man. The second indicator lies in the absence of the absolute teleology. As for the third indicator, it is related to the absence of freedom. It is undoubtedly true that the direct correlation between the moral issue and the problem of setting standards on one hand, and the great questions on Man's view of himself and his surroundings on the other hand, has made the focus on the havoc wrought upon the ethical dimension and its governing system an important area of discussion for the potential that religion (as a reservoir of values) can bestow upon the system of modernism (or postmodernism, if appropriate).

behavior was also enriched by contribution from other branches; in particular, mathematics intended to provide a quantitative description of a fundamental aspect of human behavior, which is isolated and studied in abstract form. Neoclassical economic work contemplates a simple and abstract rational "economic man" who lacks social, ethical and political dimensions, and who is not a creature of habit, hunches or impulses. The sequence methodological individualism results in that the development of society is the result of actions of individuals, from which we can see "natural" laws of development. Thus, the separation of economics from the social and historical is becoming increasingly pronounced, and the neoclassical economic approach dominates. The social and political connections are considered as derivatives from this sphere. This trend was expressed by a firm conviction that economic values are the most important, and the restructuring of society expressed that valuation. Economics thus became an ideology expressed by the move from a market economy to a market society as form of "market fundamentalism."

The expansion of capitalism in the early seventeenth century has been associated with the retreat of other cultural models and the exacerbation of their internal crises. This, in turn, resulted in making the cultural process in other world civilizations revolve around the dominant Western style and created a never-ending questioning regarding what happens inside and outside non-Western culture. Perhaps the best case in point for the presence of this methodology is what has been written on economics that has a direct role in the life of mankind. We can also say that writings in this field have taken a one-way direction that strikes a comparison between what is called the "economic heritage"[2] of different civilizations and peoples and the outcome of the Western economic experience summed up in the modern economic thought. Although this methodology has prevailed and continues to prevail in many academic spheres, some scholarly arenas have witnessed, as part of the criticism faced by some circles within the human sciences, the emergence of calls for revolt against two critical issues.

First, the reduction of all social facts (Durkheim 1982) to the economic dimension, the blind faith in an "invisible hand" in which supply and demand are the only important factors in decisions, had paved the way to a deep critique of "capitalism as the ultimate way for humanity." Thus, dissenting voices try to keep the relationship between economics, sociology and history alive.

Second, fascinated by the market as social regulator, (mostly Western) specialists from different fields did not pay adequate attention to other societies classified as "pre-capitalist" or "underdeveloped." As D.F. Eickelman stated:

> Modernization theory framed not only the work of social theorists but also blocked historians from imagining the possibility that "traditional" empires, societies, and religious formations could be as dynamic as their presumed "modern" counterparts. (Eickelman 2002)

For instance, history of economic thought does not accord great importance to the pre-capitalist era. In this context, the history of non-Western societies is simply overlooked. As a concrete example, the economic heritage of Islamic societies is ignored. Through their analysis of economic thought, economists perpetuate J.A. Schumpeter's (1883–1950) "great gap thesis."[3] They usually refer to

---

2   This heritage is classified through a selective process for books and manuscripts which do not carry the terms used in the modern economic dictionaries. In the case of Islamic civilization, tackling Islamic economic heritage is done through reference to books related to trade, contracts, sale, agriculture, money, etc.

3   In his important work on the history of economic thought Schumpeter focuses on the intellectual efforts that men have made during 2,000 years (from the beginning until the publication of Adam's Smith book *Wealth of Nations*).

the Greek and Roman civilizations, but they do not accord any significance to the booming era of Islamic Empire. As S.M. Ghazanfar (1991) pointed out:

> [according to Schumpeter's analysis] more than five years prior to writings of Scholastics, nothing of any significance to economics was said or written anywhere else, as though the period of Europe Dark's Ages was a universal phenomenon that extended over the intellectual evolution of the rest of the world.

As a response to this reductionism, many contemporary scholars call for a better attitude to rethink and to understand the economic contributions of societies classified as "underdeveloped" by according the adequate importance to the cultural reservoir of nations and overcoming the demeaning categorizations of the old, "traditional" and "primitive." Methodologically, this trend substitutes a single view of social phenomena with a multidimensional approach with the aim of assimilating their density (Bartoli 1994), and consequently making use of all the intellectual and material potentials owned by nations, regardless of their economic development figures or the income rates of their individuals. This matters for legal development because, at least in the economic area, it seemingly would lead away from an overly heavy emphasis on law and economics, or transaction cost-based approaches.

This chapter seeks to contribute to a "reconstruction" of Qur'anic perspective in dealing with the place and role of economy in society by highlighting the function of Islamic percepts and values and legal scholarship in shaping the explanation of socioeconomic phenomena. Beginning with an overview of critics of the self-regulating market assumption, the chapter emphasizes the degree to which many authors, such as Karl Marx, Max Weber and Karl Polanyi, developed a theoretical framework that break different paths in explaining economic phenomena. It then demonstrates the extent to which the Qur'anic framework could be an alternative. Focusing on the idea of man, the Qur'an refers to the signs of reality in the various phenomena of the universe, relates stories of bygone nations, criticizes the beliefs, morals and deeds of different peoples, elucidates supernatural truths, and discusses many other things. All this the Qur'an does, not in order to provide instruction in physics, history, philosophy or any other particular branch of knowledge, but rather to push people to develop and use these "knowledge tools" in order to think about the misconceptions that they could have about reality and to make that reality manifest to them.

Through the overarching themes that emerge from this historical reconstruction, the chapter sets out to explore the extent to which Islamic principles may contribute specifically to constructing a socioeconomic approach "analytically-integrated," as well as certain theoretical connections between Islamic and contemporary frameworks.


## Critique of Economics: Beyond the One-Dimensional Man

Capitalism is one of many types of social formation that societies have experienced during their long histories. Karl Marx, Max Weber, Karl Polanyi and others share the same idea about the peculiarity of capitalism. For Marx (1818–1883), capitalism was a particular "mode of production" that had been created in Western Europe (between the fifteenth and eighteenth centuries). Marx highlighted the creation of a "free" labor force, which paved the way for the expansion of market forces, money and production for exchange rather than for immediate consumption. Thus, growing trade and commerce was seen as one of the major propelling forces. The "circulation of commodities" was the starting point of capital. The major change is seen in the manner that people are related in the productive process. In capitalism, there is a full development of individual, private property. No longer is property communal, owned by community or family, but it is fully owned by the individual. This applies not only to real estate but to the ultimate "property" of an individual, his labor power. In capitalism, all becomes alienable. Everything is a commodity to be traded on the market, and people can buy and sell objects, as well as their own and each other's labor. All is apparently set "free" and given a monetary value.

According to Marx, the power of money is one of the most brutal expressions of this capitalist quantification. It distorts all human qualities, by submitting them to the monetary measure. The quantity of money becomes more and more the unique and powerful property of the human being. At the same time, it reduces all being to its abstraction, and it reduces itself in its own movement to a quantitative being. Money is confused with social power.

In the same context, Max Weber (1864–1920) perceived capitalism as a system where impersonal relations replace the personal relations of dependence, and where the accumulation of capital becomes a largely irrational end in itself. For Weber, the peculiar irrationality formed within the process of rationalization appears in terms of this relation between means and ends and is the basis for the concepts of rationality and freedom—namely, in terms of a reversal of this relation. Means as ends make themselves independent and lose their original "meaning" or purpose. Thus, they lose their original purposive rationality oriented toward man and his needs. This reversal marks the whole of modern civilization, whose arrangements, institutions and activities are so "rationalized," that whereas humanity once established itself within them, now they enclose and determine humanity like an "iron cage." Human conduct, from which these institutions originally arose, must in turn adapt to its own creation, which has escaped the control of the creator. Weber declared that the real problem of culture, rationalization toward the irrational, becomes most clearly evident when it occurs in exactly the type of activity whose innermost intention is to be specifically rational, namely, in *economically* rational activity. Precisely here, it becomes plainly apparent how and why behavior which is purely purposeful and rational in intention turns inexorably into its own opposite in the process of its rationalization.

For his part, Karl Polanyi (1886–1964) started from the idea that economy was not primarily controlled by the market but was embedded in society and culture. As he stated, "No society could, naturally, live for any length of time unless it possessed an economy of some sort; but previously to our time no economy has ever existed that, even in principle, was controlled by markets" (Polanyi 1944). He argued that reciprocal and redistributive forms of integration have been much more common in human history than "self-regulating" market systems. Polanyi's argument comes from the history of humanity thus far in which *Homo sapiens* never lived in a pure market economy until recently. Polanyi looked at different societies from Polynesian tribes to Egypt and Rome and found not one use of a self-regulating market economy. Relationships were characterized by reciprocity and redistribution. Instead of the profit motive, social needs dictated exchange in reciprocal form. Social obligation was the glue cementing people together in society, not the interconnected network of the market. He became a critic of the Austrian School of Economics focused on individual agents as a close cousin of modern neo-liberal economics.

Polanyi focused with his pivotal idea on what has happened with the advent of capitalism and how the economic field became independent and tried to dominate all other constituents in society. He analyzes the economic and social changes brought about by the "great transformation" of the Industrial Revolution. His analysis explains the deficiencies of the self-regulating market as the greatest change that befell the economic activity in human history (Polanyi 1944). This charge has also been an exception to all other human communities where such activity was harmoniously blended with the other elements of the social fiber. Families, kinship, beliefs and diverse social relationships, along with other levels influencing such clusters, embrace within them in different degrees the economic elements. This happens while the economy undertakes its responsibility in meeting human needs without working independently or forming a pressuring trend. Polanyi closely related the hegemony of this economic field over all other social aspects on one hand (Latouche 1995)[4] and the destructive consequences resulting from the experience of this paradigm on the other, not only on the level of economic injustice covering most of the populations all over the world but also on other levels other than the economic field that witnesses the eruption of racist and Fascist trends in the West (having fled Nazi Europe in the 1930s).[5]

These ideas have prompted very important changes in dealing with ancient societies; the most important of which is to dispel the aura of holiness that guards certain postulates, mainly the maxim "self-regulating market" heralded by J.B. Say, M. Walras and A. Smith, among others. They believed that the market is the normal place for any economic activity and that it has a self-generated mechanism— "hidden mechanism" as Say puts it—that enables it to arrange originally discordant behaviors and regulate their activities[6] until we reach social equilibrium.

The anthropologic critique of market ideology has concluded that the market, as a regulating mechanism, cannot include all that can come under "economic activity." However, the "self-regulating market" is not a scientific concept and is immensely colored by ideology. Economic activity has not necessarily passed through centralized mechanisms (empires and sultanates) because of the weakness of their political authority and because the nature of economic activity is different from what was known two centuries ago as economics. Economic activity in such societies, usually referred to as "primitive" and "backward," was influenced by the social, cultural and environmental surroundings, and was consequently part of a multifaceted model. Humanity, however, did not see the horizon of the "one-dimensional man" (Marcuse 1969)[7] until the emergence of capitalism and its concomitant intellectual establishment as well as the rise of the economy as a single façade of social regulation.

---

4 This trend cannot be restricted in criticizing the development paradigms and their negative consequences to the third-world countries because it is related to the modernity paradigm itself and all the havoc wrought by the economic field (in its independent and dominant form) in marginalizing other civil establishments in the society (politics, sociology, aesthetics, etc.).

5 Polanyi's ideas have been transmitted through different followers. Among them, Moses Finley's works on Greco-Roman economy tried to provide an analysis that showed the adverse inner principles of capitalism by emphasizing the conceptual universe of the Ancients themselves rather than the modern way of thinking. Moses Finley, the author of *The Ancient Economy*, unveiled a view of the economic underpinnings of ancient economies in which markets and economic motivations played little if any role. Status and civic ideology governed the allocation of scarce resources. He showed the misguided application to ancient society of modern theories of investment, banking and credit; the absence from ancient society of conglomerations of interdependent markets, and of anything like "economic policy"; and the absence from Greek literature of economics. Instead of using economic models, he attempted to prove that the ancient economy was largely a byproduct of status. In other words, economic systems were not interdependent, they were embedded in status positions.

6 Some economists will go beyond this to list any human activity under economic activity. In this attitude, they depended on two main considerations; the first sees the consumer as a producer (who produces to achieve satisfaction) while the second lists the family (the only social part in all the sectors) under the economic structures on the basis that marriage originally is built on sharing life expenses. Gary Becker, one of the most prominent members of Chicago School, has been the most active of economists calling for this idea, especially in his book published in 1964 and in one of his articles that appeared one year later.

7 Since the 1960s, some Western intellectuals and philosophers have analyzed this trend which dominated the track of industrial societies since the first decades of the twentieth century.

This critical trend does not stop at a theoretical critique of Western schools in viewing the consequences of the economic field, but is part of a strategy, a confrontation (i.e., M.A.U.S.S.)[8] and refutation of the view being circulated day and night that capitalism is the end of history and the only available choice for all the people of the world. Although the political gains of this trend are still very limited, its scientific and academic aspect is bravely dynamic, especially through the calls for combating the utilitarian trend that dominates the course of social and human sciences. This critical approach is related to the reconsideration of certain research topics that were removed from the focus of interest in human and social sciences as they were labeled studies of the "religious," "magical" and "irrational." This opens up the possibility for alternative standards of value.

Several authors tend to tackle this issue in terms of the requirements of modern society, specifically the exacerbation of the social alienation of individuals which emanated from the decrease of social solidarity (Godelier 1996).[9] Others linked this to the global resurgence of religion since the late twentieth century. They argue that religion could bring another way we deal with the "malaise of modernity." Religion furnishes a comprehensive vision of the meaning and purpose of life. It offers guidance for a people's way of life and values to guide its future. In this regard, we think that Islam has a rich social and economic history that has produced different patterns of "economic institutions" where values and moral prerequisites played a significant role without altering need satisfaction. These values are embedded in concepts like Islamic economics or finance, and we explore those Islamic concepts as we try to move toward our own concept of how to regulate social relations, including law.


**Islam and Man**


The Qur'an addresses the world at large and creates the basis for the relationship among human beings according to the principles of human nature, which God has ingrained into mankind. This universal nature transcends all the barriers of beliefs, ethnicities, and geography and even turns such differences into a basis through which people may know one another. God says "O mankind! We created you from a single (pair) of a male and a female, and made you into nations and tribes, that ye may know each other (not that ye may despise (each other))" (QS Al-Hujurat 49:13).

On the same basis, religion in the Islamic perspective has come for the benefit of Man and his prosperity as Man is superior to all other creatures. However, this superiority has to be understood within the framework of God and His creation because all of God's creatures are interdependent. The Prophet Muhammad (PBUH) believed that the true believers should be handling everything with ultimate mercy and said, "there is an act of rewarded charity in every act of kindness that you do to any living being on the earth" (Al-Nawawi 1999, Hadith No. 13, narrated by Abu Huraira).

Each created thing is endowed with a definite and defined nature which constitutes an ordered form of existence. All created things have an inherent nature and are subject to laws of behavior that God endowed them with. The Qur'an states, "Everything has been created by us according to a measure" (QS Al-Lail 92:49). All existence is contingent and finite, and it is God alone who is self-sufficient, necessarily existent, and unlimited. It is God's wisdom that has made bearing

---

8    *Mouvement anti-utilitariste dans les sciences sociales* (Anti-utilitarian movement in the social sciences). Under this headline come different political movements (religious, environmental, leftist, etc.) and diverse intellectual trends. However, the common target of them all is to find an alternative model. In this respect, we can refer to what is done in France.

9    Maurice Godelier, a French sociologist, has focused one of his studies on the anthropological analysis of the Donation philosophy with ancient populations.

trust associated with the existence of Man on earth. This explains the reason why the Qur'an has always mentioned Man within his own social milieu, so that he may not be seen as an individual self isolated from all around him, but rather identifies him with one family: the multiform human family that has similar objectives. In this context, diversity becomes the way through which one person can integrate with his fellow human beings, strengthening the relation between people and God who has made them equal and superior to all other creatures. "We have honored the sons of Adam" (QS Al-Isra 17:70). This honoring constitutes a central part of the Islamic vision that Man is the only creature who is able to understand through reflection, and this certainly is the main quality that renders him eligible to social action in the universe that has been harnessed for his benefit. In addition, this conception has become part of the culture that prevailed in Muslim societies for a long period of time before they suffered from enervation and weakness. It is an open culture that revolves around Man with his different dimensions and choices. Ali Bin Abi Talib had clearly demonstrated this point when he advised one of his governors: "Remember, Maalik, that amongst your subjects there are two kinds of people: those who have the same religion as you have; they are brothers to you, and those who have religions other than that of yours, they are human beings like you" (*Ali Ibn Abi Taleb*, 535).

The concept and purpose of worship in Islam combines the mundane with the spiritual, the individual with the society, and the internal soul with the external body. Worship has a unique role in Islam, and through worship, a person accords his entire life to the Will of God. In this context, we can look at worship as social symmetries that help direct, develop and adjust human behavior and the relationship among individuals, pushing it forward to ensure that God is worshipped on earth. Islamic *Shari'ah* has set several mechanisms aimed at building a society whose members have mercy on one another, show sympathy toward each other, and try to bring to bear the concept laid down by Prophet Muhammad (PBUH), who describes the unified society "like the building whose bricks are pressed tightly together." Worship is among the most important mechanisms, or the secondary value orders, laid down by God, the Legislator, in order to create the true link between heartfelt belief and the practical faith through action. The Islamic conception of belief and the duties of worship it entails do not restrict such duties to "inner" dimension but rather associate them with continuous preparation for the individual in his behavior and dealing with others. Consequently, the outcome of such duties of worship in life is directly reflected on people. From this point, we can grasp the answer given by Prophet Muhammad (PBUH) to Abu Amr bin Sufian Al Thaqafi who asked the Prophet about something authoritative in Islam. The Prophet said "Say: I believe in God and thereafter be upright."[10] It is a perfect prophetic instruction that links the belief felt in the heart with the life and the behavioral order reflected through the movement of sentiments settled in conscience.

The bases, dictates and regulations of Islam work in this direction, each according to their peculiarity, timing and relation with the needs of Man and to which extent he has adapted to them. However, all of these bases, dictates and regulations have the same outcome: turning the inner belief into upright, straightforward deed from which an individual can derive benefit.

The social approach of the five pillars of Islam enables us to recognize the roles they play and the great potential they provide for the individual who is part of a larger human community. Such pillars have been always a good and sincere image for the value of self-motivation and spiritual upbringing in building societies and directing the human behavior toward the well-being of

---

10   The Hadith as narrated by Muslim: "On authority of Sufian bin Abdullah, may God be pleased with him, I said, O Messenger of God, tell me something about Islam which I can ask of no one but you. He said, Say: I believe in God, and thereafter be upright" (Hadith 23, in Al-Nawawi 1999).

mankind. Therefore, the pillars of Islam (the two testimonies, prayer, *Zakat* [the alms tax], fasting and pilgrimage when able to do so) will continue to be the basis on which the total conception of the Islamic society is built. However, these pillars need some complementary touches in order for society to take its final shape. According to this rule, dealing with people becomes very important as it represents the real yardstick of the duties of worship, and their direct outcome is reflected upon one's relationships with his brethren in religion and humanity.

The Islamic cultural environment has been reflected, in its continuous assiduity and interaction with other civilizations, on the creativity of some social establishments which strengthened the economic, social and cultural relationships among individuals and gave a broader sense of human dimensions, especially in specifying rights and duties which became an integral part of the Islamic social network. This result has materialized through regulating contracts as a procedural, yet basic, behavior that fortifies and protects human relationships from any injustice or violation. This is reiterated in what God has mentioned in this verse "O You who believe, fulfill any contracts (you may make)" (QS Al-Maidah 5:9). Relationships in Islam have been built on contracts from belief in God, which is a contract between Man and his Creator, and the social establishments to economic transactions. It is also very important to note that Islam, in its view of the state and political system, has unmistakably sided with the society and called for stabilizing its sources of power in a way that makes the state at the society's disposal. Therefore, the society has to be organized, creating establishments that ensure its existence regardless of the state's approach and notwithstanding its strength or weakness.

Various institutions and organizations have emerged in Islamic societies to place the protection of individuals as a top priority and enable individuals to form organizational networks through which they can jointly face the state. Therefore, trade guilds have been one of the economic features in the Islamic civilization as they tried to develop the workers themselves by maintaining higher rates of productivity and quality to ensure the continuity of the profession and to protect the interests and rights of the workers in the face of the state and help solve any problems that may arise among them or between them and the state.[11] Such guilds have always been trying to achieve social balance, which mainly relies on the mechanisms of human solidarity. It is the human characteristic which Ibn Khaldun has creatively interpreted when he made Man's civilization a basic condition for forming human community.

Perhaps Abdul Rahman Ibn Khaldun's (1332–1406) precedence was the main reason Arnold Toynbee considered his *Introduction* (*Muqaddimah*) to be "the best book in its genre created by a person anytime and anywhere" (Toynbee 1962). Ibn Khaldun concluded that it is a true interpretation of the social experience based on the Qur'anic view of Man and the attempt to explain how such a vision is stable within the human framework (Khaldun 1958). However, Ibn Khaldun has found rational proof that human gathering is a natural phenomenon that has its rules and laws which vary according to behavioral values and criteria based on family relationships. Furthermore, people's needs (one's need to his fellow human beings) lead to some sort of regulation in the relationships within the community and the emergence of authority whose legitimacy is based on the community's customs and traditions. In this context, Ibn Khaldun has been able to analyze the network of social relationships and mediums which were instrumental in forming the behaviors of individuals within the social framework, and the creation of varied coexistence

---

11   Bernard Lewis (1937) states: "Unlike the European guilds, which were basically a public service, recognized, privileged and administered by public authorities, seigniorial, municipal or Royal, the Islamic guild was a spontaneous development from below, created not in response to a State need, but to the social requirements of the laboring masses themselves."

forms and establishments that congruously linked the intellectual questioning on one hand and the dynamics of reality and the various daily transactions and behaviors it entails on the other hand.

Islamic identity has played a great role within a large swathe of the Muslim world as it helped spread the social and economic mediums and enabled them to have a role in Muslim society. Therefore, the socioeconomic institutions such as guilds worked toward collective expression, and protected society against any individual or institutional detrimental trend. The Islamic conception of the individual in his social milieu is associated with giving significance to the existence of "the other." On this basis, the latter turns into a value and self-motivated power that shakes the ego and ingrains within it psychological and educational mechanisms that take the ego to elevation and overcome all the obstacles laid on its way to worshipping God, the Almighty. It is the self-ability through which one could seek the help of others to overcome all the hindrances impeding the worshipping of God on earth and through which Man could be psychologically prepared for the human psyche and surmount all the impediments on its way. It is the process of passing the steep path mentioned in the Qur'an, "But he has not attempted to pass the path that is steep" (QS Al-Balad 90:11), which prevents Man from realizing the philosophy of worshipping. Moreover, the Qur'an shows the best way to get through such obstacles and challenges "It is: freeing the bondman; Or the giving of food in a day of privation; to the orphan with claims of relationship; or to the indigent (down) in the dust" (QS Al-Balad 90:12–16).

The obstacles that come between Muslims and Heaven need, according to the Qur'an, a kind of psychological and mental upbringing on how to accept rather than dispense with "the other." An individual should be aware of the importance of others in realizing the objectives of one's own worship. Therefore, Islam seizes all and every moment in one's life to turn it, according to time and place, into an opportunity to deal with one's fellow human beings. In this sense, overcoming obstacles may be associated with solving Man's problems. A case in point is the pillars of Islam, such as prayer, *Zakat*, fasting and pilgrimage, which translates worship duties into an adjustment of the human psyche to coexist with others, and to consolidate human relationships. We understand religion and worship as a collective activity.

According to this process, the idea of volunteering throughout Islamic history has developed where individual responsibility correlates with social responsibility. This behavior has never been an attitude brought to bear according to the mood or the state of mind, but has always been associated with a social necessity based on a vision that human relationships cannot be maintained in essence unless through solidarity and cooperation.

The most important aspect in the experience of volunteering in Islam is the vital role it plays in reining in economic activity and neutralizing its ability in the reification of human relationships. However, it is unquestionable that economic activity has been associated with Man's existence on this earth, and consequently became concomitant with Man's social nature. But this concomitance has not meant for the pre-capitalist human societies an isolation of the economic phenomenon from all other phenomena. The marginality of the economic field and its correlation with the intense social blend had caused the economy—as an independent and then dominant field—to be absent from such societies. However, this absence has not been in contradiction with the existence of other economic phenomena that are interwoven into the inclusive social blend, and this makes it embedded within institutions and not in the first place "economic." Islamic civilization has not been an exception to this trend, although it reached high levels of financial progress and economic accomplishment. Economy remained an integral part of this civilization's social life, flowing into it without hegemony and entwined with its different expressions without independence or a subjective logic through which it prevails over all other fields.

## Economics in Islamic Perspective

Islam respects economic activity as it represents Man's endeavor to meet his means of livelihood, but encloses this activity with rules so that such competition will not be an end in itself, but a means to ensure security for the individual and the community. The Qur'an warns people against treasuring wealth in order to avoid a situation in which few people possess vast wealth without sharing it with others: "It may not become a fortune used by the rich among you" (QS Al-Hashr 59:7).

Perhaps one of the most important principles is related to spending such wealth on the needy, such as the poor and wayfarers, or even on relatives, as this may eventually develop strong social and human relationships while harnessing wealth to have a balanced society. So we consider wealth to be subject to redistribution to build social relationships. Ultimately, that implies a much greater emphasis on the collective rather than the individual human being. "Give them something yourselves out of the means which God has given to you" (QS Al-Nur 24:33).

Islam has been always trying to achieve integrity in social relationships through helping the members of the society, according to the circumstances of time and place, reasonably make both ends meet. In order to reach this aim, Islam has always tried to arrange this important part of economic activity through setting the necessary mechanisms of acceptable competitiveness and giving wealth a positive role, as long as such wealth has been gained through legal means.

Social justice, as part of the comprehensive concept of justice which Islam is calling for, is an important issue in the field of economic behavior. For this reason, the Islamic vision was not restricted in conceptualizing the role of economic activity to the limits of market and the laws of supply and demand, but it added to it parallel mechanisms that helped create some sort of balance within the economic activity itself. This is achieved through directing part of this activity toward the classes of people who cannot live a decent life. The Islamic experience, therefore, has been able to feed the society with models of livelihood that allowed for meeting the needs of individuals in diverse ways.

In this framework, Qur'anic dictates have laid the basics of altruism in order to arouse the spirit of solidarity among the members of the society. The intellectual background established by the Qur'an has been instrumental in this achievement, as the value of solidarity has emanated from two interrelated processes.

The first process is calling people to interact with one of God's universal norms which makes people in need of one another and feel responsible toward one another so that the society will be viable enough to reflect God's honoring the sons of Adam. In this context, the Qur'an links donation and giving charity with piety: "So he who gives (in charity) and fears God" (QS Al-Lail 92:5) and, at the same time, it links miserliness to self-centeredness and ignoring others: "But he who is a greedy miser and thinks himself self-sufficient" (QS Al-Lail 92:8).

On a second level, the Qur'anic context has developed the concept of altruism into a methodical, flexible state of man's openness to others, to the extent that a smile to others is considered a kind of charity, and the half of a dry date is one of the biggest charities. "They ask thee how much they are to spend; Say: What is beyond your needs" (QS Al-Baqarah 2:219). "But give them preference over themselves, even though poverty was their (own lot)" (QS Al-Hashr 59:9).

The two above processes have enabled Muslims to give beyond what Islam requires from them as a duty. Islamic history is full of such examples where individual responsibility interrelates with society. This behavior has never been an attitude brought to bear according to the mood or the state of mind but has always been associated with a social necessity over centuries based on a vision that human relationships cannot be maintained in essence unless through solidarity and cooperation.

Inside this solidarity sphere, *waqf* (roughly, an Islamic foundation) emerges as the main tool of the process of institutionalizing voluntary giving. The word *waqf* is used for charities and gifts that have permanence and continuity, so that people can benefit from them for years, generations or even centuries. In a well known *hadith*, the Prophet Muhammad (PBUH) labeled *waqf* as "the lasting charity:" "When a human being dies, his work for God comes to an end except for three: a lasting charity, knowledge that benefits others, and a good child who calls on God for his favor" (narrated by Al-Bukahri).

The permanent nature of *waqf* resulted in the accumulation of properties all over the Muslim lands, and the variety of its objectives provides support for widespread religious and philanthropic activities. The size of *waqf* and its objectives play an essential role in the sociopolitical life of Muslim societies and communities. Among these crucial tasks, *waqf* contributed greatly in organizing the dialogue between the local community and its rulers. *Waqf* appears to be a major factor in the shaping Islamic societies' public sphere. The institutionalization of *waqf* transforms the religious precept of charity to a sustainable socioeconomic practice which becomes an integral part of the vast social neighborhood. The integrity of the *waqf* objectives, the quality of services it offered, and transparency in its functioning, was possible in large part because of the effectiveness of *waqf*-generated civil society institutions. Miriam Hoexter concluded her scrupulous investigation of *waqf* practice in Islamic history, by stating:

> The waqf's contribution to the shaping of the urban space can hardly be overestimated ... A major part of the public environment in (Islamic) towns actually came into being as a result of endowments. (Hoexter 2002)

A "public sphere" as such had not only come into existence but had also been rendered more consonant with urban Islam's notions of morality and good order. Different economic and social communities emerged as *waqf* capital grew considerably, providing them with a degree of economic independence from the central government as well as social legitimacy. A network of small endowments was offered not only by the rich, but also by people from all levels of the social order. Moreover, recent research suggests that women in Islamic societies during long historical periods, were deeply involved in the management of their own wealth, particularly the active creation and administration of *waqf* institutions.

In this large context, we can say that *waqf* as a charity would help the needy and the poor, but such tasks will always remain one part of the philosophy through which the endower recognizes his social responsibility and his own role as a member of society. There should be a sense of giving more than what is required in the form of *Zakat's* 2.5 percent tax on wealth each year in order to reach the great diversity of social needs which range between maintaining Man's dignity and showing clemency to animals. Actually, the development and the diversity of *waqf* in Islamic societies reflect the complexity of Muslims' simultaneous attitude toward the Qur'anic references and social outcomes.[12]

---

12    It is important to wonder how cultural behavior can reach such levels where people create endowments for children's milk, migrant birds (to provide them with the food supplies they need upon traveling from one country to another), or the endowments of aged animals that are unable to work (to provide them with pastures), or the utensils broken by children, or when servants break things while buying them from the market.

**The Qur'anic Concept of Economic Embeddedness**

One of the most important benefits of an endowment is its ability to prevent what we might otherwise call economic imperatives from controlling society. The Qur'an has been able to appreciate Man's cooperation with others and highly value such solidarity. Endowments, therefore, became part of the economy in such societies, and there have been great and numerous examples of this throughout Islamic history. Projects such as the building of schools, hospitals, streams, insurance cooperatives and other endeavors are some examples of the solidarity created by the system of endowment which is one of the major strategic tools of Islamic civilization.

The decision to make an endowment places two kinds of responsibilities on the endower. The first is how to achieve a balance between the social and economic levels and the need to transfer part of his wealth to others, and the second is how to choose a certain group of people who will benefit from the endowment.

Being a perpetual form of charity, endowment needs greater effort from the endower to protect it and maintain its economic role as it combines both the saving process and the investment process in addition to providing social services. This combination, therefore, is one of the greatest outcomes of this endowment experience which could lead to a self-financing, sustainable economic process directly related to social priorities.

The historical experience of endowments is not restricted to a narrow utilitarian logic, but it has been of great social help to the beneficiaries, even beyond economic benefits. Endowments in education, for instance, have been very beneficial in protecting education from the influence of the state. They rendered it impervious to the political turbulence that has swept through such societies.

**Conclusion**

This chapter focused on elements of the Islamic vision of the human dimension in societies, and we tried to recognize some of their potential and how they can provide a unique methodology in developing social relationships. Islamic experience has provided a sophisticated mechanism for economic performance, with special care in order to avoid the reification of Man and his social dimensions. The essence of this mechanism is related to the kind of the solidarity relationships which Man creates within his societal network. So we look to neither efficiency, nor utility as such as the be all and end all. This kind of discourse may seem odd to Western scholars asking where is "law" in such an approach, but we think questions of governance surrounding social and economic relations lie at the core of law from a human perspective. Western scholars would abstain from such a discussion in assuming market fundamentalism resolves all questions. Our view of developing law is more tied to institutions and human relationships rather than economics in the neo-liberal sense, so to us, the concept of modernization premised on industrialization is simply beside the point. There is also no doubt that a greater part of the above could lay the basis for a serious discussion of values in our modern life in a bid to help man return to his religious and ethical values, which have been overlooked for far too long.

# References


Al-Nawawi. 1999. *The Forty Hadith of al-Imam al-Nawawi*. Abul-Qasim Publishing House.

Bartoli, H. 1994. L'économie multidimensionnelle. *Economica*, Paris, France.

*Ali Ibn Abi Taleb, Nahjul Balagha (Peak of Eloquence), Sermons, Letters and Sayings*, Published by Tahrike Tarsile Qur'an, Elmhurst, New York, 1996, letter 53 to Maalik al-Ashtar, p. 535.

Durkheim, E. 1982. *The Rules of the Sociological Method*. New York: Free Press.

Eickelman, D.F. 2002. Foreword: The Religious Public Sphere in the Early Muslim Societies, in *The Public Sphere in Muslim Societies*, edited by M. Hoexter, S.N. Eisenstadt and N. Levtzion. Albany: SUNY Press, 1–2.

El-Ansary, W. and Linnan, D. 2010. *Muslim and Christian Understanding: Theory and Application of a Common Word*. New York: Palgrave Macmillan.

Ghazanfar, Shaikh M. 1991. La science économique scolastique et les savants arabes, une remise en question de la thèse du grand vide, in *Diogène*, 154, 121.

The Glorious Qur'an, the City (Al-Balad 90).

The Glorious Qur'an, the Cow (Al-Baqarah 2).

The Glorious Qur'an, Exile (Al-Hashr 59).

The Glorious Qur'an, The Inner Apartments (Al-Hujurat 49).

The Glorious Qur'an, The Night Journey (Al-Isra 17).

The Glorious Qur'an, the Night (Al-Lail 92).

The Glorious Qur'an, the Table Spread (Al-Maidah 5).

The Glorious Qur'an, the Light (Al-Nur 24).

Godelier, M. 1996. *L'énigme du don*. Paris: Edition Fayard.

Hoexter, Miriam. 2002. The waqf the public sphere, in *The Public Sphere in Muslim Societies*, edited by M. Hoexter, S.N. Eisenstadt and N. Levtzion. Albany: SUNY Press, 129.

Khaldun, I. 1958. *The Muqaddimah: An Introduction to History*. Volume I, II, III. Translated by F. Rosenthal. London: Routledge & Kegan Paul.

Latouche, S. 1995 *La mégamachine. Raison techno scientifique, raison économique et mythe du progrès, La Découverte*. Paris : M A.U.S.S.

Lewis, B. 1937. The Islamic guilds. *The Economic History Review*, 8(1), 35–6.

Marcuse, H. 1969. *L'homme unidimensionnel*. Paris: Minuit.

Polanyi, K. 1944. *The Great Transformation*. Boston: Beacon Press.

Toynbee, A. 1962. *A Study of History: The Growths of Civilizations*. Volume 3. New York: Oxford University Press.

# Chapter 8

# Rules and Behavior in Judging *Shari'ah*: A Woman's Perspective

Lily Zakiyah Munir

The compatibility of *shari'ah* and secular, national law as part of modernization has been a long-standing debate within the Islamic world. Meanwhile, dependency theory often mixes with explanations of specifically Islamic approaches to development as result of a perception that the Islamic world has lagged behind the West. This matters for the modernization concept itself, because it has led to a fractured response within the Islamic world under which, at one extreme, some abandoned religion as cultural hindrance to development (for example, Kemal Attaturk as aggressive secularist in Turkey), while at another extreme others have rejected all things Western, seeing heightened attention to Islam and concepts like specifically Islamic sciences as the answer, which folds back on itself as an entire debate within Islam about authenticity and interpretation (bin Muhammad 1996; El-Ansary and Linnan 2010). So the whole concept of modernization itself has a special significance in the Islamic world in political and legal terms.

The two practical poles of the *shari'ah* interpretive debate are that, in the alternative, approaches must be tied in particular to a more literal, textually-based interpretation of the Qur'an and hadiths (stories of the Prophet's life, PBUH, as model) as the original sources, versus a focus on the basis of *shari'ah* more in ethical principles lying behind the texts (with the result, technically speaking, that secular law based upon ethical principles could in theory satisfy *shari'ah* requirements). There are two further qualifications to be noted. First, the concept of *ijtihad* as interpretive mode is traditionally applied to determine answers under *shari'ah* to issues not directly addressed in the Qur'an and hadiths. But to avoid a proliferation of schools of Islamic law (beyond the mainstream four *sunni* classical schools: Hanafi, Shafi'i, Maliki and Hanbali), *ijtihad* theoretically was declared complete or closed circa 1000 CE. Second, *shari'ah* itself is considered God's law as broader concept, which we explore subsequently, while its human, or narrower, interpretation by man is merely fallible *fiqh*, or *shari'ah* as applied to particular facts and circumstances. This also explains why some Muslims talk about *shari'ah* per se as a moral rather than legal compulsion.

It is actually a misnomer when people talk about implementing or enacting *shari'ah* in the modern setting under secular, national law. They would at best be implementing *fiqh*. In the national law (especially constitutions) of most Islamic majority countries, you would find a requirement merely that secular legal principles be *consistent* with *shari'ah*. However, that simply presents the question of its proper interpretation. More conservative, textually-oriented *shari'ah* interpretation is the rule, although Western preconceptions about adulterers being stoned, or thieves having their hands cut off, are wildly overstated. But it does make a difference, ultimately, whether one bases interpretation literally on texts addressing customs of the Arabian Peninsula in the sixth century CE, versus distinguishing the older (social) practices as outdated in detail but constituting the framework for ethical principles in a more modern society. Examples from a modern Muslim majority society can be gleaned from Julia Suryakusuma's chapter describing Indonesian affairs (Chapter 11, this volume), noting her characterization of "Arabization" versus her view of authentically Indonesian Islam. Textual emphasis is not just a Muslim issue, considering different schools of sometimes literal biblical interpretation within Christianity.

Many Muslim legal scholars, particularly in the Middle East, are criticized for having alienated themselves from the changing conditions of contemporary life. They have been unable to relate the primary and secondary sources of *shari'ah*, the Qur'an and hadiths, to current conditions and achieve the ultimate goal of *shari'ah*, namely *maslahah* (public benefit). The technical issues result largely from the purely textual focus of interpretation and views of *ijtihad*, which produce the criticized distance from contemporary life. But there is a further problem of interest, namely the extent to which social views may be confused with religion (the tribalism problem, bearing in mind that the Prophet himself, PBUH, brought reform in opposition to tribal custom in his own time). The response to the above perceived shortcomings is arguably the alternative interpretive approach, but that is the debate within Islam about authenticity and interpretation. In practice, the fault line often lies in the law's view of women.

The relatively poor status of women under law for those governments formalizing *shari'ah* may be cited as an example of how politicized *shari'ah* has been devised to curtail women's freedom and control their sexuality. History notes that in countries adopting *shari'ah* as the positive law, women have almost always become the first target for (re)islamization. In Afghanistan, once the Taliban enforced *shari'ah*, they banned women from performing activities in public. Schools for girls were closed, and women professionals such as doctors and teachers were not allowed to work. In Nigeria, Amina Lawal, a woman who got pregnant out of wedlock, was nearly stoned to death, while nothing was done to the man. In the province of Aceh in Indonesia, for example, once the province gained its special autonomy status and formalized *shari'ah* in 2000, women were obliged to wear veils, as if it were the biggest and most critical issue in women's lives. More substantive women's issues such as poverty, violence in the public and domestic spheres, poor education and health status, are not the concern of political *shari'ah*. Cases of injustices and control of women under *shari'ah* are documented in Abou El-Fadl's passionate 2001 book *Speaking in God's Name*. El-Fadl compiled *fatwas* (verdicts) of the Saudi's CRLO (Council for Scientific Research and Legal Opinions), from the ban of women's driving, to the restrictions governing women's clothing, to support his argument that divinely ordained law is often misinterpreted by Muslim authorities at the expense of certain groups, especially women (El-Fadl 2001).

A major problem of *shari'ah* in staying current with modern law is its rigid and textual understanding. The alleged closure of the door of *ijtihad* is held accountable for the gap between Islamic law and its sources on the one hand, and changing society on the other. There is hegemony of *ahlul hadith* (people of the text) over *ahlur ra'yi* (people of the ratio, meaning thinking or ethically-based interpretation) after the alleged closure of the door of *ijtihad* has shrunk Islam into a religion of rigid and stagnant nature. The quest for better solutions and alternatives to keep *shari'ah* compatible with contemporary issues lies at the very heart of *ijtihad*, which must, according to the formulation of classical *Ushul Fiqh* (Roots of Islamic Law), never be allowed to stop. *Ijtihad* is a collective obligation of the Muslim community and its scholars to exert themselves in order to find solutions to new problems and to provide new guidance in matters of law and religion (Kamali 1991).

To appreciate Islam as a religion for humanity, a comprehensive understanding of *shari'ah* including its ultimate goal, which is geared toward achieving benefit and well-being for all beings, is of paramount importance. The gap between Islam's teachings on ethical and moral values and their realities within Muslim societies, I submit, is caused by lack of appreciation of this dimension of humanity of the religion. This chapter explores, *inter alia*, the ultimate goal of *shari'ah*, to which all legal formulations should refer. It also discusses the contingencies applicable to human agents in the determination of laws. These are human beings who invariably represent and negotiate the authoritativeness of God (in practical terms, those who deliver *fatwas* as legal opinions concerning *shari'ah*). Finally, this chapter reflects on the formalization of *shari'ah*, which tends to perpetuate discrimination against women.

## *Maqashid Shari'ah*: Islam as a Source of Well-Being

*Shari'ah* is often understood as Islamic jurisprudence. While this meaning is not completely untrue, *shari'ah* also refers, in its wider sense, to other elements or dimensions of the religion. Imam Shatiby, a Maliki jurist, in his magnum opus, *al-Muwaffaqat fi Ushul-alShariah,* elaborates about the general framework of *shari'ah*. He affirms that within *shari'ah* there are variants that should be understood comprehensively, which include the law, ultimate goal of *shari'ah*, textual justification (*dalil*), and *ijtihad*. Thus, *shari'ah* should not be understood just as a law. There are other important elements such as the main purpose of why *shari'ah* was revealed (*maqashid 'ammah*). Not only that, Imam Shatiby expounded that law cannot be presented in a rigid way as it needs *dalil* and careful process of *ijtihad*.

Such an opinion reflects an openness in viewing religious doctrines. Imam Shatiby has brought new lights to *shari'ah*, making it an open corpus which is open to reinterpretation. He contends that religion should not emphasize ritual worship aspects (*al-ta'abbud*) only, but should bring the mission of well-being for the entire human being *(al-maslahat al-'ammah).*

Imam Shatiby divided *maslahah* into three levels: primary (*al-dharuriyah*), that is to say *maslahah* which becomes the main reference in the implementation of *shari'ah*. Absence of this level of *maslahah* will create imbalance and injustices, which may undermine the social system. This primary level of *shari'ah* constitutes five basic principles of human rights: freedom of faith and religion, protection of one's life and dignity, freedom of thinking and expression, respect to human descendants, and their property. These five principles (*al-kulliyatul khams*) constitute the fundamentals of the religion.

The second level of *maslahah* deals with the principle of easiness and how the exercise of Islamic law can be made less burdensome or severe *(al-rukhsah al-muhaffafah)* for those who find difficulties. For example, travelers, sick, or old people are given the facility or ease in practicing their ritual worship that can be regulated in *fiqh*. This secondary *maslahah* implies the message that even in the implementation of ritual worships there is this spirit of ease, enjoyment, and less burden to Muslims; and, hence, there is no feeling of being forced or burdened.

The third level of *shari'ah* is supplementary in nature, in the sense that it adds up to the beauty of *shari'ah* (*al-tahsinat*). It gives attention to the dimension of ethics and aesthetics, such as Islamic teachings on cleanliness, grooming, or giving to charity and other humanitarian actions. This tertiary level of *shari'ah* is important because it adds up to perfecting the primary and secondary *maslahah*.

## Broad Meaning of *Shari'ah*

The problem with *shari'ah* is that it has been given diverse meanings, mixing between the broad *shari'ah*, which derives from God and is sacred, universal and unchangeable, and the narrow one, so-called *fiqh*, which is the product of a human intellectual exercise and is contextually bound. Citing Muhammad Ali al-Tahanawi, an Islamic legal scholar who carefully studied terminology,

Jamal Al-Banna (1996) broadly defines *shari'ah* as whatever is ordained by Allah to human beings on laws passed on through God's messengers including Prophet Muhammad, PBUH. Thus, we have *shari'ah* of other prophets such the *shari'ah* of Prophet Abraham, etc. This broad meaning of *shari'ah* encompasses three disciplines: (1) *fiqh*, which deals with matters pertaining to the methods of performing rituals, (2) *ilm kalam*, which deals with matters pertaining to faith, and (3) *ilm akhlaq*, dealing with matters related to ethics. Thus, in this context, *shari'ah* is equal to the religion itself.

*Shari'ah* pertaining to the methods of performing rituals is closely related to the *aqidah*, under the domain of *ilm kalam*, which deals with faith. *Aqidah (*faith) and *fiqh* (rituals) are two essential teachings of Islam, without which Islam would be meaningless. These teachings will be meaningful only if we focus our mind, heart and our life on both of them, not just on either of them (Syaltut 1980). They are interrelated, with one being able to strengthen or weaken the other. Their relationship is hierarchical: the *aqidah* as the foundation (*ushuliyah)* and, thus, permanent and unchangeable, and *fiqh* as the branch (*furu'iyah*) and, thus, contextual and changeable.

The above hierarchy finds its support in the Qur'an (QS al-Maidah 5:48), where the notion of *shari'ah* is mentioned with a special meaning.[1] The verse confirms that every *ummah* (community) has a law from Allah which differs from one another. The laws change following changes in life. So, religion in the sense of *shari'ah*, as the branch and not the fundamental, may change and differ from one another. Even within the same religion there can be a changing legal process, which goes in line with the changing situation and condition. An example that can be cited from the Qur'an is on the prohibition of *khamar* (alcoholic drinks). The banning of alcohol did not happen all at once. It was gradual, through a process which reflected the Muslims' progress of awareness of the matter. This flexibility is even more important in the exercise of an *ijtihad*, which depends on human thoughts in pursuing public benefits as the ultimate goal of *shari'ah*.

So in this latter context, *shari'ah* or *fiqh* is flexible and changeable. What remains untouchable and unchanged in spite of the changing situation, condition, place and time is the *aqidah*, which is related to faith. The belief in One God is eternal and unchangeable, no matter what changes happen. This may be called the eternal *shari'ah*. Meanwhile, the "branch" *shari'ah* which constitutes the legal foundation for the laws in the society, which leads to humans' safe life in this world and in the hereafter, should encompass justice, blessings and public benefit. Thus, every matter which shifts justice into tyranny and injustices, blessings into miseries, and benefits into disadvantages is not derived from *shari'ah*. *Shari'ah* is justice, blessing, salvation, goodness and blessings from Allah, the Creator (Al-Banna 1996: 35).

*Shari'ah* laws are different from *fiqh* laws in the sense that they derive from religious texts, the Qur'an and hadiths. These laws are applicable to everyone in any circumstances. They are binding and will not change. These laws are fundamental values and principles which apply universally. One example is teachings concerning equality between women and men in the sight of God. What counts is their good deeds and piety. Each human being, woman and man, is responsible for what they have done. Other principles are like justice (*'adalah*), freedom (*hurriyah*), public benefit (*maslahah*), etc. In exercising these laws, human beings can follow the principle of ease and flexibility when encountering difficulties, as prescribed in the Qur'an that "Allah intends every facility for you; Allah does not want to put you to difficulties" (QS al-Baqarah 2:185). Another verse

---

1    The verse is "To each among you have We prescribed a Law and an Open Way. If Allah had so willed, He would have made you a single People, but (His Plan is) to test you in what He has given you; so strive as in a race in all virtues. The goal of you is to Allah; it is He that will show the truth of the matters in which you dispute."

affirms that "And strive in His cause as you ought to strive (with sincerity and under discipline). He has chosen you and has imposed no difficulties on you in religion" (QS al-Hajj 22:78). Along this line, the Prophet Muhammad, PBUH, also stated that one needs "to always make things easy and not difficult."

The laws of *fiqh* are at the lower, operational level and derive from human *ijtihad*. The *mujtahid* (scholars who perform *ijtihad*) may have different opinions because of the differing depth and breadth of their knowledge, the different atmosphere of their environments, and different viewpoints concerning the goal of the law. As human intellectual product, *fiqh* laws are not sacred, and their truthfulness is time-bound. They are practical, instrumental and contextually bound laws and are not binding except to those who have similar views. Thus, there is no compulsion to follow the lead of those who have different opinions. Because of this nature, there are often different views about certain problems. For example, concerning women's clothing, how much of a woman's body can remain uncovered, should a woman cover herself from head to toe, or can an adult woman marry herself without a *wali* (guardian)? These are issues under the domain of *fiqh*, which need to be dynamic to reflect on the principles of *fiqh* on *maslahah*, equality and justice.


## Agency and Contingencies to Authoritativeness

God's Sovereignty as reflected in the sources of *shari'ah*, the Qur'an and hadiths, do not communicate without agents, and the agents are, for better or worse, human beings. The authoritativeness of God is represented and negotiated by human beings. In his passionate book *Speaking in God's Name*, Abou El-Fadl argues that this negotiative process will inevitably involve an intricate balance between an authoritativeness and an authoritarianism (El-Fadl 2001). El-Fadl classifies the agents into common agents (believing, pious Muslims) and special agents (those having special competence in understanding and analyzing God's instructions). For the jurists (special agents) to avoid acting *ultra vires* and violating the trust placed on them, El-Fadl proposes five contingencies that will define a relationship of trusting authoritativeness. The five contingencies that constitute a trusting authoritativeness are as follows (El-Fadl 2001):

*Honesty:* the jurist should be truthful and honest in all matters in the representation of God's instructions. She should not intentionally conceal, and for whatever reasons, replace God's instructions. She will not pretend to know what she does not know and will be forthright about the extent of her knowledge and abilities.

*Diligence:* the jurist should reflect on the problem at hand, and expend a conscientious effort in investigating, studying and analyzing God's instructions. The Qur'an condemns those who make claims about God or on behalf of God without a basis in knowledge, but on the basis of wishfulness, arrogance, or self-interest. The standard of diligence is what permits people to claim that they are being honest in claiming knowledge of God's law.

*Comprehensiveness:* the jurist should try to be as thorough as possible in investigating God's instructions, make an assiduous effort to acquire all the pertinent instructions, and not negligently decide not to investigate or pursue certain lines of evidence for the sake of convenience.

*Reasonableness:* the jurist should make an effort to interpret and analyze God's instructions in a sensible fashion. She should not "over-interpret" the text by forcing upon it an inconsistent fictitious text. She should not read God's instructions in such a way as to impose upon them the instruction that the reader would have liked to see, rather than the instructions that in fact exist.

*Self-restraint:* the jurist should exhibit a considerable degree of modesty and restraint in representing the will of God. The jurist should exercise particular care to avoid usurping, or the appearance of usurping, the role of God. She must be cognizant of the limits of her role.

These contingencies, El-Fadl further asserts, are the implied terms that define the relationship between jurists and the general *ummah* (community of Muslims). These implied terms justify the reliance of the *ummah* on the jurists, and therefore they have every right to expect the jurists to have observed and to continue to observe these terms on every issue and at all times.

## Formal *Shari'ah* and Discrimination Against Women

We can witness in many parts of the world that *shari'ah* has become a significant part of public related issues. *Shari'ah* deals not only with personal matters on individuals' piety, but also politics and positive law related issues. Therefore, *ulama* or jurists who are deemed authoritative in interpreting texts play a significant role. Their views are often equated to the *shari'ah* itself; and *shari'ah* is viewed as God's word. The legal determinations they issue are uncontested and unchallengeable. There appears an unwritten consensus that since *shari'ah* holds a strategic position, the state has a big stake in making it an important icon.

But this is not without risks. *Shari'ah* on the surface appears idealistic and perfect, but as a matter of fact hides a great deal of serious problems. The way *shari'ah* is viewed, exclusive and rigid, has been the main cause of the problem. *Shari'ah* is not understood as a "way" and "morality" but as particular laws codified centuries ago. So, what happens is not formalization of *shari'ah*, but formalization of *fiqh*. Why so? Because *shari'ah*—a set of teachings containing principles of justice, peace, civilization and equality—when reduced and formalized has often appeared the opposite. *Shari'ah* is viewed not in its capacity as a set of universal values applicable in all times, places, religions, ethnicities and races, but as an interpretation and *fiqh* of certain place, time, race, religion and ethnicity.

The reproduction of *fiqh*, and not *shari'ah* in its broader meaning, can be observed from two general tendencies. First, is the tendency to make *shari'ah* a positive law applied under the state's political authority. *Shari'ah* is to be formalized while the kind of *shari'ah* or how it should be formalized to achieve its goal of *maslahah* and justice is still debatable. *Shari'ah* is viewed as the state's responsibility, in spite of the Islamic teaching that every individual is accountable directly to God for whatever she or he has done. The state and *ulama* have a dominant role in determining what type of *shari'ah* is to be adopted. The ultimate question, however—also an interpretive matter once "*shari'ah*" becomes positive law—is who controls interpretation: civil servant judges paid by the state, or religious scholars at the mosque?

Second, there is the tendency to use symbols of Arab culture as part of formal *shari'ah*. The most obvious signifier of this tendency is the control of women, as can be observed in countries or regions formalizing *shari'ah*. For fear of women's destructive sexual capacity, which also ruins morality, women are to be controlled. Their freedom of movement in the public sphere needs to be limited, their garments regulated, and their domestic roles highlighted. The stereotypical view that women are a source of *fitna* or temptation is used as a ground for controlling them, to prevent further moral erosion incurred by modernity (interpreted often to involve loose or Western morality in the modern globalization context; Facebook has been "banned" under a *fatwa* in Indonesia, on the theory that social networking will encourage illicit relationships). Permissiveness and declining morality should be fought, and at the cost of women's freedom. Formal *shari'ah*, which appears noble on the surface, actually hides a series of critical interpretations because of its political and symbolic nature.

## Conclusion

*Shari'ah*, in its broader sense, is holistic, pluralistic, gender sensitive, and encompasses values on freedom, equality and justice to pursue its ultimate goal of *maslahah* for all human beings. The primary level of *maslahah* is composed of five basic principles and rights from freedom of faith, freedom of thinking and expression, protection of life and dignity, to the protection of property and of progeny. In reality, the noble vision of *shari'ah* is difficult to realize because of its often narrow understanding. *Shari'ah* is viewed narrowly in terms of its legal aspect—the domain of *fiqh*—and devaluing its other components of *aqidah* (faith) and *akhlaq* (ethics). The reliance of *shari'ah* on religious texts entails a set of contingencies on the side of the jurists in their legal determinations. These include honesty, diligence, comprehensiveness, reasonableness and self-constraint. In reality, the beautiful face of *shari'ah* is stained by its politicization and symbolization as adopted by countries or regions adopting formal *shari'ah*. In this situation, women have become the easiest target, thus perpetuating discrimination against women.

Returning to our "chicken or egg question," those pursuing strictly textual interpretative approaches to *shari'ah* seem to assume that articulating textually derived rules will change behavior (for example, eliminating Facebook would eliminate, or at least substantially decrease, illicit relations). Meanwhile, those believing that *shari'ah* should follow an ethical or moral interpretation seemingly believe that ethical beliefs must underpin social behavior, rendering it a precursor to changing behavior (because behavior only follows ethical precept). So the two differing approaches to interpretation seemingly parallel the chicken or egg question itself, perhaps more because one concentrates on forms (of behavior), while the other concentrates on the ethical interpretative inquiry itself as forming behavior (because formulating rules of behavior is only possible after there is consensus on its ethical basis). So the predominant approach in the Islamic world simply assumes that law dictates behavior, which may account for part of the fervor beyond religion when textualists assert the effect of enforcing *shari'ah* as a way of life.

## References

Al-Banna, J. 1996. *Nahwa fiqh gadid: fi talata agza' 1 Muntalaqat wa-mafahim, fahm al-hitab al-Qur'ani*. Cairo: Dar al-Fikr al-Islami.

bin Muhammad, G. 1996. *The Crisis of the Islamic World*. London: Islamic World Library.

El-Ansary, W. and Linnan, D. 2010. *Muslim and Christian Understanding: Theory and Application of A Common Word*. New York: Palgrave Macmillan.

El-Fadl, K.A. 2001. *Speaking in God's Name: Islamic Law, Authority, and Women*. Oxford: Oneworld.

Kamali, M.H. 1991. *Principles of Islamic Jurisprudence*. Cambridge: Islamic Texts Society.

Syaltut, M. 1980. *Al-Islam Aqidah wa Syariah*. Cairo: Dar al-Syurq.

Chapter 9

# Jewish Law Reform in Nineteenth-Century Europe

Peter J. Haas

Modernization and legal development are not particularly modern problems. The Jewish communities in Western and Central Europe in the late eighteenth and early nineteenth centuries offer a model for reflecting on the larger issues under consideration at the time, as well as their abandonment of legal pluralism for the modern (secular) unitary law of the nation-state. In broad terms, this period was a time in the West in which the older feudal structures of law were being set aside in favor of new models of governance, often based on notions of "nationality" and the expression thereof in the political structure of the "nation-state." The original idea was that each "people" or "ethnic group," however these might be defined, constituted a distinct "nation," meaning a community of people sharing a common history, culture, language and set of cultural traits (which we might deem a "tribe" in modern ethnographic terms). An urgent issue was to adduce how such "nations" related to the political entity of the state, since simple geographic location or fealty to a particular ruler was part of the old feudal order.

## The "Jewish Question" as Nineteenth-Century Modernization Exercise

For many, the obvious preference was for each "nation" to have its own state, but the demographic fact remained that many states contained a variety of "nationalities." This reality led to a variety of solutions in different regions of Western and Central Europe (and later in Eastern Europe as well), from attempts to create a "pure" nation-state, to endeavors to engineer multi-national states (the Austrian–Hungarian Empire is the flagship example) to questions of minority rights within someone else's nation-state. In these processes, one common topic was the so-called "Jewish Question," that is, how to manage the up-to-now distinct population of the Jews into the new political entities that were being formed (Erspamer 1997; Rena 1994; Robertson 1999). The Jewish Question was peculiar because Jews, somewhat like Gypsies, were to be found scattered throughout Europe.

If we view Jewish populations as ethnic "tribes," they faced choices in various guises not unlike those confronting traditional societies today dealing with modernization in the form of secular national law in Asia or Africa. To what extent should legal status and family law questions in particular be determined by traditional (religious) law as opposed to the newfangled (secular) national law? The Jewish population is an interesting point of study for two further reasons. One is that different states related to "their" Jews in different ways. The other is that the Jews were in constant contact with each other, and so were constantly affected by what went on elsewhere. As the process of Jewish "emancipation" matured during the course of the nineteenth century, fissures opened up among the Jews themselves, as to whether emancipation was good or bad, the role of traditional religion, how to deal with the seductions of assimilation, how to deal with fellow Jews who were now citizens of enemy countries, and of particular relevance, how Jewish religious law (*halachah*) was to be maintained in this new environment (Ellenson 2004). Overall, then, the internal discussions among Jews offer an interesting insight into how the process of nation-state building affected minority populations, and in particular, how it impacted traditional law.

I focus in particular on the rather pointed experience of one particular Jewish community, that of Napoleonic France. My focus will be more particularly on the "Paris Sanhedrin" of 1806–1807 (Schwarzfuchs 1979). Like all other Jewish communities in Europe, the Jews in France lived a separate corporate existence with their own language, religion, calendar, laws, customs and governing structures. These communities were often founded by specific royal charters and granted considerable internal autonomy. This arrangement worked well within the feudal structure of the Middle Ages. While there was a general consensus that the coming of the modern "nation-state" rendered such individual communal arrangements obsolete, it was far less clear as to what should follow.

In the case of the "Paris Sanhedrin" the assembled Jewish delegates were presented with a stark choice: either abandon traditional Jewish law altogether and become French in every way, or remain loyal to Jewish law and tradition and therefore be shut off from French citizenship, with all the rights and duties that implied (translations of Napoleon's instructions to the Assembly, and the reply can be found in Mendes-Flohr and Reinharz 1995). To be sure, variations of this proposition faced Jewish communities all across Europe in the nineteenth century. The Sanhedrin was distinctive, however, in that it was so early in the process of the Jewish emancipation and because it was so absolutely blunt. Napoleon, you might say, cut immediately to the chase. For its part, the French (and Alsatian) Jewish community found itself suddenly and starkly confronted with a radical legal proposition that was at the time without precedent. How was this to be handled? How could the delegates declare that Jewish law, which had been handed down to Moses and was developed by nearly 2,000 years of sacred rabbinic thought, was simply to be tossed aside? In the end, of course, the delegates gave Napoleon the answer he wanted, and the Jews became French citizens. The Napoleonic new order prevailed (Berkovitz 1989). But how was this radical change in law understood and accepted in the minds of the delegates? To what extent did legal theory on the one side, and socio-political changes on the other side, interact to make the Sanhedrin's answers possible? The interplay here is our entrée into the "chicken or egg question" in the modernization context.


## Paris Sanhedrin of 1806–1807

There are really two axes for analyzing the events surrounding the Paris Sanhedrin of 1806–1807. On the one hand, there is the synchronic context. What Napoleon was doing was forced from the top, and his "ultimatum" to the Jewish community was clearly part of a larger program he had in mind for forging the new French regime and its law. In this regard the Jews of Alsace were in fact a particular problem since they were regarded (by themselves and others) as more "German" than "French" (Hyman 1991). There are arguments to be made that a good deal of the driving force behind the Sanhedrin was in fact to emancipate and integrate the Alsatian Jewish community. In any event, the Sanhedrin had two consequences. One was that its declarations encompassed all Jews in France, and forged a common French Jewish identity and community (the Alsatians included). The second was that it spread the idea of Jewish emancipation (French-style, as opposed to the Austrian–Hungarian process) more into the center of the German-speaking world, with, for example the expansion into Westphalia. This, in turn, provoked reactions—positive and negative— among German-speaking Gentiles and Jews that played out in complicated patterns across Europe.

In German-speaking lands, the result produced a series of German Jewish "synods" of the early 1840s that in essence institutionalized Reform Judaism as a modern denomination.

The other axis is the diachronic. The demands of Napoleon came upon a Jewish community that had (depending on how one counts) over 600 years of a separate and distinct corporate identity in the areas that were now becoming modern France. This community was hardly monolithic, and the first tectonic plate shifts of emancipation were already being felt. But as a general rule it is fair to say that Jewish law (*halachah*) was regarded by the Jewish masses as divine, having been given at Mt Sinai, and had over the millennia become a finely honed system that had regulated and guided all of Jewish life in Europe, North Africa and the Middle East for generations. European legal theorists (Grotius, Kant, Hegel, later von Savigny, Jhering, etc.) might have been thinking about the basis of Gentile law, but these ruminations were both irrelevant and entirely unknown within the European Jewish communities, especially its rabbinic elites.

On the other hand, the social situation of the Jews in Europe was undergoing profound changes. The Jewish delegates who assembled at the Sanhedrin were fully aware that they were living in the "post-Middle Ages," that there was a much broader and attractive world out there. It was becoming painfully clear that the web of medieval restrictions on the ghettoized Jewish community was no longer serviceable. There was a dawning realization that Jews were being invited to step into a new and highly desirable reality, but one that was going to profoundly change Jewish communal life (a more general depiction of the process of emancipation across Europe can be found in Birnbaum and Katznelson 1995).

We should consider what the delegates to the Sanhedrin faced in their own minds. First of all, the name "Sanhedrin" itself is significant. According to both Jewish and Christian tradition, the Sanhedrin was, in Greco-Roman times, the supreme judicial body for determining Jewish law and its application (Seltzer 1980; Columbia Electronic Encyclopedia 2009). Whether such a Sanhedrin did in fact ever exist or function in the way it was thought is an entirely different issue. What is important is the perception that this was so, and that this modern-day "Sanhedrin" was supposed to have the power to rule on, in fact substantially change, and even overrule, medieval rabbinic law. This was no small matter.

When the Sanhedrin got underway, the delegates were presented with 12 questions to which they were asked to respond. This list included, for example, a question as to whether or not it was lawful for Jews to have more than one wife. The true *halachic* answer here would have been that it is indeed lawful for Jews to have more than one wife, although this practice had been in abeyance in Europe since the issuance of a ban on the practice by R. Gershom of Metz in about the year 1000 (Wikipedia 2009). The delegates answer was that polygamy was in fact outlawed since the decree of Rabbi Gershom. While stretching matters a bit, the delegates were at least arguably staying within the *halachah*. This was not true of subsequent questions.

The second question was "Is divorce allowed by the Jewish religion? Is divorce valid, although pronounced not by courts of justice but by virtue of laws in contradiction to the French Code?" The true *halachic* answer would be that divorce is completely allowed by Jewish law, and that certainly Jewish divorces granted up to now would be considered valid. The delegates, however, ended up declaring that Jewish divorce is only valid after civil courts have ruled. This might be technically correct under the principle of *dina d'malkhuta dina* (the law of the realm is the law), but still constitutes a major compromise of the applicability of Jewish law.[1] Marriage and divorce

---

1   A contemporary discussion of this legal principle from a traditionalist point of view can be found at Kasdan (2009).

have a significant impact, after all, on inheritance and even more important, perhaps, on the Jewish status of subsequent children.

The third question asked was if "a Jewess may marry a Christian, or a Jew a Christian woman? Or does Jewish law order that the Jews should only intermarry among themselves?" Jewish law is clear that Jewish marriage only applies to two Jews, that is, people under the jurisdiction of the *halachah*. The Sanhedrin announced that Jewish marriage could proceed only after a civil marriage had been effected. Again, this amounts to a significant retreat of Jewish law as regards civil status within the community. And so the process went.

My claim here is that when confronted with these questions, the delegates composed the answers they did on purely pragmatic grounds. They clearly—and blatantly, in my view—misstated, misrepresented or downright contorted *halachah* with at best a half-hearted, and generally unconvincing, attempt to justify what they did. There was no appeal to any legal theory. This was so in large part, I would argue, because there simply was no Jewish communal leadership at the time that had both rabbinic training (and so credibility) and any but the most passing awareness with outside, "secular" debates about law and the like. In other words, the delegates could neither justify what they said on the basis of Jewish law, nor did they have access to outside theories. The Sanhedrin, maybe as intended by Napoleon all along, simply posited a new interpretation of the Jewish legal tradition. Their invention of a new interpretation of Jewish law was then institutionalized and enforced by the French authorities.

A new type of Jewish leadership, conversant in both Jewish law and outside legal theory, did emerge in the wake of the Sanhedrin. Crucial to this was the founding of the University of Berlin in 1815 and its policy of allowing Jews to matriculate (Pickus 1999). It was in this school that the first "modern" body of Jewish intellectuals emerged, people who had both classical rabbinic training and a sophisticated secular education. This group, which created what was called "*Die Wissenschaft des Judenthums*" (the scientific study of Judaism), was already active by 1820. When the first "national" gatherings of German Jewish intellectuals took place in the 1840s to establish a sound basis for Jewish religious and social reform, the discussion was at a much more profound level, informed by the philosophical and jurisprudential discourses of the day. This is in sharp contrast to what happened in 1806–1807 in Paris.

I would like at this point to sharpen the parameters of the conundrum with which the Sanhedrin delegates were faced. It has to be noted at the outset that one of the striking features of the early nineteenth-century Jewish debate over the role of "national" law within the community was the rapidity and urgency which characterized the discussion. Although secular considerations concerning the nature and theory of law were part of the intellectual life of Europe at least as early as the Renaissance these discussions barely penetrated the Jewish communities. Very roughly, the Jews who lived in Europe were legally members of, or part of, semi-autonomous, somewhat self-governing religious/legal corporations. This arrangement served the needs both of the local rulers, who in a sense "owned" the Jews (who were often labeled explicitly as *servi camerae*, that is, servants of the court), and of the Jews themselves who could then organize their communal life around rabbinic (holy) law (Cohen 1995). When the legal "emancipation" of the Jews began to take shape in the late eighteenth and early nineteenth centuries, it confronted these Jews with the possibility of becoming free citizens of secular, liberal, non-Jewish states.

In many cases, such as in Napoleonic France and certain parts of German-speaking Europe, this change was mandated from above such that Jews found themselves abruptly moved from their medieval status to that of citizens within the course of a generation. In other areas of central Europe the process of emancipation was contentious, politically fraught and dragged on for decades (Robertson 1999). As anyone familiar with the tumultuous history of "the Jewish Question" in the nineteenth century knows, the change in status was laden with controversy, both in the larger Gentile society, and within in the Jewish community itself. Much of the ensuing debates revolved around the status of the Jews—were they a distinct nation or "just" a religion, and in either case were they subject to specific laws, and if so, how did these fit in with the laws of the larger host nation-state?

Within the Jewish communities, the legal discussion focused around the question of whether or not, and if so how, the Jewish normative tradition—*halachah*—was to be accommodated in the social and political status. The arguments concerned not only the details of this or that law, but also—and herein lies the relevance—how such change could be instituted in an authentic way. What precisely was the basis of this law and how could it be changed to take account of changing historical realities? And who had the authority to make these kinds of changes? This was precisely the question that European jurists had been dealing with for centuries already in their ongoing shift from medieval to "modern" law, although in the case of Jewish law the gap to be negotiated was large and the time period for the transition compressed.

Complicating the issue of change in Jewish law was the fact that not all Jews agreed that such change was possible or even desirable. After all, for a religious community believing itself to be living according to the divine will as instituted in its law, any change was virtually by definition a rejection of the divine. In the end a small minority accepted no change at all and become the core of modern Jewish Orthodoxy. A fairly large minority accepted the changes and became the core of modern "progressive" Judaism(s). Perhaps as much as a majority thought the whole question was irrelevant and simply abandoned Jewish law to become "secular" or "national" Jews, or just plain generic citizens.

The conflict can be seen in the very name of the convocation. From the point of view of Napoleon, the question was whether or not the Jews of France (especially the Alsatian Jews) could or should be made into "Frenchmen" at all. For this to happen, Napoleon seemed to reason, the Jews had in essence to revoke *halachah*, at least as far as it impacted the public sphere. The mechanism for so doing was to reconvene the ancient "Sanhedrin." From the point of view of the assembled representatives of the French Jewish community, the question was how to take advantage of the chance to move out of the medieval legal and social ghetto without abandoning Judaism. As far as they were concerned, however, no so-called "Sanhedrin," especially one called by an outsider had the authority to overturn 2,000 years of rabbinic law. Be that as it may, the delegates found themselves confronted with the option of either affirming that French secular law now was to take precedence over Jewish law, or of maintaining that the divine law as revealed in the Torah and interpreted by the rabbis was still binding. If they abandoned Jewish law in favor of the Napoleonic Code, they were promised full and equal citizenship with all the rights and duties thereunto appertaining.

It was not explicitly spelled out in the directions given to the Sanhedrin what would happen if the delegates choose the later, i.e., the continued validity of Jewish law, but the implication is more than clear. The Jews would not become French citizens and (presumably) medieval law on Jews (including ghettoization and the like) would continue. The agenda set for the Sanhedrin was purely legal in language, but it was obviously posing as well an existential question: are you Jewish, or are you French?

**Religious Law as Law**

The Paris Sanhedrin's work was over relatively quickly and the emancipation of French Jewry continued apace.[2] But the waves produced in its wake continued to rock the boat of Gentile–Jewish relations in Europe for well into the twentieth century (and in some sense down to our own day). What the Sanhedrin decided by fiat became the subject of fierce internal debates with central European Jewry over the next several decades, leading to the denominalization of Judaism into Reform, Orthodox and eventually other movements. These divisions came into being almost entirely over issues not of theology or philosophy, but of law and the nature/status/application of *halachah*. A few of these themes can be spelled out in greater detail (Katz 1998).

One of the major controversies concerned the question of where does law come from in the first instance, that is, is it divinely revealed, the traditional legacy of a people, or rationally adducible? In terms of the Jewish community by the middle of the nineteenth century, the question could be boiled down to whether the ultimate authority for how I understand good and right comes from Moses as font of religious law, or from Kant as font of secular Continental law. This was for the Jewish community more than just an exercise in legal reasoning; it was an existential question cutting to the core of Jewish identity. The Jewish community understood itself as the direct descendant of the Mosaic covenant of biblical times. It was created by the will of the divine and in the divine image. To use Christian terminology, the *halachah* was the Kingdom on Earth. The switch from Moses to Kant, as I over simplistically have phrased it, thus has cosmic significance.

Two, to what extent do rabbis (and by extension any judge or legislative body) have the authority to change *halachah* in drastic and sudden (and arbitrary) ways (see Chapter 12 for the analogous problem under customary *adat* and religious *shari'ah* law)? By this I am referring not to administrative "tweaks," or rulings dealing with new technologies, but to foundational and wholesale changes in values and perceptions. What the delegates to the Paris Sanhedrin were confronted with were very stark changes; changes that even impacted the very status of who is a Jew.

This question of change engendered some further questions. If we grant that Jewish law is changeable at all, how does this change happen? Is it to be evolutionary change, the organic outgrowth of the Jewish people's experience over time, or can it be revolutionary *à la* the Paris Sanhedrin? Jewish law in itself does recognize that law can change and evolve over time. There is a sense in all legal systems that such change is usually organic, that it grows out of previous decisions, precedent, and simply applies stable values to new situations. What the Sanhedrin was asked to do was something else entirely. It was asked to overturn, in fact reverse, whole areas of law overnight, as it were. Even those who could abide change in the *halachah* could find the demands of the Sanhedrin to be of another type entirely.

A third issue is what does this mean for one's personal legal status in the family and in the social group. Traditional Jewish law, for example, treats women differently from men. This is in essence no different than traditional Christian or Muslim law. In concrete terms, does adoption of secular law mean that a woman, in a Jewish family, can give her husband a divorce or become a rabbi? Does it mean that a non-Jewish woman can marry a Jewish man and agree to raise the resultant children as Jews, and that such children will be recognized as such? The question cuts the other way as well. Can a person simply decide to ignore his or her secular French legal status and

---

2    To be sure the integration and assimilation of the Jewish community into France had its own difficulty. The outbreak of rabid anti-Jewish riots in Paris and elsewhere during the "Dreyfus Affair" of the late 1890s, led the then-newspaper reporter Theodore Herzl to question whether assimilation by Jews into European society was possible at all. Herzl went on, after his witness of the anti-Jewish riots, to convene the First World Zionist Congress in 1896. For the Dreyfus affair, see Bredin (1986).

choose to conform to a traditional lifestyle? Does this person by virtue of that decision then give up French citizenship and become a foreign resident alien? In the terms I lay out here, you might say there is a choice between a society based on religious truths or secular values. For example, Napoleon questioning whether it is permitted for Jews to marry other French persons is as radical a questioning of the meaning of *"kiddushin"* ("marriage") in Judaism as asking today whether two people of the same gender can be wedded to each other is questioning the traditional meaning of the word "marriage."

## Jewish Experience and the "Chicken or Egg Question"

Faced with the above questions before they had the legal theory to deal with them, the delegates at the Sanhedrin did what they did, and it is a matter of historical record. In this light, I want to return to my claim that the historical experiences of the Jewish communities in confronting these questions, as in the case of the Napoleonic Sanhedrin, throws a stark light on the larger issues of legal reform that were going on, and still are ongoing. In what way, and to what extent, can the Jewish situation throw light on what has been called the chicken-or-egg question—that is, does the chicken of social change come first, giving birth to the egg of legal inscription of that change; or, does the egg of legal prescription come first, hatching the chicken of a new social and communal reality? Or, in the barnyard of history, does the distinction really have meaning at all?

To answer these questions, I need to make a couple of assertions about what actually did happen in the Jewish chicken coop. If I am right in asserting that the experience of the Jews is but a microcosm of the larger macrocosm, then what happened in the Jewish case should shed some light on the larger processes. It is of course entirely possible that the Jewish case is just that, the Jewish case, and does not tell us anything beyond that. Or maybe it serves as a model for how religious minorities react to outside changes, but does not say anything about the dynamics of the outside changes themselves. For now, however, I proceed as though the Jewish case is paradigmatic of something larger. Although the actual processes varied quite considerably from time to time and place to place—France in 1806 was different from Prussia in the 1840s—the outcomes were remarkably congruous.

I begin with the egg-answer provided by France. At the end of the process Napoleon got the answers he wanted, and the Jews of the French Republic were accorded full rights as citizens. Further, the community was reorganized at a national level in a series of *"consistories."* This was all accomplished by a decree from the top, and seems to have been more or less readily accepted by the majority of the population, Jewish and non-Jewish alike, with little fanfare or resistance. To be sure there were lingering doubts on both sides. Some proportion of French Jews, and for historical accuracy I must note we are mostly discussing Alsatian Jews here, determined to remain "Torah-True" and formed a core of Orthodoxy that looked at all other Jews as apostates. But they were and remain a distinct minority, 10–15 percent at most.

The other seven-eighths of French Jews made the transition quickly, apparently painlessly and maybe even with some eagerness. It is important when evaluating this meaning to remember that the communities from which the delegates to the Sanhedrin came were still "medieval" traditional communities, as were the delegates themselves. They all grew up in a pre-Napoleonic world. Yet the decision from the top did not seem to spark any significant rebellion in the Jewish communities. There was some lingering anti-Semitism among the French elite as well, such as in the army, the Church and what remained of the aristocracy, as reflected in the "Dreyfus Affair." But for most French citizens, Jewish and non-Jewish alike, the Napoleonic decree emancipating the Jews was accepted more or less at face value, and society changed accordingly. So here, the egg of legal prescription seemed to give rise to the chicken of social change, even though it seems that the delegates were prepared to do what they did because they saw their own social situation in new terms.

The German-speaking lands seem, however, to present us with the inverse, the chicken-answer, as it were. Here the Jewish communities were organized into government recognized communal structures, or "*Gemeinde*" which were supported, and of course supervised, by the government. Such *Gemeinde*, it needs to be pointed out, not only controlled the communal budget but set synagogue policy and hired, supervised and paid the rabbi(s). When "Reform" began to make itself felt in the German-speaking Jewish communities, it not only did not grow out of government decree, but was in fact largely opposed by the ruling authorities. It was a process of taking over the local *Gemeinde*, which often was supported by the conservative-leaning government. Subsequently, change in Jewish religion and communal practice came from below, from lay Jewish businessmen in cities like Berlin, Frankfurt and Hamburg, who needed to be able to participate more fully in the developing economic lives of their regions.[3]

Such people wanted, even needed, to be free from attending synagogue three times a day, to be able to travel on the Sabbath, to be able to attend business lunches, to dress and act like their business peers and competitors, and so forth. They also had the French example in front of them. When such lay leaders tried to push through changes in their local *Gemeinde*, the traditional power holders in the *Gemeinde* were usually able successfully to delay these developments by pointing out to the governing authorities that the idea of reforming Judaism was really a kind of liberalism, and even worse, a French kind of liberalism, and so should be regarded as revolutionary. The result was that the governments of German-speaking central Europe were constantly getting themselves involved in local Jewish communal politics in such a way that reform in general, and Reform Judaism in particular, was generally contained. Reformers at first succeeded only by withdrawing from the *Gemeinde* entirely and forming their own voluntary associations.

The history of this struggle in the 1820s–1840s is the history of how reforming groups gradually, one by one, came to have a majority vote and so could take over the various *Gemeinde*. They won grudging official recognition for themselves only after the fact. By the 1840s, demographic realities overtook ideological purity and more and more *Gemeinde* found themselves in the hands of reformers, or at least in the hands of those open to some reform. As votes in the *Gemeinde* shifted, various innovations were approved in the Jewish liturgy, more reform-minded rabbis were hired, so other changes were authorized, and more and more communities found themselves advancing down the slippery slope. In other words, at some point in the 1840s a tipping point appears to have been reached, possibly linked to a generational change, and the traditionalists were the ones now leaving the community.

To be sure, this transition was hardly quick and never easy. An iconic illustration of this change was the situation in the *Gemeinde* of Breslau in the 1840s. As it happens, the chief rabbi of Breslau, Solomon Tiktin, was a staunch and highly regarded defender of Orthodoxy. In 1838, the *Gemeinde* hired an assistant, a young university trained rabbi named Abraham Geiger. Geiger was one of the intellectual founders of what we now call Reform Judaism and editor of one of its leading theological journals (Wiener 1962). You can imagine the communal politics involved in that election. Tiktin, of course, was furious and managed to muster virtually the entire German-speaking Orthodox world, along with the conservative Prussian bureaucracy, against his hapless assistant. Geiger was finally able to assume his post in 1840, but the fight continued unabated until

---

3   This is a complex story. One brief overview is provided by Lowenstein (1992). Also see Meyer (2001).

Solomon Tiktin's death in 1843. At this point, Geiger became the head of the community and, with popular support, moved Breslau into the Reform camp. About 10 years later, Breslau became the home of the first modern Reform Jewish seminary. The Orthodox now found themselves on the outside, ultimately deciding to secede and form their own counter-*Gemeinde*. The community eventually agreed, under Solomon Tiktin's son, to maintain two separate religious structures, one Reform and one Orthodox. The Orthodox congregation remained a minority.

What we see in the German story is that the change in Jewish law and practice did not come from the top down, but was rather a lay movement that gradually gained social and political traction and replaced the top, at times even over the general opposition of the government itself. The synods of the 1840s did not initiate the changes so much as verify, justify and ground them *ex post facto*. At the end, about 10–15 percent of German-speaking Jews formed a sect they called "Orthodox," and the rest became "Germans of the Mosaic Persuasion" or sometimes just "Germans." By 1860 or 1870, the legal demographics of the German Jewish community and the French Jewish community were hardly distinguishable. So the French legal egg yielded a social chicken, and the German social chicken yielded a legal egg.

So what can we conclude from all this? Perhaps the chicken-or-egg question is the wrong one. It seems that Napoleon's proclamation of Jewish emancipation was possible only because deep down the French Jewish community, or at least its "leadership," was ready to accept it, and the triumph of the largely lay-led Reform movement in Germany was successful because it was finally able to get the establishment to accept its changes. Although the historical order was different in the one place as compared to the other, both ended with the same result. Chicken and egg evolved together.

Let me end by saying that the situation was of course much more complex. The French Jewish community was deeply influenced by what was going on in the German-speaking lands, and the Jews in the German-speaking lands were deeply influenced by questions of law that were swirling around them. In the wake of Napoleon and in the struggle to create a modern German state, there were many questions as to what authentic German law should be and where it should come from. Should such law be folk law or should it grow out of some philosophical abstract principle (or principles)? Should there be Common Law, as the English thought, or should there be a code, as the French thought? Kant and Hegel, and Hume and Austin, were widely discussed, both by German secular legal scholars and, in time, by their counterparts in the internal Jewish debates. All of what I have briefly alluded to took place within the context of a much broader debate about the roots, character and authenticity of modern legal systems as new nation-states were emerging. The Jewish discussions, as I noted at the beginning, can best be seen as a microcosm of this. In so far as this is in fact the case, it does not offer an answer to our chicken-or-egg question. History, I would suggest, does not seem to allow for any easy answer to this question, at least from the Jewish experience.

These debates about the nature of Jewish law were not finally resolved, but continue to animate discussions about the very nature of Jewishness and Judaism down to our own day. The basic differences between the three main Jewish "denominations" in North America—Orthodox, Conservative and Reform—are really not so much theological but legal, the status of *halachah*. The raging debates in the Orthodox community, and the emerge of ultra-Orthodoxy, all revolve around which rabbis have the authority to declare *halachic* decisions. Israeli society is struggling with what role Jewish law (or, as it is sometimes called by Jewish secularists "Hebrew law") should have in a modern, multi-cultural democracy (Elon 1999). To what extent should Turkish law (mostly regarding land ownership), British Common Law (left over from the Mandatory Period) or Knesset law be binding on Jews as Jews living in the state of Israel (as opposed to as Israelis)?

There are now, for example, ultra-Orthodox communities in Israel that refuse to recognize the authority of Israeli law (except for purely pragmatic cases) for precisely the same reasons that they would have rejected the proclamations of the Paris Sanhedrin 200 years ago. The process unleashed by the Sanhedrin is very far from playing itself out. The discussion within the Jewish community continues unabated and with increasing heat in the Israeli context. Rapid changes in social reality and the strong attraction of tradition—the chicken and the egg—are still locked in contention as modernization continues.

## References

Berkovitz, J. 1989. *The Shaping Of Jewish Identity In Nineteenth-Century France*. Detroit: Wayne State University Press.

Birnbaum, P. and Katznelson, I. 1995. *Paths of Emancipation: Jews, States and Citizenship*. Princeton: Princeton University Press.

Bredin, J. 1986. *The Affair: The Case of Alfred Dreyfus*. New York: George Braziller.

Cohen, M. 1995. *Under Crescent and Cross: Jewish Life in the Middle Ages*. Princeton: Princeton University Press, 1995.

Columbia Electronic Encyclopedia, 6th Edition. 2009. *Sanhedrin*. Available at: www.encyclopedia. com/topic/Sanhedrin.aspx [accessed: August 18, 2009].

Ellenson, D. 2004. *After Emancipation: Jewish Religious Responses to Modernity*. Cincinnati: Hebrew Union College Press.

Elon, M. 1999. *Jewish Law (Mishpat Ivri): Cases and Materials*. New York: Matthew Bender.

Erspamer, P. 1997. *The Elusiveness of Tolerance: The "Jewish Question" from Lessing to the Napoleonic Wars*. Chapel Hill: UNC Press.

Hyman, P. 1991. *The Emancipation of the Jews of Alsace: Acculturation and Tradition in the Nineteenth Century*. New Haven: Yale.

Kasdan, I.Y. 2009. A Proposal for P'sharah: A Jewish Mediation/Arbitration Service. *Jewish Law Articles*. Available at: www.jlaw.com/Articles/psharah2.html [accessed: August 18, 2009].

Katz, J. 1998. *A House Divided: Orthodoxy and Schism in Nineteenth-century Central European Jewry*. Hanover, NH: University Press.

Lowenstein, S. 1992. *The Mechanics of Change: Essays in the Social History of Germany Jewry*. Atlanta: Scholars Press.

Mendes-Flohr, P. and Jehuda Reinharz, J. 1995. *The Jew in the Modern World: A Documentary History*. 2nd Edition. Oxford: Oxford University Press.

Meyer, M. 2001. *Judaism Within Modernty: Essays on Jewish History and Religion*. Detroit: Wayne State University Press.

Pickus, K. 1999. *Constructing Modern Identities: Jewish University Students in Germany, 1815–1914*. Detroit: Wayne State University Press.

Rena, R.A. 1994. *The "Jewish Question" in German-Speaking Countries, 1848–1914: A Bibliography*. New York: Garland.

Robertson, R.R. 1999. *The "Jewish Question" in German Literature, 1749–1939: Emancipation and its Discontents*. Oxford and New York: Oxford University Press.

Schwarzfuchs, S. 1979. *Napoleon, the Jews, and the Sanhedrin*. London: Routledge & Kegan Paul.

Seltzer, R.M. 1980. *Jewish People, Jewish Thought*. New York: Macmillian Publishing Co.

Wiener, M. 1962. *Abraham Geiger and Liberal Judaism; The Challenge of the Nineteenth Century*. Translation from the German by Ernst J. Schlochauer. Philadelphia: JPS.

Wikipedia. 2009. *Gershom ben Judah*. Available at: http://en.wikipedia.org/wiki/Gershom_ben_
Judah [accessed: August 18, 2009].

# PART III
## *Shari'ah*, Customary and Secular National Laws' Interplay in the World's Most Populous Islamic Country

# Chapter 10
# Islam and Constitutionalism in Indonesia

Robin Bush

The role of Islam, and its effect on constitutional development, has been one of the most central and difficult issues to resolve in Indonesian society dating back to the colonial era. Erman Rajagukguk's chapter (Chapter 12) explores the social complications of Islamic versus *adat* or national law on a legal ethnographic basis looking at inheritance in Lombok. We address many of the same themes looking at the historical record surrounding the formation of Indonesia's constitution(s), which were born in intense debate and internal conflict. Even today, after four constitutional amendments in recent years, the relationship of the Indonesian state to Islam is an issue hotly debated both in the formal political arena as well as the public domain. The role of Islam and its ambiguous position under Indonesia's 1945 Constitution reflects our "chicken or egg" question in the Indonesian context, insofar as it represents the juncture of society and governance under law.

## Pre-Independence Background

Islam was first brought to Indonesia by Arab traders via India during the eighth century, but it was not until approximately the thirteenth century that large-scale conversions took place. The variant of Islam exported from India was suffused with mysticism and Sufism, and thus did not create much tension with the Hindu-Buddhist tradition existent on Sumatra and Java.[1] But the spirit of Muslim reformism spreading across the globe in the early twentieth century did not bypass Indonesia, and in 1912 the Muhammadiyah movement began in Central Java as a vehicle for "modernist" expressions of Islam. With their call for a purification of Islam by following "only the Qur'an and *sunna*," and with their promotion of *ijtihad*, the urban-centered modernists threatened and in some instances directly opposed many of the practices and norms of "traditional" Islam dominant throughout Java.[2]

In 1926, in response to this development, Nahdlatul Ulama (NU) was formed to preserve and protect the pesantren based (Islamic boarding school) "traditional" Muslim practices prevalent in the interior, rural areas of Java, which included adherence to the classical texts of the "middle

---

1 For historical accounts of the origins of Islam in Indonesia, see Ricklefs (2001), Baloch (1980), and Riddell (2001).

2 "Modernist" and "traditionalist" are problematic, but widely used, labels to describe the two main "streams" of Islam in Indonesia. I use them in this chapter chiefly because these are the labels most commonly used by Indonesian Muslims within the groups discussed. "Modernists" (also known as reformists) refer to largely urban-based Muslims, who refer only to the Qur'an and *hadiths* for divine guidance, while "traditionalists" are largely rural-based Muslims, who adhere to decisions of *ulama* from the classical era, as handed down within the four primary Sunni *madzhab*. The historical and cultural details as they relate to relations among Islamic groups and other Indonesians are infinitely more complex. See Ricklefs (2008), but our analysis is more oriented to political science and law, rather than culture as such.

age" of Islam, and which were more permissive toward the pre-Islamic rituals of the Javanese.[3] Long before NU was established as a formal organization, traditionalist Islam was the predominant expression of Islam, especially on the island of Java. The relatively peaceful infiltration of Islam throughout the archipelago was achieved in many instances by integrating pre-existing beliefs and customs, rather than wiping them out—which may partially account for the seemingly counterintuitive pluralist nature of traditionalist Islam in Indonesia. The arguable reason the *Syafi'i madzhab* (the approach to Islam of one of the four classical schools of *Shari'ah*) has predominated traditionally in Indonesia as the prevailing source of *fiqh*, especially among traditionalist circles, is due to its ability to flexibly accommodate pre-existing traditions (Suprapto 1987).

As with most other Muslim nations in the region, colonialism had a dramatic secularizing impact on the social order of Indonesia. Orientalist articulations of Islam and fears of its potential to mobilize unrest led Dutch colonial administrators to implement two major policies regarding Islam which were to have significant impact on later notions of Indonesian national identity and, indirectly, the Indonesian state. Firstly, Dutch colonial discourse articulated a distinction between the "authentic" traditional essence of Indonesia and Islamic belief and practice (visible in the *receptio* versus *receptio a-contrario* theories of *adat* reviewed in Chapter 12), which was portrayed as a foreign import. This was reinforced by the colonial policy of implementing its administration through the *priyayi* (Javanese bureaucratic elite, largely only nominally Muslim), which affected the increasing Westernization and secularization of this class, in turn resulting in a growing tension between the *priyayi* and Islamic elite.[4] A second mechanism of colonial control and construction of Indonesian Islam was implemented by Snouck Hurgronje, Dutch scholar of Islam and internal affairs advisor to the colonial government from 1889 to 1906. Hurgronje distinguished between cultural or spiritual elements within Islam on the one hand, and political Islamism on the other— encouraging the former and not tolerating the latter.[5] These two policies—colonial constructions of Indonesian Islam as "inauthentic" to both Indonesia and to Islam, as well as distinctions between political and religious Islam, were to have long-lasting impact, not only on early Indonesian nationalism, but also on state–Islam relations to this day.

In the late colonial era, a growing split emerged between a group of young nationalists whose Western education and class background infused them with ideals of secularism and modernism, and an equally fervent group of Muslim nationalists galvanized by the desire to rid their land of

---

3    The conflict between the modernists and the traditionalists escalated in the 1920s, during a series of Al-Islam Congresses in Java, in which the two groups clashed over theological issues of *ijtihad* vs. *taqlid* as well as issues such as pesantren vs. modern educational systems. It was the rise to power of Wahhabi leader, Ibn Saud, however, and the fears of the traditionalist *ulama* that their practice of Islam would soon be restricted, which provided the impetus for the loosely associated groups of *ulama* to organize themselves into the Nahdlatul Ulama. Specifically, the absence of a traditionalist on the delegation formed in February 1926 to attend the World Islamic Congress in Mecca, spurred the *ulama* into the formation of a Hijaz Committee which would represent the newly formed NU and traditionalist Islam in Mecca. Beyond this immediate and short-term goal, however, NU soon developed into an organization with broader goals of promoting traditionalist Islam and protecting their domain against modernist encroachment. For an examination of the early modernist-traditionalist conflict, and background on the origin of NU, see Haidar (1998: Chapter III).

4    See Benda (1958: 13–18). See also Florida (1995). Nancy Florida makes the important point that part of the colonial project of "rewriting" Javanese culture involved the construction of this *priyayi* vs. Islam dichotomy in which *priyayi* were presented as anti-Islamic, an identity reinforced by colonial and postcolonial historians.

5    Thus while under his policy many Indonesian Muslims were free for the first time to make the pilgrimage to Mecca, any sign of Muslim political incitement would be immediately suppressed (Benda 1958: 20–9).

the foreign Christians and see Islam returned to its rightful position of dominance in society. The fundamental ideological and political split between these two groups re-emerged in many shapes and forms throughout modern Indonesian history, becoming perhaps the most crucial conflict that Indonesians have had to deal with to the present day; playing a central role in the development of constitutionalism in Indonesia. At the same time, in spite of this split over the proper role of Islam in the new state, both groups were committed to and deeply involved in the process of constitutionalism. So Indonesia has a long-standing history of religious and nationalist elements engaging precisely over constitutional questions.

## Birth of the 1945 Constitution

The Japanese during their 1942–5 occupation of the Netherlands East Indies actively recruited Muslim leaders to assist in their administration. Muslim leaders, for the first time, were placed in positions of responsibility and given authority over administrative institutions created by the Japanese (Benda 1958).[6] This gave Muslim groups visibility and a voice in the ongoing process of formulating what an eventual Indonesian state would look like—a process theretofore dominated by "secular"-oriented nationalist leaders since the 1920s. Japan's promise of "eventual" independence at the outset of its 1942–5 occupation of the Dutch East Indies further galvanized Muslim leaders. In the last months of Japanese occupation, however, the Western-educated nationalist elite were able to re-establish a dominant position within the struggle over the state-to-be.

In April 1945, the Japanese established the BPUPK (Investigating Committee for the Preparation of Independence). The first session of the BPUPK dealt with what was to become the most problematic issue faced by the nation's founders, which was the basis for the state. The primary conflict, alluded to above, was between the two main nationalist groups—the "secular" nationalists and the "Islamic" nationalists. "Secular" nationalists were represented most visibly by leaders like Soekarno, Soepomo, Muhammad Hatta, and Muhammad Yamin. These men were all Western-educated, well read in European and American political and social literature, and committed to the ideals of progress, modernization and secular government.[7] Meanwhile the "Islamic" nationalists, who made up only 15 of the 62 members of the BPUKP (Anshari 1976), were represented by Muslim leaders such as KH Wahid Hasyim, Prof. Kahar Muzakkir, H. Agus Salim, and KH Mansur. These men were not only Islamic scholars but also leaders of the largest Muslim organizations, Nahdlatul Ulama, Muhammadiyah, Masyumi, and the earlier Sarekat Islam. Sarekat Islam, and Islamic nationalism more generally, had actually pioneered the nationalist movement in Indonesia, maintaining dominance among the many nationalist groups that subsequently emerged until the 1920s.

The Islamic nationalist leaders were also well educated men (some, like Agus Salim, had also received European educations), familiar with theories of socialism and nationalism. They felt, however, that these were the wrong foundations upon which to build a nation, and that Islam offered a much more complete and solid social order than individualism and religious/political

---

6　But see O'G. Anderson (1966: 13–50), especially pages 17–20 arguing that this was more a matter of appearances than a substantial departure from the Dutch strategy of ruling through the *priyayi*.

7　It should be noted that the grouping "secular" nationalists is a somewhat artificial one which actually encompasses a range of groupings and nationalist movements variably influenced by ideas of Marx, Western European parliamentary democracies, and European Enlightenment. "Western educated" also does not necessarily mean they were educated overseas, since some were educated only in Dutch schools in Java and Sumatra.

separation, which these "secular" ideologies required (Hefner 2000). It should be noted that the primary conflict was not between Muslims and non-Muslims—Soekarno, Soepomo, and Hatta all self-identified as Muslims.[8] This represents a consistent historical pattern in Indonesia, that debates about the proper relationship between Islam and the state overwhelmingly take place within the Muslim community. Bearing in mind the "chicken or egg" question, to that extent they are as much social as political or legal debates, and Islam in Indonesia arguably has no more monopoly on arguments about the role of religion, morality, and law than religions and laws within other societies.

The debate that was waged in the BPUPK from March through August 1945 concerned the role that Islam was to play in the political system of the new nation. The "secular" nationalists called for a state founded upon the "high ideals of Islam," but in which religious matters were completely separate from the state apparatus. This was articulated passionately by Soepomo in a famous speech to the BPUPK on May 31, 1945:

> Do we want to create an Islamic state in Indonesia? I have already reminded you of the advice of the [Japanese] Government that we should not simply follow the example of other states, but must be aware of the real identity of Indonesian society ... Indonesia has a character different from countries such as Iraq, Iran, Egypt or Syria ... gentlemen, creating an Islamic State in Indonesia would mean that we are not creating a unitary state ... Although an Islamic State will safeguard the interests of other groups as well as possible, these smaller religious groups will certainly not be able to feel involved in the state. Therefore the ideals of an Islamic State do not agree with the ideals of a unitary state which we all have so passionately looked forward to.[9]

Thus the opposition to creating a formal Islamic state was openly articulated in terms of safeguarding the interests of non-Muslim minorities. However, echoes of Dutch and Japanese discourses of "authenticity" could also be heard in the arguments of some calling for the formation of a state that was rooted in "Indonesian civilization" and not borrowed from other societies.

The next day Soekarno consolidated the "secular" nationalist position by articulating the concept of the Pancasila—the state philosophy arrayed against the possibility of an Islamic state in Indonesian political discourse to this day.[10] He outlined five principles upon which the state was to be based—nationalism, humanitarianism, mutual deliberation by representatives (commonly understood as democracy), social welfare, and belief in God. He emphasized the final point involved both freedom to worship according to one's own religion, as well as mutual respect for other religions (Boland 1982). It was rather the third point, that of democratic representation, where Soekarno saw a role for Islam.[11] Thus the "secular" nationalists had a vision of a state based on freedom of religion, with opportunity accorded for the Muslim majority to implement their demands through the democratic apparatus of parliament.

The "Islamic" nationalists at that first committee meeting rejected nationalism (*kebangsaan*) as a basis for the state and proposed instead Islam (Anshari 1976). These were leaders of Muslim organizations who saw themselves as the vanguard of nationalism in Indonesia—a nationalism

---

8    Soekarno, in fact, studied Islam intensively, and for a period of time was an instructor at a Muhammadiyah school, and contributor to Muhammadiyah journal *Panji Islam* (Legge 1972: 141).

9    Soepomo's speech recorded in full in Yamin (1959–60: 109–21).

10    Numerous scholars have noted that the principles of the Pancasila were actually laid out in a speech by Yamin a few days earlier. Nevertheless, history has accorded Soekarno the honor of being considered the author of the Pancasila. See Boland (1982: 17) and Anshari (1976: 13).

11    Soekarno's speech is quoted in part in Boland (1982: 22).

that meant freedom from foreign oppression and freedom to become a fully Muslim nation. In the words of Muhammad Natsir, prominent Masyumi leader, "The aim of the Muslims in fighting for independence is for freedom of Islam in order that Islamic rules and regulations be realized for the wellbeing and perfection of the Muslims as well as of all Allah's creatures" (Anshari 1976). They did, however, see Soekarno's fifth principle, belief in God, as being derived from comments made by Islamic leaders during the committee meeting about the Muslim concept of *Tauhid* (belief in the oneness of God), which was to allow room for future compromise (Anshari 1976).

After this initial meeting of the BPUPK, a small subcommittee was formed to seek a solution to the faceoff between the "secular" and Islamic nationalists.[12] The resulting agreement was in the form of a proposed constitutional preamble, which was to become known as the Jakarta Charter (*Piagam Jakarta*). This short document affirmed Indonesian independence and intention to establish a constitution:

> which ... shall establish a Republic of the state of Indonesia in which the people are sovereign and which is based upon: Belief in the One Supreme God *with the obligation to carry out shari'ah for adherents of Islam* [italics added], a just and civilized humanitarianism, the unity of Indonesia, and a Democracy guided by wisdom arising from consultation and representation, which democracy shall ensure social justice for the whole Indonesian people.[13]

Soekarno presented this draft preamble to the second plenary session of the BPUPK which met from July 10 to 16, 1945. During this time, participants heatedly debated the phrase "with the obligation to carry out the shari'ah for adherents of Islam." The ambiguity of these words in Indonesian rendered it unclear whether the obligation to enforce the *Shari'ah* was that of the state, or that of individual Muslims, and both Muslims and non-Muslims objected to the state being given power to enforce religious beliefs. On the other hand, other Muslims thought the clause was not strong enough—Hadikusumo from Muhammadiyah wanted to omit "for the adherents of Islam," while NU's Wahid Hasyim insisted that a clause be added requiring the president to be a Muslim (Anshari 1976). In the end all members accepted a draft constitution that included articles stating that the president must be a Muslim, and that adherents of Islam must practice Islamic law.

As World War II ended, on August 17, 1945, Indonesia's declaration of independence was issued, and the next day a new Preparatory Committee for Independence (Panitia Persiapan Kemerdekaan Indonesia) met to finalize the constitution. Muhammad Hatta reported that in the previous month, much private negotiation and communication had taken place. He warned the members that the predominantly non-Muslim eastern islands of Indonesia threatened not to join the nation if the constitution stood as it was, and also conveyed warnings from the Japanese that the constitution was unacceptable to non-Muslim portions of the new nation (Boland 1982). Because Hatta had previously carried out extensive negotiations with the Muslim leaders, the committee relatively quickly (given the torturous debates of the BPUPK) accepted his proposed changes to delete the requirement that the president be a Muslim, and to remove the contentious phrase regarding the state and the *Shari'ah*, and to expand the phrase "Belief in God" to "Belief in the One and Only God" (*Ketuhanan yang Maha Esa*).[14] In the classic formulation "the new Indonesia came

---

12    The subcommittee members were: Soekarno, Hatta, Yamin, A.A Maramis, Kahar Muzakkir, Abikusno Tjokrosujoso, Agus Salim, Achmad Subardjo, and Wahid Hasyim.

13    Jakarta Charter is reproduced in full in Nasution (1992: 436).

14    This latter clause, regarding "Belief in the One and Only God" was more than just a token concession to the Muslims. Muslim leaders took it seriously, interpreting it as acceptance of a central Muslim precept, which allowed them to save some face in the light of other losses in the constitutional battle. At the same

into being neither as an Islamic State according to orthodox Islamic conceptions, nor as a secular state which would consider religion merely a private matter" (Boland 1982).


**1950s Constituent Assembly and Rebirth of the 1945 Constitution**

The 1945 Constitution was viewed as provisional, and, upon presenting it to the Committee for the Declaration of Independence, Soekarno promised that once the Indonesian state was firmly established, an elected representative body would meet to fashion "a complete and perfect constitution" (Nasution 1992, quoting Yamin 1959–60). There were two intervening constitutional documents,[15] but in 1955 general elections were held to form the Constituent Assembly (*Konstituante*), as the body charged with formulating a new constitution. These elections were marked by the same heated ideological Islamic vs. "secular" polemic that colored the formation of the 1945 Constitution, and the resulting Constituent Assembly nearly split between those who advocated Pancasila as the basis for the state and those who wanted an Islamic state, with a small minority focused on a third possibility of a socialist economy as core concept (Nasution 1992).

The Constituent Assembly began meeting in November 1956, but almost immediately this ideological issue became a stumbling block. The two main debates that emerged over meetings in 1957 were over the basis of the state (*dasar negara*) which was seen as determinative of the rest of the constitution, and human rights. Debates during the last three months of that year over the basis of the state were so "ideological, absolutist and antagonistic" that the members agreed to postpone further discussion on this topic until a subcommittee could find a mechanism for compromise (Nasution 1992), but deterioration of the nation's economy, and increasing regional unrest and the resulting threat of national disintegration, moved matters quickly in another, more authoritarian direction.

After the 1955 elections, Soekarno had become increasingly disenchanted with the parliamentary and party system. In 1957, he proposed his concept of "Guided Democracy" which entailed the replacement of parties and the consolidation of power in the hands of the executive. By 1958, General Nasution, Chief of the Armed Forces, had convinced Soekarno to call for a return to the 1945 Constitution, which would allow him to reinforce the unitary state and cut off growing federalist sentiment, as well as settling the Islam vs. Pancasila debate once and for all in favor of Pancasila (Lev 1964). Soekarno faced a battle getting his cabinet to accept this proposal, with

---

time, Boland (1982: 38–9) argues that it was more than just a "deconfessionalized Muslim concept" made palatable for non-Muslims—it was a "multi-interpretable formula" which did not presume that all religions were ultimately the same, but rather allowed for "a real possibility for people to agree while disagreeing." This ability to create enough ambiguity to allow for deep conviction to coexist with sharp differences is a quality that emerges time and time again throughout Indonesian history. Some would say it is detrimental to any definite progressive movement, but it may be the only way that a nation as diverse and plural as Indonesia can remain intact.

15   It should be noted here that during the span of those 10 years two other constitutions were formed, namely the Constitution of 1949 which was drafted by a joint Indonesian–Dutch committee and served as recognition of Indonesia gaining its sovereignty from the Dutch after a four-year war, as well as establishing Indonesia as a federal state; and the Constitution of 1950, which accomplished several things—established Indonesia as a unitary state, replaced a foreign influenced constitution with a purely nationalist one, and added substantial provisions for attention to human rights and civil rights. Nevertheless, this constitution was not written by an elected representative body, hence the need for the Constituent Assembly and the proposed Constitution of 1955.

the most adamant opposition coming from NU ministers, who realized that acceptance meant the dissolution of the Constituent Assembly and any hope of establishing a state based on Islam.[16] They did however manage to elicit a face-saving agreement from Soekarno that the Jakarta Charter would be recognized as the "soul" of the 1945 Constitution.

With a (reluctantly) unanimous cabinet and the military not merely supporting, but strongly pressuring Soekarno to return to the 1945 Constitution, there was only one more step to be taken in order to make it "constitutional." This step involved having it passed by the Constituent Assembly. Soekarno presented his proposal to the Constituent Assembly on April 22, 1959, then departed for a two-month overseas trip,[17] leaving even those who supported the return to the 1945 Constitution frustrated at the thought of throwing away the past two years of backbreaking constitution-making. Within the Constituent Assembly the debate again returned to the central sticking point of the role of Islam and specifically the position of the Jakarta Charter. An NU representative demanded that the original Jakarta Charter (including the contentious words removed in the 1945 Constitution) be given legal significance and used as a source of law for Muslims, while both Catholic and Protestant members insisted that it be considered merely a historical document and not given force of law.

Muslim representatives raised the stakes by demanding that the Jakarta Charter be made the official preamble to the Constitution and, in case some might then argue that a preamble is not legally binding, they further insisted that the requirement for Muslims to follow *Shari'ah* be added to the body of the Constitution (Boland 1982; Lev 1964). The common wisdom is that the intransigence of the Muslim leaders within the Constituent Assembly was a direct result of their feeling of having been "tricked" with regard to the Jakarta Charter in the finalization of the 1945 Constitution, and a refusal to lose face, and ground, on this issue again (Effendy 1998). With this final deadlock, the Constituent Assembly was dissolved, and on June 5, 1959, Soekarno issued a decree declaring a return to the 1945 Constitution.[18]

During the formation of the 1945 Constitution, Muslim leaders were willing to sacrifice their ideals of a more prominent role for Islam within the state for the sake of independence and national unity. During the Constituent Assembly, however, they were unwilling to make similar sacrifices even when threatened with a more authoritarian government. This apparent intransigence on the part of the Muslim leaders stemmed from a variety of factors. One was, of course, ideological conviction. All of the Muslim organizations represented in the Constituent Assembly professed a

---

16    Finally, however, they were induced to cooperate largely due to the persuasive threat of prosecuting corruption charges pending against several elite NU leaders (Lev 1964: 321).

17    This trip, during which Soekarno visited nations in Europe, Latin America, North America, and Asia, had been planned for several months and was one of Soekarno's yearly international sweeps designed to raise Indonesia's visibility abroad. Lev (1964: 371 n. 48) argues that Soekarno probably especially wanted to be abroad at this time, partially to avoid responsibility if chaos broke out at home, and partially because he felt distance would give him a better perspective from which to assess the situation.

18    However, even in this apparently most decisive action, the issue of the Jakarta Charter was left ambiguous. In his Decree of July 5, Soekarno listed five considerations that had informed his decision to dissolve the Constituent Assembly and return to the 1945 Constitution—the fifth of which was that the Jakarta Charter had "inspired the 1945 Constitution and formed a unity with that Constitution" (Boland 1982: 100). Secular nationalists argued that Soekarno's meaning was "perfectly clear from his earlier speeches," which was that the Jakarta Charter was merely a historical document and had no legal force (Boland 1982: 101). Islamic nationalists on the other hand interpreted Soekarno's explicit inclusion of the Charter into the Decree as giving it legal significance and allowing for enforcement of the *Shari'ah* for Muslims. For example, noted law professor Ismail Suny (1966: 134) has argued that the Presidential Decree of June 5 transformed the Jakarta Charter (understood by him to signify the acceptance of Islamic law for Muslims) from a "persuasive source" to an "authoritative source" of law within the legal system.

commitment, at least ideally, to making Islam the *dasar negara* (basis of the state) and to promoting Islamic values and teachings throughout Indonesia. Political realities in the young state had forced most of these organizations to downplay such ideals however their ideological commitment to them was certainly a factor. Another factor was political expedience. All of the Muslim leaders in the Constituent Assembly represented parties and groups that campaigned both in the parliamentary elections of September, 1955, and in the general Constituent Assembly elections, on the basis of Islam. They felt their own political standing was in jeopardy if they could not make good on their campaign promises in some way. It has been argued that much of the insistence within the Constituent Assembly on establishing Islam as the basis of the state was not so much about commitment to that particular objective, but rather that by setting that as their asking price, Muslim leaders felt they might have a realistic chance at winning lesser goals such as the legalization of the Jakarta Charter (Effendy 1998). Thus, political interests and religious or ideological ideals were indistinguishable as motivating factors for an apparently intractable political commitment to Islam.

## Islam in the Authoritarian New Order 1966–98

Soekarno's Guided Democracy period (1957–65), did not end well in either political or economic terms, so that he was displaced in a violent political convulsion pitting the military and Islamic groups in particular against a perceived conspiracy of the left. During the 1966 transition to President Suharto's New Order (1966–98), Muslim leaders again called for the legalization of the Jakarta Charter as the preamble to the Constitution, however they were rebuffed. This led to a change of tactic whereby Muslim leaders argued that the Jakarta Charter was compatible with Pancasila as official state ideology, and therefore could be legalized without changing the basis of the state (Hefner 2000). But in 1968, after an attempt by Muslim leaders to legalize the Charter again at a Special Session of the MPRS (Peoples' Consultative Assembly), the military closed the door once and for all to any further public discussion of the issue, saying it wished to avoid the ideological divisiveness of the Soekarno era (Effendy 1998).

Over the next decade and a half Suharto was to implement a policy remarkably similar to colonial policy under Hurgronje in which "cultural" expressions of Islam were permitted and even encouraged, while any hint of a political role was firmly controlled. In 1971, Suharto ended the 30-plus-year long domination of NU (which was a political party at the time) over the Ministry of Religion, by appointing as minister a modernist with no political party affiliations. In 1973, Suharto merged all of the existing Islamic parties into one umbrella party, the PPP (United Development Party), which was labeled an "opposition" party. The forced cohabitation of modernist and traditional elements within this party was not harmonious, and in 1984 NU withdrew from PPP in a move which significantly undermined PPP's ability politically to counter Golkar, Suharto's political vehicle. The late 1970s and early 1980s also witnessed New Order crackdowns on several outbreaks of what it called "Islamic militancy."[19] In what was perhaps the low point of Islam–state relations from the point of view of the Islamists, the New Order regime in 1985 passed a law forcing all political parties and social organizations to adopt Pancasila as their "sole ideological foundation," thereby removing Islam as a potential basis for political activism.

The result of this political regulation and repression was a shifting of energy and focus among Muslims from the political realm to the "cultural" or spiritual realm. That is, Indonesia experienced a revival of outward expressions of piety and devotional activities. Islamic clothing took on a newly

---

19   For details on this period of the New Order, see Effendy (1998: 111–24).

fashionable cachet, the levels of haj pilgrimages skyrocketed, public breaking-of-the-fast events during Ramadan were held at five-star hotels, and construction of new mosques (funded both by the government and privately) boomed.[20] This development was partially due to the eagerness of Indonesians to publicly identify themselves as religious and distance themselves from communism following 1965's political convulsions, but also that it was the emergence of a very sincere spirituality that was for the first time considered "safe" due to its depoliticized nature (Lev 1997).

In the wake of the very real resurgence of Islamic sentiment, the Suharto regime shifted strategies. It took a much more conciliatory approach to Islam in the last decade of the New Order. In the early 1990s, Suharto lifted the ban on *jilbab* (headscarves) for women in the bureaucracy and in state schools, he greatly expanded the IAIN (State Institute for the Study of Islam) system, allocated more funding toward the building of mosques, and, in what was seen as a landmark event, sanctioned the establishment of ICMI (Institute of Indonesian Muslim Intellectuals). These developments, especially the last, were widely regarded as relatively transparent attempts at cooptation of Islam, though some modernist leaders who were the recipient of presidential favors and resources, declared a new and sincere Islamization of the New Order regime (Kadir 2001). In spite of this apparent reconciliation with Islam, and irrespective of its spiritual or political motivations, it was not until Suharto's downfall in May of 1998 that the issue of the Jakarta Charter and an Islamic basis for the state was publicly revived.

## Contemporary Developments

Between 1999 and 2009, Indonesia experienced a series of four constitutional amendments, three general parliamentary elections (1999, 2004, and 2009), three rounds of direct presidential elections (July and September 2004, and July 2009), and began a process of 440 direct regional elections. The role of Islam in the constitution and in the legal system was a central point of debate in both the constitutional reform and electoral processes, in interrelated ways. The two main points of contention were: (1) whether the Jakarta Charter should be reinstated into the constitution, and (2) whether *Shari'ah* should be formally adopted in legislation.

The immediate post-Suharto era saw an explosion of interest and activity in political Islam, unsurprisingly given that Islamist activists were silenced during the New Order.[21] This explosion was evidenced institutionally in the mushrooming of Islam-based parties in Indonesia from one to 42, 21 of which fulfilled the requirements for participation in the general elections on June 7, 1999. Public discussions exploring the possibilities of an Islamic state and problematizing the identity of Indonesia as a secular state proliferated.

Of the 21 Islam-based parties participating in the 1999 general elections, only four parties wanted to establish Indonesia as an Islamic state, and 14 campaigned on a platform of reinstating

---

20   Hefner (2000: 120–1) reports that from 1979 to 1991, the number of students enrolled in the IAIN (State Institute of Islamic Study) quadrupled, and that from the same time period, the level of mosque construction in Central and East Java nearly doubled.

21   William Liddle (1996: 284), among other scholars, predicted this development when he warned in 1996 that the substantialist (as opposed to scripturalist) dominance of Islamic discourse during the New Order was artificially propped up by Suharto, and that "[i]n a more open or democratic political climate, on a more level playing field, it is probable that the scripturalists would have many more political resources, in mass acceptance of their ideas, organisation, allies, media, and access to politicians, than they have now." This is precisely what happened when Suharto fell and the "fever of democracy" (*demam demokrasi*) swept through Indonesia, allowing, among many others, political Islamic groups to have a public voice long denied them.

the Jakarta Charter and giving the state the right to enforce *Shari'ah* for Muslims. Further, of these 14, 13 felt that the first step in the process of enforcing *Shari'ah* for Muslims should be the extension of authority to religious courts to try criminal cases—while still differentiating between Islamic criminal law and state criminal law (Liddle 1996). In the 1999 elections, the parties desiring Indonesia as an Islamic state took only 4 percent of the vote, while what are sometimes called "formalist Islamic parties"—those seeking integration of Islamic law through constitutional and parliamentary processes—took 21 percent of the vote (Salim 1999).

Despite low levels of electoral support for reintegration of the Jakarta Charter into the constitution and for enforcement of *Shari'ah* for Muslims, an Islamist public discourse gained momentum in the late 1990s. This fueled efforts to bring the issue of the Jakarta Charter into the constitutional amendment process. From 1999 to 2002, the 1945 constitution was amended four times—bringing about sweeping changes in the nature of the Indonesian state and its institutions. The fourth amendment, completed in August of 2002, formally rejected the proposal on the part of some Islamist parties to reinsert the Jakarta Charter into the constitution, and determined that further amendments to the constitution would require a two-thirds vote in the MPR, essentially ensuring that this proposal would not pass in the foreseeable future.[22]

This effort to revive the Jakarta Charter yet again had been driven by two parties—PBB (Crescent and Star Party) and PPP (United Development Party)—who had proposed in parliament to add the seven words of the Jakarta Charter ("with the obligation for adherents of Islam to follow shari'ah law") to Article 29 of the constitution, which stated "the State shall be based on the belief in the One and Only God." While this move sparked hot public debate and mobilized fringe militant groups to gather thousands of supporters outside the MPR building, it was not supported by mainstream organizations, Nahdlatul Ulama or Muhammadiyah, nor any of the mainstream Islamic parties. Given this lack of support, the proposal was rejected in committee within the MPR, and never actually came to a formal vote. The PBB and PPP acknowledged their lack of support and did not push for a plenary vote. During debate on this matter at the committee level within the MPR, mainstream Islamic parties PKB (National Awakening Party), PAN (National Mandate Party), and PKS (Justice and Welfare Party) proposed compromise language for Article 29: "with the obligation upon followers of each religion to carry out its religious teachings." The PBB and PPP, however, rejected this wording, saying that "the famous seven words represent a symbolic defeat of the Muslim struggle in Indonesian history to enforce Islamic law" (Hosen 2005: 432, quoting Lukman Saifuddin). With this refusal to compromise, the move to incorporate the Jakarta Charter into the 1945 Constitution appears finally, and definitively, to have been put to rest at the national level. Meanwhile, with a view specifically to continuing efforts to enact *Shari'ah*-inspired social regulations on a local basis, certain local politicians' efforts to align themselves with efforts to adopt *Shari'ah* as law seem inspired as much in the alternative by electoral pandering to social conservatives, or politicians seeking to reinforce their Islamic credentials to increase their general political prospects (Bush 2008).

On the heels of this resounding defeat in the constitutional amendment process, the general elections of 2004 further reinforced the electorate's disinterest in formalizing *Shari'ah* within the legal system in Indonesia. At first glance, it appears as though Islam was growing in importance within the political landscape—the total vote for all Islamic and Islamist parties increased from 37.9 percent in 1999 to 38.3 percent in 2004, and the vote for the Islamist

---

22   For an in-depth accounting of the efforts to re-integrate the Jakarta Charter into the constitution during the amendment process, see Hosen (2005).

parties increased from 14 percent in 1999 to 20 percent in 2004.[23] However, in both cases, these gains were almost entirely due to the extraordinary performance of the Islamist PKS (Justice and Welfare Party) whose portion of the vote grew from less than 2 percent in 1999 to 7.3 percent in 2004. These gains for PKS were widely attributed to the virtual elimination of the pro-Islamic state plank of PKS's platform prior to the 2004 elections, when the party campaigned heavily on an anti-corruption and justice platform. PKS was not the only party to tone down its Islamist angle—PBB and PPP also did not have a pro-*Shari'ah* law platform in their campaign in 2004, differently to 1999, and downplayed Islamic issues across the board. Thus, while the Islamic and Islamist parties made gains in the 2004 elections, they did so by low-pedaling or completely erasing Islamist agendas and emphasizing anti-corruption, justice, economic reform, and governance generally. This pattern held true for the 2004 direct presidential elections, in which none of the five presidential candidates supported *Shari'ah* law, and the two candidates with Islamic party affiliations got the smallest portion of the vote.[24]

In the 2009 parliamentary elections Islamic parties fared poorly compared even to 2004 (Sukma 2010), followed by (secular) nationalist President Bambang Susilo Yudhoyono's landslide re-election victory in the single round presidential election, in which Islamic parties were perceived to have played a minimal role. On the level of political consultants, current talk is of "mainstreaming" Islam in the traditional secular parties (as a kind of values politics for the vast majority of Indonesian voters who are Muslims voting for secular parties, rather than identity politics under formal Islamic parties) (Sukma 2010). Meanwhile, Julia Suryakusuma's chapter (Chapter 11, this volume) notes the parallel to the "religious right" in American Republican party politics.

Aceh is *sui generis* as the only case in which *Shari'ah* law is currently implemented in Indonesia beyond family law. As part of Law 19/2001, which accorded Aceh "special autonomy" status following the Helsinki MOU ending its long-running insurgency, Aceh was granted a province-level *Shari'ah* court, and its regional legislature was given the power to pass qanun (or the local Acehnese variety of Islamic law). However, the *Shari'ah* court still falls under the ultimate authority of the Indonesian Supreme Court, and the maximum penalty allowed to the court in enforcing the qanun are six months of imprisonment and fines up to IDR 50 million (Al'Afghani 2005). Five qanun have been passed, regulating alcohol, gambling, *zakat* (religious taxes), worship rituals, and *khalwat* (segregation of unmarried couples). The most visible effect of the implementation of *Shari'ah* is enforcement of the veiling of Muslim women, and the Arabicizing of street names, shop name boards, etc. Despite the fact that nine years have passed since *Shari'ah* was formalized in Aceh, there is still a great deal of confusion about the extent of the jurisdiction of the courts and enforcement mechanisms.

Thus, with the possible exception of Aceh, we see a picture of very strong resistance to a formalization of *Shari'ah* at the constitutional and national electoral politics level, but claimed support for *Shari'ah* influenced legislation by local politicians. This complexity is also borne out in the debate and discourse on the issue amongst political leaders and elites. Even the pro-*Shari'ah* Islamist leaders do not have a vision of Indonesia as a full-blown Islamic state. For example, Solahuddin Wahid, an Islamist leader from the Nahdlatul Ulama, argued that a call for the *Shari'ah* to be integrated into national law was not that radical a concept, as much of the language in the 1945 Constitution derived from the *Shari'ah*, such as the belief in One God, and establishment of

---

23  www.indonesiamatters.com/97/2004-election-results.

24  The five candidates were Susilo Bambang Yudhoyono (who ultimately won the presidency), Megawati Soekarnoputri, General Wiranto, Amien Rais, and Hamzah Haz. For a breakdown of the votes received by each, see www.indonesiamatters.com/97/2004-election-results.

a nation based on justice and freedom. Furthermore, he rejected both the establishment of a formal Islamic state in Indonesia, as well as a completely secular state, calling for a middle road that would allow for religious values, especially the "universal" values of Islam to inform the political system and society of Indonesia (Wahid 1998).

This position seemingly exemplifies the majority of the mainstream Islamist opinion in Indonesia. While voices and stances within this general position vary, of course, a prevailing understanding has emerged among proponents of political Islam, advocating a strongly influential role for Islam within the political system, while stopping short of calling for an Islamic state. As Yusuf Hasyim, another Nahdlatul Ulama leader stated, "We must prevent this nation from becoming a secular nation. For that reason we have a heavy responsibility to make sure that the aspirations of the Islamic people are reflected in our legal system." He went on to emphasize, however, that while he was urging Islamic parties to work together to achieve a greater political role for Islam, he was not calling for an Islamic state. "We are not aiming to create an Islamic state—do not misunderstand us," he says (Hasyim 1999). Similarly Deliar Noer (2000: 6), modernist Islamist leader, insists that while a full-fledged Islamic state is not appropriate for Indonesia right now, a stronger political and legal role for Islam is, and would not conflict with the pluralist character of Indonesia because it espouses tolerance, justice and welfare for all. PKS party leader Zulkieflimansyah, responding to charges that the PKS's shift away from a pro-Islamic state agenda is just a temporary tactic to get them into power, at which point they will revert to their original intent, states:

> From all indications thus far it is unlikely that this party will undermine the democratic process. Firstly, its Islamist framework does not necessarily preclude support for the democratic process, though admittedly more can be done in terms of the party's approach to issues of plurality and on the role of women in the public sphere. Party leaders are already cognizant of the issues they have to address as they adapt themselves to the prevailing process. There are no indications of wanting to subvert the system but rather of learning and finding the balance between the Islamist model they began with and the existing system of the modern, globalized world. (Zulkieflimansyah 2005)

These positions are actually consistent with positions and objectives of Muslim leaders from the beginning of Indonesia's statehood. Very rarely has the term *"negara Islam"* (Islamic state; sometimes within Indonesian constitutional discourse opposed to the *negara hukum* or secular *Rechtstaat* in Western human rights terminology) been used, even in the heated debates of the Constituent Assembly. Rather, the preferred term has generally been *"negara yang berdasarkan Islam"* (a state based on Islam)—a term which allows more room for ambiguity and flexible interpretation. This ambiguity has been the downfall of the various Islamist efforts in Indonesia, however, because there been no reachable consensus among Muslim groups about what precisely the phrase entails. Also, except for early in the New Order and immediately following Suharto's downfall, there has been remarkably little public debate and discussion of the idea. Repeated attempts, in the post-Suharto era, of the formalist Islamic and Islamist parties to merge into one, more politically powerful, party, or even to establish a coalition, have failed partially due to different understandings of what this catchphrase means.

Other voices are also heard within the discourse on *Shari'ah* law in Indonesia. These are voices that claim that formalizing *Shari'ah* within the legal system will only limit the room for the range of religious practice allowed by the four schools of Islamic law within the Sunni tradition. In the words of Ulil Abshar-Abdallah, founder of the Liberal Islam Network (Jaringan Islam Liberal):

> Within Islam itself there are multiple perspectives, and different *mazhabs*. Therefore, when we seek to regulate our lives [through formalizing Islamic law], we face the choice of which *mazhab* to follow. This dilemma shows that the notion of an Islamic state must be rejected … We cannot ask the state to regulate religion, because the state is an institution belonging to the public. (Abshar-Abdallah 2005)

Another point that is frequently made is the differentiation between *Shari'ah* and *fiqh*, in which the former is identified as divine but cannot be codified, and the latter can be codified but is the work of humans and therefore not attributable to the divine. For example, in the words of Prof. Zainun Kamal of Paramadina University:

> Other than Allah and the Prophet, there is not a single person who has power of religion over another. Therefore, there is not even one shari'ah law that can be forced upon a person or institution by another. When people speak of applying "shari'ah law", they are really talking about fiqh law, which are laws that are the result of the ijtihad of the mujtahid. Fiqh that is the result of this kind of ijtihad cannot be enforced in the name of religion, because it is an earthly law, the product of human minds, and contextualized within the context of a particular nation state. The nature of this law is not eternal, divine, or sacred, but ever-changing from one state to another. (Kamal 2005)

## Issues in Constitutional and Legal Interpretation

As Erman Rajagukguk's chapter (Chapter 12, this volume) notes, the only area over which the Islamic courts have jurisdiction is family law. While often discounted as being less important due to its personal nature, many scholars have noted that it is precisely in the area of family law that some of the most intense contestations for power take place between the state and religious leaders (Kandiyoti 1992; Tetreault 1993). This is especially the case in Muslim societies, where the family is regarded as a microcosm of the larger social order, and is an important site to control (Eickelman and Piscatori 1996: 83). Indonesia follows this pattern, and indeed some of the most virulent conflicts between the state and usually accommodative *ulama* have been over the issue of marriage and family law. I discuss marriage and inheritance issues below, paralleling Rajagukguk's legal ethnographic analysis of inheritance.

### Marriage Law

The contestation between the state and religion over marriage law began shortly after Indonesia established its own sovereignty. In 1950, the governor of Sumatra proposed draft legislation that would standardize marriage regulations irrespective of religion. This proposal was met with such opposition from Muslim groups that he was forced to restart the draft process, this time with specific legislation for each religious group. In 1958, parliament received draft legislation from his committee on Islamic marriages, as well as a counterproposal from the "secular" nationalist group. In a substantial repetition of the Jakarta Charter and Constituent Assembly conflicts, parliament deadlocked over these proposals, and both were tabled (Noer 1978).

This process was repeated in 1968, when two vying pieces of draft legislation on marriage were submitted to parliament—one specifically for Islamic marriages, the other a more general bill. Again, deadlock occurred, this time because of a small Catholic minority (eight out of 500 representatives) who were able to halt proceedings because at the time the parliament was operating on the consensus system (Noer 1978). In 1973, the Department of Justice submitted a draft proposed marriage bill, which was formulated largely without any input from the Department of Religion, and was effectively driven by presidential advisor Major General Ali Murtopo and the Catholic-led CSIS (Center for Strategic and International Studies) in an effort to counter political Islam (Cammack 1997). This bill not only provided for standardized marriage regulations for all citizens irrespective of religion, but placed all control over issues of marriage, divorce, and polygamy in the hands of the civil courts, which effectively eliminated the caseloads, and therefore reason for existence, of the Islamic courts in Java and Madura. Protest against this bill on the part of Muslim groups was, as might be expected, vociferous. At one point the parliament building was "occupied" by hundreds of Muslim students, and the military was brought in, not only to restore order but also to negotiate compromise with Muslim leaders in informal extra-parliamentary meetings. Finally an agreement was reached which substantially changed the original spirit of the bill. Muslim leaders agreed to legal restrictions on polygamy and divorce procedures, especially for civil servants, in exchange for the preservation of the authority of the Islamic courts (Cammack 1997).

This compromise was approved by Suharto as the 1974 Marriage Act, however, as with many other seemingly conclusive decrees and regulations discussed above, the significance of this Act varies widely depending on with whom you talk. Muslim leaders emphasize what they see as the first formal recognition of Islamic law as national law, for example because the Act allows for the validity of marriages performed according to religious law. Other civil jurists as well as officials in the Department of Religion point out that by requiring civil authorization of divorce and polygamy, the Act significantly alters Islamic law (Cammack 1997).

The question of divorce has been another site of struggle between the state and Islamic leaders. The 1974 Marriage Act is somewhat obscure on the issue, recognizing *talak* (a husband's oral, extrajudicial repudiation of his wife as effective divorce under traditional Islamic views) as a valid means for dissolving a marriage, however requiring for it to be witnessed by an Islamic court for certification of the divorce (Cammack 1997). The question of whether an extrajudicial *talak* is valid is left ambiguous. The 1989 Religious Judicature Act was also unclear on this matter, though Muslim party officials issued "official" interpretations that retained the validity of the extrajudicial *talak*, while the Armed Forces countered with a commentary on the Act arguing that the language contained therein could only mean that *talak* had to take place in court to be valid (Cammack 1997).

The 1991 Compilation of Islamic Law is much more definite on this issue, stating that a valid *talak* is one conducted "in the presence of members of the court" (Cammack 1997). The Compilation is another government regulation which is seen by some as further attempt at control of Islamic law, and seen by others as further legitimizing and strengthening the role of Islamic law within national law. This Compilation was a six-year project carried out under the leadership, and upon the original initiative, of Supreme Court Justice Busthanul Arifin. Arifin argued that the system of Indonesian Islamic courts was in sad disarray, with over 13 classical texts being used as primary resources for decision-making. Thus began a mammoth undertaking of consulting Indonesian Islamic jurists from both traditional and modernist backgrounds, classical Islamic texts, prior decisions reached by the Islamic courts, and legislation from other Muslim countries. President Suharto signed the Compilation into existence with an executive order in June of 1991, and the Department of Religion distributed and publicized it as being *the* definitive manual for use by all Islamic court judges (meanwhile Islamic courts were under the jurisdiction of the Ministry of Religion until 2003, when supervision was transferred to the Supreme Court).

The Compilation's development has important implications, not only for the integration of Islamic law into national law, as Muslim leaders prefer to view it, but also for the absorption of national law into Islamic law. In theory, if the 1991 Compilation is understood as new jurisprudence, and also as the most correct interpretation of scripture as approved by Islamic jurists, then the foundation of dual validity mentioned earlier (in which a distinction is made between validity in the eyes of the state and validity in the eyes of the religious community) disappears. The state then could be seen to be imposing its views on the issue of religious interpretation of scripture (Bowen 1998).

*Inheritance Law*

Debates over inheritance law in Indonesia also provide insight into the continually evolving content of "Indonesian Islamic law." They have less to do with direct struggle for power and influence between Muslim leaders and state interests than the marriage law issues discussed above. But, as visible in Rajagukguk's chapter, they reflect an internal push and pull between the concept of "Indonesianness" and "pure" Islamic doctrine that is also implicit in the state–Islam conflicts. One of the most contentious aspects of Islamic *Shari'ah* with regard to inheritance for Indonesian Muslims has been the 2:1 gender ratio allowing male children a portion of the inheritance rights twice as large as that given to female children. Many Indonesian Muslims, even devout religious scholars, while acknowledging the Qur'anic teachings dictating a 2:1 ratio for inheritance, have often circumvented this particular principle by passing on their wealth equally to sons and daughters as *hibah* (gift) rather than inheritance.

In the 1950s–1960s, University of Indonesia Law School Professor Hazairin S.H. argued for the establishment of an "Indonesian *madzhab*" which would allow equal distribution of inheritance, based on the argument that universal principles of justice and fairness were more relevant than specific regulations derived from Arab culture. Hazairin's argument spawned a great deal of heated debate, and was never adopted; however, his students and followers have continued to advocate similar principles, on a lesser scale. In 1984 then-Minister of Religion, Munawir Szadjali made a (largely unsuccessful) argument along similar lines as Hazairin, that Indonesian *fiqh* should be adapted to allow for equal distribution, again based on principles of justice and fairness (Abdillah 1998).[25] This parallels Erman Rajagukguk's observation in the Lombok context that the Indonesian Supreme Court is seemingly more willing to modify what is recognized as *adat* inheritance law influenced by *Shari'ah*, as opposed to decisions formally delivered under Islamic law.

Debates along these lines reappeared in the formation of the 1991 Compilation, in determining stances on issues like the 2:1 ratio and inheritance rights for orphaned grandchildren, etc. Law professor Muhammad Daud Ali, one of the formulators of the Compilation, argued that in addition to Qur'an and *hadiths*, jurists also took into account principles of justice and equality that can "be found in the adat of Muslim Indonesians and lives in the legal consciousness of Muslim society in our country" (Bowen 1998). Intense debate on these issues took place, in which those arguing for an equal ratio did so using a variety of doctrinal methods that were generally rooted in the contradiction between principles of justice and withholding equal wealth from women who played (at least) equal roles in income generation and society generally. Meanwhile those who argued for the 2:1 ratio did it on the basis largely of the direct and clear nature of the textual teaching within the Qur'an. Ultimately the 2:1 ratio was retained in the Compilation, largely it seemed because ignoring the rule was easier than rewriting it.

---

25   Most local Islamic scholars of the time opposed him, on the basis that the Qur'anic text on the 2:1 ratio was not *zanni* (relative or interpretable) but rather was *quathi* (certain or non-negotiable). Szadjali tried to counter this by using the method of *naskh* (abrogation of law), but this was not accepted by the majority of Islamic scholars at the time.

*Revision of 1991 Compilation of Islamic Law*

In October 2004, a group operating within the Ministry of Religious Affairs, called the "Gender Team," released what it called a "Counter Legal Draft." It was an alternative version to the 1991 Compilation, which they claimed updated the Compilation and brought it in line with principles of gender equity and religious pluralism. The release was strategically timed, as there was a movement within the Ministry to submit the 1991 Compilation to parliament for codification into positive law (Mulia 2005). According to Musdah Mulia, the Gender Advisor to the Minister of Religious Affairs and head of the "Gender Team" that produced the revision, the 1991 Compilation was in need of revision because, first, it did not reflect either the empirical realities or contemporary values of equity and pluralism within Indonesian society; second, in some instances it conflicted with basic principles within Islam of justice (*al-adl*), welfare (*al-maslahah*), and equity (*al-musawah*); and, third, in some instances it was claimed to conflict with existing Indonesian laws such as CEDAW-related Law 39/1999 on the elimination of discrimination toward women (Mulia 2005), with a collateral issue being whether religious judges (as government officials) in Islamic courts should be required to acknowledge and follow non-*Shari'ah* based national legislation such as prohibitions on domestic violence (generally, to what extent sitting Islamic judges were required to take judicial notice also of non-Islamic, secular national law).

The process of revision was a lengthy one, taking over a year and multiple roundtable type consultative fora with a range of stakeholders—Ministry officials, religious scholars, women's activists, *ulama*, and legal scholars—the group released its draft to the public in October 2004. The draft revision consisted of 116 articles on marriage law, 42 articles on inheritance law, and 20 articles on wakaf (religious foundations and charitable donations). Some of the more significant proposed revisions to the 1991 Compilation included:

1. women over 21 years old could marry without a *wali* (guardian);
2. registration of marriage would be required for its validity;
3. women were to be allowed to serve as witnesses for a marriage;
4. 19 would the minimum age for marriage (in the 1991 Compilation it was 16 for women);
5. interfaith marriages would be permitted;
6. polygamy (having more than one wife) would be forbidden; and
7. inheritance rights for male and female children would be the same (not divided according to the traditional 2:1 ratio).

These innovations were defended one by one in a series of "expert roundtables" in which religious scholars brought forward texts from the classical *fiqh*, the Qur'an, and *hadiths*, for or against each article, and they were each debated at length.

Despite this approach, the release of the revised draft Compilation sparked a huge controversy within Indonesia, and it was immediately attacked by conservative Islamic groups ranging from the MMI (Indonesian Mujahiddin Council), Hizbut Tahrir, Sabili, and Hidyatullah. The general complaint was that the revisions departed from the "true" teachings of Islam, though no point-by-point refutation of either the articles or their scriptural bases were made. Given the high profile controversy, then Minister of Religious Affairs, Said Agil Munawar, withdrew his support for the revision, and it was shelved. The next Minister of Religious Affairs, Maftuh Basyuni, went further by actually "banning" the draft revised Compilation.[26] Here it becomes difficult to separate the political and religious strains, since the political uproar led to consequences outside a legislative framework (reflecting the fact that the 1991 Compilation itself retains a curious existence as direction to Islamic judges from the executive branch, not to mention the question of who determines what the law means (religious scholars at the mosque versus government-appointed judges)). The proposed revisions may have been a bridge too far, but evidence the problematic social and legal overlap visible in Islamic law in Indonesia: whose view of Islam will prevail on mixed social and legal questions?

## Conclusion

Debate and contestation over the appropriate role for Islam within the political and legal system in Indonesia remains active. The fact that this issue has returned time and time again in different shapes and forms throughout Indonesia's history speaks to the complexity of Indonesian attitudes toward religion. Religion is obviously an issue on which feelings run deep, and the Muslim community has often felt that it has not received the political recognition it is due.[27] At the same time, Indonesians of all religions are strongly proud of, and committed to, the pluralist nature of their society, which has come to be symbolized in peoples' minds by Pancasila. While Pancasila was certainly used as an instrument of control during the New Order, significantly there have been no serious attempts to remove it since 1998.

The overwhelming message sent by the 1999, 2004, and 2009 election results was that Indonesian people wished to retain and protect their pluralist identity. Thus, there appears to be almost no serious desire for the establishment of an Islamic state, and very little political will even for the enforcement of Islamic law by the state at the national level. At the same time, and probably due to the legacy from both Suharto's New Order and Dutch colonial policy, there is a strong political will for increased public expression of Islam, and for increased integration of "Islamic values" into the political system. How this plays out will reverberate not only throughout Indonesia, but also through many other parts of the Muslim world. This process of integrating Islamic values seems a prime example of the "chicken or egg" question in non-Western legal development.

---

26   After the dust settled a bit however, "secular" women's groups like the National Commission of Women came out in support of the revision, bestowing an award on Musdah Mulia for her "bravery" in bringing these crucial issues of family law to the forefront of public debate. Noted human rights lawyer and activist Todung Mulya Lubis (2005) had this to say about the draft revised Compilation, "Even though the legal draft of the KHI has sparked controversy, its emergence is very refreshing because it is in conformity with (the demands of) human rights. This document offers an alternative legal standpoint that can serve the needs of the varied and pluralist Indonesian context using a gender perspective."

27   As late as 1972, Dan Lev (1972: 242) wrote that Islam in Indonesia "has always suffered from a kind of minority status. Despite the fact that Muslims are a numerical majority, Islam in Indonesia represents what is basically an under class." This is no longer the case, as from the mid-1980s on Islam became culturally and socially much more visible in society, and after Suharto's fall it took a prominent place on the political landscape as well. Today Indonesia continues to move in a direction of Islamization on many levels, a social change which will undoubtedly impact the political institutions and structures that are currently the target of efforts of *reformasi* (reformation). Thus we may see democratization and reformation of the Indonesian political system resulting in more Islamically-oriented political and legal institutions.

## References


Abdillah, M. 1998. *Islamic Legal Thought and Practice in Contemporary Indonesia*. PROSEA Occasional Paper No. 14. Jakarta: State Institute for Islamic Studies-IAIN, April.

Abshar-Abdallah, U. 2005. Perkara Penegakan Syariat Islam di Indonesia, in *Menjadi Muslim Liberal*. Jakarta: Penerbit Nalar.

Al'Afghani, M.M. 2005. Limited implementation of *Shari'ah* in Aceh. *The Jakarta Post*, July 13.

Anshari, S. 1976. *The Jakarta Charter of June 1945: A History of the Gentlemen's Agreement between the Islamic and the Secular Nationalists in Modern Indonesia*. Kuala Lumpur: Muslim Youth Movement of Malaysia.

Baloch, N.A. 1980. *The Advent of Islam in Indonesia*. Islamabad: National Institute of Historical and Cultural Research.

Benda, H. 1958. *The Crescent and the Rising Sun: Indonesian Islam under the Japanese Occupation, 1942–1945*. The Hague: W. Van Hoeve.

Boland, B.J. 1982. *The Struggle of Islam in Modern Indonesia*. Revised reprint. The Hague: Martinus Nijhoff.

Bowen, John R. 1998. Qur'an, Justice, Gender: Internal Debates in Indonesia Islamic Jurisprudence. *History of Religions*, 38(1).

Bush, R. 2008. Regional *Shari'ah* Regulations in Indonesia: Anomaly or Symptom?, in *Expressing Islam: Religious Life and Politics in Indonesia*, edited by G. Fealy and S. White. Singapore: ISEAS, 115–36 (2007 Indonesia Update).

Cammack, M. 1997. Indonesia's 1989 Religious Judicature Act: Islamization of Indonesia or Indonesianization of Islam? *Indonesia*, 63, 143–68.

Effendy, B. 1998. *Islam dan Negara: Transformasi Pemikran dan Praktik Politik Islam di Indonesia*. Jakarta: Paramadina.

Eickelman, D. and Piscatori, J. 1996. *Muslim Politics*. Princeton: Princeton University Press.

Florida, N. 1995. *Writing the Past, Inscribing the Future*. Durham, NC: Duke University Press.

Haidar, A. 1998. *NU dan Islam di Indonesia: Pendekatan Fikih dalam Politik*. Jakarta: Gramedia Pustaka Umum.

Hasyim, Y. 1999. Indonesia Jangan Jadi Negara Sekuler. *Republika*, March 24.

Hefner, R.W. 2000. *Civil Islam: Muslims and Democratization in Indonesia*. Princeton: Princeton University Press.

Hosen, N. 2005. Religion and the Indonesian Constitution: A Recent Debate. *Journal of Southeast Asian Studies*, 36(3), 419–40.

Kadir, S. 2001. *Indonesia's Democratization Dilemma: Political Islam and the Prospects for Democratic Consolidation*. Paper presented to the Consolidating Indonesian Democracy Conference, Columbus: Ohio State University, May 11–13.

Kamal, Z. 2005. Kontekstualisasi Syariat Islam, in *Islam, Negara dan Civil Society: Gerakan dan Pemikiran Islam Kontemporer*, edited by K. Hidayat and A. Gaus. Jakarta: Paramadina.

Kandiyoti, D. 1992. Women, Islam and the State: A Comparative Approach, in *Comparing Muslim Societies: Knowledge and the State in a World Civilization*, edited by J. Cole. Ann Arbor: University of Michigan Press.

Legge, J.D. 1972. *Sukarno: A Political Biography*. Sydney: Allen & Unwin.

Lev, D.S. 1964. *The Transition to Guided Democracy in Indonesia, 1957–1959*. Microfilm. Dissertation presented to Cornell University. Ithaca: Cornell University.

Lev, D.S. 1972. *Islamic Courts in Indonesia: A Study in the Political Bases of Legal Institutions*. Berkeley: University of California Press.

Lev, D. 1997. *On the Religion of Politics in Indonesia*. Paper presented at the Jackson School of International Studies, Seattle: University of Washington, October 10.

Liddle, R.W. 1996. *Leadership and Culture in Indonesian Politics*. Sydney: Allen & Unwin.

Lubis, T.M. 2005. Speech presented at Hotel Aryaduta, Jakarta, February 13.

Mulia, M. 2005. *Muslimah Reformis: Perempuan Pembaru Keagamaan*. Jakarta: Mizan.

Nasution, A.B. 1992. *The Aspiration for Constitutional Government in Indonesia: A Socio-legal Study of the Indonesian Konstituante, 1956–1959*. Jakarta: Pustaka Sinar Harapan.

Noer, D. 1978. *The Administration of Islam*. Ithaca: Cornell Modern Indonesia Project, Southeast Asia Program.

Noer, D. 2000. Umat Islam di Tengah Pluralitas Bangsa. *Republika*, March 11.

O'G. Anderson, B.R. 1966. Japan: The Light of Asia, in *Southeast Asia in World War II: Four Essays*, edited by J. Silverstein. New Haven: Yale University Southeast Asia Studies, Monograph Series No. 7, 13–50.

Ricklefs, M.C. 2001. *A History of Modern Indonesia Since c. 1200*. 3rd edn. Stanford: Stanford University Press.

Ricklefs, M.C. 2008. Religion, Politics and Social Dynamics in Java: Historical and Contemporary Rhymes, in *Expressing Islam: Religious Life and Politics in Indonesia*, edited by G. Fealy and S. White. Singapore: ISEAS, 115–36 (2007 Indonesia Update).

Riddell, P. 2001. *Islam and the Malay-Indonesian World: Transmission and Responses*. Honolulu: University of Hawaii Press.

Salim, A. 1999. *Partai Islam dan Relasi Agama-Negara*. Jakarta: Puslit IAIN, Jakarata.

Sukma, R. 2010. Indonesia's 2009 Elections: Defective System, Resilient Democracy, in *Problems of Democratisation in Indonesia: Elections, Institutions and Society*, edited by E. Aspinall and M. Mietzner. Singapore: ISEAS (2009 Indonesia Update).

Suny, I. 1966. Kedudukan Hukum Islam dalam Sistem Ketatanegaraan Indonesia, in *Dimensi Hukum Islam Dalam Sistem Hukum Nasional*, edited by A. Ahmad. Jakarta: Gema Insani Press.

Suprapto, B. 1987. *NU, Existensi, Peran dan Prospeknya*. Malang: Lembaga Pendidikan Ma'arif.

Tetreault, M.A. 1993. Civil Society in Kuwait: Protected Spaces and Women's Rights. *Middle East Journal*, 47(2), 275–91.

Wahid, S. 1998. Pancasila, Jalan Tengah Kita Menanggapi kembali Tanggapan KH Abdurrahman Wahid. *Media Indonesia*, November 4.

Yamin, M. 1959–60. *Naskah Persiapan Undang-undang Dasar 1945*. Jakarta: Jajasan Prapantja.

Zulkieflimansyah. 2005. Overcoming the Fear: PKS and the Democratization Process in Indonesia. *The Jakarta Post*, December 13.

# Chapter 11

# From Both Sides Now: *Shari'ah* Morality, "Pornography" and Women in Indonesia

Julia Suryakusuma

On October 30, 2008, after more than 10 years of debate, the Indonesian House of Representatives (*Dewan Perwakilan Rakyat*, or DPR) ratified a new far-reaching Anti-Pornography Law, No. 44 of 2008, in an attempt to introduce conservative interpretations of *shari'ah* by stealth. If fully enforced, the new Law could criminalize much sexuality, tightly censor the arts and media, prohibit much traditional cultural expression, and force women to cover up almost completely, thus largely excluding them from public space. Indeed, on New Year's Eve 2009, a few months after the Law was enacted, four female dancers (and two men, namely their agent and the club manager) were arrested for "dirty dancing" in a Bandung nightclub act and later sentenced to two-and-a-half months' imprisonment. They were probably the first ordinary Indonesians to be tried under the Law, and it has since been applied to celebrities in the high profile "Ariel/Peter Porn" sex video incident (Suryakusuma 2010).[1] What does this all mean for Indonesia and the broader "chicken or egg" question about the relationship between law reform and social change that is a key theme of this volume?

The political phenomenon at play here is similar to that driven by the Christian Right and "social values" voters in the United States. These consist of a wide spectrum of right-wing Christian social and political movements characterized by their strong support for conservative social values and, as a result, the Republican Party. The Christian Right has been increasingly vocal in reacting to a series of United States Supreme Court decisions regarding pornography, abortion, prayer in public schools, textbook content (concerning evolution vs. intelligent design), homosexuality and sex education. The Christian Right in the United States has the ability to organize, and influence politicians and political institutions, think tanks, media institutions, and grassroots organizations, and to mobilize parts of the electorate to influence the formation of legislation.

Indonesia's Anti-Pornography Law is the result of the same sort of activism by Muslim conservatives. Indonesia can thus be said to be similarly experiencing its own culture wars, albeit conducted against an Islamic background (Bayuni 2006). Unlike the debate in the United States, however, the culture wars in Indonesia are not just about religious versus secular cultures but also involve a heated argument *within* a religion, namely Islam. This conflict is about what moderate Muslims would call the attempted "Arabization" of Indonesian views of Islam, traditionally more relaxed and far less orthodox than in the Middle East. This is particularly apparent as regards

---

1   In late June 2010, Nazril Irham, better known as Ariel (many Indonesians only use one name), a popular Indonesian rock singer with the band Peter Pan, was charged under the Anti-Pornography Law in relation to a privately-recorded video of him having sex (separately, and on different occasions) with Luna Maya (his girlfriend, an artist) and Cut Tari (a TV presenter). The video had been uploaded without his consent and went viral on the Internet. On January 31, 2011, Ariel was sentenced to three-and-a-half years' imprisonment and was fined Rp. 250 million (US\$ 28,000) (www.thejakartapost.com/news/2011/01/31/three-years-and-six-months-jail-term-ariel.html).

the way the so-called Anti-Pornography Law deals with women. Is it, in fact, aimed against "pornography" or is it really directed against women and the freedoms won through post-Soeharto democratization? The Law, I will argue, is, in fact, based on a social construction of "morality" and womanhood that masquerades as religion but which is, in fact, a potent combination of social conservatism and political opportunism. This is hardly surprising. Throughout Indonesian history, patriarchal power elites have always attempted to define, use and abuse women to suit their ends. The Anti-Pornography Law is just the latest example of this.

To make these points, this chapter will first consider interpretations of history in the Indonesian context, and how women are defined by them. It will then examine the 'war' over these definitions in the context of the phenomenon of creeping "*shar'iah*-ization" (legal Islamization) through *Perda* (*Peraturan Daerah* or regional regulations passed by dozens of local governments across Indonesia) (Bush 2008) and how the Law defines "pornography." I will argue that this war is a reaction to the re-engagement in public life post-1998 under so-called *Reformasi* (Reformation) of both Islamic and women's groups on issues including gender bias in pesantren texts, domestic violence, reproductive rights and polygamy, among others (Anshor and White 2008). Finally, this chapter will assess what the debate about the Anti-Pornography Law—as opposed to the substance of Law itself—means for the future of the women's movement and for democratization in Indonesia. I will conclude that it involves the drawing of the ideological battle-lines that will dominate the next decade of law reform and social change in Indonesia.

## Historical Interpretations and Social Constructions of Womanhood

Across history and geography, women are often socially constructed as repositories of morality. When moral panic breaks out, or when male-dominated factions engage in political power plays, issues centered around women quickly become an arena for debates and struggles that are ostensibly about "morality" but which are, in fact, usually a guise for the vested interests of the groups involved. This is certainly true in Indonesia, where since the onset of the *Reformasi* movement in 1998, women have been at the center of political development, as actors, pawns and victims, buffeted by the social and political forces unleashed as a result of the lifting of the 32 years of authoritarian rule imposed by Soeharto's military-backed New Order (1966–98).

The common perception is that this movement was instigated by students. Popular analysis waxes lyrical about them as being "the heroes of *Reformasi*,"[2] telling stirring tales of their occupation of the legislature in May 1998 as the key to the end of the New Order. The counter-argument is that the students were only able to enter the legislature complex because it suited the military. Like the mobs and militias that were bussed around at the same time, students were once again pawns of elites who often determined when they could mobilize, and when they were to stop.[3]

---

2   At least four students were shot dead during a demonstration on May 12, 1998 at the Trisakti University, apparently by military snipers. Their deaths became one the main grounds for according status as "heroes" of *Reformasi* to students in general, although the many other casualties of the violence that erupted as the New Order collapsed (including urban poor and ethnic Chinese rape victims) have never been accorded similar status.

3   The manipulation of students by elites at times of political crisis is a long-standing historical pattern in Indonesia. In 1966, in an attempt to oust the then President-for-Life Sukarno, the student movement unwittingly made a pact with the devil, and ushered in the military dictatorship of Soeharto. Decades of hindsight now make it clear that the 1966 student movement was exploited and manipulated by the military. Students were pawns who, in the end, lost the freedom they thought they were winning.

It would be more historically accurate to cite women as being at the forefront of *Reformasi*. On February 23, 1998, for example, 3 months before Soeharto's resignation, a group of women—activists, intellectuals, ordinary women, mothers—took to Jakarta's streets during a special legislative session. They were breaching clear prohibitions against demonstrations to initiate one of the first of the now-common public demonstrations that differentiate the *Reformasi* from the New Order. Known as *Suara Ibu Peduli* (SIP, or the Voice of Concerned Mothers),[4] these women were not backed or manipulated by the military (indeed, that first demonstration ended in their arrest). Nor were they motivated by idealism or a new ideology, rather they were alarmed at how the spiraling costs of milk (up by 400 percent) and other basic commodities were affecting ordinary families, and children in particular. SIP retained its original humanitarian orientation but produced spin-offs that were more self-consciously political, notably the Women's Coalition for Justice and Democracy (KPI), among many others. Women actvists were, however, quickly overshadowed by the student movement and the rise of a strangely familiar "new" political elite, especially at the district level.

In many cases these elites were, in fact, old elites redux, that is, traditional (local) leaders pushed to one side under the New Order reasserting themselves three decades later. The issues behind the rise of the new elites go even further back in Indonesian history, however. In preparing for Indonesia's independence, politically-minded Muslims wanted to include in the preamble to the 1945 Constitution a phrase making *shari'ah* applicable to Muslims. The seven additional words they sought translate into English as "with the obligation to live according to Islamic law for Muslims." This would have given the state an explicitly Islamic basis, as more than 80 percent of the Indonesian population are Muslim. The "Jakarta Charter," as the seven words became known, was hurriedly deleted immediately before Independence was declared on August 17, 1945, following behind-the-scenes intervention by secular nationalist leaders who feared its inclusion would keep non-Muslim Eastern Indonesia out of the new-born Republic. The Jakarta Charter question was revived after Sukarno's fall, only to be rejected again early in the New Order. It then largely disappeared from public debate, excluded by the authoritarian and repressive policies that prevailed under Soeharto. This, however, never stopped the Jakarta Charter (and the idea that the state should be based on *shari'ah*) from being a sore point for political Islam.

With *Reformasi* and the freeing up of political life, the issue made a return to the political stage, with conservative Muslims again calling for Islamic law to be made formally binding for Muslims. This proposal was rejected decisively by the highest national legislature, the MPR (*Majelis Permusyawaratan Rakyat* – People's Consultative Assembly) in 2002 during amendment of the Constitution, and it instead became a basis for the rise of the "new" elites at the local level. This is because the massive decentralization and the devolution of power to Indonesia's many regions that followed Soeharto's fall in 1998 created a new basis for the rise to power of many traditional and religious leaders. Like their New Order military counterparts, one of the ways these leaders asserted themselves was by promises to deliver moral reform, only now these were framed by reference to conservative Islam rather than the New Order "secular religion" of development and security. More specifically, many of these new leaders revived the debate from 1945 about whether Islam should be enforced under state law. What easier way to air these new sources of legitimacy than to impose revanchist social constructions of womanhood expressed in conservative Islamic terms?

Women are easy targets because they comprise half the population but they are also strategic targets, as they exist across classes and other social divides, with links to men, each other and children. They also have their own social networks. Women are nurturers and educators who are

---

4   *Sip* is also a colloquial Indonesian term for "ready," or "prepared."

expected to transmit social and moral values. Like the New Order state, which created a top-down, fascist militaristic system to "domesticate" women, the revived traditional political elite began using conservative, even reactionary, religious interpretations of the Qur'an and *Sunnah* for very similar purposes. There is thus a remarkable consistency in much of modern Indonesian history, and the sidelining of the women's movements is part of it.

This was as true after Independence in 1945 and under the New Order as it has been under *Reformasi*. In all periods, women have been subjected to definitions of womanhood that conveniently allocate them a subordinate role. They exist to serve the political, ideological, economic, social and sexual interests of the male patriarchal oligarchy, to ensure the hegemony of that oligarchy. For example, as part of the systematic and violent annihilation of the Indonesian Communist Party (PKI) after 1965, military historians constructed a false but highly persuasive image of members of *Gerwani* (the women's organization affiliated with the PKI), portraying them as lewd, immoral, evil and demonic.[5]

Since the onset of *Reformasi*, some revisionist history books have sought to present a different interpretation of the alleged Communist coup of 1965 (known by its acronym, the G30S movement) and the role of General Soeharto and the military in the coup and killings that followed it. They have done this despite three decades of saturation myth-making about these events intended to legitimize Soeharto's rule.[6] Perhaps now it is also time to rewrite Indonesian history from a feminist perspective, fairly and squarely placing women in the picture, rather than relegating them to the sidelines, as is usually the case.

In the New Order (1966–98), womanhood was constructed in accordance with the prevailing authoritarian political ideology. Women were defined primarily as wives and mothers, there to serve their men, families, community, nation and state. Corporatist state organizations were created to contain and control them. Although the mere fact of this was a tacit acknowledgment of their power, almost all women's organizations and movements were firmly under the thumb of military might, legitimized by a fascist political ideology reminiscent of Europe in the 1930s–1940s (with its attendant sexism), and the active dumbing-down (*pembodohan*) of the masses through indoctrination and repression (see Suryakusuma 2011).

In the post-Soeharto Reform Era, the ideological basis for the New Order's social construction of womanhood began to dissolve but was quickly supplanted by the "Islamic" social construction of women described earlier that is just as, if not even more, repressive. As in the Soeharto era, the new (or revived) construction led by the new post-Soeharto elites was part-and-parcel of a long tradition of repression of Indonesian society by prevailing power groups.

---

5   Falsified reports described them engaging in orgies and mutilating the bodies and genitals of the seven army officers who were murdered and dumped into *Lubang Buaya* (Crocodile Hole) on the outskirts of Jakarta under the New Order foundational myth. The stigmatization of Gerwani members is a grim story of myth and misogyny produced to justify patriarchal military rule. See Drakeley (2007).

6   The official story is that G30S was an attempted Communist (PKI) takeover prevented only by Soeharto taking aggressive military action. This became the foundation myth that legitimized the New Order, helping it maintain its hold on the Indonesian people for 32 years. History, after all, is written by the victors, who often maintain their grip on their version of the truth by distorting, manipulating, banning, blacklisting, imprisoning or even killing. Losers are excluded or demonized, and history becomes the monopoly of those with political power.

## The Hard-line Islamist *Perda* Movement

The Reform movement created opportunities, but it also opened a Pandora's box from the past. What emerged were the political Islamic groups who, since Independence in 1945 (and, in fact, well before then), have sought to claim their place in the Republic, although their ultimate—if highly unlikely—goal has always been to create an Islamic state. In the early years after Independence in 1945, these groups had to vie for power with the military, the Communists and the nationalists. During the New Order, they were repressed and persecuted. *Reformasi* meant they could finally come out of the box, and in the regions they did so with a vengeance.

Invariably members of the new regional elites are male, and often they draw their authority from traditional local sources. In other words, new local leaders tend to look for legitimacy to conservative and socially-regressive value systems linked to local identity. This may be *adat* (traditional custom) but is usually intertwined with religion, and in most (but, significantly, not all) areas, that religion is Islam. In many regions, these groups or their proxies replaced Jakarta-endorsed bureaucrats who had once ruled at Soeharto's pleasure, without much reference to local needs. Most of the New Order bureaucrats, whatever their many failings (including entrenched corruption), had a strongly secular nationalist bent, and many had some level of commitment to a modernizing agenda. The old-for-new elites who emerged after Soeharto shared many of the flaws of their predecessors but rarely that modernizing agenda. Most, in fact, want to revive aspects of what they see as the traditional past to build their local legitimacy. They are now influencing local policy right across the country, even in areas where they have not won office, but are nonetheless potent social voices.

How did this happen? A series of local elections through to late 2005 seeking to implement post-Soeharto democratization and decentralization delivered dramatic political change in Indonesia, cementing a broader social process underway across the archipelago since 1998. The result was a wave of attempts to introduce conservative interpretations of *shari'ah*-derived moral norms through local regulations and by-laws, known as *Perda* (*Peraturan Daerah*, or regional regulations). This occurred most obviously in the autonomous province of Aceh, where it led to some social disruption, although many of the norms underpinning that province's new *shari'ah* system were long ago internalized, in part at least, by many Acehnese. *Shari'ah*-influenced *Perda* have been even more disruptive in other areas with greater religious and social plurality. These include West Java, West Sumatra and South Sulawesi, and, especially, urban Tangerang, on the outskirts of Jakarta, to give just a few examples of regions where "Islamizing" regulations have been proposed or introduced amid controversy.

That some of these new regulations are inspired to some extent by Muslim "hard-line" (*garis keras*) groups is clear. The drafting of the Acehnese laws, for example, drew inspiration from radical and very controversial *shari'ah* codes introduced by Malaysia's conservative rural Islamist party, PAS (Parti Islam Se-Malaysia) in Kelantan and Trengganu. Likewise, a local Congress that led to the drafting of a proposed law for South Sulawesi in 2001 was attended by Abu Bakar Ba'asyir, then recently returned from Malaysia. Ba'asyir is, of course, the alleged leader of the terrorist organization Jemaah Islamiyah and founder of *Majelis Mujahidin Indonesia* (Indonesian Jihad Fighters' Council).

Although the *Perda* movement is relatively new in Indonesia, the political ideas behind it are not, and they are linked to political Islam's repeated failure since 1945 to revive the Jakarta Charter as discussed in Chapter 10. When conservative Islamist parties were soundly defeated in the MPR in 2002 in their attempts to insert a clause similar to the Jakarta Charter into the Constitution, a proposal for which radicals, including Ba'asyir, had campaigned hard, their defeat led them to renew efforts to introduce legal grounds for *shari'ah* implementation at the local level. This they did through the *Perda* movement. Invigorated by success at the local level, the Islamist conservatives then came back at the national level. The Anti-Pornography Law is, in fact, the local *shari'ah* regulations writ large and is, to that extent, an attempt at *"shari'ah*-ization" of the Indonesian state by stealth. Like many of the *Perda*, the Anti-Pornography Law bans modern social behavior that offends conservative Islamic cultural norms. As originally proposed, it prohibited forms of expression that its supporters consider *pornoaksi* (pornographic actions). This covers sexually suggestive performances but it is interpreted loosely to include even public displays of affection such as spouses kissing in public or simply women's self-expression.

The first draft of the Law emerged around 1998 (10 years before the bill was ratified) but as a result of waves of protests it was repeatedly rewritten under the oversight of a special legislative committee (*Pansus*) headed by Balkan Kaplale. He argued that the final version of the Bill took into account all the original objections, chiefly by watering down over-regulation of clothing and the prohibition of *pornoaksi*. These were highly controversial provisions that many feared would ban sensual or sexually provocative movements, turning Indonesia's hugely popular *dangdut* singers,[7] with their gyrating hips, pouting lips and suggestive lyrics, into criminals, to give just one example. Despite Kaplale's claims, massive protests continued against the Bill, including in central Java, Bali and several times in Jakarta,[8] with counterattacks from the Muslim conservatives in the form of *fatwas*, public disparaging remarks and similar public rallies.[9] The protests against the Bill were justified, and Kaplale's claims that the Law as passed was substantially changed from the version contained in the earlier Bill were largely inaccurate.


**Indefinite Indecency**

The problem starts with the basic definition of "pornography" in article 1 of the Law as passed:

> Pornography includes pictures, sketches, illustrations, photographs, writings, vocalizations, sounds,
> moving pictures, animations, cartoons, conversation/dialogue/discussion, lewd sexual gestures, or

---

7    *Dangdut* is a genre of Indonesian pop music developed in the 1970s, partly derived from Malay, Arab and Hindustani music. It typically consists of a lead singer, often female, backed by a band.

8    Demonstrations against the Anti-Pornography Bill included the following: on March 15, 2006, thousands of artists in Solo staged a colossal art performance called *Gelar Seribu Tayub* ("A Thousand *Tayub* Performances," *tayub* being a sensual traditional Javanese dance, with hints of exoticism, sex and even prostitution); on April 22, 2006 thousands of people participated in a cultural carnival called *"Bhinneka Tunggal Ika"* (Unity in Diversity, Indonesia's national motto) in Central Jakarta; on May 13, 2006 dozens of artists calling themselves *"Masyarakat Bhinneka Tunggal Ika"* (Unity in Diversity Community) staged performances and poetry readings.

9    Demonstrations in support of the Pornography Bill included the following: on May 21, 2006, Muslim figures, including artists, and members of Muslim organizations calling themselves *"Aksi Sejuta Umat"* (The Demonstration of a Million Ummah) convened around the Hotel Indonesia roundabout; on May 27, 2006, the Muslim Council of Ulamas (MUI, *Majelis Ulama Indonesia*) issued a *fatwa* calling for the Bill to be enacted immediately; on June 1, 2006, Sinta Nuriyah, wife of former president Abdurahman Wahid, reported Fadholy el Munir, a member of the *Forum Betawi Rembug* (FBR, the Betawi Brotherhood Forum, a hardline vigilante gang which rules the Jakarta underworld) to the police for having insulted the female members of the Bhinneka Tunggal Ika carnival (mentioned in the previous notes) as being "corrupt, satanic women who destroy the morality of Indonesians." Fadholy had also threatened to attack the carnival and run its participants out of Jakarta.

messages in other forms made in any communication medium and/or public shows/exhibitions/ performances, that represents lewdness, salaciousness or obscenity, or sexual exploitation, that can arouse sexual desires and/or violate public moral values.[10]

This very broad definition covers sexually-oriented material generally—visual, written, auditory, verbal, movements—so long as it can be said to "arouse sexual desire" or offend "public moral values." But whose desire? Whose morals? Are bikinis now banned from the pages of women's magazines? Does this mean that telling a dirty joke to your friend becomes a criminal offense? And what of a news report of a DPR member cavorting naked with his *dangdut* singer girlfriend in a widely distributed cell phone video (yes, our politicians behave that way too)? The terminology of the definition is broad, vague and extremely subjective, and its application is therefore unpredictable in practice. In the first draft, public displays of affection (such as kissing or holding hands) were criminalized, as were exposing "sensitive" body parts such as breasts, thighs, belly and navel, as well as, incredibly, hair, shoulders and legs. In the Law as passed, these were eliminated, but the definition remains so dangerously vague and subjective that the law resembles a Rorschach test in practice and would likely still catch those things deleted from the first draft.

This was well understood in non-Muslim regions of Indonesia such as majority-Hindu Bali, where the locals voiced their objections loudly and frequently while the Law was still being debated in the DPR. For example, at a street rally on September 23, organized by the Bali Peoples' Component (*Komponen Rakyat Bali*, KRB), KRB Coordinator I Gusti Ngurah Harta denounced the bill forcefully, saying that it discriminated against women and, indeed, Hindu Balinese in general. Made Mangku Prastika, the governor, even sent a letter to President Susilo Bambang Yudhoyono (SBY) and House of Representatives Speaker, Agung Laksono, explaining why the Balinese were so opposed to the bill.

His points were well made. As with Papuans (who are mainly Christian or Animist), a lot of Balinese culture—dances, art, religion—involves the exposure of bodies, and many sacred Hindu symbols involve nudity—even their gods. Never mind tourist breasts and bellies on the beaches, images of *lingga-yoni* (penis and vagina in today's parlance) abound in Balinese art, and indeed, in much of this archipelago's pre-Islamic culture, with the famously erotic fifteenth-century Hindu Candi Sukuh (Sukuh Temple) in Central Java being one of the best-known examples.[11]

The Balinese protesters also argued that the Anti-Pornography Bill would put their livelihoods on the line. The beleaguered Balinese tourist industry, then devastated by the terrorist bombings aimed at tourist targets and Avian flu scares, would suffer again. None of these arguments were enough, however, to dissuade the national legislature from passing the Law in a form that, if enforced, could criminalize much of Bali's tourist industry and religious practice. The problem is, of course, even more significant for penis gourd-sheathed Papuans, at the far eastern end of the Indonesian archipelago, where traditional life often involves nakedness—if not every day, then certainly in ritual activity.

---

10    "Pornografi adalah gambar, sketsa, ilustrasi, foto, tulisan,suara, bunyi, gambar, bergerak, animasi, kartun, percakapan, gerak tubuh, atau bentuk pesan lainnya melalui berbagai bentuk media komunikasi dan/ atau pertunjukan di muka umum, yang memuat kecabulan atau eksploitasi seksual yang melanggar norma kesusilaan dalam masyarakat" (Law No. 44/2008: article 1(1)).

11    Candi Sukuh is a fifteenth-century Javanese-Hindu temple on the slope of Mount Lawu on the border between Central and East Java. It has a single pyramid surrounded by tortoises and a male figure grasping his penis. One of the statues, a giant 1.82 meter phallus with four balls representing penile incisions, was relocated to the National Museum of Indonesia, making it formally part of Indonesia's national heritage.

Articles 18 and 19 of the Anti-Pornography Law are also of concern. These give local governments authority to block Internet sites. With all the reports of bribery and incompetence at the district level in Indonesia, there is surely real danger in allowing local politicians to decide which websites can be accessed. And who will coordinate it? Quite apart from the obvious logistical problems in granting local government authority over the Internet (which transcends national boundaries with ease), these provisions are surely a recipe for corruption, or chaos at best.

Then there are articles 21 and 22, which deal with how the public can report, press charges, "socialize" people on the law and conduct *pembinaan* (supervision, support). Although the government has on several occasions said that these articles do not allow the community to take the law into their own hands as vigilantes to support the enforcement of the new anti-pornography provisions, the popular perception of their effect is precisely the opposite. In fact, articles 21 and 22 might as well be titled the "Defend Thuggery and the FPI (*Front Pembela Islam*, Islamic Defenders' Front)" clause. Hard-line Muslim groups who reject democracy[12] and smash up bars and hotels in Indonesian urban centers can rely on these clauses—or popular understandings of their effect, at any rate—to justify their violent, criminal brand of vigilantism in the name of protecting Islam.

A recent example involving religious freedom was an unprovoked and brutal attack by the FPI and other allied groups on unarmed men, women and children gathered in the park around the National Monument (*Monumen Nasional*, Monas, comparable to the Washington Monument in the United States) in downtown Jakarta on June 1, 2008.[13] The victims of FPI's violence at Monas were members of the AKKBB (*Aliansi Kebangsaan untuk Kebebasan Beragama dan Berkeyakinan*, the National Alliance for Freedom of Religion and Belief). Most were mainstream Muslims who came with their families to commemorate 63 years of Pancasila, the state ideology, which espouses religious pluralism, among other things. They felt that Indonesia's national motto *Bhinneka Tunggal Ika* (unity-in-diversity) was besieged by Muslim radicals. They also wanted to show solidarity with members of Ahmadiyah,[14] a marginal Muslim sect accused of doctrinal deviancy and now facing persecution as a result of a government clamp-down on the proselytizing of their beliefs. Unfortunately, articles 21 and 22 of the Pornography Law have the potential to be used in the future to authorize these sorts of attacks, which go much further than stopping pornography. They do, in fact, threaten the political settlement reached in 1945 by which the essentially secular nature of the state as expressed in the Pancasila became a guarantee of religious freedom, a settlement that still lies at the heart of the modern Indonesian polity.

It is not unreasonable for the legislature to want to take further steps to combat Indonesia's out-of-control pornography industry, which has earned the country the dubious honor of being the world's No. 2 "porno heaven" after Russia. But isn't the obvious solution just to enforce the existing law on pornography? As it stands now, the penalty for pornography under the Criminal Code (KUHP) is grossly inadequate: a maximum term of one-and-a-half years' imprisonment and a fine of just Rp. 4,500 (less than US$ 0.50). Surely toughening up the existing law and enforcing it—challenging though that would doubtless be—would be better than pandering to hang-ups about sexuality, religious difference and dissent generated by the far right of Indonesia's Muslim

---

12   Compare Hilmy (2010).

13   The attack was carried out by about 200 members of the Islamic Defenders Front armed with bamboo sticks, stones, swords and broken glass (see www.indonesiamatters.com/1797/aliansi-kebangsaan/).

14   Ahmadiyah is an Islamic group founded by Mirza Ghulam Ahmad in India in the 1880s, and which has since split into two groups. The first, Ahmadiyah Lahore, is the more moderate group and accepted Ahmad as a reformer, but not a prophet. They are more often accepted by mainstream Islam. The second, Ahmadiyah Qadiani, is considered more radical because it is believed to accept Ahmad's claims that he was a prophet after the Prophet Muhammad.

community? So how did the Bill get passed and made into law despite vociferous protests from all over the nation? After all, there was strong opposition from Yogyakarta, North Sulawesi and East Nusa Tenggara, and Balinese and Papuans even threatened to secede from the Republic.

The personal moral and social conservatism of the current president, Soesilo Bambang Yoedhoyono, is one reason the Law was passed. Political expediency is another. Prior to the presidential elections in July 2009, the president felt he needed the support of the Islamist Prosperous Justice Party (Partai Keadilan Sejahtera, PKS) (Hilmy 2010), which was pushing for the Pornography Bill. When Yudhoyono signed it into law on November 26, 2008, he said that he did so after having "examined" it and finding that it "guaranteed freedom of expression and protected traditional customs," although, in fact, it does neither of these things in any meaningful way. The president did, however, receive firm PKS support in his successful bid for re-election in July 2009, six months later.


## Fighting Back

Regardless of why the Law was passed, implementation has so far been minimal (consisting to date only of the arrest of those involved in the Bandung "sexy dancing" incident,[15] and the prosecution of Ariel, the male rock singer who appeared in the widely-circulated "Peterporn" celebrity sex video and a few others involved in this incident) (see Suryakusuma 2010). Resistance to the Law has also been strong. Many groups said they would challenge the validity of the Law if it were enacted,[16] and there have been three applications to Indonesia's new post-Soeharto Constitutional Court (*Mahkamah Konstitusi*) by a total of 43 groups, all seeking constitutional review of the Anti-Pornography Law. The Court eventually upheld the controversial Law in a 405-page opinion. It implied an exception for "traditional culture" or performance but left objecting groups dissatisfied because of fears about the Law's vagueness and apparent breadth. Tellingly, only the Court's sole female justice (who is also a Christian) dissented, stressing the Law's vagueness and its consequent lack of legal certainty. The Court's decision is binding, however, and cannot be appealed. It therefore drew immediate declarations from provincial governments in majority non-Muslim areas including Bali and Papua that it would simply be ignored and not be enforced.


## "If You're Not for Us, You're Against Us"

Often what becomes a social or political issue depends on who takes the first step to define it as one. This was the case with the issue of pornography in Indonesia. It was socially conservative Muslims—particularly hard-line Islamists—who first raised publicly the dangers and destructive nature of pornography, claiming it threatened the moral fiber of society, and therefore the integrity of the nation. Through decades of agitating, they have become more adroit at identifying issues and running socio-political campaigns than the pro-democracy camp (including women's groups),

---

15   "Bandung Sexy Dancers Busted for Stirring Desires," *The Jakarta Globe*, January 6, 2010, www. thejakartaglobe.com/home/bandung-sexy-dancers-could-face-15-years-in-jail-police/350979.

16   For example, I Made Mangku Pastika, Governor of Bali, said in late December 2008 that he would support any effort to challenge the Law in the Constitutional Court. Likewise, Cirylus Bau Engo of the Nusa Tenggara Timur (NTT) parliament said the people of NTT didn't want the Law. Andrikus Mofu of the Council of Churches in West Papua, a Christian organization, has also said his organization would sponsor a class action against the Law.

which has been publicly active only since 1998. The hard-line Muslim groups had much experience over the decades since 1945 in manipulating imagery and terminology to their advantage, and so they were able early on to impose their own understanding of what constitutes "pornography." In doing so, they won control of the very definition of the term itself, thus obtaining a huge advantage in the battle to pass the Law.

Pornography is difficult to define. One person's pornography is another's erotica, and in the case of Indonesia, our culture and tradition is, as mentioned, replete with sexual symbols, and sensual expressions in the arts, both performative and visual. For many socially conservative Muslims in Indonesia, however, the issue is often not one of substance. They do not propose to emulate the Taliban at Bamiyan by destroying national heritage but rather aim to identify an issue they feel will resonate with many, act as a rallying point and allow them to publicly identify themselves as "guardians of morality."

According to Neng Dara Affiah, a commissioner of the National Commission on Violence against Women (see www.komnasperempuan.or.id/), and Head of Research and Development of the Fatayat NU, the women's wing of Nahdlatul Ulama (NU—the world's largest Muslim organization), the Islamists' strategic use of language enabled them to polarize the debate into simple extremes. Whoever was not with them against pornography, was, in their terms, against them—and thus for pornography. At one point, Affiah herself was summoned by the Central Board of NU, and questioned. "You wear a *jilbab* [headscarf] and are from a *pesantren* [traditional Muslim boarding school]," they said, "How can you reject the Pornography Law? You should repent!" (Affiah 2009a[17]).

Another example of conservative Islam's manipulation of meanings relates to the word "liberal." This has been stigmatized as something created by the West, and therefore evil and immoral. In this way, the progressive Liberal Islam Network (*Jaringan Islam Liberal*, JIL: see http://islamlib.com/en/pages/about/) has been branded as an enemy of not just Muslims but seemingly of all Indonesians. JIL is, in fact, a group of progressive Muslim scholars who believe in individual freedoms and that Muslims in a plural society like Indonesia should not be tied to literal interpretations of the scriptures. Instead they argue for more relative interpretations, based on social contexts and realities. Members of JIL are few, and they have little social, let alone political, power although they do have some intellectual clout. Yet at the grassroots level rejection of JIL has been widespread and uncompromising, due to the very negative connotations that the conservatives have now been able to attach to the term "liberal" (Neng Dara Affiah 2009, personal communication March 16).

Similar strategies were used during debate over the Anti-Pornography Bill, and the substance of the drafting quickly became much less significant than the polemics involved. Affiah has, for example, recounted how at a public dialogue that formed part of the process of the drafting of the Bill, her attempt to discuss the critical issue of the definition of "pornography" was summarily cast aside. What was important for the Islamists was the political battle and the symbolic struggle they saw themselves as engaged in. The nuances of definitions were a distraction, and so they actively sought to exclude their opponents from the drafting processes.

In this way, the conservative anti-democratic groups put the pro-democracy groups—including women's groups—at a huge disadvantage. Alarmed but helpless, they could only intervene after the drafting process was already well advanced, and were therefore able to make only superficial changes. This was ironic, because international regulations on anti-trafficking, especially child

---

17   Affiah is the author of a recent memoir: *Muslimah Feminis: Penjelajahan Multi Identitas* (A Muslim Feminist: an Exploration of Multiple Identities) (Affiah 2009b).

trafficking and child pornography, have long been a central part of the agenda of the Indonesian's women's movement.

## Men on Women

It would be a mistake to think that the women's movement consists only of women, or that only women have opposed recent efforts at legal Islamization. Men are also involved and the case of Kyai Haji Husein Muhammad is a particularly interesting one.[18] The head of the Al-Tauhid Al-Islami Arjawinangun pesantren in Cirebon on the north coast of Java, Kyai Husein is also founder of three Muslim feminist organizations, one of which, Fahmina, is also located in Cirebon.[19]

Kyai Husein's views on women are as progressive as one would expect from a secular, Western-style feminist despite his extensive use of the *Kitab Kuning* (literally, "yellow books," the classical texts approved by the Ministry of Religion for teaching in the pesantrens, some medieval in origin). In fact, Kyai Husein draws upon the *Kitab Kuning* to produce a feminist interpretation of Islamic *fiqh*, or jurisprudence (see Husein 2009). In this way, Kyai Husein is a personification of progressive Islam, and living proof that Islam, pluralism, feminism and male authority can, in fact, be compatible.

This, of course, is not a popular combination so far as conservative Islamists are concerned, especially in the dramatically polarized climate created by the controversy over the Anti-Pornography Bill. On May 21, 2006, for example, the vigilante group Islamic Brotherhood Forum (FUI, *Forum Ukhuwah Islamiyah*) and a coalition of Islamic organizations in Cirebon, demanded that Fahmina's office be closed down. It happened to be Sunday, and no one was present except an office boy, so the 30 protesters picketed the building. They carried placards saying "Fahmina Asia Foundation poisonous NGOs," "Fahmina is a lackey of foreigners" (meaning the West)[20] and "Closed down for selling Allah's verses very cheaply. Closed down in the name of Muslims who support the Anti-Pornography Bill."[21]

Fahmina had not made any official statement on the Bill, so it was strange that they were attacked in this way. Personally, Kyai Husein agreed with the broad aims of the bill but the drafts were problematic, he felt, as they could extinguish Indonesia's social and religious pluralism, and victimize women—precisely the group whom the Bill should, in fact, protect. In 2006, he therefore wrote an article (Husein 2006a) and an unpublished paper (Husein 2006b) containing strong arguments against the Bill as it stood, saying that it was too vague and open to interpretation, would curtail Indonesia's rich cultural diversity and would criminalize women.

In his article "Perempuan Menari" (Dancing Women) (Husein 2006a) talked specifically about the Anti-Pornography Bill prohibiting sensual and elegant movements in traditional Indonesian

---

18　*Kyai* is a Javanese title loosely indicating that a person is an *ulama* (alim), or Muslim religious scholar. It is often used for the head of a pesantren (traditional Islamic boarding school). A *haji* is someone who has gone on the *hajj* pilgrimage to Mecca.

19　For a more detailed account of Fahmina see http://fahmina.or.id/en/. The two other organizations are Rahmina (www.rahima.or.id/) and Puan Amal Hayati (www.puanamalhParagraphi.or.id/), both in Jakarta (Puan Amal Hayati has branches across Java). All now work closely with pesantrens and other religious institutions, mainly at the grassroots level.

20　Fahmina receives some of its funding from The Asia Foundation (http://asiafoundation.org/country/overview/indonesia).

21　Interview with Kyai Husein Muhammad by Yerry Niko Borang, Voice of Human Rights, Human Rights News Centre, May 23, 2006.

dances, like *jaipong* from West Java, and others from Bali. In this article, he recounted a visit he made to Cairo in 1998 to attend an international conference for Muslim countries on reproductive health. The conference, which was opened at Al Azhar, one of the world's most prestigious Islamic universities, was attended by *ulamas* (religious scholars) and reproductive health experts from all over the globe. At the end of the conference, the participants were invited to a dinner cruise on the Nile. In the middle of the dinner, as they were enjoying a meal, music and beautiful moonlit scenery, a belly dancer suddenly appeared. Dressed in a flowing chiffon skirt fastened very low on the hips, her breasts were covered by a revealing bra-top—standard belly dancer attire. She swayed her hips in what would be considered an extremely sexually provocative way according to the Indonesian Pornography Law, and made sensual movements with her arms, chest and eyes. The only response she got was pleased smiles and thunderous applause.

Kyai Husein and the other Indonesian participants looked at each other, and then at their Egyptian hosts, highly-regarded *ulama*, who were calmly enjoying the show. Kyai Husein recounted he was trembling because he was afraid the dancer would approach and ask him to dance. So he sneaked out and watched with pleasure from behind the safe cover of a window until the dance was over. He wrote in his article, his tongue firmly in cheek, that "after dinner we went home, and had no intention at all after watching the dance to commit any act of violence against women." From this experience Kyai Husein reasoned that if the *ulama* of Cairo who taught Islam to aspiring religious scholars from all over the world, including Indonesia, could not only accept but enjoy an extremely sensual dance, with much of the woman's body exposed, why could we not do the same in Indonesia, where dancers' clothing is usually much more modest?

**When is a Spade not a Spade?**

The Anti-Pornography Law is not really about pornography. It is about denying women and sexuality public space. It uses pornography as an excuse, equating expression of sexuality outside the marriage bed—even the very presence of women outside the home—with obscenity and criminality. And it would lock up artists and writers who present these themes, as do many artists in most societies, including Indonesia.

The irony is thus that reforms intended to give democracy and the right to a voice to millions of Indonesians silenced for decades under Soeharto may now strip away from half of them some of the few rights they enjoyed under his rule. While decentralization may deliver political democracy to the regions, it can also deny social democracy—at least for women and non-Muslims. So far, however, this hasn't happened in a widespread or consistent fashion, but there is a real *Kulturkampf* in progress.

It is true that the Indonesian government is driven by a kind of panicky political fear of offending the 80 percent-plus Muslim electorate, and so it becomes the dog that is wagged by the tail of minority Muslim radical conservatives and hard-liners. The result has been much moralizing rhetoric and, of course, the Anti-Pornography Law itself. But the government also cannot ignore protests by artists, activists, intellectuals, some Muslim religious leaders and many members of non-Muslim ethnic groups, including some regional leaders, all of whom see the Law as a direct threat to the diversity and democracy at the heart of new post-Soeharto "*Reformasi*" Indonesia. The government's reaction so far has therefore mainly been to simply ignore the Law. Aside from Ariel, no artist has yet been arrested under the Law and neither has any member of a religious minority, while hard-core pornography continues to be widely available in all shapes and form. There is, in fact, as mentioned, a huge market for pornography in Indonesia, which it seems, few really want to eradicate—not the consumers, and certainly not the producers and marketers or those who profit from its existence (including, of course, corrupt police and politicians).

Regulating moral behavior by fiat is something that most authority figures erroneously believe is easy. Here we see the "chicken or egg" question in practice. They pass a law, impose a regulation or pronounce a *fatwa* (legal opinion of an Islamic religious scholar) and believe that will do the job. Not in Indonesia! In fact, this country is a perfect example of the shortcomings of law as a means of social engineering. Like the recent anti-smoking ban first introduced in February 2006 in metropolitan Jakarta, the Anti-Pornography Law has had little impact on people's behavior. So, for example, the opening film at the widely-publicized 'V Jakarta International Women's Film Festival' held in April 2009 included full-frontal nudity that was advertised in advance, and it did not attract any attempt at enforcement of the Anti-Pornography Law by either state or religious authorities. On the other hand, the Q! Film Festival (see www.qfilmfestival.org/), encountered resistance from the Islamic Defenders Front (FPI) from the moment it began in 2002. Somehow the organizers of the festival were able to persuade the FPI to leave them alone until 2010, when the Q! Film Festival again received violent protests from the FPI, as well as calls from the Indonesian Ulama Council (MUI, *Majelis Ulama Indonesia*) for its banning.[22] Despite all this, the Q! Film Festival continues to be held and the Anti-Pornography Law has not been invoked to stop it.

## National Identity and Weapons of Mass Distraction

In the midst of the many far more pressing problems that Indonesia faces, and the fact that the issues meant to be covered by the Anti-Pornography Law were already covered by the Criminal Code, broadcasting laws, and laws on child protection, it seems the debate over the Law is now a largely symbolic one. And interestingly, despite their success with the passing of the Anti-Pornography Law, conservative Muslims still face strong resistance from mainstream liberal and tolerant thinking, from non-Muslim minorities, from a popular dislike for moral authoritarianism, and from an increasingly prosperous middle-class that fears a religious or repressive government. For these groups, as for the conservative Muslims, the Law remains a proxy for a broader and persistent debate: should Indonesian Muslims be forced to follow *shari'ah* law and, if so, whose version of *shari'ah*? Disagreement was intense among Indonesia's founding fathers in 1945 and there is no sign that much has changed after 50 years of debate—except that now women are part of the argument too.

In fact, the debate today is far more complex that it has ever been before. For the 32 years of Soeharto's repressive New Order, Islam in Indonesia was cloistered and controlled, its expressions watchfully—sometimes violently—monitored by the state. Since 1998, however, the modernization, globalization and the democratization accelerated by the openness and political deregulation of post-Soeharto *Reformasi* have liberated a multitude, both reactionary and conservative Muslims, as well as those who support the new liberal democratic system. The result is that today Indonesian Muslims of all persuasions can play out their faith in many spheres—political, economic and popular—in myriad ways unimaginable before.

Some of the results are conservative, dogmatic, reactionary, or progressive and liberal, and others are outright weird and wacky, but all show creativity and adaptability, as new ways are found to express old beliefs. This type of hybrid, localized faith has always been a feature of

---

22    See Suryakusuma (2009). See also Giado (2010).

Indonesian Islam, and it has made Indonesia a showcase of Muslim diversity. Given its ethnic, cultural and social plurality, is that surprising?

Yes, Indonesia has hard-liners who use religion to justify destructive and atrocious acts of violence but it also has influential liberal intellectuals and long-established, softer Sufi (mystic) traditions, as well as syncretic groups (mixing Islam with local animistic and pagan beliefs), and, of course, political Islam, already a fixture of our rowdy, adolescent democracy. Now add to this potent brew the new savvy preacher-businessmen. They use commercial methodology and the latest information technology to mass-market their wares to eager consumers, hungry for instant, pre-packaged *nafkah batin* (spiritual sustenance) in an increasingly materialistic, chaotic and confusing world.

One product of this new industry celebrity (television) preachers, exemplified by the controversial Aa Gym,[23] with his theatrical but down-to-earth style. Newfangled *da'i* (preachers) like him are all the rage, providing religious advice, solace and entertainment. And why not? If Indonesians have infotainment and edutainment, why not "*dakwah-tainment*" too? After all, *dakwah* or "call" (to religion) is compulsory for all Muslims. Traditionally it referred to preaching, predication and Islamic outreach, but now even activities with no primary religious meaning can be considered *dakwah*. Performing one's vocation, carrying out family duties, doing business, art and even fashion shows all qualify. Needless to say, Muslim fashion in Indonesia means fancy, funky, elaborate and often extravagant designs, and, of course, a riot of colors. This is Indonesia's creative conservatism at its best and it enables women to follow what they see as spiritual dictates but still feel sexy.

There are also the phenomena of Internet *fatwa* shopping; Googling a *kyai* (religious scholar); alms-giving via mobile phone; mass religious rallies in soccer fields; glossy Muslim women's magazines (as well as hard-line jihadi ones); Islamic medical treatments; a booming *halal* industry; multi-level marketing of *halal* products; and fast-growing *shari'ah* banking services as well as Islamic microfinance as well. These are just some of the manifestations of a new consumer-oriented approach to Islam.

Sometimes the new modi operandi interact with more traditional expressions of faith, and sometimes they replace them. Overall, the (very visible) trend is the commodification of piety and an extraordinary conflation of the sacred, mundane and profane. It is hard to imagine a televangelist in the West delivering sermons in *sinetron* (Indonesian TV soap operas) style, sprinkled with humor and even sexually-suggestive jokes, or serenading his wife during a mass sermon with the Everly Brothers' "Let It Be Me." These things could probably only happen in Indonesia, which has always displayed an eclectic character and an ability to comfortably combine the sacred with the mundane and the religious with the sensual and sexual.

The obvious conclusion to be drawn is that the post-Soeharto re-engagement of Islam and public life in Indonesia has changed Indonesian society but it has also changed Indonesian Islam. It is democratic and exciting, but sometimes it can be anarchic too, with anyone able to issue *fatwa* online, and religious consumers shopping around for whatever answer suits them. The truth is that after 32 years of repression and 10 years of euphoric freedom, Islam in Indonesia is still trying to find a balance, and some wobbling along the way is inevitable. It is quite possible that the Anti-Pornography Law is just part of that wobble but it is not to be dismissed as nothing more than that,

---

23    Aa Gym is the popular name of Abdullah Gymnastiar, a popular Muslim cleric, who developed significant commercial interests around his media, preaching and educational activities, especially at his base Pondok Pesantren Darut Tauhid in Bandung. In 2006, he took a second wife contrary to his own previous support for monogamy, thus damaging his previously extremely high popularity.

for two reasons. The first is that it while conservative Muslims have been given a symbolic victory, the Law is still there for anyone to invoke. The second is more a question than a reason: what long-term real effect will the Anti-Pornography Law and the conservative Islamic movement have on the social construction of womanhood, and on the women's movement?

### *Cherchez la Femme*: What are Women Doing About It?

Pornography, in the conventional sense of the word is a more-or-less inevitable product of the free-market, of Indonesia's engagement in the global economy. It has long been present in Indonesia but, as I argued in the opening to this chapter, that is not what the Anti-Pornography Law is really about. Rather, it is a regressive attempt to create a social construction of womanhood aimed not just at containing and controlling women, but also at creating a society that is in line with a particular vision of what an Islamic society should be—one that would be very different indeed to Islamic society as it currently exists in Indonesia. The hard-liners on the Muslim right apparently believe that changing law will change behavior, despite all the evidence to the contrary presented by Indonesian history. In terms of modus operandi, the Anti-Pornography Law thus smacks very much of New Order ways, when state ideology on womanhood was a means to buttress state ideology and power, as well as the systematic repression of civil society. The New Order believed firmly in social engineering by law, and this is a local tradition that the Islamists seem to have inherited.

But if in the New Order tensions and conflicts were vertical, they are now decidedly horizontal, playing out between a politically motivated and very vocal "religious" minority, and the rest of Indonesian society, who are usually much less ready to voice their views. The Anti-Pornography Law has, however, been a trigger for the latter group to rise up and express powerful resistance in the form of demonstrations, petitions, letters to the DPR, street rallies, discussions, talk-shows, Internet blogs and so on.

What are women doing in the midst of all this? While there are similarities between the process of controlling women between the New Order and the Reform Era, there is one major difference: Indonesia is now a democracy. The women's movement has had a chance to wake up from its 32-year slumber and many women are not willing to passively accept this revival of old tactics by new groups. The women's movement in Indonesia is, however, by no means monolithic. There are, in fact, many who agree with the Anti-Pornography Law, including Meutia Hatta, the Minister of Women's Affairs. She has even claimed that the passing of the Anti-Pornography Bill was a "historic moment in Indonesia's democracy and its aims were noble."[24] Her views have won support from both secular and religious women's groups. This is partly because of the manipulation of the term "pornography," discussed at the beginning of this chapter,but also because of a lack of gender awareness among many women.

The groups that oppose the Anti-Pornography Law are also made up of both secular and religious women's groups. The former include, among others, LBH APIK, *Solidaritas Perempuan* (Women's Solidarity), *Komnas Perempuan* (short for *Komisi Nasional Anti Kekerasan Terhadap Perempuan*, National Commission on Violence against Women), KPI (*Koalisi Perempuan Indonesia untuk Keadilan dan Demokrasi*, the Women's Coalition for Justice and Democracy),

---

24   Meutia Hatta even went so far as to "guarantee" that the Pornography Law would not oppress women at all, and in fact was a means for the state to "protect its citizens." She also said that it would in no way be a threat to Indonesia's pluralism (see www.kompas-tv.com/content/view/7569/2 and http://beritasore. com/2008/11/03/meutia-hatta-uu-pornografi-tak-diskriminatif/).

SPEK-HAM (*Solidaritas Perempuan untuk Kemanusiaan dan Hak Asasi Manusia*, Women's Solidarity for Humanity and Human Rights), and others. The latter, Islamic-based, groups, include some of those mentioned earlier (Rahmina, Fahmina, Puan Amal Hayati), as well as individuals who work within Islam, such as Musdah Mulia,[25] Ciciek Farha,[26] Neng Dara Affiah and Kyai Haji Husein Muhammad. A unique case is Affiah's Fatayat NU, the women's wing of the Nadhlatul Ulama (see Candland and Nurjanah 2004), the only Muslim mass organization that is publicly opposed to the Law.

These Islamic women's groups—which include men as well— confront huge challenges in pursuing their opposition to the Anti-Pornography Law, as they face accusations that by doing so they are "betraying their faith." But just as it brings challenges, so the new Law also brings opportunities. Women's resistance to the Anti-Pornography Law provides a lens through which to see the rise of women since the onset of *Reformasi*, and their active involvement in areas as diverse as politics (in both the executive and legislature), law, literature, performing arts, the media, human rights, and social activism, among others (Allen 2009). Ironically, the Anti-Pornography Law has given women—both secular and religious—the opportunity to rally for, and defend, their rights by engaging in a public discourse that directly involves them, their bodies and their sexuality. This would have been difficult to do prior to controversy emerging over this Law. In fact, according to Mariana Amiruddin, editor-in-chief of *Jurnal Perempuan*, a feminist journal, the Anti-Pornography Law is the first regulatory instrument in which women's bodies are overtly identified as the problem— the cause of moral degradation (Allen 2009). The debate over the Anti-Pornography Law has thus publicly demonstrated the feminist dictum "the personal is political" in a way that has never happened before in Indonesia.


**Conclusion: A Polarized Future**

In this sense, the debate and controversy surrounding the Anti-Pornography Law is a manifestation of democracy in action in Indonesia, and a sign that Indonesia's newly revived civil society is, in fact, thriving, despite more than 30 years of repression and domination by the state. *Reformasi* gave repressed Muslim groups the chance to come out of the woodwork but it gave the same opportunity to the women's movement as well. *Reformasi* has, in fact, been witness to the resurrection of the women's movement, and of women's consciousness in general, whether or not identifying with the women's movement. In this way, the Anti-Pornography Law has served to clarify the issues that matter to women activists and intellectuals. It has thus defined the battlefield between them and the forces of patriarchal religious conservatives more clearly.

The lessons in terms of the "chicken or egg question" addressed by this volume are mixed. On the one hand, conservative Muslim groups that supported the Anti-Pornography Bill debate alternated between treating the Law as symbolic discourse exercise (hence resisting discussion of gritty details like definitions) and viewing the law as social engineering specifically intended

---

25    Siti Musdah Mulia is a well-known Muslim intellectual, a professor at the Islamic State University (Universitas Islam Negeri, UIN, in Jakarta) and an adviser to the Minister of Religion. In 2004, she led a team that drafted a controversial and progressive "Counter Legal Draft" to replace the national Compilation of Islamic Law. The draft was rejected. In 2007, the United States awarded her an International Woman of Courage award.

26    Ciciek Farha (Farha Abdul Kadir Assegaf) was head, and is now board member, of Rahima, a progressive Muslim NGO. She is a highly-regarded gender researcher and scholar working on women in radical Islamist organizations.

to change behavior. On the other hand, groups opposing the Anti-Pornography Bill regarded it as an extremist attack on women and diversity, treating it as threatening behavior even if non-enforcement seems the short-term policy response. While women and (non-Islamic) minority groups were most vocal in their opposition, the debate over the Anti-Pornography Bill was always more of a *Kulturkampf* within Indonesian Islam. This suggests that Indonesian society for "chicken or egg question" purposes is more often heterogeneous than homogeneous and the underlying question raised by the pornography debate is, whose society is it, really?

To answer this, it is important to look at the performance of Islamic political parties. The trend since the end of the Soeharto era in 1998 is clear. In 1999, the first free elections of the Reform Era, Islamist parties (which include the nationalist Islamic parties, see Fealy 2009)[27] gained 35 percent of votes in total. In 2004, the figure was still a close 33 percent, but in the April 2009 legislative elections, they secured only 25.5 percent. When this is compared to the 44 percent they won in 1955, the decline seems greater still. The trend clearly indicates that historically Islamization and *shari'ah*-ization are not what the electorate wants. This suggests that the Muslim social conservatives in Indonesia are, in fact, merely a minority with declining electoral clout. Like their Christian Right counterparts in the United States their efforts to gain political control lead them to mix law, morality and "religion," and, in the process, create much unrest, as well as resistance from those who are, in fact, the majority. [28]

There is also a fundamental difference in the constellation of forces in *Reformasi* as opposed to the period before 1998. If in the past, the state stood above and dominated civil society, in post-Soeharto Indonesia, the state stands in the middle, mediating and moderating the pro-democracy camp, the anti-democracy camp, and the forces of globalization, which include the free market. In the pro-democracy camp are the secular, the religious, politicians, activists, intellectuals, the press, artists and women, but in the anti-democracy camp you find exactly the same combination. The legal restrictions on so-called "pornography" so fiercely debated in the public arena in connection with this new Law are thus not solely a moral issue but also a vital source of legitimacy for social conservatives. "Pornography" is used by the anti-democracy camp to hold Indonesia back, making it a state akin in many respects to the New Order but this time imbued with their notion of "Islamic values" and thus under their control. They must now contend, however, with a multitude of other genies released from the same *Reformasi* bottle, including civil society groups that have also woken from their fear-and-repression-induced slumber, just like the Muslim groups.

Since 1998, the conflict between these groups has become more polarized. Conservative groups under the banner of Islam now face women's groups and their other progressive allies. This will not be easy for the conservatives. For them, women's power symbolizes a progressive force, one that they dismiss as liberal, Western, immoral, and with which they are distinctly uncomfortable. For the pro-democracy forces, however, the issue not just about women's bodies, but also about a

---

27    The two nationalist, sometimes also called pluralist, Islamic parties are the National Awakening Party (PKB) and National Mandate Party (PAN), who, unlike the pure Islamist parties such as the United Development Party (PPP) and the Crescent Star Party (PBB), do not call for the implementation of *shari'ah* in Indonesia.

28    Rick Santorum, an American politician and candidate for the Republican Party presidential nomination, is a prominent example of this. He holds socially highly conservative positions, including opposition to contraception (saying "It's a license to do things in a sexual realm that is counter to how things are supposed to be."), abortion (even for rape victims), same sex marriage, and separation of state and church. In fact, he said John F. Kenedy's famous 1960 speech that religion should be separated from politics makes him want to 'throw up' (http://www.politico.com/blogs/politico-live/2012/02/santorum-jfk-speech-makes-him-115569.html)

body politic—be it gendered, ethnic, or religious—that refuses to be subjected to the dictates of a conservative few, who, like the New Order apparatchiks before them, are motivated by power. In this sense, the battle over the issues raised by the Anti-Pornography Law is far from over.

In fact, it may have only just begun. We now live in interesting times—and in Indonesia that is not always a curse.

**References**

Affiah, N.D. 2009a. Focus Group Discussion, at the *National Commission on Violence against Women*, March 16.

Affiah, N.D. 2009b. *Muslimah Feminis: Penjelajahan Multi Identitas*. Jakarta: Penerbit Nalar.

Allen, P. 2009. Women Gendered Activism and the Anti-Pornography Bill. *Intersections: Gender and Sexuality in Asia and the Pacific*, Issue 19. Available at: http://intersections.anu.edu.au/issue19/allen.htm.

Anshor, M.U. and White, S. 2008. Islam and Gender in Contemporary Indonesia: Public Discourses on Duties, Rights, and Morality, in *Expressing Islam: Religious Life and Politics in Indonesia*, edited by G. Fealy and S. White. Singapore: INSEAS.

Bayuni, E. 2006. Porn Bill Exposes Culture War Fault Lines. *The Jakarta Post*, 27 March.

Bush, R. 2008. Regional Sharia Regulations in Indonesia: Anomaly or Symptom?, in *Expressing Islam: Religious Life and Politics in Indonesia*, edited by G. Fealy and S. White. Singapore: ISEAS, 174–91 (2007 Indonesia Update).

Candland, C. and Nurjanah, S. 2004. *Women's Empowerment through Islamic Organizations: The Role of Indonesia's "Nahdlatul Ulama" in Transforming the Government's Birth Control Programme into a Family Welfare Programme*. Available at: www.wellesley.edu/Polisci/Candland/KBIndonesia.pdf.

Drakeley, S. 2007. *Lubang Buaya*: Myth, Misogyny, and Massacre. *Nebula*, December, 11–35. Available at: www.nobleworld.biz/images/Drakeley.pdf.

Fealy, G. 2009. Indonesia's Islamic Parties in Decline. *Inside Indonesia*, May 11.

Giado, S. 2010. Long-Running Gay Indonesian Film Festival Faced Attacks. *Illume*, October 19. Available at: www.illumemagazine.com/zine/articleDetail.php?Long-running-Indonesian-Gay-Film-Festival-Faced-Attacks-13350.

Hilmy, M. 2010. *Islamism and Democracy in Indonesia: Piety and Pragmatism*. Singapore: INSEAS.

Husein, M. 2009. *The Women's Movement*. Available at: http://fahmina.or.id/en/index.php?option=com_content&view=article&id=593:womens-movement&catid=15:articles&Itemid=74.

Husein, M. 2006a. Perempuan menari. *Kompas*, March 11. Available at: http://khhuseinmuhammad.blogspot.com/2011/02/perempuan-menari.html.

Husein, M. 2006b. *RUU Pornografi dan Pornoaksi: Sebaiknya Bagaimana*? Unpublished paper delivered at a seminar on the Pornography Bill, Sumenep, Madura, February 27.

Law No. 44/2008. Available at: www.lbh-apik.or.id/uu-pornografi.htm.

Puan Amal Hayati. Available at: www.puanamalhParagraphi.or.id/.

Rahima. Available at: www.rahima.or.id/.

Religious Rights Groups Demand Litmus Test for Supreme Court. 2001. *Church and State*, 54. Available at: www.thefreelibrary.com/religious+right+Groups+Demand+Litmus+Test+For+Supreme+Court.-a079515428.

Schwartz, H. 2003. *The Rehnquist Court: Judicial Activism on the Right.* New York: Hill and Wang.

Suryakusuma, J. 2009. Thank Q! The Gayest Indonesian Film Festival. *Garuda Inflight Magazine*, September. Available at: www.juliasuryakusuma.com/column.php?menu_id=3&year=2009&month=9&column_id=270.

Suryakusuma, J. 2010. "Dirty Dancing" or "The Sound of MUI-sic"? *The Jakarta Post*, January. Photographs available at: http://jendralberita.wordpress.com/2010/03/08/foto-penari-striptis-di-bel-air-cafe-bandung/.

Suryakusuma, J. 2011. *State Ibuism: The Social Construction of Womanhood in New Order Indonesia.* Jakarta: Komunitas Bambu.

# Chapter 12
# Legal Pluralism and the Three-Cornered Case Study of Women's Inheritance Rights Changing in Lombok

Erman Rajagukguk

Indonesia enjoys a pluralistic legal system, particularly in family law areas like divorce and inheritance. The reasons for this are formally the continuation of ethnically-based personal legal jurisdiction principles reaching back to Dutch colonial times. So we face under differing circumstances Islamic law, customary or ethnically-based *adat* law, and secular national law in inheritance matters. For our purposes, we can precisely trace the details of our "chicken or egg" question because the treatment of women in inheritance matters traditionally differs according to which legal approach is applied, but shows development in the practical overlap.

Our inquiry proceeds via an examination at the "ethnographic" ground level involving the *Sasak* ethnic group living on Lombok Island, Indonesia. We focus on how shifts occur between and within these three legal jurisdictions (Islamic, *adat* and national law). This allows insight into the three-cornered discourse under which law as social engineering sometimes appears to shape behavior (particularly under national or secular law), and social behavior sometimes seems to change legal interpretation (particularly under *adat* law), but it matters equally who articulates the law (national secular or religious courts, versus Islamic scholars under local forms of alternative dispute resolution [ADR], versus ethnically-based closed local village societies where neither formal litigation nor ADR in a religious mode occurs). Our conclusion is that both Islamic law as reform element (enjoying significant social support), and national law under general equal protection approaches (as the sovereign's apparent command), have under many circumstances altered both the rules and outcomes involving customary law. Interestingly, discussions with senior members of the *Sasak* ethnic group in question indicate an acceptance on their part of the sociological basis of the changes (so customary or *adat* law itself is acknowledged as having changed to fit new social circumstances).

Secular law and Islamic law run through different court jurisdictions in Indonesia, meeting at a higher reviewing level in the Supreme Court or Makamah Agung. The interesting point is that the Supreme Court is visibly reluctant to "modernize" outcomes under Islamic law in the same fashion as it seems willing to change ethnically-based customary law when acting in cassation. The applicable lesson there seems to be that, given an assumption of stronger social support for the Islamic or religiously based rules (as opposed to ethnically-based *adat* rules), the Indonesian Supreme Court has specifically chosen *not* to attempt what we might call social engineering via secular, national law when faced with what it perceives as a pre-existing legal structure incorporating religiously mandated social norms. This is presumably since the fiqh they represent finds textual support in Al Qur'an and the hadiths, or stories and sayings attributed to the Prophet Mohammed, although religious positions are almost invariably subject to counterarguments (commonly accepted [human] theologies are not written in stone, since as Muslims say by way of general exception, God knows better than any human being). So it appears there are practical limits, at least in Indonesian judges' eyes, concerning the extent to which judicial decisions can or must engage in social engineering via legal decisions, at least in the face of perceived religious counter pressure.

## Background

The *Sasak* ethnic group inhabits Lombok, an island best known for its immediate proximity to the east of the island of Bali. The Balinese are ethnically Hindu, and represent in an historical sense demographic remnants of Indonesia's former predominantly Buddhist-Indian Majapahit culture reaching back over 1,000 years, with Islam arriving in full force in Indonesia less than 500 years ago. This mosaic of religions and cultures is characteristic of Indonesia's diversity, which for our purposes finds its expression also in legal pluralism. Currently, Lombok's *Sasak* ethnic group follows Islam as its religion, with a total population at present of 2,878,917 people.[1]

Islam began to arrive on Lombok only in the sixteenth century, after the fall of the Java-based Majapahit kingdom. Islam was brought by the followers of *wali* (sometimes translated as "saints," but more properly pious Muslim religious leaders, here functional missionaries) from the nearby island of Java. Lombok's inhabitants are currently renowned as particularly pious Muslims, and Lombok is often referred to as the "island with thousands of mosques." The number of mosques on the whole Lombok was 3,975 in 2007,[2] so that as a matter of simple arithmetic there is a mosque for every 724 of Lombok's *Sasak* inhabitants. Notwithstanding Islam's strong presence on Lombok, however, in respect of women's inheritance rights the *Sasak* community theoretically remains subject to three legal systems: customary or *adat* law, Islamic or *Shari'ah* law taken from Al Qur'an and the hadiths (as understood by religious practitioners, but also formally applied as law by Indonesian judges in state-sponsored religious courts), and state or secular law taken from judicial decisions of Indonesia's three levels of national or secular courts.

Under customary or *adat* law, a *Sasak* woman traditionally would have no right to inherit her parents' assets. This is a consequence of the *Sasak* character as a patriarchal community, namely a community that derives succession according to father's lineage. As might be imagined in terms of religion or even "forum shopping," however, many *Sasak* women think themselves instead subject to Islamic law which divides inheritance unequally into two portions for sons and one portion for daughters under classical fiqh. All decisions of Indonesia's Islamic religious courts comply with Quranic principles in inheritance matters (meaning that bringing an inheritance action in the Islamic religious court results automatically in the application of Islamic inheritance law rules). Meanwhile, the Indonesian Supreme Court declared in a 1978 decision and repeated in a 1982 decision, that rights of women and men under modern law are equal, with the result that *Sasak* women should have the same rights in inheriting an equal share of their parents' assets, insofar as the case is pursued in the secular courts.

Courts in Indonesia have at their apex the Supreme Court of the Republic of Indonesia or Makamah Agung. The ordinary lower courts include both appeal courts (both secular and religious Pengadilan Tinggi) and the district court courts (Pengadilan Negeri as the court of first instance). In terms of special jurisdictions they coexist among others with Islamic religious courts, military courts, and the state administrative courts.[3] The district courts have jurisdiction to hear and examine

---

1 Data of Statistic Centre Bureau, office of Department of Religious Affairs, West Nusa Tenggara, 2007.

2 Data of Statistic Centre Bureau, office of Department of Religious Affairs, West Nusa Tenggara, 2007.

3  The military courts have jurisdiction to try military personnel who commit crimes, while state administrative courts hear cases involving the actions or decisions of a state official (following continental or Civil Law models, from which Indonesia also borrowed in creating a Constitutional Court in 2003). Labor

civil and criminal cases for ordinary people. The Islamic religious courts have jurisdiction for cases of marriage, divorce, child adoption, inheritance and Syariah civil dispute cases for Muslims (and are in practical terms among the busiest courts in terms of caseload, because most ordinary people are likely to see the inside of a court room only in cases such as divorce, rather than in criminal proceedings or large scale commercial litigation). The possibility of forum shopping exists for inheritance matters, but the issue is complicated by the question of the legitimacy of any court's decision in society's eyes. This raises the question whether an objectively more favorable decision from a less respected judicial source would find social acceptance at the village or town level, since social relations are different in rural village or small town Lombok, as compared with Jakarta as Asian megacity.

## Colonial Tradition of *Adat* Law versus Islamic Law

*Adat* law under the Indonesian traditional definition is an ethnic group's customary law that has sanctions for members of the *adat* law community who violate it. *Adat* law is characteristically unwritten (although captured since the Dutch colonial period in academic treatises), but lives in the social practices of the ethnic community. Under Dutch colonial law, *adat* law was officially recognized as the prevailing law for indigenous Indonesians (current terminology usage would be pribumi Indonesians) with the enactment of article 131 of *Indische Staatregelling* in 1925. That article mentions, "For native Indonesians and foreign Easterners, the legal regulations valid for them are the laws based on their religions and traditions." At that time the population in the Indonesian Dutch colony was divided into three groups, namely the native Indonesians (now pribumi), Europeans (now we would say Westerners) and foreign Easterners (now we would say non-pribumi Asians, normally ethnic Chinese but encompassing in fact other distinct groups like Japanese and Arabs too). *Adat* law was applied to the native Indonesian population; meanwhile the European population was subject to Western (meaning Dutch) law. The foreign Easterners such as Chinese and Japanese were made subject to Western law too, and what was then Dutch or Western law has evolved into modern (secular) Indonesian law.

The exact role of Islamic law was always a problem for political reasons during the colonial period, because Islam itself was perceived by the Dutch as the incipient rallying point for any opposition to colonial control. Snouck Hurgronje, perhaps the most famous nineteenth-century Dutch legal expert qua colonial bureaucrat, performed legal research on *adat* law and Islamic law from 1884 until 1892. He articulated a theory that Islamic law could only be applied *if* it had been adopted by *adat* law (known as the *receptie* or reception theory in terms of conflicts of law approaches). This position was naturally opposed by Islamic religious leaders with *receptie a-contrario* theory, maintaining that *adat* law could only be applied as long as it was not in contradiction with Islamic law. This principle took its example from Minangkabau *adat* law (from West Sumatra) which states, "Adat Bersendikan Syariah, Syariah bersendikan Kitabulah" (*adat* is based on Islamic law, Islamic law is based on Al Qur'an as Holy Book). This kind of juxtaposition lives on in modern practice, because in reality the courts do not always apply Islamic law to Muslims, but quite often they apply *adat* law on the ground that in a specified geographic area the

---

courts hear disputes between workers and employers, or disputes between labor unions. Finally the taxation (dispute) court hears tax-related cases. Meanwhile, at a more detailed level, commercial courts and labor courts do not have appeal tribunals, but (case) cassations move directly into the Supreme Court. Taxation (dispute) court treats the district court as the court of appeal, and after that cassation goes to the Supreme Court. But such details are not at issue in the inheritance matters of interest in this chapter.

prevailing law is *adat* law rather than Islamic law. So modern Indonesian law preserves something like what would be recognized as a nineteenth-century-style consular approach to jurisdiction in family law matters, overlaid with conflicting religious law elements.

## Legal Pluralism and Ethnography in Lombok

We now shift our focus to what we shall call the ethnography of legal pluralism as it affects inheritance on Lombok, shifting as called for between the three sources of law potentially governing inheritance for women on Lombok. This has been developed by the author in intensive interviews with various members of the *Sasak* ethnic community, research on local religious court (Pengadilan Agama) decisions, the decisions of the local district court of first instance (Pengadilan Negeri), high appellate courts (Pengadilan Tinggi), and finally the Indonesian Supreme Court (Makamah Agung).

*Sasak Customary Law with Patrilineal Characteristics at the Village Level*

According to traditional *Sasak* customary law, the *Sasak* ethnic group draws its line of descent in inheritance matters from the man (so patriarchy). But where can we find today the living *Sasak adat* law? The author conducted research in the village community of Sade, a small and still traditional Lombok village located in the Central Lombok rural countryside close to the town of Praya.[4] Although all Sade's inhabitants are Muslims, they consider themselves still subject to traditional *Sasak* customary law (Interview October 17, 2007). According to the customary law in this village, women can receive no inheritance when their parents die. Basically, the *Sasak* community of Sade village operates on the traditional patriarchal system, so that lineage (and inheritance) follows from the man's or father's side. A daughter upon marriage is considered to leave her family and enter into her husband's family, because she follows her husband after she marries.

When a woman in Sade village marries she lives with her husband's family. Consequently, the only goods that are hers will be in the nature of dower, since she may bring along jewelry made from gold or silver in the forms of rings, earrings, necklaces and bracelets. She would not receive a piece of land or a house from her birth family. Land and houses are only for sons (Interview October 17, 2007). Sade village has a history of 15 generations, and currently consists of approximately 150 family heads or 750 persons. During my conversation with one of the village residents, interfamily marriage, for example, between nephews or nieces, was identified as a habit to maintain the descendant line.

Sade is a farming village working at subsistence levels. The men, with women's help, cultivate their rice fields. Additionally, the women weave cloth, such as making sarongs, shawls, and neck-cover-cloth for sale, using very simple looms. The women make threads from cotton planted in their paddy fields, together with rice plants. Most of them also buy threads of various colors in the local market. A woman from Sade village must marry a man of the Sade village. If she nonetheless marries a man from outside Sade village, that woman has to leave the village. Similarly the man who gets married to a woman from outside the village must also leave. There have been no inheritance

---

4   In the aristocratic level of the *Sasak* ethnic group, women are given the title of Baiq and men have the title of Lalu. But in lower levels of society, women as well as men have no noble title, but the women are called Inaq and the men Amaq. The *Sasak* community in Sade village, for example, has no aristocratic society members. All of its residents are from the lower level of the *Sasak* community. Readers can glean something of the social status of disputing parties subsequently through attention to social titles.

disputes from Sade village brought into the courts up to now (Interview October 2, 2008), with the result that the self-enforcing traditional *Sasak adat* law remains in place. So the customary law rights in Sade village follow the traditional customary law pattern, also for Muslims, without the interposition of religious (Islamic) figures or the courts.

*Inheritance under Islamic Law among the Sasak*

The majority of the Lombok *Sasak* community follows Islamic law as found in Al Qur'an and the hadiths.[5] The relevant principles of Islamic law on inheritance are taken from the Al Qur'an Sura An-Nisa verse 11, which states: "God regulates for you (on distribution of inheritance) to your children, the portion of a son is the same as the portion of two daughters." In the *Sasak* language it is said that the portion of a woman is referred to as *"sepersonan"* namely one portion of goods put on top of a woman's head. The corresponding portion of man is *"sepelembah,"* or as much as a man has who carries two wooden baskets suspended from a pole placed over his shoulder.

In the author's interview with a woman at Banyu Muleh village, Kediri sub-district, West Lombok, a man gets two portions and a daughter receives one portion following the rule of *"sepelembah sepersonan."* If there is no son then the whole inheritance shall go to the daughter. If there is more than one daughter, the inheritance assets shall be divided equally among them. The inheritance shall not be given to any brothers of their late father (NB, the patrilineal principle is effectively gone). If the daughter is the only child the whole inheritance shall go to that only daughter. The Banyu Muleh village is famous for pottery making which is not only marketed in Lombok, but also in the Bali area and exported to various countries, with the result that, unlike Sade village, it seemingly does enjoy a cash economy.[6]

At Cemara Beach, a fishing village in the Lembar sub-district, West Lombok, its inhabitants also follow Islamic law in inheritance issues. If there is no son, all inheritance assets shall go to the daughter. Inheritance assets shall never be distributed to the brother of her father (as would presumably occur in a purely patrilineal system). In this village disputes concerning inheritance are very rare. But if a dispute does arise, such dispute is settled by a sub-village head (*Dusun*) rather than the parties going to any court. Family law disputes at Cemara Beach that are brought to a religious court only involve divorce (Interview October 5, 2008). In Sembalun village (Central Lombok), Rinjani mountain area, the whole *Sasak* ethnic group in this area are Muslims, and distribution of inheritance again complies with Islamic law, referred to in the local language again as *"sepelembah sepersonan"* or two portions for a man and one portion for a woman (Interview October 10, 2008).

---

5    Most people in the *Sasak* ethnic group are common Muslims, although some of them, in small groups in some Lombok towns such as Bayan, Kopang, Narmada and Lingsar apply *Islam Waktu Telu* (a somewhat heterodox sect). These followers of Islam Waktu Telu pray three times, or in the *Sasak* language *Telu*, a day, rather than the orthodox five times at dawn (*Subuh*), noon (*Zuhur*), *Ashar* (at about 3 p.m.), sunset (*Magrib*) and at night (*Isya*) as the general Islamic practice. Such five prayers are only obligatory for their religious leaders and not for commoners in the eyes of practitioners of Islam Waktu Telu. However, the Indonesian government tries to influence them to follow the general Islamic teachings, namely praying five times, and fasting during the *Ramadhan* (fasting month) (Department of Education and Culture 1977–8: 75).

6    The women are called *"Inaq"* or *"Umi"* when they have become hajjah, which means that they have gone on a pilgrimage to Mecca, and so enjoy special repute in Islamic terms. The father is called *"Amaq"* (Interview October 17, 2007). Again, attention to these terms supplies some insight into the social standing of parties in the cases that follow.

In my interview with a woman in Kediri village, located only 5 kilometers from provincial capital city of Mataram (West Lombok), the woman said that she had just received the whole inheritance of assets from her late parents (because she was the only child). The inheritance was in the form of two hectares of rice fields and a house (one hectare equals 2.47 acres). The inheritance case was settled after obtaining guidance from the *Tuan Guru*, or the Islamic religious leader in the village. (Tuan Guru in local Lombok usage literally means "Mr. Teacher" in Indonesian, with the more common Indonesian term for an Islamic scholar being a *kyai* or *ulema*.) According to my interview of a seller of rimless Muslim caps (*kopiah*), which is a typical product from that village, the majority of Kediri residents are Muslims who distribute inheritance assets again under the system "*sepelembah sepersonan*" in the local language, namely two portions for a man compared with one portion for a woman (Interview January 26, 2009).

However, inheritance disputes within such *Sasak* small towns are quite often brought to the religious court, allowing a further exploration of actual cases. According to 2008 data for Lombok, the Mataram Religious Court (West Lombok) settled six disputes, Praya Religious Court (Central Lombok) settled 29 disputes, and Selong Religious Court (East Lombok) settled 58 disputes. Up to May 2009, Mataram Religious Court (West Lombok) examined two cases, Praya Religious Court (Central Lombok) seven cases, and Selong Religious Court (East Lombok) 38 cases.[7] The data shows that Selong Religious Court examined the greatest number of inheritance cases. Asked for an explanation, some local people opine that such condition is probably due to the fact that Selong constitutes a center of Islamic religious scholars (Tuan Guru), so that the women in that area claimed their Islamic (half share) inheritance right, to which, according to the traditional *Sasak* customary law as practiced in Sade village, they should have no right. Other local people said that many inheritance disputes come through Selong Religious Court because of advocates (not necessarily lawyers in terms of members of the bar) who exist and walk into the villages explaining inheritance rights of men and women according to Islamic law (Interview in Mataram July 17, 2009). So knowledge of Islamic inheritance rules seems to trigger formal disputation, if informal mediation is unsuccessful.

Here we give some examples of inheritance cases decided by the Lombok religious courts. They demonstrate a variety of Islamic inheritance rules as applied to children and widows. The Praya Religious Court (Central Lombok) in 2007 examined the case of *Amirah v. Ande et al.* The position of the case was derived from the death of Mia in 1966 and also his wife Sadiah in 2005. They were survived by three children, respectively Ilah, a daughter (defendant 5), Amirah, a daughter (claimant), and a son, Sahan, who had died in 1991. Sahan left his wife Ande (defendant 1), and three children respectively Azhar (a son, as defendant 2), Ramdan (a son, as defendant 3) and Marini (a daughter, as defendant 4). The deceased Mia and Sadiah left inheritances in the forms of a garden plot, rice fields and plantation land.

The Praya Religious Court in its decision quoted Al Qur'an—verse 11 of the An-Nisa Chapter: "God regulates for you (distribution of inheritance) to your children, the portion of a son is the same as the portion of two daughters," and articles 176 and 185 of the Indonesian Compilation of Islamic Law (*Kompilasi Hukum Islam*, a kind of authoritative secondary source for Islamic law approved by the Indonesian Ministry of Religion). As a result, the Praya Religious Court decided the portions of each beneficiary as follows:

---

7    Data from the High Islamic Court of Mataram, June 2009.

1.  Ilah (daughter) 1/4 portion
2.  Amirah (daughter) 1/4 portion
3.  Sahan (son) 2/4 portion, for each of the three children from the inheritance assets, and especially for Sahan's double portion because he had died and was substituted for by his inheritors, namely were received:
    a.  Ande (wife) 1/16 portion
    b.  Azhar (son) 6/16 portion
    c.  Ramdan (son) 6/16 portion
    d.  Marini (daughter) 3/16 portion. (*Amirah v. Ande et al.*; see also *Sumenah v. Inaq Sini et al.*)

This case demonstrates the standard Islamic rules for sons and daughters being applied in the mixed *per stirpes* setting including distribution to grandchildren.

The Selong Religious Court (East Lombok) examined an inheritance dispute in the case of *Amaq Munasih et al. v. Amaq Subur et al.* The case involved the inheritance from the late Papuq Sap, who died in 1964, and his wife Inaq Herman, who also died in 1981. These grandparents had five children, namely Amaq Inah, Inaq Samiah, Inaq Nang, Amaq Kesim and Amaq Munasih, but all of these children had died so that now those who would be the beneficiaries were the grandchildren. The grandparents left two parcels of rice fields amounting to 1.34 hectares. The lands were now controlled by the defendants, who were also the ancestors' beneficiaries' grandchildren. The claimants were also the ancestors' grandchildren asking for the distribution of the inheritance asset.

The Selong Religious Court stipulated the portions of each deceased child as beneficiaries in line with Islamic law, namely Amaq Inah 2/7, Inaq Samiah 1/7, Inaq Nang 1/7, Amaq Kesim 2/7 and Amaq Munasih 2/7. Their own children who were women received one portion and men received two portions, calculated on a *per stirpes* basis (*Amaq Munasih et al. v. Amaq Subur et al.*). At the appeal level the Mataram Religious High Court affirmed the decision of the Selong Religious Court.[8] At the cassation level the Supreme Court stated, that the courts were not wrong in implementing the law.[9] This simply reflects the application again of the Islamic law rules at the grandchildren's level, to the extent the suit arose after the children's generation had already passed away. But the point is that the religious courts will often reach back 20 years or more to correct inheritances already in the hands of the second and even third generations.[10]

The Praya Religious Court (Central Lombok) also decided the case of *Inaq Suni et al. v. Hj. Salmah et al.* The dispute arose after the husband Syamsudin died. His wife Salmah (as defendant 1) had three natural brothers/sisters, respectively who were Inaq Kamariah (a woman, as defendant 2), Inaq Kamran (a woman, as plaintiff 2), and Inaq Suni (a woman, as plaintiff 1). The late Syamsudin and his wife did not have children, but Syamsudin left rice fields totaling 1.452 hectares, which were controlled in turn by Hj. Salmah (defendant 1) in the amount of one hectare and Inaq Kamariah (defendant 2) in the amount of 0.452 hectares. The plaintiffs had often requested from the defendants their portions peacefully through familial meetings, but the defendants did not want to give them property without any clear reason.

The Praya Religious Court initially found that the rice field of 1.4520 hectares located in Setumbak, Jelatik village, Jonggat sub-district, Central Lombok Regency was the asset originally of from the late H. Syamsudin (rather than constituting at all originally the property of the wife) (*Inaq*

---

8   Mataram Religious High Court, No. 37/Pdt.G/2007/PTA.MTR.
9   Indonesian Supreme Court, No. 121 K/AG/2008.
10  Indonesian Supreme Court, No. 121 K/AG/2008. See also *Lalu Purwadi v. Baiq Nursam et al.*

*Suni et al. v. Hj. Salmah et al.*). Thereafter, the Praya Religious Court in its decision determined the beneficiaries namely:

1. Hj. Salmah (wife) got 1/4 portion or 3/12 portion.
2. Inaq Kamariah (sister) got 3/12 portion.
3. Inaq Kamran (sister) got 3/12 portion.
4. Inaq Suni (sister) got 3/12 portion.

The Islamic law principle applied was that of 1/4 interest in property as widow's share, with the balance divided equally among the female siblings.

It is also not uncommon for the decisions of religious courts to be appealed to the appellate instance of the High Religious Court, even all the way to the level of the Indonesian Supreme Court. For example, in 1992 the Mataram Religious Court heard the dispute of *Inaq Putrahimah et al. v. Amaq Mukminah et al.*, concerning which the Supreme Court of the Republic of Indonesia at cassation level expressed the opinion that, as long as there were any son or daughter of deceased parents, then their other (male) family members had no right to inherit. The case was initiated from the claim of Nursaid et al., the grandchild of Amaq Triawan who had passed away in 1930. The defendant was Le Putrahimah, the daughter of Amaq Nawiyah who died leaving inheritance assets in the forms of two plots of plantation land of six hectares. Nursaid's parents themselves died in 1950. At the time Amaq Nawiyah died, Le Putrahimah was still a child so that the land was controlled by Nursaid together with his brothers and sisters.

The Mataram Religious Court was of the opinion that the boundaries of the land in dispute could not be proven by the plaintiffs, while the defendant had showed *pipil garuda* (a stamped land tax receipt, customarily employed as preliminary proof of ownership under *adat* law in the absence of further documentation) as the evidence of the defendant's ownership. Therefore, the Mataram Religious Court rejected the initial claim of the plaintiffs (*Inaq Putrahimah et al. v. Amaq Mukminah et al.*). The Mataram Religious High Court decided that actually the disputed plantation lands belonged to Amaq Nawiyah and its apparent ownership had been changed by Le Putrahimah's daughter in obtaining *pipil garuda* in her own name. The disputed land had not yet been divided according to inheritance system between Le Putrahimah and her father's brother or her uncle Amaq Itriawan. Amaq Itriawan had died in 1930 so his portion went to his children. His children had also died so the inheritance asset went to the grandchildren of Nursaid et al. The Religious High Court then decided the plantation land No. 2534/7002, Lot No. 375 of 3.260 hectares and the plantation land No. 2532/7002, Lot No. 375 of 3.440 hectares located in Malimbu sub-village, Pemenang Barat village, Tanjung sub-district, and West Lombok Regency was the inheritance asset of Amaq Nawiyah that had not yet been distributed. Therefore, Inaq Putrahimah as the daughter of Amaq Putrahimah (the defendant) also received a half portion of the two plantation land pieces, but because the beneficiaries included a wife, three sons and four daughters, they each received an eighth.[11]

At the cassation level, the Indonesian Supreme Court opined as long as there was a son or a daughter, then no right existed to inherit by a more distant male relative who had a blood relationship with the deceased. For that reason, the Supreme Court decided Inaq Putrahimah as the defendant was the one and only beneficiary.[12] This represented formally a problem in Islamic law

---

11    Mataram Religious High Court, No. 19/Pdt.G/1993/PTA.Mtr.
12    Indonesia Supreme Court, No. 86 K/AG/1994.

terms of the inheritance of property by a single child, with complications arising from the fact that the land had been managed by other parties initially due to the child being a minor.

Jurisdictional determinations also play a distinct role in inheritance cases. In 1997, the Religious Court in Praya (Central Lombok) examined the case of *Amaq Rede v. Serem et al.* This case began from the claim of Amaq Rede as the son of Amaq Rabik, who died in 1947. Amaq Rabik had a son, Amaq Rede, and also his brother Amaq Gande. Amaq Gande eventually passed away leaving 10 children, who became the defendants. In 1996, the defendants directly took over the rice field and plantation land totaling 1.0768 hectares, then being cultivated by the mother of the claimant Inaq Rabiq together with the plaintiff.

The Assembly of Judges of the Praya Religious Court gave advice to both parties to settle the case peacefully, but to no avail. The Assembly of Judges carried out a local inspection of the property on April 19, 1997, and listened to witness' testimony. They were assured that such plantation lands belonged to Amaq Ribiq and were not any inheritance from Amaq Gande. Because Amaq Ribiq had died then his portion went to Rabik and Amaq Rede. After Rabik died the portion of Rabik went to Hamsiah (a woman) and Nuriah (a man). That the rice field and plantation belonged to Amaq Rabik that had not yet been distributed – should be distributed to the beneficiaries according to Islamic Faraid Law, namely:

1. Rice field:
    a. Rabik gets $1/2$ X $\pm$ 1,000 ha = $\pm$ 0.500 ha
    b. Amaq Rede gets $1/2$ X $\pm$ 0,0768 ha = $\pm$ 0.0384 ha.

Stipulating the portion of each beneficiary of Rabik:

2. Rice field:
    a. Hamsiah = $1/3$ X $\pm$ 0.500 ha = $\pm$ 0.1666 ha
    b. Nuriah = $2/3$ X $\pm$ 0.500 ha = $\pm$ 0.0512 ha
3. Plantation land:
    a. Hamsiah = $1/3$ X $\pm$ 0.768 ha = $\pm$ 0.0258 ha
    b. Nuriah = $2/3$ X $\pm$ 0.768 ha = $\pm$ 0.0512 ha. (*Amaq Rede v. Serem et al*)

At the appellate level the Mataram Religious High Court stated that the subject of dispute was whether the rice field of one hectare belonged to the plaintiff's father or defendant's father. Then under the article 50 of Law Number 7 of 1989, it was not the jurisdiction of the Religious Court, but such dispute was the jurisdiction of District Court (treating it as a land ownership dispute belonging in the secular courts, rather than an inheritance dispute belonging in the religious courts). Therefore, the Mataram Religious High Court did not agree with legal opinion of the Praya Religious Court and canceled its decision.[13]

The Supreme Court at the cassation level stated that the Mataram Religious High Court had wrongly applied the law, because the dispute about inheritance assets did not fall into category of an ownership dispute.[14] Here the rule applied was more a simple jurisdictional one, that the jurisdictional rules ordinarily consigning property ownership disputes to secular courts did not apply to ownership disputes arising out of inheritance questions.

---

13   Mataram Religious High Court, No. 2/Pdt.G/1997/PTA.MTR.
14   Indonesia Supreme Court, No. 111 K/AG/1998.

In 2006, the Praya Religious Court (Central Lombok) examined the case of *Ishak et al. v. Mahyin et al.* The position of the case was Ishak et al. had filed a suit against Mahyin et al. because the defendants controlled one rice field plot and three pieces of plantation land. The plaintiffs had repeatedly asked for their portions amicably through familial representations to the defendants with the help of village and sub-district heads, but were unsuccessful in resolving the dispute. The Praya Religious Court then, in its decision dated September 5, 2005,[15] granted the claim of the plaintiff in part. It decided that the beneficiaries of Amaq Sediah were Amaq Nursidah (son), Amaq Mun (son), Amaq Muriah (son), Raminah (daughter) and Amaq Darsiah (son). The Praya Religious Court also stipulated the portions of each beneficiary as follows:

1. Amaq Nursidah received 2/9 portion, further it was inherited by his children *per stirpes* with reference to his son receiving two times the daughter's portion.
2. Amaq Mun received 2/9 portion, further it was inherited by his children with reference to his son receiving two times the daughter's portion.
3. Amaq Ariah received 2/9 portion, further it was inherited by his children with reference to his son receiving two times the daughter's portion.
4. Raminah received 1/9 portion as daughter, further it was inherited by her sole child.
5. Amaq Darsiah received 2/9 portion, further it was inherited by his children with reference to his son receiving two times of the daughter's portion.

At the appellate level, the Mataram Religious High Court canceled the decision of the lower Praya Religious Court.[16] The Indonesian Supreme Court at the cassation level affirmed the decision of the Religious High Court because the Praya Religious Court had been wrong in its legal consideration. According to the Religious High Court and the Supreme Court a question remained whether the subject of dispute constituted Amaq Sediah's inheritance assets or property belonged to the child and/or grandchild of Amaq Sediah, because it could not be proven during examination process that Amaq Sediah was leaving inheritance assets that had not yet been distributed, and the Praya Religious Court only had authority to determine who were the beneficiaries of Amaq Sediah. Therefore, because the subject of dispute in this case was related to rights of ownership, it was within the jurisdiction of the (secular) District Court.[17]

In 2008 the Selong Religious Court heard the inheritance dispute of *Rohini et al. v. H. Sajidi*, that involved joint inheritance assets of ancestor and of his wife. H. Faturahman had passed away in 1981, and left a wife and four children, namely Redah (wife), Rohini, Hj. Rehanah, H. Sajidi and Hj. Nurhasanah. H. Faturahman left them rice field and plantation land as common assets. Plaintiffs tried to settle this case amicably through familial negotiations, but were always rejected by the defendant who controlled the land. Thereafter, the plaintiffs requested the Religious Court to distribute the inheritance according to Islamic law, that first the asset be split between the husband and his wife (because it constituted a joint asset as a product of the marriage). The Selong Religious Court in its decision decided that a half of the joint asset constituted the right of Redah, the deceased's wife, and the other half was the right of the late H. Faturahman as father, that had to be distributed to all beneficiaries. The Selong Religious Court then decided the portions of each beneficiaries of the late H. Faturahman, namely:

---

15	Praya Religious Court, No. 61/Pdt.G/2005/PA.PRA.

16	Mataram Religious High Court, No. 18/Pdt.G/2006/PTA.Mtr.

17	Supreme Court, No. 368 K/AG/2006. See also *Inaq Illah et al. v. Lemin et al.*, raising change of religion upon subsequent remarriage as jurisdictional defense.

1.  Redah (wife) got 1/8 of the whole inheritance asset.
2.  Rohini (daughter) got 1/5 X 7/8 of the inheritance asset.
3.  Hj. Rehanah (daughter) got 1/5 X 7/8 of the inheritance asset.
4.  H. Sajidi (son) got 2/5 X 7/8 of the inheritance asset.
5.  Hj. Nurhasanah (daughter) got 1/5 X 7/8 of the inheritance asset. (*Rohini et al. v. H. Sajidi*)

At the appeal level the Mataram Religious High Court corrected the decision of the Selong Religious Court and decided each of the beneficiaries as the following:

1.  Redah (wife) got 5/40.
2.  Rohini (daughter) got 7/40.
3.  Hj. Rehanah (daughter) got 7/40.
4.  H. Sajidi (son) got 14/40.
5.  Hj. Nurhasanah (daughter) got 7/40.

Furthermore the Mataram Religious High Court also decided the proceeds of Redah (wife) was 1/2 of the joint asset plus 5/40, Hj. Rehanah was 7/40 subtracted by Rp. 75,000,000 and H. Sajidi was 14/40 plus a portion of Rp. 75,000,000.[18]

The Supreme Court at the cassation level listened to the request of the defendant, who in his cassation memorandum argued:

1.  Judex facti (judges in high court) in their legal considerations had merely taken over the legal considerations of Selong Religious Court, that did not take into account the real facts occurred between the parties and the legal facts disclosed in the court sessions, that the Selong Religious Court did not contemplate completely on the entire legal facts.
2.  The legal issue between the parties in dispute should be considered in accordance with the sense of justice and facts on the genuineness of what had happened formally as well as substantially between the two parties. The reality was the opposing party, i.e., the plaintiff, previously had agreed and accepted the offer from the party requesting cassation, i.e., the defendant, in the forms of yields (crops from the fields) from the disputed properties. In other words, he was willing to receive some parts of the disputed subject yields, not to obtain the land but enough for the yields thereof, as customary practice at Pringgajurang sub-village. The descendants or only men had the right to the land, whereas the daughters were only to get the yield of their parents' inheritance land (NB, apparently introducing *adat* law elements into the case).
3.  In this case, the Judge Assembly of Selong Religious Court as well as the Mataram Religious High Court had not considered that the excess of the portion sold by one of the parties in the case should also be held accountable at the acting party's expense.

The Indonesian Supreme Court opined without necessarily taking into account the cassation reasons formally submitted. According to the Supreme Court, the Mataram Religious High Court had been wrong in applying the law under the following considerations:

---

18    Mataram Religious High Court, No. 64/Pdt.G/2007/PTA.MTR.

1.  The subject of dispute in the claim document in the forms of 33 acres of rice field that had been sold by defendant I to defendant II should be calculated as the joint asset between ancestor (H. Faturahman) and Raedah.
2.  The subject of dispute had also to be distributed between the ancestor (H. Faturahman) and Raedah.
3.  1/2 (a half) of portion of ancestor (H. Faturahman) of the disputed subject constituted inheritance asset that had to be distributed to his beneficiaries.
4.  Solution of sale of the subject of dispute constituted the business between the defendant I and defendant II.
5.  Because the subject of dispute constituted a dowry that had to be determined as a dowry of the ancestor (the late H. Faturahman) that had to be distributed to his beneficiaries.

The Supreme Court finally decided, among others:

1.  To stipulate 1/2 (a half) of the inheritance asset constitutes the right belonged to Redah and the other 1/2 (half) becomes the right of the late H. Faturahman that has to be distributed to his beneficiaries.
2.  To stipulate the portions of each beneficiaries of H. Faturahman as the following:
    a.  Redah (wife) got 1/8 of the whole inheritance asset.
    b.  Rohin (daughter) 1/5 X 7/8 of inheritance asset.
    c.  Hj. Rehanah (daughter) 1/5 X 7/8 of inheritance asset.
    d.  H. Sajidi (son) 2/5 X 7/8 of inheritance asset.
    e.  Hj. Nurhasanah (daughter) 1/5 X 7/8 of inheritance asset.[19]

In this case the Supreme Court seemingly rejected *adat* law claims within the case brought before the Islamic Religious Court, instead affirming solely Islamic law principles to decide the case.

*Settlement of Inheritance Disputes in the (Secular) District Courts*

Although *Sasak* ethnic communities are Muslim, its members disputing inheritance matters do not always go to the religious courts where Islamic law would apply, but may also seek justice in a District Court where *adat* or national law would be recognized. The Indonesian Supreme Court arguably has changed *Sasak* women's rights to inherit under something approaching an equal rights analysis under its decision in *Inaq Rasini v. Amaq Atimah et al.* (1978). The Supreme Court decided that equal treatment in accordance with its jurisprudence concerning the inheritance rights of a daughter in Tapanuli (North Sumatra), should also be the rule in Lombok. In order to be fair, the daughter was named as beneficiary, so that in this case the daughter as only child should inherit the whole of her father's estate (in opposition to the traditional *Sasak adat* law rule that would deny her any inheritance).

The Indonesia Supreme Court had previously effectively changed Batak Karo customary law applicable in North Sumatra (in a challenge to patrilineal descent analogous to the traditional *Sasak adat* rule in the 1961 case of *Sitepu v. Ginting*). According to the current views of Batak Karo customary law, in accordance with principles of the patrilineal community inheritance was only for sons. However, the Supreme Court at cassation level decided to annul the lower court decisions applying the traditional Batak Karo *adat* law, deciding that a daughter should receive a portion

---

19   Supreme Court, No. 515 K/AG/2008.

of the inheritance. According to the Supreme Court, under principles of humanity and general justice on the essence of equality of rights between man and woman as the living law in Indonesia (without formal reference to the 1945 Constitution in Indonesia as a Civil Law jurisdiction where separation of powers principles rendered it difficult for courts to apply the constitution directly, but seemingly contemplating its third party effects), a daughter and son of someone leaving inheritance equally had the rights to the inheritance, in the sense that the portion of a son should be the same as the daughter's. This Supreme Court decision initially shocked the Batak Karo community in North Sumatra, but received a warm welcome from women's society there. This decision was considered in Indonesian law to be a historical milestone in the struggle for legal equality between women and men. With this decision the Supreme Court made new law in the area of inheritance formally only in Tapanuli (North Sumatra) under local *adat* law, but the principle could be extended more broadly under a kind of nationalized approach to *adat* law.

With that in mind, we can return to the decision of the Indonesian Supreme Court for Lombok in *Inaq Rasini v. Amaq Atimah et al.* The Supreme Court simply quoted its decision in *Ginting v. Sitepu* for Batak Karo, saying that *Sasak* women in Lombok were also the beneficiaries of their late parents, fully entitled to inherit under now current *Sasak adat* law views. The question is whether this decision of the Supreme Court would actually be accepted in the *Sasak* law community, given that the Supreme Court was not part of the community (even though it had formal jurisdiction to decide *adat* law matters).

In the case of *Inaq Supar et al. v. Amaq Mali et al.*, the Supreme Court again stated that women were beneficiaries of their late parents. In this case Inaq Supar (a woman) and Inaq Kamar (a woman) lived in Peresak village, Narmada sub-district, West Lombok, and filed suit against Amaq Mali (defendant 1, a man), Amaq Sani (defendant 2, a man), Amaq Su (defendant 3, a man) and Amaq Mulinah (defendant 4, a man). The position of the case was Amaq Siti (a man) had died and had a brother Amaq Ipah (a man) and a cousin Amaq Radiah. The plaintiffs' grandfather had left to them inheritance assets in the form of 1.060 hectares of rice field which was controlled by defendant 1, and 1.225 ha of plantation land controlled by defendants 2, 3 and 4. The plaintiffs had asked for the portions of the lands properly, but were rejected. The Mataram District Court in its legal considerations, among others stated that for the *Sasak* ethnic group in West Lombok, based on jurisprudence and also the reality of the living customary law, which was still changing, constituted the basis of the inheritance dispute settlement. According to present *Sasak* customary law, the court acknowledged that a daughter could be a beneficiary/inheritor. This was confirmed in February 1974 by the research of the West Nusa Tenggara High Court concerning inheritance customary law in West Lombok.

The reasoning was that Amaq Siti who passed away in 1956 did not have offspring other than Le Siti who had died at an earlier time. Le Siti before she died married and had two daughters, Inaq Supar and Inaq Kamar, the plaintiffs. Therefore, the plaintiffs were the grandchildren of the late Amaq Siti. If Le Siti was still alive and Amaq Siti died earlier, then according to *Sasak* customary law, Le Siti was the only inheritor of the late Amaq Siti. Because the plaintiffs were the grandchildren of the late Amaq Siti, then the plaintiffs were the legitimate beneficiaries of Amaq Siti.

The plaintiffs since Amaq Siti was still alive and after the death of plaintiffs' mother (Le Siti), had never benefited from (in terms of receiving crops) or utilized the inheritance assets of the late Amaq Siti. The plaintiffs were the legitimate beneficiaries of the assets left by Amaq Siti, despite the fact that the circumstances of their life were very miserable. Their condition became wretched, because they did not have the benefit of the assets left by the late Amaq Siti, which was perceived as unfair.

Because the defendants had benefited from and utilized the inheritance assets of the late Amaq Siti, even to the extent that from the yield of such assets they could purchase new rice fields. The Court opined that it was very fair given the time of taking benefit or utilizing the assets left by the late Amaq Siti. They could purchase in the interim their own rice field from the yields of such assets as portions of the defendants, so concerning the assets left by the late Amaq Siti, the defendants had no further right and had to return the disputed lands in this case to the plaintiffs as the legitimate inheritors of the late Amaq Siti who had the right to possess such disputed lands.

Under the said considerations, the claim of the plaintiffs had to be granted. Finally the Mataram District Court stated, because the dispute was concerning the issue of right, namely under the above considerations that the plaintiffs were the party having the rights and the owners of the disputed lands. The Denpasar High Court at the appeal level in its decision dated June 27, 1977 affirmed the decision of Mataram District Court, and stated that the plaintiffs were the beneficiaries of Amaq Siti.[20] The Indonesian Supreme Court at the cassation level declared that the Denpasar High Court was not wrong in applying the (*adat*) law and affirmed the decision, which meant the plaintiffs, namely Inaq Supar and Inaq Kamar, had the right to the said inheritance land.[21]

The Selong District Court in 1977 in *Baiq Fadlah et al. v. Baiq Saeah* stated that the plaintiff and defendant as daughters had the right to inherit a half portion, according to *Sasak* customary law principles of "*sepersonan*" (NB, bearing in mind that this appears to be *Sasak adat* law as affected by Islamic law principles under the *receptio a-contrario* theory, rather than "pure" traditional *adat* law as we saw in Sade village). The position of the case was Baiq Fadlah and Lalu Ahmat who lived in Labuhan Village, East Lombok filed a suit against their relative Baiq Saeah who also lived in the same area. The dispute arose when the plaintiffs and defendant's mother passed away leaving rice field plots and plantation lands.

Following a special funeral ceremony in 1977 40 days after the mother's death, it turned out that the total 5.670 hectares of rice fields and 2.200 hectares of plantation lands had been transferred by their mother in a donative transaction before she died because of the defendant's enticement, Baiq Saeah, and without the plaintiffs' knowledge. The plaintiffs then did not receive the inheritance assets. According to the plaintiffs, under the *Sasak* customary law (as affected by Islamic principles, at least to the extent of the *receptie a-contrario* theory) the man would get *sepelembah* or two portions, and the woman would get *sepersonan* or one portion. The defendant plead that under *Sasak* customary law a woman did not receive any inheritance (the traditional, patriarchal *Sasak adat* rule still visible in Sade village) and the bequest (*hibah*) was carried out wholeheartedly without any duress by their own mother when he treated her during the sickness ending in her death.

The Selong District Court in its decision stated that according to a general principle of law, a bequest could not create any harm to a legitimate beneficiary (NB, not treating it formally as what might be viewed as an undue influence case under Western law, but more like a transfer void under public policy). Therefore, the bequest document was nullified by the court and the plaintiffs were also declared as beneficiaries. The Selong District Court distributed the inheritance asset following "*sepelembah sepersonan*" or two portions for a son and one portion for a daughter. The Denpasar High Court at the appeal level supported the decision of the District Court.[22] The Indonesian Supreme Court also affirmed the decision of Denpasar High Court stating that it was in accordance

---

20    Denpasar High Court, No. 102/PTD/1977/Pdt.

21    Indonesia Supreme Court, No. 853 K/Sip./1978.

22    Denpasar High Court, No. 187/PTD/1977/Pdt.

with local customary law (thus seemingly reaffirming the *Sasak adat* law rule as now presumably affected by Islamic law principles, rather than in its Sade village traditional *adat* law form).[23]

A 1982 decision of Selong District Court contemplated that *Sasak* women were not only able to inherit, but also should receive the same portion as the men. This decision was received enthusiastically among *Sasak* women in Lombok. In *Inaq Sanah et al. v. Kadirun et al.*, the Selong District Court in East Lombok stated that it was necessary to review the sociological background of the *Sasak* ethnic group's customary law on Lombok Island, especially customary inheritance law in the East Lombok area. It could not be denied by anyone in this area, specifically *Sasak adat* law community members, that in the past three decades many advances had been made in their lives and livelihoods in the social, economic, cultural and educational areas. According to the Selong District Court, the above advances actually had significantly influenced the pattern and way of thinking of *Sasak adat* law community members.

The Court opined that the status of women and their treatment under *adat* law had experienced changes, namely they had become equal to men. Equivalent opportunity was given to obtain education to both boys and girls, which was followed also by equal opportunity and rights in obtaining employment and the like. It was not surprising that various public positions and professions were filled by women of this ethnic group. It was logical and reasonable this situation should be followed by equal rights and positions in the law, especially in inheritance law.

According to Selong District Court, *adat* law constituted an empty illusion unless it reflected living conditions and values. The old, obsolete customary law was out of date, so that it was no longer suitable for the needs and character of the present era, neither was it in accord with sense of legal justice of the *Sasak adat* law community itself in the present era. To the extent that there were people who claimed that the values of older inheritance law (presumably like that practiced in Sade village) were still vibrant and maintaining themselves, it only reflected some individuals' mindset. These were people whose intentions were materialistic, who aimed merely to acquire inheritance assets for themselves (without giving the right to inherit to their daughters and sisters).

The Selong District Court also quoted research entitled *Sasak Customary Law Development* (undertaken in 1979 by the Mataram University Faculty of Law, Lombok). Since 1951, especially in the Masbagik sub-district (East Lombok), there had been a shift in values under the *adat* inheritance law, especially concerning the position of daughters. Under the traditional *adat* law view, a daughter did not have any right to inherit fixed assets such as land. But at the present stage in its development, *Sasak adat* law recognized that women could be beneficiaries and as a matter of right also was eligible to inherit her parents' assets jointly with her brothers.

The above conditions should be interpreted as there had been a shift of attitude within members of this ethnic group as a matter of modernization. From the customary law community viewpoint, philosophically it can be understood that equality of rights, status and position of sons and daughters had changed from traditional views. A daughter was no longer always behind a son's prime standing. Instead, both had equal rank and dignity. From the legal viewpoint it seems the *Sasak* customary law community had experienced quite rapid development. This social development and growth actually was followed also by appropriate legal changes. Within this customary community, a shift in social values, specifically in their legal values, had occurred. The *Sasak adat* law community's situation and condition nowadays had changed. In reality in the midst of this customary law community had grown new legal values, which were in line with the needs of the concerned community itself. It simply felt unjust for a daughter to be ineligible to be

---

23    Indonesia Supreme Court, No. 2014 K/Sip/1979.

a beneficiary. A daughter at present has been recognized as a beneficiary generally, so that as a logical consequence then she should be given the right to inherit her parents' assets.

With a starting point of equal rank and dignity, and equality of right and position of every citizen before the law, in accordance with our state philosophy *Pancasila* and its description in the articles of the 1945 Constitution and also in view of general sense of justice, and the living values and their applications adhered to within the concerned community (living law), then in this case the Court was of the opinion that it was reasonable to get guidance from the fixed jurisprudence of Indonesia Supreme Court legally binding on the whole of Indonesia, dated November 11, 1961, No. 179 K/Sip/1961, which provides: "A daughter and a son of an ancestor's inheritance jointly have the right to the inheritance asset in the sense that the portions of the son and daughter are the same" (the *Karo Batak Ginting v. Sitepu* decision).

There is no formal doctrine of precedent in such cases (because of Indonesian law's Civil Law roots). It is, however, helpful to review the jurisprudence of Indonesia Supreme Court applied in this Lombok Island area, in the case between *Inaq Rasini v. Amaq Atimah et al.*,[24] with the content as follows: "In accordance with jurisprudence of Indonesia Supreme Court for a daughter in Tapanuli, also in Lombok, it is only fair for a daughter to become inheritor, so that in this matter the plaintiff of cassation as the only child, should inherit the whole assets left by her father."

The Court in this case through its decision tried to fulfill the legal needs of the concerned customary community, and could also satisfy the sense of justice of the people constituting the customary community concerned. Through a judge's decision which constitutes a source of law, it attempts to position the law as a social engineering tool. Following from the above considerations, especially the two opinions of Indonesian Supreme Court, then the Selong Court in this case was of the opinion that it had been proper and just to give equal right to all natural children or descendants of the late Amaq Seniah to inherit the disputed rice fields and plantation land left by him. That meant in this case equal portions for the son and the daughter. The most accurate method to carry out distribution of the inheritance of disputed lands was first returning it to the original position of the inheritance owner (the late Amaq Seniah). After that it could be equally distributed to all of his natural children, and further each portion was distributed to the next descendants *per stirpes*.

The Court concluded that the plaintiff had been able to prove the grounds of her claim, therefore the claim of the plaintiff reasonably had to be granted. The Selong District Court finally decided that both parties were the beneficiaries of the late Amaq Seniah, and had the right to inherit the disputed rice field and plantation land under an equal distribution. At the appellate level, the West Nusa Tenggara High Court followed the reasoning and conclusions of the Selong District Court and affirmed its decision.[25] At the cassation level, the stated objections to the lower court decisions were:

1. On Lombok Island, in East Lombok specifically in Sukamulia sub-district, in Padamara village a woman could not be a beneficiary, because they adopted a marriage system drawn from the male descendant line, embracing a patrilineal system. A woman could not inherit family assets from parents, whether in the form of rice fields or plantation land. A woman could only inherit limited kinds of movable assets, such as jewelry and daily utensils.
2. The basis of judge's decision which equalized the position of women and men was only based on the claimed advancement of the modernization era. According to the cassation application, regardless of modernization, whatever it meant, women could not become the

---

24    Indonesian Supreme Court, No. 1589 K/Sip/1974, dated February 9, 1978.
25    Mataram Religious High Court, No. 17Pdt/1984/PT.NTB.

head of the family and this position was always held by men. Based on this premise, then there emerged dissimilar rights to inherit the core family assets.

3. If viewed more deeply, the decision of the District Court was in violation of inheritance law as regulated in verse 11 of the An Nissa Sura of Al Qur'an, and based on the two legal sources, namely viewed from *Sasak* customary law as well as Islamic law viewpoints, then the lower courts had been wrong in their legal conclusions generally, not to mention that their view was inaccurate for East Lombok. Especially in Padamara village, the customary law as well as Islamic law were still strongly implemented until now (at that time) and that the inheritance law used to distribute inheritance asset being applied was customary law (NB, rather than national law).

Directly facing these arguments, the Supreme Court affirmed the lower courts' decision.[26] Following publication of this Supreme Court decision, other inheritance cases are being brought to the Lombok District Court in increasing numbers (Interview July 17, 2009). I separately interviewed men of the *Sasak* ethnic group to ask them in particular about the Supreme Court's original 1974 decision in *Inaq Rasini v. Amaq Atimah et al.*, in which the Supreme Court quoted its 1961 *Ginting v. Sitepu* decision establishing gender equality under Batak Karo (Sumatra) *adat* law, extending its principles to Lombok (*Sasak* ) *adat* law. The *Sasak* group men whom I asked about the Supreme Court decision were of the opinion that it was fair and accurate (Interview October 4, 2007). At present, *Sasak* women also worked, had careers comparable to those of men, and financed household needs, so that it was correct also in their eyes for *Sasak* women to inherit from their parents. On that basis, it would appear that the judicial opinions in question accurately capture the current sense of a majority of the *Sasak adat* law community.


## Conclusions

The *Sasak* community divides into three groups in inheritance matters. The first represents those who remain in compliance with traditional customary law's purely patrilineal system characteristics. In this community, women are ineligible to receive any inheritance in the form of real property or similar core family goods. Although this group has been reduced to small numbers (like all residents of Sade village in Central Lombok), this *adat* system is still authoritative within that village. The second community group represents those Muslims who express loyalty to Islamic law's inheritance views, under which a daughter should receive one portion compared with two portions for her brother. Religious courts in Lombok always firmly adhere to such a distribution of inheritance under Islamic law. The Indonesian Supreme Court in its decisions has never changed the distribution of inheritance carried out by this Religious Court at cassation level. The Supreme Court seems to be very cautious if confronted with the Islamic law based on Al Qur'an and hadiths. Third, there is a part of the Muslim *Sasak* community willing to bring their inheritance disputes to the (secular) District Courts. The District Court in one decision expressed the opinion that women's status has been the subject of a social change in Lombok.

At present, according to the District Court under its decision, the inheritance rights of women and men are the same (with ratio of 1:1). This decision was affirmed at the appellate and cassation levels by the High Court and the Indonesian Supreme Court. Nonetheless, no similar examination at the cassation level has been made of any decision of Religious High Court and the Religious

---

26   Supreme Court, No. 2662 K/Pdt/1984.

Court of the first instance, so here the Supreme Court appears to still follow the classical Islamic law view contemplating unequal inheritance distributions. However, the cassation examination by the Supreme Court against *adat* law inheritance cases asserting the "*sepelembah sepersonan*" view (as apparently influenced by Islamic law under the *receptio a-contrario* theory) coming from the High Court and District Court, has applied a decision that a woman and man have equal rights, each to receive equal portions in inheritance matters. In the *Sasak* community itself it has happened that a man pitied his poor sister, so that his sister obtained a bigger portion of inheritance assets. There was also the example of a father who loved his daughter more so that when he was still alive, he gifted his daughter with his assets.

Legal changes prevail qualitatively, not quantitatively. It means simply one decision of the Indonesian Supreme Court at the beginning signifies legal changes have occurred, such as the decision of the Supreme Court to Batak Karo community in Kabanjahe. It can be said, however, that changes at the level of legal pluralism in inheritance for *Sasak* women in Lombok have become increasingly visible over the past several years. It would appear social change accompanies the legal changes, but legal changes may be "uneven" to the extent in a case like Sade village one finds the population apparently following the traditional *adat* law views, and simply making no recourse to the courts (or for that matter following Islamic law's precepts, despite the fact that the village's inhabitants are Muslims). Meanwhile, strictly speaking, Islamic law inheritance rules differentiating between sons' and daughters' shares in inheritance as applied by the Lombok religious courts have not been challenged by the Indonesian Supreme Court, even while *adat* rules consistent with the *receptie a-contrario* theory (meaning arguably influenced by Islamic law) have been altered so that women's and men's inheritance shares under Lombok *adat* law have been equalized under the Supreme Court's jurisprudence.

The twist in terms of our "chicken or egg" question is that, based upon the author's interviews, the prevailing view in the *Sasak adat* law community itself arguably is that daughters should receive equal shares, not the unequal shares under the traditional Islamic rules, so the question becomes why do more people not "forum shop" in pursuing inheritance cases in the district court rather than the religious court? One should acknowledge the continuing tension of different social views, captured already in nineteenth-century colonial discourse under the opposition of the *receptio* and *receptio a-contrario* theories. Under diverse Indonesian circumstances, current "modernization" patterns visible in development of women's inheritance rights under legal pluralism reflect older divisions carried forward. The deeper question here may be how to deal with legitimacy issues as they affect individual choices about things like "forum shopping" options in the face of competing social views, since social change is a dynamic rather than static exercise (meanwhile, the "chicken or egg" question is arguably phrased more in a static fashion).

## References

*Amaq Munasih et al. v. Amaq Subur et al.* Selong Religious Court, No. 407/Pdt.G/2006/PA.SEL, dated March 29, 2007.

*Amaq Rede v. Serem et al.* Praya Religious Court, No. 45/Pdt.G/1997/PA.PRA., dated May 21, 1997, *nullified by* Mataram Religious High Court, No. 37/Pdt.G/2007/PTA.MTR, *nullification reversed in cassation*, Indonesian Supreme Court, No. 111 K/AG/1998.

*Amirah v. Ande et al.* Praya Religious Court, No. 262/Pdt.G/2006/PA.PRA., dated April 4, 2007.

*Baiq Fadlah et al. v. Baiq Saeah*, Denpasar High Court, No. 187/PTD/1977/Pdt, dated April 11, 1979, *upholding District Court determination, confirmed also by* Indonesian Supreme Court, No. 2014 K/Sip/1979, dated May 19, 1981.

Denpasar High Court, No. 102/PTD/1977/Pdt., dated June 27, 1977.

Denpasar High Court, No. 187/PTD/1977/Pdt, dated April 11, 1979.

Department of Education and Culture. 1977–78. *History of the West Nusa Tenggara*. Centre for Research and Culture, Research Project and Documentation.

*Inaq Illah et al. v. Lemin et al.* Mataram Religious Court, No. 144/Pdt.G/PA.MTR, dated February 22, 2006, nullified by Mataram Religious High Court, No. 38/Pdt.G/2006/PTA.MTR, dated July 19, 2006, affirmed in cassation by Supreme Court, No. 15 K/AG/2007, dated May 30, 2007.

*Inaq Putrahimah et al. v. Amaq Mukminah et al.* Mataram Religious Court, No. 85/Pdt.G/92/PA.Mtr., dated November 5, 1992.

*Inaq Rasini v. Amaq Atimah et al.* Indonesia Supreme Court, No. 1589 K/Sip/1974, dated September 2, 1978.

*Inaq Sanah et al. v. Kadirun et al.* Selong District Court, No. 164/P.N.Sel/1982/Pdt., dated December 27, 1982.

*Inaq Suni et al. v. Hj. Salmah et al.* Praya Religious Court, No. 306/Pdt.G/2007/PA.PRA, dated March 17, 2008.

*Inaq Supar et al. v. Amaq Mali et al.* Decision of the Mataram District Court, No. 049/PN.Mtr./Pdt/1970, dated December 27, 1976.

Indonesia Supreme Court, No. 853 K/Sip./1978, dated April 29, 1981.

Indonesia Supreme Court, No. 2014 K/Sip/1979, dated May 19, 1981.

Indonesia Supreme Court, No. 2662 K/Pdt/1984, dated November 26, 1985.

Indonesia Supreme Court, No. 86 K/AG/1994, dated July 27, 1995.

Indonesia Supreme Court, No. 111 K/AG/1998, dated September 13, 2005.

Indonesia Supreme Court, No. 121 K/AG/2008, dated June 6, 2008.

Indonesia Supreme Court, No. 515 K/AG/2008, dated March 6, 2009.

*Ishak et al. v. Mahyin et al.*, Praya Religious Court, No. 61/Pdt.G/2005/PA.PRA, September 5, 2005, *nullified by* Mataram Religious High Court, No. 18/Pdt.G/2006/PTA.Mtr, March 21, 2006, *nullification affirmed by* Indonesian Supreme Court, No. 368 K/AG/2006, January 3, 2007.

*Lalu Purwadi v. Baiq Nursam et al.* Selong Religious Court, No. 121/Pdt.G/2005/PA.SEL., dated September 21, 2005, approved by Mataram Religious High Court, No. 11/Pdt.G/2006/PTA. MTR., February 23, 2006 and Indonesia Supreme Court, No. 387 K/AG/2006, May 5, 2008.

Mataram Religious High Court, No. 17/Pdt/1984/PT.NTB, dated March 26, 1984.

Mataram Religious High Court, No. 19/Pdt.G/1993/PTA.Mtr., dated September 15, 1993.

Mataram Religious High Court, No. 72/Pdt.G/1997/PTA.MTR., dated October 13, 1997.

Mataram Religious High Court, No. 18/Pdt.G/2006/PTA.Mtr, dated March 21 2006.

Mataram Religious High Court, No. 37/Pdt.G/2007/PTA.MTR, dated June 28, 2007.

Mataram Religious High Court, No. 64/Pdt.G/2007/PTA.MTR, dated November 15, 2007.

Praya Religious Court, No. 61/Pdt.G/2005/PA.PRA, dated September 5, 2005.

*Rohini et al. v. H. Sajidi.* Selong Religious Court, No. 118/Pdt.G/2007/PA.SEL, dated July 19, 2007.

*Sitepu v. Ginting.* Indonesia Supreme Court, No. 179/Sip/1961, dated January 11, 1961.

*Sumenah v. Inaq Sini et al.* Praya Religious Court, No. 30/Pdt.G/2005/PA.PRA, dated August 22, 2005.

# PART IV
## Japan's Once and Future
## Legal Modernization Narrative

Chapter 13

# Japan's Legal Technical Assistance:
# A Different Modernization Narrative?[1]

Veronica L. Taylor

Scholarship examining the legal transplantation phenomenon suggests we are witnessing a continuum of five distinct periods of foreign aid or donor-propelled legal reform worldwide, namely: a pre-history of colonial legal development (to the 1960s); the inaugural moment of US legal development cooperation (1965–1974); the critical moment (1974–1989); the revivalist moment (1989–1998); and the "post" moment (1998 to the present) (Newton 2006). Similarly, but employing a slightly different taxonomy, one of the American protagonists in the "inaugural moment" has declared this present period to be a "third moment" of Law and Development (Trubek 2006). I would argue that both views are too narrow and fail to capture the complexity and breadth of 21st century donor-driven legal reform.

Each of the "moments" sketched by Newton above is underpinned by an assumption shared by many policy elites in the West—that legal reform assistance serves development and modernization of the target countries. In the "post" moment, what had been called "law and development," is increasingly labeled "rule of law" and the contours of that renamed field remain contested (Taylor 2009c). Less remarked upon, however, is the reality that Western industrialized states no longer have a monopoly on ideas about legal and political development and their relationship to modernization. There are now a significant number of well-funded non-Western players on the field of legal development assistance, both as bilateral donors and as funders of multilateral entities such as the World Bank and IMF. Who are these non-Western players, what are they doing, and what motivates their agendas about legal and regulatory reform in countries that are important to them?

Most of these non-Western efforts at legal and political development come out of Asia, broadly understood. The rise of Asia is crucial (Berger 2004), both as a target region for contemporary rule of law assistance, and as a source of distinct models of legal reform, whether domestic or as part of donor-funded assistance. These new—or newly prominent—streams of rule of law assistance from and within Asia prompt a specific query. Is there any necessary link between rule of law assistance in Asia and "development" or "modernization" as framed in earlier "moments" of Western legal intervention?

Responses may vary according to where one sits within the Asian matrix of rule of law assistance, and whether we employ the conventional Western/global framework of analysis, or adopt local perspectives (see, for example, Peerenboom 2004; Perry-Kessaris 2008; Gillespie and Peerenboom 2009; Bergling, Ederlöf and Taylor 2009; Perry-Kessaris 2009). In this chapter I suggest that, regardless of one's preferred normative stance, the empirical reality of legal technical assistance originating in Asia represents a challenge to the view that legal development is a Western or American enterprise, an assumption arguably underlying much of the law and development

---

1   This chapter is an adapted and re-edited version of Veronica L. Taylor (2009a).

scholarship canon (see, for example, Trubek and Santos 2006). I illustrate this question by exploring Japan's evolving experience as a rule of law donor. Japan's experience is particularly salient because it was the first of the "Asian miracle" economies, matured as an industrial power, and is now a stagnant post-industrial state that provides legal development advice and support to other Asian countries. That Japan's own state building paralleled its economic and technological flourishing in the later 19th century (the 1868–1912 Meiji era) is itself an important component of the Japanese legal development narrative.

## Japan as Pre-History for Modern Asian Legal Development

Japanese legal elites describe the rise of legal technical assistance through three different narratives: Government sponsored stories about law in the service of Japanese modernity; Japan's response to recipient countries' desire for a non-Western version of legal reform; and questions about how to reconcile Japan's own reception of modern law and its new role as provider of legal technical assistance. Running parallel to these discourse threads is a self-critical comparison with Western bilateral and multilateral donors.

### *Law in the Service of Japanese Modernity*

Japan's nineteenth century Meiji era is sometimes understood in the West as episodes from Puccini's opera *Madama Butterfly*. The story is that Japan was a closed traditional (non-Western) society, which was forced to open in 1868 by the famous "black ships" of American Commodore Mathew Perry. So technology forces the opening of a traditional Asian society, short term tragic dislocation ensues, but Japan ultimately adopts Western ways (industrialization), and experiences booming economic development, becoming strong and independent as a result.

Japan modernized between 1868 and World War I, drawing on endowments like political revolution, widespread literacy, established technologies and an awareness of the threats posed by Western powers. It emerged in the early twentieth century as a modern industrial economy with conglomerate corporations—*zaibatsu*—that assumed great importance as trading enterprises. Japan's economic and political growth was accelerated by wars of expansion – defeats of China over Korea in 1894–1895 and Russia over Manchuria in 1904–1905. The latter war saw the Japanese navy sink Russia's imperial fleet at the Battle of Tsushima in 1905. The ultimate policy goal was political independence and the ability to absorb and improve know-how from the West— themes that resonate with political and legal policies being pursued today in the places such as the People's Republic of China and Vietnam.

The "legal" version of this history found in Japanese government sources, and in some scholarly writing, is more selective. It begins with the foreign legal experts invited to Meiji Japan (1868–1912) in the latter half of the nineteenth century, to teach law and advise on the drafting of European-style codified positive law (for example, Riles 2001). Japanese political leaders during the same period dispatched their best and brightest young men to Europe, in order to make an exhaustive study of comparative legal models. Decades of laborious statutory drafting and redrafting followed, resulting in the promulgation of hybrid Codes that drew on multiple sources. Then followed decades of "reception" of the new legal concepts, professionalization of the bench and bar, and then legal self-reliance.

Over the period 1868–1912, Japan imported a great deal of development "software" in the form of the Civil Law system—predominantly, but not exclusively, drawing on German models.

The nineteenth century Japanese reformers deliberately chose Civil Law over Common Law on which to model their country's legal system, because they judged it a better "fit" with their view of politics and the proper relationship between individuals and the state (see also the chapters of John Haley, and Kent Anderson and Peter Kirby). This pattern continues in much of Asia today; where countries such as the PRC have the scope for choice, a version of Civil Law is often the preferred reform vehicle.

The Civil Law institutional choice becomes important again in the twenty-first century when Japan emerges as a legal technical assistance provider within a region in which the majority of Asian jurisdictions share a Civil Law doctrinal base and distinctively civilian approaches to institutional design—including the judiciary, traditions of scholarship, public law, and even conceptions and forms of democracy. For Japanese civilian lawyers, for whom the Codes are constitutive of the legal system and quasi-constitutional in importance, it makes complete sense to contribute to legal technical assistance through Code-drafting.

In Cambodia, for example, the Japanese Taskforce on the Civil Code was chaired by Professor Morishima and the Japanese Taskforce on the Civil Procedure Code by Professor Takeshita. Morishima and Takeshita placed great emphasis on the orderly development of law, beginning with the Code framework for private and commercial law. Critical of other donors, who encouraged patchwork development of specific legislation aimed at attracting foreign investment, Japanese actors maintained that specific laws on security interests in property, or on insolvency, could only make sense once the Code framework was established (Taylor 2005).

The unspoken premise is that Japan's nineteenth century codification served the country well, at least until the post-World War II Occupation reforms of the 1950s, and then until the intensive statutory reforms of the 1990s and 2000s. Thus, conversational claims such as that (Professor) "Morishima is the Boisonnade of Vietnam" explicitly tie together the "foreign legal advisor," Code-drafting and voluntary adoption of modern Continental European law as phases of Japan's state-building, with an implicit expectation that the rapid military and economic development of the twentieth century that followed in Japan can be emulated. This is a mythic narrative of abstracted modernity in which the key themes are self-reliance, collaboration, and voluntary choices by local decision-makers, elements that seem subordinated in twenty-first century rule of law assistance (Taylor 2009a). This is expressly not the same thing as local "buy in" to foreign designed and organized programs such as those pursued by many contemporary bilateral and multilateral donors.

This historical discourse also weaves in cultural attributes, such as a Japanese "preference" for alternate dispute resolution, which marks Japan as an "Asian" country, well-placed to assist neighbors seeking to avoid the litigious excesses of the United States. As system insiders know, however, the historical pattern in Japan is that ADR was created and manipulated by the state to curb citizen litigation during economic downturns and social crises (Tanase 2001; Haley 1991; Upham 1998). This is an invented tradition of non-litigiousness.

The sanitized legal development narrative also conceals Japan's historical use of law as a tool of social control, both at home and during its colonization of Asia. In the early twentieth century, this meant implementing variations of newly-minted Japanese law in the colonies of Korea, Formosa and Manchuria, while carefully studying local law and custom in order to create concentric circles of indigenous, local colonial and imperial law (Wang 1992; Dudden 2004). Not all Japanese colonial legal reform, of course, was coerced. Thailand drew heavily on Japanese expertise in the course of undertaking its own autonomous codification and legal modernization drive in the 19th century (Kagawa 2002). The narrative also disregards the embarrassing interlude of the nominally anti-colonial "East Asian Co-Prosperity Sphere" and World War II, which began for Asia in 1931 with the Japanese conquest of Manchuria. It incorporates an unspoken assumption that the post-

1945 Occupation, and General Macarthur's efforts to rewrite the Japanese constitution returned Japan to a Western "rule of law." More recently this was echoed in American claims that Iraqi "nation-building" including the re-establishment of rule of law, should and could be as successful as what had been pursued in Germany and Japan following World War II (rebutted in Dower 2003).

Nor was Japanese legal development tempered and gradual. The historical narrative is largely silent about the way in which war, social conflict and the toxic side effects of modernization influenced the trajectory of the legal system. Convulsive legal change occurred, for example, when the post-World War II Occupation introduced market-oriented commercial law, as well as democratic institutions that created new possibilities for challenging the state. Regulatory law was subordinated to the needs of big business during the economic take-off period of the 1950s and subsequent high growth from the 1960s to the 1980s, and consumer protection and fully-developed intellectual property rights were delayed until the 1990s (Hirowatari 2000). However, legal (and litigated) clashes between citizens and the government continued to target regulatory lapses and harmful business practices in areas such as the environment, labor, gender equity and civil rights during the twentieth century, in some cases successfully (Feldman 2000). Even today, the statutory gaps that remain in respect of protection from discrimination, redress for wartime wrongs and protection of human rights are routinely challenged through public interest litigation.

Having rebuilt its own economy in the second half of the twentieth century—initially with multilateral financing and foreign aid assistance—Japan grew to become the world's second largest economy. By the 1990s it had begun to export rule of law assistance to Asia—but with what characteristics? While they were familiar with the approaches of other multilateral and bilateral donors, Japanese governmental and legal elites initially avoided the formulations "law and development" and "rule of law," opting instead to label their activities "legal technical assistance" [*hōseibishien*]. A distinctive national discourse developed about the origins, aims and characteristics of Japanese legal technical assistance which was, in its "first moment" not framed in policy terms as either economically oriented or as explicitly developmental in nature (so the Washington Consensus was mostly prominent in its absence).

By 2008, Japan had entered its "second moment" as a donor. A new political debate about the definition, delivery and geographic targets for legal technical assistance has emerged. There are indications that some elites wish to recast the activity as a more explicitly economic initiative and locate projects within the multilateral donor discourse of "rule of law assistance." At the same time, a recurrent thread in the policy discourse underscores the need for "Japanese-style assistance" (Kurokawa 2008). Japan's "first" and "second" moments of legal technical assistance contain a very different mix of elements from those sketched in the traditional Western rule of law typology. Japan clearly monitors the dominant Western donor initiatives and discourses in legal reform, but is forging a rather different path, substantively and geographically.


**The Japanese Trajectory of Rule of Law Assistance**

Japan is a relatively late entrant to the rule of law assistance surge of the late twentieth century. Its formal program of Overseas Development Assistance or ODA-funded legal technical assistance began in 1996. It was targeted at developing economies in Asia that were commercially important markets for Japan, particularly Vietnam, Cambodia, Indonesia and China. Although Japan's status as the world's largest bilateral provider of ODA has fallen, it remains a dominant source of development funding in Asia and Central Asia. It is the primary shareholder in the Asian Development Bank, and the second largest shareholder in the World Bank after the United States.

The domestic mandate for Japan's move into legal technical assistance derives from Japan's ODA Charter, first approved as a Cabinet policy directive in 1992 and then significantly revised in 2003 to deliver better "strategic value, flexibility, transparency and efficiency" in Japan's ODA spending (Official Development Assistance Charter [ODA Charter] 2003). Newly incorporated in those revisions was an explicit reference to requiring recipient countries to exercise good governance, and a commitment to providing cooperation "for institution building including development of legal systems." The policy priority areas identified in the 2003 revision were poverty reduction, sustainable growth (explicitly defined to include protection of intellectual property rights and standardization); global issues such as terrorism and international organized crime; and peace-building. The priority regions for Japanese ODA were defined as Asia (particularly South Asia, Central Asia and the Caucuses); Africa, the Middle East, Latin America and Oceania (ODA Charter 2003). However, to date legal technical assistance has been carried out primarily in Southeast Asia and Central Asia.

The 2003 revision was driven by rapid geo-political changes in the 1990s, including a policy switch by multilateral development banks from Washington Consensus-style neoclassical economic policies to poverty reduction. During the same period, Japan experienced a prolonged recession of historic severity, and public support for ODA dropped from 43.2 percent in 1990 to 19 percent in 2003 (Sunaga 2004). Some factions of the ruling Liberal Democratic Party began to push for an ODA policy emphasizing national interest, and Japan's private sector continued to lobby for a return to tied aid so as to better align with national commercial interests (Keidanren 2007). Japanese NGOs, on the other hand, remained strongly in favor of both continuing and increasing the value of untied ODA. The 2003 Charter attempted to strike a compromise, paying some deference to the ruling party's views but preserving untied ODA (Sunaga 2004).

The 2003 Charter ensured that the status of legal technical assistance was boosted, and its future was secured, when it established "institution building including development of legal systems" as an ODA priority activity. In so doing, it bolstered recommendations in a policy document issued in 2001 by the Justice System Reform Council. The Council was created in 1998 as part of the most intense domestic legal reform for Japan since the Occupation (1947–1953) and Meiji (1868–1912) periods. Under the heading "Legal technical assistance for developing countries should be promoted," the document points out that:

> … Utilizing its own experience in having adopted modern legal systems from other countries and having established the legal system as well as the administration of that system in conformity with the circumstances of the country, Japan has been providing legal technical assistance by accepting trainees from Asian and other developing countries, dispatching professionals and conducting on-site seminars in the fields of civil law, commercial law and criminal justice. Such assistance is important in order for Japan to play a positive role as a member of the international society and also to contribute to the development of smooth economic activities in private sectors in the advancing globalization of society and the economy. Therefore, the government, lawyers and bar associations should cooperate as appropriate and continue to actively promote support for legal technical assistance for developing countries (Justice System Reform Council 2001).

Inscribed into both justice system reform policy and the revised ODA Charter, legal technical assistance—a modest voluntary effort by a small number of Japanese legal academics and government lawyers—now had secure ongoing government funding.

*Japanese Rule of Law Actors and Projects*

Japan's legal technical assistance funding comes primarily from an ODA budget that is distributed across multiple government Ministries and agencies. The Ministry of Foreign Affairs (MOFA) administers more than half of this. Its agency, the Japan International Cooperation Agency (JICA) is one of several direct recipients and a key umbrella for legal technical assistance projects. Programming in this area involves multiple government and non-government players, including: the Cabinet Secretariat, Ministry of Foreign Affairs, JICA, the Ministry of Justice, the International Civil and Commercial Law Centre (ICCLC, now Foundation); Ministry of Finance, the Ministry of Economy, Technology and Industry (METI); the Japanese Federation of Industries (Keidanren 2007); the Japan Federation of Bar Associations (Nichibenren 2012); the Supreme Court, and Japanese university law faculties, particularly the regional national universities, Nagoya, Kyushu and Kobe.

As the list suggests, legal technical assistance in Japan is predominantly a public sector-led enterprise, although the government does solicit financial support from the private sector. Business, in turn, is able to call for project priorities. Legal technical assistance projects have, at least until 2008, been treated as pro-bono or public service for the purposes of staffing. The national development agency, JICA, has relatively few legally-trained staff so must co-opt academics, prosecutors, judges and attorneys. Despite (or perhaps due to) the small size of the Japanese legal professions, volunteering for legal technical assistance work is the norm. The projects and their implementers build on the self-perception of legal professionals as an elite corps, charged with the support and advancement of a national mission. In the case of attorneys, this fits well with the foundational provision Article 1(1) of the Practicing Attorney Law (1949, as amended), which explicitly defines the mission of Japanese attorneys as public service and the upholding of human rights. Furthermore, the legal technical assistance wave is exciting for Japanese lawyers, prosecutors and judges because it offers an opportunity to be internationally engaged and important without directly incurring the systemic capital expense of increasing the size of the legal profession or establishing global legal practices.

The combination of a small-scale legal profession and a unitary legal system facilitated a high degree of interpersonal cooperation during Japan's "first moment." JICA convenes several legal coordination committees with outside membership. The universities sponsor frequent seminar series and symposia on law and development. The Ministry of Justice publishes a regular newsletter for the field *ICD News: Law for Development.* These players also coordinate the staffing of projects, allowing what one commentator calls the "all Japan" approach to delivering the necessary mix of legal professionals to counterpart countries (Inaba 2008). In private, Japanese legal professionals engaged in legal technical assistance are dismissive of American rule of law delivery (characterized as corporate in nature, since rule of law work constitutes a major for-profit consulting industry), believing their "national" Japanese model to be more altruistic and responsive. The Ministry of Justice has, based on the national experience of the Meiji era, aimed at not directly transplanting the Japanese national legal system, but—through repeated consultative interactions with the counterpart country—sought to effect the "unforced legal technical assistance" suited to the needs and conditions [of that country]. Due to appreciation and understanding of this approach, among the many donors that conduct legal technical assistance, Japanese believe their national assistance is particularly highly valued by target countries (Kurokawa 2008).[2]

---

2   Japanese altruism may indeed be the overriding norm here, but the mode of delivery is also structurally induced by the limited supply of legal professionals. The national bar pass rate is artificially pegged to just

A consequence of expanded aspirations regarding legal technical assistance is that the modalities may need to change. A key issue for Japan is insufficient personnel. The short-term "fix" proposed is to ease personnel regulations for judges and dig deeper into the public service to court clerks and institutional staff, in order to populate projects (Kurokawa 2008) while "hoping" that more volunteers will appear (Yabuki 2008).

The *ad hoc*, voluntary responses to recipient requests that characterized the launch projects in Vietnam and Cambodia described below are likely to be replaced with Japanese diagnostic determinations about what is needed, a more strategic deployment of resources and a formal mechanism for interagency cooperation established at the Cabinet level (Kurokawa 2008).

*Launch Projects and Characteristics*

Japan's official contemporary legal technical assistance commenced with the work of Emeritus Professor Akio Morishima, former Dean of the Law Faculty of Nagoya University. An acquaintanceship with the Minister of Justice in Vietnam led to a request to provide advice on legislative drafting, which he did under the auspices of cultural exchange in 1992 (Morishima 2000). This was followed by training courses for Vietnamese officials in Japan from 1994 and the formal commencement of legal technical assistance to Vietnam as ODA in 1996. The core of the Vietnam project in its first phase was a ten-member Japanese team on Civil Code drafting chaired by Morishima and working with Vietnamese counterparts. The final draft of the Civil Code was adopted by the National Assembly of Vietnam in May 2005, replacing the Civil Code of 1995. Further requests followed from Cambodia and from Mongolia in 1994 to the Japan Federation of Bar Associations and from the Ministry of Justice in the Lao PDR in 1996. In 1999, the Japanese and Cambodian governments agreed to draft a new Civil Code and Code of Civil Procedure for Cambodia.

Individual Japanese projects during this first moment were broadly similar to those supported by other donors, including the usual components of legislative drafting; institutional support for economic policy, such as direct assistance to the competition authority in Indonesia; judicial training on decision-writing and the selection and publication of case decisions; law enforcement mechanisms, especially in relation to intellectual property rights; computerization and legal education, including short-course training in-country, project based skills transfer, and scholarship support for advanced legal study in Japan (Taylor 2005). In scale and significance, however, the Code drafting projects in Vietnam and Cambodia were the most important legal technical assistance projects carried out by Japan (Yamashita and Tanaka 2003), and they established what Japanese commentators see as distinctive characteristics and national practices.

**Responding to a Call for a Non-Western Version of Legal Reform**

Japanese legal technical assistance projects, of course, are intended to stabilize rather than challenge the local system. Common to these projects is a strong emphasis on recipient autonomy in selecting and requesting the form of assistance. The projects in Vietnam and Cambodia took several years

---

above replacement levels in all branches of the profession and, while the 70 percent of legally educated applicants who are *not* permitted to pass each year would be prime candidates for building out new areas of legal practice and/or consulting, there is no sign that legal elites in Japan plan to loosen their grip on the definition or accreditation of "lawyers".

of round-table collaborative discussion before the Japanese partners were satisfied that their local counterparts had sufficient understanding of the laws and the drafting issues to make informed choices about what their Code provisions should contain (Taylor 2005). This echoes a kind of legal "memory" of Japan's nineteenth century (Meiji) legal modernization, instituted as a result of American gunboat diplomacy, sketched earlier in this essay, but then implemented autonomously. Japanese participants place a high value on the freedom to fashion a national legal identity, or "independent development" (*jiritsu hatten*) (Inaba 2008).

Not surprisingly, a core theme of the launch projects has been an emphasis on legal education. On the Japanese side, the foundations of this approach lie in the 1980s policy outlined by then Prime Minister Nakasone which emphasized development of human resources within Japan's strategically important markets. Student scholarships in law at Japanese universities that are targeted at Central Asian republics such as Mongolia and Uzbekistan and the newly marketized economies of China and Vietnam are illustrative (Aikyo 2008). The content of customized programs at the graduate level for these students has tended to be doctrinal and/or practical. At Nagoya, for example, the LLM and PhD programs have been delivered in English, with a long-term plan to build cohorts of graduates who are also fluent in Japanese and able to use Japanese legal materials at an advanced level. Although some "perspectives" courses are available, there has been relatively little theoretical "law and development" content and branding. This is both a pragmatic choice, given the educational backgrounds of the students, and also probably reflects some Japanese ambivalence about American "law and development" scholarship, the degree to which it reflects Japanese policy priorities and its applicability in an Asian context.[3]


**From Receiver of Law to Provider of Legal Assistance**


The third strand of legal technical assistance discourse in Japan is linked to the Justice System Reform policies of the late 1990s. A clear theme in this policy initiative is the charge that the rule of law never really took root in Japan, either during Meiji, or after the Occupation reforms (compare Haley and Taylor 2004; Hamada 2008). Not surprisingly, thoughtful academics in Japan have tremendous difficulty reconciling the apparent contradiction of their own country's justice system "failure" and the success of its economy with the standard American rule of law claim that highly developed legal systems are indispensable elements in economic growth. Providing an account of modern law as the central, propelling factor in Japan's industrialization is taxing, largely because this is a modernist fiction. Certainly Japan had sophisticated civil, commercial and procedural law, and plenty of it, but as Haley (1991) and Upham (1987) have argued, it was the strong reliance on informal means of ordering and the government control of formal law and processes that really distinguished Japan until at least the mid-twentieth century.

Japanese legal history raises real questions about how much law is necessary for development (or modernization) and at what point, and how much predictability business really seeks (as opposed to claiming that it seeks) in a transitional economy. Leading Japanese legal sociologist

---

3   The educational emphasis within legal technical assistance in the 1990s also supported the emergence of "Asian law" as a formal field of research and teaching in Japanese universities. To be sure, Japanese legal scholars do not see Asian law and legal technical assistance as fungible fields (Imai, Morigiwa and Inoue 1999; Yasuda, 2000 and Kaneko, 1998). But there is no doubt that government funding for ODA also played a role in universities hiring young faculty in law with backgrounds in Asian languages and/or area studies; the establishment of the Center for Asian Legal Exchange (CALE) at Nagoya University, the Asian Law Center at Kyushu University and the Faculty of International Cooperation at Kobe University are leading examples.

Takao Tanase argues that "law was not a precondition of the modernization in Japan, at least to the degree that the sweeping statement of 'the law as a prerequisite for modern society' implies" (Tanase 2001). Rather, he suggests, that the Justice System Reform narrative employs a standard modernist technique: simultaneous denial and affirmation of (Japanese) legal culture and legal institutions. This leads to, and indeed requires, more modern law (Tanase 2001).

This tension between the historical development narrative in Japan and Western donor rhetoric of rule of law assistance runs through Japan's first "moment" of legal technical assistance. The tension involves self-critique, as well as considerable ambivalence about Western donor approaches. A common self-criticism by Japanese practitioners during this period is that Japan's legal technical assistance lacks clear objectives and measurable outcomes. By this, they often mean a clear normative statement of priorities. For example, Japanese legal technical assistance to date is noticeably agnostic on economic theory, particularly neo-liberal or new institutional economics (NIE) ideas embedded in international financial institutions' frame of reference (see Sakumoto, Kobayashi and Imaizumi 2003; Kobayashi 2001). Instead, Japanese lawyers in the field seem to accept the market economy as meaningful, but also to understand the diverse and hybrid features of American, European and Japanese capitalisms (Hall and Soskice 2001). They have been reluctant to present the evolution of Japanese commercial law as a causal factor in Japan's rise as an economic superpower, being more concerned with how law and legal institutions in Japan were historically molded to the political and economic priorities of the day (Hirowatari 2000).

The lack of a dominant economic theory in Japanese legal technical assistance is not simply a normative preference. Legal education in Japan is not interdisciplinary at either the undergraduate or graduate level, so few lawyers are trained in economics. Similarly, Japan's legal technical assistance projects are seldom staffed with members from a business background, although they may utilize the local presence of entities such as the Japan External Trade Organization (JETRO) or Japanese businesses. The implicit Civilian character predominates, and law and economics in the American doctrinal sense accordingly is absent.

A further domestic criticism by Japanese business and taxpayers has been that the ODA efforts are invisible and lack direct, tangible benefits for Japan. Japanese legal technical assistance is vulnerable to this claim in part because projects to date have not focused on metrics in the style of other donors (Taylor 2007). Nor do they employ elaborately designed project evaluation. The absence of a rigid or normative framework can, of course, be useful. If, for example, you want to engage with Myanmar on legal reform, not having an overarching concern with human rights norms would be convenient. But it can also be felt as a void. So, for example, the Scandinavian design elements of gender equity and human rights which are clearly tracked in Japan's evolving ODA policy (JICA, 2003) are also attractive to some Japanese legal technical assistance academics and practitioners (Nagoya University Center for Asian Legal Exchange, undated). Japan's pragmatic, low-profile approach is also vulnerable to the charge that insufficient attention is given to partnering with NGOs, both at home and abroad (Kawai and Takagi 2001). The tripartite analysis of the state, "society" and the individual, which underpins much NGO involvement in much Western bilateral donor-sponsored legal development work, is missing on a technical level, and Japanese legal technical assistance is accordingly very much a state to state exercise.


**New Global Pressures and Japan's "Second Moment"**

Since 2008, the beginning of what we could call Japan's "second moment," the political nature of Japan's technical legal assistance has become more apparent. Japan's first moment practitioners sometimes claimed in conversation that Japan's ODA (including legal technical assistance) was distinct from that of other countries because it had no instrumental motive. It was a response to a genuine request from recipients. To the extent that rule of law assistance is a form of ODA, however, it is more accurate to view it as having multiple main purposes: diplomatic (including security), developmental, humanitarian relief, commercial and cultural (Lancaster 2006). Since the 1990s, bilateral aid has also performed the additional tasks of promoting economic and social transitions (including legal reform), promoting democracy, addressing global issues, mitigating conflicts and managing post-conflict transitions (Lancaster 2006).

Donors mix, shift and frequently obscure the nature and relative priority of their goals. Japan's "first moment" of legal technical assistance could be coded as mix of cultural (student scholarships and in-country training) and economic transition—providing foundational legal infrastructure such as Codes. However, policy discourse suggests that a "second moment" of legal technical assistance has begun since 2008, as part of which policy objectives become more sharply defined.

The first indicator of a shift to a second moment was the geographic expansion of Japanese legal reform projects. Work in Vietnam, Cambodia, Lao PDR, Indonesia and China is now joined by a significant focus on Central Asia and a projected build out to Africa. All of these countries and regions appeared in the revised ODA Charter of 2003, but the Central Asian focus was underscored in the "Silk Road" policy launched in 2004 with (then) Foreign Minister Yoriko Kawaguchi's visit to the region and then the conclusion of a series of bilateral trade agreements with governments in that region (Len et al. 2008).

The second indicator that legal technical assistance in Japan was changing was when it became the focus of the ruling Liberal Democratic Party's Legal Affairs Committee, which unveiled "Strategic Vision for Our Country's Legal Technical Assistance that we can take Pride in Before the World" in June 2007 (Liberal Democratic Party 2007). This subsequently fed into Cabinet policy deliberations and reappeared in the Cabinet-level 13th Annual Forum on Economic Cooperation, held in January 2008, at which legal technical assistance was recognized as "an important form of foreign economic cooperation, which going forward, requires strategic attention" (Inaba 2008). The keyword in these policy documents is *economic* cooperation, a bilateral aid objective that was not prominent in "first moment" projects. An immediate practical example is given in the White Paper on Official Development Assistance, which describes capacity building for young bureaucrats in Tashkent and the development of an Uzbekistan commentary on bankruptcy law and strengthening of civil and administrative statutes in order to support business activity (White Paper on Official Development Assistance 2007).[4]

At the trade policy level, it has been suggested that Japan in the last decade has sought to enhance its trade competitiveness by engaging in "aggressive legalism" (Pekkanen 2008). Exporting legal

---

4   A project that illustrates the convergence between commercial and educational interests is the Legal Information Research Center, home of an East Asia legal translation database being developed at Nagoya University in cooperation with the Ministry of Justice (Aikyo 2008:23). Initially a Japanese Government attempt to respond to the demands of Japanese business exporters for reliable official translations to English of Japan's key statutes, the project became a platform for developing an interoperable database of statutes and legal terminology in Japanese, Chinese, Korean and English. An important feature is the ability to add annotations to statute provisions, and so in effect, create a narrative of statutory and legal system history around shared doctrinal areas of law (Keidanren Sub-Committee 2004). A related project based at Nagoya is the build out of a collaborative library collection and catalogue covering legal materials from Asia (Aikyo 2008:20–23). Again, these are both cultural and educational projects but are intended to furnish important commercial intelligence about key markets in Asia, and to promote Japanese law as a relevant resource and standard.

services and technical know-how through legal technical assistance is not "aggressive" in the sense of juridifying trade disputes and manipulating rules legalistically for national advantage. However, it is an alternative example of harnessing law as a technology to improve the business environment for Japanese companies in Asian emerging markets.

The continued emphasis on education in this second moment of legal technical assistance is consistent with cultural objectives of bilateral aid—that is, positioning Japan as an "Asian" donor and emphasizing the cultural similarities and complementarities between the Japanese and recipient legal systems and institutional counterparts. Running through much of the new programming is a nationalist sense that "[i]t is important for us to try to extract ourselves from the 'Leave Asia, Enter Europe' situation" (Aikyo 2008). Allied with this is a keen understanding that at least some of the "wider diffusion of the rule of law being proposed, while laudable, is in essence a new plan for the worldwide export of American lawyers" (Hamada 2008).Viewed politically, the second moment projects in legal technical assistance are intended to help Japan assert its "global player" role in relation to other world powers, particularly China, by emphasizing its Asian credentials. By directing legal technical assistance towards Central Asian countries that remain relatively low priorities for the United States (Len 2005), Japan gains "market share" in a region that is proximate to China and Russia. Importantly, it also contributes to the legal infrastructure in places where Japan—and its competitors—have a direct interest in securing natural resources and bolstering their own energy security.

Thus far, the "second moment" looks endogenous, with Japanese elites independently determining the new policy direction. However, woven through the second moment conceptions is a clear sense that legal technical assistance is also a forum for global competition and policy dialogue. So, legal technical assistance and capacity building formed part of the Justice and Interior Affairs meeting agenda at the June 2008 G8 meeting, requiring Japan to show strategic thinking and commitment (Kurokawa 2008). The sense of global competition also comes through in Kurokawa's observation—as a key policy player in the Ministry of Justice—that legal technical assistance has the advantage of being a type of ODA where "[y]ou can see the international assistance provider's face" (Kurokawa 2008).

## Whose "Moment"?

The Japanese trajectory of legal technical assistance suggests that experience of "law and development" in Asia may vary, depending on the actors. Within the United States, of course, "law and development" resonates with academic lawyers both as an established field of study, and as the lived experience of first-generation practitioners (as "old guard" and this chapter's point of departure). At the same time, neither scholarship nor practice have remained static, so the formula has been displaced in rhetoric and practice by "rule of law assistance." Trubek as a 1970s co-founder of the law and development movement concedes this by sub-titling his "third moment" of law and development "Rule of Law II" (Trubek 2006), and by recognizing that:

> The contemporary "Rule of Law" enterprise took shape in a very different *conjuncture* [from that of the development policy of the 1950s and 1960s]. By the 1990s when ROL really became big business, major changes had occurred in the world economy and world politics. International trade had grown substantially. The spread of industry in the "third world" and the success of export-led growth in Asia, plus the globalization strategies of major transnational corporations and rapid deregulation of capital markets, significantly increased the degree of world economic integration.

... The vision of a world of partially closed national economies and state-controlled national markets gave way to a vision of a fully open global economy with minimal state involvement and free flows of goods and capital across national boundaries. This vision affected thinking about development in very profound ways, creating a new development paradigm with important implications for the law reform agenda (Trubek 2006).

Trubek is primarily thinking of how the World Bank operationalizes multiple versions of rule of law internally, but of course "rule of law" as label and construct has a life independent of international financial institution usage.

The diversity of circumstances in which rule of law assistance is deployed is very visible in Asia, where disaster relief, post-conflict peace keeping, post-conflict reconstruction, institutional reform and democratization and ratification of global trade agreements are all drivers for donor-assisted legal reform. Although we may, following Trubek, continue to classify the donor intervention as "development assistance," a better working hypothesis for the twenty-first century might be that rule of law assistance has become decoupled from *development* as the sole or primary objective, and that security, commercial, humanitarian and cultural outcomes benefiting the donor may be equally, if not more, important (Taylor 2009c).

Japan's legal technical assistance over the last two decades would seem to support that hypothesis. This empirical reality, of course, is unlikely to affect the taxonomy of the field in the United States, where the "third moment" of law and development also functions as intellectual branding by energetic scholar-entrepreneurs. However, at the very least, it should alert us to the possibility that a "third moment" is not universal, and that developments in Asia bear closer analysis precisely because they do not converge with Western experience.

## References


Aikyo, M. 2008. Nagoya daigaku to hōseibishien jigyō / kenkyū.[Nagoya University research and initiatives on legal technical assistance]. *Jurisuto [Jurist]* 1358, June, 17–25.

Ministry of Foreign Affairs Japan. 2010. Gijyutsukyôryoku hōseidoseibishien ni kansuru kihon hôshin [Basic policy direction on technical cooperation on legal system assistance, http://www. mofa.go.jp/mofaj/gaiko/oda/seisaku/keitai/gijyutsu/houseido.html [Last accessed 9 February 2012].

Berger, M.T. 2004. *The Battle for Asia: From decolonization to globalization.* London and New York: RoutledgeCurzon.

Bergling, P., Ederlöf J., and Taylor V.L. 2009. *Rule of Law Promotion: Global Perspectives, Local Applications.* Uppsala: Iustus.

Dower, J. 2003. A Warning From History: Don't Expect Democracy in Iraq. *Boston Review.* Available at: http://bostonreview.net/BR28.1/dower.html [last accessed: February 9, 2012].

Dudden, A. 2004. *Japan's Colonization of Korea: Discourse and power.* Honolulu: University of Hawaii Press.

Feldman, E.A. 2000. The Ritual of Rights in Japan: Law, society and health policy. Cambridge: Cambridge University Press.

Gillespie, J. and Peerenboom, R. 2009. *Regulation in Asia: Pushing Back on Globalization.* London: Routledge.

Haley J.O. and Taylor, V.L. 2004. *Rule of Law in Japan*, in *Asian Discourses of Rule of Law*, edited by R. Peerenboom. New York, London: RoutledgeCurzon, 440–68.

Haley, J.O. 1991. *Authority without Power: Law and the Japanese paradox.* Oxford: Oxford University Press.

Hall, P.A. and Soskice, D. 2001. *Varieties of Capitalism.* Oxford: Oxford University Press.

Hamada Kunio. 2008. Nihon ni okeru hō no shihai ni tsuite [On the Rule of law in Japan]. *NBL,* 873.

Hirowatari, S. 2000. Post-war Japan and the Law: Mapping Discourses and Legalization and Modernization. *Social Science Japan Journal,* 3(2) 155.

Imai Hiromichi, Morigiwa Yasutomo, Inoue Tatsuo. 1999. *Henyō suru ajia no hō to tetsugaku [Asian law and Philosophy in Flux].* Tokyo: Yuhikaku.

Inaba Kazuo. 2008. Hōseibishien jigyō no ima [Current legal technical assistance initiatives]. *Jurisuto [Jurist],* 1358(June 2008): 2–8.

JICA: Japan International Cooperation Agency. 2003. *Japan International Cooperation Agency Annual Report 2003.* Available at: http://www.jica.go.jp/english/publications/reports/annual/2003/index.html [last accessed 9 February 2012].

Justice System Reform Council. 2001. *Recommendations of the Justice System Reform Council – For a Justice System to Support Japan in the 21st Century English Translation of the Final Report.* Available at http://www.kantei.go.jp/foreign/judiciary/2001/0612report.html [last accessed 9 February, 2012].

Kagawa, K. 2002. *Masao Tokichi den: hōseibishien kokusaikyōryoku no senkusha [Biography of Tokichi Masao, Pioneer in International Cooperation and Legal Technical Assistance].* Tokyo: Shinzansha.

Kaneko Yuka. 1998. *Ajiahō no kanōsei [The Potential for Asian Law].* Okayama City:Daigakukyōikushuppan.

Kawai Masahiro and Takagi Shinji. 2001. Japan's Official Development Assistance: Recent Issues and Future Directions 4 (World Bank Policy Research, Working Paper No 2722). Available at: http://papers.ssrn.com/sol3/papers.cfm?abstract_id=634433 [accessed: May 4, 2011].

Keidanren. 2007. *Nippon Keidanren [Japan Business Federation]: Recommendations on Japan's International Cooperation Policy and Expectations on the new JICA.* Available at: http://www.keidanren.or.jp/english/policy/2007/040.html. [last accessed 9 February 2012].

Keidanren Sub-committee on Corporate Law. 2004. *The Benefits of Translating Japanese Laws into Foreign Languages, Committee on Economic Law, Nippon Keidanren [Japan Business Federation]* [Provisional English translation]. Available at: http://www.keidanren.or.jp/english/policy/2004/051.html http://www.keidanren.or.jp/english/policy/2007/040.html [last accessed 9 February 2012].

Kobayashi Masayuki. 2001. *Ajiashokoku no shijōkeizaika to shakaihō [Market Transitions in Asian Countries and Social Law].* Tokyo: Institute of Developing Economies.

Kurokawa, H. 2008. Ōkiku kawaru hōseidoseibishien [Major changes to Legal technical assistance]. *ICD News: Law for Development,* 36(September 2008),1–4.

Lancaster, C. 2006. *Foreign Aid: Diplomacy, Development, Domestic Politics.* Chicago: University of Chicago Press.

Len, C. 2005. Japan's Central Asian Diplomacy: Motivations, implications and prospects for the region. *The China and Eurasia Forum Quarterly,* 3(3), 127–149.

Len, C., Uyama, T., and Hirose T. (eds). 2008. *Japan's Silk Road Diplomacy: Paving the Way Ahead, Central Asia-Caucasus Institute and Silk Road Studies Program.* Available at: http://www.isdp.eu/publications/books-and-monographs.html [last accessed 9 February 2012].

Liberal Democratic Party. 2007. Sekai ni hokoru, Wagakuni hōseibishien no senryaku bijiyon [Strategic Vision for Our Country's Legal Technical Assistance: {One that} we can take

Pride in Before the World]. Available at: http://www.jimin.jp/jimin/seisaku/2007/seisaku-012. html [Last accessed August 2007] See also Liberal Democratic Party *Policy Manifesto 2010*. Available at: http://www.jimin.jp/policy/manifest/index.html [last accessed 9 February 2012].

Morishima, A. 2000. Hōseibishien to nihon no hōritsugaku [Legal Technical Assistance and Law Studies in Japan]. *Hikakuhō kenkyu*, 62(issue), 120 – 36 as cited in Y. Shio, Japanese Legal Technical Assistance: Basic Codes Drafting Assistance and the Discourse of Japanese Legal Modernization (unpublished, on file with author).

Nagoya University for Asian Legal Exchange. Undated. *Legal Assistance in Asia: Structuring a paradigm for countries in transition*. Available at: http://tla.nomolog.nagoya-u.ac.jp.

Newton, S. 2006. The Dialectics of Law and Development, in *The New Law and Economic Development*, edited by D.M. Trubek and A. Santos. Cambridge: Cambridge University Press, 174–202.

Nichibenren [Japan Federation of Bar Associations]. 2012 *Kokusaikôryû no tame no katsudô* [Activities relating to international exchange] Available at: http://www.nichibenren.or.jp/ activity/international/interchange.html [last accessed 9 February 2012].

Official Development Assistance Charter (Unofficial Translation). 2003. Available at: http://www. mofa.go.jp/policy/oda/reform/charter.html [last accessed 9 February 2012].

Peerenboom Randall. 2004. *Discourses on Rule of Law in Asia*. London, New York: RoutledgeCurzon.

Pekkanen, S.M. 2008. *Japan's Aggressive Legalism: Law and foreign trade politics beyond the WTO*. Stanford: Stanford University Press.

Perry-Kessaris, A. 2009. Editor *Law in Pursuit of Development: Principles into Practice*. London: Routledge.

Perry-Kessaris, A. 2008. *Global Business, Local Law: The Indian Legal System as Communal Resource in Foreign Investment Relations*. Aldershot: Ashgate.

Pistor, K., and Wellons, P. 1999. *The Role of Law and Legal Institutions in Asian Economic Development*. New York: Oxford University Press.

Practicing Attorney Law (or Lawyers' Law). 1949, as amended. *Law No. 205 of 1949*. Available at: http://www.nichibenren.or.jp/en/about/pdf/practicing_attorney_law.pdf.

White Paper on Official Development Assistance. 2007. *Seifu kaihatsu enjo (ODA) hakusho 2007ban: 'Nihon no kokusai kyōryoku' [ 2007 White Paper on Official Development Assistance (ODA): 'Japan's International Cooperation']*. Available at: http://www.mofa.go.jp/mofaj/ gaiko/oda/shiryo/hakusyo/07_hakusho_pdf/pdfs/07_hakusho_020203.pdf [last accessed 9 February 2012].

Riles, A. (ed.) 2001. *Rethinking the Masters of Comparative Law*. Oxford: Hart Publishing.

Sakumoto, N., Kobayashi, M., and Shinya Imaizumi. 2003. *Law, Development and Socio-Economic Changes in Asia*. Tokyo: Institute of Developing Economies.

Sunaga, K. 2004. *The Reshaping of Japan's Official Development Assistance (ODA) Charter, FASID Discussion Paper on Development Assistance No 3*. Available at: http://www.mofa. go.jp/policy/oda/reform/charter.html [last accessed 9 February 2012].

Tanase, T. 2001. *The Empty Space of the Modern in Japanese Law Discourse* in *Adapting Legal Cultures*, edited by D. Nelkin and J. Feest. Oxford: Hart Publishing, 187–98.

Taylor, V. 2009a. *Rule of Law Assistance Discourse and Practice: Japanese Inflections, in, Law in Pursuit of Development: Principles into practice?*, edited by A. Perry-Kessaris. London: Routledge-Cavendish, 161–79.

Taylor, V.L. 2009c. Frequently Asked Questions about Rule of Law (Why the Answers Matter and Why they are so Elusive) *Hague Journal of Rule of Law*, 1, 46–52.

Taylor, V.L. 2007. *The Law Reform Olympics: Measuring Technical Legal Assistance in Transition Economies, in Law Reform in Developing and Transitional States*, edited by T. Lindsey. Abingdon: Routledge, 83–105.

Taylor, V.L. 2005. New Markets, New Commodity: Japanese Legal Technical Assistance. *Wisconsin Intl. L. J.* 23(2), 251–281.

Trubek, D. 2006. *The "Rule of Law" in Development Assistance: Past, Present and Future, in The New Law and Economic Development: A Critical Appraisal*, edited by D.M. Trubek and S. Alvaro. New York: Cambridge University Press, 74–94.

Trubek, D.M. and A. Santos. 2006. *Introduction: The Third Moment in Law and Development Theory: the Emergence of a New Critical Practice, in The New Law and Economic Development: A Critical Appraisal*, edited by D.M. Trubek and A. Santos. New York: Cambridge University Press, 1–18.

Upham, F.K. 1998. *Weak Legal Consciousness as Invented Tradition, in Mirror of Modernity: Invented Traditions of Modern Japan*, edited by S. Vlastos. Berkeley: University of California Press, 48–64.

Upham, F. 1987. *Law and Social Change in Postwar Japan.* Cambridge, Massachusetts: Harvard University Press.

Yabuki, K. 2008. Nihonbengoshi rengōkai to kokusaishihō shienkatsudō [Japan Federation of Bar Associations and International Activities to Support Justice]. *Jurisuto [Jurist].* 1358(June 2008), 9–16.

Yamashita Terutoshi and Tanaka Kazuko (2003) *Brief Introduction of Japan's Legal Assistance and the ICD, Available* http://www.moj.go.jp/ENGLISH/RATI/ICD/icd-02.pdf [last accessed 9 February 2012].

Yasuda Nobuyuki. 2000. *Tōnanajiahō [An Introduction to Southeast Asian Law].* Tokyo: Nihonhyōronsha.

Wang Tay-Sheng. 1992. *Legal Reform in Taiwan under Japanese Colonial Rule (1895-1945).* Seattle: University of Washington Press.

# Chapter 14

# Japan: A Society of Rights?

John O. Haley

Any serious discussion of the relationship of law to economic and political development requires some tentative identification of law-related features shared historically by most if not all advanced industrial democracies. Japan's relevance in this endeavor requires little explanation. Japan was the first and the most successful independent state to restructure its legal system based on Western law.[1] It was also the first and most successful non-Western industrial democracy. Aside from the decade of ultra-nationalism and war from the early 1930s to the end of World War II, few can reasonably question Japan's record as a prosperous, politically stable, and institutionally advanced state. Unless law's contribution to development is to be treated as a uniquely Western phenomenon, the question to be answered is what if any aspects of law and legal processes does Japan historically share with its industrial democratic peers.

The endeavor to identify common features of law Western law with Japan's particular legal tradition historically as well as contemporaneously leads almost inexorably to the issue of whether Japan has ever fully shared the West's notion of legal "rights," either in conception or application. Moreover, as evidenced by other chapters of this book, the role of rights in economic and political development generally has become a significant and often contested issue. For many concerned with reduction of transaction costs, effective recognition of private law rights—especially contract and property rights—has become almost an article of faith. With respect to Japan in particular, for example, Veronica Taylor argues that Japan appears to disprove the idea that a legal system with strong protection of both private and public law rights is a precondition to economic growth. To such observations Kent Anderson and Peter Kirby add, noting that Japan is arguably presently engaged in attempting to encourage a society of "rights" as opposed to a traditional approach of informal social control. We may thus appropriately begin discussion of the relationship of law to political and economic development in Japan by exploring the nature and place of legal rights first as developed in Western Europe and then received in late nineteenth-century Japan. In Western Europe several significant legal developments accompanied economic and political change. Economic growth coincided with the development of representative government and the related expansion of popular participation in political processes. Incessant warfare and the related need for additional revenue may be the more directly related causal factor,[2] but such arguments presuppose gains in wealth that were otherwise unavailable to those who governed. In other words, during the formative period of European economic and political development, the ruling elites lacked the capacity to capture and fully redistribute gains in wealth made by its producers. Lacking such means, within the most successful states, a balance was achieved between competing demands and

---

1   Japan, it should be noted, is one only a handful of countries that has not been at any time subject to colonial rule. By the end of the nineteenth century only five major countries aside from those enveloped within the Ottoman and Russian Empires had been able to resist West European colonial rule: China, Ethiopia, Japan, Korea, and Thailand. Korea was soon to join Taiwan as a Japanese colony.

2   On the relationship between warfare and the development of representative government in Western Europe, see Bisson (1966), Dowling (1989), Kiser and Linton (2001) and Stasavage (2009).

claims on resources and revenues. In the end the taxing authority and powers of rulers required some manner of political consent by an increasingly greater proportion of those they ruled.

The gains in wealth were not simply, however, a consequence of hard work, thrift, and ingenuity. Entrepreneurial activity expanded in the context of a common European belief system in which law had a prominent role. The development and acceptance of law as a system of rights was a significant factor. Following the lead of Nobel laureate Douglass C. North (1981) the significance of predictably enforceable private law rules is widely acknowledged. The availability of formal and informal means for the enforcement of contracts, as well as the recognition of property and its transfer, fostered shared expectations that facilitated the formation and investment of capital into productive enterprises as well as the expansion of trade and commercial activity. Law enforcement, however, first required the conceptualization of contracts and property within a system of legal rules and principles that were enforceable as private law rights. Otherwise claims arising from proprietorship and commercial undertakings would have been left to various means of private ordering or, as in imperial China, the interstices of an administrative and penal law system (Huang 1996). If the rules and practices of merchant communities had not been conceived as private law and had their enforcement been left entirely to guilds and other means employed by merchants themselves, they would have remained informal, customary rules within what we would refer to today as a purely private ordering system. Instead, however, the rules and practices of the merchant community were viewed as law—the *lex mercatoria*—that allowed their incorporation and enforcement within the legal structures of the emerging states of Western Europe. As a result, both political constraints and legal protections functioned in tandem, warranting belief in the realization of future reward for economic productivity that in turn encouraged and stimulated economic activity in a spiral of mutually reinforcing patterns of behavior. At the core was belief in law as a system of private law rights.

Our use of the term "rights" today is uniquely linked to such historical antecedents in the Western legal tradition. The contemporary conception of "rights" developed in Western Europe from the eleventh century.[3] As Western law spread globally, that conception of "rights" also became universally predominant. In contemporary legal systems worldwide, law is understood fundamentally as a system of rights combining three disparate notions. This tripartite combination is best revealed in the words used for "law" in the original Latin (*ius*) as well as French (*droit*), German (*Recht*), and Spanish (*derecho*) to name only three of many continental European languages that absorbed the Latin term. In each, the word also denotes "rights" as legally enforceable private and public law claims. It also encompasses the more problematic notion of what is "correct and just," a conception of rights as moral entitlements that the contemporary state is (and earlier European rulers were) morally and politically obliged to honor and protect.

In private law—itself another uniquely Euro-Roman law conception—the holders of "rights" are empowered to enforce claims recognized in substantive law against others, who have correlative duties. Common law jurisdictions, in which notions of sovereign immunity still prevail, may have to distinguish between claims against the state but generally the rules of contract, tort, as well as property apply to both private and governmental actors. In Japan as a civil law system, the state does not enjoy sovereign immunity. To the extent it acts as a private party in contract and under both constitutional and statutory provision, private parties have extensive "rights" to compensation for tortuous conduct by government actors (Haley 1987). Our contemporary conception of private law and private law rights is a direct and unique legacy of the reception of Roman civil (private) law via the *Corpus Juris Civilis* in the eleventh and twelfth centuries. To my knowledge, no analogous

---

3	See Haley (2011).

conception of private law and private law "rights" developed in any other legal tradition. Islamic law, it should be noted, also has foundations in Roman law (Schacht 1950).

A second category of "rights" encompasses claims by the citizens against the state acting in its governmental capacity. As such they might best be described as "public rights" although "civil rights" is the more common English term. Although for the most part sourced today in constitutions and treaties, the idea of public or civil rights as enforceable claims against governments is also an intellectual legacy of the late Middle Ages, particularly the contributions of canon law jurists and theologians from Gratian to Aquinas, and the resulting transformation of natural law into a theory of natural law rights (Tuck 1979).

Natural law theory also produced a closely related notion of "rights" and correlative "duties" as moral entitlements of those subject to governmental authority and the correlative obligations borne by those in authority. In effect, such inchoate rights represent political claims to governmental action. Natural law thus posited "rights" as both legal and moral claims. To the extent that "rights" recognized under natural law theory were not enforceable in positive law, they remained moral claims. As expressed in the word "justice," this notion of "rights" represented the fusion of law and political morality. Thus the normative claims of "justice" were equated with political demands for positive law recognition as enforceable rights. The "discourse of rights" in the Western tradition and political system influenced by Western conceptions of law and morality represent in essence efforts to induce political regimes to create enforceable civil rights.[4] By the end of the eighteenth century these notions fused with a political ideology that gave individual liberty priority over collective societal claims.

To describe Japan as a "society of rights" is another matter. For many such an assertion would be at best a largely rhetorical affair. A dismissive reaction, however, would be a mistake. To be sure, much of the discussion does concern what some might term a "discourse" of rights, but a few basic historical observations may be helpful to indicate more significant revelations about Japan, legal rights, and both economic and political development.[5]

Western conceptions of "rights" were first introduced in Japan in the late nineteenth century. Japan, however, had long replicated much of the European experience with adjudicatory institutions and organizational structures.[6] By the end of the eleventh century, for example, in a uniquely Japanese institutional evolution, imperial offices (*shiki*) with entitlements to the produce from specifically designated cultivated land had become transferable entitlements to such revenue divorced from the office itself. The recognition of such entitlements essentially represented the "privatization" of taxation. This development coincided with the evolution of judicial functions within an otherwise administrative state. At the end of the twelfth century the imperial regime established the Bureau of Records (*Kirokujo*). It had administrative functions as an office for record keeping and documentation, including formal recognition of documented claims to imperial grants of offices, land, and related entitlements (Kiley 1982). Consequently, as *shiki* evolved, the *Kirokujo* began to adjudicate completing claims to these entitlements. It thereby progressively acquired judicial functions and soon became the office for civil suits. With jurisdiction for all criminal matters, the Bureau of Police (*Kebiishicho*) in contrast functioned along familiar imperial Chinese patterns as a criminal court (although, unlike imperial China, criminal law enforcement was never a defining feature of Japanese governance). In Japan as in Europe adjudication of

---

4   For an eloquent critique see Glendon (1991).

5   For a provocative study of the relationship between legal language and the legal culture and the legal institutions and structures they spawn, see Gu (2006).

6   See Haley (2010).

warrior-vassal claims to land became a prominent feature of Japanese medieval governance (Mass 1979). With the establishment of stable warrior rule at the dawn of the seventh century, these structural features of Japan's legal order solidified, becoming even more prominent. Over the course of five centuries of warrior rule, Japan developed a well-established and well-used system of adjudication of private claims within which previously recognized rules and precedent produced predicable outcomes.[7] By the end of the eighteenth century Japanese enjoyed legal recognition in all but name and protection of a wide variety of property, contract, and commercial rights. Eighteenth-century edicts recognized four categories of suits to be processed administratively as minor, "adversarial" disputes. They included "main suits" (*honkuji*), those related to land and water *(ronsho)*, "money suits" (*kanekuji*) and mutual affairs (*nakama-goto*) (Henderson 1965; Hiramatsu 1981). *Honkuji* was a generic category for all private law claims other than those that came within one of the three particular categories. *Ronsho* cases had special importance for the regime since these suits covered disputes over irrigation entitlements. *Kanekuji* were essentially claims by creditors seeking to collect on defaults of loans with or without collateral but in context they involved various commercial transactions and instruments (Hiramatsu 1981). The availability of adjudicatory processes for such claims led to such a frequency of similar claims that a system of private law rules established by precedent developed. By the end of the seventeenth century, Japan had developed "by judicial precedent," in the words of John H. Wigmore, "a body of native law and practice, which can only be compared with the English independent development after the 1400's" (Wigmore 1928). Indeed the remarkable coincidence of firmly established medieval legal practices continues to amaze (West 2005).

Such institutional experience enabled Japan to assimilate with notable success Western judicial institutions and civil (private) law grounded in a conceptual system of "rights." Even within traditional patterns of adjudication, under the apparent influence of imperial Chinese law, some private law claims were "minor matters" that did not necessarily mandate adjudication and enforcement (Hiramatsu 1981).[8] An emphasis on resolution of such disputes through conciliation and compromise meant that some private claims could be properly repressed.[9] Especially discouraged were assertions of claims challenging community solidarity, for example, *nakama-goto* suits considered best resolved within the guild or other cooperative, communal organization.

No native parallels existed, however, to Western conceptions of either "natural law rights"— enforceable against those who ruled—or a conception of rights denoting inchoate claims to political recognition. Community consensus and "harmony" (*wa*) represented overriding social and political values. The Chinese characters translated into English as "justice" (*seigi*) had no legal nexus or nuance. Even the terms "public" (*kō*) and "private" (*shi*) had radically different meanings. The ideogram for "private" denoted unworthy selfish conduct while that for "public" represented the public good and general welfare. For the ruling administrative officials of the Chinese imperium, the ideology of public authority representing the common good in opposition to private, selfish interests had obvious appeal and utility. Within the sinofied political orders of East Asia, the very idea—much less rhetorical value—of justice in terms of private claims against public authority could hardly be expressed. The introduction of Western conceptions of "rights" thus challenged the deeply rooted and widely shared habits, beliefs, and values—in other words, the prevailing ideology of the Japanese community general and political elites in particular.

---

    7   See Steenstrup (1991, esp. pp. 71–159), also Haley (1991: 51–65).

    8   For the parallels in imperial Chinese law, see Huang (1996).

    9   On this topic the seminal work is Henderson (1965).

Predictably the holders of private rights articulated in the provisions of the new codes—particularly household heads and landlords—acted accordingly and began to seek judicial enforcement of their claims, together with the social and economic changes produced by emerging entrepreneurs, in doing so they further disrupted established relationships and established patterns of community life.[10] Political elites also reacted as might be expected. Within two decades political demand increased both to redefine landlord rights, to mitigate the decisional authority of household heads and to provide alternative judicial mechanisms with emphasis on conflict-avoiding resolution of civil disputes instead of enforcing legally recognized claims. However, as new measures were enacted first to enable and then to require formal conciliation for more and more categories of civil disputes, the number of ordinary lawsuits as well as conciliation proceedings increased (Haley 1982). The resulting tensions culminated in the mid-1930s. By 1934 more lawsuits per capita were filed in district courts than at any time in modern Japanese history until the late 1990s (Haley 2002).

Official concern for public welfare (the common good) versus pursuit of private (selfish) interests underpinned what Carol Gluck labels the social ideology of the early twentieth century, "an ethos of that reinforced deep vales associated with the village and familial collectivities" (Gluck 1985). The events of the first decades of the century served to reinforce these concerns as intellectuals overwhelmingly embraced and reshaped Marxist views with a toxic ultra-nationalism into the prevailing ideology of prewar Japan. Collectivist ideals had, in the words of Ronald Dore and Tsutomu Ōuchi, "a transcendent moral authority … not matched in any other industrial country." With the rise of "revisionists" within the civilian and military bureaucracies, condemnation of party politics, the emerging "money cliques" (*zaibatsu*), and individualism (*kojishugi*) became even more pronounced (Dore and Ōuchi 1971).

The most conspicuous of these values appear to have been transformed or at least diluted by war, occupation, and unprecedented economic growth. Official hostility to litigation has at least waned. At Japanese insistence over objections by occupation officials, the postwar constitution guarantees the right of citizens to sue for compensation for any tortuous acts by government officials, including, by statute strict liability for any "defect" in the management of public facilities. Assertions of legally enforceable rights are no longer condemned as litigation rates reach historic levels and reforms are implemented to dramatically increase the number of lawyers. Legal scholars on both sides of the Pacific speak about a "discourse of rights" in Japan.

At least a significant residue of these values remains in spite of both significant institutional and cultural change. During the past two decades in particular, they persist albeit frequently redefined as communitarian concerns. I especially question whether the "discourse of rights" in Japan also encompasses the idea of rights as moral claims. Let me posit three examples.

The first is the persistence of official emphasis in the criminal justice system for what is commonly referred to today as "restorative justice." I have described the attitudes and approach of police, prosecutors, and judges on numerous occasions (Haley 1999). At each stage in the formal criminal process from the identification of the offender, the decision to prosecute to final sentencing, confessions with apology, expression of remorse and willingness to compensate the victim for harm done by the offender is generally greeted by those in authority with a willingness to be lenient as the law allows. In response to offender contrition, however, officials routinely encourage victims to pardon. Similar attitudes favoring lenient treatment for confessing offenders are not necessarily shared generally by the Japanese public. Empirical evidence suggests that Japanese harbor as retributive sentiments as their counterparts in the United States at least with respect to

---

10   On community disruption from absentee landlords and their defense of rights, see Waswo (1977).

strangers (Hamilton and Sanders 1992). I believe that the process itself—especially the need for offenders through go-betweens and other means to negotiate for victim pardon, itself reduces victim demand for retribution by establishing personal connections—mutual friends and community acquaintances—linkages that tend to reduce the sense of estrangement and reinforce community. On the basis of such observations of the Japanese experience, the Australian criminologist, John Braithwaite, constructed a seminal argument for restorative justice (Braithwaite 1989).

Whatever the broader merits of restorative justice, the approach exemplifies an essentially communitarian approach to criminal justice. It requires victims and offenders to abandon "rights" in favor of offender reintegration and restoration of community cohesion. What is most significant about the Japanese experience is the degree to which restorative approaches to criminal justice reflect official rather than popular attitudes. David Johnson's exhaustive study (Johnson 2002) of Japanese prosecutors, their work and attitudes is particularly revealing. He found that they consider offender remorse and victim offender reconciliation to be among their highest professional priorities (Johnson 2002). Presented with a similar list of possibilities, King County, Washington, prosecutors placed both at the bottom (Johnson 2002). It is doubtful that, had the questionnaire not listed both, the US prosecutors would not have even considered either as aims. At least in the early postwar years, Japanese progressives viewed such attitudes and responses as a remnant of traditional "feudal" values (Haley 1998).

A second example is the judicial invocation of "the sense of society" (*shakai gainen*) to define the scope of enforceable legal claims. Illustrative are the decisions in a wide variety of contexts in which the courts denied the enforceability of an otherwise manifest legal right on grounds that its exercise was improper and invalid as an "abuse of right." Dan Foote describes the cases invalidating unilateral employment termination without cause as an example of judicial "activism" (Foote 1996). Taken together in all contexts the "abuse of rights" cases have two common features. First, the doctrine is used to disallow the involuntary expulsion of individuals from the community in question—villages, family, landlord–tenant relationships, as well as employment. Second, in each case, the court grounds its decision on its "sense of society" (Haley 1998). In stark contrast, is the dearth of decisions in which the court has similarly protected the individual exercise of rights within the relationship or the community against the collective interest or consensus (Haley 1998).

My final example is the use of litigation to produce a political response in what appears overtly to be an assertion of "rights" but, I believe, is more accurately explained as private appeals for official responses based on shared communitarian values. Some in Japan, especially those influenced most by Western conceptions of law, commonly use the language of "rights" in political discourse. The question remains, at least to me, whether this tendency represents a more traditional appeal of communitarian values or a fuller assimilation of Western notion of rights as moral entitlements. Litigation has a political aspect in Japan as elsewhere but with a subtle difference. Lawsuits are prosecuted against private and government acts or omissions both to secure personal redress and as a means to activate community concern and judicial action against alleged injuries to collective community welfare in the United States as well as Japan. Yet in Japan the goal of judicial action is less pronounced. Rather the motive—at least for some litigants and lawyers—appears to be to embarrass the judiciary and the government, to seek admissions and apology for wrongs, and to stimulate community demands for responsive governmental change. The governmental response is equally telling. The pollution cases provide a classic example. From the *Ashio Copper Mine* case (Notehelfer 1975) through the pollution litigation of the late 1960s and 1970s, lawsuits provoked officials to respond with ameliorative legislation and administrative solutions (Upham 1987). As more recently shown by Eric Feldman, the tainted blood and tobacco litigation had similar aims and consequences (Feldman 2000). The emphasis, I suggest, was on injury rather than right. What matters was the harm to the community not the right of the individual. The pursuit of selfish, private interests—including private law rights—that produces severe community harm is the underlying story. In the face of such harm the common good requires official intervention to prevent its recurrence and restore and heal the social wounds.

Despite their diversity as welfare states and degree of bureaucratic control, today all industrial democracies share certain basic features. By all measures they are the wealthiest and the most equalitarian, the least corrupt, and the most technologically advanced. Nearly all are in Western Europe or the predominately English-speaking nations that share a common British colonial heritage. Beyond these with few exceptions, only Japan and recently its two former colonies—South Korea and Taiwan—share the status and the features of industrial democracies, although many could reasonably argue that China may soon join their ranks. Within the community of major industrial democracies, Japan remains exemplary, however, as second only to the United States in per capita wealth[11] and without peer in terms of its equal distribution.[12] The question remains whether these are effects of a society of rights or more its communitarian orientations.

## References


Bisson, T.N. 1966. The Military Origins of Medieval Representation. *The American Historical Review*, 71(4), 1199–218.

Braithwaite, J. 1989. *Crime, Shame and Reintegration*. Cambridge: Cambridge University Press.

Dore, R.P. and Ōuchi, T. 1971. Rural Origins of Japanese Fascism, in *Dilemmas of Growth in Prewar Japan*, edited by J.W. Morley. Princeton: Princeton University Press.

Dowling, B.M. 1989. Medieval Origins of Constitutional Governance in the West. *Theory and Society*, 18(2), 213–47.

Feldman, E.A. 2000. *The Ritual of Rights in Japan: Law, Society, and Health Policy*. New York: Cambridge University Press.

Foote, D.H. 1996. Judicial Creation of Norms in Japanese Labor Law: Activism in the Service of Stability. *UCLA Law Review*, 43(3), 635–710.

Glendon, M.A. 1991. *Rights Talk: The Impoverishment of Political Discourse*. New York and Toronto: Free Press.

Gluck, C. 1985. *Japan's Modern Myths: Ideology in the Late Meiji Period*. Princeton: Princeton University Press.

Gu, S. 2006. *The Boundaries of Meaning and the Formation of Law*. Montreal: McGill–Queens University Press.


---

11   With a population a third larger than Germany and twice as large as France and the United Kingdom, at $28,000 in 2004 Japan's per capita GNP was higher than any of the three largest European nations. In Europe only Luxembourg ($55,100), Norway ($37,800), Switzerland ($32,800), Denmark ($31,200), Austria ($30,000), and Belgium ($29,000) had higher per capita incomes. Although the difference is slight Japan's per capita income is higher than the United Kingdom ($27,700), Germany ($27,600), France (27,500), Italy ($26,800) as well as Sweden ($26,800) (www.worldfactsandfigures.com, last accessed January 14, 2007).

12   As measured by OECD Gini indices measuring the distribution of household wealth, Japan ranks slightly behind the welfare states of Europe: www.oecd.org/dataoecd/12/4/35445297.xls (last accessed February 7, 2007). UN data are even more positive. They rank Japan just behind Denmark and Finland, just ahead of Norway and Sweden. At worst the household distribution of wealth in Japan is on par with Canada and the United Kingdom. http://hdr.undp.org/reports/global/2003/indicator/indic_126_1_1.html (last accessed January 14, 2007).

Haley, J.O. 1982. The Politics of Informal Justice: The Japanese Experience, 1922–1942, in *The Politics of Informal Justice, Volume 2*, edited by R. Abel. New York: Academic Press, 125–47.

Haley, J.O. 1987. Toward a Reappraisal of Occupation Legal Reforms: Administrative Accountability, in *Eibeihô ronshû* (Essays on Anglo–American Law), edited by Fujukura. Hideo Tanaka Festschrift, 543–67.

Haley, J.O. 1991. *Authority without Power: Law and the Japanese Paradox*. New York and London: Oxford University Press.

Haley, J.O. 1998. *The Spirit of Japanese Law*. Athens, GA: University of Georgia Press.

Haley, J.O. 1999. Apology and Pardon: Learning from Japan, in *Civic Repentance*, edited by A. Etzioni. Lanham, MD: Rowman & Littlefield Publishers, Inc., 97–120.

Haley, J.O. 2002. Litigation in Japan: A New Look at Old Problems. *Willamette Journal of International Law and Dispute Resolution*, 10(1), 121–42.

Haley, J.O. 2009. Comment on Using Criminal Punishment to Serve Both Victim–and Social Needs. *Law & Contemporary Problems*, 72(2), 219–25.

Haley, J.O. 2010. Rivers and Rice: What Lawyers and Legal Historians Should Know about Medieval Japan. *Journal of Japanese Studies*, 36(2), 313–49.

Haley, J.O. 2011. The Evolution of Law: Political Foundations of Private Law in Medieval Europe and Japan, in *Law and Long-Term Economic Change: A Eurasian Perspective*, edited by Debin Ma and Jan Luiten van Zanden. Stanford: Stanford University Press, 19–45.

Hamilton, V.L. and Sanders, J. 1992. *Everyday Justice: Responsibility and the Individual in Japan and the United States*. New Haven: Yale University Press.

Henderson, D.F. 1965. *Conciliation and Japanese Law*, volume 1. Seattle and Tokyo: University of Washington Press and University of Tokyo Press.

Hiramatsu, Y. 1981. Tokugawa law. *Law in Japan: An Annual*, 1.

Huang, P. 1996. *Civil Justice in China: Representation and Practice in the Qing*. Stanford: Stanford University Press.

Johnson, D.T. 2002. *The Japanese Way of Justice: Prosecuting Crime in Japan*. New York: Oxford University Press.

Kiley, C.J. 1982. The Imperial Court as a Legal Authority in the Kamakura Age, in *Court and Bakufu in Japan: Essays in Kamakura History*, edited by J.P. Mass. New Haven and London: Yale University Press.

Kiser, Edgar and Linton, April. 2001. Determinants of the Growth of the State: War and Taxation in Early Modern France and England. *Social Forces*, 80, 411–48.

Mass, J.P. 1979. *The Development of Kamakura Rule, 1180–1250*. Stanford: Stanford University Press.

North, D.C. 1981. *Structure and Change in Economic History*. New York: W.W. Norton & Company.

Notehelfer, F.G. 1975. Japan's First Pollution Incident. *Journal of Japanese Studies*, 351(1), 351–83.

Schacht, Joseph. 1950. Foreign Elements in Ancient Islamic Law. Journal of Comparative Legislation and International Law, 32, 9–17.

Stasavage, David. 2009. War, Geographic Scale, and Constitutional Control. Unpublished manuscript, January. Available at: http://politics.as.nyu.edu/docs/IO/5395/geographic_scale.pdf.

Steenstrup, C. 1991. *A History of Law in Japan*. Leiden, New York, Copenhagen and Cologne: E.J. Brill.

Tuck, R. 1979. *Natural Rights Theories: The Origin and Development*. Cambridge and New York: Cambridge University Press.

Upham, F.K. 1987. *Law and Social Change in Postwar Japan*. Cambridge, MA: Harvard University Press.

Waswo, A. 1977. *Japanese Landlords: The Decline of a Rural Elite*. Berkeley, Los Angeles and London: University of California Press.

West, M. 2005. *Law in Everyday Japan: Sex, Sumo, Suicide, and Statutes*. Chicago and London: University of Chicago Press.

Wigmore, J.H. 1928. *Panorama of the World's Legal Systems*. St. Paul: West Publishing Co.

Chapter 15

# Lessons from History: Japan's New Quasi-Jury System (*saiban-in seido*) and the Jury Act of 1923

Kent Anderson and Peter Kirby

On August 3, 2009, Japan experienced its first jury-like trial in over 65 years. The media hype around the event was significant; the story led the television, print, and Internet news for a week.[1] Enacted five years earlier in May 2004[2] after a long gestation period, the government promotes the new system and its objectives of delivering better justice and more civic engagement of the populace (Anderson and Ambler 2006). The question debated by everyone from housewives to Supreme Court justices with the new system is simple: will the Japanese people embrace direct lay participation—this time?[3]

Japan has tried it before, and it didn't work. In 1928, after a five-year preparatory period preceded by a long fermentation, Japan rolled out a jury system with equal hype,[4] but by 1943 the courts were hearing an average of only three trials per year (Anderson and Nolan 2004). Proponents and sceptics alike have put forward a multitude of reasons for the old system's failure. Reasons for the 1923 Act's failure remain significant, both because they inform the latest enactment as part of Japan's current "third wave" of law reform[5] fully to entrench a liberal rights-

---

1   See, e.g., "Citizen Judges Hear Their First Case," *Asahi Shimbun*, August 4, 2009; "Lay Judges Find Their Voices on the 3rd Day," *Yomiuri Shimbun*, August 6, 2009; "Saiban-in Saiban: shinken-ni kiiterureta … shuttei no mokugeki-shōninra kōkan" [Lay Judge Trial: They Listened in Earnest … A Favorable Impression made on Witnesses Appearing in Court], *Mainichi Shimbun*, August 8, 2009; and Kamiya (2008).

2   Saiban'in no sanka suru keiji saiban ni kansuru hōritsu [Act Concerning Participation of Lay Assessors in Criminal Trials], Law No. 63 of 2004. The Act is hereinafter referred to as the "Lay Assessor Act." For an English translation, see Anderson and Saint (2005).

3   This chapter considers the historical experience of the Japanese Jury Act of 1923 and sets that against the new Lay Judge Act of 2004. This is not a novel project. Many commentators in both English and Japanese, including Anderson (Anderson 2004; Anderson and Nolan 2004), have done this in the past (Dean 1995; Kiss 1999; Kowata 2008; Maruta 2001). What this project brings new to the exercise is a wider and more focused consideration of the Imperial jury system with more tolerance for multiple overlapping and subtle explanations of events, rather than a blinkered, single dominate interpretation.

4   On October 1, 1928, Emperor Hirohito visited the Court of Cassation, the Tokyo Court of Appeal and the Tokyo District Court. Altogether 71 prominent legal officers—ranking members of the Ministry of Justice, the judiciary and public prosecutor's office—had been assembled to receive the Imperial visit. In an Imperial edict issued on the same day, the Emperor urged: "Now you are assembled on the day in which the Jury Law becomes operative. All the more serve loyally and work hard" (Röhl 2005). The Imperial visit was the culmination of five years of preparation to ensure that Japan's jury system would succeed. During that time, the Ministry of Justice alone spent five million yen promoting the system. Eleven movies and 2,840,000 pamphlets were produced, and on 3,339 separate occasions, a combined total of 1,240,000 people gathered to hear lectures on the topic (Japan Federation of Bar Associations 2006).

5   Law reform during the Meiji Era as discussed in Chapter 13 constituted the first wave under this view, and post-World War II legal reforms under the American Occupation constituted the second wave.

based democracy, and because they represent a failure in Japan as the original Asian testing ground for legal development, as discussed in Chapter 13. If one learns more from failure than success, this allows us to examine the "chicken or egg question" with some historical perspective in a sophisticated non-Western society.

As many others have noted, the *Saiban-in* Act is the crown jewel in Japan's major third wave law reform movement. Already some backtracking from those ambitious reforms has occurred. Historically whether the suite of reforms will be judged as a success or futile exercise will largely be based on whether the jury system will be able to "stick" this time. That, in turn, will depend on whether policy-makers and the public are convinced the system is able to deliver the objectives of better justice and more civic engagement which are the only justifications for the accompanying costs, confusion, and delay that will necessarily accompany introducing a new system that injects amateurs into what is unavoidably a complex and detailed legal process.

This chapter seeks to place a contemporary law reform project—the introduction of the quasi-jury system in Japan—within its historical context—the failure of the 1923 Japanese jury system—and thereby provide insight into the likelihood that the current project has for delivering better justice and greater civic engagement outcomes. The first section of this chapter reviews in detail the historical background of the Imperial jury system and its demise, highlighting the various theories observers have used to explain its failure. The second section reviews the historical developments that led to the enactment of the new system, briefly introduces the basic elements of new *saiban-in seido*, and applies the variety of the historical explanations concerning the old jury system to the new procedure. The chapter concludes by arguing that the new *saiban-in* system and those responsible for its implementation have learned enough from history to ensure that this time it will succeed.

## Jury Act 1923

*Historical Context*

The Jury Act 1923 came into effect on October 1, 1928 (Kowata 2008; Maruta 2001).[6] Although explained in the limited English literature as the product of a period of growing liberalism and democracy in Japan coinciding with the reign of the Taishō Emperor (the so-called Taishō Democracy),[7] this understanding fails to appreciate the long gestation period for the reform. The 1923 Act was the culmination of efforts to introduce the jury that began in the earliest years of modernization in Japan, during the early Meiji Period (Japan Federation of Bar Associations 2006; Mitani 1979).[8]

---

6    Baishin hō [Jury Act], Law No. 50 of 1923.

7    As used by historians, the term "Taishō Democracy" conventionally refers to the period stretching from the political agitation protesting the treaty that ended the Russo-Japanese War, towards the end of the Meiji Era in 1905, to the demise of party led cabinets, at the beginning of the Shōwa Period in 1932 (Gordon 2009: 161).

8    Scholars writing about lay participation in Japan have tended to afford the historical build-up to the 1923 Jury Act only a cursory treatment (see, e.g., Kiss 1999; Lampert 1992; Landsman and Zhang 2008; Wilson 2007). This is regrettable as, in addition to providing a valuable insight into the motives behind the introduction of the jury system, such details undermine Orientalist notions that Japanese society was historically neither pluralist nor rights conscious.

Draft constitutions incorporating the jury system formed part of the debate leading up to the promulgation of the Constitution of the Empire of Japan in 1889 (the Meiji Constitution) (Japan Federation of Bar Associations 2006; Mitani 1979). The French jurist Gustave Boissonade, who was invited by the Japanese government to assist in drafting a new criminal code for Japan, had championed the system (Dean 1995; Kowata 2008). He included provisions establishing a jury system in the 1879 draft of the Code of Criminal Instruction. Boissonade argued that if the purpose of Japan's adoption of Western legal ideas was modernization, then Japan would benefit from adopting a lay participation system to bring itself into conformity with advanced industrial nations in Europe and the United States. Furthermore, it was argued, adopting such a system was an essential step toward revising the unequal treaties and restoring the integrity of the Japanese justice system. Foreign powers, he reasoned, could hardly complain at their nationals being tried using procedures comparable to that in their own countries.

Despite Boissonade's advocacy, after passing through the review board almost untouched, the jury provisions were struck from the draft of the Code of Criminal Instruction during Cabinet deliberations (Kowata 2008). The rationale for the decision was that citizens lacked the capacity to make judicial rulings. The decision, however, was also influenced by a desire on the part of the new Meiji elite to see opposing forces judged harshly.

Under the patronage of one of the most influential figures in early twentieth-century Japanese politics, Takashi Hara, the push to introduce the jury system again gathered momentum in the first decade of the century. In February 1910, over two years before the end of the Meiji Era, Home Minister Hara introduced into the Diet a "Motion on Establishing a Jury System" (Japan Federation of Bar Associations 2006). This motion passed with the unanimous assent of the House on March 3 of the same year.

Beyond the general trend toward greater civic participation in government and liberalism, which characterized the Taishō Democracy, the success of the Hara motion was a response to concerns over the power of the judiciary and the increasingly interventionist stance taken by prosecutorial authorities in political graft cases. The political parties were particularly outraged by the detention and interrogation of Diet members that occurred as a result of political bribery allegations in the Japanese Sugar Refining Scandal of 1909, which they argued were an abuse of human rights (Japan Federation of Bar Associations 2006). Hara was similarly concerned with the closed court hearings that were used to try the 26 socialists prosecuted for plotting the assassination of the Meiji Emperor, in the High Treason Incident of 1910 (Japan Federation of Bar Associations 2006; Kowata 2008). The introduction of the jury, it was reasoned, would counter the tendency for the courts simply to endorse the results of prosecutorial investigations by requiring prosecutors to prove their case in court before the jury. This would also restrain prosecutorial attacks on party politicians (Mitani 1988). In other words, the jury was seen as a systematic way to address structural biases in the justice system at the time by delivering "better justice" for Japan.

Due to the division of powers created under the Meiji Constitution, the limited influence of the Hara's party in both the House of Peers and the Privy Council, and a change in political fortunes of the same party in the House of Representatives, the next major push to introduce the jury system had to wait until Takashi Hara's own term as Prime Minister, commencing on September 29, 1918. In May 1919, the Hara Cabinet endorsed legislating for a jury system (Japan Federation of Bar Associations 2006; Kowata 2008). A Special Deliberative Council on the Legal System answering to Prime Minister Hara was established in the same year and, from November, concrete studies into jury systems, including the dispatch of fact-finding missions to America and seven countries in the Europe commenced (Japan Federation of Bar Associations 2006; Kowata 2008; Maruta 2001).

Although the Special Deliberative Council on the Legal System was set-up by the Hara Cabinet, its membership was split evenly between proponents of the jury system and those antagonistic to it. The central issue of contention was whether a jury system would be constitutional under the Meiji Constitution. Tatsukichi Minobe, the leading constitutional theorist of the day, developed an argument against the constitutionality of the jury system based on the absence of an express jury provision in the Constitution and Articles 24 and 57 of the same document (Kowata 2008). Article 57 was interpreted as restricting the exercise of judicial power exclusively to officers of the court.[9] Meanwhile, Article 24 was interpreted as guaranteeing subjects the right to trial by judge alone.[10] Legal scholar and practicing lawyer Makoto Egi advanced a counter-argument (Kowata 2008). He argued for a more functional interpretation of the Constitution that would allow for the introduction of the jury system on the basis that it was the determiner of facts rather than law. Egi's constitutionality argument was ultimately strengthened by the right for defendants to waive trial by jury under the 1923 Act,[11] thereby voiding the argument based on Article 24.

The presence of opposing arguments in the Special Deliberative Council on the Legal System resulted in compromise. This compromise was reflected in the "General Statement of Principles on the Jury System," which became the basis for the Jury Act 1923 (Kowata 2008). Importantly, it was instrumental in defining the role of the jury as responding to questions about the facts rather than providing general verdicts of guilt or innocence, a role that was left to the judge.

After the debate in the Special Deliberative Council on the Legal System, Prime Minister Hara anticipated that the draft of the Jury Bill would meet with little opposition in the Privy Council. On this point, he was sorely mistaken. The Privy Council remained under the control of Aritomo Yamagata, one of the Meiji Restoration's founding fathers, and a bastion of anti-political party sentiment (Mitani 1988). More importantly, six out of nine members of the Privy Council's Jury Bill Examination Committee were opposed to the jury system (Kowata 2008).[12] Hara was forced to call on his political acumen to find common ground with opposing forces and navigate the passage of the draft Bill.

On January 17, 1921, Prime Minister Hara, appearing before the first session of the Privy Council's Jury Bill Examination Committee, outlined the rationale for the introduction of the jury system (Japan Federation of Bar Associations 2006). The Prime Minister noted that the Diet had been established and the people enfranchised, but the justice system alone allowed for no form of citizen participation. Thirty years after the promulgation of the constitution, it was only natural that the people be empowered to participate in the administration of justice. He argued that should Japan fail to take the opportunity to put the jury law in place, considerable harm to the development of the state would eventuate. The Prime Minister added:

---

9 Article 57 of the Meiji Constitution states: "The Judicature shall be exercised by the Courts of Law according to law, in the name of the Emperor. The organization of the Courts of Law shall be determined by law."

10 Article 24 of the Meiji Constitution states: "No Japanese subject shall be deprived of his right of being tried by judges determined by the law."

11 Baishin hō [Jury Act], Law No. 50 of 1923, Arts. 2, 3 and 6.

12 Elder statesmen Miyoji Itō led the opposition to the draft Jury Bill. Thirty years earlier, Itō had accompanied Hirobumi Itō, another of the Meiji Restoration's founding fathers, on his tour to investigate constitutions and governmental structures in Europe. As one of the three secretaries subsequently charged with drafting the Meiji Constitution, Miyoji Itō possessed an intimate knowledge of the intent of the framers of the Constitution. His opposition was, accordingly, a formidable obstacle for the sponsors of the Jury Bill to overcome.

I want the people to put their faith in the administration of justice, and to eradicate the alienation between government and the people and the influence of lingering resentment.[13]

In short, one of the primary rationales for the jury system was that it would foster a more civically engaged and democratic society. Despite his advocacy, Hara never saw the fruition of his years of labor in trying to introduce the jury system into Japan. On November 4, 1921 he was assassinated at Tokyo Station. A third draft proposal of the Jury Bill by that time had already been presented to the Privy Council (Kowata 2008).

The death of the jury system's great political advocate did not mark its demise. On November 13, 1921, the Hara Cabinet was reconstituted as the Korekiyo Takahashi Cabinet. Work thereafter continued on the third draft proposal for the Jury Bill in an effort to gain Privy Council approval. Finally, on February 27, 1922, the Privy Council approved the amended draft of the Bill by a margin of 14 to four (Kowata 2008). The Bill that emerged from the Privy Council departed significantly from the draft first presented by Hara. Most notably, the Bill provided that judges were not bound by the jury's factual determinations.

Privy Council approval did not mark the end of the saga to enact the jury system. The Bill soon became mired in the Diet, through the delaying tactics of opposition members, and was defeated with the collapse of the Takahashi Cabinet on June 12, 1922 (Kowata 2008). It was thereafter reintroduced by the Tomosaburō Katō Cabinet, which secured its passage through the House of Peers on March 21, 1923 (Kowata 2008). The law was promulgated on April 18 of the same year. It is one of the great ironies of the Imperial jury system that the passage of a law, which was designed to promote better democracy, was itself secured by a non-party Cabinet predominantly composed of non-elected bureaucrats and members of the House of Peers (Gordon 2009; Mitani 1988).

*Details of Jury Act of 1923*

The alterations made to the original draft of the jury law did not change the fundamental structure of the system. The jury law was not based on a continental European model for lay participation in mixed courts, which may have been expected considering Japan's earlier adoption of the Civil Law from France and Germany (Dean 1995; Röhl 2005). Instead, the Imperial jury system was based on the Common Law jury systems in Britain and the United States (Dean 1995; Lampert 1992; Maruta 2001; Wilson 2007). Typical of most of Japan's foreign receptions, the system, however, was not a straight adoption. Rather, it incorporated a number of features designed to address constitutional limitations or otherwise facilitate use within the existing legal framework. Accordingly, the Imperial jury system had a number of novel elements that set it apart from jury systems in use in other parts of the world.

The Imperial jury system was composed of 12 jurors selected at random from eligible voters.[14] Voting, of course, was limited at this period to literate male citizens over 30 years of age who over the preceding two years had been resident in the same village, town or city and paid at least three yen in direct national taxation.[15] The eligibility requirements, while seemingly excessive by modern standards, were comparable to racial and property based restrictions on jury participation

---

13    Miyoji Itō, "Notes of the proceedings of the Jury Bill Examination Committee," 1st Session, January 17, 1921, *Itō Miyoji Related Documents*, 2981i, in the possession of the Constitutional Government Reference Room of the National Diet Library (quoted in Japan Federation of Bar Associations 2006).

14    Baishin hō [Jury Act], Law No. 50 of 1923, Art. 12.

15    Baishin hō [Jury Act], Art. 12.

in Britain and the United States. As a result, the jury system was not broadly representative of society, but comparable with other lay participation systems of the time.

Trial by jury was only available in criminal cases, and then only for serious offenses. There were two categories. Where the maximum penalty was life imprisonment or death, trial by jury was mandatory unless waived by the accused.[16] Where the offense carried a minimum term of not less than a year and a maximum term of three or more years, trial by jury was at the discretion of the accused.[17] A number of offenses otherwise fitting the criteria were exempt from the provisions of the Jury Act 1923 (Dean 1995).[18] These included crimes against members of the Imperial Family, riot with the purpose of overthrowing the government, espionage, violation of electoral laws and breaches of the Peace Preservation Act 1925. In cases where the accused exercised the discretion for trial by jury, the accused bore the cost of the jury's empanelment if subsequently found guilty.[19]

During the course of proceedings, jurors had the right, with the prior approval of the presiding judge, to ask defendants, witnesses, and expert witnesses relevant questions (Dobrovolskaia 2008).[20] The jury deliberated by itself, but did not return general verdicts of guilty or not guilty. Instead, the jury made special verdicts on matters of fact, by providing yes or no answers to factual questions submitted to them by the judge.[21] Although there is debate over why this approach was adopted, the constitutional basis for the decision was Article 24 of the Meiji Constitution, which provides that "no subject shall be deprived of his right to being tried by judges determined by law." Article 24, it was argued, prohibited anyone other than judges making findings of guilt or innocence.

The special verdicts on matters of fact did not have to be unanimous: a simple majority of seven of 12 jurors was sufficient to answer a question.[22] Moreover, the presiding judge was not bound by the jury's findings. However, judges could not simply replace the jury's answers with their own. They could only declare that there was no basis in the evidence for the jury's findings and order a retrial.[23] In other words, the extent of the judge's discretion was limited to making rulings similar to judgments notwithstanding the verdict (JNOV or *judgment non obstante veredicto*) in US civil jury trials (Anderson and Nolan 2004).

No appeal on questions of facts was available from a jury trial, although it was still possible to appeal on questions of law.[24] Although this is the same as the present Common Law rule on appealing jury verdicts, it was a significant departure from Japan's standard *kōso* or cassation practice, which continued to apply to non-jury trials. The *kōso* rule is based on the argument that appellate judges are in as good or better position to make factual determinations as trial judges. While the rationale for not permitting appellate review of jury determined facts is based in the belief that jury determinations better reflect community standards than those of the judiciary, who as a group are not broadly representative of society. Moreover, the jury will have had the advantage of witnessing testimony first-hand unlike the appellate court.

---

16    Baishin hō [Jury Act], Arts. 2 and 6.
17    Baishin hō [Jury Act], Art. 3.
18    Baishin hō [Jury Act], Art. 4.
19    Baishin hō [Jury Act], Art. 107.
20    Baishin hō [Jury Act], Art. 7.
21    Baishin hō [Jury Act], Arts. 29, 77, 88, 91.
22    Baishin hō [Jury Act], Arts. 29, 77, 88, 91.
23    Baishin hō [Jury Act], Art. 95; for a translation of the relevant provision see Dean (1995: 379, 387, fn 47).
24    Baishin hō [Jury Act], Arts. 101–3.

*Experience under the 1923 Jury Act*

The Imperial Jury System was suspended in 1943 with the stated goal of freeing the manpower necessary to maintain the system at a time when World War II was intensifying (Urabe 1976).[25] This rationale masks the reality that trial by jury was faltering long before the tide of the Pacific War turned against Japan.

The Imperial Jury System had an initially promising start, with 173 cases tried under the new law in the first 15 months of its operation (Dean 1995; Kowata 2008). However, it soon went into decline. From October to December 1928 there were 31 cases of trial by jury, 143 in 1929, 66 in 1930 but a mere two in 1942 (Dean 1995; Lampert 1992). Between October 1928 and April 1936, 443 jury trials were conducted, with 15 out of 51 district courts having more than 10. In the same period, the discretion to have trial by jury, for offenses carrying a minimum penalty not less than a year and a maximum of three or more years, was exercised on only 12 occasions (Röhl 2005). In the last five years of the law only 15 juries were empanelled. By the time the Jury Act was suspended in 1943, only 484 jury trials had been performed since the law came into operation on October 1, 1928 (Anderson and Nolan 2004).

Despite the earlier mentioned figures, the acquittal rate of 16.7 percent for jury trials was significantly better than the conviction level for non-jury trials (Japan Federation of Bar Associations 2006).[26] The rate of acquittal and the disparity in outcomes between jury and non-jury trials was particularly high in murder and arson trials—two of the most serious matters in early modern Japan. In murder cases, jury trials resulted in not guilty verdicts 63 percent of the time compared to only 0.07 percent of the time for non-jury trials (Maruta 2001).

The discretion afforded to judges to order a retrial on the basis of the jury's findings was exercised on 24 occasions between 1928 and 1943 (Maruta 2001). Each of those occasions concerned jury determinations leading to not-guilty verdicts. On 16 of those 24 occasions, retrial resulted in conviction for the accused (Maruta 2001).

Based on these statistics it is possible to draw two conclusions. Firstly, through non-use and obscurity, the Imperial Jury System became marginalized toward the end of its life to the extent that it featured only as a procedural step in which the right was waived (Anderson and Nolan 2004). As a result, the 1923 Jury Law's lofty goals of delivering greater civic participation and better justice were not realized. Accordingly, Japan's first attempt to introduce broad-based mass participation into the criminal justice system must be regarded as a failure. The second conclusion that can be drawn is that the marginalization of the jury system occurred despite affording defendants a better chance at acquittal.

---

25   "While the number of jury cases are decreasing, there is a need, as the war intensifies, to curtail the manpower necessary to maintain the jury system (such as the administrative burden of drawing-up lists of nominees and registers of qualified jurors by municipalities)." Masao Okahara, "'Baishin-hō no Teishi ni Kansuru Houritsu' ni Tsuite [About 'A Law on the Suspension of the Jury Act']" (1943) 24(4) *Hōsōkai Zasshi* (quoted in Japan Federation of Bar Associations 2006).

26   Some authors cite a slightly lower figure of 15.4 percent (see, e.g., Kiss 1999: 264 fn 33; Landsman and Zhang 2008: 182).

*Lessons from the Past*

On three separate occasions between December 1933 and March 1938, a Jury Act Reform Bill was introduced into the House of Representatives of the Imperial Diet.[27] These Bills sought to remedy those parts of the Act that encouraged defendants to either waive or not exercise the right to trial by jury. They are evidence that long before the suspension of the Imperial jury system there were those who attributed the decline in trial by jury to structural problems arising from the 1923 Act. In addition to this argument, commentators have advanced a number of other theories to explain the failure of the Imperial jury system. These arguments may be grouped into four lines of thought, which neatly align with the four schools in the paradigms of Japanese law debate (Port and McAlinn 2003); namely, that the failure of the jury system was due to: structural defects, cultural disinclination reasons, the rational response to the rise of militarism and fascism in Japan, or opposition from legal elites, including judges, prosecutors and defense lawyers. These explanations are important for two reasons. Firstly, the experience under the Imperial jury law heavily influenced the drafters of the *saiban-in* Law (Anderson and Nolan 2004). This helps to explain some of the otherwise surprising policy choices made by these later policy-makers. Moreover, as these conclusions are accepted as common truths, it is likely those assumptions will influence and inform the courts as they interpret the new law. Second, the historical experience and the lessons drawn from it provide a useful roadmap of potential problems and cautionary tales to assist in applying the law and running the new mixed courts.

The structural explanation for the Imperial jury's failure is captured in statements made by Professor Nobuyoshi Toshitani (Urabe 1976). He suggested no one should be surprised at the failure of the Imperial jury system, but rather at the remarkable success of the various devices built into the system to stop it from functioning smoothly. There are broadly two sub-strands of thought in the structural explanation. The first attributes the failure of the Imperial jury system to the model of lay participation that the Diet eventually adopted. According to exponents of this line of reasoning, the adversarial model of lay participation did not function well within the French and German inspired Civil Law system in Japan (Dean 1995; Urabe 1976). The inquisitorial role played by judges, in particular, emerged as a problem. This inquisitorial function created the impression in the minds of jurors that judges were prosecutors, rather than independent decision-makers, and encouraged juror identification with the accused. The observation of Justice Ikeuchi, indicating that he was only able to gain the confidence of jurors by conducting proceedings as close to an adversarial model as possible under a basically inquisitorial framework, lends weight to this argument (Urabe 1976).

The structural explanation's second line of reasoning attributes the failure of the Imperial jury system to defects flowing from the 1923 Act, rather than to the adversarial model on which the law was based. The Jury Act Reform Bills earlier referred to were designed to address a number of these perceived defects. The Bill introduced into the 65th Imperial Diet, for example, contained provisions that made all jury trials payable on the national account and permitted *kōso* appeal on questions of fact (Ichihara 1993). These proposed amendments addressed two key criticisms of the Act. The first is that the financial burden imposed on defendants found guilty after exercising the discretion for trial by jury was a disincentive to exercise that right. The second criticism is that

---

27　"Attempts to overcome the defects that the same law [the Jury Act] possessed through law reform can be seen in the introduction of the 'Jury Act Reform Bill' into the House of Representatives for the 65th Imperial Diet (26 December 1933 – 3 March 1934), the 71st Special Session of the Imperial Diet (25 July 1937 – 7 August 1937) and the 73rd Imperial Diet (26 December 1937 – 26 March 1938)" (Ichihara 1993: 67).

the lack of a *kōso* appeal, in circumstances where there was a tendency for appeal courts to reduce sentences, was an incentive to elect for trial by judge alone.

Other criticisms of the 1923 Act are that it made no provision for prosecutors or defense lawyers to object to the judge's instructions to jurors and denied potential users access by excluding political crimes. The scope for prosecutors to frustrate the system, for example by initiating proceedings in a Ward Court rather than a District Court, has also been criticized (Urabe 1976). Perhaps the biggest criticism of the Act, however, has been directed at the discretion afforded to judges to order a retrial on the basis of the jury's findings. This, it is argued, created the impression that despite the presence of the jury it was the judges alone who were determining guilt or innocence. In other words, the presence of the jury was merely shop dressing. It is significant that the 1933 Bill also contained a provision abolishing this discretion (Ichihara 1993).

The cultural explanation for the failure of the Imperial jury system is built on claims that Japanese people have a preference for trial by "those people above" rather than "their fellows" (Kiss 1999; Urabe 1976). The basis for this claim itself rests in two assertions. The first is that Japanese society was, and remains, strictly hierarchical. Speech, particularly honorific speech; seating arrangements; and bowing are all pointed to as manifestations of the hierarchical nature of Japanese society (Kiss 1999). The second assertion reflects the reasoning of leading postwar sociologist of law Takeyoshi Kawashima. In the 1960s Kawashima argued that Japanese people possessed a "weak legal consciousness." This weak legal consciousness resulted in a tendency for individuals to submit to the will of the group and social superiors and to forego asserting legal rights (Fukurai 2007; Kawashima 1963). This borders on the Japanese interpretation of "rights" reviewed in Chapter 14.

Many scholars have treated the cultural explanation for the failure of the Imperial jury system with skepticism. This is understandable, as the explanation on occasion appears to be based on notions that Japanese people have a genetic predisposition to trial by "those people above." Kawashima's cultural theory explaining low litigation levels in Japan at least recognized that the ways citizens interact with the legal system was evolutionary and changeable. Moreover, it alludes to the possibility that although Japanese citizens may not have been culturally ready for lay participation in the 1880s or 1930s, they may be now.

There are indications to suggest that cultural factors did play a part in the demise of the Imperial jury system. For example, commentators have noted that defendants were reluctant to exercise the right to trial by jury as it displayed distrust for the presiding judge.[28] There is likewise evidence to suggest that, despite the campaign to promote the system, the workings of the jury system remained a mystery for many citizens (Dobrovolskaia 2008). On occasion it appears to have constituted a source of shame. The reference in *The Jury Guidebook* to the man who asked how he could return to his village after being excused from jury service is a case in point (Dobrovolskaia 2008). Despite this, there is also evidence demonstrating that ordinary Japanese citizens adapted to introduction of the jury system and, as jurors, were not cowed into silence by socially superior judges (Dobrovolskaia 2008). *The Jury Guidebook* even notes that, in the early days of the Imperial jury system, jurors raised highly relevant questions about important evidence to the astonishment of judges (Dobrovolskaia 2008).

The rise of militarism and fascism in Japan as an explanation for the demise of the Imperial jury system is a deceptively simple one. During the 1930s Japan experienced the downfall of party cabinets and the re-emergence of bureaucratic and military elites. These elites saw themselves not

---

28　"Moreover, the selection of trial by jury, before the trial, signifies distrust for the presiding judge" (Japan Federation of Bar Associations 2006).

as servants of the people but rather as shepherds of the people (Berger 1977; Brown 2009; Garon 1987; Gordon 1991). The rise of the military and bureaucratic elites, and the general shift toward a statist solution for the problems facing Japan, was facilitated by international developments. Frustrated with Britain and the United States, Japan moved from a policy of cooperation in the 1920s to one of increasing hostility toward those powers in the 1930s (Berger 1977; Kasza 1988; Kato 1974). This trend was exacerbated by the emergence of fascist states in Italy and Germany. The apparent success of Mussolini's Italy and Nazi Germany in combating the depression, at a time when the great liberal-democratic states seemed to be floundering, encouraged a belief in the inherent weakness of democratic institutions and a commitment to a state-centered approach to dealing with the problems besetting Japan (Garon 1987; Gordon 1991). The times were, therefore, very much against the jury system. That system challenged the right of court officials to "shepherd the people." It was moreover a "weak" liberal-democratic institution adopted from the enemy states of Great Britain and the United States.

At its heart, militarism and fascism as an explanation for the demise of the Imperial jury system reflects the position held by many Common Law jurists that trial by jury is itself a "lamp that shows that freedom lives" (Devlin 1966). The reason, according to Lord Devlin, is because "no tyrant could afford to leave a subject's freedom in the hands of twelve of his countrymen" (1966). Research from Spain supports this assertion. There is a consensus amongst Spanish jurists that the jury was invariably adopted by liberal or progressive regimes and abolished or suspended by repressive regimes (Gleadow 2001). The problem with carrying the Spanish experience over to Japan is that, although the jury was suspended at a time of authoritarianism, the decline in trial by jury began at a time when Japan still had party cabinets, in the early 1930s. The argument is more persuasive when it takes into account the Peace Preservation Law 1925 and its amendment in 1928, the exclusion of political crimes from the Jury Act, and the first mass arrest of communists in 1928, the year the Imperial jury system became operative. It then becomes clear that structure of the Jury Act itself reflected a growing intolerance within the Imperial state for dissent.

The legal elite's explanation for the failure of the Imperial jury system is premised on the notion that judges, prosecutors and, to a lesser extent, defense lawyers engaged in conduct designed to limit the number of jury trials. There are certainly indications that judges encouraged defendants to waive, or not elect, trial by jury (Maruta 2001). There is likewise evidence that public prosecutors, in particular, were adverse to the system. Beyond the sheer unfamiliarity of the system, the higher acquittal rate of 16.7 percent for jury trials has been pointed to as an explanation for the antipathy of the judiciary and prosecutorial authorities toward the system. The rate of acquittal introduced an element of uncertainty into criminal proceedings that had the potential to encourage more defendants to contest their guilt. This in turn had the potential to raise the cost of deterrence. The antipathy of the judiciary and public prosecutors for the system does not, however, explain why defense lawyers did not embrace the system. The answer here perhaps lies in the unfamiliarity of the system and structural factors, such as the absence of appeals on questions of fact and the discretion of judges to dismiss the findings of the jury.

The explanations for the demise of the Imperial jury system point to a number of lessons for policy-makers. The structural argument emphasizes the importance of adopting a system of lay participation that functions effectively within the existing legal framework and urges caution in legislating to avoid incorporating disincentives into the system. The cultural argument points to the importance of taking cultural norms into consideration and stresses implementing public relations and education campaigns, both before and after any change, to both inform and engage participants. The explanation based on the historical shift toward authoritarianism is more problematic, but perhaps alludes to the need for the system to apply as broad a range of offenses as possible to avoid marginalization. The argument warns that the goal of greater civic participation, in particular, is undermined by removing serious cases based on political dissent from the scope of the system. Lastly, the legal elite's explanation emphasizes that for any system to work effectively it must enjoy the support of the legal profession broadly defined, particularly the judiciary and the prosecutorial authorities.

Taken as a group, the arguments' applicability to the "chicken or egg question" may reflect the concept that there are numerous players and institutional aspects which may affect the failure of a legal innovation. So success or failure in law shaping behavior may be a relative judgment subject to a number of factors embedded in the social setting, or, in the alternative, the social setting may be more or less receptive to legal innovation ex ante in the modernization context.

## Current *Saiban-in* System

In this section, we turn to consider the new *saiban-in* system. We first describe the period leading up to the law's enactment, which bears a number of relevant similarities to the political developments that resulted in the Imperial Jury Law. We then briefly introduce the basic elements of the new system. Following this, we apply the identified historical lessons from the 1923–1943 experience to the new *saiban-in* system.

### *Historical Context*

The 1943 Act Regarding the Suspension of the Jury Act, and statements made at the time the Bill was introduced into the Diet, raised the strong possibility that at some time in the near future after the end of the Pacific War trial by jury would once again return to Japan.[29] Despite these indications, and the continuing presence of the Jury Act on the statute books, the re-emergence of broad-based lay participation was to take over half a century. As had been the case in the lead-up to the Imperial Jury Law, the calls for such a system would be driven by concerns over the investigative powers of public prosecutors and the independence of the existing trial system as a forum for determining facts, and by a belief that lay participation would foster a more civically engaged and democratic society. Also reflecting earlier developments, the system ultimately adopted would be the product of a compromise between powerful stakeholders.

The right to trial by jury contained in the Sixth Amendment to the United States Constitution was not one of the procedural rights that the US framers of Japan's postwar constitution sought to impose on the Japanese government (Dean 1995; Lampert 1992; Wilson 2007). Despite this, there were nevertheless attempts made by the Occupation to incorporate the right to trial by jury within Japan's ordinary body of statute law. The Courts Act of 1947 made provision for the return of juries,[30] perhaps anticipating that the system would be included as part of the Code of Criminal Procedure. The first draft of that law did provide for jury trials but in the face of strong opposition

---

29    "The Jury Act will be made effective again after the end of the present war at a date as proscribed by accompanying Imperial order." Baishin hō no teishi ni kan suru hōritsu [Act on the Suspension of the Jury Act], Law No. 88 of 1943, Art. 3. The government, at the time the Suspension Bill was introduced, explained: "The enforcement suspension is appropriate in light of various circumstances that become strained in times of war. We can, however, say that the principle of the system is desirable as soon as there is peace. Therefore, the Jury Act is being suspended not repealed. We will consider enforcing the Act once more after the war" (Japan Federation of Bar Associations 2006).

30    Saibansho hō [Courts Act], Law No. 59 of 1947, Art. 3(3).

from Japanese members of the drafting committee, a group dominated by central-rightists retained from the war period elite, the provisions were removed (Dean 1995; Maruta 2001). Those members placed particular emphasis on the fact that the Imperial jury system had undoubtedly failed to justify excluding the jury provisions in the revised framework. For their part, the US members of the drafting committee were willing to accept that the jury was an institution alien to the inquisitorial system of justice or Japanese culture. Moreover, prominent members believed it counterproductive to force the Japanese to work with a system that differed fundamentally from what they experienced until that time. Trial by jury, as provided for under the draft, presumably marked such a departure. As a result, the Code of Criminal Procedure of 1948 did not provide for trial by jury.

As had occurred in the aftermath of failed attempts to incorporate the jury into the Constitution and Code of Criminal Instruction during the early Meiji Period, debate over whether Japan should have a system of lay participation as part of its justice system disappeared from the mainstream of political and legal debate for a time during the 1950s, 1960s, and 1970s. Only in US-occupied Okinawa did the jury system continue to feature as a significant part of the prevailing legal landscape, and then only on 10 occasions between 1963 and 1967 (Dobrovolskaia 2007).

This is not to suggest that calls for some form of lay participation disappeared altogether. Indeed, every few years some scholar or group would suggest such a proposal. One prominent advocate even used his own experience as a juror under the system that had been in force in US-occupied Okinawa to write a prize-winning autobiographical novel pointing to the virtues of the trial by jury (Isa 2001).[31] Although helping to explain why lay participation was subsequently accepted so readily as a reform capable of effecting institutional change, these proposals did not enjoy the support necessary to influence policy-makers until the 1980s at the earliest. In that decade, the retrial and acquittal of a number of death row inmates rocked the Japanese criminal justice system. The movement leading to the eventual introduction of the Lay Assessor System was to ride the wave of consternation, criticism, and anger that emerged in the wake of those decisions.

On July 15, 1983, the Kumamoto District Court acquitted Sakae Menda, who had been convicted for the hatchet murder of a 76-year-old prayer reader on March 23, 1953, and sentenced to death.[32] This decision was the first of four cases involving the retrial and acquittal of death row inmates. On all four occasions, the retrial courts found that in the absence of any corroborating evidence the defendants' confessions were an insufficient basis to support conviction. Prior to being released, the defendants served a combined total of 130 years in prison. For a time Menda had also held the dubious honor of being the longest serving death row inmate in the world.

There had been major cases involving miscarriages of justice prior to the Menda decision, but these cases had not involved the death penalty (Dean 1995). Thus, the events were shocking both for the realization that there had been people who had lived in prison awaiting execution for crimes they did not commit and that the prosecutors who had been entrusted with almost unlimited powers could not unconditionally be relied on to discover the truth. This in turn provoked almost unprecedented scrutiny of the justice system and reinvigorated calls for lay participation in the trial process.

In the year preceding the Kumamoto District Court decision in the Menda case, the first postwar organized civic movement to reintroduce trial by jury into Japan was formed in Hitotsubashi, Tokyo. The Research Group on Jury Trial included Chihiro Isa, the author of the Okinawan juror

---

31   Isa (2001). For further information about Isa's advocacy of the jury system, see: Dobrovolskaia (2007); Fukurai (2007).

32   *Japan v. Menda* (the Menda Case), 1090 *Hanrei jihō 21* (Kumamoto Dist. Ct., 15 July 1983). For English language accounts, see Foote (1992a); Kiss (1999).

autobiography, law professors, private lawyers, and a few liberal judges. Significantly, many of the members had first-hand experience working on wrongful convictions cases, including Tetsuya Kurata who was the chief defense lawyer in the Menda case.

As initially constituted, the Research Group on Jury Trial was a typical Japanese "study group" that sought to promote a cause—re-establishment of the jury system—with organization research and periodic meetings on the subject. With this aim in mind, from December 1982 the group published an official bulletin called *Jury Trial* (Fukurai 2007). In subsequent years the organization went on to encompass branches outside Tokyo and with increased membership to attract distinguished guests and speakers, including a former Chief Justice of the Supreme Court of Japan (Fukurai 2007). Unifying the membership of the Research Group on Jury Trial was a belief in trial by jury as an effective mechanism to deliver better justice by reducing wrongful conviction levels.

By the late 1980s the sense that the Japanese criminal justice system was not infallible had become widespread. Japan's abnormally high conviction rate of 99.7 percent and the prevalence of confessions in securing convictions increasingly came to be seen as proof of a system designed to secure conviction rather than justice (Lampert 1992). The circumstances under which confessions were made and the reliance placed on such confessions by judges came under particular scrutiny. A report by a committee established by the three Tokyo Bar Associations at the time arrived at the conclusion, after interviews with 30 victims of miscarriages of justice, that interrogation practices employed by authorities to secure confessions during protracted periods of pretrial detention were in breach of Japan's obligations under the International Covenant on Civil and Political Rights (Dean 1995). Menda's confession, for example, had come after almost 80 hours of questioning, during which time he had not been permitted to sleep (Foote 1992a).

The most damning attack on the reliance placed by judges on factual determinations arrived at by prosecutors and confessions came from within the judiciary itself. In a speech delivered at the Hokkaido University Faculty of Law on October 27, 1989, Justice Takeo Ishimatsu of the Osaka High court raised the question whether criminal defendants in Japan were truly receiving trial by judges (Dean 1995; Kiss 1999).[33] Answering his own question, the judge described a system where proceedings in court were "merely a formal ceremony" to confirm conclusions arrived at by prosecutorial authorities, which were contained in the dossier presented to the court and supported by now circumspect "confession" (Dean 1995).

For critics, a familiar systemic solution was close at hand: lay participation in the justice system. Freed from day to day interaction with the prosecutors, government influence and the conservatism of the Supreme Court, lay participants, it was reasoned, would not simply endorse the results of prosecutorial investigations but require cases to be proven in court. This, as Takashi Hara had argued before the Privy Council in 1921, would restore public confidence in the legal system and deliver "better justice" for Japan.

Any doubts that lay participation was once again on the agenda as a serious proposal for law reform was dispelled in 1988. In that year, Kōichi Yaguchi, Chief Justice of the Supreme Court of Japan, announced that the court was examining ways to incorporate lay participation into trial processes (Dean 1995; Fukurai 2007). As elsewhere, the court had primarily become interested in lay assessment as a mechanism for combating wrongful convictions (Fukurai 2007). However, later comments made by the court indicate it was also mindful that lay participation had an important role to play in the democratic administration of justice. In *Justice in Japan*, the court noted, when referring to the (lay) Judicial Commissioner, the Expert Commissioner, the Family

---

33    The speech was subsequently published, see Ishimatsu (1989).

Court Councilor and the Conciliation Commissioner, that "[t]hese systems surely contribute much to the democratic administration of justice in our country."[34]

The late 1980s to the 1990s saw further activity by the Supreme Court, the bar associations and the Research Group on Jury Trial. Similar to study missions in Japan's legal modernization a century before, the Supreme Court dispatched judges to the United States and the United Kingdom to investigate the jury system. The court also sent judges to Germany and France to observe the workings of mixed jury systems. The Supreme Court was not alone in its interest in lay participation systems in other jurisdictions. A subcommittee of the Osaka Bar Association's Committee for Judicial System Reform also toured the United States, Germany, and the United Kingdom. Closer to home, the bar associations and the Research Group on Jury Trial were active in conducting mock jury trials. The public response to calls by the Osaka Bar Association was such that it was able to run three jury trials.

Although lay participation was back on the agenda, it was far from a foregone conclusion that Japan would have such a system anytime soon. It was the "serendipity of events" leading to the development of the Judicial Reform Council (*shihō kaikaku shingikai*) that paved the way for the introduction of a new system of broad-based lay participation (Anderson and Nolan 2004). Within the space of two short years, calls for a new system, first raised in the Council's interim report in 1999, was transformed into a proposal for a particular type of system: the *saiban-in* system (Anderson and Ambler 2006; Anderson and Nolan 2004).

Although recommending the introduction of a *saiban-in* system, the Judicial Reform Council's final report did not proscribe the specific content of that system. The report was more remarkable for saying what the system was not. It was neither an Anglo-American style jury, nor a continental European mixed court of lay and professional judges (Anderson and Ambler 2006). Nor were these details contained in the Justice System Reform Promotion Act, which established the Office for Justice System Reform to give effect to the report's recommendations.[35] The resulting ambiguity meant that between the adoption of the final report by Cabinet on June 12, 2001, and the winding-up of the Office for Justice System Reform in December 2004, through operation of sunset provisions in the enabling legislation, there was an opportunity for powerful stakeholders to influence the specific content of the system (Anderson and Ambler 2006).

The battle over the shape of the *saiban-in* system was to be waged in the Lay Assessor/Penal Matters Investigation Committee, which was charged by the Office for Justice System Reform with implementing the proposal for the *saiban-in* system. Professor Masahito Inoue, Dean of the Tokyo University Law School, chaired the committee. As a criminal procedural law expert fluent in English, he was exceedingly familiar with both Japan's experience under the 1923 Jury Act and how juries operate overseas. Indeed, the term *saiban-in* itself had first emerged in a book presented by Professor Inoue in March 2001 (Anderson and Ambler 2006; Fukurai 2007).

If the saga to establish the Imperial jury system has but one lesson it is that when the interests of powerful stakeholders clash against a backdrop of an unstoppable push for reform compromise will eventuate. The powerful stakeholders in this instance were the Ministry of Justice, the Supreme Court, and the Japanese Federation of Bar Associations. These bodies notionally represented the vested interests of prosecutors, judges, and defense lawyers respectively. Although a number of arguments were put forward by each of these groups to advance their position, the central argument soon boiled down to the composition of mixed panels under the *saiban-in* system. The Japanese Federation of Bar Associations argued for panels consisting of nine lay people and a solitary judge,

---

34   *Justice in Japan* (1990) Tokyo: Supreme Court of Japan (quoted in Dean 1995).
35   Shihō seido kaikaku suishin hō [Justice System Reform Promotion Act], Law No. 119 of 2001.

whilst the Supreme Court argued for panels with three judges and three jurors (Anderson and Ambler 2006; Gotō et al. 2004; Japan Federation of Bar Associations 2003). The Ministry of Justice for their part adopted the consensus-seeking model suggested by Professor Inoue of three judges and between four to six lay participants (Anderson and Ambler 2006; Gotō et al. 2004; Investigation Committee 2003). This, however, merely marked the next phase in the struggle over the *saiban-in* system.

In early 2004 the process to establish the *saiban-in* system moved to the legislative phase. Although the model of three judges and four lay people enjoyed the support of the senior partner in the government coalition, the Liberal Democratic Party (LDP), it was not supported by the coalition's junior partner, the Kōmeitō. Nor was the LDP's position supported by the then opposition the Democratic Party (DPJ) (Anderson and Ambler 2006; Gotō et al. 2004). Kōmeitō supported panels consisting of two judges and seven lay people, whilst the DPJ advocated panels consisting of one judge and 10 lay people. The LDP was left with no other choice but to seek a compromise. On January 26, 2004, the two partners to the coalition government announced that they had reached a compromise: *saiban-in* panels would consist of three judges and six lay people in contested cases, and one judge and four lay people in cases where the commission of the crime was not in dispute.[36]

The compromise reached between the coalition partners was immediately incorporated into the Bill for the *saiban-in* system, which was endorsed by Cabinet on March 2, 2004 (Anderson and Ambler 2006).[37] The Bill was subsequently introduced into the Diet on March 16 and passed through the Lower House with the unanimous assent of its members on April 23. On May 21, the Upper House passed the Bill by a margin of 180 to 2. The law was proclaimed on May 28, 2005.[38]

As had been the case for the Imperial Jury Law, legislators provided for five years to implement the system.[39] During this time, the structural changes and procedures needed to implement the law were put in place and an education and public relations campaign was undertaken to promote the system (Anderson and Ambler 2006; Kamiya 2009; Wilson 2007). The new system came into effect in May 2009, with the first trials taking place in early August of the same year.

In sum, the long gestation of the *saiban-in* system bears remarkable similarity to the development of the original jury system in Japan. Both were nascent ideas, long fermenting. Both were drafted in government deliberative councils informed by foreign experience. Both were enacted at a secondary stage after the main thrust had waned, but serendipity provided a window of opportunity. Most significantly, the final version of both the Imperial jury system and the modern *saiban-in* system were the product of political compromise that produced structural elements that the pure reformers would have liked to avoid. For the 1923 Jury Act, these included elements such as the discretionary yet user-pays nature of trial by jury, the limited appeal rights, and the purely advisory effect of the jury's decision. Cognizant of these historical limitations, all have been avoided by the drafters of the new law. The modern political process, however, has produced its own compromises, introduced below. Critics argue that these new limitations will equally obstruct this system from delivering the promised better justice and more civic engagement (Jones 2008

---

36   "Three Judges, Six Lay Assessors Deliberation: Coalition Party Reaches Agreement on System Design," *Asahi Shimbun*, January 27, 2004; "Lay Judges Accord a Compromise," *Yomiuri Shimbun*, January 28, 2004.

37   "Japan's Cabinet Approves Overhaul of Judiciary," Agence France Presse, March 2, 2004.

38   Saiban'in no sanka suru keiji saiban ni kansuru hōritsu [Act Concerning Participation of Lay Assessors in Criminal Trials], Law No. 63 of 2004. Referred to in this chapter as "Lay Assessor Act."

39   Lay Assessor Act, Supplementary Provisions, Art. 1 [Enforcement Date].

and 2009). We suggest enough has been learned that most major problems will be avoided, though not all promises will be able to be delivered.

*The Lay Assessor Act 2004*

This section briefly introduces the basic elements of the *Lay Judge Act of 2004* by addressing six questions: what cases are heard, how lay judges are selected, what is the composition of the courts, what are the lay judges charged with doing, how are decisions made, and what are the protections provided for the system. As the *saiban-in* trials have only just begun at the time of this writing, there is almost no experience to inform this discussion; rather, we rely primarily on the text of the law and its accompanying rules, extensive interviews with the involved legal actors, and the few trials that have occurred. The experience under the Jury Act is used a point of reference along the way.

Very similar to the Imperial jury system, *saiban-in* trials are limited to serious criminal cases divided into two categories. Unlike the old jury system, there is no blanket exception for the most serious crimes and, directly in response to the prewar experience, no right to waive a *saiban-in* trial. The subject cases include those which are punishable by death or imprisonment for an indefinite period or with hard labor,[40] and those in which the victim has died due to an intentional criminal act.[41] As eligibility is not waivable and prosecutors determine what crime a defendant is charged with, the prosecutors will be the gatekeepers to the new system much as they were with the old. Thus, similar to the previous complaints regarding the practice of bringing suits in the Ward Courts to avoid a jury, there is the potential with the new system for the prosecutors to manipulate the charges to avoid the process. Alternatively, prosecutors can also oversubscribe the new system by including *saiban-in* trial claims with lesser charges, as mixed proceedings which are heard by the lay judges.[42]

At 2007 criminal rates, the courts are anticipating roughly 3,600 trials per year.[43] This is one of the most obvious places where the old Jury Act's lessons have been learned. Marginalization of the original jury system represented by the 484 juries under the 15 years of that system, or the 10 trials under the four years of Okinawa's occupation by the United States, will be surpassed in the first few months of enforcement of the new Act. Indeed, the more likely problem seems to be the inverse—a judicial system overwhelmed with the cost and logistics of processing so many novices through their short study-tour of judicial system.

The lay judges are to come from a random selection of those people listed on electoral rolls within the municipal jurisdictional divisions.[44] Therefore, lay judges will all be Japanese citizens at

---

40    Lay Assessor Act, Art. 2(i) [Subject Cases and Composition of a Judicial Panel]. The law covers cases listed in Art. 26(2)(ii) of the Courts Act, namely crimes punishable by death, indefinite imprisonment, penalties of minimum of one-year imprisonment and above, hard labor. For example, this would cover murder, arson of an inhabited structure, destruction by explosives, etc. See Penal Code, Law No. 45 of 1907, Arts. 199, 108, 117.

41    For example, this would cover inflicting bodily harm resulting in death, dangerous driving resulting in death, robbery or assault resulting in death (see Shinomiya et al. 2005).

42    Lay Assessor Act, Art. 4 [Handling of Concurrently Pled Cases]. In addition, if the prosecutors change the charges to a non-*saiban-in* offence after a *saiban-in* panel is underway, the lay assessor panel, at the court's discretion, may still determine the issue. Art. 5 [Handling of Cases Following Changes in the Criminal Charges].

43    "Top Court Seeks Lay Judge Budget," *Japan Times*, August 27, 2008.

44    Lay Assessor Act, Arts. 20 [Notice and Allocation of the Number of Lay Assessor Candidates]; 21 [Preparation of the Proposed List of Lay Assessor Candidates].

least 20 years of age.[45] While this is a significant advancement on the Imperial jury systems limits of eligibility that excluded women and were restricted to those rich enough to pay substantial taxes, the *saiban-in* definition does exclude the large population of Korean and Chinese permanent residents who have chosen not to take Japanese citizenship. Perhaps ironically, these are people who would have been eligible jurors under the former system as they were citizens of the greater empire at the time.

A variety of other people are excluded from this general eligibility rule. First, those who have not completed compulsory education through Year 9; those who have been subject to imprisonment; and those who would be significantly burdened in their execution of lay assessor duties are disqualified.[46] Second, almost all people pursuing some form of a legal profession such as lawyers, patent attorneys, and politicians are exempt.[47] Third, people aged 70 years or older, currently enrolled students, and people who have served as a lay assessor in the past five years may decline to serve if they so choose.[48]

In addition to these automatic exemptions, discretionary exemptions are available upon application to the court. Thus, the court may excuse a person on the basis of serious illness or injury; family childcare or nursing commitments; important work obligations; or the very culturally defined "unavoidable social obligations such as attendance at a parent's funeral."[49] While excessive exemptions have not been cited as a problem under the Imperial jury law, the framers of the *saiban-in* system were very aware of that failure of other systems to maintain representativeness, and thereby promotion of the civic engagement objective. Thus, the Supreme Court Rules on granting discretion construct a conservative test,[50] but only time will tell if the court system's practice and subsequent handbook guidelines will follow that line.

The new *saiban-in* trials will be heard predominately by panels of three professional judges and six lay judges.[51] For all of the serious crimes captured within the new Act, presently the norm is a trial in front of three professional judges.[52] The law also provides for some cases to be heard by one judge and four lay judges where there are no facts in dispute and all parties agree.[53] This smaller panel was a key compromise in the drafting process, and in light of the over 90 percent confession rate (Johnson 2002) and concerns about the efficiency of the whole judicial system to handle the 3,000 plus cases a year, it might be expected that a large number of cases will proceed through this expedited process. This, in turn, would raise historical concerns of the marginalization seen in the prewar jury system where given the opportunity parties opted out of the lay trials. Cognizant of the risk it seems, the involved parties say the default will be set for the larger panels and the smaller panels will be used sparingly (Anderson and Ambler 2006). The first *saiban-in* case supports that

---

45   Kôshoku senkyo hō [Public Election Act], Law No. 100 of 1950, Art. 9.

46   Lay Assessor Act, Art. 14 [Reasons for Disqualification].

47   Lay Assessor Act, Art. 15.

48   Lay Assessor Act, Art. 16 [Reasons to Decline].

49   Lay Assessor Act, Art. 16; *Saiban'in no sanka suru keiji saiban ni kansuru hōritsu dai jūroku jō dai hachi gō ni kitei suru yamu wo enai jiyū wo sadameru seirei* [Cabinet Order prescribing the unavoidable circumstances provided for in Article 16, Item 8 of the Law Concerning the Participation of Lay Assessors in Criminal Trials], Cabinet Order No. 3 of 2008.

50   Saiban'in no sanka suru keiji saiban ni kansuru kisei [Rules Concerning Participation of Lay Assessors in Criminal Trials], Supreme Court Rules No. 7 of 2007 (as amended by Supreme Court Rules No.5 of 2008 and No.1 of 2009).

51   Lay Assessor Act, Art. 2(2) [Subject Cases and Composition of a Judicial Panel].

52   Saibansho hō [Courts Act], Law No. 59 of 1947, Art. 28(3).

53   Lay Assessor Act, Art. 2(3) [Subject Cases and Composition of a Judicial Panel].

with a full six lay judges empanelled even though the defendant had confessed and the only issue at question was the weight of the sentence he would receive (Johnson 2009).

Most significantly, unlike the separate jury and judge deliberations under the Imperial Jury Act, the *saiban-in* system has the professional judges and lay judges deliberating together. Moreover, the Act stipulates that the professional judges and lay judges are to reach a verdict on the basis of recognition of the facts of the case and application of relevant laws and ordinances, and then sentence accordingly.[54] The Act further clarifies, however, that only the professional judges are to interpret the law, though the lay judges may question and comment on those issues.[55] Interestingly, the lay judges may also question witnesses, victims, and the defendant during the trial.[56] Thus, when contrasted to the old jury system, the lay judges have lost their monopoly on factual determination, thereby avoiding the need for the judicial opt-out clause, but the judges have lost their monopoly on sentencing and have conceded some space in legal determinations as well.

The law and the accompanying court rules do not provide guidance on how the actual deliberations will be handled. Given the cultural critiques of the prewar Jury Act about jurors' deference to authority, this is a surprising omission. The positive news is the Supreme Court is highly cognizant of the critique and has been training its professional judges to be sensitive to deliberation dynamics within the cultural context that they operate.

Despite the cultural theorists' arguments about a consensus based society, the law does not require unanimity in decisions. Rather, the political compromise resulted in a complex majority rule that preserved a higher value vote for the professional judges. Decisions are by a simple majority but must include at least one professional judge.[57] As a simple majority could numerically be formed without any of the professional judges, this rule gives priority to the professional judges' votes. Arguably this preference is based on the same rationale that gave Imperial judges the right to overrule juries in the old system: the risk that amateurs may produce a factual determination that cannot be supported consistent with the law. Stated differently, the special majority rule avoids the possibility of jury nullification that worries pure lay jury systems elsewhere.[58]

Reminiscent of the juror under the 1923 system who asked how he could return to his village after having served, the new law goes to great extents to protect lay judges and their identities. Indeed, it goes so far that one of the areas that has provoked the strongest critique of the law are the privacy protections and penalties (Levin and Tice 2009). The *Saiban-in* Act protects lay judges from any information being disclosed about them or them being contacted about the trial by others.[59] The trouble is that in trying to protect the lay judges' identity, the system has been enveloped with a layer of opaqueness that prevents scrutiny of deliberations, confirmation of the accuracy of written judgments, and post-service counseling (Levin and Tice 2009). All recognize that a balance should be found between transparency of process and protection of the lay judges' privacy. The Imperial jury system experience cautions, however, against setting that balance too far in favor of secrecy. If the rationale for the actions being made cannot be revealed, even if they

------

54    Lay Assessor Act, Art. 6(1) [Powers of Judges and Lay Assessors].

55    Lay Assessor Act, Art. 6(2) [Powers of Judges and Lay Assessors].

56    Lay Assessor Act, Arts. 56 [Questioning of Witnesses], 57 [Witness Questioning Outside the Court]. Art. 58 [Questioning of Victims]. Art. 59 [Questioning of the Defendant].

57    Lay Assessor Act, Art 67.

58    "Jury nullification occurs when the jury rejects or ignores the court's instructions on the law in reaching its verdict. The term is typically applied in criminal cases on account of the fact that, in such cases, jurors have the acknowledged power to acquit for any reason. Such acquittals are unreviewable on appeal" (Hardwick 1996).

59    Lay Assessor Act, Arts. 100–2, 106–9.

are legitimate and defensible, they will become circumspect. With that in mind, the surprising post-trial television interview of five of the six lay judges in the first *saiban-in* trial in August 2009 was a positive development.

With the benefit of introducing outsiders not beholden to the existing order, the *saiban-in* system resembles the classical jury system. The political compromise has hedged against the greatest risks of that system by having the professional and lay judges act together. Whether that avoids the problem as supporters suggest or gives rise to a new set of capture problems will only be told in time.

*Applying Historical Lessons to the New System*

Recall that commentators have asserted four reasons for the failure of the original Japanese jury system: structural problems, cultural issues, rational reaction to political incentives, and rejection by the relevant elites. Applying those rationales against the new system portends both risks and optimism.

The specific structural issues under the Imperial jury system have all been consciously avoided in the *saiban-in* law. Proceedings are compulsory to avoid defendants opting out and marginalizing the process. The more lenient *kōso* appeal practice has been retained and there is no cost to the defendant for using the new process. Finally, decisions by the lay judges are binding. Interestingly, it is exactly these structures, as modified to satisfy political compromise, that appear to present the most difficulty in the new system delivering the better justice and more democracy promised.

Because defendants cannot opt out of the *saiban-in* system like they could under the jury system, one of the greatest risks of the new procedure is that it is simply too ambitious. The ongoing cost of running nearly 4,000 trials with lay participants a year is enormous. This is exacerbated by the infrastructural pressure caused by having the candidate lay assessors, alternative lay assessors, and lay assessors themselves coming to courthouses not designed for these volumes. Moreover, the financial demands will be made during perhaps the greatest government budgetary crisis since the financial demands that contributed to the suspension of the original jury system. The structural solution of making the new procedure compulsory also is of questionable value. First, the compulsory nature passes the overall regulator of the flow of cases from defendants to the prosecutors (Johnson 2009). This may have a positive effect on prosecutorial charging practice, but it might equally have prosecutors either under-charging to avoid the process or over-charging to flood the system. In either case, it takes away from the democratic ideals sought to be promoted by the new system. Second, with over 90 percent of trials being based on confessions, a large majority of the compulsory trials simply will not deliver any different judgment than fully professional panels. This was indeed the case with the first well publicized *saiban-in* trial where the lay judges were only asked to contribute to the sentencing determination, an area where Japan has led the world and been able to produce the greatest reform records (Foote 1992b; Johnson 2002). In other words, it is not clear that the costs of the compulsory rule is justified by its likely return on improved justice. Rather, it seems more likely that systemic pressure caused by the compulsion, perhaps exacerbated by new charging practice of the prosecutors, will be the first item cited by those who seek to rollback the reform.

The decision to include a *kōso* or cassation appeal heard solely by professional judges was insisted on by those who wanted to avoid the limitations of the Imperial jury system. The problem is it creates a logical tautology. Allowing three appellate judges to overrule a mixed court on matters of fact, does not recognize the expertise that the lay judges bring to the process. Moreover, while this decision was a political compromise won by the liberals seeking to avoid the jury system faults, it in fact is not compelled by the historical experience since the *saiban-in* trials are compulsory. Similarly while it makes sense that the new law has avoided the old requirement that a defendant had to pay for the procedure, the process fee and the revised appeal will have no real impact as the compulsion of the new system means internal disincentives to electing the procedure are irrelevant.

Structurally the chief complaint regarding the Imperial system was that jury decisions were merely advisory. Thus, the new system makes them mandatory, but the compromise the process produced was that determinations are drawn together collaboratively with the professional and lay judges, and that the professional judges collectively have a veto. Research shows that professionals and lay people can work extremely effectively together (Anderson and Nolan 2004; Fujita 2003; Kaplan and Martin 1999). Nevertheless, the deliberation room is the lynchpin element both for delivering better justice and engendering more public engagement with the legal process. If satisfying cross-communication occurs, as the research suggests it might, the experiment will succeed. If the professional judges dominate or lay judges are passive, then all of the naysayers' predictions will come true.

As discussed below and argued previously,[60] we have confidence in both the professional judges to try sincerely and earnestly to make this work, and the citizens' confidence and engagement to participate actively. The structural impediment in seeing this succeed, however, is that the privacy rules have been set so strictly that the deliberation room must remain opaque. The results for the entire process will remain suspect without the transparency to test objectively whether the deliberation room is working, or to confirm subjectively with the lay judges that it was a real process (and they agree with the outcome). Put more bluntly, without more transparency of the internal processes the detractors will be perpetually armed with the argument that the entire process is "mere window dressing" not delivering the reform goals and therefore not worth the costs.

The cultural lessons from history should portend more optimism as Kawashima's cultural argument always assumed that culture was evolutionary and time would bring more convergence with rights-based approaches. In other words, the argument suggests that while Japan might not have been ready for lay participation before the war or immediately after it, by the twenty-first century it has developed to the stage where lay participation is likely to get social traction. Some, however, have used the current public opinion polls that show 70 percent of Japanese to be hesitant to serve as lay judges as evidence to show the cultural evolution still has not occurred (Onishi 2007; Tabuchi and McDonald 2009). Other so-called rights-based countries also have similar figures regarding the public's willingness to serve (Fukurai 2007). What is interesting culturally is to compare the primary reasons for reluctance.

In Japan, the primary concern is a hesitancy to judge others (Anderson and Ambler 2006; Fukurai 2007), while in the other countries there appears to be little hesitancy to judge one's neighbors, but more concern with the pragmatic cost of the exercise (Fukurai 2007). Generalizing, the Japanese rationale is encouraging in that it suggests people take seriously the responsibility and plan to exercise, albeit reluctantly, active engagement with the process. Meanwhile, the alternative rational suggests a cynicism with the process that more likely will lead to passive participation or avoidance. That being said, Japan's reason for personal hesitancy in serving as a lay judge does seem to be culturally different in a way that is more difficult to address structurally. As such, the historical lessons about the importance of a sustained education campaign appear relevant.

---

60    Historical experience and the results of mock trials indicated that once empanelled as lay judges the general public would engage in fulfilling its role (Anderson and Ambler 2006). Reports from early trials indicate that this has indeed been the case (Johnson 2009).

It is hard to apply directly to the new *saiban-in* system the relevance of the historical lessons concerning rational actors' response in the prewar period to the changed broader environment as part of the demise of the jury system. The Imperial jury system arose under Taisho Democracy, and the leaders of the day bet on liberal-democratic ideals as the path to future prosperity. The jury system's demise followed when different political forces, namely the military and the bureaucracy, were able to use international developments and the apparent success of a rival model of governance in Italy and Germany to sell a vision of society where experts directed the efforts of the people toward the achievement of national aspirations. In this sense, the *Saiban-in* Act drafted in the midst of hand-wringing in Japan during its Lost Decade and the United States hegemonic lead at the turn of the twenty-first century reflects the ideals of the time. In a different future world, with the Global Financial Crisis pointing out cracks in a simple liberal democracy model, the potential for an alternative paradigm to arise exists. If rational actors find it in their interest to lobby from that basis for change of the *saiban-in* system, that may be persuasive. Predicting too far along this unknown trajectory, however, is more risky than useful.

Finally, the historical experience of the Imperial jury system teaches that support of the elite is crucial. A simplistic analysis along these lines might suggest judges and prosecutors may very well collude silently to undermine the new system and bring about its demise. Similarly, the same analysis might suggest it will be the private defense bar who will work hardest to ensure the success of a system that creates the smallest chink in the existing Teflon armor of the current criminal system (Anderson and Ambler 2006; Johnson 2002). Our sense after talking with many judges, prosecutors, and private lawyers over the past six years, however, is the opposite (Anderson and Ambler 2006; Johnson 2002, 2009).

The original strongest holdouts against the *saiban-in*—the courts—are now its strongest allies. The judges know the new system will bring their practices into the open, but they also know that its success or failure will be judged against them based on whether they can manage the logistics of implementing the new structure, the new trial procedures, and the new deliberations within the mixed panels. As such, the courts have wholeheartedly prepared and are committed to the system. Similarly the prosecutors, while not as exposed as the judges, are keen not to be at fault for any failings in the new system. They have their nearly perfect conviction rates on the line, as well as their long held assertion that this record is not due to tacit collusion with the judges but due to their high quality interrogation, preparation, and courtroom practice.

Counter-intuitively, it is the private defense lawyers who are the weak link in the new system. With the exception of a handful of dedicated advocates, the private bar as a whole has little incentive to make the *saiban-in* system work. These cases will be more trouble, take more time and thereby be worth less money than the present system. Further, unlike the courts and prosecutors who have a national mandate to invest in preparing for the new system, the private bar has no compulsion to be prepared and so has not undertaken any comprehensive preparation for the new system. Indeed, this might be a case of the present explaining the past, that is, why defense lawyers under the jury system did not counsel more of their clients to elect juries when the acquittal rates were so much higher. Whether the private bar plays their role successfully, we believe, presents the greatest risk to the new system.


**Conclusion**

The background to the Jury Act of 1923 and the Lay Judge Act of 2004 are remarkably similar. Both were subject to a long gestation period and eventually enacted in a reform wave supported by a liberal-democratic ideal. Both expressly sought to deliver better justice by putting checks on the state legal organs, and better democratic engagement by involving the general public in one of the cornerstones of democracy, the justice system. Both benefited from a five-year lead-up to the implementation of the systems for an education and preparatory campaign. Both have been subject to immense mass media scrutiny.

The 1923 experiment, however, failed. It was suspended in 1943 having failed by marginalization. Different commentators have attributed the demise to various factors. Some focus on the structural limits of the jury system, in particular its ability to be waived by the defendant and the advisory nature of the jury decisions. Others focus on cultural elements suggesting the Japanese people in the prewar era were not inclined to judge others and preferred to have top-down delivered justice. Historians also remind that most Taisho Democracy innovations were not able to survive the new paradigm of an Axis-centric world. Finally, those who focus on a political economy analysis note that the legal elites did not sufficiently support the system. With the possible exception of the cultural arguments, however, these explanations lie outside the general "chicken or egg" question.

Does history predict the future for the *saiban-in* system? Without giving dominance to any single interpretation, we suggest history is a useful analytical tool for critiquing the new law. The drafters have worked hard to avoid the historical structural problems, but the political process and the compromises it requires have created new structural issues, in particular the compulsory nature of the new trials and the lack of transparency. The cultural interpretation when unraveled suggests fewer obstacles than many would suggest. Whether this is due to an evolution of the Japanese people or flaccid original analysis is arguable. The rationale actor's response to the times provides a historically bound interpretation of limited immediate application, but also a cautionary canary for monitoring larger geopolitical trends. Finally, a subtle analysis of elites suggests both reasons for optimism regarding the courts and prosecutors, but the largest concern in developing an engaged defense bar.

With only a handful of trials completed to date, the easiest and safest statement is to say that only time will tell whether the *saiban-in* system has learned the lessons of the jury system. Being more adventurous, we are willing to suggest that the early signs, when measured against the historical teachings, are optimistic. No doubt that there are serious issues of concern such as moderating the flow of cases, controlling the cost of the system, ensuring the effectiveness of the deliberation process, promoting more transparency, and maintaining the support of the defense bar. But, a number of positive signs exist: marginalization of the process is not a concern, cultural obstacles appear overstated, the general global climate supports such liberal-democratic developments, and the majority of legal elites are working toward its success. On balance, while like any other good system we expect it will be refined over time, we are willing based on a historical critique, to be cautiously optimistic regarding the prospects of the new Japanese lay judge system.

## References

Anderson, K. 2004. *Gaikoku no jōshiki kara mita saiban-in seido* [The Lay Assessor System Viewed from a Foreign Commonsense Perspective]. *Hōritsu Jihō* 37.

Anderson, K. and Ambler, L. 2006. The Slow Birth of Japan's Quasi–Jury System (Saiban-in Seido): Interim Report on the Road to Commencement. *Journal of Japanese Law*, 11(21), 55–80.

Anderson, K. and Nolan, M. 2004. Lay Participation in the Japanese Justice System: A Few Preliminary Thoughts Regarding the Lay Assessor System (*saiban-in seido*) from Domestic

Historical and International Psychological Perspectives. *Vanderbilt Journal of Transnational Law*, 37(4), 935–92.

Anderson, K. and Saint, E. 2005. Japan's Quasi-Jury (Saiban-in) Law: An Annotated Translation of the Act Concerning Participation of Lay Assessors in Criminal Trials. *Asian-Pacific Law & Policy Journal*, 6(1), 233–83.

Baishin hō [Jury Act], Law No. 50 of 1923.

Baishin hō no teishi ni kan suru hōritsu [Act on the Suspension of the Jury Act], Law No. 88 of 1943.

Berger, G. 1977. *Parties Out of Power in Japan 1931–1941.* Princeton: Princeton University Press.

Brown, R.H. 2009. Shepherds of the People: Yasuoka Masahiro and the New Bureaucrats in Early Showa Japan. *Journal of Japanese Studies*, 35(2), 285.

Dean, M. 1995. Trial by Jury: A Force for Change in Japan. *International and Comparative Law Quarterly*, 44(Pt. 2), 379–404.

Devlin, P. 1966. *Trial by Jury.* London: Stevens & Sons.

Dobrovolskaia, A. 2007. An All-Laymen Jury System Instead of the Lay Assessor (*Saiban-in*) System for Japan? Anglo-American-Style Jury Trials in Okinawa under the U.S. Occupation. *Journal of Japanese Law*, 12(24), 57–80.

Dobrovolskaia, A. 2008. The Jury System in Pre-War Japan: An Annotated Translation of "The Jury Guidebook" (*Baishin Tebiki*). *Asian-Pacific Law and Policy Journal*, 9, 231–96.

Duus, P. 1988. *The Cambridge History of Japan; Volume 6: The Twentieth Century.* Cambridge: Cambridge University Press.

Foote, D.H. 1992a. From Japan's Death Row to Freedom. *Pacific Rim Law & Policy Journal*, 1(1), 11–103.

Foote, D.H. 1992b. The Benevolent Paternalism of Japanese Criminal Justice. *California Law Review*, 80(2), 317–90.

Fujita, M. 2003. *Can Japanese Citizens Play Active Roles in "Saiban'in-Seido"? [Japanese New Mixed Jury System]: Survey Research with Mock Mixed Juries*, Poster Presented at the Psychology & Law International, Interdisciplinary Conference, Edinburgh (July 7–12).

Fukurai, H. 2007. The Rebirth of Japan's Petit Quasi-Jury and Grand Jury Systems: A Cross-National Analysis of Legal Consciousness and the Lay Participation Experiences in Japan and the U.S. *Cornell International Law Journal*, 40(2), 315–54.

Garon, S. 1987. *The State and Labor in Modern Japan.* Berkeley: University of California Press.

Gleadow, C. 2001. Spain's Return to Trial by Jury: Theoretical Foundations and Practical Results. *Saint Louis-Warsaw Transatlantic Law Journal*, 57–74.

Gordon, A. 1991. *Labor and Imperial Democracy in Prewar Japan.* Berkeley: University of California Press.

Gordon, A. 2009. *A Modern History of Japan: From Tokugawa Times to the Present.* 2nd Edition. New York: Oxford University Press.

Gotō, A., Shinomiya, S., Nishimaru, T., and Kudō, M. 2004. *Jitsumuka no tame no saiban-in hō nyūmon* [A Practitioner's Introduction to the Lay Assessor Act]. Tokyo: Gendaijin-Bunsha.

Hardwick, L.B. 1996. Juror Misconduct or Juror Accountability? *Litigation*, 22(4), 19–26.

Ichihara, Y. 1993. 1923-nen Bashin-hō no Kōzōteki-kekkan to Sono-kokuhuku – Dōhō-shikkōki oyobi Sengo-kaikakuki wo Chūshin toshite [A Historical Survey of Attempts to Eliminate the Structural Defects from the Jury Law of 1923]. in Kansai University: Jury System Study Group.

Investigation Committee 2003. *Saiban-in seido ni tsuite* [Concerning the Lay Assessor System]. [Online]. Available at: www.kantei.go.jp/jp/singi/sihou/kentoukai/saibanin/dai13/13siryou1.pdf [accessed: October 16, 2009].

Isa, C. 2001. *Gyakuten: Amerika shihaika, Okinawa no baishin saiban* [Turnaround: A Jury Trial in Okinawa under American Rule]. Tokyo: Iwanami Shoten.

Ishimatsu, T. 1989. Are Criminal Defendants in Japan Truly Receiving Trials by Judges? *Law in Japan: An Annual*, 22, 143–56.

Japan Federation of Bar Associations. 2003. *Saiban-in seido "tatakidai" ni tai suru iken* [Opinion Regarding the "Sounding Board" on the Lay Assessor System] May 30. Available at: www. nichibenren.or.jp/ja/opinion/report/data/2003_23.pdf [accessed: October 16, 2009].

Japan Federation of Bar Associations. 2006. *Nihon demo baishin-seido ga okonawareteita!* [The Jury System was also Performed in Japan!]. Available at: www.nichibenren.or.jp/ja/citizen_ judge/about/column2.html [accessed: June 11, 2009].

Johnson, D.T. 2002. *The Japanese Way of Justice: Prosecuting Crime in Japan*. New York: Oxford University Press.

Johnson, D.T. 2009. Early Returns from Japan's New Criminal Trials. *The Asia-Pacific Journal: Japan Focus*, 36(3), September 7. Available at: www.japanfocus.org/-David_T_-Johnson/3212 [accessed: October 20, 2009].

Jones, C. 2008. *Amerikajin Bengoshi ga Mita Saiban'in Seido* [An American Lawyer's View of the Lay Judge System]. Tokyo: Heibonsha.

Jones, C. 2009. Big Winners in "Jury" System may be Judges, Bureaucrats. *The Japan Times*, March 10.

Kamiya, S. 2008. Lay Judges Relieved Case Over but Enthusiastic about Experience. *The Japan Times*, August 7.

Kamiya, S. 2009. Day of Public Reckoning in Criminal Trial Process Looms. *The Japan Times*, May 12.

Kaplan, M.F. and Martin, A. 1999. Effects of Differential Status of Group Members on Process and Outcome of Deliberation. *Group Processes & Intergroup Relations*, 2(4), 347.

Kasza, G.J. 1988. *The State and the Mass Media in Japan, 1918–1945*. Berkeley: University of California Press.

Kato, S. 1974. Taishō Democracy as the Pre-stage for Japanese Militarism, in *Japan in Crisis: Essays on Taisho Democracy*, edited by B.S. Silberman and H.D. Harootunian. Michigan: University of Michigan Press.

Kawashima, T. 1963. Dispute Resolution in Contemporary Japan, in *Law in Japan: The Legal Order in a Changing Society*, edited by A.T. von Mehren. Cambridge, MA: Harvard University Press, 41–60.

Kiss, L.W. 1999. Reviving the Criminal Jury in Japan. *Law and Contemporary Problems*, 62(2), 261–83.

Kōshoku senkyo hō [Public Election Act], Law No. 100 of 1950.

Kowata, Y. 2008. Baishinhō to Saibanin-Seido—Minshushugi-Kokka to Shukensha—Kyōiku-Hoshō e no Kakyō toshite no Saiban-in Seido [The Jury Act and the Saiban-in System: The Saiban-in System as a Bridge to a Democratic State and a Guarantee for Educating People as Sovereigns]. *Shakaihukushi-Kenkyuu*, 10, 13–22.

Lampert, R. 1992. A Jury for Japan? *The American Journal of Comparative Law*, 40(1), 37–71.

Landsman, S. and Zhang, J. 2008. A Tale of Two Juries: Lay Participation Comes to Japanese and Chinese Courts. *UCLA Pacific Basin Law Journal*, 25(2), 179–227.

Levin, M. and Tice, V. 2009. Japans New Citizen Judges: How Secrecy Imperils Judicial Reform. *The Asia-Pacific Journal: Japan Focus* [Online], 19(6). Available at: www.japanfocus.org/-Virginia-Tice/3141 [accessed: October 20, 2009].

Maruta, T. 2001. The Criminal Jury System in Imperial Japan and the Contemporary Argument for its Reintroduction. *International Review of Penal Law*, 72(1–2), 215–24.

Mitani, T. 1979. Nihon ni okeru baishinsei-seiritsu no seijishiteki-imi (ni) [The Significance in Political History of the Establishing of the Jury System in Japan (2)]. *Kokka Gakkai Zasshi*, 92(5–6), 357–437.

Mitani, T. 1988. The Establishment of the Party Cabinets, 1898–1932, in *The Cambridge History of Japan; Volume 6: The Twentieth Century*, edited by P. Duus. Cambridge: Cambridge University Press.

Onishi, N. 2007. Japan Learns Dreaded Task of Jury Duty. *The New York Times*, July 16.

Port, K.L. and McAlinn, G.P. 2003. *Comparative Law: Law and the Legal Process in Japan*. Durham, NC: Carolina Academic Press.

Röhl, W. 2005. *History of Law in Japan Since 1868*. Leiden: Brill.

Saiban'in no sanka suru keiji saiban ni kansuru hōritsu [Act Concerning Participation of Lay Assessors in Criminal Trials], Law No. 63 of 2004.

Saiban'in no sanka suru keiji saiban ni kansuru kisei [Rules Concerning Participation of Lay Assessors in Criminal Trials], Supreme Court Rules No. 7 of 2007 (as amended by Supreme Court Rules No.5 of 2008 and No.1 of 2009).

Saiban'in no sanka suru keiji saiban ni kansuru hōritsu dai jūroku jō dai hachi gō ni kitei suru yamu wo enai jiyū wo sadameru seirei [Cabinet Order prescribing the unavoidable circumstances provided for in Article 16, Item 8 of the Law Concerning the Participation of Lay Assessors in Criminal Trials], Cabinet Order No. 3 of 2008.

Saiban-in Saiban: Shinken-ni Kiitekureta ... Shuttei no Mokugeki-Shōninra Kōkan [Lay Judge Trial: They Listened in Earnest ... A Favourable Impression Made on Witnesses Appearing in Court]. 2009. *Mainichi Shimbun*, August 8.

Saibansho hō [Courts Act], Law No. 59 of 1947.

Shihō seido kaikaku suishin hō [Justice System Reform Promotion Act], Law No. 119 of 2001.

Shinomiya S., Nishimura T., and Kudō, M. 2005. Moshimo saiban-in ni erabaretara: Saiban-in Handbook [What if You were Chosen to be a Lay Assessor: The Lay Assessor Handbook]. Tokyo: Kadensha.

Silberman, B.S. and Harootunian, H.D. 1974. *Japan in Crisis: Essays on Taishō Democracy*. Princeton: Princeton University Press.

Tabuchi, H. and McDonald, M. 2009. In First Return to Japan Court, Jurors Convict and Sentence. *The New York Times*, August 6.

Tanaka, H., assisted by Smith, Malcolm D.H. 1976. *The Japanese Legal System: Introductory Cases and Materials*. Tokyo: University of Tokyo Press.

Urabe, M. 1976. Wagakuni ni Okeru Baishin Saiban no Kenkyū [A Study on Trial by Jury in Japan], in *The Japanese Legal System: Introductory Cases and Materials*, edited by H. Tanaka. Tokyo: University of Tokyo Press, 483–91.

von Mehren, A.T. 1963. *Law in Japan: The Legal Order in a Changing Society*. Cambridge, MA: Harvard University Press.

Wilson, M. 2007. The Dawn of Criminal Jury Trials in Japan: Success on the Horizon? *Wisconsin International Law Journal*, 24(4), 835–70.

# PART V
# Latin America, Post Conflict and the Judiciary

Chapter 16

# Institutional Factors Determining the Gap between Laws in the Books vs. Laws in Action: An Analytical Framework for Improving Judicial Effectiveness

Edgardo Buscaglia

This chapter aims at identifying the necessary conditions for the more effective implementation of laws, thus reducing the gap between *the laws in the books and the laws in action*. We understand the "chicken or egg" question in this context, assuming an interest in whether law can be used as a means of social engineering, capturing the essence of "on the books" versus "in action." A case study and jurimetrics-based analysis of impact indicators of judicial reforms are presented below detailing the factors enhancing effective legal implementation within the counter-organized crime judicial domain.

The modernization of economic life entails increasingly complicated interactions among individuals and organizations at national and international levels. Furthermore, the mix of deregulation, liberalization of international trade, and the privatization of state enterprises undertaken in many countries have intensified the need for legal frameworks with clear rules for economic interaction (Buscaglia 1997). For example, the increasing permeability of national frontiers to international trade and ideas is so great that it has forced national authorities to consider the adoption of international best practices for protecting intellectual property rights (Buscaglia 1997). Within criminal jurisdictions, the dark side of globalization, combining an increasing cross-border porosity with the use of advanced technologies by criminal enterprises, has generated a bonanza for organized crime and public sector corruption (Buscaglia 2001). All suggest a wider and international impact of laws (in terms of scale and scope) on socio-economic interactions and vice versa. In this context, there is an increasing need for legal rules to be designed, interpreted, and enforced in a consistent, coherent, and predictable manner within nation states and across international borders in order to enhance risk management and foster wealth generation in an increasingly complex world (Buscaglia 1994).

Strengthening the rule of law with the aim of generating economic prosperity requires securing property rights and contractual enforcement while making the exercise of the state's power more coherent, more predictable, and more consistent with the needed incentives to foster investment and promote economic growth. In order to comply with these requirements, a rule of law state makes governments subject to laws while every person (regardless of socio-economic status, ethnicity, or gender) is treated with equal rights within a judicial system that is feasibly accessible to all. As a result, a rule of law state consists in providing enactment, interpretation, and enforcement of laws in a coherent, consistent, and predictable manner through effective and efficient judicial systems (Buscaglia 1994). In short, economic progress requires legal rules to be clearly defined, made public, while also interpreted and enforced by a judicial system immune to systemic abuses of substantive and procedural discretions.

Yet high costs for delineating and protecting property and contractual rights are still common in many developed and developing countries' jurisdictions. Many countries still present a picture of unpredictable regulatory frameworks and multiple, high, and unanticipated taxation applied to the same bundle of property rights. All these pernicious effects are sometimes compounded by an inconsistent application of the laws worsened by judicial ineffectiveness and, worse, corrupt practices within the state. As a result, societal transaction costs (reflecting the costs of acquiring information, negotiating complex transactions, and monitoring compliance of agreements in society) are increased to levels that make it unprofitable to invest by those demanding and supplying goods and services within a market.

Abundant empirical research has shown significant links between strengthening the rule of law and greater economic growth (Buscaglia 1994; Buscaglia and Dakolias 1999; de Soto 1996; Maoro 1995;). Accordingly, many developed and developing countries have attempted to reform their laws and judiciaries as a result of their political and social efforts to strengthen democracy in order, to enhance the protections of human rights and to foster private investment. Yet, an international comparative analysis demonstrates that legal and judicial reforms have shown mixed results around the world (Buscaglia and Dakolias 1999). Dysfunctional laws and limited judicial capacities within the police, prosecutorial, and judicial domains are the common denominators of failed legal and judicial reforms worldwide where serious impediments to enhancing public sector governance block economic growth (Buscaglia 2001). A short account of the factors explaining these mixed results will be covered below.

In this context, the analytical framework presented here is provided by the discipline known as law and economics of development and growth. This discipline aims to identify changes in laws, improvements in interpretation and enforcement mechanisms that, within the socio-legal tradition of each country, are able to enhance sustainable economic development. One key aspect in the literature applied to this chapter identifies the characteristics of a legal and judicial system that foster economic growth and social prosperity (Buscaglia 1997). Within this discipline and based on empirical studies performed during the past 10 years, the notes below aim at accounting for the necessary conditions within the law-making process and within the judicial systems' functioning which need to be present in order to promote a welfare-enhancing impact of laws.


## Sources of Law-Making and Economic Growth

One recently emergent line of research in the law and economics of development literature concentrates on the socio-economic foundations of the sources of those rules that will allow the law and its enforcement mechanisms to adapt to a modern economy and, by adapting to it, foster economic growth. This topic explored by Cooter (1996) in a theoretical manner argues that efficiency is enhanced by a "bottom-up" process of capturing evolutionary successful social norms that are already in place as "informally" relevant in human interaction. Norms are understood here as coordinating mechanisms for social interaction. This decentralized approach to law-making stands in sharp contrast to the centralization proposed by the first Law and Development school that during the 1960s and 1970s proposed a clear centralization and "modernization" of the laws through legal transplants. The most important contribution in this first movement can be ascribed to Seidman (1978), who sponsored a comprehensive, centralized, and top-down legislative reform aimed at modernizing the public and private dimensions of the law. The Common Law or judge-made law sustained by *stare decisis* has suffered from the significant expansion of administrative law. In this scenario, administrative law, as the top-down framework establishing the rules to be followed in the relationship between the state and private individuals, has been the by-product of the expansion of the government role in Western societies.

On the other hand, the Civil Law systems are currently facing a choice between either legalizing and enforcing social norms within a bottom-up approach by following the policy prescriptions of Hayek (1973), or generating laws and regulations in a centralized top-down manner. For example, the civil code can either capture the norms of local and international business communities or simply impose rules on a top-down approach. Following Hayek (1973), one could argue that the higher information constraints that are the product of added social complexity within modern societies require public policy to decentralize law-making by capturing norms and thus reduce market transaction costs. As Cooter (1996) states, "efficiency requires the enforcement of customs in business communities to become more important relative to the regulation of business." As Cooter (1996) also argues, "customs arise when external effects align with incentives for signaling." From this perspective, the irrelevance of the civil and commercial laws enacted by legislatures in many countries must be understood as a reflection of the lack of links between the essence of what the law stipulates and the social norms followed by people and businesses in their daily life. When regulations or laws show this lack of compatibility, the costs of complying and enforcing the law become higher. These are the so-called "bad laws" mentioned by de Soto (1996) in which he identifies a deficient rule by comparing the approximate transaction cost of complying with the law against the transaction cost of following the social norm within an informal market. In de Soto's 1996 piece one can observe that these higher transaction costs are rooted in the drive of governments to centralize law-making without regard to the true social practices followed by people. Only when the laws and regulations reflect these practices, will transaction costs of the social interactions affected decline and a movement toward efficiency occur. From de Soto's (1996) perspective, the size of many informal sectors around the globe is intimately related to the way laws and regulations fail to capture the social practices followed by society. When this occurs, Buscaglia (1997) shows that an increasing gap between law in action and law in the books will emerge.

By here applying the studies by Cooter (1996) and Mattei (1994) we could argue that generating obedience to laws requires a compatibility between the substance and procedures of these laws and the ethical code prevailing in society. Individuals in social frameworks seek the level of predictability that will tend to increase their capacity to generate wealth through their interactions. The state of nature or "grab what you can" is not a priori desirable or compatible with long-term survival under a "veil of ignorance." Different levels of concentration of political and economic power may be compatible with predictable rules of the game. Yet for all levels of concentration of political and economic power that countries may choose to live by, when social norms and values support the prevailing and predictable rules of political and economic interaction, allocative efficiency and equity in the interpretation and application of these laws would be enhanced by the reduced transaction costs of social interaction. In this scenario, societal norms must be found by public institutions and transformed into formalized legal rights and obligations within each branch of the law. One could extend Cooter's 1996 analysis and state that, in order to enhance the effectiveness in the application and execution of laws, politics must follow not just the market but also the non-market social norms. In a more comprehensive fashion, civil society's market and non-market rules for social interaction provide a law-making guide for the legislature and the judiciary. By making laws familiar to the individual, the transaction costs of human interactions decrease and allow society to achieve legal effectiveness and efficiency in its market and non-market activities. The evolution of intellectual property laws worldwide provides a good example of how legal transplants provided a channel through which national laws started to capture business practices and social norms.

Within this context, it has become clear that a centralized and discretionary "top-down" approach to law-making has resulted in a general rejection (or in the best case scenario, irrelevance) of the formal legal systems in many countries (Buscaglia and Stephan 2005). In these cases, it is frequent to find large segments of the population perceiving themselves as "divorced" from the formal framework of laws generated by legislative bodies in a "top-down" manner. This institutional "divorce" reflects a gap between the "formal law in the books" and the "law in action" that is frequently found in many countries. Because of this gap, large segments of the population, who lack the information or resources to surmount significant substantive and procedural barriers to access, pursue informal means to interact or redress their grievances. For example, the relationship between socio-economic barriers to access court systems and the growth of alternative dispute resolution has been empirically verified in 17 countries (Buscaglia and Stephan 2005). In practice, informal institutions provide an escape valve for certain types of conflicts, in part, due to the states' lack of ability to secure access to formal dispute resolution mechanisms. Yet, many other types of disputes, involving fundamental rights and the public interest, go unresolved. This state of affairs undermines the legitimacy of the state, hampers economic interactions, and disproportionately burdens the poorest segments of the population.

**Legal Transplants and Economic Efficiency**

Let us now address the analysis of legal effectiveness in cases of international legal transplants. There are two main choices for a country when selecting the source of its laws. A country can adopt a law from within the evolution of its own socio-juridical tradition implemented through its own institutional mechanisms, or it can transplant rules from outside its political-legal zone of dominance. A key need in the analysis of legal reforms is to determine a framework for predicting which of the two options is the most effective to enhance the expected impact of the law. Watson (1978) has shown that most legal reforms are due to legal transplants. Therefore, one should also aim at explaining why, from an international pool of laws available for transplant, certain rules and institutions are commonly used and later enacted in different jurisdictions while others are rejected. For example, why is it that most countries adopt (e.g., through the ratification of international conventions) certain rules and standards to protect intellectual property, while also reject others? In more fundamental terms, we should also explain why some countries adopt adversarial judicial systems and oppose inquisitorial systems, or separation of powers as opposed to parliamentary systems. One reason could be simply national prestige. Yet, national prestige is not a measurable variable and, thus, is difficult to verify the hypothesis in a scientific manner.

The economic analysis of the law, on the other hand, can provide an explanation and guide transplants by applying tests to determine if the legal rules transplanted are also the most effective choices for efficient implementation. In other words, an inter-temporal cost–benefit analysis may provide an explanation of why some legal rules and systems are adopted and others rejected. Within this scenario, Eggertsson (1990) indicates that the economic efficiency hypothesis proposes that different legal systems may compute the costs and benefits of legal rules for the same situation differently because real economic and legal factors (such as national resource endowments or socio-juridical culture) are different across different regions and nations.

At the same time, it is also true that legal reforms are subject to the political supply and demand exercised by pressure interest groups from within the state or from outside the state. In other words, professional private interests groups, states, or even international organizations (e.g., UNODC) that may be threatened or benefit from any profound alteration in the incumbent legal system from which they have previously benefited, or domestic public officials' interests (that determine the successful implementation of any legal reform) are all ultimately partly responsible for the effective legal application, interpretation, and enforcement of new laws compatible with international best practices.

A case study of legal transplants from best-practice countries can be provided by the generation of the existing international legal framework to counteract organized crime. As stated in the introduction, transnational organized crime has experienced a bonanza due to a mix of increasing international cross border technological improvements and the liberalization of commerce. Given that transnational organized crime represents what economists call an inter-jurisdictional (i.e., international) negative externality or "public bad," an initial group of pioneer countries such Italy and the United States found no other choice than to seek a common international legal framework to be transplanted to other countries in order to combat criminal enterprises through common operational mechanisms. However, the very legal definition of organized crime represented at first a barrier to an international agreement.

In the legal domain, a few countries successfully pioneered the enactment of legal measures that criminalized conspiracy to commit a crime (e.g., the United States) and, as a result, these countries successfully reduced the scale and scope of organized crime. Other countries criminalized membership or participation in criminal enterprises (e.g., France) and, as a result, also reduced the scale and scope of organized crime in a significant manner. Illicit association as a form of criminal activity has been introduced into many criminal codes around the world, in particular in France, Italy, Spain, and Latin America. Other countries have established as criminal offences crimes committed by groups. In Italy these are called "associated crimes" or "Mafia-type crimes." In the United States, legislators have enacted the Racketeer Influenced and Corrupt Organizations Statute (the so-called RICO statute), which prohibits engaging in an enterprise involved in a pattern of criminal activity (racketeering). In that case, judicial rulings indicate that a "RICO enterprise" entails an organizational structure that carries on its business by means of activities that are primarily criminal and where there is a high degree of probability that the criminal activities will continue in the future. In all of the country-specific laws, the judicial capacity to dismember a criminal organization has been greatly enhanced by the enactment of innovative statutes.[1] At the same time, law enforcement agencies in Europe developed a number of operational definitions of the term "organized criminal group." Those definitions agreed on the following crucial elements: such a group must be structured, must possess some degree of permanence and continuity through time, must commit serious crimes for profit, must use violence, must corrupt public officials, must launder criminal proceeds, and must be found to reinvest in the licit economy.

As a result, during the 1990s, 135 country-delegations seeking legal transplants generated the United Nations' Convention Against Transnational Organized Crime (also known as the Palermo Convention). The Palermo Convention defines an organized criminal group as "a structured group, committing serious crimes for profit" (Palermo Art. 1). That very broad definition was favored over the listing of the most common types of organized crime such as trafficking in drugs, arms, persons, stolen cars or protected species and terrorism. The Convention thus focused on the same types of group as are targeted by law enforcement agencies using the Falcone checklist, which was

---

1   For participation in a criminal association, see the French Criminal Code, Title V, articles 450–1–450–4; the Italian Penal Code, Royal Decree No. 1398 of October 19, 1930, articles 416, "Association for purposes of committing offences," and 416 *bis*, "Mafia-type association"; and the Spanish Criminal Code, articles 515 and 516, on illicit association.

later incorporated into the so-called Falcone framework.[2] This is evident from the three protocols supplementary to the Convention, dealing with trafficking in persons, smuggling of migrants, and trafficking in firearms (General Assembly resolutions 55/25, annexes I and II, and 55/250, annex), as well as from provisions in the Convention dealing with such secondary characteristics of organized crime as the use of corruption, violence, money-laundering and reinvestment in the licit economy. As a result of the above, we find now that 125 countries have transplanted legislative frameworks compatible with the Palermo Convention.

## Legal Effectiveness and the Judicial System

International experience shows that the sustainable consolidation of democracy and the rule of law requires an effective judicial system composed of judges, prosecutors, police, and administrative staff who resolved issues in a predictable, consistent, and coherent manner (Buscaglia 1994). A democratic system is composed of public institutional mechanisms serving the purpose of translating social preferences into public policies. These public policies are embodied in laws and regulations that must be subject to interpretation and enforcement by the judicial system. The rule of law requires governments themselves to be bound by laws while every person is treated with equal rights within a judicial system that is feasibly accessible. As a result, democracy and the rule of law both require that enacted laws by legislatures be subject to effective judicial systems (Buscaglia 2004). For the judicial systems to perform these roles effectively, courts, prosecutors, and police domains need to be accountable through performance indicators, while also enjoying a strong degree of judicial independence and accountability within their decision-making, financial, career appointment, career promotion, dismissal, and disciplinary domains.

When a legislature aims at designing and drafting new statutes, it is always necessary to account for the evolution of institutions in charge of implementing legal frameworks within any chosen jurisdiction. This is clearly useful in order to avoid a clash with the socio-legal-judicial tradition of the jurisdiction that will interpret, apply, and execute a new stature. By taking into account this institutional "path dependence," countries can avoid any future divorce between proposed statutes and the organizational values-practices present within socio-legal-judicial tradition of a country.

As stated above, this chapter aims at accounting for the necessary conditions within the law-making process and within the judicial systems that need to be present in order to enhance the originally-intended impact of laws. The components of this assessment must therefore include judicial functioning and operational capacities of the judicial actors and police, the quality and quantity of human capital available within the judiciary, efficiency aspects of the courts, their transparency habits and procedures, and their capacity to provide effective access as conditions for guaranteeing judicial effectiveness. In this context, any assessment of a systems' capacity to interpret, apply, and execute laws must aim at providing an account of judicial effectiveness by examining a required core of components and domains.

In order to assess the process of modernization of judicial capacity to implement laws within any chosen jurisdiction, one needs to provide an objective analysis of the institutional *effectiveness* of the court, prosecutorial, and police subsystems.

---

2    The Falcone checklist provides an operational account of organized criminal groups operating within a certain jurisdiction by describing the composition, structure, modus operandi, licit/illicit linkages, and other important aspects necessary for the investigation and prosecution of criminal networks. For more details, see Gonzalez-Ruiz and Buscaglia (2002).

An assessment of *effectiveness* must use a model (such as the one with components 1 through 8 below), capable of providing analysis of the following domains:

1.  institutional-organizational design;
2.  abilities, incentives, and capacities of officials;
3.  infrastructure compatible with 1 and 2 above;
4.  the ability of the judicial system to address cases of social relevance and to provide access to redress grievances in case-types relevant to all socio-economic, ethnic, and cultural groups in society;
5.  processing capacity (e.g., procedural times and caseloads);
6.  the legal profession's abilities and capacities;
7.  the quality of judicial decisions as a result of 1 through 6 above (e.g., quality of court rulings); and
8.  legitimacy of public institutions in charge of implementing laws as a result of 7 above.

As can be seen above, components 1 through 8 constitute a model of understanding for the analysis of "legal impact effectiveness" in any given jurisdiction. Unless 1 through 8 are specifically analyzed one by one (including the interactions among the eight components), one cannot claim that an evaluation of "legal impact effectiveness" is actually performed. For example, evaluating the quality of judicial decisions (i.e., rulings) is the main test of court performance and it represents the main output of any court system. One could argue that all the other domains within the legal impact effectiveness categories 1 through 6 above are just inputs aimed at enhancing the quality of judicial decisions and the effectiveness found within their execution.

Obviously, the quality of judicial rulings cannot be assessed through subjective perceptional governance indicators, to the extent that one needs the results of this assessment to design specific remedies as part of legislative proposals and policy reforms. Therefore, methodologies currently available and currently used for the objective analysis of labor, civil, and criminal court effectiveness must be implemented in order to assess the feasibility and impact of newly enacted laws (Buscaglia 2001). Despite the necessary margin of allowed judicial discretion, there are certain methodologies that have been used with success during the process of evaluating the presence of abuses of judicial discretion (i.e., the lack of proper foundation and motivation of court decisions that need to be considered).

In this context, the impacts of investments made in judicial infrastructure, organizational improvements, and human capital need to be assessed not just in terms of improved selectivity, better institutional design, better processing capacity, and enhanced geographic access to the courts. In addition, the assessment of abuses of substantive and procedural discretion (past and present) need to be delved into through the use of a proper methodology.

Furthermore, lack of proper access to justice is key to understanding the lack of legitimacy experienced by court systems. Any evaluation of court systems must address the causes of lack of access within a clear methodology founded on legal science combined with interdisciplinary approaches. This is not just a theory. Such court-related evaluations were already performed by the United Nations (Buscaglia 2004). Within this framework, the following considerations are proposed:

*   Any evaluation of legal implementation capacities needs to adopt an implicit or explicit (qualitative or quantitative) model in order to understand and diagnose judicial effectiveness (such as the model with components 1 through 8 above).

- The interactions among the eight components explaining judicial effectiveness should be identified and analyzed explicitly, including monitoring indicators for each of them and an explanation of how each of these components—interactively—affect the quality of judicial services, in particular, and judicial effectiveness, in general.
- An explicit methodology is needed to assess quality of judicial decisions and judicial services.
- A methodology is needed to assess access to justice going beyond geographic indicators by also addressing socio-economic, cultural, and ethnic factors.

Many developed and developing countries have attempted to reform their judiciaries as a result of their political and social efforts to strengthen democracy, to enhance the protections of human rights and to foster private investment. As an illustration, an international comparative analysis demonstrates that these court reforms have shown mixed impact (Buscaglia and Dakolias 1999). Yet, limited judicial capacities are the common denominator in all judicial reforms worldwide where there are serious impediments to enhancing public sector governance and economic growth (Buscaglia 2001). If barriers to the judicial system, caused by backlogs or corruption, affect the population and business life, one can anticipate greater social and political conflict, social interaction becomes more difficult, and disputes become more costly. Moreover, public perceptions of the courts' ineffectiveness and corruption grow whenever penal and civil courts experience increasing and unjustifiable backlogs and delays (Buscaglia 2001).

Empirical evidence shows that specific factors contribute to a low quality of legal interpretation, enforcement, and execution around the world (Buscaglia and Dakolias 1999). Namely, low quality judicial systems are characterized by politicized merit-less appointments, lack of case management systems, lack of modern court administrative practices (e.g., a high burden of administrative tasks falling on judges themselves), lack of quality controls standards applied to work performed by judges and other judicial system personnel, lack of proper requirements for career promotions, lack of steady funding for capital budgets allocated to training, infrastructure, and technologies; and lack of a practical model against which to assess the character and psychological suitability of those applying for a judicial position. Countries correctly addressing these problematic areas have shown relative success in improving judicial performance (Buscaglia 2001; Buscaglia and Dakolias 1999). For example, Botswana, Chile, Costa Rica, Singapore, and South Africa all stand out as best-practice countries (Buscaglia 2004; Buscaglia and Dakolias 1999). Yet, failures of judicial reforms during the implementation stage abound. Despite huge sums of money spent on higher salaries and additional staff in a majority of the countries sampled in recent studies (Buscaglia and Dakolias 1999), the persistence of pernicious incentives faced by judges and court personnel is still at the heart of the problems linked to court ineffectiveness and ineffective legal implementation.

In order to enhance court performance, judicial reforms have been implemented through a mix of national and international efforts focused on areas such as:

- drafting improved codes to better address substantive legal matters (e.g., reforming civil and criminal codes);
- establishing better systems to hire and train court, prosecutorial, and police personnel, linking periodic technical proficiency evaluations of court personnel to merit-based career paths;
- establishing an improved system to hire more and better prosecutors and public defenders;
- modernizing judicial infrastructure and administrative management, including the judiciaries' ability to install modernized budget/planning systems and up-to-date case

processing/management styles (e.g., this entails reducing the administrative burden within the judges' and police domains by shifting responsibility to professional administrators);
- enhancing the operational role of civil society in fostering improvements in judicial and administrative performances within the executive domain;
- establishing systems of internal and external controls in order to foster consistent, predictable, and unbiased judicial and administrative rulings; and
- supporting alternative dispute resolution mechanisms (Buscaglia and Dakolias 1999).

Moreover, an intense hiring and continuing training of judicial administrators is needed in all low performance countries within the industrialized and developing world alike. For example, court administrators require key competencies such as basic levels of knowledge in areas such as organizational performance of court systems; budget and financial management; information technology management; quality control techniques; public information; strategic planning; case-flow management; human resources training; human resources management; financial investigative techniques; and institutional leadership (Baar 1999).

Several empirical studies have measured how these institutional reforms enhance the desirable impact of new statutes within criminal jurisdictions by focusing on clearance rates (i.e., percentage of cases filed that were subsequently disposed of during a certain period of time), procedural times, and the frequencies of abuses of substantive and procedural discretion exercised by each stage of the judicial system (Buscaglia 2004). In these empirical studies, indicators of judicial performance also addressed access to justice, equality, fairness, integrity, independence, accountability of the executive, legislatures, and judiciary, the judiciary's own technical proficiency, and public trust in state institutions (Buscaglia 2004).


## Case Study: Laws in the Books against Organized Crime vs. Laws in Action

The identification of pernicious factors expanding the gap between the law enacted in the books and the law in action must be the focus of legislators' attention when designing and drafting organized crime legislation. Figure 16.1 establishes a relationship between the frequency of organized crime (objectively measured) and the quality of judicial rulings measured by the frequency of abuses of substantive and procedural discretion exercised by sentencing judges within drug trafficking case-files in those countries mentioned within the figure (where the United Nations' Convention Against Organized Crime addressed above has been ratified).

To measure the prevalence of organized crime on the vertical axis of Figure 16.1, Buscaglia and van Dijk (2003) used an index combining objective factors linked with complex crimes. The development of an international index of organized crime obviously had to start from a universally agreed upon definition as described above in the previous section. For the purposes of calculating the organized crime index used here, the extent of organized crime in a country was assessed on the basis of indicators of the various defining elements contained both in operational investigations conducted by law enforcement agencies (e.g., the Falcone checklist)[3] and in the United Nations' Organized Crime Convention and its protocols. It was also concluded that official data on police

---

3    The Falcone checklist provides an operational account of organized criminal groups operating within a certain jurisdiction by describing the composition, structure, modus operandi, licit/illicit linkages, and other important aspects necessary for the investigation and prosecution of criminal networks. For more details, see Gonzalez-Ruiz and Buscaglia (2002).

records of criminal activities offered little reliable information on the extent of organized crime activity in a country and that other sources would have to be found or developed. One potentially relevant source was the World Economic Forum's survey of business aimed at measuring the costs imposed by organized crime on firms, which provided an estimate of the extent of victimization of businesses by organized crime. The country ranking based on the World Economic Forum's index was subsequently correlated with indices for corruption and violence (homicide). The three indices were found to be highly correlated across the large group of countries presented in Figure 16.1 and, as a result, a composite index of non-conventional crime was constructed.

It was subsequently decided to seek additional available country data on the core activities of organized criminal groups such as credit card fraud and trafficking in drugs, persons, firearms, stolen cars, and cigarettes.[4] The indicator for drug trafficking (police seizure data) did not show any correlation with the other organized crime factors mentioned above and was subsequently excluded from the analysis. Finally, a composite index was constructed that included indicators of five core activities (trafficking in persons, firearms, stolen cars, and cigarettes and fraud) and four secondary factors (costs for business, extent of the informal economy as a proportion of gross domestic product, violence, and money-laundering). This composite index of organized crime is used in Figure 16.1. It should be noted that although the composite index has proven to be robust and not greatly affected by the inclusion or exclusion of individual indicators, efforts are nevertheless ongoing to add further statistical indicators.

The measures of abuses of discretion were calculated after reviewing a sample of between 10 and 12 percent of all annual flows in organized crime (drug trafficking) case-files in each country. The horizontal axis on Figure 16.1 measures consistency and coherence of judicial rulings by identifying the most frequent abuses of procedural and substantive discretion. The most frequent abuses included contradictions in the value or weight attached by the judge to the evidentiary material that represented a contradiction with the prevailing jurisprudence. Another frequent substantive abuse of judicial discretion included case-files where the criminal acts did not fit the criminal code-related categorization of the indicted crimes subject the final sentencing stage within the ruling. Other abuses included unjustified procedural delays, contradictory uses of the jurisprudence within the same case-types found within the same court, and the use of irrelevant jurisprudence or unrelated (i.e., incorrect) laws to support judicial rulings.

As one can see from Figure 16.1, there is a clear cause–effect relationship between more consistent and more coherent judicial rulings linked to drug trafficking and lower levels of organized crime (e.g., Austria, Denmark, and Finland). This improved consistency and coherency

---

4   In particular, data was compiled on smuggling of firearms (taking into account data on manufacturing, sales, imports, and exports already computed by the United Nations), estimates on smuggling of cigarettes, car theft, and consumer fraud victimization (the International Crime Victim Survey), number of homicides (the United Nations, the International Criminal Police Organization (Interpol), and the World Health Organization), size of the informal economy and the business sector's perceptions of organized crime prevalence (World Economic Forum), inflows of laundered money in millions of dollars per year as a proportion of gross domestic product (the Walker index), and trafficking in persons in terms of nationalities of suspects (human trafficking database of the United Nations Office on Drugs and Crime). The index presented here ranked each country for each variable in order to compute the composite organized crime index as an average of the rankings that each country showed for each item mentioned above. Each component showed strong correlations with the index, with costs to business, homicide, and money laundering being the best predictors. The index considered here only included those countries for which there were at least three observations out of which at least two were "core activity" factors. Higher values corresponded to greater prevalence of organized crime (Buscaglia and van Dijk 2003).

is assured by effective control systems applied to rulings by either judicial councils or appellate court systems. On the other hand, those countries found to lack consistency and coherence in their rulings (i.e., high frequencies of abuses of judicial discretion) are also countries where organized crime tends to grow (e.g., Colombia, Indonesia, and Venezuela). These results found in Buscaglia and van Dijk (2003) are founded on United Nations databases.[5]

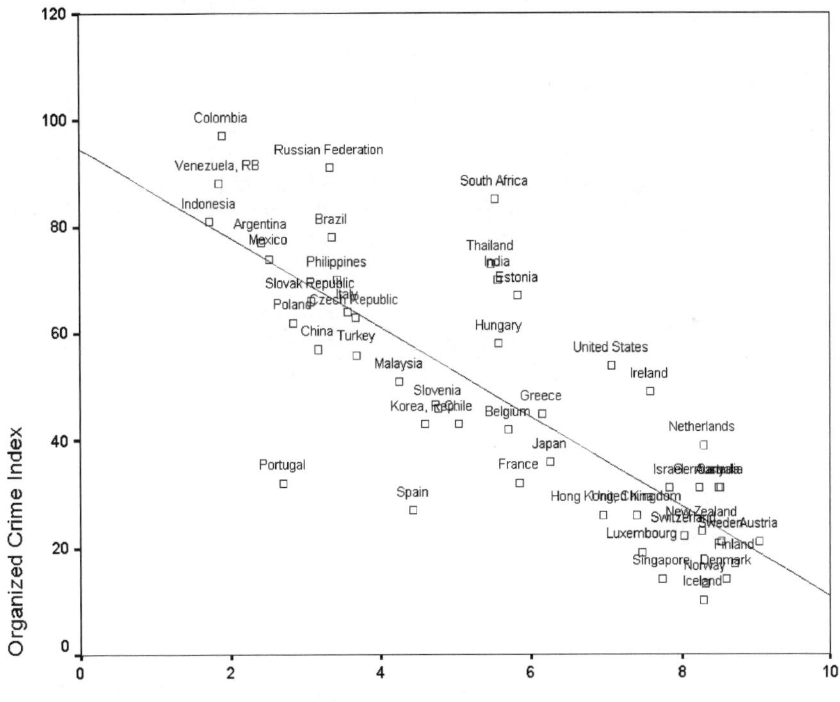


**Figure 16.1 Relationship between judicial capacity to implement laws against organized crime and levels of organized crime**

Case-file analysis performed in 67 countries by Buscaglia (2001) shows that measuring the systemic lack of a proper foundation and motivation found in a high frequency of court rulings (measured through case files objectively *in situ*) within criminal and civil jurisdictions explains the growth of organized crime (measured through a weighted average of 25 crime indicators associated with organized crime gathered by Interpol). These types of assessments within criminal, civil, and labor jurisdictions have identified high frequencies of rulings (within the same case-types) where a contradictory/incoherent application of jurisprudential criteria is present within the same court or within courts corresponding to the same jurisdiction in each sampled country. Moreover,

---

5   Statistical tables showing the results of the study presented here can be found at: hwww.unodc.org/unodc/crime/crime_cicp_publications_forum.html.

substantive flaws are found during audits of court rulings where, for example, case-related facts are systematically not adjusted to the required categorization stipulated within the criminal or civil codes. These and other types of abuses of judicial discretion constitute the main factor hampering effective legal implementation, therefore causing an increasing gap between law-in-the-books and law-in-action. Within this framework of analysis, any court evaluation needs to address the frequencies of each type of abuse of judicial discretion through judicial audits of court rulings, prosecutorial strategies, and police investigations within each case-type.

**Table 16.1 Regional-based jurimetic indicators**

| Area | Terrorism-related violence (UN measure of % annual change 2000–2006 (% change)) | % quality of judicial rulings found in organized crime and terrorism case files (% change 2002–2005) | Organized crime (UN objective indicator 2000–2006 (% change)) |
|---|---|---|---|
| Central and Eastern Europe | 0.5 | 0.3 | 1.5 |
| Central Asia | 18.9 | -17.7 | 23.6 |
| South East Asia | 11.5 | -12.1 | 15.7 |
| Latin America | 4.2 | -4.4 | 11.3 |
| Middle East | 22.4 | -23.6 | 34.2 |
| North and SS Africa | 45.8 | -46.8 | 58.2 |

Table 16.1 shows a regional-based analysis presenting jurimetric indicators of the 2002–2006 percentage changes in the quality of sampled court rulings linked to organized crime and terrorism-related violence. Non-parametric analysis shows that these regional indicators of the quality of court rulings exercise a strong causal influence on the 2000–2006 percentage increases in terrorism-related violence—measured through the UN Terrorism index—and with the 2000–2006 percentage increases of the regional levels of organized crime.

The analysis shown in Buscaglia and van Dijk (2003) also demonstrates that judicial independence is strongly related to levels of organized crime. Additionally, results show a strong relationship between the perceived independence of the judiciary and the perceived extent of judicial corruption. Furthermore, statistical analysis in Buscaglia and van Dijk (2003) confirmed that independent judges were less vulnerable to corruption and better able to implement laws against organized crime, even when the political system and other areas of the state had been captured by organized crime. In the context of the analysis of all those countries included in Figure 16.1, corrupt judges were found to abuse their substantive and procedural discretion through rulings that slowed down or obstructed law enforcement in organized criminal cases (Buscaglia and van Dijk 2003). Among the factors enabling organized crime to capture the court system, the most significant were procedural complexity and abuses of substantive judicial discretion (Buscaglia and van Dijk 2003). Those links were verified (e.g., that higher degrees of procedural complexity were linked to judicial corruption and to higher levels of organized crime) (Buscaglia and van Dijk 2003). The link between the abuse of substantive judicial discretion on the one hand and judicial corruption and increases in organized crime on the other were confirmed through another empirical analysis.

To measure the prevalence of organized crime, the study used an index that combined objective factors linked with complex crimes.[6] The development of an international index of organized crime obviously had to start from a universally agreed upon definition. During the 1990s, law enforcement agencies in Europe developed a number of operational definitions of the term "organized criminal group." Those definitions agree on the following crucial elements: such a group is structured, has some permanence, commits serious crimes for profit, uses violence, corrupts officials, launders criminal proceeds, and reinvests in the licit economy. The United Nations Convention against Transnational Organized Crime (General Assembly resolution 55/25, annex I) defines an organized criminal group as "a structured group, committing serious crimes for profit." That very broad definition was favored over the listing of the most common types of organized crime such as trafficking in drugs, arms, persons, stolen cars or protected species and terrorism. The Convention thus focuses on the same types of groups as are targeted by law enforcement agencies using the Falcone checklist, later incorporated into the so-called Falcone framework.[7]

In order to identify which of the many correlates of organized crime found are the best predictors of the levels of organized crime within a large sample of national jurisdictions, multiple regression analysis was applied, with the organized crime index as the dependent variable. The recommendations made below are based on the strongest variables as determined by the correlation analyses (appendix A, table 18). The selection of independent variables was guided by the need to include as many of the areas considered above as possible (i.e., socio-economic factors, the political sphere, the criminal justice system, private sector governance, public sector governance, and independence and integrity of the judiciary). The choice of variables was also supported by the results of the factor analyses. Variables that best represented their particular domains were chosen for inclusion in the regression models. Several regression models were able to explain 50 percent or more of the variance in the organized crime index scores. A multiple regression model including the human development index (representing socio-economic factors; also included as control variable), independence of the judiciary (representing the judicial integrity area) and police protection of property rights (representing the effectiveness of the criminal justice system) explained 72 percent of the variations in the organized crime index, as shown in Table 16.2.

---

6   Statistical tables showing the raw data for this study presented here can be found at www.unodc.org/unodc/crime/crimen and are referred to in parentheses in the present chapter.

7   The United Nations Convention against Transnational Organized Crime and the protocols thereto are available at www.unodc.org/unodc/crime_cicp_convention.html. The Falcone checklist provides an operational account of organized criminal groups operating within a certain jurisdiction by describing the composition, structure, modus operandi, licit/illicit linkages and other important aspects necessary for the investigation and prosecution of criminal networks.

**Table 16.2 Multiple regression analysis of organized crime**

| Variables | Independence of the judiciary | | Police protection | Human Development Index |
|---|---|---|---|---|
| Beta (standard coefficient) | -0.378 | | -0.437 | -0.236 |
| Significance | 0.008 | | 0.001 | 0.065 |
| **Model summary**[a] | | | | |
| | *Model* | *R* | *R square* | |
| | 1 | 0.718[b] | 0.515 | |
| | 2 | 0.825[c] | 0.681 | |
| | 3 | 0.849[d] | 0.720 | |

*Notes*

[a] Dependent variable: organized crime index.

[b] Predictors (constant): independence of the judiciary from political pressure.

[c] Predictors (constant): independence of the judiciary from political pressure and poice protection of property rights from criminal action.

[d] Predictors (constant): independence of the judiciary from political pressure, police protection of property rights from criminal action and Human Development Index 1999.

In this context, the lack of judicial independence, the poor police protection, and poor rankings within the UN Human Development Index are causal factors explaining higher levels of organized criminal activities.

Although higher expenditure on justice systems does not per se ensure better legal implementation of laws, it is clear that the justice systems of many countries are critically under-funded. The differences in the current and capital levels of spending between developed and developing countries show expanding gaps. For example, developing countries spend an average of $5–$10 on criminal justice per citizen (Gonzalez-Ruiz and Buscaglia 2002). On the other hand, highly developed economies spend over $165 per citizen on their police, prosecutors, and judges. The analysis showed that many of the low- and middle-income countries in the sample did not even allocate enough resources to keep their criminal justice systems running at a functional level. Besides overall budget increases, reallocations of current budget resources may be warranted in many of these countries where the police receive a disproportionate share of overall funding, while the prosecutorial services and the courts suffer acutely from lack of basic operational resources. Without functioning prosecutorial and judicial systems, law enforcement alone cannot contribute effectively to better conditions for implementing laws and thus combating complex crimes.

The Table 16.3 provides a jurimetric account of the impact of judicial reforms. Specifically, the main areas of reforms in the seven sampled Colombian and Jordanian pilot courts included:

- An improved, uniform and comprehensive case management system coupled with transparent and consistent rules for the assignment of cases.
- The implementation of uniform and predictable administrative (i.e., personnel- and budget-related) measures founded on rewards and penalties driven by performance-based indicators, with a consequent clarification of the career paths for judicial and law enforcement officers.

- Specific reforms of the organizational structure of the justice system, including the introduction of category-specific organizational roles for judicial, prosecutorial, and police personnel in order to secure their own internal independence.
- The enhancement of the capacity of the judiciary to review the consistency of its own decisions in court rulings by improving the effectiveness of judicial (appellate-based) reviews but also by allowing for the monitoring of civil society-based social control mechanisms working hand in hand with the media.
- Governance-related improvements in the links between the political sphere and the judiciary in accordance with the preconditions described above.

The examples apply to Jordan and Colombia where pilot courts introduced measures during a period of between 24 and 36 months, respectively, after conducting assessments of judicial effectiveness within the eight domains as previously described.

**Table 16.3 Impacts of judicial reforms measured as differences in percentage indicators between 1999 and 2005**

|  | Frequency of corruption | Access justice | Quality of judicial rulings | Procedural times | Organized crime (UN Index) |
|---|---|---|---|---|---|
| Jordan (3 pilots) | -0.9% | 3.1% | 9.4% | -17.6% | -6.7% |
| Colombia (3 pilots) | -5.9% | 23.6% | 16.1% | -10.7% | -10.9% |

The pilot courts in Table 16.3 also started to monitor and control the progress of cases from filing to disposition by following a group management approach, with first instance court judges and pools of prosecutors jointly managing cases. Assignment of cases to different management tracks (i.e., express, standard or complex tracks based, among other factors, on the quality and quantity of evidentiary material) can also reduce procedural times and abuse of discretion in case assignments and rulings. Such a system of proactive management was supported by computerized case-tracking technologies, which made it possible to handle case assignment and to deal with judicial officers' concerns online in real time. Technical personnel and professional staff development was therefore aimed at adopting more advanced information technologies to support case management.

In these two countries following best practices, systems to implement forfeiture and financial management of assets have been upgraded in order to include measures that are the most effective in striking at the roots of organized crime and corruption. As an incentive to achieve greater operational efficiency, law enforcement agencies could also be allowed to retain the proceeds of asset forfeiture, to be allocated to staff welfare accounts or spent on organizational improvements. (In Chile and Singapore, for example, an autonomous agency handles payment of fines and refunds of bail electronically, with payments credited to the law enforcement departments achieving predetermined levels of performance.) Previous experience reveals that higher salary levels tend to attract more qualified personnel if subject to strict performance-based indicators, thus making corrupt practices less likely. Yet structural reforms of the judicial system are needed first, including strengthening and modernizing financial management and budgeting while training and developing administrative staff.

In sum, the countries performing best legal implementation strategies within the organized crime domain have developed computerized case management processes for police, prosecutors and judges, co-developing multi-agency "task force" systems (for investigations and prosecutions) and computerizing court administration. Such reforms have made internal corruption and infiltration by organized crime less likely through the introduction of organizational re-engineering, including elimination of procedural complexity, and through reductions in the abuse of procedural and substantive judicial discretion. In that connection, legislatures must contribute to empowering the judicial system to take on new and innovative programs by amending laws, introducing electronic means of handling complex evidence linking many case files, enacting subsidiary legislation for better case management and upgrading judges' salaries.

Evidence-based results show that a balance between judicial accountability and the independence of judicial institutions from political forces is a necessary condition to achieving success in the effective interpretation, application, and execution of laws. Yet this balance between democratic accountability and institutional independence requires a basic prior consensus among the main political forces in countries undertaking judicial reforms (Buscaglia 1997). Certainly, it would be quite naïve to just think that constitutional provisions prescribing the separation of powers alone would be enough to guarantee the judicial independence required for the unbiased and transparent implementation of laws. In fact, such constitutional provisions are not even a necessary condition to attaining judicial independence: countries such as Israel, New Zealand, Sweden, and the United Kingdom—all countries with high levels of judicial independence, good records of legal design and implementation—do not possess constitutionally entrenched judicial independence. Examination of international experience shows that the political elements enhancing an independent judicial system with the capacity to effectively implement laws can be identified. For example, the cases of Colombia, Costa Rica, Jordan, and, to some degree, Italy, show that judicial systems can only enhance their capacity to interpret laws with independence and autonomy when the political concentration of power within either the legislative branch, the executive branch, or both tends to be relatively balanced such that alternation in power becomes a likely outcome of periodic elections.

To some degree, the balance of political power among truly competing political forces creates an increased willingness among politicians to give up a good part of their political control of the courts and prosecutorial decisions in order to avoid mutual assured destruction in subsequent electoral periods when the opposition may take over the reins of power. This sequential "game" between or among political forces operates as a tacit insurance that guarantees increased independence of the justice system from political whims (Buscaglia 1997). In this context, international experience shows that better governance within the political domain is required before achieving higher levels of governance within the judicial domain. Therefore, the judicial reforms described in the previous section, when applied in best practice countries, have required a background of socio-political consensus that includes the legislative, executive, judicial, and civil society domains with actors all willing and able to design, implement, and support such reforms. The gap between the enacted law in the books and the law in action will not represent a significant constraint to legal implementation whenever the political will to enact legal reforms coexists with the executive capacity to implement the aforementioned judicial reforms. Failures to fully implement much-needed legal reforms, judicial reforms, or both, have been mostly due to the lack of governmental long-term commitment, political instability, a lack of participatory stakeholders' (i.e., civil society-based) approach supporting reforms, or to the erroneous importation of foreign legal systems that may not be appropriate to the national jurisdictions undertaking judicial reforms (Buscaglia 2004). These lessons from experience must be taken into account whenever legislatures design, draft, and enact laws.

## References


Baar, C. 1999. The Development and Reform of Court Organization and Administration. *Public Administration and Development*, 19(4), 48–82.

Buscaglia, E. 1994. Legal and Economic Development: The Missing Links. *Journal of Inter-American Studies and World Affairs*, 4(35), 20–32.

Buscaglia, E. 1997. An Economic Analysis of Corrupt Practices within the Judiciary in Latin America, in *Essays in Law and Economics*, edited by C. Ott and G. Von Waggenheim. Amsterdam: Kluwer Press, 289–321.

Buscaglia, E. 2001. An Analysis of Judicial Corruption and Its Causes: An Objective Governance-Based Approach. *International Review of Law and Economics*, 21(2), 233–49.

Buscaglia, E. and Dakolias, M. 1999. *A Comparative International Study of Court Performance Indicators: A Descriptive and Analytical Account*. Legal and Judicial Reform Series, Washington, DC: The World Bank Press.

Buscaglia, E. and van Dijk, J. 2003. *Controlling Corruption and Organized Crime*. Forum on Crime and Society, Vienna: United Nations Office on Drugs and Crime.

Buscaglia, E. and Stephan III, P. 2005. An Empirical Assessment of the Impact of Formal vs. Informal Dispute Resolution on Poverty: A Governance Based-Approach. *International Review of Law and Economics*, 25, 89–106.

Cooter, R. 1996. The Theory of Market Modernization of Law. *International Review of Law and Economics*, 16(2) 141–72.

de Soto, H. 1996. Property Rights and Economic Progress in Developing Countries, in *Law and Economics of Development*, edited by E. Buscaglia, W. Ratliff and R. Cooter. New Jersey: JAI Press, 234–91.

Eggertsson, T. 1990. *Economic Behavior and Institutions*. Cambridge: Cambridge University Press.

Gonzalez-Ruiz, S. and Buscaglia, E. 2002. How to Design a National Strategy Against Organized Crime in the Framework of the United Nations' Palermo Convention, in *The Fight Against Organized Crime*. United Nations International Drug Control Programme, 23–6.

Hayek, F. 1973. *Law, Legislation and Liberty*. Chicago: University of Chicago Press.

Maoro, P. 1995. Corruption and Growth. *Quarterly Journal of Economics*, 110(3), 681–712.

Palermo Convention 2000. *United Nations Convention Against Transnational Organized Crime and the Protocols Thereto*. Available at: www.unodc.org/documents/treaties/UNTOC/Publications/TOC%20Convention/TOCebook-e.pdf.

Mattei, U. 1994. Law and Economics in Civil Law Countries: A Comparative Approach. *International Review of Law and Economics*, 14(1), 265–75.

Seidman, R. 1978. *State, Law and Development*. New York: St Martin's Press.

Watson, A. 1978. Comparative Law and Legal Change. *Cambridge Law Journal*, 37, 313–36.

# Chapter 17

# Politicization of the Latin American Judiciary via Informal Connections

Raul A. Sanchez Urribarri

Are courts mere "mouthpieces of the law" in the traditional Civil Law formulation of the separation of powers, or are they powerful agents "making law" following the Common Law view (and "agents" of whom or what)? How shall we confront this basic ambiguity for purposes of rule of law (ROL) work? While judicial reform as institutional reform lies at the heart of much ROL work, particularly in Latin America, surprisingly little attention is paid to the practical results of an "empowered" judiciary. Perhaps in Latin America the hidden issue may be the assumption that courts merely apply "norms" almost mechanically (a modern doctrinal version of those selfsame Civil Law views), without examining the "agents of whom" question from anything approaching a public choice or instrumentalism position. The problem seems to lie in institutional ROL approaches of improving the judiciary by adopting a "build it and they will come" attitude, which may or may not work in practice. The difference is already visible in this book in the contrast between Chapters 16 and 20.

Much Latin American ROL work has concentrated on judicial reform, so it is well-suited to addressing the question of how "reformed" and "empowered" judiciaries behave in practice. Latin America has formally experienced an expansion of the courts' policymaking role. This expansion has included instances in which courts openly decide salient issues against important political actors, both governmental and non-governmental. Arguably, the most important political player to be controlled is the government itself, especially in a region with a strong authoritarian past, relatively unfettered executive rule and weak enforcement of fundamental rights. Courts have been empowered precisely with this purpose (Prillaman 2000). The core argument is that institutionally powerful courts, endowed with formal guarantees for judicial independence, enough resources, and a supportive environment, will be able to contain unruly political actors and help consolidate democracy. The apparent surge of judicial power is often portrayed in an unreservedly positive light. However, in practice, there is cause for concern across the region. Most importantly, the empowerment of courts and the politicization of the judiciary are not mutually exclusive phenomena (Domingo 2004). We observe instances in which courts become apparently strong, only to discover that they are actually carrying out an exogenous agenda pushed by the executive or other powerful player, through judicial means. And this kind of departure from the traditional ROL script may not be an isolated phenomenon (Hammergren 2003).

This chapter commences with a brief review of examples of problematic judicial behavior, followed by a review of the judiciary's role in Latin America, paying special attention to past research focused on how and why judges hold governments accountable, and addressing issues of judicial independence and judicial power. Thereafter, I lay out the theoretical foundations of a *judicial loyalties* approach analyzing courts in Latin America, a discussion that includes defining and operationalizing this concept to connect it to related notions. I then address the implications of the *loyalties* thesis of judicial decision-making for our understanding of the role of courts in weakly institutionalized political systems, especially with respect to judicial decision-making and performance. This represents an additional side of the problem Chapter 20 addresses, calling into question simple "build it and they will come" ROL approaches to institutional development of any judiciary.

Parallel to ensuring the courts' independence, the last two decades have witnessed a significant number of Latin American judicial reform programs targeted at improving the courts' quality in terms of accessibility, efficiency, efficacy, fairness, professionalism, and transparency (Hammergren 2007). There are compelling reasons to argue that persistent judicial loyalties negatively influence judicial quality in the broadest sense of the term, however, and this is perhaps one of the key reasons why certain reform initiatives have failed.

## Examples in Practice

How do such examples of an "exogenous agenda" appear in practice? Recent events in Honduras, where the Supreme Court became a key tool of the coup against President Zelaya come to mind (see Ruhl 2010). For these purposes, it matters little that President Zelaya was also, in turn, breaching the Constitution by carrying out a clearly unconstitutional referendum on the modification of the no-reelection rule. Meanwhile, plans to improve the judiciary's administrative capacity do not necessarily imply greater judicial independence or the systematic display of judicial assertiveness vis-à-vis the government. For instance, the World Bank considers reforms implemented by the Venezuelan Supreme Court a successful project, especially in terms of the improvements made to the Court's technological platform. Yet, in the hands of the Chavez regime, the Supreme Court became a key tool for political domination and control of the opposition and was (and is) subject to political interference coming from other branches of government (Perez Perdomo 2005; Sanchez Urribarri 2010). Efficiency does not necessarily translate into effectiveness, and is not per se related to a stronger (independent) judiciary either. When evaluating these and other aspects of judicial reform, every one of these elements should be assessed separately (Hammergren 2007). So it may go too far to categorize all such work as "ROL"-based simply because it touches on the judiciary.

The true puzzle, however, is why the judiciary remains in control of the political class in some countries and not in others, sometimes in spite of similar institutional reforms or agendas and notwithstanding the apparent commitment of governments and external audiences to effective judicial reform. What is the root of this chronic domination of the courts? I argue that one key to understanding persistent patterns of judicial politicization in Latin America, and its pernicious effect on judicial power, lies in the existence of informal quid pro quo linkages between judges and political actors. They condition judges' willingness to exercise their prerogatives effectively against other political players. These links are not only based on the coincidences of ideological views between judges and politicians, of the kind witnessed in established programmatic democracies (for example, why American political groups argue incessantly about the "judicial philosophy" of Supreme Court nominees).

These links are rooted in particularistic connections that are part of the general informal political dynamics present throughout the political system of several countries in the region and beyond. These connections do not go so far as determining how courts function in *all* or *most* circumstances, and how judges make decisions in *all* or *most* cases, as they coexist with other sources of judicial behavior. However, judicial loyalties are critical to explain their decisions in those situations in which their intervention is most necessary – especially in cases that involve the control of key political institutions. Understanding *why* these quid pro quo political connections exist, and *how* they affect judicial behavior, may illuminate important issues. These include why judges fail to control political authority in certain contexts, in spite of being ideologically opposed to the government and enjoying several conditions that would favor their confrontation with the regime; or why judicial reform programs fail to enhance the judiciary's capacity to protect fundamental rights and adjudicate conflicts efficiently.

The effect of political connections on judicial decision-making becomes most evident in highly salient political cases, in which justices side with the political actors linked with them, often setting aside other reasons that would usually shape their decisions – such as ideological, strategic or legal considerations. Consider, for example, the decision issued by the Venezuelan Supreme Court finding grounds to authorize a criminal trial against President Perez in 1993, and the subsequent proceedings culminating in President Perez being found guilty of misappropriation of funds (Martin 1996). Pre-trial decisions of this kind can be particularly telling concerning the political arrangement in a higher court. Judging whether there is sufficient evidence to move forward with an investigation against a sitting president not only involves solving the strictly legal question of whether such evidence is valid and relevant, but also the political question of whether it is convenient to separate the president from his or her post (see Perez-Linan 2007). In this type of decision, the judges' political loyalties can become particularly visible.

Thus, from outside, the May 20, 1993 decision against President Perez was an assertive decision against an embattled president, made with the purpose of restoring the political system's popularity in a time of political turmoil vis-à-vis an extremely disappointed Venezuelan electorate and a restless military (taking also into account that Hugo Chavez's coup attempt against Perez and a follow-up attempt by other rebels had taken place in February and November 1992). However, after taking a look at who voted for impeachment and the dissents, six of the 15 members of the Plenary Chamber dissented and sided with President Perez. This group was mainly formed by justices who were appointed during past governments of Democratic Action (Perez's ruling party). Conversely, the justices who challenged Perez and opened the gate for his eventual departure from power were all justices publicly identified with the opposition, plus a small group of three justices who had just been appointed by opposition forces and were not considered politically aligned with any specific force (Sanchez Urribarri 2010).

*Theory of the Politicization of the Judiciary through Loyalty Links*

Courts are supposed to play key political roles in democratic and non-democratic societies (O'Donnell 1999, 2000). Judicial institutions can appeal to rulers across different regimes for several reasons. In addition to performing their typical inter-party conflict resolution prerogatives, they may offer a useful venue for a variety of goals, such as chastising political opponents, controlling crime, curbing corruption, or simply gaining legitimacy vis-à-vis international or domestic audiences (Moustafa and Ginsburg 2008; Shapiro 1981).

Although these matters have been extensively discussed in the context of Western democracies, they are also critical issues in the context of developing countries. The empowerment of courts can be critical to ensure the viability of new democratic regimes and provide a legitimate solution to a variety of issues that plague these governments and impair their performance – including issues of transitional justice, restoring social order, stabilizing the economy and fostering growth. This has led governments around the world to expand the realm of court action in the political arena, endowing judges with new prerogatives (especially judicial review), and theoretically ensuring that they enjoy the necessary conditions to fulfill their duties, among other institutional reforms.

In connection with this trend toward increasing the formal powers of the judiciary, a "judicialization of politics" has taken place in numerous countries (Tate 1995). Studies show that, even in authoritarian societies, judges have been able to challenge the regime in a variety of scenarios and influence political outcomes. As examples, consider the South African Apartheid regime (Haynie 2003); constitutional politics in Mubarak's Egypt (Moustafa 2003, 2007); judicial institutions in "crisis regimes" in Asia (Tate 1993); and functions of courts in Marcos' authoritarian regime in the Philippines (Tate and Haynie 1993).

Latin America has become a fertile ground for judicial politics analyses. Several countries in Latin America have experienced such a judicialization of politics (see essays in Gloppen et al. 2004; Sieder et al. 2005). This trend followed the 1980s democratization wave and the implementation of broad judicial reform agendas in these countries. Thus, a wave of works emerged, explaining the role of courts in Latin American democracies. Some assess the conditions and determinants of the courts' successful exercise of their governmental accountability functions, particularly in countries with a long-standing tradition of hyper-presidentialism, such as Argentina (Dix 2004; Finkel 2008; Helmke 2002, 2005; Kapiszewski 2007; Scribner 2004), or Mexico (Magaloni 2003; Rios-Figueroa 2007b; Staton 2006). Others focus on how and to what extent in a transitional justice mode courts make political officers accountable for past misdeeds in authoritarian polities, most prominently Argentina, Brazil (Pereira 2005), and Chile (Hilbink 2007; Huneeus 2006). Some of these works have looked explicitly at the court's influence in policymaking in a variety of areas, including Argentina (Iaryczower et al. 2002), democratic Costa Rica (Wilson 2005) and Brazil (Taylor 2008). The number of works grows as further demonstrations of judicial assertiveness take place, scholarly attention and debate increases, and more data becomes available (Kapiszewski and Taylor 2008).

In Latin America, the critical concern for analysts has been assessing judicial independence in general, vis-à-vis overzealous executives and other important actors. One aspect of the phenomenon deals explicitly with institutions. Judges need a series of formal conditions in place to be independent, especially regarding appointment rules, tenure security, and mechanisms to ensure compliance with judicial rulings. However, as the experience in Latin America suggests, the most ideal institutional design *on paper* does not necessarily lead to independent judges in practice (Hammergren 1997, 2007; Prillaman 2000). Several non-institutional factors are also relevant for this analysis. Take, for example, the political context: an environment with numerous political forces espousing different policy preferences makes it difficult for political actors to agree on staging a backlash against judicial authority (see Magaloni 2003; Rios-Figueroa 2007a). On the other hand, judges need to be willing to challenge the regime, and assume confronting the government as one of their goals. Otherwise, courts might fail to stand against political actors – as shown in the Chilean case alluded to in Chapter 18, in which a mixture of ideological conservatism and institutional isolation arguably prevented the judiciary from denouncing human rights violations under the Pinochet regime (Hilbink 2007).

Thus, even if judges are formally independent, this does not guarantee that they will rule against the rulers or uphold fundamental rights against abuses by political actors. Other circumstances that often escape the judges' control can also influence their ability to assert their authority. Formal institutions regulating inter-branch relations involving the judiciary may be poor predictors of actual behavior in (developing) countries where the gap between formal and informal politics is prominent. In countries where there is a clear coincidence between programmatic commitments and actual political behavior, in addition to taking into account their professional credentials, judges may be appointed with the purpose of reproducing the views of their appointers from the bench, on the basis of their honest ideological affinity with them (Dahl 1957; Epstein and

Segal 2005; Keck 2007; Whittington 2005). However, in political systems where ideology is less important to structure political preferences, and to translate such preferences into actual political outcomes, politicians might not appoint judges *solely* on the basis of their ideological proclivities. This might be particularly the case in those environments where particularistic or personal relations-based politics prevail and individual benefits are more common. In such circumstances, a judicial designation, just as any other positive entitlement or sanction, might be allocated as a direct, individualized and excludable benefit involving a *giver* (the person or actor responsible for making the decision that favors the individual or judge in question) and a *recipient* (the person or actor receiving the benefit). If this is the case, then it is also possible that judges may fail to rule against politicians and hold them accountable as a function of their *mutually dependent* (quid pro quo) relationship vis-à-vis their appointers, those politicians who play a role in appointing them, or other political actors able to offer them stable and long-term individualized advantages.

The basic notion that judges *may* follow individualized links should not be strange to those familiar with the broader literature on particularistic politics and personal relationships in the developing world. Students of politics have long noticed patterns of political behavior that follow individualized incentives or preferences, as opposed to following the collective good. Phenomena as varied as clientelism, patronage and corruption schemes involving tacit or express agreements between two or more people have been thoroughly researched for decades (see Roniger and Gunes Ayata 1994; Schmidt 1977). Latin America, in particular, is well known for the divorce between the formal commitments of political players, and the actual processes and outcomes that take place in the political arena (see essays in Helmke and Levitsky 2006). Claims about political behavior that cannot be consistently explained on the basis of ideological preferences are numerous. For example, Lyne (2008) and Zucco, Jr. (2009) have studied Latin American legislatures and find compelling evidence for the thesis that "something else" other than ideological commitments or purely strategic, electoral considerations to achieve such goals explains legislative behavior. This new research is theoretically and methodologically sophisticated, and has been able to shed new light on long-standing issues.

On the other hand, claims about individualized linkages between judges and political elites, and their consequence on judicial decision-making, are not new. Journalistic accounts, often lacking scientific rigor, have delved into this politicization, sometimes credibly (see, for example, Verbitsky 1993), and sometimes in a less scrupulous way (Ojeda 1995). However, the effects of these political connections on judicial behavior and other phenomena of interest for judicial scholarship are often left unattended. Yet, they can provide an important avenue of inquiry to understand a variety of judicial decision-making phenomena. The most important may be the judges' variable commitment, across countries and over time, to uphold the rule of law when deciding cases where such political actors have utmost interest. This may follow from the politicians' effort to ensure the presence of political allies in the courts at expense of the independence, professionalism and stability of judicial institutions.

The latter issue is particularly troublesome in the region, especially following changes of political direction through democratic means. Similar issues are visible within ongoing changes to the rules of the game that characterized the changes of regime that have operated in some countries where the arrival in power of previously excluded left-wing groups has taken place. For example, in Bolivia, the top echelon of the judiciary politically aligned with the previous ruling elite, with a strong *esprit de corps* that resulted from years of little involvement in political affairs, was at odds with the Morales government practically since it came to power in 2006. A stand-off between the government and the opposition led to a lack of timely replacement for justices. In a way, this lack of agreement was not new – it was part of a trend that had already taken place in the past, precisely because political forces would strive to field as many politically-aligned judges as possible, often dragging on unresolved judicial replacements for years (see Perez-Linan and Castagnola 2009). Unsurprisingly, the most recent development was the clean-slate replacement of the court system after the passing of the new Constitution in 2009 through referendum.[1]

Such a lack of judicial stability can be blamed mainly on overt political intervention of the courts. On the other hand, in Paraguay, the brisk replacement of justices of the much criticized Paraguayan Supreme Court, who theoretically enjoyed life tenure at the beginning of Nicanor Duarte's term, was portrayed to the public and the international community as an effort to clean up the judiciary (Popkin 2004). However, a stronger clue to understand the need for replacement was probably the president's need to field candidates directly connected to him and/or his faction of the Colorado Party, in order to prevent the use of the courts to hinder his political agenda and to seize the opportunity to extend his own political domain. This explanation might also help to understand the emphasis President Lugo placed on "reforming" and packing, once again, the courts after his arrival in power in 2008 – a proposition that involved a serious stand-off with a Court still dominated by the outgoing Colorado Party (an event widely reported by prominent Paraguayan newspapers). The delay in replacing judges, the discussions of appointments centered on political linkages, and the lack of respect for tenure rules should be seen, to a great extent, as by-products of dynamics of political intervention in the courts based on judicial loyalties.

In any case, high courts in Latin America typically decide thousands of cases per year. Even in the most politicized systems, it is unreasonable to think that political commitments explain *all* or even *most* of their decisions. It may well be the case that judges decide a vast majority of the court's proceedings following their ideological preferences, their strategic calculations or legal principles (for a summary of the attitudinal, strategic and legal models, see Baum 1997; Segal 2008). However, such explanations fall short in a series of cases dealing with salient political issues, that is, cases in which the crux of what is at stake are prominent political advantages for a political actor or group.

Judicial politicization – the systematic control that politicians exercise over courts and their staff, and their use by the same politicians of these courts for political gain – can take place prior to the arrival of judges in the bench; or after their nomination, that is, after judges are carrying out their duties (Brinks 2009). The first modality usually refers to the politicians' efforts to ensure that judges represent the policy preferences of their appointers, especially in the context of programmatic democracies (such as ideologically motivated examination of Supreme Court nominees in the American process). For instance, according to this view conservative politicians, other things equal, will try to appoint conservative judges inasmuch as the designation process allows for a discretionary appointment in this respect. In some countries, this may permit politicians to influence outcomes long after they leave power.

The second, post-hoc modality refers to politicians' attempts to constrain or entice judicial behavior in a way that best favors their policy-driven or personal political interests after judges are on the bench. This includes institutional modifications to jurisdictional rules (withholding jurisdiction), the size of the court (court packing), the creation of new mechanisms to hold justices accountable for their behavior, or other gross attempts against judicial independence, such as salary reduction or withholding of resources for the courts in exchange for political support. Both strategies attempt to hold governments accountable to their appointers.

---

1   For example, see www.bbc.co.uk/mundo/america_latina/2010/02/100218_2043_bolivia_justicia_jueces_evo_morales_irm.shtml.

The greater the political importance of the cases decided by a given court, the greater the institutional accountability mechanisms that will be implemented to keep judicial rulings in agreement with the preferences of the ruling political elites. Of particular interest for this analysis is the first modality, i.e., controlling the courts with likeminded judicial actors. Theories of judicial partisanship, which have always been controversial in studies of judicial behavior, have been explored as an instance of the influence of reference groups in judicial behavior in the United States (Lloyd 1995; Songer and Davis 1990). In fact, the role of judges as part of a political establishment, and their connections with a governing political coalition, has troubled scholars for a long time, especially those ascribed to the new-institutionalist tradition (see generally essays in Gillman and Clayton, 1999; see also Keck 2007; Whittington 2005). The literature on courts and "political regimes" is abundant. For instance, consider Dahl's (1957) renowned essay exploring the "counter-majoritarian difficulty," and the connection between changes in the political establishment and the US Supreme Court's proclivity to exercise judicial review. Preliminary empirical evidence allowed Dahl to infer that judges seldom decide against ruling elites, and that this pro-governmental stance resulted from the government's influence on the court by appointing ideologically sympathetic judges. The weak link in theorizing about the judiciary in ROL literature is formalism, which seemingly ignores these effects even in developed countries (meanwhile, they might be expected a fortiori in developing countries).

A major problem with the analyses mentioned above is that they do not explicitly address contexts outside of the United States, an established democracy with an independent judiciary and where the rule of law is generally upheld. In these contexts, judges are not expected to have significant ties with political elites which might systematically influence their decision-making in a way distinct from ideology. Since political processes and outcomes are structured along distinct ideological lines, the struggle for dominating the courts centers on the disagreements among political elites of certain core issues in the social, economic and strictly-political realms. Though courts will often get to decide cases where the ideological component is less relevant, especially at the Supreme Court level, the institutional conditions enjoyed by these courts and the importance of their roles (especially judicial review), will mean that ideologically-charged cases will tend to arrive at the bench (usually selected by the justices themselves thanks to their control of the docket) and be decided accordingly. Moreover, following this approach, any advantages enjoyed by specific actors, such as the Solicitor General or specific interest groups, are often analyzed in terms of their ideological agreement with political elites.[2]

Developing countries targeted for ROL work are different. The need to achieve and secure particularistic goals in weakly institutionalized democracies pervades political relations, including judges. These linkages thus have a distinct effect on the way judges behave (at the micro level) and how courts perform (at the macro level). Since these connections have been underestimated by judicial scholarship, there is a theoretical need to conceptualize these political loyalty links, to operationalize them in a way that is amenable for cross-national research, and to explore their influence on the judges' ability to hold the government accountable in spite of the pressure to favor

---

2   In addition to the *ideological* connection, recent analyses have explored the possibility that judges take into consideration politicians, their peers and other audiences due to a psychological need for approval. Thus, in *Judges and their Audiences* (2006), Baum discusses judicial decision-making from the standpoint of the judges' need to please certain individuals or groups for their own satisfaction, including other judges, interest groups, law professors or public opinion. Baum does not go as far as asserting that this could be the *main* determinant of judicial behavior in the United States, but that it still is a critical perspective to appropriately understand how and why judges act as they do. In certain instances, this need to please their audiences would drive judges to set aside other considerations and decide purely on the basis of these psychological bonds.

political allies. Within the Latin American context, my argument is not far from studies about the role of elites, and how they attain and manage political power. For example, Paige (1997) argues that revolution and governmental structure in Central America are deeply rooted in the histories of the coffee elite. Like other well-documented institutions based on informal dynamics, the existence of political ties in the judiciary adheres, in part, to cultural norms followed by political actors. Weak institutions, low levels of trust, and a culture that has traditionally assigned a long-standing importance to personal links for appointing political agents, delegating power and hold them accountable are all well-known features of Latin America's political systems.

*Assessing the Effect of Loyalties on Judicial Decision-Making*

I define *loyalty links* as commitments made by judges to individual (or collective) political players to benefit or, at least, take into consideration their interests once they ascend the bench, in cases that are politically relevant to such political players. Thus, a *loyalty link* is a conscious allegiance with a political actor to whom "fidelity is due."[3] This political actor can be a chief executive, a political party, a faction, an individual, or even a prominent corporation or interest group – as long as the said actor plays an essential role in the nation's political life.

In Latin America, judges can potentially have many relevant loyalties. With respect to the executive, judges could have connections with the president prior to his or her arrival in power, with other officers who hold important cabinet positions, or, for instance, with the military. With regards to the legislature, judges could have affiliations with political parties, factions, or even with powerful politicians. Within the judiciary, judges could develop loyalty ties with other judges, in the same judicial entity or in other bodies, at the same or at a different hierarchical level. Beyond the regime's structure, judges may develop loyalty ties with other relevant political actors, such as interest groups – like workers' unions or associations for the protection of human rights – political parties, factions or politicians with no participation in government; or even with powerful businesses. In Latin America's political systems, the president has a vast influence in the political arena, and parties often function as political machines without much concern for ideology. Thus, two loyalty ties may have great importance among the many existing links: loyalty toward the president; and loyalties toward political parties or factions.[4]

These political connections could have different sources: family ties, educational background (for example, attending similar military academies or law school), professional links, common membership in an interest group, or common affiliation to a political party, including specific factions. Other times they evolve from ongoing work and cooperation between judges and political

---

3    The use of the term "loyalty" is controversial. The common usage of the word *loyalty* refers to "the quality or state or an instance of being loyal" (Merriam Webster's). The adjective "loyal" has several meanings. According to the cited dictionary, it can mean "1: Unswerving in allegiance as: a: faithful in allegiance to one's lawful sovereign or government b: faithful to a private person to whom fidelity is due c: faithful to a cause, ideal, custom, institution, or product." Additionally, it can also mean "2: showing loyalty." So it is important to separate the notions of loyalties (the existence of the commitment to a person or group, as referred to in 1b) from "behaving loyally," which would be the result of acting on the basis of the actor's loyalties. What I explain here, then, is the effect of commitments on "deciding loyally."

4    I am aware this conceptualization may create problems, especially because the traditional separation-of-powers approach already assesses inter-branch relations from an institutional/strategic framework. Notice my approach is different in the sense that I believe that exploring personal connections between the actors is worth analyzing coupled with other approaches to have a compete panorama of judicial decision-making, especially with respect to the judge's capacity to prevent power-holders from breaching the law.

elites, allowing them to develop reciprocal trust bonds where none existed before.[5] Signs of those loyalty links are common around the region, and are not concealed from the public. Newspapers commonly report the specific actors that have prominent connections with the judges, with what groups or political parties they are affiliated, and even comment or speculate about the influence such links have on the judges' behavior.

Judges' loyalties vis-à-vis other actors can have a distinctive influence on judicial behavior that is often *independent* from political ideology, especially in societies with pervasive non-programmatic or personal relations-based politics, common in Latin America. The influence of loyalties is based on common interests between judges and political actors in attaining, keeping and making the most of political power. In less institutionalized contexts, where the politics of nomination can be at odds with formal institutions, judges depend on other people to be appointed to the bench – not any people, but usually *their* people, typically those with whom they have previously established prominent social connections. On the other hand, without *loyal* judges – judges who are conscious of the importance of the connections with politicians, and willing to act on behalf of their appointers, protectors or *patrones* – politicians lose in several ways: they cannot rely on the (legal and illegal) advantages that judges can deliver in terms of judicial decisions in political cases, cannot benefit from judicial favoritism to law firms or specific litigants, and cannot obtain judicial posts and other appointments under their control.

In fact, personal connections are crucial to understand how the legal profession is structured in Latin America. Like in many other contexts, from the moment future lawyers and judges attend law school, they not only understand and accumulate legal knowledge, but also develop common expectations about their future professional roles in different positions in the legal and judicial system. This generates important friendships and acquaintances that provide the foundations of their professional relations in the immediate future and beyond. The formation and renovation of legal elite networks begins at this stage, and evolves even further throughout the lawyer's professional life. Potential judges and lower court magistrates, in addition to proving their professional competence, need to foster and cultivate connections with other political actors in order to be appointed and/or subsequently promoted or remain in office.

Why and under what conditions do political connections influence judicial decision-making in Latin America, especially the judge's proclivity to support the government? How do these connections influence judicial decision-making? First of all, political connections influence decision-making in *salient* cases involving overt contestation for political domain. Some salient cases will deal with important policymaking issues, such as matters of economic policy, so important in Latin America during the 1990s and 2000s (see Kapiszewski 2007). Others may entail social policy issues, which have also become paramount in the region, especially in countries where courts have become very influential in the political arena and thus have the power to decide unpopular issues without fearing reprisal, such as the Colombian Constitutional Court or the Costa Rican Constitutional Chamber (*Sala Cuarta*). In such cases, the key will be to separate purely political influence from ideological or principled decision-making. Yet, in other occasions, the analysis might focus on cases of no defined ideological content, in which political forces are seeking specific advantages from the court in the struggle for political competition. This is characteristic of contexts of regime transition or in the midst of political turmoil.

---

5 These are not the same kind of loyalties addressed above, since they emerge after the judicial designation, but they can be equally important, and also signify an allegiance toward a political actor that is based on the fulfillment of mutual commitments.

From this viewpoint, the consolidation over time of a regime-friendly judiciary requires the presence of enough judges in the court to form friendly majority coalitions that rule in favor of the government and exercise their powers in favor of the regime – along with raising the costs for opposition-minded judges of ruling against the regime. In this respect, a variety of strategies may be employed to craft a supportive court. For instance, over time, increasing dominance of the political space can allow the government to employ additional opportunity windows to replace unfriendly judges with partisan supporters. Conversely, if the judiciary is dominated by political opponents as soon as the government starts bending the contestation arenas, the opposition will be tempted to use the courts to seek the support of their allies in the fight against the ruling coalition, sometimes with the genuine expectation of defeating the coalition at the bench.

We find a good example of a case in which judicial loyalties seemingly play an important role among the most prominent decisions issued by the Venezuelan Supreme Court during the consolidation of Hugo Chavez's government (early 2000s). The Constitutional Chamber of the Venezuelan Supreme Court, created to concentrate key powers of judicial review according to the 1999 Constitution, played an essential role in paving the way for the recall referendum against Hugo Chavez in August 2004. This included several critical decisions, such as filling the void of the Legislature's failure to designate the members of the National Electoral Council in 2003 (appointing their interim members, including the Council's President), to rule on the constitutionality of different decisions made by the Electoral Authority, most of which were perceived as pro-government by the opposition. Most of these cases showed a Supreme Court divided between *Chavista* and *anti-Chavista* loyalists, with little or no regard to considerations of principle (see Brewer-Carias 2004 for a summary of these controversial cases, and Sanchez Urribarri 2010 for a more extensive analysis). The effects of these political connections on judicial behavior and other phenomena of interest for judicial scholarship are often left unattended, because they do not "fit" comfortably any formalistic narrative of judicial independence, yet at the same time are hard to characterize as corruption.

*Distinguishing the Effect of Loyalties from other Covariates of Judicial Behavior*

Despite the importance of judicial loyalties in some political contexts, it is incorrect to generalize from the onset that judges do not take heed of other considerations in most cases. On one hand, the discussion in the preceding section applies to a specific category of cases: "salient" proceedings, that is to say, cases that are especially meaningful for politicians, in which judicial loyalties might have a *systematic* effect on behalf of political actors and forces. In non-salient cases, the effect of political connections might not be systematic, but sporadic and contingent on specific demands by political groups or actors, and hard to distinguish in courts with broad jurisdiction like most Latin American courts. On the other hand, it is also possible that judges systematically pay attention to *other* kinds of loyalties, in *other* kinds of proceedings, especially in judicial corruption schemes. For example, a judge may alter his or her decision or the time it takes to decide, in cases that involve a certain lawyer or business firm, as a result of their collusion or gratitude with these actors or due to their connection with the political actor in question. This might, or might not, involve bribing through giving a monetary sum. Other kinds of rewards might suffice, such as a job for a relative or a professional opportunity after leaving office.

Although the effect of political loyalties can be quite clear in certain cases, it is usually not so evident. Depending on the nature of the case, judges might also take into account their personal preferences (as the attitudinal model of judicial behavior suggests, see Segal and Spaeth 1993, 2002), the costs and benefits associated with ruling against the wish of the government and other political actors or public opinion (as the strategic perspective on judicial decision-making proposes, see for example Epstein and Knight 1998), and legal interpretations or precedents. With regards to ideology, as mentioned above, it is important to bear in mind the potential overlap or differences between judges' policy preferences and loyalties. If both ideology and the loyalty tie point in the same direction, it would be hard to tell which effect is truly driving the outcome.

The impact of loyalty links on judicial decisions could also be conditioned by strategic considerations, important in the context of change in government (compare Jensen 2003: 342). The first considerations are the popularity of the actor in question, and the ability of this actor to punish or reward the judge for her complacent behavior. This is because the quid pro quo linkage between a judge and his or her political ally is contingent on the politician's ability to deliver the promised particularistic goods. If a politician no longer carries the clout necessary to fulfill her end of the loyalty link, or if there is a serious risk of future loss, the judge might feel an incentive to seek another ally or, more importantly, rule independently and without regard for the politician's preferences. This premise is connected to Helmke's strategic defection theory (2002, 2005) which argues that judicial support for a government varies as a function of the decaying popularity of the ruling regime. The *loyalties* perspective may supplement Helmke's strategic defection theory. Judges potentially reflect the preferences of their original allies and take into consideration their links when deciding whether to defect against the government or remain loyal, especially if the government's ruling coalition is breaking down. Thus, it can shed light on the phenomenon of why some judges fail to defect and continue supporting a governmental coalition, in spite of the risk of losing or abandoning office, while other judges quickly defect as soon as the government loses political strength (a decision that might be tied to their political allies' decision to depart the coalition).

The loyalties approach can also explain why some governments decide to get rid of judges rather than keep them once they come in office, notwithstanding the judges' prior defection in prominent cases, and notwithstanding their seeming lack of commitment to any political cause. Examples abound after a change of regime or change of administration in Latin America. A loyalty perspective on judicial appointments suggests that the main reason why these processes happen in weakly institutionalized contexts concerns the surging political elites' need to appoint new officers – including judges – not only to ensure their political loyalty, but also to seek as much personal profit as possible from the bench during *and* after the transition. In fact, in systems with blatant dynamics of judicial loyalties and poor institutionalization, judges will lack tenure protection and their appointments will be "temporary," both because this helps to prevent judges from ruling against the governmental coalition and because this allows for easy replacement after the composition of the ruling coalition changes (see Hammergren 2007). Tenure instability in spite of formal tenure protection is a logical by-product of a politicized judiciary.

Additionally, legislation, legal doctrine, case-law and other *legal sources* are capable of affecting the influence of loyalties on judicial decision-making. In this respect, it is important to make a distinction between "easy" cases and difficult, "hard" cases. "Easy" cases are those in which there is a clear, unchallenged legal interpretation generally accepted as the correct solution. The latter are cases involving a harder, more contested interpretation. Deciding in a politicized manner – i.e., in favor of political allies – is easier when this is consistent with authoritative legal interpretations, or within the boundaries of fair legal discourse. Conversely, if the case is located in a grey zone or, even worse, in the event that deciding politically would be clearly at odds with prevailing doctrine, judges should be less prone to following their judicial proclivities. Judicial loyalties are presumed to have an effect on the margin.

Finally, when comparing and contrasting the influence of political connections or *loyalties* on judicial decision-making across Latin American nations, it is necessary to address the connection between loyalties and the characteristics of the regime. Loyalties can be consequential in democratic and non-democratic regimes. In Latin America, the consolidation of democratic institutions does not necessarily rule out the existence of clientelist political dynamics in the judiciary. The coexistence of particularistic and programmatic politics in Latin American democracies is possible, as it was the case in the United States and other consolidated democracies, and still is the case in countries such as Brazil or India, with well-embedded democratic institutions.

In democratic regimes, increasing fragmentation of the political arena, accommodating different political actors, can allow courts to enjoy greater independence. The more plural and fragmented the ruling coalition, the greater the number of important loyalties that tends to emerge. This, in turn, reduces the relative impact of a single loyalty on judicial decision-making. The opposite phenomenon occurs in authoritarian polities, where the nexus with a president or smaller ruling elite can trump other factors. This picture would coincide with accounts that provide a larger role for judges in polities where power is more diffuse, an explanation that has also been applied in the Latin American context (Rios-Figueroa 2007b). On the other hand, the notion of judicial loyalties also helps to explain dynamics of *apparent* judicial empowerment in a system transitioning toward authoritarianism. As courts are employed by the opposition to further political agendas against rulers, the governing elite becomes concerned with ensuring they have political agents on the court in the first place who understand the importance of ensuring their success for political survival.

## References


Baum, Lawrence. 1997. *The Puzzle of Judicial Behavior*. Ann Arbor: University of Michigan Press.

Baum, Lawrence. 2006. *Judges and their Audiences*. Princeton: Princeton University Press.

Brewer-Carias, Allan Randolph. 2004. *La Sala Constitucional versus el Estado Democratico de Derecho (El Secuestro del Poder Electoral y de la Sala Electoral del Tribunal Supremo y la Confiscacion del Derecho a la Participacion Politica)*. Caracas: Ediciones El Nacional.

Brinks, Daniel. 2009. "'Faithful Servants of the Regime:' The Brazilian Constitutional Court's Role under the 1988 Constitution." Presented at the Annual Meeting of the American Political Science Association, Toronto. In Gretchen Helmke and Julio Rios-Figueroa (eds.), *Courts in Latin America*. Cambridge: Cambridge University Press, 128–53.

Dahl, Robert A. 1957. "Decision-Making in a Democracy: The Supreme Court as a National Policy-Maker." *Journal of Public Law* 6: 279–95.

Dix, Sarah. 2004. "Breaking with Deference: Judicial Politics in Argentina." Ph.D. Dissertation, Department of Political Science, Yale University.

Domingo, Pilar. 2004. "Judicialization of Politics or Politicization of the Judiciary: Recent Trends." *Democratization* 11: 104–26.

Epstein, Lee and Jack Knight. 1998. *The Choices Justices Make*. Washington, DC: Congressional Quarterly Press.

Epstein, Lee and Jeffrey A. Segal. 2005. *Advice and Consent: The Politics of Judicial Appointments*. New York: Oxford University Press.

Finkel, Jodi. 2008. *Judicial Reform as Political Insurance: Argentina, Peru and Mexico in the 1990s*. South Bend: University of Notre Dame Press.

Gillman, Howard and Cornell Clayton (eds.) 1999. *The Supreme Court in American Politics. New Institutionalist Interpretations*. Lawrence: University Press of Kansas.

Gloppen, Siri, Roberto Gargarella and Elin Skaar (eds.) 2004. *Democratization and the Judiciary: The Accountability Function of the Courts in New Democracies*. London: Frank Cass Publishers.

Hammergren, Linn A. 1997. *The Politics of Justice and Justice Reform in Latin America: The Peruvian Case in Comparative Perspective*. Boulder: Westview Press.

Hammergren, Linn A. 2003. "International Assistance to Latin American Justice Programs: Toward an Agenda for Reforming the Reformers." In Erik G. Jensen and Thomas C. Heller (eds.), *Beyond Common Knowledge: Empirical Approaches to the Rule of Law*. Stanford: Stanford University Press, 290–335.

Hammergren, Linn A. 2007. *Envisioning Reform: Improving Judicial Performance in Latin America*. College Park: Pennsylvania State University Press.

Haynie, Stacia L. 2003. *Judging in Black and White: Decision Making in the South African Appellate Division, 1950–1990*. New York: Peter-Lang Publishing, Inc.

Helmke, Gretchen. 2002. "The Logic of Strategic Defection: Court-Executive Relations in Argentina under Dictatorship and Democracy." *American Political Science Review* 96(2): 305–20.

Helmke, Gretchen. 2005. *Courts Under Constraints: Courts, Generals, and Presidents in Argentina*. New York: Cambridge University Press.

Helmke, Gretchen and Steven Levitsky (eds.) 2006. *Informal Institutions and Democracy: Lessons from Latin America*. Baltimore: The Johns Hopkins University Press.

Hilbink, Lisa. 2007. *Judges Beyond Politics in Democracy and Dictatorship: Lessons from Chile*. Cambridge: Cambridge University Press.

Huneeus, Alexandra Valeria. 2006. "The Dynamics of Judicial Stasis: Judges, Pinochet-era Claims, and the Question of Judicial Legitimacy in Chile." Ph.D. Dissertation, University of California, Berkeley.

Iaryczower, Matias, Pablo Spiller and Mariano Tommasi. 2002. "Judicial Decision-Making in Unstable Environments: Argentina 1935–1998." *American Journal of Political Science* 46(4): 699–716.

Jensen, Erik G. 2003. "The Rule of Law and Judicial Reform: The Political Economy of Diverse Institutional Patterns and Reformers' Responses." In Erik G. Jensen and Thomas C. Heller (eds.), *Beyond Common Knowledge: Empirical Approaches to the Rule of Law*. Stanford: Stanford University Press, 290–335.

Kapiszewski, Diana. 2007. "Challenging Decisions: High Courts and Economic Governance in Argentina and Brazil." Ph.D. Dissertation, University of California at Berkeley.

Kapiszewski, Diana and Matthew M. Taylor. 2008. "Doing Courts Justice? Studying Judicial Politics in Latin America." *Perspectives on Politics* 6(4): 741–67.

Keck, Thomas. 2007. "Party, Policy or Duty: Why Does the Supreme Court Invalidate Federal Statutes?" *American Political Science Review* 101(2): 321–38.

Lloyd, Randall D. 1995. "Separating Partisanship from Party in Judicial Research: Reapportionment in the U.S. District Court." *American Political Science Review* 89(2): 413–20.

Lyne, Mona. 2008. *The Voter's Dilemma and Democratic Accountability*. University Park: Penn State University Press.

Magaloni, Beatriz. 2003. "Authoritarianism, Democracy and the Supreme Court: Horizontal Exchange and the Rule of Law in Mexico." In Scott Mainwaring and Cristopher Welna (eds.), *Democratic Accountability in Latin America*. Oxford: Oxford University Press, 266–307.

Martin, Cadi. 1996. *El Juicio a CAP: Inocente o Culpable?* Caracas: Arte Fotolitografico.

Moustafa, Tamir. 2003. "Law versus the State: The Judicialization of Politics in Egypt." *Law and Social Inquiry* 28(4): 883–930.

Moustafa, Tamir. 2007. *The Struggle for Constitutional Power: Law, Politics and Economic Development in Egypt*. Cambridge: Cambridge University Press.

Moustafa, Tamir and Tom Ginsburg. 2008. "Introduction: The Functions of Courts in Authoritarian Politics." In Tom Ginsburg and Tamir Moustafa (eds.), *Rule by Law: The Politics of Courts in Authoritarian Regimes*. New York: Cambridge University Press, 1–22.

O'Donnell, Guillermo. 1999. "Horizontal Accountability in New Democracies." In Andreas Schedler, Larry Diamond and Marc F. Plattner (eds.), *The Self-Restraining State: Power and Accountability in New Democracies*. Boulder and London: Lynne Rienner Publishers, 29–52.

O'Donnell, Guillermo. 2000. "The Judiciary and the Rule of Law." *Journal of Democracy* 11(1): 25–31.

Ojeda, William. 1995. *¿Cuanto Vale un Juez?* Valencia, Venezuela: Vadell Hermanos Editores.

Paige, Jeffery M. 1997. *Coffee and Power: Revolution and the Rise of Democracy in Central America*. Cambridge, MA: Harvard University Press.

Pereira, Anthony W. 2005. *Political (In)Justice, Authoritarianism and the Rule of Law in Brazil, Chile and Argentina*. Pittsburgh: University of Pittsburgh Press.

Perez-Linan, Anibal. 2007. *Presidential Impeachment and the New Political Instability in Latin America*. Cambridge: Cambridge University Press.

Perez-Linan, Anibal and Maria Andrea Castagnola. 2009. "Bolivia: The Rise and Fall of Judicial Review." Presented at the Conference *Judicial Politics in Latin America*, March 4–8. Mexico City: CIDE.

Perez Perdomo, Rogelio. 2005. "Judicialization and Regime Transformation: The Venezuelan Supreme Court." In Rachel Sieder, Line Schjolden and Alan Angell (eds.), *The Judicialization of Politics in Latin America*. New York: Palgrave Macmillan, 131–60.

Popkin, Margaret. 2004. "Fortalecer la Independencia Judicial." En Luis Pasara, *La experiencia latinoamericana en reforma de la justicia*. Mexico, DF: Instituto de Investigaciones Juridicas de la Universidad Autónoma de Mexico.

Prillaman, William C. 2000. *The Judiciary and Democratic Decay in Latin America: Declining Confidence in the Rule of Law*. Westport: Praeger.

Rios-Figueroa, Julio. 2007a. "Fragmentation of Power and the Emergence of an Effective Judiciary in Mexico: 1994–2002." *Latin American Politics and Society* 49(1): 31–57.

Rios-Figueroa, Julio. 2007b. Judicial Independence: Definition, Measurement, and its Effects on Corruption. Ph.D. Dissertation, Department of Political Science, New York University.

Roniger, Luis, and Ayse Gunes Ayata (eds.) 1994. *Democracy, Clientelism, and Civil Society*. Boulder: Lynne Rienner Publishers.

Ruhl, J. Mark. 2010. "Honduras Unravels." *Journal of Democracy* 21(2): 93-107.

Sanchez Urribarri, Raul. 2010. "Judges and their Loyalties: A Comparative Analysis Focused on the Venezuelan Supreme Court." Ph.D. Dissertation, University of South Carolina. Columbia, South Carolina.

Schmidt, Steffen W. (ed.) 1977. *Friends, Followers and Factions: A Reader in Political Clientelism*. Berkeley: University of California Press.

Scribner, Druscilla. 2004. "Limiting Presidential Power: Supreme Court-Executive Relations in Argentina and Chile." Ph.D. Dissertation, University of California – San Diego. San Diego, California.

Segal, Jeffrey. 2008. "Judicial Behavior." In Keith Whittington, R. Daniel Kelemen and Gregory A. Caldeira (eds.), *The Oxford Handbook of Law and Politics*. New York: Oxford University Press, 19–33.

Segal, Jeffrey A. and Harold J. Spaeth. 1993. *The Supreme Court and the Attitudinal Model*. New York: Cambridge University Press.

Segal, Jeffrey A. and Harold J. Spaeth. 2002. *The Supreme Court and the Attitudinal Model Revisited*. Cambridge: Cambridge University Press.

Shapiro, Martin. 1981. *Courts. A Comparative and Political Analysis*. Chicago: The University of Chicago Press.

Sieder, Rachel, Line Schjolden and Alan Angell (eds.) 2005. *The Judicialization of Politics in Latin America*. New York: Palgrave Macmillan.

Songer, Donald R. and Sue Davis. 1990. "The Impact of Party and Region on Voting Decisions in the United States Courts of Appeals, 1955–1986." *The Western Political Quarterly* 43(2): 317–34.

Staton, Jeffrey K. 2006. "Constitutional Review and the Selective Promotion of Case Results." *American Journal of Political Science* 50(1): 98–112.

Tate, C. Neal. 1993. "Courts and Crisis Regimes: A Theory Sketch with Asian Case Studies." *Political Research Quarterly* 46(2): 311–38.

Tate, C. Neal. 1995. "Why the Expansion of Judicial Power." In C. Neal Tate and Torbjorn Vallinder (eds.), *The Global Expansion of Judicial Power*. New York: New York University Press, 27–37.

Tate, C. Neal and Stacia L. Haynie. 1993. "Authoritarianism and the Functions of Courts: A Time Series Analysis of the Philippine Supreme Court, 1961–1987." *Law & Society Review* 27: 707–40.

Taylor, Matthew. 2008. *Judging Policy: Courts and Policy Reform in Democratic Brazil*. Stanford: Stanford University Press.

Verbitsky, Horacio. 1993. *Hacer la Corte: La Creacion de un Poder sin Control ni Justicia*. Buenos Aires: Planeta.

Whittington, Keith. 2005. "'Interpose your Friendly Hand': Political Supports for the Exercise of Judicial Review by the United States Supreme Court." *American Political Science Review* 99(4): 583–96.

Wilson, Bruce. 2005. "Changing Dynamics: The Political Impact of Costa Rica's Constitutional Court." In Rachel Sieder, Line Schjolden and Alan Angell (eds.), *The Judicialization of Politics in Latin America*. New York: Palgrave Macmillan, 47–66.

Zucco, Jr., Cesar. 2009. "Ideology or What? Legislative Behavior in Multiparty Presidentialist Settings." *Journal of Politics* 71(3): 1076–92.

Chapter 18

# Criminal Law Reform after Dictatorship: Chile's Struggle to Balance Rights with Citizens' Desire for Law and Order

Lydia Brashear Tiede

Following the Pinochet dictatorship, the new democratic government of Chile modernized the country's institutions and laws, including major reforms to the criminal justice system. As such it represents an instance of transitional justice defined broadly as "the recovery of the rule of law and justice after mass violence" (Humphrey and Valverde 2008). Despite the new government's attempts to rectify the past, Chilean citizens viewed the reform agenda with skepticism. Over time there was a fundamental difference between the political leadership's ideologically inspired human rights emphasis, and ordinary citizens' perceptions concerning the effects of legal changes in the criminal justice system.

The reforms forced citizens to face how legal changes based on transparency and individual rights might negatively affect their own personal security. While authoritiarian regimes typically have abysmal human rights records, these regimes' oppressive tactics generally guarantee more order and less ordinary crime than democratic regimes (Packer 1968; Sung 2006). The issue came down to the elite's declared preference for a "due process" model upholding individual rights and personal liberties of criminal defendants as part of democratization, versus ordinary citizens' apparent preference for a "crime control" model guaranteeing more order and less ordinary crime in a fashion perhaps more at home under an authoritarian regime. So in a modern democratic society, there may be a distinctive "push–pull" relationship in which the public as the supposed object of legal changes may act as subject to "change the changes" via the political system. In criminal justice, this effect is measurable in the interplay between legislative changes, public opinion surveys, and the comparison of statistics like the difference between arrests and reports of crime.

## Democratization and Modernization as Divergent?

For us, the "chicken or egg question" is present in the apparent third party effects (and resistance) in the public when faced with the political leadership's ideologically inspired changes in the law. So the aspirations of social engineering via law may run afoul of divergent social views. The due process model finds it roots in much of the literature on democratization and the rule of law. Domestic and foreign advocates of legal reforms after a transition emphasize that such reforms will ensure that individuals are treated fairly and that actors in the legal system will respect the rights of all litigants, whether they are government actors or not.

For countries transitioning from authoritarian rule to democracy, there is no better way for the government to re-establish respect for law than by following a due process model of criminal justice and asserting the primacy of rights. By committing to rights, governments not only assert their willingness to be bound by law, but also to treat unpopular people and causes with equal respect under the law (Brunetti et al. 1997; McGuire and Olson 1996; Olson 1993; Weingast 1997, 2003). Immediately after a transition to democracy, governments and the public often see criminal law reforms as a necessary step in the transitional justice process.

In the early stages of a transition, scholars have often incorrectly analogized democratization to modernization and drawn heavily on the insights of three models which attempt to predict the effect of modernization on crime. Modernization is thought to either lower crime (i.e., the "civilization perspective" asserted by Elias 1978; Weber 1978), raise crime (i.e., the "conflict perspective" asserted by Bohm 1982; LaFree and Tseloni 2006; Taylor et al. 1973), or initially raise crime and then lower it (i.e., the "modernization perspective" put forth most notably by Durkheim 1947). Modernization referred to in these models, however, is not always comparable to democratization because modernization in traditional terms focuses on a country's industrialization, while democratization focuses on a country's movement from one political regime to another, regardless of its socio-economic level of development. For countries such as Chile, where industrialization occurred relatively late (i.e., in the 1930s), and where Pinochet's authoritarian regime in place from 1973 to 1990 based its economic policy on market-oriented reforms, modernization theory provides little purchase for understanding the effect of democratization on the behavior of individuals facing political and legal change.

Rather than using modernization theory as a way of evaluating the criminal justice system after a successful democratic transition, in the Latin American context it is more useful to evaluate the perceptions of individuals (both elites and non-elites) concerning criminal law reform in a two-step process. In the first step, immediately after a transition and for some time, criminal justice reform is seen as necessary to remedy issues of impunity and to modernize antiquated criminal justice systems which failed to incorporate international standards of due process. Post-transition politicians and their supporters generally emphasize the human rights and modernization aspects (characterized often as "international standards") of the reform as such aspects most distance them from the former authoritarian regime. While supporters of the post-transition regime revel in the reforms, others loyal to the former authoritarian regime are resistant to both the reforms and the changes that they create. As a result, the public becomes split on its perception of criminal law reform. For some, reform is seen as necessary to distance the new government from the *ancien régime*. For others, reform is seen as a threat to the former order and its insistence on control, even if such control violated human rights.

In the second phase of a more successful transition, concerns about the authoritarian past and human rights abuses become more distant. As a result, citizens tend to become more concerned about crime levels and "law and order." In line with these concerns, politicians react by changing relevant legislation introduced post transition. When democracies consolidate, politicians' approaches to crime and citizen fear often resemble those in long-standing democracies, where politicians write new legislation to appear responsive to citizens' "law and order" concerns. The level of responsiveness in turn is directly related to politicians' desire to be re-elected, because no politician wants to be labeled as soft on crime (Mayhew 1974). The surprising thing is how quickly the perception may flip post-transition as memories of the bad old days recede.

## Historical Context and Substantive Reforms

In Chile, reforms promulgated between 1995 and 2000 moved Chile's criminal law system closer to that existing in Western democracies in Europe and the United States. Prior to the reforms, Chile operated under the arcane set of criminal procedures found in its 1906 *Código de Procedimiento Penal* (CPP–1906), which was based substantially upon nineteenth-century colonial law (so barely dating back to the introduction of the modern criminal and procedure codes immediately post-Enlightenment in Western Europe under the leadership of figures like Beccaria, von Feuerbach and Mittermaier; Chilean law was 150 years behind its time in comparison to leading Western European Civil Law jurisdictions like Germany and France) (Carocca et al. 2000).[1]

In 1988 Pinochet unexpectedly failed to win a plebiscite which he instigated and consequently handed over power to democratically elected President Patricio Aylwin in 1990. One of Aylwin's first actions was the establishment of the Commission for Truth and Reconciliation (the Rettig Commission) to investigate and report human rights abuses under the Pinochet regime. In February 1991, the Rettig Commission issued its report which included a full chapter criticizing the courts during the dictatorship (*Report of the Chilean National Commission on Truth and Reconciliation* 1991). The report stated that the Chilean Supreme Court failed to protect human rights by upholding the 1978 amnesty decree. Besides suggesting that courts and legal procedures related to human rights be changed, the Commission called on the government to specifically change the constitution as well as criminal law and procedure to ensure the protection of human rights. Many of the suggestions were incorporated into subsequent criminal law reforms. Further, the focus on human rights in the criminal law reforms came directly from the Rettig Commission that emphatically suggested that international human rights standards related to criminal defendants and prisoners be incorporated into Chile's domestic law.

Following the Rettig Commission's lead and criticizing judges for their lack of "moral courage" under the Pinochet regime (*Report of the Chilean National Commission on Truth and Reconciliation* 1991), President Aylwin proposed a number of substantive changes to the legal system which included reforms to the structure of the judiciary, the criminal justice system, and an attempt to deal with past human rights atrocities. Of these reforms, only a few were enacted. Further, during Aylwin's tenure, Chilean courts were hesitant to prosecute high ranking officials under the Pinochet regime due to several factors. First, the conservative nature of Chile's judiciary prevented judicial activism in human rights (Hilbink 2007). Second, judges felt constrained by the 1978 Amnesty Law which precluded prosecution for "disappearances" occurring between 1973 and 1978, and thus applied the law inconsistently and selectively. Finally, the ability of Supreme Court justices to rank and punish lower court judges precluded any activism at the lowest levels of the judiciary who generally followed their conservative brethren in the Supreme Court (Hilbink 2007).

Building on judicial reforms introduced under Aylwin, in 1995 President Eduardo Frei Ruiz-Tagle launched a plan to reform the criminal justice system (Mensaje de Presidente 1995). Riego (2006), who was significantly involved in the reform, articulates four justifications:

---

1 In 1980, amendments to the Chilean Constitution made under the dictatorship did not specifically affect the CPP–1906, but in theory they increased the rights of defendants by incorporating rights espoused by international treaties into national law. Despite these changes, rights were seldom recognized as other constitutional amendments solidified Pinochet's presidential powers (Siavelis 2000) and marginalized the Supreme Court which shielded human rights abusers (Correa Sutil 1993; Hilbink 2007).

- establishment of standards for rights of criminal defendants more consistent with international standards (meaning those practiced in advanced democracies);
- modernization of the criminal justice process to make it more efficient;
- improvement of the image of the judicial system, as Chile had a long history of judicial impotence whereby judges had done little when faced with human rights abuses; and
- improvement of victims' rights and voice in the criminal justice process.

Further, although not mentioned by Riego, the criminal law reform paralleled the more general process of a regional criminal and criminal procedure code reform movement across Latin America in which 14 countries adopted reforms similar to those adopted in Chile and for many similar reasons (Langer 2007 provides an overview of the criminal law reforms across Latin America).

While the Chilean reforms emphasized judicial and legal actors, they did not include concurrent reforms to the police or prisons. Although not changing the internal structure or day-to-day workings of the police, reforms did affect which authorities police reported to as well as how quickly to report. Reforms to these institutions were not a priority and are only just beginning to be considered by the government.[2] However, by failing to reform the police, the government left out a significant actor in the criminal justice process. This was unfortunate as police play a vital role in crime prevention and are one of the main actors that citizens observe in the fight against crime. Further, law enforcement officials under Pinochet were considered complicit and abusive and thus including reform to the police in the overall criminal reforms would have signaled an even more significant break from the past.

Although Chile's criminal law reforms were approved by 2000, the laws themselves provided for gradual implementation by region.[3] To understand the breadth of the criminal law reforms, an understanding of Chile's pre-reform system is necessary (Duce et al. 1998). Formerly, the lower criminal courts in pre-reform Chile, *juzgados del crimen*, used only one judge, who investigated criminal cases, accused individuals, decided their culpability, and sentenced them. These pre-reform judges also made decisions regarding defendants' fundamental rights, including the duration and conditions for pre-trial release from detention. The wide range of their duties prevented lower court judges from acting quickly on cases, resulting in delays and bottlenecks in the process.

---

2   On June 5, 2009, the Ministry of Justice announced plans to reform the Chile's prisons. "Ministerio de Justicia Anuncia Consejo para la reforma penitenciaria." June 6, 2009. Available at www.minjusticia.cl/comunicado/subse/05_06_09.htm.

3   The new CPP, effective in October of 2000, allowed for the new process to be instituted in stages. In other words, the reform was implemented in certain regions over a five-year period. The first stage of the reform was implemented in region IV and region IX in December 2000. The remaining reforms occurred in regions II, III, and VII in October 2001; in regions I, XI, XII in December 2002; in regions V, VI, VIII, X in December 2003, and in Santiago in June 2005. The reform was supposed to be implemented in all the regions by 2004 with Santiago scheduled as the final region for reform. However, in August of 2001, the legislature revised the schedule of implementation, not changing the order of implementation, but extending the implementation period until 2005 (*El Mercurio* 2001a, 2001b; Ley No. 19.762). By mid-2005, the criminal law reform was fully implemented in Chile, although courts handling cases prior to the reform were being phased out as they completed their case loads. Despite the newness of the reforms, politicians were keen to react to citizens' security concerns about the reform. In 2002, they modified the laws relating to police intervention in the criminal justice process. In 2005 and again in 2008, in response to citizen outcry about the reforms, the legislature enacted additional reforms primarily dealing with pre-trial detention.

The most startling aspect of Chile's pre-reform criminal law system was the general lack of defendants' rights.[4] Not only were there few actual rights on paper, but the rights that did exist were frequently curtailed in practice, sometimes due to a lack of resources. For example, Article 19(3) of the Chilean Constitution states that everyone has the right to an attorney. However, the quality of a defendant's legal defense was based largely on his financial situation. Often law students with no practical experience represented indigent defendants in criminal proceedings, including murder trials. The result was that poor defendants were given inadequate representation, and there was a wide disparity in treatment between rich and poor defendants. In pre-reform Chile, in line with nineteenth-century inquisitorial procedure doctrine, there existed no presumption of innocence. Individual rights were further curtailed because a judge could not escape the prejudices that inevitably attach when investigating a case prior to its submission to trial. The judge was thus given the contradictory tasks of first investigating whether a crime took place and, once deciding that it had, weighing the evidence to resolve the question of guilt—a question the judge had often predetermined during investigation.

The reforms ultimately drafted by the Chileans resulted in the creation of new institutions and a new *Codigo Procesal Penal* or criminal procedure code (Ley No. 19.696) "modernizing" it in terms of moving its general tenor and provisions to something resembling leading Western European jurisdictions' criminal justice systems (e.g., Germany's). Currently, when a crime comes to the attention of the police or judge, a prosecutor with the *Ministerio Público* is immediately notified of the case, and the investigation begins with an assigned prosecutor from this agency. If a defendant is detained by the police, the police must notify the *juez de garantía* within 24 hours. The *juez de garantía* informs the defendant of the charges against him and makes decisions regarding his detention. The defendant has a right to an attorney from the moment he is arrested. There is a two-year limitation on investigations, but the defendant can request that the judge shorten the time.[5] After the investigation is completed, the prosecutor chooses whether to file a formal accusation against the defendant, dismiss the case, or agree to some type of alternative resolution. The prosecutors have the discretion not to proceed with a case if the facts do not constitute a crime. Decisions and resolutions made in the new *juzgados de garantía* are appealable (Carocca et al. 2000: 341).

While the observers of the reform saw the creation of a public prosecutor's office as significant, the reforms themselves did nothing to alter the role of the police in investigations (except for making

---

4   Under the pre-reform inquisitorial system, lower criminal courts reviewed cases in a two-step process. The first stage, or *sumario*, was an investigative phase in which the judge carried out the entire investigation, with the assistance of the police. The *sumario* often took place in secret, and defendants were unaware of the accusations against them despite an ongoing investigation. During the *sumario*, the judge could hold a defendant for an indefinite period, and defendants were sometimes held for years before being formally accused. This provided an almost Kafkaesque scenario, in which individual defendants were not informed about the charges against them and/or their detention status. If the judge decided there was sufficient evidence tying the defendant to a specific crime, he moved the case from the investigative phase to a *plenario* phase, an action that had the appearance of a tacit presumption of guilt. The *plenario* phase involved new actors, including representatives for the defendant and the government, respectively, and also attorneys for the victim, who interacted with the judge by presenting evidence in written form. After the *plenario* was completed, the same judge who conducted the investigation and made the evidentiary decisions during the *sumario* and *plenario* stages would then decide the guilt of the defendant and determine the sentence.

5   In September, 2001, the National Defender, Alex Carocca, criticized the National Prosecutor, Guillermo Piedrabuena, for instituting an alleged blanket policy in which prosecutors would request two years to investigate all crimes. Carocca charged that such a policy was "excessively ritualistic" and led to delays (Pfeiffer and Vergara 2001).

police interact with prosecutors rather than investigative judges and to ensure that individuals arrested were given proper due process). The creation of the public prosecutor more significantly altered the role of judges, who had previously conducted investigations.

Besides creating the new institutions of public prosecutor (Ley Nos. 19.519 and 19.640), public defender (Ley No. 19.718), and two new criminal courts (Ley Nos. 19.665 and 19.708), the new criminal reform substantially improved the rights of defendants by codifying new substantive and procedural rights. The most important new right for defendants is the right to be presumed innocent. Although this right appeared to have some precursor in the former Code, in practice the old process of *sumario* and *plenario* negated this important right. The new Code also provides defendants with a defense attorney from the moment the criminal process begins. The defendant also has a right to a *defender de confianza*, a public defender who is an attorney, whose services are free if a defendant cannot afford to pay. Procedurally, the defendant is also given a plethora of other rights, including a right to oral public trial, right to intervene in the entire process, and the right to immediately know the specific charges against the defendant himself. Once the defendant is aware of the charges against him, he has several rights regarding his ability to present a defense, including the right to contradict allegations in an accusation and review the prosecutor's investigation file from the outset.

The other main improvement in defendants' rights concerns pre-trial custody. Prior to the reform, defendants could be held for long periods of time while the judge investigated the case. Thus, he could be held in prison without knowledge of the case against him or the status of the investigation. Riego (2006) notes that one impetus of the reform was to reduce the number of people in lengthy pre-trial detention (*prisión preventative*). Under the new reform, the judge must speak to the defendant within 24 hours of his detention, instead of five days, and defendants have a right to be informed and have an attorney. Decisions regarding the pre-trial detention of defendants must be decided in an adversarial manner with both the defense and the prosecutor presenting evidence on this issue and only after prosecutors' formalized charges (Venegas and Vial 2008). The judge is then limited as to when he can impose this pre-trial detention by the code requirements themselves. To impose pre-trial or preventative detention, the prosecutor must show that a crime exists, that the defendant was somehow related to the crime, and that the detention will assist in the success of the investigation. As initially drafted, pre-trial detention was only to be used when other measures of personal restraint were insufficient to complete the proceedings (CPP, Art. 139) and pre-trial detention was not allowed when it would be disproportionate to the seriousness of the underlying crime (CPP, Art. 141). The new reform also increased the availability of alternative types of detention such as house arrest or other confinement within Chile.

The reforms also substantially improved victims' rights and opportunities to intervene in the criminal process. The reform required the *Ministerio Público* to represent victims' interests in individual criminal cases. Victims are now allowed to intervene in a case and have input on certain decisions regarding the progress of the case. In certain instances, a dissatisfied victim has a right to appeal a decision. The new CPP sets out six specific rights for victims including the rights to request protection from threats and attacks against himself and family members while involved in a prosecution, to pursue civil suits against defendants, to request to be heard in the case, and to challenge the case dismissal or defendant's acquittal.


**Selling the Reforms to the Public and Public Reaction**

The criminal law reforms in Chile are striking due to the breadth of changes encompassed in the reform as well as the government's commitment to the transformation of the criminal justice system. Chile's Ministry of Justice estimated that the implementation of the reform cost 341 billion pesos (approximately $617 million) broken down as follows: approximately 53 percent to the judicial branch, 38 percent to the Ministry of Justice, and 9 percent to the Public Defender (*Ministerio de Justicia* 2008). In 1999, the government estimated that 0.9 percent of the national budget had been spent on the reform. Beginning in 2000, the government indicated that it would spend 2 percent of the national budget on the reform.

The commitment by the government also was evidenced in the money spent not only in implementing the letter of the law, but also in creating new institutions and training prosecutors, judges, and public defenders. Further, the government spent money on building new courthouses to signal the transparency and newness of the reform. The *Centro de Justicia* in Santiago opened in 2005 and consists of open spaces and expansive windows. Finally, to ensure the public's acceptance of the cost and substance of the reforms, the government launched an extensive advertising campaign. The introduction of the reform in each region and the completion of the reform in Santiago were celebrated by the government in public speeches and celebrations.

Despite all of the efforts and resources expended to sell Chile's reform to the public, it was met with much trepidation. News articles and opinion pieces indicated that citizens were extremely concerned about the rights accorded to criminal defendants in the context of their own security. It was thought that citizens believed that the criminal law reform resulted in judges being overly lenient toward defendants in both the decision to detain them prior to trial and in their inclinations to convict. Further, Duce and Riego (2009), in a study on pre-trial detention, note that certain high profile cases received great negative publicity and some citizens believed that defendants who were arrested were being released rapidly. Finally, in response to the real or perceived citizen anxiety, Congress enacted additional reforms (Biblioteca del Congreso Nacional de Chile 2002, 2005, 2008).

In order to measure the prevalence of fear that permeated the news and to understand the effect of democratic reforms on public opinion, several surveys were conducted by the government as well as non-governmental organizations. Citizens' security concerns were measured by the government's Instituto Nacional de Estadísticas (INE), as well as two other non-governmental organizations: Latinobarometer and La Fundación Paz Ciudadana with Adimark. In comparing the results of the different studies that were conducted, I predict that citizen fear did not increase after the reforms, but remained largely stable. This prediction is based on the belief that citizen fear reported in the media is overblown and based on citizens' immediate reaction to a few high impact cases. To measure Chileans' perceptions of crime and the role of government in protecting citizens, each source of public opinion is analyzed separately.

First, Chile's own crime perception surveys produced by the INE attempt to measure more specifically how Chileans viewed crime. Taken in the years 2003, 2005, and 2007, the surveys include numerous questions posed to individuals and households. Figure 18.1 summarizes citizens' responses to the following question, "During the last 12 months, have you or a member of your household been a victim of any crime?" The availability of survey responses prior to the reforms limits the ability to compare citizens' opinions before and after the reform. However, during the implementation of the reform individuals reported lower incidents of victimization and this trend has continued. This in turn could over time lead to changes in attitudes and behavior about the government, law and order, and the reforms themselves. The INE's report shows that perceptions of victimization have actually decreased from 43 percent in 2003 to 35 percent in 2007 despite the citizen concerns expressed in the media.

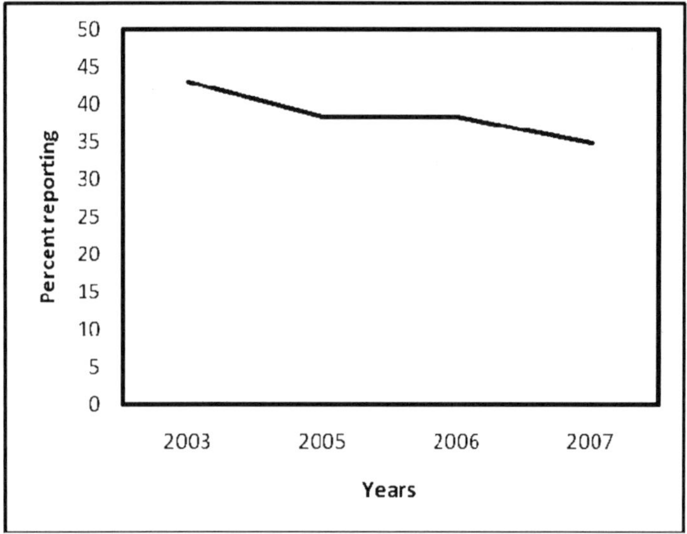



**Figure 18.1 Summary of responses to victimization**

As far as rankings concerning which government agencies should be responsible for citizen security, respondents were generally consistent over time in response to the question, "[i] n your opinion which of the following persons, organizations or instituions is the principal one responsible for the security of citizens?" As seen in Figure 18.2, about 25–35 percent believed that the *carabineros* or police were primarily responsible followed by about 15–20 percent of citizens who believed that courts were primarily responsible. Of those surveyed, less than 5 percent believed that prosecutors or Congress were primarily responsible for their security. What is striking about this analysis is that respondents overwhelmingly failed to agree on which group or agency was principally responsible for citizen security. As a result, individuals' security concerns may be tied to their confusion about which institution is primarily responsible for protecting them.

Second, Latinobarometer measures rule of law as the aggregate of whether households trust the judiciary and the police, and whether anyone has been a victim of crime.[6] Survey scores approaching one are deemed more positively. As seen from Figure 18.3,[7] citizen trust in the judiciary has decreased over time, but the decrease is relatively small occuring over 10 years. Such a decline in perception of the rule of law is troubling as the decline occurred in the same period in which major criminal law reforms were implemented and in which prosecution of human rights abusers from the Pinochet era increased. However, compared to other countries in the region, Chile's rule of law scores over time are relatively high.

---

6   Latinobarometer only provides its data commercially. As a result, the data for this analysis was obtained from the World Banks's Governance Matters (available at http://info.worldbank.org/governance/wgi/sources.htm), which provides averages of sub-indicators from Latinobarometer. The rule of law sub-indicator which measures trust in judiciary, trust in police and whether a household member was a victim of crime was available for the years 1996, 1998, 2000, 2002–2007.

7   Latinobarometer as reported by World Bank, Governance Matters.

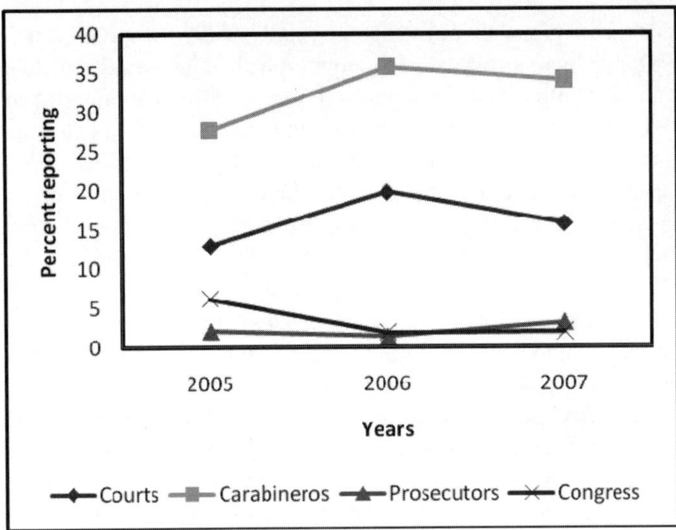



**Figure 18.2 Opinions about institutions primarily responsible for citizen security**

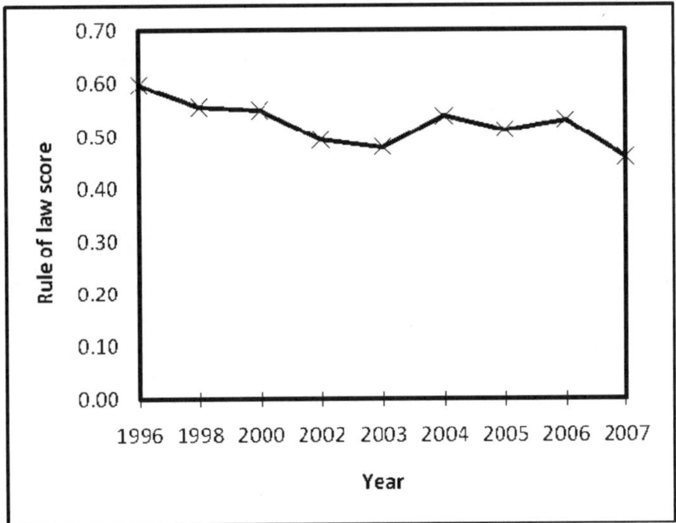



**Figure 18.3 Chile's Latinobarometer rule of law score from 1996 to 2007**

The third source evaluated is from Adimark, a German organization and Fundación Paz Ciudadana, a Chilean non-governmental organization, which analyzed survey data for the years 1993–2007 in some instances. These organizations surveyed individuals over 18 years of age who resided in homes with telephones (Adimark and Fundación Paz Ciudadana 2008). First, questions between 1993 and 2003 ask whether citizens think the quantity of crime has increased significantly in the last six months, and whether the type of crime is more violent. The responses to these questions provide a historic perspective as they go back to 1993, very close to the time of Chile's transition to democracy. Citizens' perceptions about the quantity and severity of violence were highest during the late 1990s. In 1997, 69 percent surveyed thought crime had increased, and 85 percent thought it was more violent. In 2000, after the reform was introduced, citizens' opinions began to improve— only 57 percent believed that crime was on the rise and only 63 percent believed that it was more violent. Since 2000, these perceptions have changed slightly, but citizens' perceptions regarding the quantity and quality of crime did not reach the highest levels seen in the mid 1990s (Tiede 2012). Although the above analysis provides a more historic perspective, results for this question have not been available from 2003 onward. To remedy this, Paz Ciudadana–Adimark's surveys from 2002 until 2008 included a question asking whether family members had been victims of robbery or intent to rob. Results from these questions show that the percent of individuals reporting crimes has been largely stable between 2002 and 2008, and that victimization was at its highest (around 41 percent) in 2003 prior to the reform's complete implementation nationwide.

So what do these varied public opinion results really tell us and how do they relate to the prediction that citizen fear has not increased due to rights-based criminal law reforms? In general, Chileans' opinions concerning their victimization have remained relatively stable. Opinions about the quantity and severity of crime have improved. As to government institutions, Chileans' distrust of legal and government institutions that deal with crime control has not varied considerably over time. In other words, the results generally support the hypothesis that criminal law reforms have generally not increased citizen fear overall. Indeed, there seem to be some improvements in perceptions about the incidence of citizen victimization and the prevalence of crime, but less improvement in citizens' opinions about trusting legal institutions. There is no consensus about which institution is primarily responsible for public safety, which in itself could raise concerns about government accountability.

## The Government's Response to Citizen Fear

In reaction to the public's actual or perceived concern about the interaction between rights for defendants and public security, the government began reviewing the effect of the reform by creating various expert commissions beginning in 2001. Scholars have noted that there were three subsequent major legislative changes to the new criminal procedure law reform which were tied directly to citizen security (Duce and Riego 2009). Only those changes that directly addressed issues of citizen security and that occurred through 2009 (the last year of this study) are highlighted here. The first change to the original reform involved changing how the police dealt with the detention of individuals involved in minor crimes as citizens believed that police were acting too leniently in this regard (Ley 19.789 of 2002).

The second change to the reform primarily involved amendments to change the process and considerations for pre-trial detention. The government established an expert commission to review the reforms' impact. In November 2005, after consideration of the expert commission's recommendations, the legislature amended the new CPP Articles 139 and 141 in regards to pre-trial detention (Ley 20.074 of 2005). The amended CPP Article 139 placed pre-trial decisions exclusively in the authority of the *juez de garantía* and allowed such pre-trial detentions for the express purposes of completing the proceedings or ensuring the security of the defendant or society (CPP Art. 139 amended by Ley 20.074). Amended Article 141 provides specific examples concerning when courts should order pre-trial detention. These additional reforms came only five months after the reform had been in force across the entire country. Scholars assert that "an alarmist discourse on public safety emerged" during the discussions about the effects of the new criminal law reforms due to the public's increased concerns about crime during this period (Venegas and Vial 2008). This discourse was apparently driven by Chile's political opposition, who had not been in power since the return of democratic rule and failed to voice any real concerns about the initial reforms. Despite the passage of additional reforms related to pre-trial detention, some felt that these additions were driven by politics and not by empirical data regarding the reforms' efficacy (Venegas and Vial 2008).

The third change to the reform entailed additional amendments to the law enacted in 2008 (Duce and Riego 2009; Ley 20.253 of 2008). Again, the modifications changed many provisions of the code, but the focus again was on pre-trial detention and issues of citizen security. In general, the revisions left in place the concept that pre-trial detention should be authorized in only exceptional situations that involved danger to the defendant, society, or would make the completion of the investigation difficult. However, the modifications introduced in 2008 provided more specific direction of when detention would be warranted based on a danger to society.

As shown by the above examples, Chilean politicians appear quite responsive to citizens' concerns about safety and security. However, the motivations behind this responsiveness should be explored further for their link to politics. It appears from the analysis of survey results that politicians responded to concerns of citizens that were exaggered in the media. In many democratic states, politicians use criminal law reform as a method for garnering votes. Politicians from all parts of the political spectrum are looked upon favorably when they appear tough on crime. The problem, however, with continuous reforms tailored to placate citizen concerns is that it is impossible to determine which reforms work and which do not. Further, constant reforms may have many unintended consequences.


## Empirical Analysis of Criminal Law Reforms and Behavioral Changes

Measuring the impact of the criminal law reforms on behavior other than public perception is difficult due to the limited amount of available data.[8] However, using a mixed methodology, I attempt to test whether the criminal law reform affected citizens' propensity to report crimes and the police's propensity to arrest. While reporting and arrest rates are only two measurements testing the effect of criminal law reform, they provide some evidence of whether the reform influenced the behavior of citizens and the police.

The empirical analysis in this section seeks to test two predictions relating to citizen trust and behavior of the police. First, I predict that criminal law reforms will increase citizens' reporting of crimes to official authorities. The Chilean government invested significant resources and effort to ensure that the reform was effective and well received by the public. This was accomplished by investment in training judges, lawyers, and legal professionals as well as constructing new courthouses throughout the country that would be transparent and open. Through these efforts, the government sought to change the public's image of the justice system. It expended significant sums of money to ensure that the reforms and the government's efforts were well received. I predict

---

8   Marangunic and Foglesong (2004) provide one of the few empirical studies on the effect of the reform which went beyond just descriptive statistics. This study produced by the Vera Institute in conjunction with Chile's Ministerio Público compared a sample of cases in Santiago before the reform to a sample of cases in Temuco after the reform. The authors generally find that the reform has been successful in a number of areas including resolution of cases and convictions reached in a reasonable period of time as well as an increase in conviction rates under the reformed system. Their analysis provides no controls or regression analysis nor does it compare two regions of the country that are similar. As a result, they do not formally test the effect of the reform.

that these efforts were significant enough to change citizen behavior. Specifically, citizens would report more crimes after the reform because they believe that the government's efforts are sincere not only to reform the criminal justice system, but to make it more accessible, effective, and just to everyday citizens.

Second, I predict that the reform itself has had little impact on arrest trends. Instead, I predict that police focus their arrests on those crimes that are being reported the most and that this trend has gained significance as Chile has moved away from its transition to democracy in the early 1990s. Because the reforms did not significantly change the structure and operation of the police or prisons, the reforms themselves should have little effect on arrests overall. Instead, police are incentivized to arrest individuals for crimes that appear the most prevalent in society. In this way, they enhance their reputation while also pursuing politicians' goals for improving law and order—goals that have increased as Chile has moved away in time from its transition to democracy. Although the police have incentives to make arrests in the highest demand areas, police are constrained by their knowledge that Chile's prisons are exceeding capacity.[9] Criminal reports and arrests are analyzed

---

9    For the regression analysis on crime reports, the data was compiled from several sources. The data dealing with a change in citizen crime reports to the police for the years 1997, 1999, and 2001 to 2007 came from the Instituto Nacional de Estadísticos (INE's) *Policía de Investigaciones: Informe Annual*. All the data regarding citizen reporting is measured by region, rather than nationally. The main control variable is whether the reform occurred or not in a specific region. This variable was created by reading the applicable criminal law and amendments to determine when reform was instituted in each region. If reform was implemented for only a fraction of the year, the reform variable reflected this. The regression also included a control for population. The regression testing the effect of reform on criminal reports also includes three interaction variables. The first interaction variable measures how the reform affected areas that are particularly urban (Santiago and Valparaiso). The second interaction is between the reform and whether it occurred in the region containing Chile's second largest city, Valparaiso. The third interaction term measures the effect of the reform in regions that had a population that was at least 10 percent indigenous determined using Chile's 2002 census results found in the INE's *Síntesis de Census 2002*. The interactions test whether there is a significant difference in how the reform performs in certain areas of the country. Binary variables for the regions and the years analyzed also were inserted. The regression equation is: $\text{Log(Citizen reports of crime)}_{it} = \beta_0 + \beta_1 Reform_{it} + \beta_2 \log(\text{popestimate}) + \beta_3 Reform*Urban + \beta_4 \text{Reform}* \text{Valparaiso} + \beta_5 \text{Reform}*\text{Indigenous} + \lambda \text{year dummies} + \delta \text{regional } dummies + \alpha_i + v_{it}$

While this regression analysis, testing the effect of the reforms on criminal reports, provides some indication of the reform's impact, a few concerns should be analyzed. First, endogeneity or reverse causality should be considered. While the hypothesis tested here is based on a theory that converting a legal system from a European Civil Law model to a Western adversarial system drives such things as crime reporting rates, it is possible that instead problems with crime and conviction rates caused the government to reform the system in the most problematic regions first. Based on research and interviews, the regions do not appear to be chosen due to their high crime rates, but rather due to the efforts of individuals in certain regions who petitioned the government for reform to appear in their region first for both the prestige of the reform and to prove its success. Second, as in many studies, omitted variable bias may be a concern. By using a fixed effects model and controlling for variations among the 13 regions, omitted variable bias should be minimized. Third, another challenge to this study is the small number of observations. For the quantitative analysis on arrests, I do not use regression analysis or a causal test as there is insufficient data to control for all of the factors that influence the decision to arrest. Rather, I first analyze whether arrests for certain groups of crimes are highly correlated with citizens' reports of these same crimes. High correlations between citizen reports and arrests indicate that police may be targeting arrests for the crimes that are most prevalent in society. Conversely, low correlations between arrests and criminal reports may mean that police are not responsive to citizen complaints for certain types of crimes. After analyzing correlations, I then turn to the overall trends of arrests for police for specific types of crimes to determine whether police arrest practices have changed over

for five sets of crimes including: (1) homicide, infanticide, and parricide, (2) rape, (3) drugs, (4) robbery, and (5) theft.

## Results and Implications

The results confirm the first prediction regarding criminal reports made by citizens. The reform increased the number of such reports by 8 percent.[10] None of the interaction variables involving location resulted in statistically significant coefficients. Therefore, the reform had a positive effect on citizens' reporting of crimes and the geographic location (implementation was staged by region) where the reform occurred did not influence its effect. Despite the perception that citizens fear crime, the reform seems to have improved citizens' trust in legal institutions such that they are reporting more crimes to law enforcement.

Further, the results partially confirm the predictions that law enforcement arrest trends have changed over time and seem to mirror the prevalence of crime in society. As shown in Table 18.1, reports for drug crimes, robbery, and theft are highly correlated (i.e., greater than 0.84) with arrests for these same crimes as predicted. In other words, as crime reports for certain crimes have increased, the police have responded in kind by arresting more individuals for these crimes. Furthermore, these categories of crimes are some of the most prevalent in society and their prevalence has increased since Chile's transition to democracy.

**Table 18.1 Correlation coefficients between crime reports and arrests**

| Reports | Arrests | | | | |
|---|---|---|---|---|---|
| | Drugs | Robbery | Theft | Homicide etc. | Rapes |
| Drugs | 0.86 | | | | |
| Robbery | | 0.84 | | | |
| Theft | | | 0.98 | | |
| Homicides | | | | 0.39 | |
| Rapes | | | | | -0.65 |

---

time. The data for this analysis was compiled using the *Fundación Paz Ciudadana's Anuario Estadísticas Criminales 2008*. This publication is based on information from Chile's *carabineros* or police.

10   The regression results are as follows:

$$\text{Log (Citizen reports of crime)}_{it} = \beta_0 + \beta_1 Reform_{it} + \beta_2 \log(\text{popestimate}) + \beta_3 Reform*Urban +$$
$$-9.52 \quad \textbf{0.08**} \quad 2.54 \quad -0.01$$
$$(8.94) \quad (0.02) \quad (1.59) \quad (0.05)$$
$$\beta_4 Reform* Valparaiso + \beta_5 Reform*Indigenous + \lambda \text{year dummies} + \delta \text{regional } dummies + \alpha_i + v_{it}$$
$$-0.06 \quad -0.02$$
$$(0.04) \quad (0.04)$$

**p<0.01. N=104; R–squared = 0.99.

The coefficients (and standard errors in the parentheses) are listed under the variables in the above regression. The bold face coefficient for reform is statistically significant which in this case means that we can reject the null hypothesis that the reform had no effect.

Although drugs, theft, and robbery showed high correlations, crime reports and arrests for homicide were weakly correlated (i.e., 0.39). This means that reports for homicides, infanticides, and parricides are not strongly associated with the arrests for these same crimes. Although this may appear a negative result to some, the number of these kinds of crimes compared to all others in Chilean society is very low. For instance, in 1988, there were 292 reports of these crimes nationwide, while in 2007 there were 299 reports of these same crimes. Similarly, although arrests for homicides, infanticides, and parricides have decreased, the numbers are again quite small ranging from 760 in 1988, to 307 in 2007.

The correlations between crime reports and arrests for rape also ran counter to the prediction. Rape reports were negatively correlated with arrests (i.e., -0.65). In the case of rape, as the number of rape reports has increased, the arrests for this crime have generally decreased. It appears that until 2006, police decreasingly arrested suspects for rape although the reports for these crimes had increased. Further, like homicides, there are very few rape cases in society. The number of rapes nationwide is relatively small ranging from 766 reports in 1988 to 908 reports in 2007 and 748 arrests in 1988 to 127 arrests in 2007.

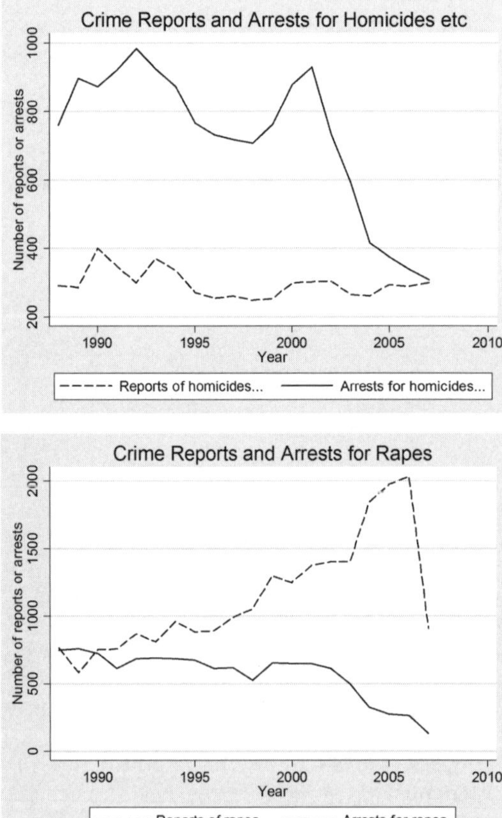

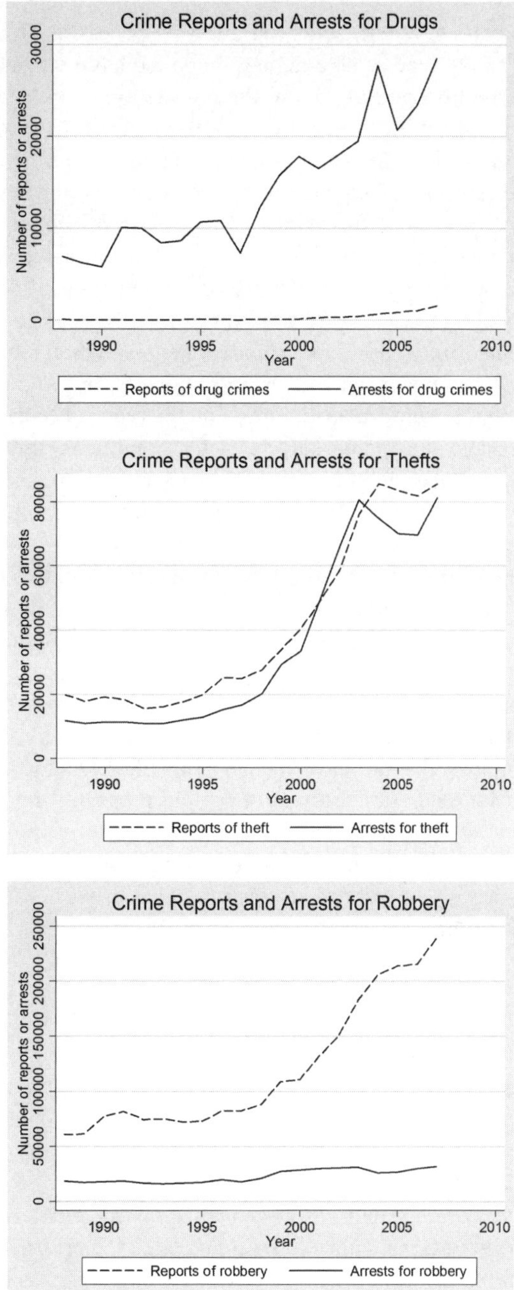


**Figure 18.4 Crime report and arrest trends 1988 to 2007**

Besides analyzing correlation coefficients, an analysis of arrests from 1988 to 2007 shows several interesting trends in the type of arrests that the police have pursued over time (see Figure 18.4). Similar to the information revealed from the correlations, arrests for drugs, robbery, and theft have all increased at a steep rate since the mid-1990s. Arrests for robberies have increased only slightly in comparison to the number of reports. Counter to this, arrests for homicides have generally decreased since the mid-1990s although there was a slight upsurge in the early years of the twenty-first century. The trend for reports of rapes has been more complicated revealing an increase in reports for rape until about 2006 when such reports decreased dramatically. This increase in reporting occurred concurrently with a decrease in arrests of defendants for rape.

In general, the data for these five categories of crimes reveals that police have increased arrests in response to an increase in crime reports for drugs, robbery, and theft since the mid-1990s. These crimes are some of the most prevalent in society and police seem to be responding to a law and order agenda by placing their law enforcement efforts on the types of crimes that warrant attention. In opposition, the police have not increased arrests for homicides, infanticides, and parricides over time, and these crimes, although some of the most serious, are some of the least prevalent in Chilean society. Only in the area of rape have reports increased while arrests for rape have decreased.

Interestingly, the crimes for which arrests have increased are those that tend not to require pre-trial detention under the new reform. As discussed above, pre-trial detention allows judges to hold defendants who have committed violent crimes or pose a serious threat to themselves or society. Unless involving violence or implicating large amounts of money, the majority of crimes for drugs and theft do not implicate the use of pre-trial or other detention. In comparison, homicides, infanticides, parricides, and rape all involve violence and thus detention at some stage in the proceeding. This suggests that police also have targeted arrests for a large quantity of crimes that did not involve pre-trial detention and would not put pressure on Chile's overcrowded and unreformed prison system. Future research on the effects of the reform on arrests might focus on the opinions of police about how the reform and overcrowded prisons affect their decisions to arrest. If police "under arrest" in response to overcrowded prisons, that implies limits on their responsiveness to public opinion.


## Conclusion

Chile's criminal law reforms were part of the ruling elites' attempts to modernize their legal system and make it consistent with the standards employed in well-established democracies. As seen from the recommendations by the Rettig Report as well as comments from politicians and scholars, criminal law reforms were seen as a way to acknowledge the abuses of the military regime, while providing a more effective legal system ensconced in rights for citizens acknowledged in most democracies. Although politicians may have initially intended the reform to rectify Chile's human rights record, as time progressed from the transition in 1990, politicians became more concerned with law and order similar to politicians in long-standing democracies. In other words, as Chilean society moved from its transition in 1990 to the present, concern about the media and citizens' perceptions about law and order affected politicians' decisions to implement further reforms based more on an agenda of security than human rights.

Although the implications of the reform cannot yet be discerned in full due to the fact that the reform has only been implemented in the entire nation since mid-2005, several lessons can still be learned from Chile's reform process. First, reforms take time and often do not have an immediate or large effect on behavior and actions. So social engineering via law is hardly instantaneous in any case. The reforms encompassed in Chile's own criminal law reform were sweeping and involved the creation of new institutions, the redistribution of power among judges, police, and the new institutions, and an entirely new view of how criminal law operates in a society. While Chile became democratic again in 1990, citizen distrust and fear from the authoritarian era could not easily be dismissed. Further, any analysis of the reform should be based on an understanding that although the reform was initially motivated by human rights concerns, it soon was informed by concerns of citizen fear and law and order. Because of this trajectory, criminal justice system reform in the transitional justice setting should be viewed as a long-term process, the success of which can only be measured after many years (so initial enactment of "due process" measures does not end matters).

Second, reform should be envisioned as something that is not inflicted by the government on its citizenry with the expectation of immediate results. Instead, policy-makers and citizens alike should realize that reform takes time and that policy-makers are unable to anticipate all of a reform's effects. Therefore, policy-makers should be sensitive to concerns from citizens and respond to them when appropriate (the push–pull effect). It appears that the Chilean government was quite sensitive to citizen concerns over security issues when it changed its original reforms. A balance, however, must be found between reacting quickly to citizen concerns and allowing time for the reform to work. Hyperbolic political statements may raise citizens' concerns about public safety. The fact that additional reforms seem to have been made without solid empirical evidence of their need is troublesome (indicating potential manipulation of public opinion). Chilean politicians should be careful not to use criminal justice policy as a tool for re-election as their counterparts in other modern democracies may do. On the other hand, as seen from the analysis of public opinion surveys by the government and various non-governmental organizations, citizens' fear has remained stable and decreased in some instances. Further, the empirical evidence suggests citizens are reporting more crimes, which also signals an increase in trust in legal institutions.

A third lesson that can be drawn from Chile's reform experience is that reform may have unintended consequences if not all institutions involved in the criminal justice process are reformed at or near the same time. For example, the reform in Chile involved the judiciary and office of the public prosecutor and defender. Despite these dramatic reforms, concurrent reforms of the police and the prisons were not instituted. Criminal law reforms in Latin America "often contain their own inconsistencies and contradictions" (Hammergren 2007) and at least in Latin America, reform has focused primarily on judges and courts and less on investigation and police. Issues of prison overcrowding and the effectiveness of the police are coming to the forefront as cases are being processed in the court system more efficiently and more quickly. Chile's government should be careful that institutions that have not been reformed, such as the police and the prisons, do not stymie the success of the reform. The failure to reform police may further fuel citizens' fears of crime and lack of trust in institutions related to criminal justice. While the new criminal law system may lead to more apprehensions in the long run, police need separate motivations to be effective and efficient. Furthermore, the size and condition of prisons have not been increased or improved. As seen in other countries, even the most well intended reform will be unsuccessful if the prisons cannot sustain their populations in a humane manner. Although the police and prison overcrowding are issues that the government must face, it seems to have acknowledged them in some reforms it made to police processes in 2008 and its new initiative in 2009 to deal with prison overcrowding. This points to the very complicated institutional interplay within any modern legal system, which may impose practical limits on social engineering via law in terms of our "chicken and egg question."

This analysis of Chile's criminal law reform provides an example of an attempt to revamp a (middle-income, industrialized) country's legal system, such that it changes the behavior of officials and citizens in a broader sense while transitioning to democracy. It is unrealistic to expect that reform can instantly change behavior, especially in a country where the criminal law system had not been changed significantly in over 100 years. Further, as Chile has distanced itself from its transition of 1990, the intention behind criminal justice system reforms has shifted from one based on concerns for human rights to one more focused on law and order. Despite such a shift, policy-makers remain cognizant of the fears and concerns of citizens (even if exaggerated by the media) when it comes to issues of personal security. A continuous dialogue between officials and citizens as well as the understanding that additional changes based on empirical evidence may be necessary to ensure that reform is legitimated in society's eyes.

## References


Adimark and Fundación Paz Ciudadana. 2003, 2004, 2008. Indice Paz Ciudadana-Adimark. Santiago, Chile. Available at: www.pazciudadana.cl.

Biblioteca del Congreso Nacional de Chile. 2002. Historia de Ley No. 19.789. Santiago.

Biblioteca del Congreso Nacional de Chile. 2005. Historia de Ley No. 20.074. Santiago.

Biblioteca del Congreso Nacional de Chile. 2008. Historia de Ley No. 20.253. Santiago.

Bohm, R. 1982. Radical Criminology: An Explication. *Criminology*, 19(4), 565–89.

Brunetti, A., Kisunko, G. and Weder, B. 1997. Credibility of Rules and Economic Growth. *Policy Research Working Paper 1760*. Washington, DC: The World Bank.

Carocca A., Duce M., Riego C., Baytelman A. and Vargas J. 2000. *Nuevo Proceso Penal*. Santiago: Editorial Jurídica Conosur Ltda.

Correa Sutil, J. 1993. The Judiciary and the Political System in Chile: The Dilemmas of Judicial Independence during the Transition to Democracy, in *Transition to Democracy in Latin America: The Role of the Judiciary*, edited by I. Stotsky. Boulder: Westview, 89–103.

Duce, M. and Riego, C. 2009. La Prisión Preventiva en Chile: El Impacto de la Reforma Procesal Penal y de sus Cambios Posteriores. La Facultad de Derecho de la Universidad Diego Portales, Santiago, Chile.

Duce, M., González, F., Jiménez, M., Riego, C., and Vargas, J. 1998. *La Reforma de la Justicia Penal: Cuadernos de Análisis Jurídico, no. 38*. Santiago: Escuela de Derecho, Universidad Diego Portales.

Durkheim E. 1947. *The Division of Labor in Society*. Translated by George Simpson. New York: Free Press.

Elias, N. 1978. *The Civilising Process 2 vols*. Translated by Edmund Jephcott. New York: Urizen Books.

El Mercurio. 2001a. Aprueban el Nuevo Cronograma de la Reforma Procesal Penal, August 15.

El Mercurio. 2001b. Postergación de reforma. August 15.

Hammergren, L. 2007. *Envisioning Reform: Improving Judicial Performance in Latin America*. University Park: The Pennsylvania State University Press.

Hilbink, L. 2007. *Judges Beyond Politics in Democracy and Dictatorship*. Cambridge: Cambridge University Press.

Humphrey, M. and Valverde, E. 2008. Human Rights Politics and Injustice: Transitional Justice in Argentina and South Africa. *The International Journal of Transitional Justice*, 2(1), 83–105.

Instituto Nacional de Estadísticas. 1997–2006. *Carabinerios: Informe Anual*. Santiago.

Instituto Nacional de Estadísticas. 1997–2006. *Policía de Investigaciones: Informe Anual*. Santiago.

Instituto Nacional de Estadísticas. 2002. *Síntesis de Census*. Santiago.

LaFree, G. and Tseloni, A. 2006. Democracy and Crime: A Multilevel Analysis of Homicide Trends in Forty-four Countries, 1950–2000. *Annals of the American Academy of Political and Social Science*, 605, 26–49.

Langer, M. 2007. Revolution in Latin American Criminal Procedure: Diffusion of Legal Ideas from the Periphery. *The American Journal of Comparative Law*, 55(4), 617–76.

Ley No. 19.519. Reforma Constitucional que crea el Ministerio Público. *Diario Oficial*, September 16, 1997.

Ley No. 19.640. Establece la Ley Orgánica Constitucional del Ministerio Público. *Diario Oficial*, October 15, 1999.

Ley No. 19.665. Reforma del Código Orgánico de Tribunales. *Diario Oficial*, March 9, 2000.

Ley No. 19.696. Código Procesal Penal. *Diario Oficial*, October 12, 2000.

Ley No. 19.708. Adecua la Ley No. 19.665, que modifica el Código Orgánico de Tribunales, al Nuevo Código Procesal Penal. *Diario Oficial*, January 5, 2001.

Ley No. 19.718. Crea la Defensoría Penal Pública. *Diario Oficial*, March 10, 2001.

Ley No. 19.762. Cambia Gradualidad de la Entrada en Vigencia de la Reforma Penal. *Diario Oficial*, October 13, 2001.

Ley No. 19.789. Introduce Modificaciones al Código Procesal Penal. *Diario Oficial*, January 30, 2002.

Ley No. 20.074. Modifica los Códigos Procesal Penal y Penal. *Diario Oficial*, November 14, 2005.

Ley No. 20.253. Modifica el Código Penal y el Código Procesal Penal en Materia de Seguridad Ciudadana y Refuerza las Atribuciones Preventiva de las Policías. *Diario Oficial*, January 30, 2008.

McGuire, M. Olson, M. Mancur, Jr. 1996. The Economics of Autocracy and Majority Rule: The Invisible Hand and Use of Force. *Journal of Economic Literature*, March, 72–96.

Marangunic, A. and Foglesong, T. 2004. *Charting Justice Reform in Chile: A Comparison of the Old and New System of Criminal Procedure*. New York: Vera Institute.

Mayhew, D. 1974. *Congress: The Electoral Connection*. New Haven: Yale University Press.

Mensaje de SE de Presidente de la República con el que Inicia un Proyecto de Ley que Establece un Nuevo Código de Procedimiento Penal. Available at: www.ksg.harvard.edu/criminal justice.

*Ministerio de Justicia de Chile*. 2008. La Reforma Procesal Penal, Inversión. Available at: www. minimusticia.cl/rpp/inversion.php [accessed July 28, 2008].

Oesterberg, E. 1992. Criminality, Social Control, and the Early Modern State: Evidence and Interpretations in Scandinavian Historiography. *Social Science History*, 16(1), 67–98.

Olson, M. 1993. Dictatorship, Democracy, and Development. *American Political Science Review*, 87(3), 567–76.

Oppenheim, L. 2007. *Politics in Chile: Socialism, Authoritarianism, and Market Democracy*. Boulder: Westview.

Packer, H. 1968. *Limits of the Criminal Sanctions*. Stanford: Stanford University Press.

Pfeiffer, M. and Vergara, P. 2001. Dura Polémica entre Fiscal Nacional y Defensor Público. *La Tercera*, September 8.

Piedrabuena, R. 2000. *Introducción a la Reforma Procesal Penal*. Santiago: Editorial Fallos del Mes Ltda.

*Report of the Chilean National Commission on Truth and Reconciliation*. 1991. Santiago: Ministerio de Secretaria General de Gobierno de Chile.

Riego, C. 2006. Introducción de Procedimientos Orales en Chile, in *Judicial Reform in Latin America: An Assessment*, Policy Papers on the Americas, Vol. XVII, Study 2. Washington, DC: Center for Strategic and International Studies.

Siavelis, P. 2000. *The President and Congress in Postauthoritarian Chile, Institutional Constraints to Democratic Consolidation*. University Park: Pennsylvania State University Press.

Sung, H. 2006. Democracy and Criminal Justice in Cross-National Perspective from Crime Control to Due Process. *Annals of the American Academy of Political and Social Science*, 605, 311–37.

Taylor, I., Walton, P., and Young, J. 1973. *The New Criminology*. London: Routledge and Kegan Paul.

Tiede, L. 2012. Chile's Criminal Law Reform: Enhancing Defendants' Rights, and Citizen Security. *Latin American Politics and Society*, forthcoming.

Venegas, V. and Vial, L. 2008. *Boomerang: Seeking to Reform Pretrial Detention Practices in Chile*. New York: Open Society Institute, 44–56.

Weber, M. 1978. *Economy and Society: An Outline of Interpretive Sociology*. Edited by G. Roth and C. Wittich. Berkeley: University of California Press.

Weingast, B. 1997. The Political Foundations of Democracy and the Rule of Law. *American Political Science Review*, 91(2), 245–63.

Weingast, B. 2003. A Postscript to Political Foundations of Democracy and the Rule of Law, in *Democracy and the Rule of Law*, edited by J. Maravall and A. Przeworski. Cambridge: Cambridge University Press, 109–14.

# PART VI
## Russia and the State: A Window on Modernization

Chapter 19

# Modernization and Legal Reform:<br>The Dilemma of the State in Russia

Gordon B. Smith

Russia has struggled to implement meaningful legal reforms from the early days of glasnost and perestroika more than two decades ago. The collapse of the Soviet Union (USSR) occurred as a culmination of the long-sought desire by many of Russia's educated population to jettison a bankrupt ideology and join the democratic West. They dreamed of Russia as a "civilized" society that would function "normally" with competitive elections, a free press, provision of social and political guarantees to its citizens, and above all rule *of* law, as opposed to rule *by* law. Rather than rule of law, democracy and an efficient market economy, however, what they experienced in the first decade following the collapse of the USSR were social and political chaos, the rapacious plunder of the prime assets of the former Soviet economy, crony capitalism, hyperinflation, massive unemployment, and a breakdown in the ability of the government to provide basic services.

Many jurists played a prominent role in advocating fundamental legal reforms prior to and following the collapse. But other jurists, often those employed in powerful law enforcement agencies such as the Procuracy, the Ministry of Internal Affairs, and the KGB, resisted the reform efforts by both overt and covert methods. The dilemma confronting Russia in the early 1990s was a familiar one—a struggle between the values of those favoring an independent legal system characterized by supremacy of law, transparent processes, judicial independence, and equality before the law, on the one hand, and those who saw law as a powerful instrument of the state supporting the state's efforts to implement a plan of modernization and social engineering, on the other hand. This duality has deep roots in Russian society and history.

The reforms of 1864 under Tsar Alexander II introduced a long list of modernizing measures largely modeled on Germany's legal system, making the Russian legal system among the most progressive in Europe, at least on paper. But the economic and political dislocations of the late nineteenth century, compounded by the repressive leadership of Alexander III, the increasingly radicalized opposition, World War I, and the revolutions of 1917, snuffed out modernizing reforms in favor of a new revolutionary and utopian concept of legality.

The fledgling Bolshevik state proclaimed a radical new vision for society: building the world's first socialist state that would free the creative and intellectual energy of the intelligentsia as well as the proletariat. So much as Veronica Taylor's chapter (Chapter 13) notes that Japan was the first successfully "modernized" Asian developing country reaching back to the nineteenth century, the USSR itself as socialist state was an early twentieth-century experiment in modernization and radical social engineering in the European context (recalling also Japan's original coming out exercise was the 1905 Russo-Japanese War, in which it defeated Russia as European power). This experiment with radical "modernization" was not without its successes. Paralleling Peter Haas' discussion of Western Europe, Jews and people of other ethnic groups, as well as women, enjoyed unprecedented opportunities to be involved in the great (social)ist experiment. Artists and writers, architects and poets took advantage of the short-lived abolition of artistic censorship to produce works of avant-garde abstraction, and also works attempting to reach and inspire Russia's rapidly increasing urban working class.

The Marxist vision predicted that with the abolition of classes under communism there would be no further need of law and law enforcement bodies, since there would no longer be a ruling class needing the law to suppress or coerce other classes. In time law and the state would wither away altogether. The Bolsheviks, led by Lenin, held a much more pragmatic and cynical view that law was a powerful tool in the hands of the Bolshevik state. In his political pamphlet, "State and Revolution," Lenin outlined the fundamental principles of revolutionary justice: smash the old state machine, set up new revolutionary tribunals; make these tribunals simple, informal and open to mass participation; subordinate the law to revolutionary goals of the Party (for all law has a class character; if it does not serve the Bolsheviks' purposes, it will be serving the purposes of counter-revolutionary elements); and use merciless force toward the eventual goal of reaching a society in which there will be no need for coercion (Lenin 1958–65).

Thus, in the early days of the Soviet regime there coexisted two countervailing trends in Soviet law: the Marxist, utopian trend, which stressed both the withering away of the state and the creation of popular, informal tribunals to administer revolutionary justice, and the dictatorial trend, which advocated the use of law and legal institutions to suppress all opposition, however brutally, and justified this approach by promising to build a modern communist society.

Stalin's consolidation of power and his schemes for the economic modernization of the country rejected earlier utopian approaches. He built on the Leninist foundations of "revolutionary justice" to harness the power of the state and law enforcement agencies in furthering his vision of building the mighty Soviet socialist empire. Despite the well-documented crimes of the Stalin era, Stalin was responsible for many remarkable achievements. The USSR rapidly expanded production of steel, heavy industrial equipment, chemicals, and armaments between 1927 and 1939. It is unlikely that the Soviet Union would have survived Nazi Germany's assault had it not been for Stalin's program of forced industrialization, mass mobilization of society, and restructuring of the Soviet government. It is often said that Stalin inherited a country of the wooden plow and left it with nuclear weapons. Even the disastrous program of collectivization of agriculture had the effect of driving able-bodied young men and women from the countryside to become the new urban blue-collar working class, Stalin's much-proclaimed "New Soviet Man."

The USSR underwent a kind of coincidental accelerated urbanization as perhaps the single most prominent twentieth-century effort to "modernize" rural areas (as collateral effect of collectivization; given Liu Dongyin's reflections on Chinese views, with the possible exception of the People's Republic of China). Looking to the rural–urban migration question, it might be viewed equally as accelerated termination of what was by Western standards still a traditional society (the rural peasantry of Tsarist Russia). Massive investments were made in education and health care under Stalin in recognition that these policy areas were vital to sustaining the Soviet Union's new urban industrial workforce, again part of USSR modernization plans.

Stalin was also the chief architect of the massive hyper-centralized state bureaucracy. Gone were the utopian references to the withering away of the state. In their place was a campaign of glorification of the state and Stalin. Under his leadership ministries and state commissions, such as GOSPLAN, the State Planning Agency, which coordinated all economic planning, flourished, and the ranks of state officials swelled. These same ministries and state committees would not only outlive Stalin, most of them remain in place today, even after the collapse of the USSR. Moreover, they continue to exhibit a culture of protecting their bureaucratic interests and resist reforms that would encroach on them.

The waxing and waning of support for legal reform in Russia illustrates the fundamental struggle between two models or sets of values. On the one hand, are those who wish to see law as autonomous, supreme, and binding on the state and state officials. Law in this perspective serves to protect the rights of individuals vis-à-vis the state; thus, it represents a diminishing of the power of the state. On the other hand, strong sentiments exist within Russian society, including among jurists in powerful law enforcement agencies, and among some political leaders, that law remains a vital tool in the state-orchestrated plan for the modernization of Russia (a stress on "policy" rather than law, not terribly unusual in the development context). These generally oppose any change that would weaken the state and threaten the dominance of their powerful bureaucratic interests. And so bureaucratic resistance to reforms may, in the alternative, represent the influence of petty corruption (as described in Chapter 21), or institutionalized resistance perhaps based upon ideology (as described in Chapter 20).

The ghosts of this history still haunt Russian society and some reformist jurists. They remember the brief period after Stalin's death when Nikita Khrushchev permitted an opening for legal reforms. New criminal and civil codes were enacted, as well as codes of criminal and civil procedure. Extraordinary tribunals were abolished and attempts were made to rein in the powerful NKVD. A new Constitution that included a presumption of innocence was under discussion. However, Khrushchev was removed in disgrace before more substantive reforms could be realized.

The Gorbachev modernization reforms harkened back, however briefly, to the Khrushchev era. Gorbachev came to head the USSR as a moderate reformer, a law school graduate who wanted to engage a public rapidly losing faith in the fundamental goals of the society, after 18 years of the stodgy, bureaucratic, and conservative leadership of Brezhnev and his two short-lived successors. A wave of enthusiasm, even euphoria, swept over Russian society toward the end of the 1980s. Many Soviet lawyers expressed the hope that at last Russia was on the path to joining Western "civilized nations." One Russian jurist even predicted that the country would be "like Finland within the span of just seven to ten years." When faced with surprise and skepticism, he revised his estimate and said, "[w]ell, then at least like Ireland or Portugal!"[1]

That Russia's inflated hopes have only been partially realized over the past two decades of wrenching economic, political, and social change has resulted in widespread cynicism among the public. The Yeltsin years are seen not as a flourishing of multiple political parties, constitutional reforms, privatization of the economy, a largely unfettered press, freedom to travel abroad, and acceptance into the G-8. Rather Yeltsin is viewed as an out-of-touch leader whose policies led to the collapse of the state, hyperinflation, massive unemployment, weakening of the military, rampant crime and corruption, and friends and insiders who became billionaires overnight. The hands-off approach of the Yeltsin Administration empowered provincial governors and mayors to assert unprecedented independence resulting in corruption, rent seeking, a breakdown in public services, and passage of thousands of laws and regulations contradicting the Constitution and federal laws.

One can view the entire sweep of events from Gorbachev's glasnost and perestroika to the collapse of the USSR and the ensuing failure of many of Russia's government institutions, economic collapse, the rise of the Mafia, the inability of the state to garner taxes or provide for basic services including protecting the safety of citizens on the streets, the health, education and

---

1   From my personal conversation with a Russian legal scholar, Institute of State and Law, Moscow, 1988.

public order as a massive loss of state capacity.[2] By the end of the Yeltsin presidency, the Russian government was largely unable to perform the functions that citizens expect governments to do.

The public mood by the mid-1990s was one of exhaustion. People proclaimed that they were tired of being guinea pigs in one social experiment of modernization after another. They wanted stability and a return to normalcy. The most pressing priority confronting the new Putin Administration in 2000 was to reassert the power of the state and restore its ability to meet the public's expectations. In his address upon assuming office on December 31, 1999, Putin observed: "For Russians a strong state is not an anomaly which should be got rid of. Quite the contrary, we see it as a source and guarantor of order and the initiator and main driving force of any change."

Vladimir Putin entered the scene in 1999 as a largely unknown career law enforcement official, determined to stabilize Russia, to recentralize state administration, restore order and predictability in government, renationalize prime sectors of the economy that had been fraudulently handed to Yeltsin's inner circle, revitalize Russia's lagging economy, and renew a pride in Russia as a powerful nation with an honorable history and culture. In eight years, Putin largely succeeded in these ambitious endeavors and left office with an unheard of degree of popularity, over 70 percent approval ratings.

Thus, the post-communist transition in Russia represents a sweeping redefinition of the proper scope of the state's activity. As the state has withdrawn from vast areas of social, economic, and political life, so too have we witnessed an erosion of the power of the state and a lack of consensus about what the proper boundaries of state activity should be in the new Russia. Jurists have struggled to reform Russia's legal system in the midst of these volatile swings in Russian society and fundamental clash of competing value systems. Collectively, Chapters 20–22 illustrate that much work remains to be done even while much progress has been realized in drafting new laws, modernizing and streamlining regulations, standardizing laws across Russia's many regions, and bringing more openness and predictability to the judicial system. This is especially true in insuring enforcement of judicial decisions and in overcoming the insidious resistance and foot-dragging among bureaucrats, who view legal reforms as a threat to their interests and to the power of the state. While a separate description of regional (European) international human rights law, Angelika Nussberger's description of the collision between the European Human Rights Convention and Russia's *nadzor* system reflects the same tensions (much as does Michael Kubiciel's chapter touching on anti-corruption efforts in Eastern Europe under treaty law).

The recurring theme in each of this part's chapters is Russia's struggle to resolve the dilemma of state power. There is evidence of efforts to undertake meaningful legal reforms that would empower the courts as independent entities and citizens as possessors of rights. Yet we also see a state unable to enforce its own laws and court decisions, whether due to weakened capacity or to a culture of resistance, subversion, and sabotage. We also still find political leaders unwilling to relinquish control over legal institutions, because they still harbor hopes of mobilizing the powers of a strong state to socially engineer yet another modernization scheme for Russia. It remains an open question whether Russia can forge a conception of the state that is both strong and effective, yet able to grant independent powers to the courts and enforceable rights to its citizens; a state that grants to regional and local authorities appropriate powers under the Constitution and holds officials at all levels accountable for being responsive to the public.

---

2   State capacity has been prominently featured in the literature of comparative politics beginning with Gabriel Almond and Bingham Powell in the 1960s and more recently in the works of Charles Tilly, Theda Skocpol, Joel Migdal, and Stephen Krasner, to name a few. For a discussion of state-building in Russia, see: Smith (1999: 3–16).

Taking the long view, Russia has its own history of successive attempts at "modernization." Peter the Great is known for his eighteenth-century efforts to bring Russia into Europe, which were followed in the nineteenth century by Alexander II's 1864 reforms targeting much the same purpose, which were followed by early twentieth-century efforts under socialism to create a "new" kind of human being, and, finally, ongoing post-glasnost and perestroika, law reform efforts. What is striking in terms of the "chicken or egg" question is the pattern of repeated efforts. In Russia, there seems to be currently a certain skepticism, if not outright fatigue, surrounding efforts to use law for purposes of social engineering. There is now readiness for experimentation and fondness for "international standards" in the legal setting, but little eagerness in the short term again to embrace "big bang" or social engineering exercises. The serial attempts carry their own judgment in Russians' eyes.

## References

Lenin, V.I. 1958–65. *Polnoe sobranie sochinenii*. 4th edition, vol. XXXVI. Moscow: Politizdat.
Putin, Vladimir. 1999. Russia at the Turn of the Millennium. In *Vital Speeches of the Day* 66/8. New York: City News Pub. Co. Available at: http://pravitelstvo.gov.ru.
Smith, Gordon B. 1999. *State-Building in Russia: The Yeltsin Legacy and the Challenge of the Future*. Armonk: M.E. Sharpe.

# Chapter 20

# Can Weak States Have Strong Courts?
# Evidence from Post-Communist Russia

Alexei Trochev

Law and development scholars increasingly turn their attention to the role the state-building processes play in making or breaking the legal order in post-authoritarian societies. Drawing on the experience of post-communist Russia this chapter argues that without a capable state, there is little that the enforcement of law can do to transform lives of ordinary citizens. Busy courts and impartial judges can accomplish little if successful litigants face the rest of the government apparatus that has neither willingness nor capacity (or both) to carry out judicial decisions.

Judicial empowerment crucially depends on the extent to which the government bureaucracy is "friendly" to court decisions. Nonetheless, we know very little about what actually happens after the court has issued a decision that requires action on the part of the government officials, be it returning overpaid taxes, issuing a license or transferring property. The core argument of this chapter is that post-communist bureaucracies are not court-friendly. They lack the capacity to implement unfavorable judicial decisions (court cases that the government lost). This lack of bureaucratic capacity to obey judicial decisions stems from both the Soviet past, in which judiciaries did not figure highly in the power map of socialist governance, and from the post-Soviet experience, in which courts failed to gain real authority due to the mix of three factors: the unwillingness of the rulers to share power, bureaucratic sabotage, and the public disaffection with courts. Non-compliance of governmental officials at all levels with judicial decisions partially explains the paradox of waning public trust in post-Soviet courts.

- In Georgia, after the Rose Revolution of November 2002, in which month-long peaceful protests over rigged parliamentary elections forced President Shevardnadze to resign, public trust in courts declined from 50 percent in 2004 to 21 percent in 2007 and rose to 54 percent in 2011 (International Republican Institute 2004, 2007, 2012). Although, according to official court statistics, the government lost half of non-criminal court cases in 2008, many of these court victories remained largely unenforced.[1]
- In Ukraine, after the Orange Revolution of November–December 2004, in which peaceful protests against fraudulent presidential elections led to the victory of the opposition candidate, public trust in the judiciary fell from 21 percent in February 2005 to 3 percent in 2011 (Razumkov Centre 2011). Yet the litigation rates are growing, and government

---

1   The Human Rights Information and Documenation Centre (2007: 25) reported that only 4 percent of court decisions were enforced by government agencies in 2006. Official statistics of the Justice Ministry show that, in 2008, bailiffs were mainly busy with enforcing court-ordered monetary compensation issued in favor of private entities between 2004 and 2007. In mid-2011, the National Enforcement Bureau had some 80,000 judicial decisions due for enforcement yet it enforced 25,500 decisions, about a 30 percent enforcement rate (Statistics of National Bureau of Enforcement 2011).

    loses 87 percent of court cases, in which it is named as defendant. But these court victories against the government remain on paper in 60 percent of cases (Onishchuk 2008).

- In Russia, in 1995, about a half of Russians reported they trusted courts (Colton 2000), by 2002, only 3–5 percent of surveyed said they trusted courts (RTR-Vesti 2002; FOM 2002). During the same period, however, all Russian courts experienced an explosion in litigation rates. Moreover, the chances of successfully suing the state were growing and reached some 70 percent by 2003 (Solomon 2004). At the same time half of judicial decisions are enforced while "creditors typically receive only 20 percent of what they are owed" (Orttung 2009). Meanwhile, thousands of ordinary people complain about Russia's chronic inability to enforce court decisions to the European Court of Human Rights.[2]

To explain how bureaucratic incapacity hinders judicial empowerment and rights revolutions in post-communist societies, this chapter is divided in four parts. First, I explain the relationship between judicial empowerment, bureaucratic capacity and public perceptions toward courts. Next, I examine the evidence from the public opinion surveys in the past decade to show that Russians increasingly distrust their judiciary yet they hold dear the abstract notions of judicial independence and the rule of law. Then, I discuss the actual judicial behavior to argue that the explosion of litigation rates in Russia and the high chances of successfully suing the state go hand in hand with declining public support for the judiciary. Finally, I explore what happened with these court victories to assess the actual impact of judicial decision-making on Russia's public governance. Exploring how Russians sue their government and demand monetary compensation, I argue that post-communist citizens are cynical about their courts because the state officials often fail to implement court-ordered policies.

## Impact of State Capacity on Public Perception of Courts

Waning trust in stronger courts is a puzzling relationship for students of post-authoritarian transitions, who view the rule of law institutions, like independent courts, as essential elements of the democratic consolidation processes (Linz and Stepan 1996). According to some observers, citizens in post-authoritarian societies, at least those who successfully sue the state in courts, should view the powerful and independent judiciary as a highly legitimate institution of new post-communist regimes. This is because stronger courts are supposed to uphold democratic values, protect individual rights, and serve as a bulwark against the return to the totalitarian past. Some even argue that by subjecting their policy choices to judicial review, post-communist rulers demonstrate their commitment to democracy and the rule of law to their domestic constituencies and to the rest of the world (Thorson 2004). In short, this theory predicts that citizens in countries like Russia should increasingly approve of judicial empowerment in the process of democratic consolidation.

    Facing the Russian reality, "transitology" scholars could argue that Russians increasingly distrust their judiciary because it lacks power, impartiality and independence. By using the YUKOS affair, citing Vladimir Putin's retreat to authoritarianism and referring to numerous Soviet-era legacies of powerless bench, the critics could argue that the Russian judges are not there yet. They

---

2    Former Deputy Chairman of the Russian Supreme Court Viktor Zhuikov complained that "non-enforcement of court decisions today is one of the most acute and dangerous diseases of our government" (Nikitinskii 2006). The Higher *Arbitrazh* Court (2009) reported that in 2008, 40 percent of the *arbitrazh* court decisions were implemented. See Higher Arbitrazh Court of Russia (2009).

lack powers, discretion and authority necessary to champion the rule of law. However, as I will discuss below, Russian judges at the top and the bottom do behave independently, possess a wide degree of discretion and do not hesitate to rule against the state.

Some scholars, who view democracy as simple majority rule, suggest one possible solution to this puzzle. They argue that the review of government actions by non-elected judges is essentially anti-democratic (Sadurski 2003). When the judges strike down government policies as unconstitutional, such judicial decisions run against the will of the majority of citizens, who, in turn, treat such anti-majoritarian judicial behavior with suspicion. Therefore, the more often the courts rule against government, the less likely the voters trust in an unelected judiciary. This approach assumes that post-communist voters hold dear democratic values similar to the citizens in advanced democratic polities.

Historical-culturalist scholars question this assumption. They suggest that post-communist voters, who had little or no experience with democratic rules and procedures during the centuries of autocracy and arbitrariness, simply have distaste for democracy and judicial empowerment. The more these voters experience democratization, the less and less they tend to trust democratic institutions, including strong courts. Indeed, Russian folklore does not have a single proverb that would positively describe judges and courts. Evidence from numerous public opinion surveys, however, shows that the Russians hold in high esteem abstract commitments to judicial independence and the rule of law. The steadily growing litigation rates in the post-communist Russia also show that individuals and NGOs increasingly use courts to try to achieve social change.

I suggest that Russians increasingly distrust their courts because:

- people do not know much about the trends in judicial decision-making and about their chances of successful litigation; and
- the state authorities fail to implement unfavorable court decisions and create a public perception that going to court is a waste of time.

My chapter suggests that the possible answers to the above-mentioned puzzle are incomplete because they assume that post-communist voters easily receive and understand judicial decisions, and that the state automatically implements each and every court decision. I argue that these assumptions may not pertain in the actual dynamics of post-communist governance.

The answer to this paradox of declining trust in stronger courts may lead us to take a serious look at the machinery of governance, namely the state capacity to inform the public about unfavorable judicial decisions and to carry out court-ordered policies. Lacking both the power of the purse and the power of the sword, most courts, be it high constitutional tribunals or local Justices of the Peace, depend upon the cooperation of other government bodies. Patterns of this cooperation or the lack thereof, depend in turn, less on the formal institutional arrangements, which are fragile in nascent post-authoritarian regimes. Rather, the structure of informal sanctions and incentives influences the extent to which bureaucrats are willing and capable of carrying out judicial decisions. The chronic non-implementation (defiance or the lack of capacity to enforce) of court decisions may make voters more cynical about the judicial branch of government.

Just like the rule of law, state capacity is both a buzzword for international development agencies and a "black box" for political scientists. This chapter deals with only one dimension of state capacity, namely with the extent to which the institutions of public governance are "court-friendly." Are public agencies open to judicial intervention? Are bureaucrats prepared to comply with court orders and judge-made rules? Are there real mechanisms of external accountability of government officials? Such "court-friendliness" of public bureaucracies is the capacity of government agencies to respect and implement judicial decisions. This aspect of state capacity is only one element of the Weberian vision of formal-rational law-abiding governance and constitutes a part of what has been called an *infrastructural* power of the state—the capacity to actually penetrate civil society and to implement political decisions throughout the realm (Mann 1988).

Traditionally, political scientists have studied the role of courts in governance by focusing solely on the judgments of top national, and most recently, supra-national courts and their impact on public policies (Hirschl 2004). Scholarly discussions, however, rarely discuss the role of courts in strengthening or weakening of state capacity. A generation ago, Charles Tilly and his colleagues regretted the omission of judicial system from their analysis of state-building in Western Europe. Tilly warned, "it is easy to forget how large a part certain kinds of courts played in the day-to-day construction of Western states" (Tilly 1975). Recently, some scholars include the judicial system in the analysis of governance and state capacity by exploring how these courts created and enforced the rules of the political game in developing countries (Grindle 1996; Hyden et al. 2004).

My vision of court-friendliness of bureaucracies is broader and consists of three interconnected components:

- the capacity to obey policies, as pronounced by the high national courts;
- the ability to be accountable for its activities before the courts; and
- the ability to enforce everyday judgments of local courts in civil and commercial disputes.

Thus, using recent scholarship's elements of state capacity, a court-friendly bureaucracy must possess not only *institutional* capacity to govern under the court-mandated rules, but also *political* capacity to mediate disputes with citizens through the judicial system, and *administrative* capacity to implement mundane judicial decisions on a daily basis. For example, in cases of illegal occupation of land, courts should have the resources to compel other government officials to evict the defendants and remove all illegally built properties on that land, as happened in Mexico (Staton and Vanberg 2008). Moreover, the court-friendliness in cases of administrative justice requires government agencies to do more than penetrate civil society. It requires government departments responsible for the enforcement of court decisions to penetrate other government agencies, which violated individual rights. For example, in cases of illegally issued traffic tickets, court bailiffs must have the resources necessary to force the municipality to pay back the value of the traffic ticket to the driver, who successfully sued the city parking office. This *administrative* capacity (or its absence) to enforce the routine court decisions influences public perceptions about the effectiveness and impartiality of judicial system no less than the landmark judgments of high national courts because this is where ordinary citizens meet face to face with the state apparatus, and where successful litigants see (or fail to see) that their court victories really protected their rights.

Exploring the successes and failures of high and local Russian courts to have their anti-government judgments respected by state agencies is a challenge. Few of these agencies openly defy judicial decisions while many bureaucracies secretly sabotage them.

Judges, litigants, scholars and the general public can rarely access this information. Exploring the structure of informal sanctions and incentives within any organization is a daunting task. However, not all government agencies disobey court decisions. Also, Russian bureaucrats tend to comply with anti-government verdicts in some public policy areas faster and fuller than in others. In this chapter, I investigate how Russian bureaucracy, from top to bottom, responded to judicial decisions which involved financial penalties for the state authorities at the federal, regional and municipal level. I do not explore compliance with court decisions in politically sensitive cases because governmental defiance in such cases rarely depends on the capacity of the state bureaucracy.

If most low-key judgments, which carried financial penalties for the state budget, were enforced and the plaintiffs received compensation through courts, then my thesis that Russians disapprove of their courts because the judiciary is ineffective in protecting their rights, is wrong.

In short, when evaluating the work of courts, ordinary citizens also express their opinions about the court-friendly capacity of the state. But this capacity depends on the degree of cooperation between courts and other government departments, or the extent to which the rest of the executive branch of government is court-friendly. As Timothy Frye (2004) powerfully argues, at "a minimum, reform of the judiciary should proceed hand in hand with the efforts to build the capacity of state police and bureaucracies" (see also Chapter 18, this volume). Russia's failures to build an effective court bailiffs agency and to make the top-level and street-level bureaucrats more court-friendly shows how difficult it is to make the rights revolutions real. To be sure, the chronic incapacity of public officials to carry out court decisions may fuel the growing public skepticism toward judicial performance, a subject to which I turn next.

## Public Distrust in Russian Courts

Just like citizens in other countries, Russians are being increasingly polled on many issues of their lives. What do public opinion surveys tell us about Russian attitudes toward courts? (Satarov et al. 2010). This question is important because evidence from these surveys, however imperfect it is, often serves as the crucial indicator of the state of the judicial system.[3] The Russian judicial system consists of the federal Constitutional Court, commercial (*arbitrazh*) courts in charge of business disputes and business–government disputes, and courts of general jurisdiction handling the rest of the cases. I examine attitudes toward each branch of the judiciary separately because each branch operates differently according to separate procedural codes and dealing with different audiences.

Public opinion surveys reveal that the social demand for independent and powerful courts is present in Russia, even if it is hidden under cynicism about the current state of the judicial system. After all, as I will explain in the next section, every year the Russian courts hear thousands of cases against the government and side with private litigants.[4] Indeed, since the beginning of the 1990s, three-quarters of Russians have believed that a "judicial system that treats everyone equally" is important for democracy, and that the right to judicial protection is a "very important" right (Mikhailovskaia et al. 1997; Millar and Wolchik 1994). Similarly, surveys of normative attitudes of ordinary Russians reveal a consistent respect for the rule of law in the past decade, on a par with other European nations (Gibson 2003). This is why two out of three Russians consistently supported judicial reform as a way to get rid of the corruption of the Soviet-era legal system (Strana.Ru 2001). Surveys also show that Russia's high courts have the potential power to persuade Russians (Baird and Javeline 2007). Moreover, despite the high popularity of President Putin, public opinion polls conducted by the FOM polling center in 2004 and in 2008 show that the same proportion of Russians (40 percent) agreed that "courts while administering justice should be independent from the leadership of the country" as the proportion of those (37 percent) who believed that "courts should be under the control of the leadership of the country" (FOM 2008).

---

3   Due to the lack of reliability of polling data in Russia, recognized by both Western and Russian experts and Russian judges, I provide survey data on public attitudes towards courts from both Western and Russian sources. On the challenges of conducting reliable public opinion research in Russia, see, e.g., Gerber and Mendelson (2003: 187–8) and Konygina (2003).

4   For an insightful analysis of the lack of correlation between the attitudes toward the law and the litigation behavior, see Hendley (2001: 74).

At the same time, over half (56 percent) of those surveyed by the Levada Center in 2007 believed that "the judiciary should be wholly or partly controlled by the executive arm of the Government" (Ordzhonikidze 2007).

## Distrusted Constitutional Court[5]

This abstract support for judicial independence spills over to the Russian Constitutional Court (RCC), a separate constitutional review tribunal that was created shortly prior to the break-up of the USSR at the end of 1991 (Trochev 2008). According to the 1998 survey, excluding those with no opinion, 77 percent of Russians surveyed during Yeltsin's presidency believed that their government should obey the RCC. Similarly, surveys of Russian elites, carried out under both Yeltsin and Putin in 1998 and 2000, show overwhelming support for a strong constitutional review: only 3–4 percent of elites in Moscow and the regions agreed with the statement that "the President shall be able to overrule the Constitutional Court."

This consistent public support for abstract judicial empowerment, however, does not imply that the RCC enjoys stable support in the society. If anything, survey data show the decline of public support for the tribunal. In the mid-1990s, only 22 percent of Russians distrusted the Constitutional Court. At the time, a much larger proportion of both left-wing and right-wing voters distrusted both the president and the Russian parliament. But by the fall of 2000, according to the nationwide Russian Citizen Survey of 1,804 persons, one-half (50.7 percent) of those surveyed reported distrust in the RCC with 8 percent of respondents reporting strong trust in the tribunal. According to the British-based New Russia Barometer, between 2001 and 2003, about 25 percent of Russians trusted the Constitutional Court as compared to 55 percent of respondents who reported no trust in the RCC. According to one survey by the then authoritative All-Russian Center for the Study of Public Opinion (VTsIOM), between February 2001 and September 2002, the RCC, like other Russian courts, received 2.77–2.91 marks on a five-point scale, trailing behind the president, the federal Cabinet, the army, the security services and the law-enforcement agencies (Sedov 2002).[6]

According to the 2003 poll, only 14 percent of the St. Petersburg residents reported that that the RCC "worked well" in 2002–2003. In February 2006, only 20 percent of Russians surveyed by VTsIOM reported that Valerii Zorkin, the Chief Justice of the RCC (who also headed the Court between 1991 and 1993) "worked well." According to the New Russia Barometer, in 2001, 29 percent of surveyed Russians thought that the RCC had a "strong influence" on their lives, while 44 percent thought that it had a "little influence." Russians accorded similar low levels of importance to political parties, the State Duma, police and newspapers, while President Putin, regional governors and magnates were believed to be much more important (Rose 2001). Five years later, the public perception did not change much: one out of three Russians thought the RCC played a big role in the life of the nation, another third believed otherwise, and another third had no opinion. When asked whether they thought the RCC was completely independent, 12 percent of Russians answered positively as compared to 18 percent who thought the opposite. Meanwhile, 28 percent thought that the Court "aspired to act independently but it was not always possible." Note that ordinary Russians increasingly give a failing grade to the RCC albeit they, unlike politicians and high government officials, know very little about the work of this tribunal. In fact, two out of three residents of St. Petersburg, the second largest city in Russia, surveyed in June 2003, reported that

---

5    This section is based on Trochev (2008: 247–52) and sources cited therein.

6    Russian schools use this 5-point scale with 1 (fail) and 5 (excellent), 3 being a passing grade.

they knew nothing about the work of the RCC. By February 2006, the same proportion of Russians reported the same lack of knowledge about the work of the tribunal, and 95 percent of them could not name even a single case decided by the 14-year-old Constitutional Court.


## Distrusted Judicial System

The zigzagging pattern of public trust in Russian courts is even more dramatic. At the end of 1995, 45 percent of Russians said they trusted the courts and 39 percent said they did not (Colton 2000). In 1998, according to the New Russia Barometer, the only institution that surpassed courts in the degree of public trust was the military. Back then, Russians trusted their courts as much as they trusted the church and the people (Mishler and Rose 2001). But by early 2000, half of Russians reported distrust in courts (Petrova 2000). In the fall of 2000, according to the nationwide Russian Citizen Survey, 71.4 percent of Russians had low or no trust at all in Russian courts as compared to 4 percent of respondents who reported very strong trust in courts in general (Jonsson 2002: 20). In the spring of 2001, when Vladimir Putin announced his plans for judicial reform, another nationwide survey poll found that only 18 percent of Russians, as compared to 20 percent of Ukrainians and 28 percent of Belarussians, trusted the courts (White and McAllister 2004: 84). By October 2002, polling agencies reported that only between 2 and 5 percent of Russians trusted courts (FOM 2002). If in 1996, according to a survey of 3,000 Russians, 41.3 percent said that they would turn to a court if any authority took a decision violating their rights, in April 2004, only 1 percent of those surveyed was prepared to challenge the government actions in court (Solomon and Foglesong 2000; Samarina 2004: 2).

Since then, public attitudes toward courts gradually improved. According to the VTsIOM (2006, 2008) surveys conducted between 2006 and 2009, slightly more than a quarter of Russians trusted courts. Data from the 2006 round of the Russian Longitudinal Monitoring Survey (RLMS) conducted by the Institute of Sociology of the Russian Academy of Sciences indicated that a quarter of Russians trusted courts with two-thirds of those surveyed having mentioned that the "non-implementation of judicial decisions" was the reason for not going to court. According to this survey, 91 percent of respondents believed that the courts would always rule in favor of government in a dispute with an ordinary person (Kozyreva and Smirnov 2008). The 2007 Levada Center poll asked respondents to report their trust in courts in criminal cases and in civil cases and found no difference between these two categories of cases. Of those surveyed, 47 percent reported distrust in courts handling criminal cases and 46 percent in civil cases (Rimskii 2009). The FOM polls conducted in 2004 and 2008 show that 26–28 percent of respondents positively evaluated performance of the judiciary with 39 percent of respondents giving negative evaluation (46 percent—in 2004). According to these polls, in 2004, 39 percent of Russians believed that "it was necessary to go to court in conflict situations" while 44 percent believed in "avoiding courts in conflict situations." By 2008, according to the FOM (2008), this pattern changed very little: 34 percent of those surveyed were in favor of going to court as compared to 39 percent who preferred avoiding courts. The Levada Center (2008: 30, 103) surveys conducted in 2008 revealed that 21 percent of respondents believed that resorting to litigation was the "fastest way for Russian citizens to resolve their problems" and 22 percent of those surveyed said that they would sue their employer if the latter violated their labor rights.

As in the case with the Constitutional Court, Russians do not know much about the actual performance of the judiciary. Indeed, in the mid-1990s, one-half of Russians reported that they have never heard of the Russian Supreme Court (Gibson et al. 1998). At the end of 2004, according to VTsIOM (2005), only 10 percent of surveyed Russians reported that they knew a lot about the work of courts, while one-third of those surveyed said that they knew nothing about the work of courts. The above-mentioned 2006 RLMS poll found that 12.5 percent of respondents knew about courts from personal experiences, and another 18 percent knew about courts through friends and relatives. Over 85 percent of respondents learned about courts from the mass media reports (Kozyreva and Smirnov 2008: 100). The 2007 Levada Center poll found that 71 percent of Russians never went to court for help (Rimskii 2009). The FOM surveys conducted between 1997 and 2007 indicate that two out of three Russians have never taken part in judicial proceedings (FOM 2007), while the 2008 FOM survey found that 80 percent of Russians said that they never filed a lawsuit.

Finally, surveys of business firms operating in Russia provide a glimpse into their views of the commercial (*arbitrazh*) courts. According to a survey of 500 firms conducted by VTsIOM at the end of 2000, 44 percent of firms that had a dispute with the local or regional government over the last two years turned to the *arbitrazh* courts to resolve at least one conflict. In contrast, two out of three managers who had recently experienced a property rights violation by a business partner took at least one dispute to court, indicating a greater willingness to use courts in cases involving private rather than state entities (Frye 2004). Evidence from this survey shows that 76 percent of managers expected commercial courts to protect their interests in cases against other private businesses, but only 39 percent of managers said that courts could protect their interests in cases against the local or regional government. Twenty-eight percent of surveyed managers said that the courts would be able to ensure compliance of local and regional governments with unfavorable judicial decisions while two out of three managers reported that the courts would be able to enforce decisions against private businesses (Frye 2004). The surveys of Russian companies by the Moscow-based INDEM conducted between 2001 and 2005 revealed a non-linear trend: in 2001, 74 percent of surveyed firms reported that the "ineffectiveness of the judicial system" was an obstacle for doing business; in 2002, 56 percent indicated so; and in 2005, 72 percent. The same trend was captured by the question whether "poor performance of the *arbitrazh* courts" impeded business activities: in 2001, 24 percent of surveyed companies said that it does not impede; in 2002, 52 percent; in 2004, 42 percent; and in 2005, 28 percent said so (Rimskii 2009).

The EBRD–World Bank Business Environment and Enterprise Performance Surveys (BEEPS) of Russian firms conducted in 2002, 2005 and 2008 show a growing proportion of firms indicating that the "functioning of the judiciary" represents a problem for doing business: from 27 percent in 2002 to 31 percent in 2005 to 44 percent in 2008 (World Bank 2005, 2010). About 28 percent of firms polled by the BEEPS have been in court, and about 38 percent of firms with overdue payments used the courts to solve an overdue payment. However, when asked in 2005 about specific problems of the judiciary, a larger proportion, as compared to 2002 BEEPS, of all surveyed firms and those that used courts reported that the judiciary was "able to enforce its decisions," "affordable," "quick," "honest/uncorrupted" and "fair and impartial." For example, during the 2002 BEEPS, 20 percent of surveyed companies (and 25 percent of those that used courts) said that courts were able to enforce their decisions. In the 2004 round of BEEPS, 41 percent of surveyed companies (and 37 percent of those that used courts) said the same. In the 2008 round of BEEPS two-thirds of surveyed companies (and 70 percent of those that used courts) said the same (World Bank 2011: 54). It is possible that businesses are more optimistic about judicial power due to the easier procedure of implementing decisions of the *arbitrazh* courts and due to more knowledge about the work of courts (Hendley 2004). That the better views about the specifics of the work of courts go hand in hand with more critical views of the overall functioning of the judiciary may mean that the progress in judicial performance is not fast enough to keep up with the demands of the business world.

To sum up, these public opinion surveys tell us that once-respected Russian courts are losing their legitimacy even though the public does not know what courts are doing on the ground. Russians increasingly distrust their judiciary not simply because they distrust all other political institutions. In addition to viewing courts as biased and corrupt, citizens appear to distrust their courts because litigation does not deliver expected results to successful litigants. This pattern of waning confidence in the judicial system goes hand in hand with the growing perception among voters that suing the state in Russian courts is a waste of time. The more deeply the Russians distrust their judicial system, the less likely they are ready to turn to their courts, regardless of their chances of winning against the government, and the less likely they are to learn about the impartiality and independence of the judicial branch. Thus, the Russian judiciary faces the challenge of informing the public about its decision-making. This task of spreading reports about judicial neutrality, impartiality and independence is daunting in the context of waning public confidence in this institution as well as in the rest of the judicial system. Repairing the reputation of courts involves both supplying positive information about their performance and increasing the demand from the public to strengthen the legal accountability of political branches.


**Russian Courts in Action: Administrative Justice**

This disappointing view of judicial legitimacy runs in the face of the official court statistics. While at the beginning of the millennium at least three out of four Russians believed that courts would fail to protect their rights against the government, the regular and commercial (*arbitrazh*) courts increasingly exercised judicial review of governmental actions and ruled against the government in about 80 percent of cases (Solomon 2004). According to the Russian Finance Ministry (1999), in 1998 alone, courts heard over 4,500 lawsuits against federal government and awarded about 80 million rubles to the successful litigants. I consider how each of the three branches of the Russian judiciary dealt with the lawsuits against the state at the time when the public was turning more and more skeptical about judicial performance.

The courts of general jurisdiction that hear all cases outside the jurisdiction of other courts, consist of a traditional hierarchy of about 2,500 district courts, 89 regional courts, and the Russian Supreme Court (to which were added, in 2000, a new lower rung, the Justices of the Peace), and a separate hierarchy of 151 military courts. Their caseload has been growing every year since the early 1990s. In 2004, regular courts heard some 10 million cases, including 583,000 lawsuits against the government. Among these were some 80,000 complaints against illegal administrative actions by government officials of all ranks. In 2008, regular courts heard 1.1 million criminal cases, 10.6 million civil cases, and 5.4 million administrative offenses. Among them were 82,400 complaints against illegal administrative actions by the government officials, 3,200 lawsuits against tax authorities, 77,000 lawsuits against the Pension Fund, 107,000 social benefits cases, 521,000 lawsuits against the government, and 3,100 electoral disputes.[7] On average, the success rate of such complaints never went below 67 percent, which means that two out of three complaints against government action are won in Russian courts. In 2002, courts awarded a total of 135 million rubles to those who successfully sued the government; in 2004, 266 million rubles; and in 2006, 351 million rubles (Biianova 2006). Moreover, the average amount of the court award in such cases jumped from 1,000 rubles in 2002 to 7,000 rubles in 2006. When it comes to the lawsuits over illegal actions of the law-

---

7 Official court statistics are published by the Judicial Department of the Russian Supreme Court and are available at http://cdep.ru/index.php?id=5.

enforcement agencies, such as illegal detention and seizure of property, plaintiffs consistently win at least 70 percent of cases. In 2008, according to the official statistics, courts awarded the total of 3.36 billion rubles to the victims of illegal action by the law-enforcement agencies.[8] More importantly, courts of general jurisdiction actively reviewed the legality of governmental regulations: in 2002, they heard 5,500 challenges to regional laws and gubernatorial decrees and struck down 4,700 of them (85 percent). Two years later, in 2004, the probability of successful challenge to a legal enactment in regular courts stood at 67 percent (Rabota sudov Rossiiskoi Federatsii v 2002 godu 2003: 71; Mikhailina 2004; Kucher 2005). In 2006, this probability was even higher at 71 percent (2,500 cases) (Biianova 2006).[9] Similarly, military courts have handled about a million complaints against administrative decisions of military officials in the past decade and consistently found in favor of complainants in 80 percent of cases (Solomon 2004).

The *arbitrazh* courts, established in 1991 to hear disputes among firms and between firms and the government, exist at the trial level in 81 regions, 20 appellate circuits of three to five regions (introduced in 2003), 10 cassation circuits of eight to 10 regions (added in 1995), and the Higher *Arbitrazh* Court. Their caseload has been growing by 15–20 percent each year. By 2004, it reached 1.2 million cases, two-thirds of them involving disputes between businesses and the government.[10] In 2008, the *arbitrazh* courts received 1.1 million lawsuits, roughly half of them being disputes between businesses and the government. That year, these courts handled about one million cases, one half of which had a government agency (tax service, Pension Fund, bailiff service, customs committee and anti–monopoly service) as a plaintiff or defendant. Similar to their colleagues in regular courts, *arbitrazh* judges also appear to adjudicate in an impartial manner. For example, they did not hesitate to rule against the federal government in economic disputes between the Federation and the regions, and in disputes over taxes they sided with taxpayers in 70 percent of the cases, and tended to award larger sums to private firms as compared to tax authorities (Hendley 2002; Solomon 2004). In 2008, these courts heard 17,854 cases brought by procurators and ruled in favor of them in 51.5 percent of cases (53.5 percent in 2007). When businesspeople contested the legality of imposed fines in these courts, they won in 59.4 percent of the cases in 2008, up from 55.7 percent in 2007. However, when the government agencies brought businesses to courts, they won in 66 percent of cases in 2008. That year, the *arbitrazh* courts handled 39,505 complaints against government action (except tax service), half of them being addressed to the federal government agencies, and ruled in favor of plaintiffs in 33 percent of cases. When these courts reviewed the legality of federal and local legislation in the total of 1,304 cases, they struck it down in 21 percent of cases. According to official court statistics, when taxpayers sue to recover excessive tax payments from the federal budget, they win in 77 percent of cases. Businesses also win two out of three lawsuits (66 percent) brought against customs officials. In sum, in 2008, the *arbitrazh* courts appear to be less deferential to the government side as compared to 2007.

The 19-member Russian Constitutional Court (RCC), with narrowly defined jurisdictions, stands alone and does not form a hierarchy with regional constitutional courts. Between 1992 and 2008, this Court received over 180,000 petitions from individuals, corporations, regions, other courts and politicians, and issued some 4,000 decisions, a significant share of which reversed federal and regional policies.

---

8   Official court statistics for 2008, http://cdep.ru/statistics.asp?search_frm_auto=1&dept_id=8.

9   In 2008, regular courts exercised judicial review of legislation in 6,800 cases.

10   The Higher *Arbitrazh* Court of Russia collects judicial statistics from the *arbitrazh* courts and publishes them on its official website at www.arbitr.ru/press-centr/news/totals.

Between 1995 and 2006, the Constitutional Court struck down 141 laws, offered its own binding statutory interpretation in 200 cases, and ruled in favor of the petitioner in 1,105 cases. The Court issued most of these decisions at the request of individuals (Trochev 2008) and repeatedly ordered the federal government to respect judicial decisions (Biianova 2006).

Russia's regions do not have their own separate judicial systems, although federal law empowers regions to set up their own constitutional courts and Justice of the Peace courts. As of summer 2009, only 15 out of 89 regions actually staffed their constitutional courts, emulating German *Laender* with their own constitutional courts.

Contrary to theories that link democratization and vibrant "electoral market" with judicial empowerment, these courts were created and persisted in the regions with authoritarian political regimes, and failed or were not created in the regions with high electoral uncertainty (Trochev 2004). These tribunals determine whether regional and local laws and decrees comply with the regional constitutions through a posteriori abstract and concrete constitutional review procedures. Between 1992 and November 2003, these courts issued over 330 decisions on the merits of the case, having struck down about equal proportions of executive and legislative acts in 60 percent of the cases, which included numerous politically charged disputes between regional legislatures and governors over fiscal policies, electoral procedures and socio-economic rights (Trochev and Solomon 2005).

To sum up, the Russian judiciary appears to be both active and activist in its willingness to address numerous important issues of public policy, a serious achievement for courts in a post-authoritarian state (Solomon 2004). To be sure, many Russian judges are still Soviet; yet others draw on the 1950 European Convention on Human Rights to rule in favor of citizens (Hendley 2007; Trochev 2009). Many Russian judges are biased, dependent and corrupt; yet others are not afraid of ruling against the powerful. This judicial activism together with the statutory expansion of judicial authority and high rates of successful litigation against the government runs counter to the widespread cynicism about courts. Russian judges use their discretion and do not hesitate to rule against the government albeit their high success rate in suing the government may indicate that citizens bring strong cases to courts. However, ordinary citizens fail to appreciate these advances in judicial performance. How we could explain this gap between negative public attitudes and actual judicial behavior? As I will argue below, Russians do not feel the impact of this judicial independence in action because the federal and local governments consistently fail to implement court decisions, the major reason for this failure being the lack of *administrative* capacity of the Russian state.


### "The Court Has Ruled ..." What Next?


The question of carrying out court decisions constitutes the greatest test for judicial power. We can understand the role the courts play in governance only if we know how and why public officials reacted to judicial decisions. Because judges lack the "the sword and the purse," successful judicial empowerment depends on the capacities of states to operate under court-ordered rules, like allowing same-sex marriages, and to implement routine court decisions in the variety of cases, like transferring property or assets to the winning party in the litigation. As Justice Stephen Breyer of the US Supreme Court famously put it, "the paratroopers and the judges must cooperate" (Breyer 1998). Researching compliance with court decisions is difficult: from defining it (what constitutes compliance?) to measuring it on the ground to deciphering the long-term impact (if any) of judicial decisions. In this chapter, I will deal with litigation against Russian government because it simplifies the task of studying bureaucratic compliance.[11] I will focus on the areas of the litigation, in which courts order the transfer of monetary awards from the state coffers to private litigants, many of whom found themselves poor during the unprecedented collapse of Russian economy in the 1990s. Unlike protecting due process rights of criminal defendants, which is unpopular in the context of surging crime rates, protecting the right to fair taxation or to job-related benefits should be popular among voters. Also, Russian law provides sanctions for non-compliance with judicial decisions. For example, Article 315 of the Russian Criminal Code makes non-compliance punishable by up to two years' imprisonment, Articles 17.14 and 17.15 of the Code of Administrative Offenses impose the maximum 100,000 rubles ($3,300 USD) fine for non-compliance with court enforcement orders. How did public officials react to landmark and routine judgments of top and lower courts in post-communist Russia?

## Constitutional Court: Taxpayers' Rights Revolution Unfulfilled

Consider how Russian bureaucracy responded to the set of new rights of taxpayers created by the Russian Constitutional Court (Trochev 2008). Indeed, taxation cases occupied a central place on the docket of the Constitutional Court, partly because the Court had to defend its vision of fair taxation against the rest of the government. The series of cases on the concept of the bona fide taxpayer illustrate how difficult it is to make judge-made concepts work in practice. In October 1998, just a few months after a nationwide financial crisis brought down Sergei Kirienko's Cabinet, the Constitutional Court boldly ruled that the taxpayer's obligation to pay taxes ended at the moment that the tax amount was deducted from the account of the taxpayer in good faith.[12] On paper, this legally sound judgment overruled the practice of the federal Tax Ministry and the Higher *Arbitrazh* Court, which believed that the tax obligation ended only after the tax amount had been deposited in the state coffers. In the context of widespread "bank runs," this unconstitutional practice meant that if, for any reason, the tax payment did not reach the state coffers on time it was OK for the revenue agency to deduct the same tax again in a single tax period. The RCC disagreed and ruled that the taxpayers could not be held responsible for the illegal behavior of banks, which delayed the transfer of tax payments to the state budget. Moreover, Article 45 of the Russian Tax Code, which entered into force in January 1999, copied the wording the RCC decision: "the tax obligation ends when the tax amount is deducted from the account of the taxpayer."

On the ground, however, this RCC judgment made little difference. Although the federal Pension Fund and several federal ministries reimbursed those who paid their taxes twice, the State Customs Committee in February 1999 issued a secret letter, which banned customs officers from clearing the goods unless the customs duties have been deposited in the state budget. The Russian Supreme Court approved this non-compliance by ruling that the customs clearance of goods should be done only after the "real payment of customs duties," that is, after the payment had been deposited to the state coffers. Thus, deduction of customs duties from the account of the payer ends the obligation to pay the duties, but it does not bind the customs officials (Pepeliaev 2000). Moreover, in May 1999, the Russian Tax Ministry issued a secret letter, in which it banned tax officers from applying this RCC judgment retroactively. In practice, this meant that all taxpayers who were taxed twice

---

11   To be sure, my focus on administrative justice leaves out most of the cases that the Russian judiciary handles and does not analyze the capacity of Russia's Bailiffs Service, a division within the Justice Ministry in charge of enforcing judicial decision. See, e.g., Kahn (2002: 148–81).

12   RCC decision 24–P of October 12, 1998, *VESTNIK KONSTITUTSIONNOGO SUDA RF*, no. 1 (1999), pp. 10–17, English translation in *Statutes and Decisions*, no. 5 (2000).

before October 12, 1998, the date of the RCC decision, would not receive a refund. The Higher *Arbitrazh* Court upheld the legality of this secret letter and consistently refused all lawsuits, in which taxpayers sought to recover taxes paid twice (Pepeliaev 2000).

As expected, aggrieved taxpayers flooded the RCC with complaints, trying to recover their taxes, and in July 1999, the RCC defended their right to fair taxation by ruling that its October 1998 decision applied to all payments of taxes, fees, and duties to the state budget.[13] At the same time, the Enforcement Department of the RCC contacted the legal office of the Tax Ministry, but to no avail. The Procuracy also refused to act on behalf of these taxpayers. Numerous publications in the mass media about this unconstitutional behavior of the bureaucracy and the judicial branch did not help either. In May 2000, the RCC again clashed with the *arbitrazh* courts by ruling that its October 1998 decision was to be applied retroactively to remedy the rights of the "good faith" taxpayers.[14] All in all, by March 2001, the RCC, in 23 decisions, insisted on its own definition of the timing of tax payments, which, of course, the aggrieved taxpayers extensively used in trying to recover the unconstitutionally paid taxes between 1994 and 1998. The *arbitrazh* courts, however, launched a unified front to defend the budget against this flood of lawsuits (Boikov 2001: 51–4). These courts had the support of the federal Tax Ministry, which complained that by mid-2001, the Russian budget had lost 31 billion rubles as a result of the October 1998 RCC decision (van den Berg 2002: 471, fn.6).

In July 2001, the RCC appeared to have given up its "taxpayer rights" revolution. As Justice Gadzhiev recalled, his colleagues had asked the Tax Ministry to petition the Court to "clarify" its October 1998 decision (Gadzhiev 2004). The Tax Ministry could not refuse such a tempting offer from the guardians of constitutional order, and the RCC promptly issued a "clarification" ruling in which it restricted the application of its October 1998 judgment only to the taxpayers "in good faith" and essentially gave a free hand to the revenue agencies to determine the "good faith" element.[15] According to the RCC, instead of assuming that the taxpayers behave in "good faith," revenue agencies have to check the "good faith" of both the taxpayers and the banks that delay the transfer of tax payments from the payer's account to the state budget. In a sign of clear deference to the executive, the Court held that the tax authorities had to impel the "good faith" taxpayers to pay their taxes in full and on time. Moreover, in the Court's view, the "good faith" taxpayers ought to pay their taxes through the banks, which are "approved" by the local branches of the Tax Ministry. It should be noted that the Russian Tax Code does not define "good faith" behavior—it presumes that all taxpayers are bona fide, and, therefore, street-level tax authorities faced virtually no checks on the abuse of their authority to separate "reliable" banks from "bad" ones and "good" taxpayers from malicious ones.

The Higher *Arbitrazh* Court developed its own test to determine "good faith" taxpayers: they had to ask tax authorities if their bank was reliable and efficient in transferring payments to the state budget (Skliarova 2004). The flood of complaints against the abuse of this authority, by and large protected by the *arbitrazh* courts, prompted the RCC to issue yet another decision in October 2003. Here, the Court changed its July 2001 decision by ruling that government agencies, including the *arbitrazh* courts, had to presume the "good faith" behavior of the taxpayers and could not

---

13　RCC decision 97–O of July 1, 1999, *VESTNIK KONSTITUTSIONNOGO SUDA RF*, no. 5 (1999), pp. 37–9, English translation in *Statutes and Decisions*, no. 1 (2002).

14　RCC decision 101–O of May 4, 2000, *VESTNIK KONSTITUTSIONNOGO SUDA RF*, no. 6 (2000), pp. 21–5.

15　RCC decision 138–O of July 25, 2001, *VESTNIK KONSTITUTSIONNOGO SUDA RF*, no. 2 (2002), pp. 27–30.

impose on them obligations not authorized by tax statutes.[16] In essence, the RCC required the tax authorities to behave in "good faith," thus, inserting the "good faith" principle in the Russian tax law (Gadzhiev 2004). Following this decision, the Russian Tax Ministry still resisted presuming innocent all corporations whose tax payments did not reach the state coffers on time and, throughout 2004, attempted to change the Tax Code in its favor (Gradova 2004; Skliarova 2004).

The Kremlin-approved "tax collection" campaign against YUKOS, at the time the Russia's largest private oil exporter, only strengthened this stance of the Tax Ministry and the *arbitrazh* courts. As expected, the YUKOS lawyers complained to the RCC against a whopping 99.4 billion rubles (US$3.4 billion) tax bill imposed in back taxes for the year of 2000 by the tax authorities and approved by the Moscow *Arbitrazh* Court in 2004. In January 2005, the RCC responded with a Solomonic judgment. The Constitutional Court blasted the Moscow *Arbitrazh* Court judge for abusing the concept of a "good faith" taxpayer and upheld the three-year statute of limitations on back tax claims, as provided by Article 113 of the Tax Code. Yet the RCC stopped short of ordering the rehearing of the YUKOS case and dismissed the complaint.[17]

But just a few months later, in another Solomonic decision involving the same back tax claims against YUKOS and the same legal issues, the RCC changed its position. In a 16–3 vote, the Court changed the meaning of the three-year statute of limitations on back tax claims by allowing tax authorities to pursue claims indefinitely if they can prove "obstruction" on the part of the taxpayer.[18] The RCC ruled that the statute did not apply to "dishonest taxpayers," which acted illicitly for the purpose of dragging out tax audits. The Court observers agreed that the full impact of the ruling would hinge on how the *arbitrazh* courts and the tax authorities interpret what constitutes proof of obstruction (Fak 2005). Deferring to the executive and other courts again proved dangerous to the constitutional court. In October 2006, after a prolonged debate, the Higher *Arbitrazh* Court rejected the good faith concept stated previously by the RCC and established a brand new concept of unjustified tax benefit. This innovation is binding on all *arbitrazh* courts and targets good faith taxpayers, who may be accused of tax optimization or utilization of tax planning schemes or interaction with bad faith taxpayers. For example, any tax benefit related to transactions with shady business or any incomplete, inaccurate or inconsistent information in primary or supportive documents may mean a tax benefit is unjustified. A taxpayer must justify a business rationale for the questioned operation and its consistency with true economic intent (Smirnov 2006).

In summary, these judgments of the RCC created a "quiet revolution" in Russian taxation. These judgments repeatedly surprised both tax authorities and taxpayers, as the head of the Russian Tax Ministry Legal Department delicately put it in August 2004 (*Dvoinaia zapis'* 2004). Yet, on the ground, short-term political campaigns against oligarchs, the defiance of the bureaucracy and the rest of the judiciary have mitigated the impact of this "taxpayer rights" revolution and forced the RCC to change its mind in its approach to the fair taxation. Meanwhile, year after year, the newspapers run stories about bureaucratic defiance of the Constitutional Court decisions and publish interviews with its Justices and clerks who complain about disrespect for the Constitutional Court on the part of the rest of the government apparatus (Getman 2005; Ivanov 2007). In a word, Russian public officials lack the capacity to operate under the judge-made rules of the fair taxation of businesses.

---

16   RCC decision 329–O of October 16, 2003, unpublished, available at www.ksrf.ru.

17   RCC decision 36–O of January 18, 2005, *VESTNIK KONSTITUTSIONNOGO SUDA RF*, no. 3 (2005), pp. 108–12.

18   RCC decision 9–P of July 14, 2005, *VESTNIK KONSTITUTSIONNOGO SUDA RF*, no. 4 (2005), pp. 67–102 (Gadzhiev, Iaroslavtsev and Kononov, dissenting).

## Administrative Justice and Unaccountable Bureaucracy

Similarly, the Russian government has been disregarding unfavorable judicial decisions of courts. Russia does not have sovereign immunity, as it is viewed as a Soviet-era mechanism of placing the rulers above the law. Article 1071 of the Russian Civil Code makes government agencies liable for the damage caused by illegal actions and decisions of these agencies and officials. Successful plaintiffs in these cases or courts themselves must send judicial decisions directly to the Finance Ministry or another federal agency for their enforcement. Bailiffs, officials within the Justice Ministry in charge of enforcing judicial decisions, are not involved in the enforcement procedure, as they successfully lobbied for excluding them from it. According to Tatiana Neshataeva, Judge of the Higher *Arbitrazh* Court, bailiffs did not want to interfere with the Finance Ministry, and since 2002, the annual federal budget law contains a provision that bailiffs had no power over enforcing successful lawsuits against federal government (Karchevskaia 2004: 6: Biianova 2006). The Finance Ministry argued that the absence of bailiffs in the enforcement procedure automatically made the compliance with unfavorable court judgments a voluntary process, in which clerks of this Ministry decide whether such judgments would be enforced and victorious litigants would receive actual court-awarded compensation (Karchevskaia 2004: 6; Saul 2005: 1). Needless to say, these clerks have more power over ordinary Russians who proved in court that they suffered from the illegal actions of government officials. Not counting tax disputes, Chapter 24 of the Russian Budget Code distinguishes two sorts of judicial decisions against federal government: against federal treasury and against specific federal agencies. Lawsuits against illegal actions and decisions of federal officials (police) belong to the first category, while the employment-related and social benefits cases belong to the second one. I briefly describe how government bureaucracy responded to each of these categories of lawsuits below.

The Russian Finance Ministry is a defendant in cases against federal treasury and is directly responsible for paying out compensation to those who prove in court that they have been victims of illegal actions of government officials. As explained in the previous section, Russian courts frequently rule in favor of the victims and order the federal government to pay out appropriate compensation. According to the Russian Accounting Chamber, a monitoring arm of the Russian parliament, in 2002, Russia's Finance Ministry received 2,175 judicial decisions, which ordered it to pay out 914 million rubles in compensation. The Ministry chose to focus on minor cases and implemented 808 decisions by paying out 199 million rubles to the victims of government abuse (Accounting Chamber of the Russian Federation 2003: 290–1). Facing more litigation and more losses in courts, the Ministry allocated only 117 million rubles to the payment of compensation in cases against federal treasury in 2003 (Accounting Chamber of the Russian Federation 2004: 21). However, the propensity of Russian courts to rule against the government forced the Finance Ministry to increase this amount drastically. Russia entered 2004 owing one billion rubles of unpaid court-ordered compensation. That year, courts ordered the federal treasury to pay 2.8 billion rubles more. The Finance Ministry paid out 1.9 billion rubles (Accounting Chamber of the Russian Federation 2006: 130–1). As a result, Russia started 2005 with 1.8 billion rubles of unpaid court-ordered damages in 3,656 cases against federal treasury. That year, courts issued 5,842 decisions in which they ordered the Finance Ministry to pay out the total of 2.1 billion rubles, and the latter paid out 1.4 billion rubles of compensation to successful litigants in 2,366 cases (Accounting Chamber of the Russian Federation 2007: 144–50). Russia began 2006 with 10,330 non-implemented court decisions, in which the Finance Ministry had been ordered to pay the total of 5.3 billion rubles. That year, it lost 11,058 cases with the total amount of 10.8 billion rubles in court-awarded compensation. The Finance Ministry sent back to plaintiffs or successfully appealed 6,512 cases with the total 4.3 billion rubles.[19] It paid out 5.8 billion rubles (28 percent of the total court-ordered amount against the federal treasury) in the total of 7,377 judicial decisions (26 percent of the total judicial decisions received in 2006). As a result, by the end of 2006, there remained outstanding 7,499 judicial decisions in the total amount of almost six billion rubles. In 2007, the Finance Ministry lost 19,240 cases against federal treasury, which amounted to over 11 billion rubles. That year, the Ministry sent back or successfully appealed 8,468 cases (6.8 billion rubles), and paid out 8.3 billion rubles in the total of 11,992 judicial decisions. As a result, Russia entered 2008 with non-enforced 6,279 court judgments against the treasury totaling in 1.9 billion rubles (Accounting Chamber of the Russian Federation 2008: 319–23). In short, the dramatic increase in the litigation against federal government went hand in hand with the bureaucratic defiance of unfavorable judicial decisions in the context of an economy growing at the rate of 7 percent annually, budget surpluses, and the creeping authoritarianism of Putin's regime.

The second category of court cases against federal government involves employment-related litigation against federal government agencies, such as lawsuits of soldiers and police officers for various perks and benefits. According to the Russian Accounting Chamber, in 2002, all federal agencies received 45,300 judicial decisions, which ordered the total of 11.2 billion rubles to be paid from the federal budget. Agencies responded by enforcing 18 percent of judgments (7,900) and paying out 23 percent of the total court-awarded compensation (2.6 billion rubles) (Accounting Chamber of the Russian Federation 2003: 70–1). In 2003, according to the Finance Ministry data, the Defense Ministry lost 50,000 cases yet it failed to comply with 23,000 of them amounting to 5.15 billion rubles; the Ministry of Internal Affairs, which controls the police, lost 20,000 cases yet it failed to enforce 12,000 of them in the total amount of 1.66 billion rubles; other federal ministries failed to enforce 393 judicial decisions by failing to pay the total of 192 million rubles (Panov and Onegina 2003). By April 2004, Russia accumulated a record six billion rubles ($200 million US) in unpaid awards after losing 34,000 completed court cases to private individuals and corporations.[20]

Two federal departments, Internal Affairs and Defense, topped the list of the least court-friendly agencies by refusing to pay the total of some 2.2 billion rubles in unpaid awards. All in all, according to the Russian Finance Minister Alexei Kudrin, citizens who successfully sue federal government have to wait at least four years before they receive court-ordered payments (Lenta.Ru 2004). However, Kudrin's complaints fell on deaf ears, in part because government officials faced no punishment for disrespecting court decisions. Thus, the Russian federal government entered 2005 with unpaid 5.6 billion rubles owed to successful litigants. That year, courts ordered federal agencies to pay out 19.2 billion rubles, and the latter paid out 17.5 billion rubles in court-ordered compensation. As a result, at the end of 2005, the federal government owed 7.3 billion rubles due to lost court cases, a 30 percent increase (Accounting Chamber of the Russian Federation 2006: 135). In 2006, Russian courts ordered federal agencies to pay the total of 16.9 billion rubles to successful plaintiffs, and the latter paid out the total of 10.3 billion rubles. This resulted in arrears of 17.3 billion rubles, a 90 percent increase! (Accounting Chamber of the Russian Federation 2007: 152). In 2007, courts ordered federal agencies to pay out the total of 16.2 billion rubles, and the latter complied by paying out 18.1 billion rubles to successful plaintiffs. As a result, Russia was able to reduce the amount of court-ordered arrears to 11.3 billion rubles by the end of 2007 (Accounting Chamber of the Russian Federation 2008: 326).

---

19   The Finance Ministry can send back court documents if they "do not comply with the proper rules of submitting enforcement documents as established by the Russian legislation." Unfortunately, official statistics do not separate this number from the number of successfully appealed cases.

20   By "completed court cases," I mean cases that cannot be any longer appealed or re-opened.

To be sure, federal officials blame the Ministry of Finance for allocating insufficient amounts to them for the purpose of complying with judicial decisions. For example, in 2004, the Defense Ministry was required to pay out 2.8 billion rubles in the total of 37,500 completed court cases, which it lost to officers and soldiers (Vyskubin 2008). In the first nine months of 2006, the figure jumped to 5.57 billion rubles while the 2006 federal budget allocated only 3.05 billion rubles for the Defense Ministry to pay out court-ordered payments (Vyskubin 2008). This budgetary allocation would cover less than a half of what the courts ordered the Defense Ministry to pay out that year without counting the arrears it had already accumulated! All in all, by the beginning of 2008, the federal government failed to implement tens of thousands of judicial decisions, in which courts ordered 13.2 billion rubles in compensation to be paid out from the federal budget.

Regional and local governments fare no better: only in mid-2003 did they begin to define rules of complying with court judgments against them. For example, in 2000, in the Voronezh region (300 miles south of Moscow) the court bailiffs enforce less than 13 percent of court decisions in cases where citizens have successfully sued the government on social service issues (Egorov 2001). Not surprisingly, the Voronezh region holds the top spot in number of complaints to the European Court of Human Rights against Russia, most of which have to do with the unwillingness and inability of the federal and regional governments to carry out court-ordered payments to pensioners and single mothers.[21] According to the Moscow Division of the Federal Bailiffs Service, a unit that receives court enforcement documents against the federal budget and the budget of the Moscow City, in 2005, it received over 8,000 non-implemented final judicial decisions with the total of 1.4 billion rubles to be recovered from the federal and Moscow City governments (Regions.Ru 2006). In 2008, the Russian Supreme Court estimated that at least 3,800 judicial decisions will remain non-implemented in Russia each year and proposed the federal government to allocate an additional 420 million rubles for compensating victorious plaintiffs in these cases (Supreme Court of the Russian Federation 2008). There is no doubt that this "administrative justice delayed" creates the perception that suing public officials is not the speedy way to hold the government accountable.

Readers need to be aware that the Russian judicial system is not the only victim of bureaucratic sabotage. The Russian presidency also suffers from the bureaucratic non-compliance. In 2002, when President Putin was well entrenched in his office, he discovered that only 48 percent of his executive orders were implemented (*Izvestiia* 2003: 3). By 2005, the rate of implementation declined so dramatically that Putin was forced to hold weekly meetings with the federal Cabinet just to track how the federal government carried out his orders (*NewsProm.Ru* 2005). Later, in 2009, when Vladimir Putin went on to become prime minister, he proudly announced that the federal Cabinet would have ceased to exist long ago if he did not personally persuade Ministers to carry out his presidential orders (Putin 2009).[22] Putin's successor, Dmitrii Medvedev, also discovered that only 30 percent of orders he gave during the 2008 financial crisis were implemented (Medvedev 2009).

In sum, Russian bureaucracy is not court-friendly. But average Russians tend to blame the judiciary for this incapacity. If they fail to collect court-awarded monies from the government, then they perceive courts as biased and dependent on the authorities.

---

21   Active human rights NGOs also contributed to this transnational litigation. See Trochev (2009) and Zviagina (2006).

22   *Izvestiia* (2003: 3), Kommersant-vlast (2003: 10), *NewsProm* (2005), *Gazeta.Ru* (2005) and Putin (2009).

## Conclusion

Russians deeply distrust their judicial system not because they abhor judicial independence or because they can't access it or because most judges are dependent and biased toward the government. Just like many European nations, Russians value independent courts and use them in increasing numbers to settle their disputes with other citizens and the government. Judges, on the other hand, do not hesitate to rule against officials most of the time and order the Russian government to pay billions of rubles to private litigants each year. However, public distrust in Russian courts is reaching new heights. I have shown that, in part, deepening distrust in the judicial system stems from the inability of the winning party to secure court-awarded victory in successful citizen vs. government lawsuits. Federal and local governments make these victories unfulfilled because bureaucracies lack capacity to operate under the rules elaborated by top courts and to implement routine judgments of lower courts. This secret sabotage of the court-ordered rules has not gone unnoticed by the public. Although Russians, just as other European nations, value judicial independence, they increasingly distrust their courts, including the Constitutional Court. Having learned that a police officer or finance minister can openly disobey judicial decisions without being punished, Russians appear to consider litigation as an inefficacious option to defend their rights. Meanwhile, the RCC redirects the majority of individual complaints to these distrusted regular courts. Naturally, it breeds even more disappointment with the judicial system regardless of the fact that the Russian courts have been consistently ruling on behalf of individual complainants against state officials. Moreover, bureaucrats exploit this public distrust and further refuse to obey the judicial decisions. Breaking this vicious circle is an arduous task that should begin with informing the public about the essence of court decisions in plain language. This is an important educational responsibility of judges in those societies with thin constitutional traditions (Sadurski 2003).

By drawing on the successes and failures of high and local Russian courts to have their anti-government and pro-government judgments respected by the state agencies, this chapter assesses the real impact of post-communist courts on public policies and provides insights to the study of government accountability in comparative contexts. First, it contributes to the growing literature on comparative constitutionalism by bringing state capacity into the business of "rights revolutions." Numerous law and society scholars have argued that the bills of rights, accessible and independent courts, and the legal complex are crucial for the protection of basic rights (Halliday et al. 2007). Recent research on legalization of public policy-making in the United States and Britain shows that bureaucratic capacity is also vital for entrenching rights and improving accountability of bureaucracies (Epp 2009). I argue that in heavily bureaucratized post-authoritarian societies achieving the effective protection of constitutional freedoms is impossible without having a usable bureaucracy. If government officials are not willing or able to change public policies according to the court guidelines, then, judicial decisions and court victories remain on paper rather than on the ground. This is not identical to the "chicken or egg question" as such, but it does demonstrate that institutional resistance, presumably based upon the bureaucracy's perception of its own interests, can so slow down implementation as to undercut courts' legitimacy (when they are no longer viewed as effective). State incapacity does not allow law and courts to effectively regulate the relations between the state and an individual.

Second, my analysis adds an important dimension of the interplay between ideas (rule of law and judicial independence), economic interests and institutions (courts and bureaucracies) to the literature on public policy-making during democratization processes. Many approaches to democratization recognize the importance of usable bureaucracy to successful democratic consolidation yet very few of them explore the actual functioning of post-communist governance.

The novelty of my approach lies in the investigation of the complex interaction among the values and the litigation behavior of the voters, and bureaucratic behavior in response to unfavorable judicial decisions. My study provides insights into how and why the government officials from top to bottom respond the way they do to court-mandated changes in public policies in the context of democratization. In Putin's Russia, bureaucratic defiance of judicial decisions went hand in hand with enviable economic growth and budget surpluses.

Third, my analysis of growing distrust in empowered courts contributes to the research on the legitimacy of political systems. Russian experience with distrusted yet empowered courts demonstrates that the voters must be educated about the actual performance of government institutions. Judges in post-authoritarian societies must advertise their anti-government decisions to ensure that the general public knows them (Staton 2010).

Although such "public relations" campaigns by judges would be declared as improper in advanced democracies, making the court decisions visible is crucial in the context of the instrumental use of courts by ever-myopic Russian elites and the ensuing decline in the reputation of courts in the eyes of the public. Judges must maintain the link between the Olympus of abstract constitutional principles and the everyday needs of broad groups of Russian society so that ordinary Russians, who hold abstract commitments to the rule of law, can learn the benefits of having a powerful and independent judiciary. If judges fail to inform the voters, nobody else will because the rest of the state apparatus will be secretly defying the court verdicts. If the voters do not know much about the practice of judicial independence, courts cannot please them and cultivate their own institutional legitimacy. Moreover, the political branches of government can easily thwart judicial empowerment in the context of widespread public cynicism toward the judiciary.

## References


Accounting Chamber of the Russian Federation. 2003. Zakliuchenie Schetnoi palaty Rossiiskoi Federatsii po otchetu Pravitel'stva Rossiiskoi Federatsii ob ispolnenii federal'nogo biudzheta za 2002 god, predstavlennomu v forme proekta federal'nogo zakona "Ob ispolnenii federal'nogo biudzheta za 2002 god." Available at: www.ach.gov.ru/userfiles/tree/posl2003-tree_files-fl-37.pdf.

Accounting Chamber of the Russian Federation. 2004. Zakliuchenie Schetnoi palaty Rossiiskoi Federatsii po otchetu Pravitel'stva Rossiiskoi Federatsii ob ispolnenii federal'nogo biudzheta za 2003 god, predstavlennomu v forme proekta federal'nogo zakona "Ob ispolnenii federal'nogo biudzheta za 2003 god." Available at: www.ach.gov.ru/userfiles/tree/posl2003-tree_files-fl-37.pdf.

Accounting Chamber of the Russian Federation. 2006. Zakliuchenie Schetnoi palaty Rossiiskoi Federatsii po otchetu Pravitel'stva Rossiiskoi Federatsii ob ispolnenii federal'nogo biudzheta za 2005 god, predstavlennomu v forme proekta federal'nogo zakona "Ob ispolnenii federal'nogo biudzheta za 2005 god." Available at: www.ach.gov.ru/userfiles/tree/posl2005-tree_files-fl-36.pdf.

Accounting Chamber of the Russian Federation. 2007. Zakliuchenie Schetnoi palaty Rossiiskoi Federatsii po otchetu Pravitel'stva Rossiiskoi Federatsii ob ispolnenii federal'nogo biudzheta za 2006 god, predstavlennomu v forme proekta federal'nogo zakona "Ob ispolnenii federal'nogo biudzheta za 2006 god." Available at: www.ach.gov.ru/userfiles/tree/posl2006-tree_files-fl-35.pdf.

Accounting Chamber of the Russian Federation. 2008. Zakliuchenie Schetnoi palaty Rossiiskoi Federatsii po otchetu Pravitel'stva Rossiiskoi Federatsii ob ispolnenii federal'nogo biudzheta za 2007 god." Available at: www.ach.gov.ru/userfiles/tree/percent202007-tree_files-fl-45.pdf.

Baird, V. and Javeline, D. 2007. Persuasive Power of Russian Courts. *Political Research Quarterly*, 60(3), 429–42.

Biianova, N. 2006. Zasudit' ministra. *Vedomosti-Smart Money*, October 30. Available at: www. smoney.ru/print.shtml?2006/10/30/1608.

Boikov, O. 2001. Postanovleniia Konstitutsionnogo Suda Rossiiskoi Federatsii v deiatelnosti arbitrazhnykh sudov [Decisions of the RF Constitutional Court in the Activity of the Arbitrazh Courts], in *Problemy ispolneniia federalnymi organami gosudarstvennoi vlasti i organami gosudarstvennoi vlasti subektov Rossiiskoi Federatsii reshenii Konstitutsionnogo Suda Rossiiskoi Federatsii i konstitutsionnykh (ustavnykh) sudov subektov Rossiiskoi Federatsii*, edited by M. Mitiukov, S. Kabyshev, V. Bobrova and S. Andreev. Moscow: Formula prava, 50–5.

Breyer, S. 1998. Comment: Liberty, Prosperity, and a Strong Judicial Institution. *Law & Contemporary Problems*, 61(3), 3–6.

Colton, T. 2000. *Transitional Citizens: Voters and What Influences Them in the New Russia*. Cambridge, MA: Harvard University Press.

*Dvoinaia zapis'*. 2004. VAS i KS – ukaz MNS. Nalogoviki o nalogovykh sporakh [The Higher *Arbitrazh* Court and RCC Must be Obeyed by the Tax Ministry. Tax Officials about Tax Disputes]. *Dvoinaia zapis'*, August 3.

Egorov, S. 2001. Voronezh. Sostoialos' soveshchanie sluzhby sudebnykh pristavov, posviashchennoe itogam raboty v 2000 godu. *Regions.Ru*, February 13.

Epp, C. 2009. *Making Rights Real: Activists, Bureaucrats, and the Creation of the Legalistic State*. Chicago: University of Chicago Press.

Fak, A. 2005. Uncertainty Lingers Despite Tax Ruling. *Moscow Times*, July 18, 6.

Finance Ministry. 1999. Letter No. 01–01–10 "Ob obzore praktiki rassmotreniia v sudakh sporov s uchastiem Ministerstva finansov Rossiiskoj Federacii po zashchite interesov kazny Rossiiskoj Federatsii i Pravitelstva Rossiiskoj Federacii za 1998 god." June 28. Unpublished document.

FOM. 2002. *Indikatory*, October 31. Available at: http://bd.fom.ru/report/cat/power/pow_rei/dd024305.

FOM. 2007. *Rossiiskie sudy v zhizni in a teleekrane*, August 16. Available at: http://bd.fom.ru/report/cat/power/pow_jus/d073324.

FOM. 2008. *Otnoshenie k sudebnoi sisteme*, June 12. Available at: http://bd.fom.ru/report/map/d082322.

Frye, T. 2004. Credible Commitment and Property Rights: Evidence from Russia. *American Political Science Review*, 98(3), 453–66.

Gadzhiev, G.A. 2004. U nas ogromnyi potok zhalob nalogoplatelshchikov, i on vriad li umenshitsia v obozrimom budushchem [We Have a Huge Stream of Complaints from Taxpayers, and This Will Unlike to Subside in the Foreseeable Future]. *Rossiiskii nalogovyi kurer*, 24, 2–5.

Gazeta.Ru. 2005. Revoliutsiia dvernykh tablichek. *Gazeta.Ru*, May 17.

Gerber, T. and Mendelson, S. 2003. Research Addendum. *Post Soviet Affairs*, 19(2), 187–8.

Getman, E. 2005. Chinovnik glavnee Konstitutsii. Kto i pochemu ne vypolniaet resheniia glavnogo suda strany [Officer Is Above the Constitution. Who Does not Carry Out Decisions of the Highest Court of the Land and Why]. *Rossiiskaia gazeta*, August 9.

Gibson, J. 2003. Russian Attitudes Towards the Rule of Law: An Analysis of Survey Data, in *Law and Informal Practices: The Post-Communist Experience*, edited by D. Galligan and M. Kurkchiyan. New York: Oxford University Press, 77–91.

Gibson, J., Caldeira, G. and Baird, V. 1998. On the Legitimacy of National High Courts. *American Political Science Review*, 92(2), 343–58.

Gradova, M. 2004. MNS vystupaet za zakonodatelnoe reshenie problemy s "zavisshimi platezhami" [Tax Ministry Stands for the Legislative Solution to the Problem of "Stuck Tax Payments"]. *RIA Novosti*, February 12.

Grindle, M.S. 1996. *Challenging the State: Crisis and Innovation in Latin America and Africa*. Cambridge: Cambridge University Press.

Halliday, T., Karpik, L. and Feeley, M. 2007. *Fighting for Political Freedom: Comparative Studies of the Legal Complex and Political Liberalism*. Portland: Hart Publishing.

Hendley, K. 2001. "Demand" for Law in Russia – A Mixed Picture. *East European Constitutional Review*, 10(4), 72–7.

Hendley, K. 2002. Suing the State in Russia. *Post–Soviet Affairs*, 18(2), 122–47.

Hendley, K. 2004. Enforcing Judgments in Russian Economic Courts. *Post-Soviet Affairs*, 20(1), 46–82.

Hendley, K. 2007. Are Russian Judges Still Soviet? *Post-Soviet Affairs*, 23(3), 240–74.

Higher *Arbitrazh* Court of Russia. 2009. АНАЛИТИЧЕСКАЯ ЗАПИСКА к статистическому отчету о работе арбитражных судов Российской Федерации в 2008 году. Unpublished document. Available at: www.arbitr.ru/_upimg/0B081D25F0F48AE6B5FEAD937ABEDF 1F_01_itogiVAS08.pdf.

Hirschl, R. 2004. *Towards Juristocracy: The Origins and the Consequences of the New Constitutionalism*. Cambridge, MA: Harvard University Press.

Human Rights Information and Documentation Centre. 2007. *The Velvet Downfall: Human Rights Situation in Georgia in 2006*. Tbilisi: HRIDC.

Hyden, G., Court, J. and Mease, K. 2004. *Making Sense of Governance: Empirical Evidence from 16 Developing Countries*. Boulder: Lynne Rienner Publishers.

Ivanov, V. 2007. Neuvazhaemyi Konstitutsionnyi sud [Disrespected Constitutional Court]. *Gazeta* [Online, July 18]. Available at: http://gzt.ru/wallet/2007/07/18/220222.html.

*Izvestiia*. 2003. Kontrol nad glavnym. *Izvestiia*, May 15.

Jonsson, A. 2002. The Constitutional Court of the Russian Federation, 1997–2001. Uppsala University Working Papers, no. 73. October.

Kahn, P. 2002. The Russian Bailiffs Service and the Enforcement of Civil Judgments. *Post-Soviet Affairs*, 18(1), 148–81.

Karchevskaia, L. 2004. Obrashchenie vzyskaniia na kaznu. *EZh-Iurist*, 47, 6.

Kommersant-vlast. 2003. 10 November.

Kontrol nad glavnym. 2003. *Izvestiia*, May 15.

Konygina, N. 2003. Obshchestvennoe mnenie vozmut pod control. *Izvestiia*, August 6.

Kozyreva, P. and Smirnov, A. 2008. Problemy ukrepleniia doveriia k sudebnoi vlasti v sovremennoi Rossii. *Vlast'*, 8, 97–102. Available at: www.isras.ru/files/File/Vlast/2008/08/Kozyreva.pdf.

Kucher, N. 2005. Ne voevat' s chinovnikom, a suditsia. *Parlamentskaia gazeta*, May 19.

Lenta.Ru. 2004. Minfin: Gosudarstvo zadolzhalo 6 mlrd rublei po sudebnym iskam, Lenta.Ru, June 11. Available at: http://lenta.ru/russia/2004/06/11/suit.

Levada Center. 2008 *Ezhegodnik Obshchestvennoe mnenie – 2008*. Moscow: Levada–Tsentr, pp. 30, 103.

Linz, J. and Stepan, A. 1996. *Problems of Democratic Transition and Consolidation: Southern Europe, South America, and Post-Communist Europe*. Baltimore: Johns Hopkins University Press.

Mann, M. 1988. The Autonomous Power of the State: Its Origins, Mechanisms and Results, in *States in History*, edited by J. Hall. Oxford: Blackwell Publishers, 109–36.

Medvedev, D. 2009. *Meeting on Stabilizing the Situation in the Real Economy*. [Online: Speech Excerpt]. Available at: www.kremlin.ru/text/appears/2009/01/211554.shtml.

Mikhailina, Iu. 2004. Reformatory. Sudi rasskazali o prestupleniiakh i nakazaniiakh. *Gazeta.* January 28, 3. Available a:t http://dlib.eastview.com/browse/doc/5827574.

Mikhailovskaia, I., Kuzminskii, E. and Mazaev, Iu. 1997. Prava cheloveka i sotsialnopoliticheskie protsessy v postkommunisticheskoi Rossii. Moskva: Proektnaia gruppa po pravam cheloveka, 54–7.

Millar, J. and Wolchik, S. 1994. Introduction: The Social Legacies and the Aftermath of Communism, in *The Social Legacy of Communism*, edited by J. Millar and S Wolchik. New York: Woodrow Wilson Center Press, 1–28.

Minfin: Gosudarstvo zadolzhalo 6 mlrd rublei po sudebnym iskam. 2004. *Lenta.Ru,* June 11. Available at: http://lenta.ru/russia/2004/06/11/suit.

Mishler, W. and Rose, R. 2001. What Are the Origins of Political Trust? Testing Institutional and Cultural Theories in Post-Communist Societies. *Comparative Political Studies*, 34(1), 30–62.

*NewsProm.Ru.* 2005. Pravitelstvo RF na kazhdom zasedanii budet rassmatrivat porucheniia Putina. *NewsProm.Ru*, May 12. Available at: www.newsprom.ru/news/111591928520094.shtml.

Nikitinskii, L. 2006. Pristala k pristavu. *Rossiiskaia gazeta*, May 31.

Onishchuk, M. 2008. Derzhavna Vikonavcha Sluzhba na Shlyahu do Reform ta Efektivnosti. *Dzerkalo tyzhnya*, March 8–14.

Ordzhonikidze, M. 2007. Zapadnye tsennosti v vospriiatii rossiian [Western Values in the Perception of Russians]. *Vestnik obshchestvennogo mneniia* [*Journal of Public Opinion*], 2. Available at: www.polit.ru/research/2007/06/26/ordzhonikidze.html.

Orttung, R. 2009. Nations in Transit 2009 – Russia. In *Nations in Transit 2009*. Freedom House.

Panov, A. and Onegina, A. 2003. Biudzhetnikov nakazhut za neispolnenie reshenii suda [Budget Will be Punished for Failure of Court Decisions]. *Vedomosti* [Online, December 24]. Available at: www.vedomosti.ru/newspaper/article.shtml?2003/12/24/70602.

Pepeliaev, S. 2000. Kommentarii, in *Kommentarii k postanovleniiam Konstitutsionnogo Suda RF. T. 2*, edited by B. Ebzeev. Moscow: Iurist, 515–16.

Petrova, A. 2000. Nashi sudy v zerkale obshchestvennogo mneniia. *Press-release of the Public Opinion Foundation (FOM)*. March 3. Available at: http://bd.fom.ru/report/cat/power/pow_jus/of000903.

Pravitelstvo RF na kazhdom zasedanii budet rassmatrivat porucheniia Putina. 2005. *NewsProm*, May 12, Biianova. Zasudit' ministra.

Putin, V. 2009. Pochemu trudno uvolit' cheloveka. *Russkii pioner*, June 17. Available at: http://ruspioner.ru/columns/putin/613.html.

Rabota sudov Rossiiskoi Federatsii v 2002 godu. 2003. *Rossiiskaia iustitsiia*, 8, 69–78.

Razumkov Centre. 2009. *Sociological Poll: Do You Support the Activity of the Courts in Ukraine?* Available at: www.uceps.org/ukr/poll.php?poll_id=169.

RCC decision 24–P of October 12, 1998, *VKS RF*, no. 1 (1999), pp. 10–17, English translation in *Statutes and Decisions*, no. 5 (2000).

RCC decision 97–O of July 1, 1999, *VESTNIK KONSTITUTSIONNOGO SUDA RF*, no. 5 (1999), pp. 37–9, English translation in *Statutes and Decisions*, no. 1 (2002).

RCC decision 101–O of May 4, 2000, *VESTNIK KONSTITUTSIONNOGO SUDA RF*, no. 6 (2000), pp. 21–5.

RCC decision 138–O of July 25, 2001, *VESTNIK KONSTITUTSIONNOGO SUDA RF*, no. 2 (2002), pp. 27–30.

RCC decision 329–O of October 16, 2003, unpublished, available at: www.ksrf.ru.

RCC decision 36–O of January 18, 2005, *VESTNIK KONSTITUTSIONNOGO SUDA RF*, no. 3 (2005), pp. 108–12.

RCC decision 9–P of July 14, 2005, *VESTNIK KONSTITUTSIONNOGO SUDA RF*, no. 4 (2005), pp. 67–102 (Gadzhiev, Iaroslavtsev and Kononov, dissenting).

Regions.Ru. 2006. V Mosgordume obsudili problemu neispolneniia sudebnykh reshenii. *Regions. Ru*, March 21. Available at: www.regions.ru/news/1961370.

Revoliutsiia dvernykh tablichek. 2005. Available at: www.*Gazeta.Ru*, May 17.

Rimskii, V. 2009. *Obzor sotsiologicheskikh issledovanii sudebnoi sistemy Rossii? Vypolnennykh v period s kontsa 1991 goda po nastoiashchii moment* [Overview of Sociological Studies of the Judicial System of Russia, Executed in the Period from Late 1991 to Present]. [Online: INDEM]. Available at: www.indem.ru/Proj/SudRef/soc/Rim9128.htm.

Rose, R. 2001. New Russia Barometer 10: Russians Under Putin. *Studies in Public Policy*, 350.

Rose, R. 2003. New Russia Barometer XI: The End of Term Report. *Studies in Public Policy*, 378.

Sadurski, W. 2003. Book Review: The Struggle for Constitutional Justice in Post-Communist Europe by Herman Schwartz. *International Journal of Constitutional Law*, 1(2), 159–62.

Samarina, A. 2004. Sudam doveriaet lish kazhdyi sotyi. *Nezavisimaia gazeta*, April 21.

Satarov, G., Rimskii, V. and Blagoveshchenskii, Iu. 2010. *Sotsiologicheskoe issledovanie rossiiskoi sudebnoi vlasti*. St.Petersburg: Norma.

Saul, S. 2005. Biudzhet – eshche ne vsia kazna. *EZh-Iurist*, 28, 1. Available at: www.roskazna.ru/pubs_24.html.

Sedov, L. 2002. Obshchestvennoe mnenie v sentiabre 2002 goda (Public Opinion in September 2002). *VTsIOM*, October 7. Available at: www.levada.ru/press/2002100700.html.

Skliarova, I. 2004. Posmotri v moi chestnye glaza [Look in My Honest Eyes]. *Vremia Novostei*, May 17.

Smirnov, I. 2006. New Taxpaying Realities—Unjustified Benefits. *St. Petersburg Times*, December 26.

Solomon, P. 2004. Judicial Power in Russia: Through the Prism of Administrative Justice. *Law & Society Review*, 38(3), 549–82.

Solomon, P. and Foglesong, T. 2000. *Courts and Transition in Russia: The Challenge of Judicial Reform*. Boulder: Westview Press.

Statistics of National Bureau of Enforcement. 2011. *The Official Website of National Bureau of Enforcement of Georgia*. August. Available at: http://nbe.gov.ge/index.php?lang_id=ENG&sec_id=32&info_id=4212.

Staton, J. 2010. *Judicial Power and Strategic Communication in Mexico*. New York: Cambridge University Press.

Staton, J. and Vanberg, G. 2008. The Value of Vagueness: Delegation, Defiance, and Judicial Opinions. *American Journal of Political Science*, 52(3), 504–19.

Steen, A. 2003. *Political Elites and the New Russia*. London: RoutledgeCurzon.

*Strana.Ru*. 2001. Otnoshenie rossiian k sudebnoi reforme ostaetsia ustoichivo pozitivnym. *Strana. Ru*, November 15. Available at: www.cja.ru/pages/pressreview/13-17-11-01.htm.

Supreme Court of the Russian Federation. 2008. Edict of the Plenum No. 16. September 26. Available at: www.supcourt.ru/news_detale.php?id=5491.

Thorson, C. 2004. Why Politicians Want Constitutional Courts: The Russian Case. *Communist and Post-Communist Studies*, 37(2), 187–211.

Tilly, C. 1975. Reflections on the History of European State-Making, in *The Formation of National States in Western Europe*, edited by C. Tilly and G. Ardant. Princeton: Princeton University Press, 3–83.

Trochev, A. 2004. Less Democracy, More Courts: The Puzzle of Judicial Review in Russia. *Law & Society Review*, 38(3), 513–39.

Trochev, A. 2008. *Judging Russia: The Role of the Constitutional Court in Russian Politics, 1990–2006*. New York: Cambridge University Press.

Trochev, A. 2009. All Appeals Lead to Strasbourg? Unpacking the Impact of the European Court of Human Rights on Russia. *Demokratizatsiya*, 17(2), 145–78.

Trochev, A. and Solomon, P. 2005. Courts and Federalism in Putin's Russia, in *The Dynamics of Russian Politics, Volume 2*, edited by P. Reddaway and R. Orttung. Lanham: Rowman & Littlefield, 91–121.

van den Berg, G.P. Constitution of the Russian Federation Annotated. *Review of Central and East European Law*, 27(2–3).

VTsIOM. 2005. Otnoshenie rossiian k sudam i sudebnoi sisteme. *Sudia*, 1, 49–60.

VTsIOM. 2006. Rossiiane o rabote obshchestvennykh institutov: SMI – v favore, partii – v zone neodobreniia. *Press-vypusk No. 573*. 10 November. Available at: http://wciom.ru/index.php?id=268&uid=3562.

VTsIOM. 2009. Komu doveriiat rossiiane v usloviiakh finansovogo krizisa. *Press-vypusk No. 1104*. 27 November. Available at: http://wciom.ru/index.php?id=268&uid=11048.

Vyskubin, A. 2008. O nekotorykh aspektakh ispolneniia vstupivshikh v zakonnuiiu silu sudebnykh reshenii, vynesennykh v polzu voennosluzhashchikh. *Interaktivnyi pravovoi zhurnal Instituta pravovedeniia "Ra"*. October 28. Available at: www.institutra.ru/trudi-inter-2008-11.php.

White, S. and McAllister, I. 2004. Dimensions of Disengagement in Post-Communist Russia. *Journal of Communist Studies and Transition Politics*, 20(1), 81–97.

World Bank. 2005. *Russia BEEPS At-a-Glance*. Available at: http://siteresources.worldbank.org/INTECAREGTOPANTCOR/Resources/BAAGREV20060208Russia.pdf.

World Bank. 2010. *BEEPS At-a-Glance Russia 2008*. January. Available at: http://siteresources.worldbank.org/INTECAREGTOPANTCOR/Resources/704589-1267561320871/Russia_2010.pdf.

World Bank. 2011. Trends in Corruption and Regulatory Burden in Eastern Europe and Central Asia. Washington, DC: World Bank.

Zviagina, N. 2006. Problema neispolneniia reshenii suda v Voronezhskoi oblasti. *Agentstvo Sotsialnoi Informatsii*, May 10. Available at: www.soc-otvet.ru/ASI3/main.nsf/0/5576D35E7B420D99C325716A003DE54F.

# Chapter 21

# The Challenges to Deregulating Russia: Business Registration Policy and Practice under Putin

Eugene Huskey

In the West, the consensus view of Putin's Russia is decidedly negative. The initial sympathy toward a president who assumed power in a seemingly ungovernable country gave way to disappointment and in some cases outrage.[1] During Putin's presidency, Russia abandoned the election of governors, reclaimed for the state the commanding heights of the economy, prosecuted political enemies of the president, further limited press freedom, created a presidential "pocket party" that controls parliament, and witnessed the murders of numerous opposition figures. In the eyes of almost all Western observers, these policies compared unfavorably to the democratizing initiatives under Yeltsin.

The picture is somewhat different in terms of economic reform, however, inasmuch as Russia under Putin advanced certain liberalizing and "marketizing" policies, especially at the level of small businesses (as opposed to the natural resource sector, particularly hydrocarbons, where state-ownership has increased and direct political pressure is common, whether based upon claims of "looting" of state assets in their acquisition by the private sector, or changing policies concerning strategic industries or sectors of the economy). Many of the initiatives in the small business sector follow the standard international financial institution (IFI) playbook, in which league tables exist for how business-friendly a country's government apparatus is (calculated normally in terms of how long it takes and how much it costs to establish a private business in incorporated form). At the level of economics, this represents a transaction cost minimization strategy in which a host government seeks to increase economic activity by establishing a framework of publicly accessible "rules," then relies upon the market and private sector entrepreneurs for growth (in opposition to traditional ideas about centralized economic planning).

In countries whose formal rules stifle private sector business formation, international organizations typically recommend early revision via changed statute or regulation of institutional competences of the bureaucracy. Such changes eliminate discretion, typically at the level of the government's business registry, and limit the maximum processing times as a means of accelerating business formation. This is the standard policy recipe for improving (small) business formation, but the implementation question is how do subsidiary government officials administering the business registry respond in practice to quite specific substantive law changes designed to accelerate processing times. And to the extent they resist implementation, is it rooted in an attempt to extort rents in holding up processing until paid "facilitation" fees (corruption explanation); a principled disagreement with a higher government policy to transition to a market economy (ideological explanation); or simple pique at changed personal circumstances as the newly rich entrepreneurial classes run up against relatively poor officialdom (jealousy explanation)?

---

1   For a less pessimistic view of Putin by a leading Western scholar, see Solomon (2005: 3–12).

On Putin's watch, Russia introduced progressive changes in the codes on criminal procedure, land, tax, and civil law; it also made other revisions to the legal and administrative environment that were intended to improve the business climate in the country. Thus, although democratization was on the wane, Putin was interested not only in the enhancement of state capacity but the marketization of at least a portion of the economy that had been weighed down by the legacies of the Soviet and immediate post-Soviet eras. It is only by recognizing these contradictory strains in Russia's development that we can understand the role of law and institutional reform in Putin's Russia.

Its assault on YUKOS notwithstanding, a central concern of the Putin presidency was the deregulation of the economy, especially as it relates to small and mid-sized business. With presidential backing, the liberal economist, German Gref, set out the intellectual foundations for the deregulation of the economy in late 1999 and then began to push through specific reforms in his role as minister of economic development. One of the earliest and most prominent of these reforms was the 2001 Law on the State Registration of Juridical Persons, which came into effect in the summer of 2002 (O gosudarstvennoi registratsii 2001). However, because this law, like virtually all Russian laws, was not self-executing, it required the enactment of sub-statutory acts by the government and relevant ministries to assure its implementation. Where some of these norms promised to fulfill faithfully, and even extend, the liberalizing spirit of the law, others served to impede the deregulation of the economy. In the pages below we illustrate the ways in which the traditionalism and/or rent-seeking instincts of the bureaucracy have erected hurdles to the implementation of marketizing legislation. The study serves as a reminder that law reform is as dependent on the proper operation of institutions as the content of norms. The question posed by this study is why petty officialdom resists direct attempts to change their behavior in the name of improving the business climate. Is resistance rooted in corruption, left-over ideological opposition to the private sector, or simple envy of the nouveau riche private sector, or some combination of the three?

## The Introduction of the Law on State Registration of Juridical Persons

The impetus for the introduction of the 2001 Law on State Registration was Putin's recognition of the woeful state of small business at the end of the Yeltsin era. Whereas small and mid-sized business accounted for 37 percent of employment in the Czech Republic and 58 percent in Georgia, the figure was only 13 percent for Russia in 2002 (Black and Tarassova 2003).[2] Besides limited access to credit and a lack of entrepreneurial traditions, Russian small business faced relatively high transaction costs and formidable barriers to entry. If the bribes required to pay off the ubiquitous state inspectors increased the transaction costs, the complexity and expense of the state registration process raised the barriers to entry for small enterprises.[3] Before the introduction of the 2001 Law on State Registration, businesses had to submit 50–90 registration forms to 20–30 agencies, which meant an average of three months to complete registration as opposed to three weeks in Poland (Black and Tarassova 2003). Because of the registration hurdles, those forming new businesses faced the choice of hiring expensive middlemen to secure registration or devoting untold hours to standing in lines at government offices.

The 2001 Law on State Registration promised to simplify registration in two ways. First, the new registration documents were limited to a four-page application form, proof of payment

---

2    For more detail on this reform, see Huskey (2007: 149–70).

3    Many other post-communist states faced similar problems. See Suhir and Kovach (2003).

of the state license fee, the passport and notarized signature of the official representative of the firm, and documents concerning the founding meeting and capital of the business, if it was a corporation. Second, the new law required state officials to register juridical persons within five days of receiving registration documents. Failure to meet the deadline subjected state registration authorities to liability for damages. To ensure that officials did not use a rejection of registration as a means of avoiding its responsibilities, the law stipulated that there were only two grounds for denying registration: failure to submit a required document or failure to submit the documents to the appropriate registration authorities. This simplified and expedited registration was designed to minimize, if not eliminate entirely, the opportunities for rent-seeking behavior by state officials, who traditionally extracted bribes from applicants in order to complete the registration in good order and in good time.

A further streamlining of state registration came into force on January 1, 2004, when revisions to the Law on State Registration introduced a "single service point" (literally, one window, *odno okno*), where those wishing to form a new business would submit all their documents (Buravchikova 2006). This system required the state registration officials, and not the applicant, to provide the registration information to the relevant government agencies. This reform sought to change the culture of state service by adopting an approach to public administration associated with the New Public Management in the Anglo-American world, which emphasized the treatment of citizens as valued clients as opposed to supplicants. In some places, the "single service points" were introduced with much fanfare and with some of the accoutrements of Western institutions, such as the service of customers based on a number pulled from a machine on entry into the office. As we shall see below, however, the "concretization" of these laws, by which is meant its translation into working directives for the bureaucracy, created new opportunities for state officials to introduce fields of bureaucratic discretion where none were envisioned by the law itself.

**Two Steps Forward, One Step Back**

No sooner had the laws gone into effect than some state officials began to search for ways to "reregulate" the registration process. In Moscow, for example, tax officials in one borough created queues artificially so that they could sell places in them to those seeking registration. When the Moscow offices were later consolidated into a single registration bureau in 2005, the cost of bribing one's way to the front of the queue had reportedly increased to $100, while the bribe required to arrange a personal meeting with the office manager was $1,500 (Skliarova 2006a; Zinov'ev 2006). Although registration officials rarely rejected applications in the first year of the law's operation, they began to change their behavior by mid-decade. According to Michael Green, the director of Grand and Metro Consulting and a registration middleman, if one saw 42 rejections on a bad day in Moscow in 2005, it was common to see 10 times that number in 2006, a development that he associated with the desire of the tax service to fill its coffers with the $80 fine imposed on those whose applications were allegedly not in order (Zinov'ev 2006). Another businessman observed that the registration offices had begun to collect money like "turnstiles in the metro" (Davydova 2006).[4]

In many cases, the attempts to undermine liberalization did not originate with the frontline bureaucrats but with high-ranking officials in the ministries or the government. An important innovation in the Law on State Registration of Juridical Persons was the formation of a single,

---

4   This article provides a useful introduction to the problem of bribery in Russia. For a sustained analysis of informal practices in the Russian economy and society, see Ledeneva (1998, 2006).

nationwide company register, which replaced the locally-based registries of the Yeltsin era. Although this source was initially made available to all citizens free of charge, as part of a broad-based e-government initiative, by 2007 access was only available by paying a fee to the Federal Tax Service, which was thereby able to enhance its revenues and monitor the use of the site.

One of the most implacable opponents of the deregulation of the economy has been the Ministry of Internal Affairs (MVD), whose resistance to economic liberalization began in the late tsarist era. For officials in the MVD, deregulation reduces the control mechanisms that they believe to be essential to the policing function of the state. The very idea of market solutions to problems of scarcity conflicts with their paternalistic outlook on the world. It was not enough, of course, to be philosophically opposed to the Law on State Registration, which was passed by the Duma with Putin's support. In order to weaken the law, the MVD seized on what it regarded as an undesirable by-product of simplified registration: the proliferatii of companies whose sole purpose was tax avoidance or illegal takeovers of legitimate businesses. These companies, known in Russian as "one-day wonders" (*firmy-odnodnevniki*) were often involved in brazen corporate identity theft. This enabled a dummy company to temporarily take over the bank accounts of solvent businesses and drain them of their assets. According to the head of the Federal Tax Service, Alexander Serdiukov, about one half of the 2,000 juridical persons created daily have tax avoidance as their sole *raison d'être* (Visloguzov 2006).

Tables 21.1 and 21.2 capture the increase in the number of firms registering and ceasing activity in the Putin and Medvedev years.

**Table 21.1 Juridical persons registered in Russia, 2003–2009**

| Year | Juridical persons in the unified state register | Number of commercial enterprises | Number of non-commercial enterprises | Other juridical persons |
|---|---|---|---|---|
| 2003 | 2,027,385 | 1,466,963 | 480,463 | 79,959 |
| 2004 | 2,271,887 | 1,643,259 | 512,740 | 115,888 |
| 2005 | 2,240,732 | 1,648,942 | 480,183 | 111,607 |
| 2006 | 2,893,358 | 2,198,999 | 572,386 | 121,973 |
| 2007 | 3,285,730 | 2,675,166 | 610,564 | NA |
| 2008 | 3,634,821 | 3,012,835 | 621,986 | NA |
| 2009 | 3,835,965 | 3,193,659 | 642,306 | NA |

*Source*: Svedeniia o rabote po gosudarstvennoi registratsii iuridicheskikh lits po sostoianiiu (2003–2009), website of Federal Tax Service (www.nalog.ru/index.php?topic=reg_ur_lic).

**Table 21.2 The closure of commercial enterprises in Russia, 2003–2009**

| Year | Commercial organizations ceasing activity | Ceased activity due to reorganization | Ceased activity due to liquidation | Number of bankrupt firms among those liquidated | Ceased activity due to decision of registration agency |
| --- | --- | --- | --- | --- | --- |
| 2003 | 67,885 | 11,386 | 56,006 | 41,898 | NA |
| 2004 | 116,246 | 18,514 | 94,627 | 70,537 | NA |
| 2005 | 133,722 | 22,107 | 109,349 | 77,273 | NA |
| 2006 | 210,249 | 39,284 | 164,659 | 110,193 | 82 |
| 2007 | 572,301 | 64,284 | 241,787 | 97,177 | 257,165 |
| 2008 | 948,271 | 94,595 | 298,206 | 131,995 | 543,436 |
| 2009 | 1,112,085 | 109,465 | 321,433 | 138,211 | 667,706 |

*Source*: Svedeniia o rabote po gosudarstvennoi registratsii iuridicheskikh lits po sostoianiiu (2003–2009), website of Federal Tax Service (www.nalog.ru/index.php?topic=reg_ur_lic).

The MVD and their allies in the bureaucracy used the scourge of the "one-day wonders" to launch a two-pronged attack on the deregulation of company registration. They first sought to revise legislation in order to lengthen the turnaround time for registration from five days to a month or longer, to increase capital requirements for new juridical persons,[5] and to introduce measure to authenticate documents before they were submitted (Davydov 2006). Implicit in these proposals was the replacement of a presumptive automatic registration with a system of review of documents and personnel that would allow state officials to reject applicants at their discretion. Among the many checks that the MVD and their parliamentary allies wished to introduce on business reporting was the independent verification of votes of the board and meeting minutes. To ensure that company documents accurately reflected the procedures and results of its meetings, traditionalists sought to require the presence of an independent registration official at all company meetings (Rubchenko 2006).

Such proposals would not only satisfy the penchant of law enforcement agencies for stronger policing powers but also provide openings for rents that were being denied to bureaucrats under the radical deregulation regime advanced by Gref and other liberals in the Putin administration. In the view of Vladimir Pligin, an ally of the MVD and chair of the Duma's Committee on Legislation, "the influence of the state is declining on matters where it should be decisive" (Rubchenko 2006).[6] So, instead of fighting fraud by introducing stiffer penalties for the falsification of documents, an approach favored by the Minister of Revenue, the MVD and other traditionalists have sought to return to a system that seeks to assure the accuracy of all materials before they are registered.

---

5   The Federal Tax Service sought to raise the minimum amount of founding capital from 10,000 to 25,000 rubles for OOO (Limited Liability Companies) and to 100,000 rubles for OAO (Public Stock Companies) (Medvedeva 2006: 14).

6   In this interview, Deputy Pligin reveals his beliefs that Western models are inappropriate for Russia, in part because Russia has a deep-seated tradition of deciding matters not by law but by fairness (*spravedlivost'*).

Although the Duma and regional assemblies have debated proposals to extend the turnaround time for registration, the opponents of reform have not yet been successful in altering the law.[7]

The second line of attack against the provisions of the Law on State Registration of Juridical Persons did not seek to revise the law—always a politically difficult undertaking—but rather to interpret it in ways that would erode its deregulating impact. On the basis of the threat posed by the "one-day wonders," the opponents of deregulation in the Moscow branch of the Federal Tax Service succeeded in altering the established procedures for submitting documentation. Other regional offices soon followed suit. From January 2006, the chief officer needed to appear if submitting registration documents or forms that reported changes in the company address, principals, or constitutive documents (Lavrov 2006; Liashenko 2006a).[8] Although in principle submission by mail remained an option, the long delays common to the Russian postal service, combined with a lower return rate on applications sent by mail, meant that Russian business leaders were effectively forced to abandon their usual work for a day or longer and assume the role of a courier.

Despite the introduction of the "single service point" system, by the middle of the decade, as we noted earlier, lines at registration offices rivaled the queues of the Soviet era. Because Moscow consolidated its borough-based registration offices into a single citywide bureau, a CEO desiring to register his company would have to arrive before dawn and expect to wait several hours before he or she could submit the necessary documents, only to return another day to join a queue to retrieve the completed registration. And although the government allegedly introduced this procedure to discourage the creation of "one-day wonders," there is no evidence that the policy has had the desired effect, or indeed that registration personnel even check the passports of all applicants. Some reports suggest that the applicant, after waiting for hours, does not even speak with registration officials but instead drops the materials into a container, for which he or she receives no receipt.

Not surprisingly, the government edict requiring a personal appearance of the company head at the registration offices prompted a backlash, not only from the businessmen themselves but also from the firms that handled company registration for their clients. In several instances, companies whose authorized representatives were unable to submit registration documents brought suit against the registration office in commercial (*arbitrazh*) courts. Although most won their cases, and were able to use authorized representatives to submit their documents, the registration offices refused to extend the courtesy to other applicants (Liashenko 2006). As a result, one law firm with a significant company registration practice, Private Law (*Chastnoe Pravo*), brought suit in the Russian Supreme Court against the refusal of the registration offices to accept documents from the authorized representatives of a business. In August 2006, the Supreme Court decided in favor of the plaintiff (O priznanii 2006). The Federal Tax Service appealed the ruling, but the Cassation Collegium of the Supreme Court upheld the decision in late September 2006. The Courts based their decision on the agency provisions in the Russian Civil Procedure Code as well as the Federal

---

7   In some cases, however, frontline officials have taken matters into their own hands by delaying the registration of juridical persons beyond the five-day deadline. To be fair, these delays do not always represent attempts to undermine reform. Large numbers of applications come in advance of certain deadlines, which makes it difficult to adhere to the strict provisions of the law. In order to limit the number of "one-day wonders," registration offices have also begun rejecting any applications that include an address already used by 10 or more companies (Skliarova 2006: 4).

8   It should be noted that the government directive on which this strict requirement was based was introduced in 2002, but until that time registration offices had always allowed company officers to send their authorized agents to submit documents, acting on a Directive Letter of the Federal Tax Service issued on February 1, 2005 (Liashenko 2006: 9).

Tax Service's own Directive Letter of February 1, 2005, which allowed an authorized company agent to submit the required documentation (Dokumenty 2006).[9]

## Conclusion

This decision is just one skirmish in a protracted war, where law must do battle with other weapons, like informal practices and administrative discretion, which are often better suited to the intricate terrain of Russian officialdom. Laws and legal decisions have a certain force, but they do not inspire respect or deference as they would in more mature legal systems. It is not enough, therefore, to make laws or to issue court rulings. Until a new legal culture emerges, one must learn to fight in the bureaucratic trenches, which means finding ways to overcome the advantages enjoyed by officials whose livelihood and self-importance depend on limiting the rights of citizens.

The postscript to the Supreme Court victory reminds us of law's limited reach in Russia. After the Court's initial decision, registration officials in Moscow agreed to open up windows to receive registration documents from applicants, but only two windows. And whereas those company heads who appeared personally had the right to return to the bureau to obtain their registration documents directly, those sending authorized representatives had to await receipt of the documents by mail, which meant that they might not receive them at all (Liashenko 2006, 2006a).

Besides seeking to lower the barriers to entry for small businesses, legislation adopted in the Putin era also attempted to lower the transaction costs of small businesses by protecting them against unjustified state inspections, which served as opportunities for bribe-taking by officials. However, like the law on the state registration of juridical persons, this legislation was not self-executing, and there is little evidence that bureaucrats reduced their use of inspections to shake down small business owners. When businessmen and women in the republic of Buriatia were asked which state agency served as the most serious obstacle to their activities, they replied the fire marshal (22 percent of the respondents). Because legislative attempts to restrain inspections were largely ineffective, the Procurator-General, Iurii Chaika, noted in early 2009 that state agencies conducting unplanned inspections of businesses would need first to receive the permission of the Procuracy, beginning in July of that year. And beginning in 2010, the Procuracy started keeping a register of planned inspections as well (Prokurorskoe slovo i delo 2009). Such a proliferation of bureaucratic checking mechanisms is the logical result of a system where law is as yet unable to restrain officialdom.[10]

---

9   In another positive development, the Deputy Speaker of the Duma, Oleg Morozov, proposed introducing legislation that would free small businesses from intrusive state inspections for the first three years of their existence (Malyi biznes 2006: 4).

10   On the efforts to lower the transaction costs and barriers to entry for small business under the Medvedev presidency, see Huskey (forthcoming). On the links between legal and bureaucratic development in Russia, see Rowney and Huskey (2009), especially chapters 1, 13, and 19.

## References


Black, B.S. and Tarassova, A.S. 2003. Institutional Reform in Transition: A Case Study of Russia. *Supreme Court Economic Review*, 10, 211.

Buravchikova, D. 2006. Ot 'odnogo okna' v glazakh troitsia. *Argumenty i fakty*, April 5, 23.

Davydov, D. 2006. V federal'noi nalogoi sluzhbe (FNS) reshili dat' boi firmam-odnodnevkam. *Rossiiskie vesti*, March 29, 16.

Davydova, M. 2006. Komu by dat' vziatku? *Slovo*, March 10, 11.

Dokumenty. 2006. *Kommersant Daily*, September 29, 14.

Huskey, E. 2007. Lowering the Barriers for Russian Small Business: The 2001 Law on the Registration of Juridical Persons, in *Remaking the Role of Law: Commercial Law in Russia and the CIS*. Huntington: Juris Publishing, 149–69.

Huskey, E. Forthcoming. Bureaucratic Agents and Policy Implementation in Contemporary Russia: De-bureaucratizing the Small Business Sector, in Lena Jonson and Stephen White (eds), *Russian Political Modernization: Challenges and Dilemmas*. Basingstoke: Palgrave.

Lavrov, A. 2006. Biznesmenam razreshili otpravliat' khodokov. *Gazeta*, August 3.

Ledeneva, A. 1998. *Russia's Economy of Favours: Blat, Networking, and Informal Exchange*. Cambridge: Cambridge University Press.

Ledeneva, A. 2006. *How Russia Really Works: The Informal Practices that Shaped Post-Soviet Politics and Business*. Ithaca: Cornell University Press.

Liashenko, G. 2006. Biznes na doverii. *Gazeta*, September 29, 10.

Liashenko, G. 2006a. Nedoveritel'nye otnosheniia. *Gazeta*, August 30, 9.

Malyi biznes osvobodiat ot proverok na tri goda. 2006. *Rossiiskaia gazeta*, September 20, 4.

Mau, V. 2006. Malyi biznes v bol'shoi politike. *Profil'*, June 6, 44.

Medvedeva, E. 2006. Gumanizm Grefa. *Gazeta*, April 26, 14.

O gosudarstvennoi registratsii iuridicheskikh lits, Federal'nyi zakon RF ot 08.08.2001 no 129–F3.

O priznanii chastichno nedeistvuiushchim abzatsa 1 punkta 3 trebovanii k oformleniiu dokumentov, ispol'zuemykh pri gosudarstvennoi registratsii, utverzhdennykh postanoveleniem pravitel'stva RF ot 19.06.2002 N 439, Verkhovnyi Sud RF, Reshenie ot 1 avgusta 2006 g. N GKPI06–735.

Otchety o rabote po gosudarstvennoi registratsii iuridicheskikh lits na 01.10.2003, 01.07.2004, i 01.01.2005. Available at: www.nalog.ru/index.php?topic=reg_ur_lic.

Prokurorskoe slovo i delo. 2009. *Rossiiskaia gazeta*, February 25.

Rowney, D.K. and Huskey, E. 2009. *Russian Bureaucracy and the State: Officialdom from Alexander III to Putin*. London: Palgrave Macmillan.

Rubchenko, M. 2006. Razrushitel'nyi poisk spravedlivosti. *Expert*, June 19.

Skliarova, I. 2006. Adresnaia figa. *Vremia novostei*, March 27, 4.

Skliarova, I. 2006a. Nikogo lichnogo. *Vremia novostei*, August 25, 4.

Solomon, Jr. P.H. 2005. Vladimir Putin's Quest for a Strong State. *International Journal on World Peace*, 22(2), 3–12.

Suhir, E. and Kovach, Z. 2003. Administrative Barriers to Enterpreneurship in Central Asia. *CIPE*, June 30.

Visloguzov, V. 2006. Glava nalogovoi sluzhby predstavilsia Gosdume. *Kommersant Daily*, 2, March 23.

Zinov'ev, I. 2006. Pravila igry. Registratsiia iavochnym poriadkom. *Kommersant-Den'gi*, April 3, 28.

Chapter 22

# Dancing the Rumba: Federalism Reform in Russia under Putin and Medvedev

Joel H. Samuels

No single issue defines Russia, past, present, or future, more than the question of center–periphery relations. Imperial Russia faced challenges to central governance for more than a century.[1] During the Soviet period, the communist regime centralized power but created disparate regional nomenclatures, which only complicated center–periphery relations. The question remains: are there practical constraints on the governance of a large geographic expanse, divided into a multitude of culturally and linguistically distinct ethnic groups? So it was notable that, when, in December 1993, Russia ratified its first post-communist constitution, Article 1 of that Constitution proclaimed that Russia is "a democratic federal law-bound state with a republican form of government" (Constitution of the Russian Federation 2009). The question, however, is how at the legal and institutional level this federalism is articulated in practice, whether it seems to fall back into traditional Russian pathways, and why?

The 1993 Russian Constitution created an expressly federal structure, with a striking mandate to spread the power beyond Moscow. That mandate has been revisited over the past decade through a series of legislative and presidential actions that have taken on a rumba-like feel, with reforms often moving in different directions on the center–periphery power scale. Vladimir Putin and his successor, Dmitry Medvedev, have orchestrated these reforms, leading their dance partners—Russia's regions and their leaders—to react as the central authority sets the terms and pattern of reform.

The rumba is a passionate Cuban dance characterized by complex steps, in which one partner loses ground as the other gains, only to then turn the tables and push back across the dance floor. The apparently chaotic dance in fact follows rules as graceful as those of chess and lends itself to a palpable reflection of center–periphery relations in Russia. Although meaningful developments involving federalism in Russia occurred during the 1990s, this chapter largely will evaluate reform of the center–periphery relationship in Russia from late 1999 to the present (under Putin and Medvedev, making only occasional reference to Russia under Yeltsin in the immediate aftermath of the USSR's demise).[2] The past decade of rumba-like federalism reforms in Russia have followed old patterns of power politics in response to the pressures of governing a large and ethnically diverse state. While this history demonstrates that behavior (or expectations of behavior) must change before legal reform—at least with regard to decentralization reform in Russia—can have a meaningful impact, it also raises the question: to what extent is behavior learned versus being largely predetermined by the institutional constraints of history, geography, and ethnic and linguistic diversity?

---

1   For a detailed account of the center–periphery relationship during the Czarist period, see Starr (1972).

2   For an in-depth look at center–periphery relations during the 1990s, see Stoner-Weiss (2006a: 51–75). For an enlightening study of the broad and narrow issues of center–periphery relations in Russia during that same period and in the early Putin years, see also, Kempton and Clark (2002).

Russia's efforts at federalism are affected in large measure by the country's size and structure. In terms of land mass, Russia is the largest country in the world at 6.5 million square miles (17 million square kilometers), nearly double the next largest country in the world. Just as important to the complexity of federalism in Russia is the composition of the federal structure. Russia is made up of 83 sub-federal units.[3] The only country in the world that has a remotely comparable number is the United States—at 50. And in the United States, all 50 states have the same rights and are treated equally by the law.[4] The sheer number of sub-federal units is further complicated by ethnic differences, as many of those units are in fact defined by a significant single ethnic group.[5]

Dating back to Czarist times, Russia has struggled to maintain uniformity in policy across the breadth of a vast and multi-ethnic nation. Secessionist movements in the nineteenth century led to often draconian measures by central authorities in an effort to maintain the unity of the state. Tension between the center and the periphery upset the governing power structures. At the same time, the czars recognized their dependence on regional leaders to maintain order in the far-flung country. So the czars (much like their successors in the 90 years since) struggled to identify an appropriate balance between offering authority to regional leaders and maintaining control over those leaders and the territories they governed.

The Bolshevik Revolution, which overthrew the czars and installed the communist apparatus, drew strength in part from the tension between center and periphery. Once in power, though, the leaders of the Soviet Union cracked down on the power of the regions. By the end of its 70-plus year window as a state, the Soviet Union included (among other sub-federal entities) 15 different republics which made up the union. When the Soviet Union collapsed in the early 1990s, those republics broke off.[6] Today, those 15 entities, which once made up a single nation, are in fact 15 different nations.[7] Russia today largely mirrors Czarist Russia in size and scope, but the Soviet era injected additional regional considerations by making Russia at best the first among 15 equals. Moreover, the potential for a single state to fracture apart with such ease still animates Russian leaders.

--------

3   The 83 sub-federal units are divided into two primary categories—ethnically defined subjects (26) and territorially defined subjects (57). The ethnically defined subjects are further divided into ethnic republics (21) (which enjoy far greater autonomy than other federal subjects, creating the impression that some federal sub-units are more equal than others), autonomous okrugs (4) and autonomous oblasts (1) and where the territorially defined subjects (57) include krais (9), oblasts (46) and federal cities (2) (Moscow and St. Petersburg). It is worth noting that that the current number of subdivisions is down from the Soviet area, when there were not 83 but 212 subdivisions—the 15 Soviet republics (all of them now separate nations), 20 autonomous republics, eight autonomous oblasts, 10 autonomous okrugs, and 159 (rather than 57) territorially based regions. Although these 83 provinces, republics, territories, autonomous districts, and federal cities have varying constitutional status, they will be referred to collectively in this chapter as regions. Similarly, the leaders of these entities have varying titles and powers, but those leaders will be referred to herein as leaders or governors or executives.

4   It is worth noting that, in addition to the 50 states, the United States has federal relationships of a different nature with several territories, including American Samoa, Guam, Puerto Rico, and the District of Columbia.

5   Many of these ethnic sub-federal units are the remnants of Stalin-era efforts to deport or transport entire ethnic groups in the then-Soviet Union. During the 1930s and 1940s, ethnic republics were created out of ethnic groups which had previously been disparate.

6   Indeed, a colorable argument can be made that the break-up of the Soviet Union was hastened by reforms during the 1980s era of perestroika and glasnost under Mikhail Gorbachev that decentralized power and allowed the republics to gain greater power and autonomy which they ultimately used to split from the union.

7   They are: Armenia, Azerbaijan, Belarus, Estonia, Georgia, Latvia, Lithuania, Kazakhstan, Kyzgyz, Moldova, Russia, Tajikistan, Turkmenistan, Ukraine, and Uzbekistan.

In the 1990s, Boris Yeltsin (who had been the governor of Russia when it was merely a region in the Soviet Union, but who became president of a nation when the Soviet Union split and Russia became a nation-state) struggled to maintain the power of Russia while making concessions to regional leaders who had been instrumental in his rise to power. During the 1990s, Yeltsin devolved powers to the regions, even though such decentralization had caused significant problems for the country for hundreds of years. Regional governors continued to support Yeltsin but also prioritized their own local concerns over the needs of the state as a whole, reducing the efficacy of the central state and leading to misuse and at times spoliation of natural resources.

The decision by Yeltsin to decentralize went against the intent of the framers of the post-Soviet Union Constitution. The Russian Constitution of 1993 codified the historical Russian view of center–periphery relations, anointing the federal state with virtually exclusive control, subject only to its own decisions to relinquish authority. Articles 71–73 of the Russian Constitution granted the federal government expansive power over the mechanisms of governance. This left the regions to exercise their powers in only limited arenas when granted power by the federal state.

During the 1990s, the central authorities actually encouraged regional autonomy, with Boris Yeltsin notoriously telling the regions to "take as much sovereignty as they could swallow" (Erlanger 1992). Strikingly few constraints were placed on autonomy-minded governors, as 46 regions brokered bilateral treaties with Moscow, with virtually all exercising authority in areas constitutionally reserved for the federal government, including foreign policy, civil rights, tax rates, international trade, and exploitation of natural resources (Hahn 2003).[8] The regional authorities further asserted their independence from the central government by passing laws that contradicted federal law and the Russian Constitution itself.[9]

In part due to the decentralization of authority and power, the Russia that Vladimir Putin inherited in 2000 was mired in chaos.[10] Moreover, the prior decade of center–periphery relations offered something of a cautionary tale to Putin. Not only had the country fallen into chaos, but in the years before Yeltsin took over, decentralization had led the Soviet Union to break up as the regions split away. There was every reason to fear that regions within Russia would take similar steps and further erode the unity of the Russian state. Secession by even one sub-federal unit would open a gateway that would shake the foundations of the Russian state.

As described in this chapter, the Putin and Medvedev administrations have swung back in the opposite direction, centralizing power as a way of reining in the regions and providing a sense

---

8   See also Graney (2008).

9   Although a great deal has been written about these regional and local laws, it remains unclear whether the contradictory laws were motivated by the desire to flout the power of the central administration or by basic misunderstandings of the federal laws and Constitution, such that the drafters of regional and local laws did not appreciate the problems posed by their laws. Though that issue goes beyond the scope of this chapter, it raises fundamental questions about the nature of the chaos and struggle for power (with the regions) that Vladimir Putin inherited from Boris Yeltsin.

10   Recent history also affects present-day federal reform. The Russia that Boris Yeltsin inherited from Mikhail Gorbachev was the definition of a conflicted society. Indeed, he inherited a crumbling Soviet empire as well as a crumbling Russian state. So, virtually overnight Russia saw 14 of the 15 Soviet republics declare independence (with some interim efforts to keep a few of them in the fold). The Constitution aside, legal reform under Yeltsin turned more and more chaotic during his last five years in office—that is from 1995 to 1999. Notably, though, through 1995, Yeltsin passed a series of moratoriums on the election of regional governors, instead choosing to appoint the then 89 regional governors himself. It wasn't until 1999 that all of the 89 regional leaders had been elected and not appointed.

of national focus and purpose.[11] Buoyed by his overwhelming victory in the 2000 presidential elections, Putin undertook to reform the federal system in Russia.[12]

Putin has written that he believes that "from the very beginning, Russia was created as a super centralized state. That's practically laid down in its genetic code, its traditions, and the mentality of its people" (Putin 2000; Putin et al. 2000: 186). Federalist reform in Russia over the past decade has reflected that understanding of the relationship between the center and regions. Putin's vision of Russian tradition as centrist, historically and indeed genetically, has informed (perhaps even guided) Russian legal reform of center–periphery relations.

In an effort to create some order, one of Putin's first steps was to rein in the power of the regions—and in particular, the regional governors. Putin's first major reform sought to "strengthen the unity of the state" by curtailing the power of regional governors (Presidential Decree No. 849 2000). This language of unity demonstrates the underlying cultural norms that envision unity as a benefit in itself, contrasted with chaos and anarchy, which serve as an unconditional foil in the Russian psyche and which in fact flourished during the Yeltsin years.

As Putin stated in his message to the Federal Assembly[13] in 2000:

> It's a scandalous thing when a fifth of the legal acts adopted in the regions contradict the country's Basic Law [the Russian Constitution], when republic constitutions and province charters are at odds with the Russian Constitution, and when trade barriers, or even worse, border demarcation posts are set up between Russia's territories and provinces (Putin 2000).

Putin's initial reforms struck at the authority of regional governors and the power of the regions themselves. By weakening the power of the leaders of each region, Putin could diminish the power of the regions themselves. By revising the structure of the regions, Putin similarly could reduce regional political clout. Since 2000, Russia has seen at least eight significant reforms to center–periphery relations, each of which I will explore in this chapter:

1. power to remove regional governors and dissolve regional legislatures;
2. redivision of the country into seven super-districts;
3. reform of the upper house of parliament, the Federation Council;
4. creation of the State Council;
5. revised laws reducing the power of regional governors and political parties;
6. implementation of an evaluation system for regional governors;
7. Tatarstan's revised treaty with Russia; and
8. amendments expanding presidential power over regional governors and legislatures.

The chapter will focus on four central questions in evaluating the federalism reforms in Russia: what was the reform? What was the impact of the reform? What might be the external perceptions of the reform and the motivations for making the reform? What might be the effects of those perceptions on the legitimacy of the reforms?

---

11    In many ways, the last decade of reform in Russia harks back to the Czarist era when the central authorities sought to control the regions.

12    For a more detailed account of federal reform in the early days of the Putin administration, see Ross (2002).

13    The Federal Assembly is made up of two bodies, the State Duma (sometimes referred to as the lower house) and the Federation Council (upper house). Putin's remarks were made at a joint session of the two bodies in May 2000.

## Power to Remove Regional Governors and Dissolve Regional Legislatures

The first major reform to center–periphery relations occurred on the eve of Putin's ascension to the presidency, initiated by Putin and his political allies. This early reform signaled his intent to reduce the chaos that he perceived as emanating from personal fiefdoms governed by regional leaders with no sense of central (or national) priorities. In October 1999, a new law entered force, which gave the president the power to remove regional governors and dissolve regional assemblies (Ob Obshchikh Principakh Organizatsii Zakonodalet'nykh 1999). This new law signaled a clear intent to rein in the power of the periphery. The legislation also empowered central authorities—including the Duma and the Federation Council as well as the general procurator in Moscow—to recommend the removal of regional governors (Zakonodalet'nykh 1999). Demonstrating the nuance implicit (but often forgotten) in recent regional reform in Russia, however, regional legislatures were also empowered to make similar recommendations (Zakonodalet'nykh 1999).

The nuances of the law also demonstrated the first steps of the rumba that would come to symbolize federalism reform in Russia over the past decade. In addition to the nod to regional legislatures noted above, unwieldy provisions blunted the practical power of the law from Moscow's perspective. The process for a removal of a regional governor under the law is at best cumbersome:

> One, he must on two different occasions ignore presidential decrees, two, allow the passage of two bills with provisions that violate federal laws, or three, make use on two different occasions of regional acts previously denounced by the president or the courts. And, in each of these cases, a court verdict is required ruling that these actions constitute violations of federal law. (Corwin 2000)

Thus the new law required repeated repudiation by the governor of directives from the center for removal. Moreover, the law required intervention by the courts, ensuring that the president alone could not remove regional governors (Zakonodalet'nykh 1999). On its face at least, this first law reined in the power of regional governors without centralizing authority over the governors in the hands of any single central authority.

Given the complex process for removing a regional governor, the direct impact of the law itself was minor. Regional governors did not face a real threat of removal under the law; nevertheless, the threat of the law did blunt the power of regional governors and, above all, the subject matter of the law made for good headlines and sound bites. Moreover, in April 2002, the Russian Constitutional Court upheld the law and the power of the president to remove regional leaders and of the Duma to disband regional legislatures.[14] Even if the process for removal was unwieldy and unlikely to be undertaken, the message was clear: regional governors must follow the dictates of the central government or face consequences.

In this light, what might have been a clear message created mixed impressions. Internally, the legal reform was popular. Putin had a mandate to rein in the chaos of the Yeltsin years, and many viewed regional elites as one of the sources of that chaos. But abroad, observers saw the reform as an initial step at centralizing power and silencing opposition forces, many of which had bases outside Moscow. These competing perceptions led to competing views of the legitimacy of the reforms and in many ways dictated the dance that the central government has engaged in with the

---

14 For a discussion of this case, see Mikhailova (2002: 6, quoted in Ross 2005: 359): "Under this new ruling, for the removal process to begin, the law requires that the action of a governor or regional legislature must have 'caused massive and serious violations of individual and civil rights and freedoms, threatened the unity and territorial integrity or national security of the Russian Federation and its ability to defend itself, or the unity of the country's legal and economic space.'"

regions in the subsequent decade. This first law merely drew an initial line in the sand for regional power brokers. But it was only the first step in a multi-pronged attack on the periphery that took shape starting in 2000.


## Division of Russia into Seven Super-Districts

In a move that weakened the regions themselves, the second major federalism reform of the Putin years divided Russia into seven super-districts along lines that were connected more to military lines of communication and power and less to historical and ethnic connection. The districts were created by virtue of a Presidential Decree on May 13, 2000 (Presidential Decree No. 849 2000). The decree created the new districts and also empowered the president to appoint special representatives to represent the interests of the federal government in each district. Putin's creation of the seven federal districts and provisions for the special representatives complied with Article 83 of the Russian Constitution, which grants the president the power to appoint and remove "plenipotentiary representatives of the President of the Russian Federation" (Constitution of the Russian Federation 2009).

The May 13 decree tasks the special representatives with ensuring that the federal government's constitutions, laws and officials are effective in the regions. But the decree did not provide the central government representatives meaningful mechanisms to remedy problems that they identified in the regions. In spite of its broad reach, this initial reform has not proven successful in consolidating central power, largely because the presidential representatives in the super-regions had undefined powers, and as such proved unable to insert themselves into the policy-making process.

In many ways, this odd group of individuals appears reminiscent of foreign ambassadors, but instead of representing the interests of the state in foreign nations, they merely express the interests of the central administration in the periphery, without actually wielding any power to effect change. The initial appointees themselves were politically connected. Five of the seven initial appointees were former KGB officials who had known Putin from that period of his career. In many ways, these officials served as the eyes and ears of the president, much as the czars had used similar officials a century earlier.

On its face, the May 13 decree had an immediate impact on center–periphery relations in Russia. The decree regrouped the regions into districts determined by the central administration. Officials appointed by—and owing an allegiance to—Moscow governed the newly created districts. These new officials could identify and stamp out the rampant corruption by regional leaders and could impose more center-friendly tax collection policies.

This reform was met with skepticism both in Russia and abroad (Graney 2008).[15] However, the widespread skepticism did not succeed in undermining the viability of the reforms. As Cameron Ross noted, "Putin can argue that the changes brought about by the May 13 decree were simply changes in his presidential administration, and not constitutional changes to the federation itself [which would have required Constitutional amendments]" (Ross 2002). Thus, this first reform of the Putin years—a Presidential Decree not vetted by the legislature—simultaneously strengthened the power of the center vis-à-vis the periphery and weakened the legitimacy of the reforms themselves.

---

15   See also Ross (2002).

## Reform of the Federation Council

The third reform to take place emanated from the legislature and again weakened the powers of the regions. In the summer of 2000, the Duma passed a law, ratified by the Federation Council, that changed the process for membership on the Federation Council.[16] The law removed governors from the Federation Council (Russia's upper house of parliament), a role provided by the 1993 Constitution (Constitution of the Russian Federation 2009).

The Federation Council as conceived by the Russian Constitution was patterned on the German Bundesrat, where representatives of each of the 16 Länder (sub-federal regions) provide input and vote on federal laws that affect the power of the regions. In terms of composition, the Federation Council roughly mirrors the US Senate with two representatives from every one of the federal subjects of Russia, regardless of size.[17]

The Russian Constitution was silent on how to choose members of the Federation Council (Constitution of the Russian Federation 2009). During the 1990s, regional governors and their representatives populated the Federation Council, where they lobbied for their respective local interests. The federal government viewed this competition as counterproductive to the management of the state. In addition, members of the Federation Council are entitled to immunity from prosecution. Armed with that immunity, many regional governors engaged in various forms of corruption without regard to punishment or recrimination. The reform to the federation Council gave regional governors a choice—lead the region (with the prospect of facing prosecution for malfeasance) or seek appointment to the Federation Council to offer advice to the center on behalf of the regions (but with the blanket of immunity from prosecution). This new, weaker role on the Federation Council reduced the potential for corruption of officials who could not be prosecuted for their actions. This effort certainly helped to provide accountability for corrupt activities by regional leaders even though it was only one among many motives for changing the composition of the Federation Council.

As one might expect, the Federation Council resisted efforts to reform its membership. Motivated not least by self-interest but also by real concerns about the effect the proposed reforms would have in diluting the voice of the regions (the presumptive reason for having such a body as part of the constitutional division of powers), the members of the Federation Council mounted a challenge to the Duma's efforts to pass the new law that would affect the process for naming members of the Federation Council. In the end, however, having been swept to power with overwhelming public support, Putin and his political allies in the Duma persuaded the Federation Council to pass the Duma's new law.

Like the first reform of the federal system under Putin, this new law weakened the power of the periphery and centralized the power of Moscow. Unlike the first reform, this law went through the legislative approval process (although a reasonable observer might question the legitimacy of that process on the basis that the Duma appeared to follow Putin's direct orders throughout the approval). But the law did have the effect of allowing for a more uniform implementation of federal law. The delicate rumba took another step to and fro as the center reeled in its power in the name of order, and the periphery lost whatever small hand it might have had in the legislative process.[18]

---

16   See Federal Law No. 113–F3, "O Paryadkye Formorovaniva Sovyeta Federatsiya Federal'novo Sobraniya Rossiskoi Federatsii, *Rossiskaya Gazeta* 2000.

17   In other words, the Council was made up of 166 members, two from each of the 83 regional entities.

18   The powers of the Federation Council are largely circumscribed as the Duma is invested with ultimate authority to craft laws while the Federation Council is largely limited to a straight up-or-down approval of Duma legislation. (In that sense, whereas there may be a similarity in composition, the Russian

The external perception mirrored that of the earlier reform; indeed, this legislation appeared little more than an extension of the May 13 Presidential Decree. Once again, the move was driven by the central government's desire to rein in the periphery, cutting down the potential for corruption and self-dealing by regional leaders. The legal reform merely followed the ambitions of the political leadership in Moscow. And the process that started on May 13 and continued through the summer was still not complete.

## Creation of the State Council

With Moscow's efforts to pull power away from the regions in full swing, the next step of the rumba took place. On September 1, 2000, President Putin issued a new Presidential Decree on issues involving center–periphery relations, creating a new advisory body called the State Council (Presidential Decree No. 602 2000). The Council meets once every three months to advise the President of the Russian Federation. The Council is composed of the head of each sub-federal entity, with a special inner circle made up of one regional leader from each of the seven districts. Whereas the first two prongs of the federal reform stripped the regions of power, this next step had the opposite effect.

The State Council offered the regional leaders a voice in central decision-making. Skeptics argued that the State Council was a consolation prize to the regions of little real value. After all, the Council is merely advisory. Moreover, as some scholars have pointed out, having been created by Presidential Decree, the Council could just as easily be abolished. Of course, that same logic would undermine the May 13 Presidential Decree that divided the country into seven districts and many saw as the start of the consolidation of federal power. If the May 13 decree was a meaningful one, as I agree it is, then the September 1 decree deserves equal import. The first three measures for federal reform under Putin were aimed at precisely the concerns outlined in his May 2000 address to the Federal Assembly.

While some outsiders viewed this reform as a sideshow and therefore undermining the legitimacy of meaningful reform, a fair accounting would conclude that this measure offered some legitimacy to Putin's stated goal of reining in the periphery so that meaningful nationwide policies could be implemented while still offering a voice to the regional leaders. At a minimum, this September decree continued the uncomfortable dance between Russia's center and its periphery.

## Revision of Laws Governing Power of Governors and Political Parties

In the four years that followed the initial raft of reforms aimed at redefining center–periphery relations in Russia, Moscow passed a series of laws through legislative action or Presidential Decree reforming the power of the governors and regional political parties.[19] Taken together, these reforms continued to erode the power of regional elites and the power structures supporting them. External observers again perceived the reforms as illegitimate power plays by the central administration (and specifically by Putin). While understandable, this view of Putin's reforms ignores the Yeltsin-

---

legislative system contrasts starkly with the American system in terms of the powers to the Upper Body of the legislature.)

19   For example, as Elena Chebankova (2007: 288) noted, in 2002, Putin signed a new law that allowed regional administrative bodies to be suspended if the region's debt to the central government exceeded 30 percent of the region's budget. See also Sobranie Zakonodatel'stva Rossiiskoi Federatsii (2003: 6553–80).

era chaos caused in part by regional officials focused on local interests that operated at cross-purposes with the interest of the nation as a whole.

In 2004, the process for appointing regional governors was revised.[20] For the previous decade, corrupt governors, offering handouts to regional constituents, had successfully been reelected regularly across the political landscape.[21] Under the system adopted in 2004, the president would nominate a regional governor, overturning a system of direct election of regional governors that had been in place since 1996 (Soderlund 2006).[22]

Although the central government took the power of direct election away from the local population, the regions retained some power in the selection of the regional governors. The regional legislature then vetted the nominee and exercised the power to accept the nomination and elect the governor nominated by the president or to reject the choice. The president in turn was empowered to re-nominate the same candidate. However, if the regional legislature were to reject the same nominee twice, then the legislature and the president would enter a period of consultations. After those consultations take place, the president can make a new nomination, appoint an interim governor, or dismiss the legislature. If the legislature rejects the nominee a third time, the president can dissolve the legislature (Soderlund 2006).

The law also included a provision allowing the president to dismiss a governor for "lack of confidence." In light of the 2000 reforms discussed above (giving the president the power to fire a governor for wrongdoing), this new presidential authority indicates a further erosion of regional authority. The threshold for firing regional leaders had dropped. If Moscow and its regions are engaged in a dance, one might assume from the 2004 changes that the regions took several steps backwards as the Kremlin executed the first of a series of well-placed box steps.

While at first glance this reform may seem to be a hard line from the central authority, one commentator has noted the surprising alacrity with which the regional governors accepted the reforms, suggesting that governors may have increased in power in their respective regions as a result of the new alignment with Moscow (Goode 2007). Notably, Putin and Medvedev have allowed some of the most powerful executives to remain in office, seemingly at odds with a centralizing strategy (Goode 2007). At least one scholar has suggested that gubernatorial appointments could actually increase regional power, causing regions to push back against the center, much as a dance partner may gain ground with the left foot after stepping back with the right.[23]

---

20   See http://news.bbc.co.uk/2/hi/europe/3965845.stm.

21   The revised gubernatorial appointment process has not necessarily reduced levels of corruption, but, like other reforms in Putin's first five years in office, it provided accountability for regional leaders and allowed the central government to at least control the nature of the corruption taking place at the regional level.

22   See also Federal'nyi zakon Rossiiskoi Federatsii ot 11 dekabrya 2004 g. N 159–FZ O vnesenii izmenenii v Federal'nyi zakon 'Ob obshchikh printsipakh organizatsii zakonodatel'nykh (predstavitel'nykh) i ispolnitel'nykh organov gosudarstvennoi vlasti sub"ektov Rossiiskoi Federatsii' i v Federal'nyi zakon 'Ob osnovnykh garantiyakh izbiratel'nykh prav i prava na uchastie v referendume grazhdan Rossiiskoi Federatsii'. *Rossiiskaya Gazeta*, December 15, 2004.

23   See Chebankova (2006: 458). According to Chebankova, regional push-back may include an increase in regional elite unity, increased power of regional governments, advances in party development, and greater competition during regional elections.

## An Interlude: Putin Recaps Reform Through 2004

In 2004, following this spate of reforms, Putin again appeared before the Federal Assembly to explain the federal reforms he had undertaken:

> The Russian Constitution and federal laws had lost the power of supreme law in many regions. Federal laws were applied selectively, at one's discretion ... Things went so far that individual regions in effect found themselves outside the common legal, financial and fiscal system of the state, stopped contributing taxes to the federal budget, and were demanding the creation of their own gold and hard currency reserves, their own energy and customs systems and regional monetary units. (Putin 2000)

The federalism reforms pursued in Russia between 2000 and 2004 seem to promote the goals laid out by Putin in his 2004 speech to the Federal Assembly. However, even as Putin was delivering the speech, critics were challenging the reforms as an anti-democratic power grab. Those critics correctly noted that Putin had seized on the overwhelming success of his political party in legislative elections and his own high popularity ratings to redefine center–periphery relations in Russia. That perception was entirely correct. Buoyed by electoral success, Putin and his party moved to centralize power in Russia while at the same time maintaining an explanation that would legitimize the reforms.

In addition to the initial goals to centralize power, all reform of center–periphery relations in Russia since September 2004 (including the gubernatorial appointment process discussed above) has been judged through what might be called the Beslan prism. In the wake of the Beslan massacre, in which more than 300 hostages (including nearly 200 children) were killed after a terrorist group took hostages in a school in the small town of Beslan in North Ossetia (an autonomous republic) (BBC News 2004, Beslan), the central administration in Moscow took a series of measures (not limited to federalism issues) to ensure that the events in Beslan would never be repeated. While it is undoubtedly true that the horrific events in Beslan spurred Putin and his allies to act, it would be mistaken to believe that the federalism reforms since September 2004 are merely a response to those events.[24] Indeed, the law that created the gubernatorial appointment process had already been drafted and had been vetted at the time of the hostage crisis in Beslan. So even that reform, attributed by many to Beslan, would almost certainly in fact have taken place in any event.[25] However, the Beslan massacre certainly underlined the need for the center to retain control over the periphery and buttressed Putin's public campaign for control over the regions.

---

24   Compare to the (perhaps tongue-in-cheek) description in one editorial of a cause and effect relationship between the hostage crisis and the elimination of democratically elected governors, which reports that Putin "thought the country would be safer if he decided who would control the regions" (Coalson 2008).

25   Stoner-Weiss (2006b: 104) aptly described Putin's usage of the hostage crisis as "little more than a pretext for Putin's latest maneuver to recentralize and de-democratize Russia." Of course public support for the reforms certainly increased in the wake of Beslan. That tide of public support for direct central control of regional governors remained strong until recently, when new polls suggest that public support has shifted. See Petrov (2009): "According to a poll just conducted by the Levada Center, 60 percent of Russians support the return of direct elections for regional governors, while only 20 percent oppose it ... By comparison, when people were surveyed to gauge their opinions of then-President Vladimir Putin's new political program after the 2004 terrorist attack in Beslan, 40 percent of respondents were opposed to the canceling of direct gubernatorial elections, while slightly more than 40 percent were in favor. Later, people grew accustomed to the new arrangement and the number opposing the move decreased."

As discussed at the outset, preconceived notions of the proper alignment of internal power in a sprawling, multi-ethnic state guided early federalism reforms in Russia. The relevant notions were those of the party—and man—in power. Consistent with past practice in Russia, the country was guided by the political predilections of the person it had placed in power. Legal reform did not drive the change to center–periphery relations. Instead, Putin's views guided the reform, suggesting that, at least in the initial years of modern federalism reform in Russia, behavior guided the reform process, meaning that legal reform remained subject to the views of the governing elite.

Reform since 2005 has largely followed the same model as the initial Putin-era reforms that ultimately set the baseline for contemporary center–periphery relations, though additionally guided by the Beslan prism. The story of the past five years of federalism reform is really more a story of the continued dance between center and periphery, with Putin and Medvedev focused on centralizing power while offering limited power to the regions when that power is not abused.

## Implementation of an Evaluation System for Regional Governors

In 2007, President Putin announced a Presidential Decree establishing an evaluation system for regional governors (President's Decree No. 825 2007). That system, revised in 2009, gave form to the president's evaluation of governor performance, a positive change in light of the 2004 law allowing for dismissal based on "lack of confidence." The 2009 amendments focused mostly on economic performance and the effectiveness of use of regional budgets (President's Decree No. 825 2007). The Kremlin's scrutiny seems to have shifted toward fiscal responsibility as Russia tries to extricate itself from the global financial crisis.

While the evaluation system may hearken back to Soviet bureaucracy, it did not come into effect without some concessions to the regions. If nothing else, regional leadership may have an easier time staying in office by virtue of compliance with the evaluation indicators, even if standing on an otherwise anti-Moscow platform (Chebankova 2008). On the other hand, as Russia staggers from the blows of the global economic crisis, finger-pointing coupled with Moscow power-plays might motivate current president Dmitry Medvedev to sack fiscally inadequate executives. Indeed, in reference to unrest caused by St. Petersburg's crippled factory industry, Medvedev recently announced that "I want you to present this position clearly and unambiguously to the governors: Either they deal with the problems, or I will have to remove them from their offices irrespective of their merits" (Abdullaev 2009).

The economic crisis certainly catalyzed the center's scrutiny of regional economic performance, but the percolation of modernization into Russia was already apparent during the 2004 reforms discussed above. Indeed, empirical data tenuously suggest that Putin was more likely to appoint new governors in "debtor" regions (these regions may not have had the worst economies, but region to center debt reveals something about Moscow's attitude toward regional leadership) (Goode 2007).[26] One scholar has identified a "political triangle" of influence, in which corporations, regional administrations, and the Kremlin form the basis of power brokerage across Russia

---

26 While the correlation between economic performance and new appointments is tenuous, Goode acknowledges the influence of regional business on the socio-political Russian fabric: "another possible explanation concerns the type of business—state relations that predominate in the regions. In contrast to popular elections, gubernatorial appointments are less about assessing economic performance and more about relationships among elites at the central and regional levels" (citations omitted).

(Chebankova 2008).[27] Even if governors could find a silver lining in the 2004 reforms, the influx of modernization, exacerbated and complicated by the economic crisis, means the balance of power may turn on Moscow's increased pressure on governors to pay wages and keep industry afloat.


## A Special Case: Tatarstan's Revised Treaty with Russia

In 2007, the Federal Assembly passed a revised treaty with Tatarstan, an ethnic republic that has spent the post-Soviet period asserting its independence and straining to achieve sovereignty in the eyes of both domestic and international law. Because of its economic power (Tatarstan possesses between 5 and 10 percent of Russia's oil reserves) and ethnic diversity, Tatarstan managed to persuade the central administration to renegotiate the treaty between Russia and Tatarstan that had been signed in 1994 and renewed in 1999.[28]

The case of Tatarstan is particularly noteworthy because it contrasts with actions taken by the central administration from the first days of Putin's presidency. By the time that Putin took office, according to some commentators, as many as one quarter of the legal acts taken in the region (numbering more than 300,000) violated federal law.[29] Starting in 2000, the central administration launched an ambitious campaign to eradicate fundamental points of disagreement between the Russian Constitution and regional constitutions, laws, and treaties. The administration created a special commission tasked with identifying dissonance between regional laws and federal mandates. That commission worked to reduce the number of inconsistencies and drafted a law on local self-government in 2002, signed into law by Putin in October 2003 with a delayed implementation schedule.[30] The law on local self-government sought both to reduce inconsistencies between local and federal law and to curtail official corruption through legal reform.

Even as legal reform to harmonize local and federal laws was underway, the central administration sought to rescind the nearly 50 bilateral treaties that Russia had signed during the 1990s with various sub-federal entities.[31] Those treaties, signed in an effort to preserve a delicate state during its period of transformation from the Soviet Union, codified a variety of principles that violated terms of the Russian Constitution. With that in mind, the Putin administration targeted those treaties for elimination, seeing them as divisive to the unity of the nation.

---

27  For a more pessimistic discussion of the role of economic elites in post-communist Russia, see Stoner-Weiss (2006a: 11): "[T]he collusion between powerful regional political and economic elites also has a clearly negative effect on what the central state can accomplish in the periphery."

28  While the case of Tatarstan is noteworthy for the amount of bargaining power the region asserted in its negotiations with the center, the case of Tatarstan was in fact quite similar to the efforts of virtually all sub-federal entities during the Yeltsin era. During that period, regions asserted power and independence, either directly (through referenda or declarations of sovereign power) or indirectly (through legal reform of tax codes, and municipal civil and criminal laws). The case of Tatarstan is different largely because of its continued success in negotiating special deals with the central government during the Putin era, though other regions have also succeeded to lesser degrees in gaining concessions from the central government since 1999.

29  See Ross (2005: 359). Tatarstan, however, does not stand alone in its occasional insouciance toward the federal government; for examples of other regions exercising federal power or violating the constitution, see Chebankova (2007: 282).

30  Implementation of the law by the regions was originally scheduled to take place starting in January 2006. While some regions followed that schedule, others delayed implementation as the implementation period was pushed back into 2009.

31  For a review of Russia's internal bilateral treaties since 1994 see Soderlund (2006: 88). Soderlund terms the bilateral treaties "quasi-constitutional umbrella documents."

So it was all the more striking when Putin signed a renewed bilateral treaty with Tatarstan in early 2007.[32] Notably, the revised treaty recognized Tatarstan's ongoing claims to sovereignty—claims clearly at odds with the central government's desire to rein in the regions. Article 2.3 of the treaty provide Tatarstan the right to "carry out international and foreign economic relations," the hallmark of sovereign nations. The treaty includes a number of other provisions that contradict the goals of centralized authority, including provisions that allow for special language allowances (two official state languages), recognition of the need to develop Tartar culture and language, and provisions for side agreements on economic sharing, which allow Tatarstan to retain power over the alienation of its natural resources. All of these provisions ran counter to nearly a decade of federal reform under Putin.[33]

How then to explain this apparent anomaly in center–periphery policy during the first decade of the twenty-first century? One explanation would focus exclusively on the unique nature of Tatarstan, its history and its resources. However, while no doubt responsible for some of the administration's flexibility, such an explanation would be incomplete. Indeed, the experience of Tatarstan may best offer insight into the dance steps of the Putin and Medvedev administrations over the past decade.

Success in achieving harmony in national policy hinges on buy-in across the country. A country spread across Russia's land mass simply cannot afford to allow for 83 different political, economic and cultural regimes. Centralization of authority is necessary to maintain order. At the same time, the central authority must recognize exceptional cases that call for flexibility in policymaking.[34] The Tatarstan treaty is perhaps an extreme example, but the reforms over the past decade are laced with examples where the central administration has taken a hard-line public stance but created procedures that preserve a certain amount of regional autonomy. What has been described as a delicate rumba-like dance may in fact be nothing more than pragmatic politics—a government inclined to recognize nuance but also cognizant of the need to maintain a hard-line approach to avoid devolution into regional fiefdoms that threaten the unity of the state.

Here again, legal reform is guided by ideology and laws are used to enforce behavior, or expectations of behavior. But experience in Russia during the 1990s had demonstrated that regions left to their own devices would pursue policies that would (reasonably, perhaps) benefit their local self-interest at the cost of national priorities. Even federal systems must balance the interests of local communities against the needs of the state as a whole. A Western lens simply cannot appreciate the complexity of the federal struggles, certainly not when the most comparable example of a similar federal structure (the United States) boasts fewer sub-federal entities, no comparable issues of unique language and culture, and limited modern-day efforts by the sub-federal units to exert

---

32   For a more complete account of the 2007 treaty and a thorough and incisive study of center–periphery relations through the lens of the relationship between Tatarstan and Russia, see Graney (2008).

33   Graney offers a detailed account of the difficult process of ratifying the treaty. After Putin signed the treaty and submitted it to the Duma for approval, which the Duma granted, the Federation Council (ostensibly representing the interests of the regions), rejected the treaty by a vote of 93–13 with 15 abstentions. This rejection perhaps demonstrates the level of resentment held by other regions toward this special arrangement but also attests to the unique nature of the treaty. Several months later, the treaty was resubmitted and this time passed both the Duma and the Federation Council (by a vote of 122–4). See Graney (2008: 146–7).

34   The Western reader cannot be reminded too many times of the sheer vastness and diversity of Russia. Moscow steps off with a veritable leviathan when it attempts to lead the regions in its frenetic dance. See Chebankova (2008: 996–7): "We can now tentatively conclude that Putin's institutional reforms created an overly centralised federal structure that could not adequately reflect Russia's socio-territorial political realities."

sovereign authority over their internal and external affairs. And yet, even in the United States, states and the federal government continue to struggle over the appropriate balance of authority, particularly where natural resources are concerned, an issue all the more acute in Russia given its post-Soviet economic hardships. In short, the experience of Tatarstan serves as a reminder of the complex federal structure that the past decade of reform has sought to manage and control.


**Amendments Expanding Presidential Power Over Regional Governors and Legislatures**

The most recent reform to the federal structure once again demonstrates that efforts by the central authority to control regional forces will continue. On July 6, 2009, a new law took effect that expands the power of the center—and specifically of the president—over the periphery (Federal Law of the Russian Federation No. 41 2009). Under this new law, the president's authority to appoint regional governors has expanded. Under the new procedures, the political party with a majority of votes in regional elections to the regional legislative body proposes at least three candidates for the position of the chief executive of a subject of the Russian Federation. The president then has the authority to pick one of the nominees or to reject the slate and ask the regional legislature to propose a new list of at least three candidates.

The law also authorizes the central party leadership, rather than local party officials, to work with the president in filling these regional posts once the nominations have been received. Finally, the new law reinforces the right of the president to dissolve a regional parliament in the event that he rejects two different slates of nominations. This provision compromises the power of the legislature to exercise independent authority inasmuch as the legislators' jobs may depend on their willingness to propose at least one candidate who will be acceptable to the central administration. Of course, if the legislature feels confident in the odds of reelection following dissolution, it may continue to reject the president's nominees. Such a move from the nuances of the rumba to the unveiled aggression of a game of "chicken," while unlikely, is not unthinkable.

Another, seemingly smaller scale law that challenges the authority of regional leaders went into effect in April 2009.[35] The new law extends the myriad reforms aimed at regional governors. Unlike the laws on removal of regional governors, under this new law, mayors can be removed by the city council of the city where they sit (*The Moscow Times* 2009).[36] Indeed, in June 2009, the mayor of the small but historically significant town of Suzdal outside of Moscow was dismissed under one aspect of this law for "inactivity" (*The Moscow Times* 2009). The law provides that mayors can be fired for mismanaging the finances of their city (reminiscent of the grounds for removing regional governors), neglecting their duties for more than three months or losing the respect of city council members (*The Moscow Times* 2009). Some have argued that this new law is a logical extension of the reform of the gubernatorial appointment process, particularly to the extent that mayors are now the highest ranking officials who are not beholden to the center (see Petrov 2007). Under this view, Medvedev hopes to use this new law to exert control over locally elected city officials.

Once again, these reforms appear to enhance the presidency and the center at the cost of separation of powers and the periphery, respectively. Such perceptions of the reform also compromise its legitimacy. But, this simplistic analysis alone is incomplete. These reforms once again ensure that

---

35    See *The Moscow Times* (2009).

36    Around the same time this new law went into effect, the Duma passed the first read of a companion law that would empower regional governors (now appointed by the central authorities) to dismiss mayors, thus bringing local officials further under the control of the center.

the center and periphery are operating with a unified agenda and sense of purpose.[37] Regional legislatures have the power to propose at least six different candidates before any action can be taken against them, ensuring that they will have an opportunity to propose a range of candidates who they feel would represent local interest but who would also prove acceptable to the central government.

In one sense, this reform in itself paints the rumba picture—the moves of the center mirroring those of the periphery as the two shuffle back and forth. The new law provides the president with a great deal of power in appointing regional leaders, thereby undermining meaningful federalism. But the new law also helps to protect the center against the danger of far-reaching, disparate, self-interested local politicians who might hijack either natural resources or other national resources to unduly benefit local populations or themselves. Management of a nation as vast, ethnically diverse and resource-dependent as Russia requires a centralized hand to manage those resources for the benefit of the whole country and not one region. The danger, of course, of such central management is that the central authorities will also misallocate or misappropriate resources. That is clearly the concern of most Western commentators, and it is not without merit. But it also misses fundamental realities of the Russian landscape—realities that dictate a strong hand to manage the disparate interests of the regions.


## Conclusion

The legacy of the past decade of reform of federal power is of course unclear at this stage. In the short run, many of the reforms under Putin (and Medvedev) have led to greater protections of individual rights in regions where unruly regional officials had infringed on the rights of citizens. At the same time, some regions benefited from strong regional governors who could acquire what Americans like to call "pork barrel" projects. That happens far less often today than it did in 1999. But at the same time, regional leaders have far less autonomy in their decision-making, and the regions are beholden to the center for concessions.

Russia struggles with the fight between a centrifugal pull to draw power away from the center and outward toward the regions and a centripetal pull in which the center draws the regions inward in an effort to create and maintain unity. The centrifugal forces in a country as large and diverse as Russia are strong. So the center must create conditions favorable to a centripetal pull. The past decade of reform in Russia has accomplished just that—drawing the regions back into the center, under its power and influence and thus tending toward the center rather than spinning away as they had been in the decade that preceded Putin's ascension to power.

A bigger question is whether Putin's actions—regardless of their effect—demonstrate a disregard for the federalism principles outlined in the Russian Constitution. One prominent scholar has argued that the measures outlined in this chapter "make a mockery of federalism" (Ross 2003: 29). Meanwhile, as others have noted, Russia has inherited a federal structure, but it has not inherited a federal tradition.[38] That holds true in virtually every area of civil society and democratic governance. But ultimately, lessons of democratic governance must be learned by the

---

37   While the center and regions are engaged in an almost adversarial dance, the reader should not forget that a rational Moscow will not trip its partners for fear of tumbling itself. Stability, in politics as in dance, tempers aggression and lends to balance. As Chebankova (2006: 470) said of the 2004 reforms, "[i]ndeed, virtually all gubernatorial appointments were made with the aim of preserving political stability at the national level and the elite balance established in the regions during the past decade."

38   See Kempton (2001: 202).

citizens through experience. After all, at least in the case of Russia, legal reform ultimately follows from changes in behavior and those changes must take place first.

Given the size of the country, the state of the nation that Putin inherited and the number of federal subjects, allowing greater autonomy to the regions would only foster the potential for chaos. Thus, as Russia has danced its delicate rumba, back and forth in delineating the lines for regional power, the federal reforms under Putin and Medvedev have been on the whole positive to the long-term rule of law in Russia.


## References


Abdullaev, N. 2009. Medvedev Threatens to Ax Governors. *The Moscow Times*, June 11. Available at: www.cdi.org/russia/johnson/2009-109-1.cfm.

BBC News. 2004. *Russian Duma backs Putin Reforms*. Available at: http://news.bbc.co.uk/2/hi/europe/3965845.stm.

BBC News. 2004. *Beslan School Siege Special Report*. Available at: http://news.bbc.co.uk/2/shared/spl/hi/world/04/russian_s/html/1.stm.

Chebankova, E. 2006. The Unintended Consequences of Gubernatorial Appointments in Russia, 2005–2006. *The Journal of Communist Studies and Transition Politics*, 22(4), 458.

Chebankova, E. 2007. Putin's Struggle for Federalism: Structures, Operation, and the Commitment Problem. *Europe–Asia Studies*, 59(2), 288.

Chebankova, E. 2008. Adaptive Federalism and Federation in Putin's Russia. *Europe–Asia Studies*, 60(6), 967.

Coalson, R. 2008. *The Vote that Counts. Radio Free Europe Radio Liberty*. Available at: www.rferl.org/content/The_Vote_That_Counts/1362876.html.

Constitution of the Russian Federation. 2009. Available at: www.constitution.ru/en/10003000-02.htm.

Corwin, J. 2000. Vulnerability of Governors to Dismissal Questioned. *Radio Free Europe Radio Liberty Russian Federation Report*, 2(21). Available at: www.rferl.org/articleprintview/1344532.html.

Erlanger, S. 1992. Tatar Area in Russia Votes on Sovereignty Today. *New York Times*, March 21. Available at: www.nytimes.com/1992/03/21/world/tatar-area-in-russia-votes-on-sovereignty-today.html.

Federal Law of the Russian Federation (RF) No. 41. 2009. *On Amendments to the Federal Law "On the General Principles of the Organization of Legislative (Representative) and Executive Organs of the State Authorities in the Subjects of the Russian Federation" and the Federal Law "On Political Parties."* Available at: http://ar.gov.ru/en/main_menu_en/news-events/index.php?m2=all&np2=661&ps2=10&q2=corruption&sp2=1&sy2=1&ul2=http://ar.gov.ru/&wf2=2221&wm2=sub&id4=952.

Federal'nyi zakon Rossiiskoi Federatsii ot 11 dekabrya. 2004. g. N 159–FZ O vnesenii izmenenii v Federal'nyi zakon 'Ob obshchikh printsipakh organizatsii zakonodatel'nykh (predstavitel'nykh) i ispolnitel'nykh organov gosudarstvennoi vlasti sub"ektov Rossiiskoi Federatsii' i v Federal'nyi zakon 'Ob osnovnykh garantiyakh izbiratel'nykh prav i prava na uchastie v referendume grazhdan Rossiiskoi Federatsii'. *Rossiiskaya Gazeta*.

Goode, P.J. 2007. The Puzzle of Putin's Gubernatorial Appointments. *Europe–Asia Studies*, 59(3), 377.

Graney, K.E. 2008. *Of Khans and Kremlins: Tatarstan and the Future of Ethno-Federalism in Russia*. Lanham: Lexington Books.

Hahn, G. 2003. The Impact of Putin's Federative Reforms on Democratization in Russia. *Post-Soviet Affairs*, 19(2), 115.

Kempton, D. 2001. Russian Federalism: Continuing Myth or Political Salvation? *Demokratizatsya*, 9(2), 200–42.

Kempton, D. and Clark, T. 2002. *Unity or Separation: Center–Periphery Relations in the Former Soviet Union*. Westport: Praeger.

Mikhailova, S. 2002. Constitutional Court Confirms Authorities' Ability to Fire Governors. *EWI Russian Regional Report*, 14(7), 6.

*The Moscow Times*. 2009. Suzdal City Council Sues Mayor for 'Inactivity. *The Moscow Times*, June 17. Available at: www.moscowtimes.ru/article/1010/42/378821.htm.

Ob Obshchikh Principakh Organizatsii Zakonodalet'nykh (Predstavitel'nykh) I Isponitelnykh Organov Gosudarstvennoi Vlasti Subyektov Rossiiskoi Federatsii. 1999. *Rossiskaya Gazeta*.

O Paryadkye Formorovaniya Sovyeta Federatsiya Federal'novo Sobraniya Rossiiskoi Federatsii. 2000. *Rossiskaya Gazeta*, August 5.

Petrov, N. 2007. *Open Season on Mayors*. Available at: www.pressmon.com/cgi-bin/press_view.cgi?id=721572.

Petrov, N. 2009. The People Want Direct Elections. *The Moscow Times*, July 7. Available at: www.moscowtimes.ru/article/1016/42/379309.htm [accessed: July 14, 2009].

Presidential Decree No. 602. 2000. Ukaz Prezidenta Rossiiskoi Federatsii. *Rossiskaya Gazeta*.

President's Decree No. 825. 2007. On the Evaluation of Efficiency of Executive Bodies in the Constituent Entities of the Russian Federation.

Presidential Decree No. 849. 2000. O Polnomochnom Predastavitele Prezidenta Rossiiskoi Federatsii v. Federalnom Okruge. *Rossiskaya Gazeta*.

Putin, V. 2000. Television address by the Russian President to the country's citizens. *Rossiskaya Gazeta*, May 4.

Putin, V., Gevorkyan, N., Timakova, N. and Kolesnikov, A. 2000. *First Person: An Astonishingly Frank Self-Portrait by Russia's President*. New York: Public Affairs.

Ross, C. 2002. *Federalism and Democratisation in Russia*. Manchester: Manchester University Press.

Ross, C. 2003. Putin's Federal Reforms and the Consolidation of Federalism in Russia: One Step Forward, Two Steps Back! *Communist and Post-Communist Studies*, 36(1), 29–47.

Ross, C. 2005. Federalism and Electoral Authoritarianism. *Demokratizatsiya*, 13(1). Available at: www.demokratizatsiya.org/bin/pdf/DEM%2013-3%20Ross.pdf.

Sobranie Zakonodatel'stva Rossiiskoi Federatsii. 2003.

Soderlund, P. 2006. *The Dynamics of Federalism in Russia: A Study of Formal and Informal Power Resources of the Regional Chief Executives in Russian Centre–Region Relations*. Biskopsgatan, Finland: Abo Akademi University Press.

Starr, F. 1972. *Decentralization and Self-Government in Russia, 1830–1870*. Princeton: Princeton University Press.

Stoner-Weiss, K. 2006a. *Resisting the State: Reform and Retrenchment in Post-Soviet Russia*. Cambridge: Cambridge University Press.

Stoner-Weiss, K. 2006b. Russia: Authoritarianism Without Authority. *Journal of Democracy*, 17(1), 104–18.

# PART VII
## International Law as Legal Development Subject

Chapter 23

# Rebuilding the Tower of Babel—The European Court of Human Rights and the Diversity of Legal Cultures[1]

Angelika Nußberger

And they said, Go to, let us build us a city and a tower, whose top may reach unto heaven; and let us make us a name, lest we be scattered abroad upon the face of the whole earth. And the Lord came down to see the city and the tower, which the children of men built. And the Lord said, Behold, the people is one, and they have all one language; and this they begin to do: and now nothing will be restrained from them, which they have imagined to do. Go to, let us go down, and there confound their language, that they may not understand one another's speech. So the Lord scattered them abroad from thence upon the face of all the earth: and they left off to build the city. Therefore is the name of it called Babel.

Genesis 11: 4–9

In the era of globalization, international enterprises and joint ventures have proven to be capable of working together across the borders. In technology, a common language has been found. In the twenty-first century the Tower of Babel symbolizes something new—a common humanistic ideal for all the different peoples in the globalized world. Within Europe, our own recent experience has been with the re-inclusion of countries from the formerly socialist bloc within the sphere of shared European views of human rights (under the European Convention on Human Rights; joining which may be a practical adjunct to European Union membership, or simply an expression of shared beliefs). But one should not dismiss the practical challenges of harmonizing legal cultures under a regional human rights system even within Europe, even where we think we are "rediscovering" commonality after an extended separation.

This experiment began after the devastating consequences of nationalistic egoism and selfishness became evident in World War II. The first step was to work out common human rights standards after the war. Due to ideological differences this project turned out not to be sincere. Too often, human rights issues were misused in the context of the Cold War. In fact, there was no true consensus on the contents of human rights. After the Cold War ended there was a fresh start. The idea was to go beyond the mere abstract definition of standards and to emphasize enforcement and implementation. On the global level, new expert committees were set up to control the implementation of human rights treaties or start to broaden their mandate and thus to work more efficiently. On the European level, the European Court of Human Rights was established as a judicial institution accessible for every citizen. This was a truly revolutionary step. Therefore, the European Court on Human Rights in Strasbourg can be seen as the motor of rebuilding the Tower

---

1 This chapter is based on a paper presented at the Constitutional Forum in Moscow in 2006, which was dedicated to the subject "European Convention on Human Rights and Fundamental Freedoms in the XXI Century: Problems and Prospects of Implementation." A slightly different version of the text was published in Russian in *Sravnitel'noe Konstitucionnoe Pravo* 2007, No. 2, pp. 71–9.

of Babel in the realm of law. It is called upon to defend the common values of "the Europeans," if not the common values of the world community.


## Differences in Legal Cultures in Europe

It is obvious that the starting point of the work of the Court is where the story about Babel ended. In Europe, more than 40 different languages are spoken. Although legal terms can be translated, it is doubtful that the underlying concepts are understood. Legal languages have developed within specific legal cultures on the basis of specific legal theories. For example, it is well known that there is no adequate term to translate the German expression "*Nichtigkeit eines Gesetzes*" into Russian. In German constitutional law, the term is used when an unconstitutional law is declared void, i.e., "non-existing" or, to be more precise, "never existing." The Russian translation "*nedejstvitel'nyj*" literally means in German "*nicht wirksam*" and in English, "not in force." That is not exactly the same.[2] Another famous example is the translation of the French word "*spirituel*" in the Preamble to the Charter of Fundamental Rights of the European Union. Whereas the German side was eager to introduce an "*invocatio dei*" into the Preamble, this was not acceptable for the French secular tradition. The word chosen in the final version offers a sort of compromise. The French word "*spirituel*" is translated as "*geistig-religiös*" into German. This clear allusion to the religious component in the German version is neither contained explicitly in the English nor in the French version.

Even if the translation is not ambiguous, the specificity of the legal term used in one language might be lost in another language. Although legal terms have to be precise and clear, their origin can often be a metaphor like the German "*ein Anspruch geht unter*" ("a claim is drowned") or "*Knebelungsvertrag*" ("gagging treaty"). Developments in legal doctrine can be summarized in newly invented terms that function only in the legal context given. For example, a "*Verwaltungsakt*" in German administrative law is not an "*akt administracii*."

Different perceptions of what is "just" and "human" might be hidden behind the different legal terms. Legal terms form a part of what is commonly called a "legal culture." Although the dichotomy between the Civil Law tradition and the Common Law tradition is generally accepted, it is not clear how many different legal cultures exist worldwide. Patrick Glenn analyses seven different traditions in his famous book *Legal Traditions of the World*: the chthonic legal tradition, the Talmudic legal tradition, the Civil Law tradition, the Islamic legal tradition, the Common Law tradition, the Hindu legal tradition, and the Asian legal tradition (most of which are represented in one form or another in this book) (Glenn 2007).[3] But it is well arguable that other traditions cannot be taken under these headings but have to be seen as separate legal traditions. This is especially true for the Russian or the Japanese tradition. Nevertheless, however varied the number of traditions identified all these traditions are deeply rooted not only in the historical, but also in the religious heritage.

The European Court of Human Rights has to adjudicate concrete cases on potential human rights violations in the 47 national states that have ratified the European Convention on Human Rights and—to a larger or lesser extent—the relevant Protocols to the Convention. As all these

---

2   The term "*ničtožnyj*" might be used in Russian, but in Russian legal language it is only used in relation to contracts.

3   There are other approaches such as the approach of Zweigert and Kötz (1996) and David and Jauffret-Spinosi (2002).

states are part of "Europe" and adhere to the values enshrined in the Statute of the Council of Europe, it might be assumed that the Court is not confronted with a clash of legal traditions. The opposite is true. Although the dividing line is not—as might be expected—between Civil Law and Common Law systems, the Court has to accommodate a lot of deeply rooted different convictions and conceptions hidden behind specific legal regulations and institutions. Therefore the jurisprudence of the Court can be seen as a courageous, but difficult attempt to define common minimum human right standards for different legal cultures. It is a balancing act that has been generally successful so far. However, cultural relativism remains a threat to the rebuilding of the Tower of Babel.

*Peculiarities of Certain Legal Cultures*

What matters in this context are peculiarities of legal cultures, for example, typical features of some legal cultures that are not shared or even misunderstood by others.

*Nadzor system*   One famous example in the Russian context is the nadzor system, a special supervisory system over the judiciary. Some countries have abolished the system after the fall of communism, but in some countries it still exists. The nadzor system is built on the idea of establishing an extraordinary control of the judicial system in addition to the revision of judgments within the hierarchically structured judicial system. Such an extraordinary control system is possible both in criminal and in civil cases. On the basis of a so-called "protest," a proceeding can be reopened. Thereby the courts are vested with the power to award redress for violations found, including the power to quash impugned decisions. This nadzor system is based on certain elements that are different from the "mainstream" European legal cultures. First, in Civil Law matters, the outcome of the private litigation is not left entirely to the litigants; the state authorities can intervene without any specific reason. Second, the legal force of a judgment can be set aside easily, originally, even without any time limit; this applies both to civil and criminal matters. Third, action upon a "protest" is within the discretionary power of the authorities. Furthermore, whereas the court procedure has to be open and balanced, the nadzor procedure can be nontransparent and behind closed doors. Summoning of the parties to the hearing is usually a discretionary right of the court or the Presidium of the court deciding the case. Last, but not least, there is an asymmetry in the system as only the state authorities, but not the citizens, are allowed to initiate the procedure; the citizens can only request it.

Such a nadzor system was invented in Russia and transferred to the states influenced by Russian law. It is linked with the strong position of the procuracy founded by Peter the Great in 1722 (Smith 2007). It is one example of a peculiarity of a legal culture that is unknown in most of the other European legal systems. From inside, it is understood as necessary for effective supervision over the judiciary. From outside, it is seen as an arbitrary means, incompatible with the principle of legal certainty. As a matter of fact, the nadzor system is an essential part of the Russian judicial system. As the Russian judge at the European Court of Human Rights, Kovler, has pointed out, about 60 percent of the mistakes committed in judicial proceedings in Russia are corrected by this supervisory system (Kovler 2004).

*Attorneys-general*   Another example might be the attorney-general ("*avocat général*") in the French as well as in the Belgian system. He can defend the "public interest," but also takes part in the deliberations on the judgment. Such a role is unknown in the legal systems of other countries. From inside, it is understood as a contribution to efficiency and to the harmonization of the jurisprudence, especially of the highest courts. From outside, it is criticized as contrary to the principle of a fair trial.

*Different Perceptions of the Dominant Actors of Civil Society*

Furthermore, the legal systems in Europe differ widely as to the perception of the main actors of civil society such as political parties, trade unions, churches, and others. Different historical experiences usually determine the role assigned to them at present.

States with a communist past are often reluctant to allow any intertwining between state authorities and political parties. Therefore, incompatibility rules are strict and far-reaching. In many of the post-communist countries, judges are not allowed to be party members and may not engage in political activities.[4] Sometimes passive membership is allowed, but activities in favor of certain political parties are forbidden.[5] These strict regulations can be understood as an answer to the domination of party politics over state politics during the communist regime. At the same time, these prohibitions reveal a general deep mistrust of political parties.

Although Germany had bad experiences with the absolute dominance of party politics over state politics in the 1930s and 1940s as well, there are no incompatibility rules in its Constitution. Judges can be party members, although strict neutrality on the job is required (German Law on Judges § 39).[6] In practice, constitutional judges are even expected to be party members, or at least to be loyal to one of the established democratic parties represented in parliament. The electoral process for constitutional judges is structured in such a way as to allow for a balance of influence of the major parties within the Court. Although this bargaining process is vehemently criticized, in practice it does not diminish the high reputation of the Court as an impartial body (Schlaich and Korioth 2010). On the other hand, there is a tangible fear of the influence of extremist parties. Thus, civil servants are required to be loyal to the Constitution. "Extremists" can be denied access to the civil service.[7] These regulations show that there is not a general distrust against political parties, but only against extremist parties.

Historical experience has also shaped the attitude toward religious institutions. Here, too, we find a variety of solutions as to their role in state and society. On the one extreme are countries like France with a secular tradition that vigorously separates state and church. On the other extreme are countries like Greece or Great Britain with a state church system.

--------

4   Compare, for example, Article 50 of the Hungarian Constitution: "Judges may not hold membership in any party and must not carry on political activities."; cf. Article 178 of the Polish Constitution: "A judge shall not belong to a political party, a trade union or perform public activities incompatible with the principles of independence of the courts and judges"; cf. Article 100 of the Macedonian Constitution: "The performance of a judge's office is incompatible with other public office, profession or membership in a political party"; cf. Article 86 of the Georgian Constitution: "The position of a judge shall be incompatible with any other occupation or remunerative activity, except pedagogical activities. A judge shall not be a member of a political party, or participate in a political activity."

5   Cf. Article 133 of the Slovenian Constitution: "Judicial office is not compatible with office in other state bodies, in local self–government bodies and in bodies of political parties, and with other offices and activities as provided by law." Cf. Article 113 of the Lithuanian Constitution: "Judges may not participate in the activities of political parties and other political organizations."

6   "The judge is obliged to act both within and outside of his official duties, also when exercising political activities, in such a way as not to put at risk the confidence in his independence."

7   "Ban on employment."

In many countries, human rights protection is effectuated by an ombudsman that plays an important role in society. This is true, for example, for the Nordic countries, but also for many of the Central and Eastern European countries having imported this model into their legal system. In other countries, as in Germany, the institution of the ombudsman plays only a minor role as human rights protection is based exclusively on the judicial system and the Constitutional Court. In Russia, the model of the ombudsman was introduced as well, but does not seem to be as efficient as in other countries.

All these cultural differences are relevant for the interpretation of the scope of freedom of the individual, of groups and of civil society as a whole vis-à-vis the state. To a certain extent, differences may persist without endangering a common standard of human rights protection, but, if necessary, they might also have to be levelled out.

*Differences in Value Judgments*

Differences between the legal traditions in Europe have not only shaped different institutions and brought about different legal regulations of important parts of social life but are also mirrored in the value judgments given by the citizens themselves. Surveys have shown very different attitudes concerning such basic questions as the role of religion in life, the conception of family life or the roles of men and women in society. Usually, geographical patterns can be established on the basis of sociological data. Considering the EU countries as well as EU accession countries, Western Europe can be opposed to Eastern Europe, although the results for Eastern Germany are not compatible with this dichotomy (Gerhards and Hölscher 2005). The results for Turkey are significantly different. It may be suggested that a survey of the Caucasian countries, Russia as well as the Western Balkans, shows deviating results as well. It is also suggested that the differences can be correlated to the specific degree of modernization of the relevant society, the per capita gross national product, the degree of education and the average life expectancy (Gerhards and Hölscher 2005). Of course, acknowledging such differences seemingly leaves open our "chicken or egg" question to the extent the EHRC is designed more as an exercise in minimum standards rather than an effort to proscribe identical standards, successful implementation of which would be the more valid test of legal engineering as such.

**The European Convention on Human Rights: Definition of Basic Common Values**

Against this background, it seems surprising that it was possible to define common human rights standards acceptable to all Europeans despite the differences in the legal traditions. The success story of the European Convention on Human Rights began in the 1950s, although at that time, it was relevant only to the Western part of the continent. But, as it had proved to be a workable basis for human rights protection for more than 40 years, all the Central and Eastern European countries accepted the Convention without claiming the necessity to re-bargain the contents and form of the system. If reservations were made, they were usually of an only transitional character.[8] The unconditional acceptance of the human rights system of the Council of Europe was fueled not only by the wish of the former communist countries to rejoin the free and prosperous "Western world," but also by the assumption that membership in the Council of Europe was a first step toward

---

8   e.g., the Russian or the Ukrainian reservation to the ECHR.

membership in the European Union. For those countries without any option to become a member of the European Union it was important not to be excluded from the "European family."

Political calculus was not the only reason for acceptance; the Convention itself facilitated the accession. The unprecedented success story can be primarily explained by the simplicity of the basic texts containing vague and open legal concepts.

*Simplicity of the Basic Legal Texts*

The Court works with no more than three dozen human rights provisions. The essence of what is "just" is condensed in the short articles contained in the European Convention on Human Rights and the Protocols. The basic ideas can be summarized in short and precise terms such as "fair trial," "prohibition of inhuman treatment," and "freedom of expression" that are understandable to everybody.

The European Convention on Human Rights summarizes the uncontroversial core contents of the national and international human rights movement. It places the individual in the center and protects him or her against all unnecessary intrusions from outside. In line with the Aristotelian conception of the individual as a "social being" (ζῶον πολιτικόν), freedom of communication with others is protected and participation in the life of the community is guaranteed. The Committee on Legal Affairs elaborated that the Convention had decided to include only rights "which imposed on the States ... obligations, not to do things, which would thus be susceptible to immediate sanction by a court; and which were so fundamental that human dignity and democracy were inconceivable if they were not respected."

Rights that might be controversial or not universally shared are excluded from the core of the Convention. That is even true for the right to property. Although in history it was one of the first rights enshrined in human rights documents, there was no consensus on the scope and content of this right. So it was separated from the basic text of the Convention and included in the First Protocol.

Social rights were excluded as well, although their inclusion was fiercely debated at the time when the Convention was elaborated. The same is true for the right to education or the freedom to choose a profession. The explanation given for this restrictive approach clearly shows a pragmatic attitude:

> Certainly, "professional" liberties and "social" rights, which have themselves an intrinsic value, must also, in the future, be defined and protected; but everyone will understand that it is necessary to begin at the beginning and to guarantee political democracy in the European Union, and then to co-ordinate our economies before undertaking the generalisation of social democracy. (Robertson 1975)

Although the standards are deemed to be high in comparison to other international human rights instruments, sometimes the protection provided by universal instruments such as the International Covenant on Civil and Political Rights is higher (Report of Committee of Experts 1970). Thus, for example, the latter contains a generally applicable prohibition of discrimination, whereas Article 14 ECHR is restricted to the rights laid down in the Convention. In specific fields, the protection provided by other, and even older, instruments can be more far-reaching as well. One example would be Convention No. 29 on Forced Labour elaborated by the International Labour Organisation in 1930 and ratified in the meantime by 174 countries. Whereas the ECHR does not consider work required to be done "in the ordinary course of detention" as "forced or compulsory labour," as long as the procedural rights are not violated (ECHR Art. 4), the ILO Convention on forced labor allows prison work only under very narrow conditions: first, it must be carried out under the supervision and control of a public authority; and second, the prisoner must not be "hired to or placed at the disposal of private individuals, companies or associations" (Forced Labour Convention Art. 2(c)). That means that the ECHR summarizes the generally accepted, but not necessarily the highest, standards worldwide.

The structure of the human rights protection system with one basic text and additional Protocols allows for certain flexibility. Whereas it is necessary to accept all the basic rights that is not true for more controversial rights such as the prohibition of the death penalty under all circumstances (Protocol No. 13, ETS. No. 187) or a general and all-encompassing prohibition of discrimination (Protocol No. 12, ETS. 177). The elaboration of new protocols is a flexible means of broadening the human rights protection system without endangering the compromise already reached.

The human rights protection system is concerned only with human rights, not with the structure of the state organization as such. Basic democratic values are mirrored in provisions such as the freedom of assembly and association (Article 11 ECHR) or the right to free elections (Article 3 of the First Protocol). But it is not possible to find answers to concrete questions such as the structure of federal states or the rights of deputies. These restrictions also contribute to the acceptability of the Convention.

*Openness of the Legal Concepts*

At the same time, the legal concepts used in the Convention are very open. Article 3 prohibits an "inhumane or degrading treatment" without defining what might be "humane" treatment. Article 8 protects "family life" without giving any indication what might be considered a "family." Are married couples without children a "family"? Are grandparents and cousins part of the "family"? Can homosexual couples form a "family"? The Convention avoids stirring dissent by not giving any answers to these questions.

In fact, the Convention presupposes a consensus on certain notions where there is none. Article 10 and 11 allow for restrictions of the freedom of expression and the freedom of assembly and association if the restrictions are necessary for a "democratic society." The self-description of many states generally considered as authoritarian regimes or even dictatorships contains the word "democratic." Despite the danger of misinterpretation, the Convention does not explain what is meant by "democratic society." Thus, the Court has an open and vague instrument at its hands.

## Jurisdiction of the European Court of Human Rights: An Answer to the Challenges of Different Legal Cultures

On the basis of these vague and open provisions, the Court has worked out a detailed and differentiated jurisprudence. Despite its complexity, the basic ideas are simple. Some of the human rights are absolute, such as the prohibition of torture and inhuman treatment. Others can be limited. The limitations must be proportional; they must be justifiable in a democratic society. On the basis of this analytical tool, the Court manages to solve more or less all intricate human rights questions. First, it analyzes whether the interference with the right was "in accordance with the law." Second, it analyzes whether the interference was "in the public interest." And third, it deals with the proportionality of the interference, i.e., whether a fair balance is maintained between the requirements of the general interest of the community and the requirements of the protection of the fundamental rights of the individual. That is a convincing scheme that can be applied in varying forms to all the cases brought to Strasbourg.

*Autonomous Interpretation*

But for the argumentation to work it is necessary to start from generally accepted concepts. The Court derives them from the provisions of the Convention on the basis of an autonomous interpretation taking into account the different national constitutional traditions. Here the problems begin. Behind the façade of generally accepted notions there might be—and often are—different understandings hidden.

*Civil rights*   According to Article 6 of the Convention the principle of a "fair and public hearing within a reasonable time" has to be applied in the determination of civil rights and obligations. This presupposes a dividing line between Civil Law and public law cases. As a rule, the differentiation inherited from Roman law matters for access to court and for rules of procedure to be applied. But some systems, such as the Common Law systems as well as the Russian legal system do not know this basic dichotomy. Other systems like the German legal system have a very sophisticated approach to decide what public law and what private law are. From the very beginning, the Strasbourg Court has defined the term "civil rights" autonomously. This has led to a very broad interpretation of "civil rights" comprising even social security rights (*Feldbrugge v. the Netherlands, Deumeland v. Germany*) or litigation concerning the rights of civil servants (*Pellegrin v. France, Frydlender v. France, Lambourdiere v. France*). Although this interpretation does not necessitate a redefinition of the scope of public respective private law or an invention of such a distinction where it does not exist, it forces member states to adapt their claim settlement systems to the requirements laid down in Article 6 ECHR. If, for instance, in former times the settlement of pension claims was possible within an administrative procedure, such a conflict resolution would not be compatible with the Convention in the interpretation of the European Court of Human Rights.

*Property*   Another legal term that can be interpreted differently on the basis of the various legal traditions is "property." Whereas the core concept of "property" based on specific legal titles is clear, the protection of legal positions rooted in public law such as social security rights is highly controversial. Whereas acquired rights in the realm of public law are protected as property rights in Germany (BVerfG E 53, 252, 289), Ireland (*SC Cox* 1992), or in Switzerland (BGE 119 Ia 245, ErwNr. 5 b), they are denied by the Constitutional Court of Austria (VfGH v. 3.10.1989, VfSlg. 12180).

A starting point for the European Court of Human Rights is the question of whether a right is to be categorized as a "pecuniary right." In the view of the Court, this applies generally to rights to receive a pension or even to the right to social benefits irrespective of the contribution of the claimant to the existence of the claim (*Gaygususz v. Austria, Koua Poirrez v. France*). Furthermore, the Court interprets "legitimate expectations" as "pecuniary rights," whereas "the right to acquire property" does not fall under this category (*Van der Mussele v. Belgium, Slivenko and Others v. Latvia*). This distinction is especially difficult in cases of property restitution (*Broniowski v. Poland, Prince Hans-Adam II of Liechtenstein v. Germany*, Nußberger 2005). As a consequence of this jurisprudence, a broad range of rights understood as "property" in the sense of the Convention has to be protected according to the requirements of the Convention set out in Article 1 of the First Protocol.

*Press* The term "press" can be understood as comprising all printed material, whatever its contents. However, it is also possible to refer to a narrower notion and differentiate between the function of the relevant publication. That is the approach taken by the Court:

> The Court considers that a fundamental distinction needs to be made between reporting facts—even controversial ones—capable of contributing to a debate in a democratic society relating to politicians in the exercise of their functions, for example, and reporting details of the private life of an individual who, moreover, as in this case, does not exercise official functions. While in the former case the press exercises its vital role of "watchdog" in a democracy by contributing to "impart[ing] information and ideas on matters of public interest" … it does not do so in the latter case. (*V. Hannover v. Germany*)

Thus the Court chooses not to define the relevant term in the broadest sense possible but to differentiate between two forms of "press" and consequently, between two levels of protection.

All these examples show that the Court builds up a new legal terminology superseding the different national legal terminologies. While it draws on national conceptions, the aim of giving new definitions is to provide the most effective protection of human rights possible on the basis of the Convention.

## Margin of Appreciation

While the elaboration of a common European human rights terminology by the Court favors the unification and harmonization of the different legal cultures, the doctrine of the "margin of appreciation" protects national peculiarities. It allows different conceptions as well as different historical and political factors to be taken into account. But, even if the Court accords a margin of appreciation to the contracting states, it stresses that it is empowered to give a final ruling on the existence of human rights violations.

Two different decisions of the Court on restrictions of Article 10 based on specific historical and political experience can illustrate this point. Both Germany and Hungary had restricted the freedom of expression; Germany by prohibiting members of extremist parties to become school teachers or work as civil servants, and Hungary by prohibiting policemen from joining political parties. In both cases, the Court had to decide if the restrictions of the freedom of expression are "necessary in a democratic society."

In this context the German government opined that it

> had a special responsibility in the fight against all forms of extremism, whether right-wing or left-wing. It was precisely for that reason and in the light of the experience of the Weimar Republic that the duty of political loyalty had been introduced for civil servants. The civil service was the cornerstone of a "democracy capable of defending itself." Its members could not therefore play an active role in parties, such as the DKP, that pursued anti-constitutional aims. (*Vogt v. Germany*)

The Court accepted to examine the circumstances of the case in the light of the situation existing in the Federal Republic of Germany at the material time. It also accepted a certain margin of appreciation of Germany, but still came to the conclusion that the dismissal in the case was disproportionate to the legitimate aim pursued.

In the Hungarian case, the government also based its arguments on specific historical and political circumstances. It contends

> That for decades preceding Hungary's return to democracy in 1989 to 1990, the police had been a self-avowed tool of the ruling party and had taken an active part in the implementation of the party policies. Career members of the police were expected to be politically committed to the ruling party. Given Hungary's peaceful and gradual transformation towards pluralism without a general purge in the public administration, it was necessary to depoliticise, inter alia, the police and restrict the political activities of its members so that the public should no longer regard the police as a supporter of the totalitarian regime but rather as a guardian of democratic institutions. (*Rekvenyi v. Hungary*)

With regard to the specific circumstances of the case, the Court comes to the opposite conclusion from the one reached in the German case:

> Regard being had to the margin of appreciation left to the national authorities in this area, the Court finds that, especially against this historical background, the relevant measures taken in Hungary in order to protect the police force from the direct influence of party politics can be seen as answering a "pressing social need" in a democratic society. (*Rekvenyi v. Hungary*)

Thus the doctrine of "margin of appreciation" allows for a reconciliation of the general rules provided for by the Convention and the specific situation in a country. The decisive question is how far the margin of appreciation goes. That can be very controversial as in the preceding case *Vogt v. Germany*, where the decision was taken by a majority of 10 to nine votes.


**Mainstreaming Legal Cultures: *"in dubio pro libertate"***

Although the Court can mitigate the clashes between various legal cultures by allowing a certain margin of appreciation in the assessment of human rights violations, it clearly professes to the principle "*in dubio pro libertate.*" That means that restrictions on human rights are always interpreted very narrowly. Decisions on the freedom to impart information are illustrative of the overall attitude:

> According to the Court's well-established case-law, freedom of expression constitutes one of the essential foundations of a democratic society and one of the basic conditions for its progress and each individual's self-fulfilment. Subject to paragraph 2 of Article 10, it is applicable not only to "information" or "ideas" that are favourably received or regarded as inoffensive or as a matter of indifference, but also to those that offend, shock or disturb. Such are the demands of pluralism, tolerance and broadmindedness, without which there is no "democratic society." (*Tammer v. Estonia*)

This interpretation conveys the idea of a very open society that also integrates what is shocking and offending. But is this idea really accepted everywhere in Europe? Is it compatible with the concept of a "democracy capable of defending itself" ("*wehrhafte Demokratie*") developed on the basis of the German *Grundgesetz*?[9] Is it compatible with the concept of an endangered democracy developed in the jurisprudence of the Russian Constitutional Court?

---

9   See on the changes of the concept of a "*wehrhafte Demokratie*" on the basis of the jurisprudence of the German Constitutional Court as well as on different models in France, the United States and Japan (Higuchi 2007).

The decision of the Russian Constitutional Court on the admissibility of regional branches of political parties is illustrative for this point. The Russian Constitutional Court explains:

> in the current circumstances, when there are serious challenges on behalf of the separatist, nationalist and terrorist forces, who tend to abuse their constitutional rights and freedoms, and whereas the Russian society did not yet gain lasting experience of democratic life, creation of regional political parties, which aim at defending their regional and local interests, would lead to the destruction of state integrity and unity of the state governance system as a basis of the federal constitution of Russia. (Russian Constitutional Court 2005)

The picture conveyed here is that of a society forced to defend its values against attacks from outside. That seems to be a different view, perhaps not on democracy as such, but on the actual status of democracy in Russia. In this context, the European Court of Human Rights levels differences between divergent conceptions. As this is done on a case by case basis, the clashes between the different conceptions are not evident at the outset but might become more and more visible in the course of time.

*Sacrifices of Divergent Conceptions*

Furthermore, special characteristics of legal systems that are unknown in other legal systems can be "sacrificed." Examples for such sacrifices are, to a certain extent, the "attorney-general" or the "nadzor system." Both are seen as incompatible with the right to a fair trial as interpreted by the Court. The Court interprets the right to a fair trial

> in the light of the Preamble to the Convention, which, in its relevant part, declares the rule of law to be part of the common heritage of the Contracting States. One of the fundamental aspects of the rule of law is the principle of legal certainty, which requires, among other things, that where the courts have finally determined an issue, their ruling should not be called into question. (*Ryabykh v. Russia*)

The Court assumes that the principle of "*res judicata*" has to be observed in all legal systems in the same way:

> Legal certainty presupposes respect for the principle of *res judicata* … that is, the principle of the finality of judgments. This principle underlines that no party is entitled to seek a review of a final and binding judgment merely for the purpose of obtaining a rehearing and a fresh determination of the case. Higher courts' power of review should be exercised to correct judicial errors and miscarriages of justice, but not to carry out a fresh examination. The review should not be treated as an appeal in disguise, and the mere possibility of there being two views on the subject is not a ground for re-examination. A departure from that principle is justified only when made necessary by circumstances of a substantial and compelling character. (*Ryabykh v. Russia*)

On the basis of these reflections, the Court considered the nadzor system as it exists in the Russian (*Ryabykh* 2003, *Roseltrans* 2005, *Volkova* 2005) as well as in the Romanian legal system (*Brumarescu* 1999) to be incompatible with the right to a fair trial.[10]

---

10    See Iurin (2006) for more on jurisprudence for fair trials.

The disputes about the institution of an *"avocat général"* also show controversies about what is fair in judicial proceedings. The *avocat général* as a representative of the authorities is called upon to give an opinion on a judicial case. Although the opinion is objective and reasoned in law and its main function is to ensure the consistency of the court's case-law, it is—in the Court's view—nevertheless intended to advise and influence the court. For the European Court on Human Rights, it is decisive that the party cannot reply to the opinion of the *avocat général* before the end of the hearing. This is seen as an infringement of the right to adversarial proceedings. This right is interpreted as the "opportunity for the parties to a criminal or civil trial to have knowledge of and comment on all evidence adduced or observations filed, even by an independent member of the national legal service, with a view to influencing the court's decision" (*Vermeulen* 1996). Furthermore, it is seen as unfair that the *avocat général* can take part in the court's deliberations, even if only in an advisory capacity.

Although this interpretation is not unanimously accepted, states where such an institution exists are forced to adapt their system to what might be called the dominant legal culture.


## Critical Reactions of National Constitutional Courts

*Critical Reactions to the Jurisprudence of the ECHR*

It is not surprising that national courts, especially national constitutional courts, are reluctant to accept the "Strasbourg" interpretations of human rights law if they are not compatible with their own views. That is especially true if the courts understand their role not only as that of guardians of constitutionality but also as that of guardians of the respective national legal culture.

In the heavily criticized *Görgülü* case, the German Constitutional Court argued generally in favor of a strong position of the Convention in national law, but also admitted that the Convention might not be respected "if there is no other possibility to prevent a violation of the basic principles of the Constitution."[11] This statement was criticized heavily, but in fact, up to now, it is only of theoretical value. All decisions of lower courts that were in contradiction to the jurisprudence of the Strasbourg Court have been quashed. But the *Görgülü* case shows that the Constitutional Court wants to reserve the last word in controversial issues.

If the aim is to build up a common European legal culture, critical statements are necessary. But critical statements calling into question the authority of the Court are dangerous to say the least. If the architects themselves doubt that the building will be stable, it is difficult to convince those living in the building to have confidence. But what is even more detrimental to the whole project is the lack of cooperation of the national authorities, especially the reluctance to realize the structural changes demanded. The nadzor system in Russia might once more serve as an example. Although it has been changed in the newly elaborated procedural codes, it has not been adapted to the demands of the European Court (Iurin 2006). The new regulations introduce some limits to the system. But still, quashing a final judgment is possible not only in exceptional circumstances but for any violation of material or procedural law (Koroteev 2006). That is why the Committee of Ministers criticizes the violations of the requirement of legal certainty (CM Interim Resolution 2006).

---

11   Decision of the German Constitutional Court 14.10.2004, BVerfGE 111, 307; see on the decision Wol'ff (2006: 39–42).

*Integration of the Jurisprudence of the ECHR in the National Legal Culture*

But on the other side, national courts as well as national constitutional courts refer to the European Convention on Human Rights and especially to the jurisprudence of the Court more and more often. Although the quantity of citations alone is not decisive as a lot of the references might be decorative and not have any real value, it is clear that the jurisprudence of the Strasbourg Court plays a decisive role in what might be called an "Europeanization of human rights."

## Conclusion

Thus, the Tower of Babel is well on its way to being built. There are thousands and thousands of judgments showing that it is possible to find compromises in difficult human rights questions that are acceptable and accepted in 47 states. At the same time, it is fair to say that not all judgments are accepted universally and equally within the community, as regards our "chicken or egg" question. But the lesson of the Tower of Babel must not be forgotten. Such an undertaking is possible only if the partners do not want to make a name themselves and if they desire to serve a common aim. It is not necessary to deny the existence of basic differences between the various legal systems and legal cultures. But it is necessary to address the questions openly and to find common solutions on the basis of a common understanding. Slowly but steadily, it is possible to rebuild a Tower of Babel in the realm of law. It is to be hoped that the architects of today achieve their aim and do not commit the same mistakes as our ancestors in biblical times.

## References

*Broniowski v. Poland* [2004] (appl. no. 31443/96), Judgment (Merits and Just Satisfaction), June, 22, Reports of Judgments and Decisions 2004–V.

*Brumarescu v. Romania* [1999] (appl. no. 28342/95), Judgment (Merits), October 28, Reports 1999–VII.

BVerfG E 53, 252, 289.

CM Interim Resolution DH (2006), 1.

David, R. and Jauffret-Spinosi, C. 2002. *Les grands systems de droit comtemporains.* 11th edn. Paris: Dalloz.

*Deumeland v. Germany* [1986] (appl. no. 9384/81), Judgment (Merits and Just Satisfaction), May 29, Reports A 100.

*Feldbrugge v. the Netherlands* [1986] (appl. no. 8562/79), Judgment (Merits), May 29, Reports A 99.

*Frydlender v. France* [2000] (appl. no. 30979/96), Judgment (Merits and Just Satisfaction), June 27, Reports of Judgments and Decisions 2000–VII, Z. 27 et seq.

*Gaygususz v. Austria* [1996] (appl. no. 17371/90), Judgment (Merits and Just Satisfaction), September 16, Reports 1996–IV.

Gerhards, J. In cooperation wtih Michael Hölscher. 2005. *Kulturelle Unterschiede in der Europäischen Union. Ein Vergleich zwischen Mitgliedsländern. Beitrittskandidaten und der Türkei.* Wiesbaden.

German Law on Judges, § 39.

Glenn, P.G. 2007. *Legal Traditions of the World: Sustainable Diversity in Law*. 3rd edn. New York: Oxford University Press.

Higuchi, Y. 2007. Dignité humaine: universalité de la valeur et diversité des methodes constitutionelles, in *Die Ordnung der Freiheit. Festschrift für Christian Starck zum siebzigsten Geburtstag*, edited by R. Grote, I. Härtel, K.-E. Hain. T.I. Schmidt and T. Schmitz. Geburtstag: Tübingen, 791 et seq.

Iurin, M.I. 2006. *Nadzornaja instancija: vzgljad Evropejskogo suda po pravam čeloveka, Rossijskoe pravosudie*. No. 5.

Koroteev, K. 2006. *Supervisory Review Procedure in Civil Proceedings: New Reforms Needed, EHRAC Bulletin*, Summer 2006(5), 10. Available at: www.londonmet.ac.uk/library/x29082_3. pdf.

*Koua Poirrez v. France* [2003] (appl. no 40892/98), Judgment (Merits and Just Satisfaction), September 30, Reports of Judgments and Decisions 2003–X.

Kovler, A.I. 2004. *Evropejskoe pravo prav čeloveka, Žurnal rossijskogo prava* 1, 4.

*Lambourdiere v. France*, [2000] (appl. no. 37387/97), Judgment (Merits and Just Satisfaction), August 2 (not reported), No. Z. 23.

Nußberger, A. 2005. A Human Rights Perspective on the Expropriation and Redistribution of Property in Eastern Germany, *The Uppsala Yearbook of East European Law*, 110 et seq.

*Pellegrin v. France* [1999] (appl. no. 28541/95), Judgment (Merits), December 8, Reports of Judgments and Decisions 1999–VIII, RJD 1999–VIII, Z. 64 et seq.

*Prince Hans-Adam II of Liechtenstein v. Germany* [2001] (appl. no. 42527/98), Judgment (Merits), July 12, Reports of Judgments and Decisions 2001–VIII.

Protocol No. 12, ETS. 177, so far (status as of January 2012) ratified by 17 and signed by 20 member States of the Council of Europe.

Protocol No. 13, ETS. No. 187, so far (status as of January 2012) ratified by 42 and signed by 3 member States of the Council of Europe.

*Rekvenyi v. Hungary* [1999] (appl. no. 25390/94), Judgment (Merits), May 20, Reports of Judgments and Decisions 1999–III, para. 44, 48.

Report of the Committee of Experts on Problems Arising from the Coexistence of the United Nations Covenants on Human Rights and the European Convention on Human Rights: Differences as Regards the Rights Guaranteed, Council of Europe Doc. H. (70) 7 (1970).

Robertson, A. 1975. *Travaux Préparatoires*, Volume 1, The Hague, 194.

*Roseltrans v. Russia* [2005] No. 60974/00, §§ 27–28, July 21.

Russian Constitutional Court [2005] Judgment February, SZ RF 2005, Nr. 6, p. 491.

*Ryabykh v. Russia* [2003] (appl. no. 52854/99), Judgment (First Section), July 24, Final 13/12/2003, Reports 2003–IX, para. 51.

*SC Cox v. Ireland* [1992] 2 I.R. 503, 522.

Schlaich, K. and Korioth, S. 2010. *Das Bundesverfassungsgericht*. München, 34.

*Slivenko and Others v. Latvia* [2005] (appl. no. 48321/99), Judgment (Merits and Just Satisfaction), June 16 (not reported).

Smith, G. 2007. The Procuracy, Putin, and the Rule of Law in Russia, in *Russia, Europe, and the Rule of Law*, edited by F. Feldbrugge. Boston: Leiden, 1.

*Tammer v. Estonia* [2001] (appl. no. 41205/98), Judgment (Merits), February 6, Reports of Judgments and Decisions 2001–I, Final 04/04/2001.

*V. Hannover v. Germany* [2004] (appl. no. 59320/00), Judgment (Merits), June 24, Reports of Judgments and Decisions 2004–VI, Final 24/09/2004, para. 63.

*Van der Mussele v. Belgium* [1983] (appl. no. 8919/80), Judgment (Merits), November 23, Reports A 70.

*Vermeulen v. Belgium* [1996] (appl. no. 19075/91), Judgment (Merits and Just Satisfaction), February 20, Reports 1996–I, para. 33.

VfGH v. 3.10.1989, VfSlg. 12180 – Pension rights.

*Vogt v. Germany* [1995] (appl. no. 17851/91), Judgment (Merits), September 26, Reports A 323, para. 54.

*Volkova v. Russia* [2005] No. 48758/99, §§ 34–36, April 5.

Wol'ff, G.L. 2006. Evropejskij sud po pravam čeloveka i nacinal'nye sudy: delo Gergjulju, *Sravnitel'noe Konstitucionnoe obozrenie*, 1, S. 39–42.

Zweigert, K. and Kötz, H. 1996. *Einführung in die Rechtsvergleichung*, 3rd edn. Tübingen: J.C. Mohr.

Chapter 24

# International Legal Development and National Legal Change in the Fight against Corruption

Michael Kubiciel

In a world of shortage, people must compete. Ever since people have organized competition in a way structured by rules, individuals have circumvented them for the sake of rent-seeking. Free-riding has thus become a constant companion of mankind (Johnston 2004).[1] Whenever free-riding involves persons who abuse their public office or function for private benefit, we speak of corruption (compare Eser and Kubiciel 2005: 17–21, and Tanzi 1998: 564).

Corruption unfolds in different forms: "Grand corruption" involves members of the government or other high-ranking public officials, whereas "petty corruption" takes place on a lower level—often on the street. While forms of corruption are dependent upon the constantly changing normative, social and economic status of a society, international and national anti-corruption policies throughout the world have remained unaltered for a very long time. In the 1990s, however, a remarkable legal development was set off. Several international organizations developed anti-corruption conventions, nations throughout the world changed their laws, and several multinational groups were founded to monitor the efforts on the national level. The field of anti-corruption legislation is thus an ideal subject to scrutinize two fundamental questions of international law: what are the causes that can initiate and energize such a global legal development? Under which conditions can international law conventions lead to both normative and social changes on the national level? In order to find answers to these questions, this chapter will trace the long process of international law on paper, to national law in action. We understand the "chicken or egg" question in this context—assuming an interest in whether law can be used as a means of social engineering—as capturing the essence of "on the books" versus "in action." Our special focus is that this is a two-step process: first, there must be enough movement on the international level to produce treaties creating implementation obligations for international law at the level of countries; second, once the focus moves to the level of individual countries, the question is whether implementation of those obligations via domestic law is effective.

This chapter will review, in its first part, the political and historic circumstances that made the 1990s the first decade in which corruption emerged as a truly global political issue (George et al. 1999: 46; Glynn et al. 1997: 7). I will point out that international law followed a shift in political interests which led to a change in perception: corruption was no longer regarded as a useful instrument to influence politics and trade abroad; instead, it was re-conceptualized as a significant danger for the administration at home and as a barrier for European and global trade. Turning to the national level, the second part of this chapter shows that the situation in many countries is converse. Law does not follow an alteration of political interests or social perceptions; rather the new anti-corruption law itself shall effectuate a change in behavior. Contrary to a widespread technocratic assumption, criminal law and law enforcement alone cannot bring about social change, for such

---

1   For historic examples, see Jordan (2009).

a change depends on complex socio-cultural preconditions. Therefore, the third part asks which social sources are needed to energize the fight against corruption on the national level. The last section is dedicated to the role of criminal law. We will see that national law-makers should neither adopt an attitude of "technocratic euphoria" nor lapse into "normative pessimism," since criminal law can indeed contribute to a lasting social change as long as national law-makers diligently take into account the particular situation of their societies.

## How to Ignite an International Legal Development

Just like an avalanche, a legal development as broad as the one related to anti-corruption policy requires three elements: a period of stagnation, a trigger, and an energizing source.

*Legal Stagnation*

With regard to the first element, the stagnation period, the preconditions for a legal avalanche were perfect. Although waves of corruption cases came and went, several countries relied on anti-corruption norms that were in place since the late nineteenth and early twentieth century.[2] National level stagnation corresponded with an absence of initiatives on the international level. The reasons for this stagnation were manifold. Many people in Western nations had the diffuse belief that their well-organized society was rather free from a criminal phenomenon that was foremost ascribed to countries of the Southern hemisphere (compare Caiden 1988: 14; Huberts 1995: 14; Little and Posada-Carbó 1996: 2). Moreover, other topics like the Cold War, the pollution of the environment, or economic recession had conquered public attention. Thus, the fight against corruption was, if ever, a minor topic in public and political debate.[3] Not only was corruption ignored, but it was also widely misinterpreted. Many of those who had an insight into the diffusion of corruption perceived bribery to be a common and indispensable means to promote business in either highly complex or developing bureaucracies (Leff 1964; Nye 1967).[4] Accordingly, many states not only ignored corruption at home but even promoted the use of bribery as a means for domestic corporations in international business relations (George et al. 1999; OECD 1997). The situation was equally dire with regard to international organizations. Using the "C-word" in the halls of most international organizations was regarded as unseemly, although many of their own projects were riddled with corruption.[5] Finally, political pressure exerted by non-governmental organizations did not exist until the 1990s (Pieth 2007).

To sum up: a lack of public awareness, political ignorance both on the national and international level, together with companies uninterested in combating corruption were the perfect ingredients for legal stagnation. Thus, for almost 20 years the US Foreign Corrupt Practices Act (FCPA) of 1977 had been the only remarkable innovation in the fight against corruption (George et al. 1999).

---

2   For the example of Ireland, see GRECO, *First Evaluation Round, Evaluation Report on Ireland*: 3. For the "outmoded, uncertain and inconsistent" anti-corruption law in the UK, compare GRECO, *First Evaluation Round, Evaluation Report on the United Kingdom*: 4–5. For a comparative survey compare Eser and Kubiciel (2005: 22–53).

3   See Huberts (1995: 11–13), analyzing the programs of political parties in Western Europe. Compare as well George et al. (1999: 22).

4   Compare as well Davis and Ruhe (2003: 276).

5   Davis and Ruhe (2003: 276) cite a study according to which 20–30 percent of the loans granted to Indonesia by the World Bank ended up in the pockets of public officials.

## The Trigger

Although the adoption of the FCPA was a significant landmark that attracted international attention, it was not the initial shot for a multilateral or even international fight against corruption. In fact, most countries came to the conclusion that the FCPA could not be used as a model applicable to their own economic, political, and legal systems. And indeed, the FCPA is a legal instrument which was designed in a particular historical context in the United States to serve extraordinary political interests of the US government: in the aftermath of the "Watergate/Nixon" scandal the Watergate Special Prosecutor and the United States Securities and Exchange Commission (SEC) exposed corrupt practices to such an extent—one of them, the "Tanaka-Lockheed" case, even involved Japan's prime minister and a member of the Dutch royal family—that the American public insisted on firm political initiatives against corruption (Tarullo 2004). In addition, the content of the FCPA met some political interests of the US government since the Act enabled sanctions against companies whose business practices were not only unethical but also interfered with the US foreign policy and national security interests, namely in the Middle East (see Pieth 2007). Since other Western governments neither had a comparably vigilant public at that time nor persecuted parallel political interests, the United States did not find many allies in the fight against corruption until the 1990s.

Then, apparently abruptly, the international attitude toward corruption changed from an uninterested tolerance to a determined abatement in the early 1990s. Many scholars argue that this stunning turnaround was a result of the increasing pressure, which the United States exerted within and by means of international organizations (Williams and Beare 1999).[6] And indeed, the United States had rational interests in promoting an international harmonization of anti-corruption standards. Most notably, the US government sought to abolish the distortion of competition resulting from the fact that the United States criminalized and charged corrupt business practices of its companies while other governments supported their enterprises in securing international deals even by means of corruption (George and Lacey 2006: 510; The Open Society Institute 2005: 22; Tanzi 1998: 561). The US interest in harmonizing the legal standards and thus balancing the economic chances of both national and foreign companies was not, however, the decisive element that finally triggered the international legal avalanche in the 1990s. Indeed, the adverse impact of the FCPA had already been reported to the federal government in 1981 (US General Accounting Office 1981) without causing any change on the international level. In fact, several efforts to create multilateral policies, guidelines, or rules failed in the years after the passing of the FCPA (compare Hotchkiss 1998: 109). The international reluctance followed from the political scaffold of the "Cold War" world. Since several allied regimes in the Third World financed their political basis by means of corruption, closing these sources of revenue was regarded as politically inopportune by many Western governments. Economic interests of US companies were weighed and related to the strategic needs of a fragmented world. The result of this evaluation was not the aggravation of international standards but rather the diminution of importance of the FCPA (George et al. 1999; Hotchkiss 1998).

With the fall of the Berlin Wall, these global conditions changed. The end of the Cold War and the increasing globalization altered the economic and political framework in which corruption could be ignored or tolerated. Economically, the true costs of corruption became apparent as the growth of global competitors led to rising prices as a result of bribing in international procurement. Public officials in Africa, Asia, or Latin America that once charged 10 percent of a contract value were put

---

6   For the US impetus to the efforts of OECD, see George et al. (1999: 11).

into a position in which they could demand 30 percent as side payment (see Doig and Theobald 2000; Hotchkiss 1998). More and more economic leaders agreed that the costs of corruption had become unacceptably high.[7] Corruption, which for a long time had functioned as a useful tool in international business development, increasingly did not pay off anymore. The change in economic perception met a changed political situation. As long as Western governments felt the strategic need to tolerate illicit enrichment in developing countries, the "reframing of corruption as a source of economic risk" (Williams and Beare 1999: 117) was insufficient to trigger an international initiative against corruption. The "Post-Cold-War" world, however, made politics accessible for complaints (Hotchkiss 1998: 109; Hulme and Turner 1997: 222–4; Sajó 2003: 173; Tanzi 1998: 560). Several Western governments found themselves unable to explain why the interest in stabilizing a political status quo in a country outweighed the corrupt nature of the regime. Political allies hence became corrupt regimes and corruption was no longer part of a permissible political strategy but became a crucial cause of global poverty (Doig and Theobald 2000; Pieth 2007). These alterations were complemented by a significant change in criminal politics. Important Western governments came to regard transnational corruption as a danger for their own societies as growing global trade and increasing international mergers facilitated the possibility of infection with the virus of corruption (Sanyal 2005: 139). In particular the political integration in Europe has brought about the danger of the incorporation of Eastern states, infecting the European Union with corruption (compare George et al. 1999: 24).

With the end of the Cold War and the dawning of globalization, which shed light on the true dimension of corruption, perception and interests in many states changed (compare Williams and Beare 1999: 119). In this new light, US initiatives not only encountered an auspicious international policy climate but were also endorsed by many citizens in important European societies, shocked by the exposure of major corruption scandals. Once awareness had been raised, the public in many countries started to question economic and political customs formerly overlooked. Public scrutiny was promoted by a growing media market in the 1990s keen on delivering "corruption scandals" to the interested public (Blankenburg 2002: 921). Societies urged politicians to react since such scandals were increasingly rated as indications of an illness threatening the very foundations of society (ibid.). These shifts in the socio-political scaffold boosted the diplomatic pressure exerted by the US government and NGOs such as Transparency International so that their anti-corruption initiatives finally succeeded (compare Abbott and Snidal 2002: 163–5 and Androulakis 2007: 260). In 1997, 28 states signed the OECD Convention on Combating Bribery of Foreign Public Officials in International Business Transactions as the first global instrument in the fight against corruption.[8]

*The Broadening of the International Development*

After the avalanche had been set off, the international legal development quickly broadened and its speed accelerated. In Europe, the Council of Europe (CoE) took the leading role. A "Multidisciplinary Group on Corruption" was implemented in 1994 and a political strategy against corruption was developed in 1996, followed finally by two conventions in 1997: the CoE Criminal Law Convention on Corruption and the CoE Civil Law Convention on Corruption.[9] The European Union followed in 1998, the African Union in 2003. The adoption of the United

---

7　See, for example, the ICC (1996). Compare as well George et al. (1999: 17) and Davis and Ruhe (2003: 276).

8　In 1996 the (regional) Inter-American Convention Against Corruption was adopted.

9　For further information about these activities of the Council of Europe, compare Eser and Kubiciel (2005: 13–15).

Nations Convention Against Corruption (Doig et al. 2009; Kubiciel 2009) in 2003 finally marks the peak of an international development whose dimension is best reflected by the United Nations' *Compendium of International Legal Instruments on Corruption*. Although the compendium does not even include the comprehensive legal guidelines of institutions such as the World Bank, the International Monetary Fund, the Asian Development Bank, and the International Chamber of Commerce, it lists no less than 21 international legal instruments (see United Nations Office on Drugs and Crime 2005). After decades of stagnation, an impressive arsenal of legal weapons has been produced in less than 10 years. The power of this legal avalanche is indicated not only by the quantity of legal instruments but also by their quality. While the OECD Convention focused on the criminalization of those who (actively) bribe foreign public officials, subsequent conventions have adopted a wider scope. All of them provide for the criminalization of domestic bribery, but most of them go a step further.[10] For instance, the Council of Europe Convention slightly expands the scope of criminalization to trading in influence and money laundering (Council of Europe 1998) while others, namely the United Nations Convention Against Corruption (2003),[11] include a variety of corruption-related offences such as embezzlement, abuse of functions, illicit enrichment, and obstruction of justice. Moreover, several conventions and other legal instruments include provisions on law enforcement,[12] asset recovery,[13] prevention,[14] awareness-raising[15] and even the highly sensitive topic of immunities (UNCAC: article 30 (2), Resolution (97) 24: number 6).

The dimension of this development in international law raises questions for its energizing sources. Shifts in the socio-political scaffold and an altered perception in many Western countries may trigger a legal change in countries like the Netherlands and the United Kingdom, yet this does not explain why countries with completely different social and economic backgrounds and diverging political interests joined the movement. What brought transition states such as Lithuania, Romania, Bulgaria, and even under-developed states in Africa to sign anti-corruption conventions that often had been designed by Western donors or international organizations? The analysis of their interests gives the answer. In the case of many developing countries, the need for international financial aid gave an incentive to join the international development. Following the example of the World Bank—the leading think-tank for development strategies (Hulme and Turner 1997)—many other international and national donors adjusted their conditions for loans to the necessities of fighting corruption (Davis and Ruhe 2003; Riley 1998). In view of declining international financial aid (Hulme and Turner 1997) even corrupt regimes were not in the position to refuse new anti-corruption policies right away (Lawson 2009; Oelbaum and Sandbrook 1997). At least they had to pretend to cooperate by signing and ratifying conventions, whilst hoping that policies designed

---

10   An exemption is the Convention on the Fight against Corruption involving Officials of the European Communities or Officials of Member States of the European Union from 1997, which only covers active and passive bribery.

11   Of comparable scope Inter-American Convention against Corruption (1996) and African Union (AU) Convention on Preventing and Combating Corruption (2003).

12   UNCAC: articles 30, 36, and 50, CoE: articles 20 and 23, Resolution (97) 24: numbers 3 and 7, and AU Convention on Preventing and Combating Corruption: article 5.

13   UNCAC: article 31 and chapter V; OECD Convention on Combating Bribery of Foreign Public Officials in International Business Transactions: article 3, CoE: article 19 (3), AU Convention on Preventing and Combating Corruption: article 16, Inter-American Convention against Corruption: article XV.

14   See UNCAC: chapter 2, Inter-American Convention against Corruption: article III, CoE articles 20 and 23, and Resolution (97) 24: numbers 1, 9, 10, 11, 12, 14–16.

15   UNCAC: article 13, Art. 5 AU Convention on Preventing and Combating Corruption: article 5, and Resolution (97) 24: number 1.

in cool Washington offices would melt once implemented under the African sun.[16] With regard to the transition states in Europe, interests of both West European and East European countries met ideally: while East European countries needed to acquire financial and political support for their stony way of transition, the neighbouring countries in Western Europe had, and still have, a strong interest in a stable political situation in their hemisphere. Consequently, East Europe received, and still receives, support of a quality unknown to developing countries—the integration in international and supranational organizations such as the European Union and NATO. As the fight against corruption has been an important condition for becoming a member of these organizations, East European countries, unlike several West European nations,[17] signed and ratified the relevant regional conventions against corruption (George et al. 1999: 23–4; Offe 1997: 64–5; Sajó 2003: 178). Thus, the rational pursuit of interests by states and their governments energized an international legal development that today has affected literally the whole planet.

However, joining an international legal development by signing and ratifying conventions is only the first step to lasting legal and social change. The next step has to be taken on the grounds of the individual nations. Those nations must transfer the content of international law to their national law system. This task is more complex than the initiation of an international legal development. Changing the national laws according to international standards encounters serious barriers, which become obvious when we now look at a group of states that have neither benefited from the blessings of the rather constant social and economic development of many Western countries, nor have suffered under the particularly hard circumstances of many African nations: the transition states in Eastern Europe.

## Legal and Social Change in East European States

If one speaks of legal change in the field of anti-corruption policy, one primarily thinks of amendments to criminal codes. And indeed, with respect to the core criminal law, legal change in the transition countries of Eastern Europe has been successful. One reason for this success has been the peer-review processes by means of which both the Council of Europe and the OECD are monitoring the implementation of their legal instruments. The *Groupe d'Etat contre la corruption* (GRECO) monitors and evaluates the implementation of the Council of Europe's legal instruments while the Anti-Bribery-Working-Group monitors the implementation of the legal instruments provided for by the OECD.[18] Accordingly, legal change in East European transition states has been realized in two steps: the ratification of the legal instruments resulted in amendments to the criminal law. This phase is followed by a—still continuing—monitoring process which aims at disclosing legal loopholes.

In its first evaluation round, GRECO had made several rather comprehensive recommendations concerning the criminal law (Eser and Kubiciel 2005). Bulgaria, for example, had been recommended to develop an efficient anti-corruption legal framework, while Bosnia-Herzegovina had been asked to speed up the process of reform of criminal legislation. Under normal conditions

---

16   See Flanary et al. (2000: 60–1): "In terms of rhetoric, anti-corruption themes are certainly at the forefront of the movement's public pronouncements, but there is less evidence of a widespread commitment in practice."

17   Among those states that have not ratified the CoE Criminal Law Convention on Corruption are Austria, Germany, Italy, Liechtenstein, and Spain (status: October 2009).

18   For the monitoring process carried out by GRECO, see Eser and Kubiciel (2005: 16–17). For the peer-review concept and its application by the OECD, see Pagani (2002).

such substantial amendments on criminal codes take a number of years. Bulgaria (GRECO, *First Evaluation Round, Compliance Report on Bulgaria*: 4–5) and Bosnia-Herzegovina (GRECO, *First Evaluation Round, Compliance Report on Bosnia and Hercegovina*: 3–4), however, managed to follow the recommendations in a very short time. The dynamic of legal change in Eastern Europe is best reflected by the different approaches to the question of whether legal persons should be held criminally liable for corruptive business practices. Together with several colleagues in other (Western) European states, the majority of German scholars argue that corporate criminal liability is incompatible with the criminal procedure, and, even more importantly, would violate the basic principle that the individual guilt (of a natural person), rather than social utility, decides the punishment (see Weigend 2008)—a prerequisite that, according to a recent decision of the German Constitutional Court, is a crucial part of the German legal culture and the constitutional identity (*Bundesverfassungsgericht*: ¶364). German scholars and politicians hence favor a regime of administrative fines as both effective and appropriate sanctions for legal persons,[19] while reserving criminal punishment for the individuals within the legal persons who are responsible for corruptive practices. Several "new" European countries such as Croatia, Estonia, Hungary, Lithuania, Poland, and Slovenia have rejected such dogmatic concerns and implemented criminal liability for legal persons as the presumably most effective means to deter enterprises from corruption.[20]

In this respect, international organizations would assess the pragmatic criminal policy of Eastern European states as cooperative and exemplary. Amending criminal law provisions however is only the first part in the process of legal change. Law is more than mere paper. It needs to have effects on society. Therefore legal change is incomplete as long as people adhere to their patterns of behavior irrespective of amended codes. The second and more important part of legal change hence is the transformation of statutes from paper to social reality. Many criminal lawmakers underestimate the complexity of the relationship between normative standards and social reality, and usually formulate criminal rules on the assumption that rules "nearly always influence conduct."[21] This underestimation has its foundation in a legal theory that has influenced great numbers of European (and American) lawyers in the last three or four decades. According to a widespread legal functionalism,[22] law in general is an instrument for "social engineering" (Pound 1965) and criminal law in particular shall enforce "certain types of behavior as standards for … the members of society" (Hart 1968, 1997: 38) by means of punishment which is "intended to provide one motive for abstaining from these activities" (Hart 1997: 27). The quintessence of these quotations is the criminal theory of deterrence and a legal concept according to which law is able to act on society irrespective of the morality and the convictions within a society.[23]

---

19   That the German legal regime is not less effective than other legal regimes can be derived from the data presented by Wells (2009: 480). For information on loopholes in the German anti-corruption legislation, see Wolf (2006: 785–92). For a list of possible improvements, see Eser and Kubiciel (2005: 53–121).

20   GRECO, *Second Evaluation Round, Evaluation Report on Croatia*: 17; GRECO, *Second Evaluation Round, Evaluation Report on Estonia*: 15; GRECO, *Second Evaluation Round, Evaluation Report on Hungary*: 17; GRECO, *Second Evaluation Round, Evaluation Report on Lithuania*: 18; GRECO, *Second Evaluation Round, Evaluation Report on Poland*: 17; GRECO, *Second Evaluation Round, Evaluation Report on Slovenia*: 18–19.

21   Darley and Robinson (2004: 173). This is a "disturbing" and "dangerous" fact.

22   See the programmatic plead against "transcendental nonsense" and in favour of a "functional approach" by Cohen (1935: 809–49).

23   This however is the position of positivists like Hart who assumes that law may not "exhibit some specific conformity with morality or justice." See Hart (1997: 185).

These assumptions, however, do not match the complexity of the problems. With regard to the concept of deterrence it is to say, that coercion and fear of sanctions alone cannot suppress criminal behavior such as bribery. First of all, potential offenders often do not know of the legal rules. And even if they do know the law, they frequently are unable to bring this knowledge to bear in guiding their conduct, due to a variety of situational, social, cultural and even chemical factors as scholars recently explicated (Darley and Robinson 2004). Secondly, a rational analysis commonly puts the perceived benefits of corruption greater than its perceived costs, due to criminal justice realities such as low punishment rates and, in particular, the high probability that acts of corruption will not be detected. Democratic and liberal states usually are neither willing nor able to adopt even stricter measures to detect and sanction corruption than communist regimes that have lost the fight against corruption, since a tight net of control and a harsh regime of sanctions would be insufficient for technical reasons. Thirdly, and most importantly, a state which primarily relies on control and coercion would undermine individual freedom and would hence lose the support of its people. This support, however, is a crucial condition for a successful legal change. If both legal officers and the society welcome new law as corresponding with their needs, even dramatic legal change can be successful, as the Japanese example teaches us.[24] On the other hand, the manifold examples of failed legal change reveal that it is impossible to create functioning political and legal systems against the overwhelming will of the people. The German philosopher Georg Friedrich Hegel has pointed out how law depends on the public consciousness: since freedom lies in the reflection of public consciousness by the law, to him, it was only natural that the Spanish people rejected a good and reasonable constitution; it did not arise from their national consciousness, Napoleon brought it to them (Hegel 1991).[25] If neither coercion alone nor the combination of reason and coercion can create a functioning legal system, law requires additional stabilizing sources. Measures must be taken that encourage people to voluntarily comply with law.[26] This is the central and hardest challenge for every national or international legislator.

## How to Energize a National Legal Change

*Rationality and Obedience to Law*

International organizations and transition states are well aware of the fact that attempts to amend the law against the public will are likely to fail. Hence they flank criminal law with a variety of measures. For example, transition states have followed international recommendations to increase the salaries of public officials[27] or to reform the remuneration in the health-care sector.[28]

---

24   In the late nineteenth century, for example, the Japanese state and important branches of society welcomed the import of foreign law as a necessary means to promote modernization of society and to circumvent unfair treaties with Western countries. This contributed to a widely successful adoption of foreign law. Compare Oda (1999: 21–5).

25   For examples of (criminal) laws that are still in place although they are dysfunctional compare Watson (2001: 6, 76–84).

26   Hart (1997: 203–4) admits that "a necessary condition of the existence of coercive power is that some at least must voluntarily co-operate in the system and accept its rules." Moreover, he acknowledges that "the stability of legal systems depends in part upon such types of correspondence with morals."

27   GRECO, *First Evaluation Round, Compliance Report on Latvia*: 8; GRECO, *First Evaluation Round, Compliance Report on Moldova*: 8; GRECO, *First Evaluation Round, Compliance Report on Romania*: 6–7.

28   GRECO, *First Evaluation Round, Compliance Report on Hungary*: 3.

The idea behind these measures is rather simple: if salary deficiencies are reduced by the state, public officials do not have to "compensate" for lacking income by taking bribes. Simple solutions, however, do not usually solve complex problems. Increasing the wages may diminish the *necessity* to bribe, but it does not reduce the *willingness* to take bribes since corruption even pays off for adequately remunerated public officials. In Russia, for example, the remuneration of police officers has been improved significantly in the last years, and yet police violence and corruption in contemporary Russia has reached such a level that a recent study has assessed the behavior of Russian policemen as "predatory," since "police officers prey on their society by using their positions to extract rents in form of money, goods, or services from individual members of the public" (Gerber and Mendelson 2008). The fact that the inclination to take bribes does not decline automatically after a boost in wages is also reflected by reports from countries such as Croatia, according to which it is not exceptional for well-paid university professors to take bribes in exchange for grades (see NOVOTINE 2009). Thus, improving the economic situation for public officials is an indispensable yet insufficient measure. A solid and lasting success in the fight against corruption cannot be achieved through public officials or citizens who latently calculate whether corruption pays off or not since it is rational to seek advantages by breaking rules that others abide. A *Homo economicus* will always opt for "free-riding." As Thomas Hobbes (1970) has told us in his philosophical masterpiece *Leviathan*, rationality may tell people to claim rules, but it does not tell them to obey rules (Robin 2004: 32–47). Consequently, the rational pursuit of interests, the force that goaded the international legal development, is an insufficient disposition to energize legal change on the national level.

Instead, a latent integrity, the acceptance of social roles, and a minimum of civic virtue are indispensable (compare Dahrendorf 2006: 61–5 and Walzer 1990: 6–23). These pre-legal conditions, however, cannot be *enforced* by law,[29] they are rather adopted by socialization,[30] or, as Immanuel Kant has proposed, result from experience (Kant 1996: second part, introduction, XIII). Therefore citizens and civil servants of Eastern European countries who have witnessed communist parties and their functionaries use law in a purely instrumental fashion must adopt a completely different attitude toward law and institutions: law is not an instrument to enforce political aims or to gain personal profit but it is rather a precondition to stabilize the social scaffold which grants fair chances to all citizens and enables the implementation of an individual's conception of a good life. If people have accepted laws as their standards and hence, consider them as morally valid, they will obey the law long after the threat of punishment has been waived.[31] As we will now see, state measures can *support* this learning process.

---

29   In the words of the famous US Supreme Court decision *West Virginia State Board of Education v. Barnette* (at 641): "Compulsory unification of opinion achieves only the unanimity of the graveyard ... Authority here is to be controlled by public opinion, not public opinion by authority." And "[i]f there is any fixed star in our constitutional constellation, it is that no official, high or petty, can prescribe what shall be orthodox in politics, nationalism, religion, or other matters of opinion or force citizens to confess by word or act their faith therein" (*Barnette* at 642).

30   For social factors that enhance law-abiding behavior, compare LaFave (2003: 26).

31   See Fisman and Miguel (2007: 1020–48), who examined the distribution of parking tickets in New York City among diplomats enjoying immunity. The results reveal that those persons who have been socialized in consolidated countries with a stable legal system will continue to act legally even if they do not have to fear sanctions for unlawful behaviour.

*Supportive Measures: Ostracizing Corruption*

With regard to public officials, several countries believe that a Code of Ethics can support the necessary learning process of their public officials.[32] Regulation of that kind and the related training shall not only specify the rights and duties of public officials. Rather, they aim at establishing informal norms which condense to a "climate of regularity" that affects the individual public official. Such a climate of virtue is indispensable since it is impossible to supervise corrupt public officials by other officials who act corruptly themselves.[33] The success of institutions depends on informal norms that flank formal rules and create a group identity that complements primary relations to families and friends, which often result in corruption and nepotism. Such measures do not only promote the functioning of institutions. As corrupt public officials frustrate the identification of the public with its institutions,[34] codes of conduct and ethical training enhance public trust in law and state institutions. The latter is an important precondition for the functioning of a legal system in states that are unable to enforce their law solely by means of coercion and control.

With regard to the public, the best way to gain sufficient support for an anti-corruption campaign is to create a social climate that ostracizes corruptive behavior. To achieve this, transition states have implemented "awareness-raising" programs that inform about the dangers of corruption.[35] However, not every program works in every nation. If the design of a program does not reflect the particular situation of the country and its society, it will not evoke the necessary social support. Governments should hence bear in mind that it is suboptimal to simply copy foreign models. Rather, such programs must address exactly that social source that can energize the fight against corruption in the particular society.

In order to reveal possible sources to be addressed by the awareness-raising programs, we have to take a closer look at the two conceptualizations of corruption that are usually used in order to ostracize it. According to the "ethical conceptualization," corruption is an attack on the fundamental principles on which a society is founded. To societies of developed and consolidated states, corruption appears as an illness threatening the very foundations of the society (Blankenburg 2002)—the well-established, functioning political system and legal values that grant fair chances to the people and constitute the framework for individual freedom and social welfare (Eser and Kubiciel 2005: 19). The situation in developing countries is converse. In many of them, the trust in the state, its institutions and procedures, is still at a minimum level (Doig and Theobald 2000).

---

32   GRECO, *First Evaluation Round, Compliance Report on Bulgaria*: 8, paragraphs 47–9; GRECO, *First Evaluation Round, Compliance Report on Poland*: 5, paragraphs 26–8. A variety of ethical codes exist in Croatia, see GRECO, *First Evaluation Round, Compliance Report on Croatia*: 4, paragraphs 20–4. During the time of evaluation a Code of Conduct had been drafted in Lithuania, compare GRECO, *First Evaluation Round, Compliance Report on Lithuania*: 5, paragraphs 26–9.

33   See the statement of Kenya's Attorney General in Doig and Williams (2000: 34): "The Government has this morning formed an anti-corruption squad to look into the conduct of the anti-corruption commission, which has been overseeing the anti-corruption task-force, which was earlier set to investigate the affairs of a Government ad hoc committee appointed earlier this year to look into the issue of high-level corruption among corrupt Government Officers."

34   Tamanaha (1997: 134–5) who neglects this aspect when he states that it is "easy to conceive of the existence of a corrupt legal system manned by officials who take a cynical view toward the entire body of rules they administer."

35   For examples, see GRECO, *First Evaluation Round, Compliance Report on Albania*: 12; GRECO, *First Evaluation Round, Compliance Report on Bulgaria*: 3–4; GRECO, *First Evaluation Round, Compliance Report on the Czech Republic*: 2; GRECO, *First Evaluation Round, Compliance Report on Romania*: 4; GRECO, *First Evaluation Round, Compliance Report on the Slovac Republic*: 4.

Political values and legal principles such as the rule of law are weak or do not exist (Oelbaum and Sandbrook 1997). Hence, those societies will not perceive corruption as a threat to well-established values. On the contrary, many corrupt patterns of behavior are not perceived as criminal but as a part of a tradition of gifts and nepotism, which derives from the importance of tribes and kinship (Flanary et al. 2000). In view of this, it is understandable why "moral calls" from Western countries have been rejected as "ethical imperialism" (Oelbaum and Sandbrook 1997).[36] Legal change, therefore, needs a different starting point. Where the ethical source is weak, legal change can be energized by the economic conceptualization of corruption. According to that model, corruption is an impediment to the formation of an economic basis on which ethical and political values can flourish.

Turning to the transition states in Eastern Europe, we face a more complicated situation in which both the economic and the ethical source for legal change are weak. In the 1990s, these states faced a situation that, in many respects, was comparable to developing countries in other parts of the world; namely that weak state institutions met a disastrous economic situation. Yet legal change could hardly be energized by the economic conceptualization of corruption for the economic situation was the legacy of the communist regimes and not a result of corruption in the phase of transition.[37] Neither could the fight against corruption be energized by an "ethical conceptualization," since legal principles like the rule of law were weak (Karstedt 2003; Reed 1995; Sajó 2003). People in transition states had not come to value new laws and institutions for their own sake but rather had an instrumental approach toward them (Offe 1997). Because new legal instruments do not perform optimally right from the start of a transition process (Karstedt 2003), a widespread feeling of insecurity and disorientation made many people resort to the mechanisms which had already helped them to cope with the communist system.[38] They used their social capital to counterbalance the shortcomings of a state whose economic and political architecture was under construction (Karstedt 2003; Sajó 2003). Corruption and nepotism were often used as "ad hoc" means to help cope with transition. In this, however, lies the exact danger that bribery causes to transition states. Widespread corruption frustrates the firm establishment of rules, procedures, and institutions and, thus, undermines the public's confidence that transition will have a happy ending.[39] In other words, corruption perpetuates transition.[40] This being so, the fight against corruption could be fueled by the insight that bribery betrays the realization of a common, yet unfinished project. The implementation of a state in which informal solutions are substituted by formal procedures and arbitrariness is substituted by equally fair chances.[41] If awareness-raising programs emphasize the interrelation between corruption and the success of political and economic renewal, sufficient social forces could be mobilized to help transform law into social reality. We will now scrutinize how and under which conditions criminal law can support these social forces.

---

36    With regard to the FCPA, George et al. (1999: 19), Hotchkiss (1998: 111), and Salbu (1997: 240).

37    Stating this does not imply denying that many cases of corruption accompanied privatization. For lucid corruption cases during this time, compare Reed (1995: 323–37) and Grødeland et al. (2002: 560).

38    For the results of large-scale surveys of public opinion in several transition countries, see Grødeland et al. (2002: 564–5) and Karstedt (2003: 295–6).

39    For the example of the Czech Republic, see Hagan and Radoeva (1998: 200). For the example of Poland, see Kolarska-Bobinska (2002: 315–26). Compare as well Eigen (1996: 158–9) and Sajó (2003: 185).

40    See Reed (1995: 327) who cites the former Czech government that advised its Prosecutor General that "the speed of the privatization process is such that it may be necessary to bypass normal legality."

41    As surveys reveal, there never was a dispute concerning the implementation of state institutions and the rule of law. Compare Grødeland et al. (2002: 578).

## The Function of Criminal Law

We have already seen that the deterrent effects of criminal law should not be overvalued. Legal change cannot be *enforced*. These findings however do not lead to the conclusion that criminal law cannot contribute to legal and social change at all, since criminal law and punishment do not only have a deterrent effect, but rather have a communicative dimension as well. The criminalization of corrupt behavior stresses the importance of a rule of behavior, while punishment confirms that the norm is a valid standard irrespective of individual deviance (compare Jakobs 1993: 13–14 and Hirsch 1995: 120–8). Addressing society, punishment "restores" the norm, thereby preventing the validity of a norm from being questioned. This mechanism of "negating the negation" (Hegel 1991) latently keeps citizens from adjusting their standards of behavior toward the criminal examples. Criminal law and punishment hence stabilize social convictions and standards of behavior. This stabilizing effect is of particular importance in transition states in which attachment to norms and social standards is not yet well-established.

The word "stabilize" implies that criminal law primarily performs a supportive task. Therefore, the persuasiveness of the norm is decisive for the success of legal change since criminal law can only stabilize those norms which are generally accepted by the society. Accordingly, transition states should be careful when implementing international legal standards or transplanting foreign models into domestic law. On the abstract level, a law may be transferable from one state to another;[42] yet human well-being is not achieved on the abstract level but within particular forms of human associations and culture. Therefore, law must have a connection with the morality and the ethical consensus of a society.[43] However reasonable a law may be in general, however functional it may be abroad, a legal transplant is likely to be rejected if it does not pay attention to national particularities and the ethical consensus in a society (see Watson 1976). Thus, national law-makers must recognize that criminal law statutes cannot be important if they are merely "meaningless form[s] of words" (Legrand 2001: 120). For law is not paper, but shall be an "incorporative cultural form" (ibid.: 116). Law-makers must carefully evaluate which tools offered by international conventions are applicable to their society, its situation and common moral convictions.[44]

In other words, amending criminal law by importing rules from abroad or by implementing international legal raw-models always brings about the necessity of cultural hermeneutics (Samuel 2008). For example, societies with corruption problems may accept a provision that criminalizes public officials who cannot reasonably explain a significant increase in their assets. Correspondingly, governments of such countries could consider implementing Art. 20 of the UN Convention Against Corruption, arguing that this duty is merely another institutional duty that is also balanced by the remuneration, the social security and other advantages of civil servants. Other societies however may conceive the criminalization of "illicit enrichment" as an undue shift of the burden of proof that runs counter to the presumption of innocence guaranteed by the constitutions of most Western states. Therefore whether national law-makers shall opt for or against the implementation of a statute concerning "illicit enrichment" depends on the criminological findings and their specific

---

42    Legrand holds that legal transplantation is impossible for no rule can be without meaning and the meaning of a rule always is a function of the interpreter's epistemological assumptions which are historically and culturally conditioned. See Legrand (1997: 114–24).

43    See, for example, the concept of an "overlapping consensus" elaborated by Rawls (1993: 133–6, 201–2). Hart (1997: 203) admits that "a necessary condition of the existence of coercive power is that some at least must voluntarily co-operate in the system and accept its rules." Moreover, he acknowledges that "the stability of legal systems depends in part upon such types of correspondence with morals" (Hart 1997: 204).

44    Compare Selznick (1999: 32). With regard to Africa, compare as well Riley (1998: 148–9).

legal framework. Another example is that of offering a gift to an employee in the health-care sector, which in Germany could be considered as an act of bribery. In some transition states however the same behavior is in line with long-standing traditions. These states should therefore take into consideration that the enforcement of criminal law in areas influenced by tradition could undermine the acceptance of anti-corruption policy in general. Starting the fight against corruption in a countryside hospital while tolerating the embezzlement of millions of European subsidies by public officials (see *Report from the Commission to the European Parliament and the Council on the Management of EU-funds in Bulgaria* 2008), as has taken place in Bulgaria, is surely not the right strategy to win the support of the citizens. If transition states bear in mind this correlation between law and the ethical consensus of a society, new norms have a hope to be generally accepted. Where law is generally accepted, the punishment of an individual deviance symbolizes the restoration of society's law.

## Conclusion

The broad international legal development on the field of anti-corruption follows a changed perspective of corruption after the end of the Cold War. The pursuit of rational interests propelled the international legal development and it is this international legal development which must be complemented by legal change on a national level. A national legal change, however, depends on more complex conditions. In many transition states, the anti-corruption law does not follow a negative social perception of corruptive behavior, but it is rather the new law that shall change existing social standards. According to a widespread technocratic assumption, criminal law has the potential to enforce normative standards since it gives individuals an incentive to obey the law, namely fear of punishment. This assumption has proven to be simplifying. As we have seen, there is no "hydraulic relationship" between criminal law and behavior (Ashworth 2006: 16). In the words of Tocqueville, "political societies are not what their law make them, but what sentiments, beliefs, ideas, habits of the heart, and the spirit of the men who form them, prepare them in advance to be, as well as what nature and education have made them" (Tocqueville, in Robin 2004: 78). Correspondingly, criminal law is unable to *enforce* new standards of behavior that go against social convictions and traditions. Therefore, the main challenge of a successful legal change lies in the approximation of the ethical consensus and the (new) law. Since criminal law is primarily a means to *stabilize* social standards, transition states should focus on informing the public of the harm that corruption causes to society.

However, all parents know that the best education is not done through words but by good examples. In view of that, one should expect that law-makers and governments in transition countries have set good examples when it comes to their own interests. However, this expectation proves to be false when we consider that the outstanding field in which GRECO's recommendations have not yet been implemented is the one related to immunities. Several nations have been asked to reduce the list of people who enjoy immunities; however, legal change has failed widely.[45] In other states, persons who have already left office still enjoy immunity. These nations have been invited to limit the scope of immunities to persons in office as the rationale of immunities is to protect the functioning of the office, not the individual (Eser and Kubiciel 2005). Several countries

---

45   GRECO, *First Evaluation Round, Compliance Report on Poland*: 11–12; GRECO, *First Evaluation Round, Compliance Report on Albania*: 8; GRECO, *First Evaluation Round, Compliance Report on Georgia*: 17. See GRECO, *First Evaluation Round, Final Overall Assessment*: 15–16.

have not responded to these recommendations.[46] Other states have been recommended to provide for guidelines that include transparent and objective criteria for the waiving of immunities but, yet again, legal change has widely failed.[47] Without a doubt, this remarkable reluctance to improve the system of immunities is caused by the fact that granting and waiving immunities affect the personal interests of law-makers and governments. It might be true that on an international level governments must act rationally in order to balance the necessities of the nations they represent with foreign interests and demands. Whenever members of government pursue personal interests while transferring international law to the national level, this expression of rationality has to be called corruption.

## References


Abbott, K. and Snidal, D. 2002. Values and Interests: International Legalization in the Fight against Corruption. *Journal of Legal Studies*, 31(1 Pt. 2), S141–S78.

African Union (AU) Convention on Preventing and Combating Corruption 2003.

Androulakis, N. 2007. *Die Globalisierung der Korruptionsbekämpfung*. Baden-Baden: Nomos.

Ashworth, A. 2006. *Principles of Criminal Law*. 5th Edition. Oxford: Oxford University Press.

Blankenburg, E. 2002. Judicial Anti-corruption Initiatives: Latin Europe in a Global Setting, in *Political Corruption*, 3rd Edition, edited by A. Heidenheimer and M. Johnston. New Brunswick: Transaction Publishers, 911–25.

*Bundesverfassungsgericht*, judgement of June 30, 2009 (2 BvE 2/08). 62 *Neue Juristische Wochenschrift* 2267.

Caiden, G. 1988. Toward a General Theory of Official Corruption. *Asian Journal of Public Administration*, 10(1), 3–26.

Cohen, F. 1935. Transcendental Nonsense and the Functional Approach. *Columbia Law Review*, 35(6), 809–49.

Committee of Ministers of the Council of Europe. *Resolution (97)24*.

Council of Europe (CoE). 1998. Criminal Law Convention on Corruption.

Dahrendorf, R. 2006. *Homo Sociologicus*. 16th Edition. Wiesbaden: Verlag für Sozialwissenschaft.

Darley, J. and Robinson, P. 2004. Does Criminal Law Deter? A Behavioural Science Investigation. *Oxford Journal of Legal Studies*, 24(2), 173–205.

Davis, J. and Ruhe, J. 2003. Perceptions of Country Corruption: Antecedents and Outcome. *Journal of Business Ethics*, 43(4), 275–88.

Doig, A. and Theobald, R. 2000. Why Corruption?, in *Corruption and Democratisation*, edited by A. Doig and R. Theobald. London and Portland: Frank Cass, 1–12.

Doig, A. and Williams, R. 2000. *Controlling Corruption*. Cheltenham and Northampton: Edward Elgar Publishing.

Doig, A., Jorge, G., and Kubiciel, M. 2009. Criminalization and Law Enforcement, in *Technical Guide to the Implementation of the United Nations Convention against Corruption*, edited by United Nations. New York: United Nations, 80–136.

Eigen, P. 1996. Combating Corruption around the World. *Journal of Democracy*, 7(1), 157–68.


---

46   GRECO, *First Evaluation Round, Compliance Report on the Czech Republic*: 7–8; GRECO, *First Evaluation Round, Compliance Report on Romania*: 14.

47   GRECO, *First Evaluation Round, Compliance Report on the Czech Republic*: 7–8; GRECO, *First Evaluation Round, Compliance Report on Lithuania*: 8–9. Compare GRECO, *First Evaluation Round, Compliance Report on Estonia*: 10.

Eser, A. and Kubiciel, M. 2005. *Institutions against Corruption*. Baden-Baden: Nomos.

Fisman, R. and Miguel, E. 2007. Corruption, Norms, and Legal Enforcement: Evidence from Diplomatic Parking Tickets. *Journal of Political Economy*, 115(6), 1020–48.

Flanary, R., Theobald, R., and Watt, D. 2000. Democratisation or the Democratisation of Corruption? The Case of Uganda, in *Corruption and Democratisation*, edited by A. Doig and R. Theobald. London and Portland: Frank Cass, 36–65

Foreign Corrupt Practices Act of 1977 (FCPA), 91 Stat. 1494.

George, B. and Lacey, K. 2006. Investigation of Halliburton Co./TSKJ's Nigerian Business Practises. *The Journal of Criminal Law & Criminology*, 96(2), 503–26.

George, B., Lacey, K., and Birmele, J. 1999. On the Threshold of the Adoption of Global Anti-bribery Legislation. *Vanderbilt University Journal of Transnational Law*, 32(1), 1–48.

Gerber, T. and Mendelson, S. 2008. Public Experiences of Police Violence and Corruption in Contemporary Russia. *Law and Society Review*, 42(1), 1–42.

Glynn, P., Kobrin, S., and Naím, M. 1997. The Globalization of Corruption, in *Corruption and the Global Economy*, edited by A. Kimberly. Washington, DC: Institute for International Economics, 7–27.

GRECO. 2004. *First Evaluation Round, Compliance Report on Albania.*

GRECO. 2007. *First Evaluation Round, Compliance Report on Bosnia and Hercegovina.*

GRECO. 2006. *First Evaluation Round, Compliance Report on Bulgaria.*

GRECO. 2004. *First Evaluation Round, Compliance Report on Croatia.*

GRECO. 2005. *First Evaluation Round, Compliance Report on the Czech Republic.*

GRECO. 2003. *First Evaluation Round, Compliance Report on Estonia.*

GRECO. 2003. *First Evaluation Round, Compliance Report on Georgia.*

GRECO. 2005. *First Evaluation Round, Compliance Report on Hungary.*

GRECO. 2003. *First Evaluation Round, Evaluation Report on Ireland.*

GRECO. 2004. *First Evaluation Round, Compliance Report on Latvia.*

GRECO. 2004. *First Evaluation Round, Compliance Report on Lithuania.*

GRECO. 2003. *First Evaluation Round, Compliance Report on Moldova.*

GRECO. 2004. *First Evaluation Round, Compliance Report on Poland.*

GRECO. 2004. *First Evaluation Round, Compliance Report on Romania.*

GRECO. 2003. *First Evaluation Round, Compliance Report on the Slovac Republic.*

GRECO. 2003. *First Evaluation Round, Evaluation Report on the United Kingdom.*

GRECO. 2007. *First Evaluation Round, Final Overall Assessment.*

GRECO. 2005. *Second Evaluation Round, Evaluation Report on Croatia.*

GRECO. 2008. *Second Evaluation Round, Evaluation Report on Hungary.*

GRECO. 2005. *Second Evaluation Round, Evaluation Report on Lithuania.*

GRECO. 2004. *Second Evaluation Round, Evaluation Report on Poland.*

GRECO. 2003. *Second Evaluation Round, Evaluation Report on Slovenia.*

Grødeland, A., Koshechkina, T., and Miller, W. 2002. Bribery and Other Ways of Coping with Officialdom in Post-communist Eastern Europe, in *Political Corruption*, 3rd Edition, edited by A. Heidenheimer and M. Johnston. New Brunswick: Transaction Press, 559–83.

Hagan, J. and Radoeva, D. 1998. Both Too Much and Too Little: From Elite to Street Crime in the Transformation of the Czech Republic. *Crime, Law & Social Change*, 28(3–4), 195–211.

Hart, H.L.A. 1968. *Punishment and Responsibility*. Oxford and New York: Oxford University Press.

Hart, H.L.A. 1997. *The Concept of Law*. 2nd Edition. Oxford and New York: Oxford University Press.

Hegel, G. 1991. *Elements of the Philosophy of Right*. Cambridge: Cambridge University Press.

Hirsch, A.V. 1995. Censure and Proportionality, in *A Reader on Punishment*, edited by A. Duff and D. Garland. Oxford: Oxford University Press, 115–28.

Hobbes, T. 1970. *Leviathan*. Stuttgart: Reclam, 112–56.

Hotchkiss, C. 1998. The Sleeping Dog Stirs: New Signs of Life in Efforts to End Corruption in International Business. *Journal of Public Policy & Marketing*, 17(1), 108–23.

Huberts, L. 1995. Western Europe and Public Corruption. *European Journal on Criminal Policy and Research*, 3(2), 7–20.

Hulme, D. and Turner, M. 1997. *Governance, Administration and Development: Making the State Work*. London and New York: Macmillan.

ICC (ed.). 1996. *International Chamber of Commerce Rules of Conduct to Combat Extortion and Bribery in International Business Transactions*. Paris: International Chamber of Commerce.

Inter-American Convention against Corruption 1996.

Jakobs, G. 1993. *Strafrecht Allgemeiner Teil*. 2nd Edition. Berlin and New York: Walter de Gruyter.

Johnston, M. 2004. Corruption and Democratic Consolidation, in *Corrupt Histories*, edited by E. Kreike and W. Jordan. Rochester: University of Rochester Press, 138–64.

Jordan, W. 2009. Anti-corruption Campaigns in Thirteenth-century Europe. *Journal of Medieval History*, 35(2), 204–19.

Kant, I. 1996. *The Metaphysics of Morals*. 2nd Edition. Cambridge: Cambridge University Press.

Karstedt, S. 2003. Legacies of a Culture of Inequality: The Janus Face of Crime in Post-communist Countries. *Crime, Law & Social Change*, 40(2–3), 295–320.

Kolarska-Bobinska, L. 2002. The Impact of Corruption on Legitimacy of Authority in New Democracies, in *Political Corruption in Transition*, edited by S. Kotkin and A. Sajó. Budapest and New York: Central European University Press, 313–26.

Kubiciel, M. 2009. Core Criminal Law Provisions in the United Nations Convention against Corruption. *International Criminal Law Journal*, 9(1), 139–55.

LaFave, W. 2003. *Criminal Law*. 4th Edition. St. Paul: Thompson/West Publishing.

Lawson, L. 2009. The Politics of Anti-corruption Reform in Africa. *Journal of Modern African Studies*, 47(1), 73–100.

Leff, N. 1964. Economic Development through Bureaucratic Corruption. *American Behavioral Scientist*, 8(3), 8–14.

Legrand, P. 1997. The Impossibility of "Legal Transplants." *Maastricht Journal of European and Comparative Law*, 4(1), 111–24.

Legrand, P. 2001. What "Legal Transplants," in *Adapting Legal Cultures*, edited by J. Feest and D. Nelken. Oxford: Hart, 55–70.

Little, W. and Posada-Carbó, E. 1996. Introduction, in *Political Corruption in Europe and Latin America*, edited by W. Little. Hampshire, NY: Macmillan Press, 1–4.

NOVOTINE, Sofia News Agency, July 29, 2009. Available at: www.novinite.com/view_news.php?id=106319.

Nye, J. 1967. Corruption and Political Development: A Cost-benefit-analysis. *American Political Science Review*, 61(2), 417–27.

Oda, H. 1999. *Japanese Law*. 2nd Edition. Oxford and New York: Oxford University Press.

OECD. 1997. Initiatives to Fight Corruption, Note by Secretary General to the OECD Council at Ministerial Level. Paris: OECD.

*OECD Convention on Combating Bribery of Foreign Public Officials in International Business Transactions*. Available at: www.oecd.org/dataoecd/4/18/38028044.pdf.

Oelbaum, J. and Sandbrook, R. 1997. Reforming Dysfunctional Institutions through Democratization: Reflections on Ghana. *Journal of Modern African Studies*, 35(4), 603–46.

Offe, C. 1997. Cultural Aspects of Consolidation: A Note on the Pecularities of Postcommunist Transformation. *East European Constitutional Review*, 6, 64–8.

The Open Society Institute (ed.). 2005. *Legal Remedies for the Resource Curse. A Digest of Experience in Using Law to Combat Natural Resource Corruption.* New York: Open Society Institute.

Pagani. F. 2002. Peer Review. A Tool for Cooperation and Change. *African Security Review*, 11(4), 15–24.

Pieth, M. 2007. Introduction, in *The OECD Convention on Bribery*, edited by M. Pieth, L. Low, and P. Cullen. Cambridge: Cambridge University Press, 3–45.

Pound, R. 1965. *An Introduction to the Philosophy of Law*. New Haven: Yale University Press.

Rawls, J. 1993. *Political Liberalism*. New York: Columbia University Press.

Reed, Q. 1995. Transition, Dysfunctionality and Change in the Czech and Slovak Republic. *Crime, Law & Social Change*, 22(4), 323–37.

*Report from the Commission to the European Parliament and the Council on the Management of EU-funds in Bulgaria.* 2008. Brussels, July 23. COM(2008).

Riley, S. 1998. The Political Economy of Anti-corruption Strategies in Africa. *European Journal of Development Research*, 10(1), 129–59.

Robin, C. 2004. *Fear—The History of a Political Idea*. New York: Oxford University Press.

Sajó, A. 2003. From Corruption to Extortion: Conceptualization of Post Communist Corruption. *Crime, Law & Social Change*, 40(2–3), 171–93.

Salbu, S.R. 1997. Bribery in the Global Market: A Critical Analysis of the Foreign Corrupt Practise Act. *Washington and Lee Law Review*, 54(1), 229–87.

Samuel, G. 2008. Is Law really a Social Science? A View from Comparative Law. *The Cambridge Law Journal*, 67(Pt. 2), 286–321.

Sanyal, R. 2005. Determinants of Bribery in International Business: The Cultural and Economic Factors. *Journal of Business Ethics*, 59(1–2), 139–45.

Selznick, M. 1999. Legal Cultures and the Rule of Law, in *The Rule of Law after Communism*, edited by M. Krygier and A. Czarnota. Singapore and Sydney: Ashgate, 21–38.

Tamanaha, B. 1997. *Realistic Socio-Legal Theory*. Oxford: Oxford University Press.

Tanzi, V. 1998. Corruption around the World. *International Monetary Fund, Staff Papers*, 45(4), 559–94.

Tarullo, D. 2004. The Limits of Institutional Design: Implementing the OECD Convention. *Virginia Journal of International Law*, 44(3), 665–710.

United Nations Convention Against Corruption (UNCAC) 2003.

United Nations Office on Drugs and Crime. 2005. *Compendium of International Legal Instruments on Corruption.* 2nd Edition. New York: United Nations.

US General Accounting Office (ed.). 1981. *Comptroller General's Report to the Congress, Impact of Foreign Corrupt Practices Act on US Business.*

Walzer, M. 1990. The Communitarian Critique of Liberalism. *Political Theory*, 18(1), 6–23.

Watson, A. 1976. Legal Transplants and Law Reform. *The Law Quarterly Review*, 92(1), 79–84.

Watson, A. 2001. *Society and Legal Change*. 2nd Edition. Philadelphia: Temple University Press.

Weigend, T. 2008. Societas delinquere non potest? A German Perspective. *Journal of International Criminal Justice*, 6(5), 927–45.

Wells, C. 2009. Bribery: Corporate Liability under the Draft Bill 2009. *The Criminal Law Review* 2009, 479–87.

*West Virginia State Board of Education v. Barnette*, 319 U.S. 624 (1943).

Williams, J. and Beare, M. 1999. The Business of Bribery: Globalization, Economic Liberalization, and the "Problem" of Corruption. *Crime, Law & Social Change*, 32(2), 115–46.

Wolf, S. 2006. Modernization of the German Anti-corruption Criminal Law by International Legal Provisions. *German Law Journal*, 7(9), 785–92.

Chapter 25

# Shifting the Paradigm of International Environmental Law: The Precautionary Principle from a Developing Country Perspective

Marsudi Triatmodjo

Climate change presents great challenges to tropical states because they are much more exposed to its effects than those located in temperate zones. Indonesia is an archipelagic state of circa 240 million people located on the equator, so we already must look seriously at both mitigation and adaptation. The question is what to do in a legal sense, which is how we come upon the precautionary principle. There are fairness issues which we consider part of legitimacy, but we see the precautionary principle for climate change purposes also as backed up by the well-recognized *sic utere* liability principle (as in *Trail Smelter*).

The precautionary principle mandates that when an action may cause serious or irreversible harm to the environment or mankind, and no scientific consensus exists at the time regarding the certainty of harm occurring, the person or group advocating the action must prove that harm will not occur as a result of the action (Raffensperger and Tickner 1999). This implies a responsibility to prevent exposure to harm for the environment and for people where a good probability of harm exists. Yet there is a real issue concerning the precautionary principle's status as a political or, conversely, legal principle for international environmental law purposes. Already incorporated into certain treaties and declarations, the question to be addressed is whether the precautionary principle has achieved independent status either as customary law, or as a general principle of law. So we look at the precautionary principle through the lens of how developing countries view international law development now, particularly in the area of climate change.

**Indeterminacy and Four Basic Versions of the Precautionary Principle**

Arguably, no set definition for the precautionary principle exists. In fact, one study noted at least 14 different interpretations in treaties and non-treaty declarations (Vanderzwaag 1999). Another scholar has identified four basic versions of the precautionary principle: non-preclusion, margin of safety, best available technology, and prohibitory (Stewart 2002). The non-preclusion precautionary principle states that "scientific uncertainty should not automatically" prevent efforts to supervise and regulate actions that have potential to impose significant harm on others (Stewart 2002). The margin of safety precautionary principle states that regulatory attempts should include some margin of safety where actions should be "limited below the level at which no adverse effect has been observed or predicted" (Stewart 2002). The best available technology precautionary principle requires that unless an actor can prove what he is doing poses no serious harm; activities which pose an uncertain amount of harm to the environment should be governed by the standards of the best available technology (Stewart 2002). Most of the formulations allow for a cost-benefit analysis that includes weighing the value of waiting for further information before enacting regulations.

The precautionary principle also has two broad interpretations which tend to split the treaties and non-treaty declarations into two categories of strong precaution and weak precaution (Sunstein 2002: 32). Strong precaution views as essential the regulation of activities whenever any risk to human health or the environment is predicted, no matter how tenuous the scientific prediction (Sunstein 2002: 33). Strong precaution does not allow an actor to weigh the economic costs of regulation in a cost benefit analysis (ibid.).

The earliest example of strong precaution came in 1982 when the United Nations World Charter for Nature stated when "potential adverse effects are not fully understood, the activities should not proceed" (ibid.; see also United Nations World Charter for Nature). The Wingspread Declaration composed by several environmentalists in 1998 is another example of strong precaution (Sunstein 2002: 33).[1]

In contrast, weak precaution at its most extreme holds that lack of scientific certainty of harm does not automatically mean regulatory efforts should not take place if the harm that could take place would be serious or irreversible (European Environmental Bureau 1999; Science and Environmental Health Network 2000). Arguably, weak precaution is easier to justify since most people practice some form of weak precaution in everyday life.[2] The New Zealand Treasury Department released a publication describing weak precaution:

> The weak version [of the Precautionary Principle] is the least restrictive and allows preventive measures to be taken in the face of uncertainty, but does not require them (e.g., Rio Declaration 1992; United Nations Framework Convention of Climate Change 1992). To satisfy the threshold of harm, there must be some evidence relating to both the likelihood of occurrence and the severity of consequences. Some, but not all, require consideration of the costs of precautionary measures. Weak formulations do not preclude weighing benefits against the costs. Factors other than scientific uncertainty, including economic considerations, may provide legitimate grounds for postponing

---

1    The Wingspread Conference stated "[w]here an activity raises threats of harm to the environment or human health, precautionary measures should be taken even if some cause and effect relationships are not fully established scientifically" (1998 Wingspread Statement on the Precautionary Principle). This formulation raises several problems with the precautionary principle. First, this formulation requires some minimum level of scientific certainty before precautions must be undertaken (van den Belt 2003). Realistically, this is the very basic question of how to deal legally with risk and uncertainty in the regulatory context. Unfortunately, no universal test has been established to find a minimum threshold of scientific certainty of harm, with distinctions typically drawn between the evaluation (how much "risk" exists in terms of a probabilistic or scientific determination) and management of risk (how much "risk" is acceptable, viewed as political decision) (van den Belt 2003). The result is that generally any indication that harm could occur is significant enough to trigger the precautionary principle. In other words, even an isolated hint that the new technology could be potentially harmful would be sufficient to invoke the principle.

Furthermore, the usual precaution taken is a blanket ban on the use of the technology until proponents of the technology can prove that the technology does not pose a threat to the environment (van den Belt 2003). George Annas, a Boston University law professor and panelist at the Wingspread Conference, stated "[t]he truth of the matter is that whoever has the burden of proof loses" (Bailey 1999). Some environmentalists would require that proponents of a new form of technology be able to prove the technology will do no harm before the technology can be used, which comes to the fore in a practical sense in disputes between the Europeans and the United States concerning GMO technology.

2    Locking the front door of one's home before leaving for work would be an example of everyday weak precautionary measures.

action. Under weak formulations, the requirement to justify the need for action (the burden of proof) generally falls on those advocating precautionary action. No mention is made of assignment of liability for environmental harm. (Cameron 2006: 12)

In contrast, the New Zealand government stated the following about strong precaution:

Strong versions justify or require precautionary measures and some also establish liability for environmental harm, which is effectively a strong form of "polluter pays." For example, the Earth Charter (2000) states: "When knowledge is limited apply a precautionary approach ... Place the burden of proof on those who argue that a proposed activity will not cause significant harm, and make the responsible parties liable for environmental harm." Reversal of proof requires those proposing an activity to prove that the product, process, or technology is sufficiently "safe" before approval is granted. Requiring proof of "no environmental harm" before any action proceeds implies the public is not prepared to accept any environmental risk, no matter what economic or social benefits may arise. At the extreme, such a requirement could involve bans and prohibitions on entire classes of potentially threatening activities or substances. (Cameron 2006: 13 (internal citations omitted))

However, the New Zealand government did note a gradual shift worldwide toward a stronger form of precaution than that seen in the Rio Declaration (Cameron 2006). Arguably, this shift toward the strong form simply reflects the pre-existing *sic utere* rule (*Trail Smelter*). In that case, the law is consciously moving away from the various positions expressed 50 years ago in the *Nuclear Test Cases (Australia v. France)* distinguishing prior restraints from potential liability, at least in areas of core state interests such as national security (France's desire to establish and maintain its independent *force de frappe*, where fallout from atmospheric testing inevitably landed downwind in Australia). Notwithstanding the different definitions formulated by different treaties, scholars have identified six core concepts of the precautionary principle that have remained a part of many definitions since its environmental inception in the 1980s (Cameron and O'Riordan 1995). Preventative anticipation requires "a willingness to take action in advance of scientific proof of evidence of the need for the proposed action on the grounds that further delay will prove ultimately most costly to society and nature, and, in the longer term, selfish and unfair to future generations" (Cameron and O'Riordan 1995: 17). Safeguarding of ecological space requires humans to respect "margins of tolerance" by not approaching them or breaching them (ibid.). Proportionality of the response to the potentially harmful actions requires a cost-benefit analysis that includes showing that the chosen regulation "is not unduly costly" (ibid.). The burden of proof falls on the actor to show that their actions are not going to cause harm to the environment (Cameron and O'Riordan 1995). Intrinsic natural rights exist and natural processes of the environment should be legally protected and allowed to continue so that the life support system of earth remains intact (ibid.). Finally, past ecological debts accrued by wrongdoers should be paid by the wrongdoer (ibid.). These six core concepts combine different points of weak and strong precaution. These observed core concepts taken in conjunction with the New Zealand observations suggest that the current form of the precautionary principle recognized by the majority is somewhere between the two extremes of strong and weak precaution, but is moving toward strong precaution as part of its roots in the *sic utere* liability rule.

## Climate Change

The reality is that, particularly for tropical developing countries facing problems like rising sea levels and increasing storm intensities, climate change itself becomes an existential question and a "national security" problem in the international setting. One traditional criticism is that the precautionary principle is oriented more toward the environment rather than being anthropocentric, but developing states in the climate change arena reject this as a matter of how the environmental destruction will have a very adverse effect on their populations. This also reveals a hidden asymmetry in many cost-benefit calculations advanced by developed states also in negotiations. They argue about increased costs for production in terms of achieving greenhouse gas limits, even while the potential magnitude of injury to many developing states goes far beyond merely impeding economic development (the existential threat problem). One of the main criticisms of the precautionary principle is that science is limited and fallible. The principle assumes science can predict with some accuracy the effect man's activity has on the environment. Essentially, scientists have both stated and proven that they cannot anticipate in advance the potential impact that new technology will have on the environment and on mankind. Many of today's most widely used inventions such as laser technology were originally predicted to be useless (Bailey 1999). Conversely, many of today's recognized toxins such as DDT originally showed no indication when they were first introduced as pesticides that they could collect in animal fat and target non-insect beings (Bailey 1999). But that does not mean that potential liability disappears as a result of the uncertainty.

Furthermore, many people citing the precautionary principle assume scientists can offer solutions to the already created environmental problems. Unfortunately, again, scientists themselves admit the difficulty of predicting environmental behavior (see, e.g., American Association of State Climatologists, admitting to the difficulty in climate prediction). For example, regarding climate change, scientists have only predicted the effects of global warming on earth through the year 2100, but they are almost certain that the effects of global warming will continue to spread past the year 2100 based on the damage humans have already caused (Archer 2005). Furthermore, while scientists can predict an increase in temperature, increases will vary by region, and scientists have yet to pinpoint exact changes by region with accuracy, even while recognizing special problems in tropical areas (Archer 2005). Also, many treaties and non-treaty declarations discuss the importance of avoiding "irreversible" harm. The very term "irreversible" implies that scientists have found no way to solve the created problem.


## State Sovereignty

The precautionary principle in its original application was based in general Continental (German) public law approaches to executive decision-making also under environmental law, namely the principle of proportionality. Proportionality as a kind of least-intrusive-means analysis limits the discretion of the state (Linnan 1984), so that its problematic side for international law purposes would be the extent to which it runs afoul of the concept of state sovereignty. We are perhaps more interested in the question how international law is made for purposes of this chapter, but would argue on the question of the substantive standard that the precautionary principle may face technical issues in the international law sphere if viewed as prior restraint on state activity. However, it is at least an emerging principle, and the clear recognition of the *sic utere* principle (*Trail Smelter*) under customary law means that, in case of actual damages following upon disregard of the precautionary principle, state responsibility should apply under international environmental law. To that extent, developing countries see the legal development glass as half full, and some countries already accept the precautionary principle as binding either as customary law or a general principle of law among developed countries as well. Meanwhile, consensus is growing and state practice is being shaped by the principle's inclusion in treaties, with the result that it seems only a matter of time until the precautionary principle is recognized, if it is not already law. However, developing countries have a special interest in the precautionary principle in the climate change setting by virtue of the fact that much of Central and South America, Africa, and Asia are located in the tropics which suffer disproportionate harm under most global warming scenarios.

Separate scientific academies have since released subsequent reports blaming climate change on human activity, particularly greenhouse gas emissions (e.g., Network of African Science Academies 2007; Royal Society of New Zealand 2008). Unfortunately, studies have not yet established the extent of the effects of global warming. While many studies have established that the earth will experience rising global temperatures, rising ocean levels, and receding glaciers through the year 2100, the exact variance in temperature by region has not been established and beyond the year 2100 is largely a mystery (Archer 2005; Solomon et al. 2009). However, given the long lifetime of carbon dioxide emissions, scientists agree consequences will continue beyond the year 2100.

Since 2007, few, if any, scientific bodies have maintained a dissenting opinion regarding climate change and global warming (Brigham-Grette et al. 2006). The few scientific bodies that have remained noncommittal regarding global warming have merely noted the difficulty of predicting climate change while acknowledging that climate change is occurring due to human activity (AASC). However, a few individual scientists and prominent figures still express skepticism regarding the existence of global warming (De Granados 2007; Revkin 2009). With the existence of these few dissenters, public debates arise regarding whether a true scientific consensus exists regarding the existence of global warming. Significantly, however, several scientific organizations have used the word "consensus" in their statements (AAAS Board Statement on Climate Change 2006). Specifically, in 2003, the American Meteorological Society stated:

> [t]he nature of science is such that there is rarely total agreement among scientists. Individual scientific statements and papers—the validity of some of which has yet to be assessed adequately—can be exploited in the policy debate and can leave the impression that the scientific community is sharply divided on issues where there is, in reality, a strong scientific consensus ... IPCC assessment reports are prepared at approximately five-year intervals by a large international group of experts who represent the broad range of expertise and perspectives relevant to the issues. The reports strive to reflect a consensus evaluation of the results of the full body of peer-reviewed research ... They provide an analysis of what is known and not known, the degree of consensus, and some indication of the degree of confidence that can be placed on the various statements and conclusions. (Climate Change Research 2003)

Regardless of the existence of scientific consensus regarding climate change, over one-third of the international population is entirely unaware that a human created global warming problem exists (Pelham 2009). Furthermore, even where the public has been informed of scientific opinion regarding climate change, members of the public seem more likely to be skeptical of global warming than scientists.

While public reaction to climate change remains mixed and scientists struggle to develop an adequate solution, nations attempt to solve the global crisis despite conflicting political interests. As recently as September 22, 2009, world leaders have met to call for immediate action to fight the effects and eliminate the causes of climate change (CNN 2009). Unfortunately, political differences caused in part by differences in economic status make it hard for world leaders to reach a global consensus on the actions necessary to respond to climate change. Poor developing regions of the world, especially Africa, face the harshest effects of global warming despite contributing relatively little to the emissions of greenhouse gases (Revkin 2007). As a result, developing countries were exempt from the Kyoto Protocol, and this exemption prompted the United States (and, previously, Australia) to refuse to ratify the Kyoto Protocol despite each country's large contributions to greenhouse gas emissions (Australia ratifies Kyoto Protocol 2007).

Recently emerging economies further contribute to the difficulties in reaching a global consensus regarding appropriate action. China and India, in particular, strongly contest the extent to which their carbon dioxide emissions should be curtailed (Max 2009). Specifically, the United States argues that China's gross national carbon dioxide emissions exceed that of the United States, and China should, therefore, reduce their greenhouse gas emissions if the United States is required to do so (Harrabin 2008; Mufson 2007). China and India, in turn, argue that their per capita greenhouse gas emissions are lower than that of the United States (Casey 2007; IANS 2009). Furthermore, it is argued, established economies such as the United States and Western European nations contributed to greenhouse gas emissions long before emerging economies such as China and India began competing industrially.

But can we say whether social views are changing also in the United States, concerning climate change and its attendant risks? In recent years, global warming has gained prominence in the public consciousness thanks in large part to the efforts of scientists to reach the public through the media. The 2006 documentary *An Inconvenient Truth*, in particular, drew international public attention to the realities of climate change. The film brought to the public's attention a scientific concept that, in all reality, has been virtually confirmed since the beginning of the twenty-first century. In January of 2001, the Intergovernmental Panel on Climate Change (IPCC) endorsed the view that the world is undergoing climate change caused by man and released a statement proclaiming that "[a]n increasing body of observations gives a collective picture of a warming world and other changes in the climate system ... [T]here is new and stronger evidence that most of the warming observed over the last 50 years is attributable to human activities" (Climate Change 2001: 2, ix). The IPCC essentially confirmed the views of over 40 academies of science in determining that human action is "very likely" the cause of increasing temperatures, the increase in hurricane activity, and the increase in cyclone strength. In this case, "very likely" means a probability of greater than 90 percent.

## Modernization of Law

The precautionary principle was first introduced into the field of international environmental law regarding protection of the ozone layer in 1985 (addressing the original ozone hole phenomenon) (Vienna Convention 1985). While the precautionary principle has multiple formulations and definitions among multiple treaties, most definitions, including that contained in Principle 15 of the 1992 *Rio Declaration on the Environment and Development* (Rio Declaration), include a couple of key concepts. First, decision-makers need to anticipate harm before it occurs. Because of this need, actors are responsible for establishing that their actions will not harm the environment; the burden of proof falls on the actor rather than the victim. Second, a responsibility exists to avoid or minimize the harm when the existence of potential harm is high, even if no scientific consensus exists that the harm will occur (Rio Convention).

In 2000, the European Commission Communication on the Precautionary Principle as, at least, regional international law, stated that the precautionary principle applies "where scientific evidence is insufficient, inconclusive or uncertain," and where preliminary scientific evaluation indicates that "there are reasonable grounds for concern that the potentially dangerous effects on the environment, human, animal or plant health may be inconsistent with" the high level of protection chosen by the EU (Commission of the European Communities 2000: 10). Additionally the January 2000 Cartagena Protocol on Biosafety, as an amendment to the 1992 Biodiversity Convention also stemming from the Rio Conference, stated: "Lack of scientific certainty due to insufficient relevant scientific information ... shall not prevent [the Party of import] from taking a decision, as appropriate, with regard to the import of the living modified organism [in question] ... in order to avoid or minimize such potential adverse effects" (Cartagena Protocol on Biosafety). Combining all of these definitions, scientific uncertainty regarding harm does not erase one's responsibility to take precautions to prevent the harm, but a certain amount of scientific probability must exist that harm can occur.

The fact that the precautionary principle exists in the field of international environmental law causes some inevitable clashes in values. Law has been defined as "protecting public interests in the society, maintaining the rights of man, [and] realizing or achieving the justice in togetherness" (Hujibers 1982). Alternatively, law is defined as "a system of norms that regulates the behavior of men" (Kelsen 1967). Law was largely developed using an anthropocentric approach, which means that law exists largely to promote the rights and interests of man. Proponents of the precautionary principle rightly point out that the interests of man should include sustainable development and preserving the ability of earth to sustain life. Critics of the precautionary principle point out the inevitable conflict that arises when "some activities that promote human health might 'raise threats of harm to the environment,' and some activities that might be thought of as promoting the environment might 'raise threats of harm to human health'" (Bailey 1999). According to critics, the precautionary principle gives no true guidelines for dealing with this occurrence, and this dilemma occurs frequently (Bailey 1999).[3] Given that the concept of law revolves around protecting the interests of man and society through regulation of human behavior, which interest of society should law protect in these instances? Candidly, attempts to fit the precautionary principle into the general rules of law category as specific application of public law proportionality principles are largely an attempt to circumvent the state practice and *opinio juris* requirements of customary law, alongside the possibility of reservation during its period of formation.

While the existence of many treaties that include the precautionary principle helps to establish it as customary international law, the fact that the treaties have varying definitions of the precautionary principle also poses a problem. For a country to recognize the precautionary principle as binding international law, the precautionary principle would need to be well defined. Each country can state provisions and exceptions to the treaties it signs onto. Specifically, the United States has opposed the use of the word "principle" in international discussions of the precautionary principle since "principle" in the United States has the connotation of valid law (Recuerda 2008). The use of the word "principle" implies compulsory language that would make the precautionary principle as applied in certain treaties or non-treaty declarations a source of law (Recuerda 2008). The United States instead favors the use of the word "approach" (Recuerda 2008). The European Union, in

---

3 Ronald Bailey cites the example of pesticides. Pesticides arguably protect food supplies in the form of crops and prevent the spread of disease by killing the insects that spread the disease. Unfortunately, many pesticides have an adverse affect on the environment. Does one protect the environment or protect human health in this scenario?

contrast, favors the world "principle" and does consider the principle to be compulsory and a source of law (Recuerda 2008).

Central to the debate regarding the precautionary principle and its influence on the modernization of international environmental law is the notion of fairness. A question of fairness is implicit in the political arguments among nations. Why should developing countries and emerging economies be expected to curtail greenhouse gases (and the industrial progress they would make while emitting greenhouse gases) when Western countries largely created the climate change issue for the world while profiting from the industrialization that required burning of fossil fuels? The "most defensible accounts of fairness and climate change suggest that the rich countries should bear the brunt, and perhaps even the entirety, of the costs" (Gardiner 2004). Close behind the fairness argument comes the liability argument of *sic utere* (*Trail Smelter*). Meanwhile it appears that social views are now moving toward the precautionary principle even in the United States.

The adequate precautionary measures vary depending on the degree of harm likely to occur and the degree of scientific uncertainty regarding whether the harm will occur. There is also room for the recognition of state capacity in the idea that the wealthier and technically more sophisticated states will be held to a higher standard. In 1992, the Rio Conference stated in the Rio Declaration that "[i]n order to protect the environment, the precautionary approach shall be widely applied by States according to their capabilities. Where there are threats of serious or irreversible damage, lack of full scientific certainty shall not be used as a reason for postponing cost-effective measures to prevent environmental degradation" (Rio Convention, principle 15). The Rio Conference definition makes clear that scientific uncertainty alone is not a sufficient excuse for avoiding precautionary measures to prevent harm to others or the environment. However, cost may be taken into account when considering which measures to take under the Rio Conference definition.

## Implementation

Thus far, the precautionary principle has appeared in several treaties and non-treaty declarations around the world. The Montreal Protocol of 1987, the Rio Declaration of 1992, the 1990 Bergen Declaration, the 1991 Bamako Convention, the 1994 Fort Lauderdale Resolution, and the 1982 Convention on the Law of the Sea are all examples of documents that apply the precautionary principle to the environment in general and the areas of toxic materials, endangered species, and marine pollution specifically. Treaties are one way to establish international law, but unfortunately, the law only applies to countries that have signed onto and ratified the treaties. Principle 15 of the Rio Declaration of 1992 defines the precautionary approach by saying "in order to protect the environment, the precautionary approach shall be widely applied by States according to their capabilities. Where there are threats of serious or irreversible damage, lack of full scientific certainty shall be not used as a reason for postponing cost-effective measures to prevent environmental degradation" (Rio Declaration). Garcia points out "the wording, largely similar to that of the principle, is subtly different in that: (1) it recognizes that there may be differences in local capabilities to apply the approach, and (2) it calls for cost-effectiveness in applying the approach, e.g., taking economic and social costs into account" (Garcia 1995). The precautionary approach is essentially a less harsh version of the precautionary principle that uses soft precaution to allow each nation to perform a cost-benefit analysis and implement the principle to the best of that nation's ability (Garcia 1995). The problem lies in the asymmetry of the cost-benefit calculations which separate increased production costs in the producing developed country from the damages caused ultimately in the developing world.

But do any countries already view the precautionary principle as customary international law? A few countries including New Zealand, Germany, Hungary, and Ireland have declared the precautionary principle to be customary international law, but the question is whether traditional requirements of state practice and *opinio juris* are thereby satisfied. Unfortunately, customary international law is difficult to establish. Current wisdom holds that the more countries that observe the precautionary principle as binding law, the shorter the period of observation needed to establish the precautionary principle as customary international law. It bears notice also that in the so-called Hormone Beef proceedings between the EU, Canada, and the United States in the late 1990s, the EU took the position that the precautionary principle was now part of customary law (the WTO appellate dispute settlement body considered whether it could be law either as customary law or under general principles of law, but found it unnecessary to make a final determination in that appeal in resolving the question under the terms of the WTO Sanitary and Phytosanitary Agreement, noting that SPS Agreement Article 5.7 itself incorporated the precautionary principle) (World Trade Organization Appellate Body 1998).

Unfortunately, four countries (although it might be argued this should include the EU as a grouping of many more states, given its position in the Beef Hormone proceeding) declaring the precautionary principle as customary international law is not enough widespread observance to actually establish the precautionary principle as customary international law. The United States currently opposes the use of the word "principle" in international dialogues, posing a problem since a major world power clearly is not observing the precautionary principle as customary international law, but rather as compulsory law (or, in the alternative, is trying to create a reservation through consistent opposition during the formation period for the customary law rule). Also, the precautionary principle as applied to international environmental law has only been around since the 1980s. For this relatively short period of conception and observance to be recognized as enough to establish the precautionary principle as customary international law, a large number of countries would need to recognize the precautionary principle as binding law. The European Union has adopted the precautionary principle and has created a mechanism for implementing it without adopting a formal definition of the precautionary principle (Fisher et al. 2006). The United States as a country has not adopted a form of the precautionary principle although the US Clean Air Act places the burden on the actor to prove that certain chemicals will not harm the environment before those chemicals can be implemented (Carruth and Goldstein 2004). Australia has adopted the precautionary principle through case law with the landmark case *Telstra Corporation Limited v Hornsby Shire Council*. In that case, Justice CJ Preston summarized the precautionary principle by stating:

> [i]f there are threats of serious or irreversible environmental damage, lack of full scientific certainty should not be used as a reasoning for postponing measures to prevent environmental degradation. In the application of the principle … decisions should be guided by: (i) careful evaluation to avoid, wherever practicable, serious or irreversible damage to the environment; and (ii) an assessment of risk-weighted consequence of various options. (*Protection of the Environment Administration Act 1991*)

But the position of many developing states on the precautionary principle as law is simply determined by the fact that they view climate change as an existential threat (albeit perhaps to their children's children), even while it remains the province of industry lobbyists in the United States. Once characterized as a national security threat, it presumably can rise at least to the level of a Chapter VI dispute under the UN Charter, but as collective problem may present more a substantive rule of law issue.

What does this all mean for our chicken or egg question? Viewing climate change as a law-making question, it is fair to say that domestic politics drives state positions. Therefore, social opinion change in a given state must precede the creation of law by that state. On the other hand, under traditional customary law creation rules, states may become subject to new customary law by default if they do not object during the period of formation. But the ability of a state to escape any such customary law rule may be restricted to the extent that it is either viewed as *jus cogens* (because of human or national security concerns), or to the extent the rule is considered to really just be an extension of the pre-existing *sic utere* principle. And if it were to be considered to stem from *sic utere* as existing rule, it simply becomes a substantive rule of law enforcement problem, if the norm were violated.

If a strong domestic consensus exists, it may also be sufficient to provide momentum to a treaty resolution of a problem. Putting aside issues like concentrated lobbying interests, it is difficult to envision states changing their position on the creation of new international law, whether in the form of customary law or by treaty, without strong social views already in place. The difficulty is how to address differing social views of the climate change problem in differing states (a question of threat perception). But the pre-existing *sic utere* liability rule may provide guidance. To that extent, the existence of a liability rule may push to the fore the idea of prior restraint embedded in the precautionary principle. So to that extent, the existence of the neighboring *sic utere* rule (*Trail Smelter*) may positively affect the creation/recognition of the precautionary principle itself as binding international law. But beyond the technical arguments, the problem is that tropical states simply cannot accept the status quo as existential threat via climate change. That is true, and pushes them toward recognizing a change of law linked with enforcement as ROL's heart.

## References


The 1985 Vienna Convention for the Protection of the Ozone Layer.

1998 Wingspread Statement on the Precautionary Principle. Available at: www.gdrc.org/u-gov/precaution-3.html.

AAAS Board Statement on Climate Change, 9 December. 2006. Available at: www.aaas.org/news/press_room/climate_change/mtg_200702/aaas_climate_statement.pdf.

American Association of State Climatologists (AASC). 2001. Policy Statement on Climate Variability and Change. Available at: http://lwf.ncdc.noaa.gov/oa/aasc/AASC-Policy-Statement-on-Climate.htm.

Archer, D. 2005. Fate of Fossil Fuel CO2 in Geologic Time. *Journal of Geophysical Research*, 110, C09S05.1–C09S05.6.

Australia Ratifies Kyoto Protocol. 2007. *Sydney Morning Herald*. Available at: www.smh.com.au/news/environment/rudd-signs-kyoto-deal/2007/12/03/1196530553203.html.

Bailey, R. 1999. Precautionary Tale. *Reason*, April. Available at: http://reason.com/archives/1999/04/01/precautionary-tale.

Brigham-Grette, J., Anderson, S., Clague, J., Cole, J., Doran, P., Gillespie, A., Grimm, E., Guccione, P., Hughen, K., Jackson, S., Jull, T., Leavitt, S., Mandel, R., Ortiz, J., Rodbell, D., Schweger, C., Smith, A. and Styles, B.. 2006. Petroleum Geologists' Award to Novelist Crichton is Inappropriate. *Eos*, 87(36), 364–464. Available at: www.agu.org/fora/eos/pdfs/2006EO360008.pdf.

Cameron, J. and O'Riordan, T. 1995. *Interpreting the Precautionary Principle*. London: Earthscan Publications.

Cameron, L. 2006. Precautionary Principle: Origins, Definitions, and Interpretations, in *Environmental Risk Management in New Zealand – Is There Scope to Apply a More Generic Framework?* (New Zealand Treasury Policy Perspectives Paper 06/06). Available at: www.treasury.govt.nz/publications/research-policy/ppp/2006/06-06/05.htm.

Carruth, R.S. and Goldstein, B. 2004, The Precautionary Principle and/or Risk Assessment in World Trade Organization Decisions: A Possible Role for Risk Perception, *Risk Analysis*, 24(2), 491–9. Available at: http://onlinelibrary.wiley.com/doi/10.1111/j.0272-4332.2004.00452.x/citedby.

The Cartagena Protocol on Biosafety to the Convention on Biological Diversity. Available at: www.cbd.int/biosafety/protocol.shtml.

Casey, M. 2007. China Says West Should Deal with Warming. *Newsvine*. Available at: www.newsvine.com/_news/2007/12/07/1147788-china-says-west-should-deal-with-warming.

Climate Change 2001: Working Group I: The Scientific Basis, IPCC, January 2001.

Climate Change Research: Issues for the Atmospheric and Related Sciences, February 2003.

CNN. 2009. Obama Warns Recession Makes Climate Change Fight Harder. *CNN*. Available at: www.cnn.com/2009/POLITICS/09/22/obama.climate.change/index.html.

Commission of the European Communities. 2000. *Communication from the Commission on the Precautionary Principle.* Brussels. Available at: http://ec.europa.eu/dgs/health_consumer/library/pub/pub07_en.pdf.

De Granados, O.Z. 2007. The Doubters of Global Warming. *Frontline*. Available at: www.pbs.org/wgbh//pages/frontline/hotpolitics/reports/skeptics.html.

European Environmental Bureau. 1999. *EEB Position on the Precautionary Principle.* Available at: www.eeb.org/publication/1999/eeb_position_on_the_precautionary.html.

Fisher, E., Jones, J., and von Schomberg, R., eds. 2006. *Implementing the Precautionary Principle: Perspectives and Prospects.* Cheltenham, UK and Northampton, MA: Edward Elgar.

Garcia, S.M. 1995. The Precautionary Approach to Fisheries and its Implications for Fishery Research, Technology and Management: An Updated Review, in *Precautionary Approach to Fisheries, Part 2: Scientific Papers*, edited by FAO. Rome: FAO.

Gardiner, S.M. 2004. Ethics and Global Climate Change. *Ethics*, 114(3), pp. 555–600. Available at: www.jstor.org/stable/10.1086/382247.

Harrabin, R. 2008. China now Top Carbon Polluter. *BBC News*, April 14. Available at: http://news.bbc.co.uk/2/hi/7347638.stm.

Huijbers, Theo. 1982. *Filsafat Hukum: Dalam Lintasan Sejarah* (Philosophy of Law: In Historical Trajectory). Yogyakarta: Yayasan Kanisius.

IANS. 2009. *India Can't Be Exempt from Mandatory Greenhouse Gas Emission Cap: John Kerry.* Available at: www.thaindian.com/newsportal/uncategorized/india-cant-be-exempt-from-mandatory-greenhouse-gas-emission-cap-john-kerry_100151668.html.

Kelsen, Hans. 1967. *Pure Theory of Law.* Berkeley: University of California Press.

Linnan, D. 1984. Police Discretion in a Continental European State: The Police of Baden-Wurttemberg in the Federal Republic of Germany. *Law and Contemporary Problems*, 47(4), 185–223.

Max, A. 2009. China Wants Top US Technology in Climate Bargain. *The Huffington Post.* Available at: www.huffingtonpost.com/2009/06/11/china-wants-top-us-techno_n_214501.html.

Mufson, S. 2007. In Battle for U.S. Carbon Caps, Eyes and Efforts Focus on China. *The Washington Post*, June 6. Available at www.washingtonpost.com/wp-dyn/content/article/2007/06/05/AR2007060502546.html.

Network of African Science Academies. 2007. Joint Statement by the Network of African Science Academies (NASAC) to the G8 on Sustainability, Energy Efficiency and Climate Change. Available at: www.interacademies.net/file.aspx?id=4825.

*Nuclear Test Cases (Australia v. France)*, Request for the Indication of Interim Measures of Protection, [1973] I.C.J. Reports 99.

Pelham, B. 2009. Awareness, Opinions about Global Warming Vary Worldwide. *Gallup*. Available at: www.gallup.com/poll/117772/Awareness-Opinions-Global-Warming-Vary-Worldwide.aspx.

*Protection of the Environment Administration Act 1991*. New South Wales.

Raffensperger, C. and Tickner, J. 1999. *Protecting Public Health and the Environment: Implementing the Precautionary Principle*. Washington, DC: Island Press.

Recuerda, M.A. 2008. Dangerous Interpretations of the Precautionary Principle and the Foundational Values of the European Union Food Law: Risk versus Risk. *Journal of Food Law & Policy*, 4(1), 1–43.

Revkin, A.C. 2007. Poor Nations to Bear Brunt as World Warms. *New York Times*. Available at: www.nytimes.com/2007/04/01/science/earth/01climate.html?ex=1333080000&en=6c687d64add0b7ba&ei=5088&partner=rssnyt&emc=rss.

Revkin, A.C. 2009. Skeptics Dispute Climate Worries and Each Other. *New York Times*. Available at: www.nytimes.com/2009/03/09/science/earth/09climate.html?pagewanted=1&_r=1&sq=global%20warming%20skeptic&st=cse&scp=1.

*Rio Declaration on the Environment and Development*. 1992. Available at: www.unep.org/Documents.multilingual/Default.asp?DocumentID=78&ArticleID=1163.

Royal Society of New Zealand. 2008. Climate Change Statement from the Royal Society of New Zealand, Press Release, July 10. Available at: www.royalsociety.org.nz/organisation/panels/climate/climate-change-statement/.

Science and Environmental Health Network. 2000. *The Precautionary Principle: A Common Sense Way to Protect Public Health and the Environment*. Available at: www.mindfully.org/Precaution/Precautionary-Principle-Common-Sense.htm.

Stewart, R.B. 2002. Environmental Regulatory Decision Making Under Uncertainty, in *An Introduction to the Law and Economics of Environmental Policy: Issues in Institutional Design*, edited by T. Swanson (volume 20 of *Research in Law and Economics* series, edited by R. Zerbe and J Kirkwood). Oxford: Elsevier Science, 71–126.

Solomon, S., Plattner, G.K., Knutti, R., and Friedlingstein, P. 2009. Irreversible Climate Change Due to Carbon Dioxide Emissions. *Proceedings of the National Academy of Sciences*, 106(6), 1704–9.

Sunstein, C.R. 2002. *The Paralyzing Principle: Does the Precautionary Principle Point Us in Any Helpful Direction?* Available at: www.cato.org/pubs/regulation/regv25n4/v25n4-9.pdf.

*Telstra Corporation Limited v Hornsby Shire Council*, 2006 WL 754833 (NSWLEC), [2006] ALMD 6808, [2006] ALMD 6809, 67 NSWLR 256, 146 LGERA 10.

*Trail Smelter Arbitration (U.S. v. Canada)*, III R.I.A.A. 1905 (1935).

United Nations World Charter for Nature. Available at: www.un.org/documents/ga/res/37/a37r007.htm.

Van den Belt, H. 2003. Debating the Precautionary Principle: "Guilty Until Proven Innocent" or "Innocent Until Proven Guilty"? *Plant Physio*, 132, 1122–6.

Vanderzwaag, D. 1999. The Precautionary Principle in Environmental Law and First Embraces. *Journal of Environmental Law and Practice*, 8, 355–75.

World Trade Organization Appellate Body. 1998. *EC Measures Concerning Meat and Meat Products (Hormones)*. WT/DS26/AB/R & WT/DS48/AB/R. January 16. Available at: www.worldtradelaw.net/reports/wtoab/ec-hormones(ab).pdf.

# Index